WOMEN IN ANCIENT EGYPT

WOMEN IN ANCIENT EGYPT

REVISITING POWER, AGENCY, AND AUTONOMY

Edited by
Mariam F. Ayad

The American University in Cairo Press
Cairo New York

First published in 2022 by
The American University in Cairo Press
113 Sharia Kasr el Aini, Cairo, Egypt
One Rockefeller Plaza, 10th Floor, New York, NY 10020
www.aucpress.com

ISBN 978 1 649 03180 8

Library of Congress Cataloging-in-Publication Data

Names: Ayad, Mariam F., editor.
Title: Women in ancient Egypt : revisiting power, agency, and autonomy / edited by Mariam Ayad.
Identifiers: LCCN 2021055858 | ISBN 9781649031808 (hardback)
Subjects: LCSH: Women--Egypt--History--To 1500. | Egypt--History--To 640 A.D.
Classification: LCC HQ1137.E3 W67 2022 | DDC 305.40962--dc23/eng/20211201

1 2 3 4 5 26 25 24 23 22

Designed by Jon W. Stoy

Contents

Illustrations

Figures

Tables

Contributors

Clémentine Audouit is a French Egyptologist. In 2017, she defended her doctoral dissertation, entitled "Représentations et fonctions du sang en Egypte pharaonique" (under the direction of Bernard Mathieu, professor in Egyptology). After that, she continued her research and published several papers about the perceptions of bodily fluids in ancient Egypt. She also co-organized with B. Mathieu and E. Panaite the symposium "Body Fluids in Ancient Egypt and the Near East" in 2019 at Montpellier. In addition to her studies about the body, she participates in the French epigraphic study of the western face of the second pylon in Amun's Temple in Karnak (CFEETK-USR 3172).

Anne Austin received her BA in anthropology from Harvard University, and her MA and PhD in the archaeology program at UCLA. Before starting her position as an assistant professor at the University of Missouri in St. Louis, Anne completed a three-year postdoctoral program in the History Department at Stanford University. Anne's research combines the fields of osteology and Egyptology in order to document medicine and disease in the past. Specifically, she uses data from ancient Egyptian human remains and daily life texts to reconstruct ancient Egyptian health care networks and identify the diseases and illnesses people experienced in the past. While working as a member of the IFAO mission at Deir al-Medina, Anne identified the mummified remains of a woman with over thirty tattoos. Since then, she has identified several other individuals with tattoos from Deir al-Medina. Her current research project explores how the practice of tattooing in ancient Egypt connects to gender, religion, and medicine. In addition to her interest in Egyptology and osteology,

Anne also works on improving archaeological data management practices through her participation in an international, collaborative ethnographic research study on archaeological field schools called the Secret Life of Data (SLO-Data) Project.

Mariam Ayad is an associate professor of Egyptology at the American University in Cairo. In 2020–21, she was a visiting associate professor of women's studies and Near Eastern religions and a research associate of the Women's Studies in Religion program at Harvard Divinity School. Ayad studied Egyptology at the American University in Cairo (BA), the University of Toronto (MA), and Brown University (PhD), and was a tenured associate professor of art history and Egyptology at the University of Memphis, Tennessee before returning to Egypt in 2011. She is the author of *God's Wife, God's Servant: The God's Wife of Amun (c. 740–525 BC)* (Routledge, 2009) and the editor of three volumes on Coptic culture.

Romane Betbeze studied Egyptology at the École du Louvre, Paris, and has worked as an epigraphist at the Centre Franco-Egyptien des Temples de Karnak in Luxor. Specializing in material culture from the Old Kingdom, her PhD, which was devoted to the study of private tomb façades from the Old Kingdom through the notions of ostentation and addressivity, was completed under the supervision of Laurent Coulon (EPHE, Paris) and Philippe Collombert (Université de Genève); she was also assistant researcher for the SNSF project of Julie Stauder-Porchet on "Monumental Discourse in the Third Millennium BCE Egypt." Her current research focuses on tomb decoration of elite women from the same period through the lens of gender studies.

Anke Ilona Blöbaum is a research associate with the project "Structure and Transformation in the Vocabulary of the Egyptian Language: Text and Knowledge in the Culture of Ancient Egypt" at the Saxon Academy of Sciences and Humanities in Leipzig, Germany. She has studied Egyptology and Coptology in Münster and Paris (EPHE, ICP) and received her PhD in Egyptology from the Westfalian University at Münster (2006). Besides her work as researcher and lecturer, she has been involved in several archaeological missions at Thebes, Abydos, Elephantine, and Buto. The focal points of her research oscillate mainly between Egyptian philology, with an emphasis on medico-magical texts and on royal and elite self-presentation (especially from the first millennium BCE), on the one hand, and analysis and documentation of archaeological objects (especially from the Early Dynastic Period), on the other hand. Her recent publications include a study of the self-presentation of Montuemhat (with Angelika Lohwasser and Meike Becker, *Inszenierung von Herrschaft und Macht im ägyptischen Tempel. Religion und Politik im Theben des frühen 1. Jahrtausends v. Chr.*, 2020) and observations on types of sealings and sealed objects in a volume which she co-edited with Eva-Maria Engel and Frank Kammerzell, "Keep Out! Early Dynastic and Old Kingdom Cylinder Seals and Seal Impressions in Context" (Wiesbaden: Harrassowitz, 2021).

Eva-Maria Engel studied Egyptology, Near Eastern archaeology, and European prehistory at Göttingen University and the University of California, Los Angeles (PhD Göttingen, 1997). Since 1984, she has worked frequently on excavations in Egypt (Abydos, Buto, Elephantine, Qantir, Saqqara, Dahshur, Maabda, Asyut) and has taught classes on Egyptian archaeology at the universities of Münster, Göttingen, and Berlin. Her research focuses on Early Dynastic studies, architecture, and reception of ancient Egyptian motifs in Europe.

Renate Fellinger is currently writing her PhD dissertation at the University of Cambridge, investigating the legal role of women in Ptolemaic Upper Egypt as reflected in a particular type of demotic legal contract (the so-called "document for money"). Her research exploits both statistical and qualitative analysis to enhance our understanding of women's roles and ancient Egyptian society at large. Her expertise includes bringing interdisciplinary approaches—for example, methods rooted in the digital humanities—and innovative solutions to ancient Egyptian sources. Renate's interest lies in broadening the scope of the examination of women's legal roles, in both geographical and temporal terms, to include not only Egypt but also other ancient societies.

Kathrin Gabler is an academic assistant and lecturer in Egyptology at the University of Basel. She has taught courses for nonacademic audiences at the universities of Basel, HU Berlin, Liège, and LMU Munich, the State Museum of Egyptian Art in Munich, and the Antikenmuseum Basel. Trained at the universities of Munich and Leiden, her education culminated in a PhD entitled "Who's Who around Deir el-Medina." The thesis deals with the supply personnel of this extraordinary settlement from prosopographic, organizational, archaeological, and diachronic points of view. Furthermore, Kathrin was a regular member of the excavation projects at Deir al-Bachit/Dra' Abu el-Naga and of the British Museum Epigraphic and Conservation Survey at Elkab and Hagr Edfu. Her post-doctoral project, "Means of Communication with a Focus on Letters, Gender, and the New Kingdom," forms part of the "Crossing

Boundaries Project: Understanding Complex Scribal Practices in Ancient Egypt" between the Universities of Basel and Liège and the Museo Egizio Turin. In addition, Kathrin directs a digital survey in the tomb of the sculptor Ipuy, TT 217, in Deir al-Medina.

Rahel Glanzmann graduated from the University of Basel with a Master of Arts in Egyptology (major) and Ancient Near Eastern Studies (minor). Since her graduation, she has been active in various Egyptological research projects including archaeological fieldwork in Egypt. She was recently involved in the Circulating Artefacts project at the British Museum, and currently works as an independent scholar on ancient Egyptian material culture and funerary archaeology.

Izold Guegan studied Egyptology, anthropology, and archaeology at the American University in Cairo and at Strasbourg University. She received her joint PhD in Egyptology from Swansea University and Sorbonne Université in 2020 on "The xnr: Research on an Egyptian Religious Group from the Old to the New Kingdoms." Her research interests include gender studies, religious studies, anthropology, and archaeology. She has worked as an archaeologist in Egypt and Sudan, and as an editorial assistant for the publishing house Soleb, specializing in Egyptology and archaeology.

Fayza Haikal is Professor Emerita of Egyptology at the American University in Cairo. She received her BA in Egyptology from Cairo University and her DPhil in Egyptology from Oxford University. She started her academic career at Cairo University, where she taught for many years before moving to the American University in Cairo in order to establish an Egyptology program there. Haikal is particularly interested in ethno-Egyptology and the lasting impact of ancient Egypt. In 1961, Haikal became the first Egyptian woman to work in Nubia during the international salvage campaign. From 1992 to 1996, she directed the North Sinai international salvage campaign. Haikal has lectured internationally in the United States, Europe, the Far East, and Africa. As a distinguished guest professor, she taught at Charles University (Prague), La Sapienza (Roma), and Paris IV–La Sorbonne, where she was also the Blaise Pascal Chair of Research (2006–2007) at the Fondation de l'École Normale Supérieure. She is the recipient of many awards and honors including, most recently, the Knight of the Star of Italy (2020). She was presented with a festschrift in 2003, *Hommage à Fayza Haikal* (IFAO, 2003).

Jan Johnson is an Egyptologist who studies the Egyptian language, especially Demotic. She is the editor of the *Demotic Dictionary of the Oriental Institute of the University of Chicago* and author of an introductory grammar of Demotic and Egyptian grammar. She has archaeological field experience in Egypt and Jordan. She is particularly interested in women, and especially nonroyal women, in ancient Egypt, and has written on aspects of the social, economic, and legal status of women, on gender and marriage, and on "women, work, and wealth," among other topics. Perhaps the favorite lecture she has given is "Cleopatra as CEO: Bureaucracy and Scandal in the Hostile Takeover of a First-century (BCE) Multinational."

Katarzyna Kapiec is a PhD candidate at the University of Warsaw, a research assistant at the Institute of the Mediterranean and Oriental Cultures of the Polish Academy of Sciences, and a member of the Polish Centre of Mediterranean Archaeology's Polish–Egyptian Archaeological and Conservation Mission at the Temple of Hatshepsut at Deir al-Bahari, where she is responsible for the study and publication of the Southern Room of Amun.

Susan Anne Kelly is an Early Career Researcher–Egyptologist whose PhD dissertation, "Female Engagement in Domains of Social Power in Ancient Egypt's Dynasties 1–6: An Interdisciplinary Approach to Women's Titles," advanced a theoretical study of ancient biographical inscriptions that offer new perspectives into women's involvement, influence, and impact in the state's socioeconomic structure in early Egypt (conferred in June 2021); she has been granted a fellowship at Macquarie University to publish the thesis. The PhD was an extension of her master's research that identified and analyzed women of Early Dynastic Egypt from women's funerary stelae/slabs from Abu Rawash, Helwan, and Abydos. She enjoys working with the titles and inscriptional records of ancient Egypt. She has participated in archaeological fieldwork in Dendera and has presented her research at several international conferences including CRE Naples 2017; Australasian Egyptology Conference 5, Auckland; and Women in Ancient Egypt: Current Research and Historical Trends at the American University in Cairo in 2019. She became an invitational lecturer at Macquarie University for their Women and Gender in Ancient History unit in 2018 and presented to the Graduate Seminar in Oxford in 2019. Her contribution in this volume is her second publication; the first is "Women's Work in the Early Dynastic Period," *Prague Egyptological Studies* 23: 92–105. She is passionate about all things ancient Egyptian, but especially about raising the profile of women in ancient history.

AnneMarie Luijendijk is a social historian of early Christianity and a papyrologist. Much of her scholarship involves early Christianity in Egypt, especially the literary and documentary papyri from the ancient Egyptian city of Oxyrhynchus. Among her publications are *Forbidden Oracles? The Gospel of the Lots of Mary* (Tübingen: Mohr Siebeck, 2014), a book about a fifth- or sixth-century Coptic miniature codex with divinatory answers ascribed to the Virgin Mary, and *Greetings in the Lord: Early Christians and the Oxyrhynchus Papyri* (Cambridge, MA: Harvard University Press, 2008), an examination of documentary sources pertaining to the lives of Christians in Oxyrhynchus before 325. She has co-edited *From Roman to Early Christian Cyprus: Studies in Religion and Archaeology* with Laura Nasrallah and Charalambos Bakirtzis (2020); *Re-making the World: Christianity and Categories. Essays in Honor of Karen L. King* with Taylor Petrey, Ben Dunning, Carly Daniel-Hughes, and Laura Nasrallah (2019); and *My Lots Are in Thy Hands: Sortilege and Its Practitioners in Late Antiquity* with William E. Klingshirn (2018). Her current research projects are a book on the Christian literary papyri from Oxyrhynchus, *From Gospels to Garbage*, and a book on ancient shoes.

Suzanne Onstine is an associate professor in the Department of History at the University of Memphis. Suzanne received her BA in anthropology at the University of Arizona and her MA and PhD in Near and Middle Eastern Civilizations at the University of Toronto. She currently directs the University of Memphis mission to Theban Tomb 16, the tomb of Panehsy in Dra Abu-l-Naga, Luxor, and has done archaeology in Egypt for more than twenty-five years. She has published many works on religion and gender in addition to various aspects of work on TT 16.

Tara Sewell-Lasater earned a PhD in ancient history from the University of Houston, Texas. She holds two bachelor's degrees from Baylor University, one in archaeology and another in history, and a master's degree in history from the University of Texas at San Antonio. Her research interests include women in the ancient world, numismatics, and the Ptolemies. Her current research focuses on Ptolemaic queenship and the roles those royal women developed for themselves in Ptolemaic administration and society. Specifically, she strives to overturn many of the misogynistic and overly simplistic stereotypes and *topoi* that have been applied to Ptolemaic queens in previous scholarship. To that end, she is currently working on a book, *Becoming Kleopatra: The Development of Ptolemaic Queenship in Context*, which provides the first in-depth, chronological survey of Ptolemaic queens, from the first *basilissai*-consorts of the dynasty, Berenike I and Arsinoë I, to the final ruler, Kleopatra VII.

José-Ramón Pérez-Accino Picatoste is senior lecturer in Egyptology and Ancient History at the Complutense University of Madrid. He specializes in Egyptian literature, texts, and the intellectual world of the ancient Egyptians. He is the founder and director of Egiptología Complutense and he conducts fieldwork in Egypt, including at Ehnasiya al-Medina (Herakleopolis Magna) and Western Thebes, where he is co-director of the C2 Project: Royal Cache Wadi survey. He has taught Egyptology for the University of London's Birkbeck College and University College London.

Yasmin El Shazly is currently deputy director for research and programs at the American Research Center in Egypt. She previously held the positions of general supervisor of the Department of International Organizations of Cultural Heritage and International Cooperation (2016–18) and assistant to the minister for museum affairs (2015–16) at the Egyptian Ministry of Antiquities. She was also head of the Registration, Collections Management, and Documentation Department at the Egyptian Museum in Cairo (2009–16) and a member of the Museum's Board of Directors (2010–13). She has taught courses at the American University in Cairo, Cairo University, and AMIDEAST. Dr. El Shazly earned her BA from the American University in Cairo in 1998 and her MA (2002) and PhD (2009) from Johns Hopkins University. Her doctoral dissertation, entitled "Royal Ancestor Worship in Deir el-Medina during the New Kingdom," was published by Abercromby Press in 2015. She has published several academic papers and has appeared in numerous documentaries, including National Geographic's "The Silver Pharaoh: Secrets of the Dead" and "Tutankhamun: The Mystery of the Burnt Mummy," as well as the BBC documentary "The Man Who Discovered Egypt."

Reinert Skumsnes is a historian specializing in interdisciplinary research between Egyptology and feminist and anthropological theory. He also works as a field archaeologist at the site of Tell al-Amarna in Middle Egypt. Skumsnes's research focuses on social history through the lens of family and gender, with New Kingdom Egypt (1500–1000 BCE) as his specialty. He has a particular eye to alternative practices as manifest in the manifold, often contradictory expressions of family and gender, from the highly normative monumental remains to the more ephemeral nonliterary texts. He is also concerned with theoretical and methodological questions, such as relational encounters between spatially and temporally fractal positions, perspectives, and records beyond the scope of New Kingdom Egypt. Skumsnes currently holds a three-year (2020–23) international mobility grant from the Research Council of Norway for the postdoctoral project "Egyptology, Feminist Theory, and Alternative Worlds: Body/Sex/Gender in New Kingdom Egypt, and Their Affective Environments." This project is a continuation of his PhD research, but with intensified attention to the interdisciplinary potential between Egyptology and feminist theory, and between the body/sex/gender divide (present theory) and the empirical material (past practice).

Isabel Stünkel is an Egyptologist who holds both MA and PhD degrees from the University of Bonn. She is an associate curator at The Metropolitan Museum of Art, where she has held curatorial positions in the Department of Egyptian Art since 2007. She is also a member of the Museum's excavations at the pyramid complex of Senwosret III at Dahshur, where she is working on the decoration of the royal women's chapels. Before she joined The Met, she was the curator of the Egyptian Museum in Bonn.

Inmaculada Vivas Sainz conducted her doctoral research in Egyptology at the University of Alcalá in Madrid in 2004, focusing on the relations between Egypt and the Aegean area in the second millennium BCE, for which she won the PhD Excellence Award. She has enjoyed several research visits at the IFAO and at the Griffith Institute, University of Oxford. Since 2010, she has lectured on ancient Egyptian art at UNED (National Distance Education University) in Madrid, and published *Egipto y el Egeo a comienzos de la XVIII Dinastía: Una visión de sus relaciones, antecedentes e influencia iconográfica*, BARIS 2595 (Oxford: Archaeopress, 2013). Since 2017, she has been a member of the C2 Royal Cache Project in Luxor. Her research interests include iconographic interchange, innovation in New Kingdom figurative art, and the role of the ancient Egyptian artist.

Hana Vymazalová is an associate professor of Egyptology at Charles University in Prague. Her research focuses on the Old Kingdom economy, funerary cults, and ancient Egyptian science. She is a member of the Czech Mission in Abusir and a member of the Djedkare Project at south Saqqara.

Jacquelyn Williamson received her PhD in Egyptology from The Johns Hopkins University. She is a member of the archaeological expedition to Tell al-Amarna, where she directs work at Kom al-Nana, the site of Nefertiti's

Sunshade of Re Temple. She is an associate professor of ancient art and archaeology at George Mason University, and the director of the Ancient Mediterranean Art and Archaeology Minor as well as graduate studies director of the History and Art History Department at George Mason. She is the author of *Nefertiti's Sun Temple: A New Cult Complex at Tell el-Amarna* in Brill's Harvard Egyptological Studies (Leiden and Boston, 2016).

Annik Wüthrich is senior postdoctoral researcher in the ERC Starting Grant project "Challenging Time(s): A New Approach to Written Sources for Ancient Egyptian Chronology" at the Austrian Academy of Sciences and Lector of Hieratic at the University of Vienna. She studied in Geneva and Paris (EPHE) and received her PhD from the University of Geneva. She has taught and researched in Geneva, Bonn, Tübingen, Münster, and Vienna. Her research interests focus on Egyptian philology, funerary literature (especially from the first millennium BCE), the history and chronology of the Third Intermediate Period, and self-presentation in ancient Egypt. Her latest publications include *Ba-Bringer und Schattenabschneider. Untersuchungen zum sogenannten Totenbuchkapitel 191 auf Totenbuchpapyri* (2013) and *Édition synoptique et traduction des chapitres supplémentaires du Livre des Morts 162 à 167* (2015). She co-edited with Anke Ilona Blöbaum and Marianne Eaton-Krauss *Pérégrinations avec Erhart Graefe. Festschrift zu seinem 75. Geburtstag* (2018). Among her recent and forthcoming articles are "L'expression de la filiation à la 21ème dynastie: reflet d'une réalité historique ou simple effet de mode? L'exemple du Livre des Morts" in *Bulletin de la Société d'Égyptologie Française* and "The Copenhagen Wooden Stela AAd6 from the National Museum of Denmark: An Unusual Testimony of the 22nd Dynasty," in Ägypten und Levante.

Foreword

Women in Ancient Egypt: Current Research and Historical Trends

Fayza Haikal

This book is based on the proceedings of an international conference held in Cairo in the fall of 2019, in the frame of the celebrations for the centenary of the American University in Cairo. It presents a series of very interesting articles dealing with women in Egypt from the birth of the Egyptian state under the pharaohs at the end of the fourth millennium BCE to Late Antiquity and the Coptic period. The reader will find here a broad array of topics dealing with royalty as well as with the people of Egypt whose social position and agency are revealed through the titles inscribed with their (auto)biographies on the walls of their tombs or on artifacts found there.

With the new surge of feminist movements across the world during the last decades, research on women has increased noticeably. In the field of Egyptology, traditional considerations on the role of women in society, probably based on preconceptions of modern women's agency in the Middle East, are often challenged by newly discovered data and by a revisiting of ancient documentation. These now confirm that ancient Egyptian women were not just decorative elements in the royal *harim* or servants of female divinities in the temples, but that they could have access to practically all walks of life through the activities they exercised both at home and outside their houses. They were probably more active in sectors like weaving or food production, which are essential to survival and could be performed inside the home, but their titles indicate clearly that they could have access to any profession they wanted when they had the proper qualifications. It is also clear that women's contributions and visibility in society depended largely on their social class, economic power, and closeness to the pharaoh, and that their agency fluctuated according to political and historical circumstances.

That being said, one must remember that our knowledge is based on the documentation that we have and that this documentation largely depends on the hazards of excavation. The current data, for example, provide us with less material related to women from the First Intermediate Period and the Middle Kingdom than for the previous period. This could indicate that female agency, more visible during the early dynastic and Old Kingdom periods, lessened for a while during the First Intermediate Period and the Middle Kingdom only to reappear stronger afterward, as is evident from the much better documentation that we have from the New Kingdom and later periods. This, however, is unlikely as the Middle Kingdom was a brilliant period in Egyptian history, inducing creativity in all walks of life.

It is fascinating to see how history repeats itself and how Egyptian women, both royal and ordinary, have always been active in moments of crisis, again playing roles corresponding to their positions in society. We know, for example, of queens raising and encouraging troops during the wars against the Hyksos, such as Tetisheri and Ahmose-Nefertari; and ruling the country when a male heir to the throne was not immediately available, like MerytNeith, a queen of the Early Dynastic Period, and Sobekneferu, Hatshepsut, and Tawosret, to name a few. The biographies of other women of wealth mention their support and care for the poor, in this case adopting the classical phraseology used in male discourse.

From the New Kingdom onward, the much richer documentation reveals more about women's visibility and agency at all levels of the society. New titles appear, underlining the woman's position at home, where she is not only the *nbt pr* ("mistress of the house") with all the administrative and economic responsibility the role carries, but she is also called "sister" by her husband, meaning his equal. The words *akh* ("brother") and *okht* ("sister") still convey this sense of equality when used in Arabic today. Outside the home, we also find a new title: that of *ʿnḫt n niwt*, usually understood as "citizen" of a place. As for the queen, her status, already essential in the kingship ideology, is elevated further with such titles as "Wife of the God" or "Votaress of the God." This latter title gradually developed into "Hand of the God" after the New Kingdom, when it was held by a king's daughter and identified her with the goddess Hathor in the solar/Heliopolitan creation myth. During her coronation, her names were written in cartouches, clearly indicating that she held a politico-religious position similar only to that of the pharaoh whom she represented in Thebes. This position disappeared after the Twenty-sixth Dynasty, but the power and agency of wealthy women continued, as is evident from burials of that period recently discovered in Saqqara.

Unfortunately, power is often stronger than justice and beauty, and the position of women in Egypt, so avant-garde in antiquity, received its first blows from the West with the conquest of Egypt by Alexander the Great and the Hellenization of Egypt—first by the Ptolemies and their imposition of Greek laws, then later by the Romans. In neither of those cultures did women possess the same freedom and power as they had in ancient Egypt. However, genius makes itself known even in restrictive circumstances. We recall the great female scholar, Hypatia, who lived in Alexandria under Roman rule, when Christianity reached Egypt. Despite the important contributions to society by her and others, principles of modesty in the new religion imposed less visibility upon women, who were often writing from within nunneries or from their homes. In contrast, in the Oxyrhynchus papyri, for example, we encounter priestesses working as letter writers, copyists of texts, and so forth.

In addition to investigating the social position and agency of Egyptian women in antiquity, this volume also presents a number of very interesting articles related to medical care for women's health and fertility alongside medical studies related to people of both genders.

Although these papers on Egyptian women in antiquity deal with subjects up until the Arab conquest of the country, it is important to note that, contrary to what the general public may believe, prestigious and influential women continued to exist in Egypt despite their visibility being controlled. Shajar al-Durr, who ruled Egypt briefly in the mid-thirteenth century when it was fighting the crusaders, is a famous example. In modern Egypt, feminist movements have been well documented for a little over a century. The first and most famous of those was probably that of 1919 led by Hoda Sha'arawy, a young, intellectual, upper-class activist who organized the largest women's anti-British demonstration for the independence of Egypt, walking the streets of Cairo alongside men. In 1923, she founded the Egyptian Feminist Union, which she led until her death in 1947. After Sha'arawy's death, the activities of the Union slowly decreased until they finally stopped. Yet this first feminist organization incited the birth of over a thousand subsequent women's organizations across Egypt and, with the opening of the first Egyptian national university in Giza around 1925, accepting both male and female students, women began to graduate and work in all professions, including aviation and engineering. Today women are employed everywhere in Egypt and, as always in periods of crisis—as in the January 2011 upheavals—they have stood with their male compatriots on the streets. It is appropriate then that in October of that same year, the Egyptian Feminist Union was reestablished under the leadership of Dr. Hoda Badran.

Throughout the long history of Egypt, women have contributed to the maintenance, continuation, and development of their culture and society. Their visibility in the records has varied according to their social class and economic power. In periods of crisis, educated women have always stood alongside their male compatriots, faced adverse situations, and encouraged and gathered around them strong women from different backgrounds. This point emphasizes once more the importance of education and economic autonomy for the empowerment of women and for the establishment of equality between genders in modern societies.

1

Moving Beyond Gender Bias

Mariam F. Ayad

Ancient Egyptian culture is very well documented.[1] Its long history spans at least three millennia, and more if we consider cultural survivals into the Hellenistic, Roman, and Late Antique periods. Thousands of hieroglyphic inscriptions survive on temple and tomb walls, on stone slab stelae, and on various sorts of funerary equipment (offering tables, coffins and sarcophagi, canopic jars, and *shabti* figurines, to name a few). In addition to these religious texts, thousands of other texts dealing with various aspects of daily life survive on ostraca and papyrus fragments. Comprising administrative texts, personal letters, legal documents, tax receipts, and a myriad of other business-related documents, these texts are written in the cursive scripts of hieratic and demotic, and later, in Greek or Coptic. Egyptian women appear in all these texts, sometimes as the central figure in a text or on a monument, and other times less focally as a family member appearing in a tomb scene next to the tomb owner or mentioned in someone's genealogy or in personal correspondence.

Since the late 1960s, numerous studies and doctoral dissertations have focused on the role of ancient Egyptian women in their society, with books dealing with women in ancient Egypt appearing on an almost annual basis since the early 1990s.[2] With their ability to work outside the home, inherit and dispose of property, initiate divorce, testify in court, and serve on a local town council (*ḳnbt*),[3] women in ancient Egypt exercised more legal rights and economic independence than their counterparts throughout antiquity.[4] Yet we still encounter statements in current scholarship that misrepresent ancient

Egyptian women by undermining their role(s) in their society and particularly their ability to act independently. This dismissive attitude is most obvious in three areas in particular: 1) women exercising power; 2) women's economic independence; 3) and female literacy. As will be demonstrated below, this dismissive attitude and associated labels are not grounded in evidence, but reflect a modern, predominately male, scholarly bias regarding what constitutes femininity and the accompanying notions of what women could do.

Women Exercising Power

Traditional attitudes regarding women exercising power in ancient Egypt share the assumption that women held their positions and titles in name only while a male relative or high-ranking official wielded actual power or pulled strings behind the scenes. This underlying assumption has been repeated in one way or another in published scholarship almost irrespective of the surviving evidence. In the next few paragraphs, I will discuss three illustrative examples where such attitudes are most pronounced.

Hatshepsut

The clearest example of this attitude is Hatshepsut, whose transformation from royal wife and sister into a reigning king in her own right has long fascinated Egyptologists. Although recent scholarship has attempted to rectify our views of Hatshepsut,[5] Gardiner's view of her reign has dominated the field, primarily because his *Egypt of the Pharaohs: An Introduction* continues to be used as a textbook in introductory courses on the history of ancient Egypt. In it, he writes: "It is not to be imagined, however, that even a woman of the most virile character could have attained such a pinnacle of power without masculine support."[6] Echoes of that view may still be found in more recent history books. For example, we read that "during her lifetime, [Hatshepsut] faced less opposition than might have been expected . . . [having] relied on a certain number of prominent figures of whom the foremost was a man called Senenmut."[7] Senenmut held several important positions: he was the chief overseer of works of Amun in *Djeser-djeseru* (Hatsheput's funerary temple at Deir al-Bahari) and, more importantly, he was entrusted with the education of Hatshepsut's only daughter, Neferure, becoming her tutor, often appearing in statues with her on his lap or wrapped in his cloak. As chief steward of Amun, Senenmut must have also supervised the construction of the new Temple of Mut in the southern precinct of Karnak.[8] The idea that Senenmut's rise to power was a result of his "intimate relations with the queen" may still be found in history textbooks,[9] although there is no reliable evidence of such a love affair,[10] of him holding power independently of Queen Hatshepsut, or of him making or influencing important decisions. In fact, neither Senenmut's rise to prominence from obscurity nor his appointment to multiple positions in various administrative and religious spheres is unique. Hatshepsut's appointment of several other trusted officials into key administrative, religious, military, and economic positions allowed her to create overlapping and intersecting spheres of power, which in turn allowed her to insert herself in every aspect of the country's administration.[11] So, while previously the focus has been on Senenmut's rise to power as an example of how a senior male official held real power, viewing his career in a broader context as one of several senior administrators appointed by Hatshepsut illustrates not his unique power but the queen's.

Additionally, Hatshepsut implemented a very elaborate religious program that included the instigation of several key religious festivals and the promotion of the cult of the goddess Mut at Karnak.[12] In her funerary temple at Deir al-Bahari, Hatshepsut also gave pictorial form to the myth of royal divine conception and birth, wherein Amun-Re took on the form of her earthly father during a conjugal union with the queen mother. The impregnated queen later gave birth to baby Hatshepsut, who is subsequently presented to various gods. Later, that cycle of scenes was copied by Amenhotep III and inscribed verbatim on the walls of the Luxor Temple.[13] Politically and ideologically, Hatshepsut further affirmed her legitimacy to rule by claiming responsibility for the expulsion of the Hyksos more than 150 years after their departure from Egypt.[14] During her twenty-year reign, Hatshepsut mounted a seafaring expedition to the land of Punt[15] and launched four to six military campaigns, possibly leading one herself.[16] Yet her reign is often described as "peaceable," and her campaigns "few in number and . . . undertaken on a limited scale."[17] Similarly, her titulary, iconography, and textual pronouncements have been labeled as propagandistic "fabrication(s)" aimed to legitimate an otherwise unacceptable reign.[18] However, such labels may reflect a modern, predominately male scholarly bias regarding what constitutes femininity and the accompanying notions of womanly inclinations and capabilities.[19]

Hatshepsut's adoption of royal titles, regalia, and iconography were part of the legitimation process of a new king.[20] She was neither a lovestruck figurehead doing the bidding of a powerful male lover nor a manipulative usurper scheming to steal what was not rightfully hers. Instead, as Williamson suggests, Hatshepsut's ascent to power was necessitated by a compelling national crisis and the subsequent power vacuum and was thus well within the legitimate religious and political framework of her milieu.[21]

The idea that an influential woman must have been a figurehead manipulated by powerful male subordinates is not limited to Hatshepsut alone nor is it confined to older, dated scholarship.

The God's Wife of Amun

The same dismissive attitude may also be found in connection with the women who held the title of God's Wife of Amun (GWA) during the Third Intermediate and Saite periods. The title first appears in its full form, *ḥmt nṯr n Ỉmn*, at the beginning of the Eighteenth Dynasty, when Ahmose conferred the title on his Chief Royal Wife, Ahmose-Nefertari.[22] He also established an endowment associated with this office that "no future king" would be able to revoke.[23] The title continued to be held by royal wives, including Hatshepsut, who often used it as her sole title, indicating that perhaps it was her favorite title. But shortly after Hatshepsut's reign, the title fell into abeyance. Later, in the politically tumultuous Third Intermediate Period, Osorkon III of the Twenty-third Dynasty revived the title, but instead of giving it to a royal wife, his royal daughter, Shepenwepet I, became a GWA. Her appointment served to consolidate his power in the Theban region. Four more princesses became GWA: two were Nubian—Amenirdis I and Shepenwepet II—and two were Saite—Nitocris and Ankhnesneferibre. In those uncertain times of dynastic change, the GWA became instrumental in achieving a smooth transition of power in the Theban region.[24] With the position of the high priest of Amun vacant for over fifty years, the Nubian GWAs became the highest-ranking individuals at Karnak, at the head of the Theban clergy.[25] As evidenced by the Nitocris Adoption Stela, the estates of GWAs were not limited to the Theban region. Furthermore, a newly installed GWA was provided with vast amounts of daily and monthly rations.[26] As a result, the cumulative wealth of a GWA only increased with time. Despite the tremendous religious power and economic independence that these royal princesses enjoyed, their influence and effectiveness have been regularly undermined by scholars in several ways, some of which have already been discussed in the treatment of Hatshepsut.

For instance, the GWA's role in temple ritual has often been inaccurately sexualized.[27] Like other representations of musicians and dancers, scenes showing a GWA playing the sistrum before Amun-Re have been interpreted as aimed at arousing the god sexually. I have argued elsewhere against this interpretation.[28] In the Karnak chapel of Osiris, Ruler of Eternity (*ḥḳ3 ḏt*), originally built under Libyan rule and later enlarged by the Nubians, an inscription captioning a scene showing Amenirdis I playing the sistrum before Amun-Re clearly states that "her father is pleased with her," not because of her music, voice, or appearance, but rather because she had "erected her monument for her father, Osiris, Ruler of Eternity. She erected for him an august temple <for> her Lord, a place for eternity through the work of knowledgeable craftsmen in a work project for eternity."[29] Likewise, further undermining the power and influence of the GWA, Redford asserted that real power lay in the hands of the high-ranking Theban administrators in the employ of the GWA and further suggested that the GWA's court "was more a theme park than city hall."[30] This clever turn of phrase manages to trivialize the GWA by applying infantilizing language to their court, while simultaneously denying them the more official-sounding "city hall," which is, by implication, considered as a necessarily masculine space.

Similarly, a distinct aversion to using proper vocabulary can be seen when describing iconographic scenes depicting the GWA participating in what were traditionally exclusively royal rites. On the jambs leading into the Libyan section of the chapel of Osiris, Ruler of Eternity (*ḥḳꜣ ḏt*), Shepenwepet I appears four times in two sets of symmetrically opposed scenes. On the upper register of both jambs, she is suckled by a goddess, while on the lower register, Amun places elaborate crowns on her head.[31] However, when these scenes were first published, Fazzini chose to caption them as "Amun . . . adjusts or imposes the GWA Shepenwepet I headdress."[32] Fazzini's overly cautious choice of words obscures the fact that the king's crowning scenes are very similarly depicted. In fact, scenes of suckling and crowning are commonly found in the king's coronation cycle and are part of his legitimation process. The milk of a goddess was believed to imbue the king with his divinity.[33] Shepenwepet's scenes should be similarly interpreted as part of her investiture as GWA.

I have argued elsewhere that each of the five GWA built on and expanded on the legitimacy and privileges acquired by her predecessor.[34] This trend includes the gradual assumption of priestly duties,[35] which culminated in Ankhnesneferibre officially becoming the High Priest of Amun (HPA), even prior to her appointment as GWA. Notably, she is named HPA three times on her adoption stela.[36] Disregarding her attainment of the high priesthood of Amun, a privilege never accorded a woman before, some have suggested that Ankhnesneferibre's accumulation of titles and epithets was a sign of weakness, not an expression of her increasingly far-reaching powers.[37]

A Female Vizier?

Toward the end of the Sixth Dynasty, Nebet, an elite woman, held the title of vizier. She is known from a funerary stela (CG 1758) bearing her name and title, *ṯꜣtyt*, a feminized form of the Egyptian term for vizier.[38] The stela, which was recovered from Abydos, shows Nebet standing, facing right, and holding a lotus flower to her nose (fig. 1.1). Opposite her, on the right side of the stela, a man is depicted standing facing her. He is represented at a slightly larger scale, possibly to indicate his anatomically larger size or his more elevated status. Although scale was regularly used to indicate status in Egyptian art,[39] Nebet's rightward orientation breaks away from the more conventional way of depicting couples in two-dimensional art. Typically, the rightward orientation—considered to be the position of primacy—would be reserved for the man.[40]

Fig. 1.1. Nebet standing on the left, her titles inscribed in the three columns just above her figure. Stela GC 1578 from Abydos.

Explanations of Nebet's title and epithets, seemingly unique until the Twenty-sixth Dynasty,[41] are wide-ranging and occasionally contradictory. Although there is no agreement on whether the titles were conferred upon her during her own lifetime or posthumously, either way, they are considered "wholly honorific."[42] Fischer and Strudwick have assumed that if indeed Nebet held the title of vizier during her lifetime, then she would have held the title in name only, while her husband performed the duties of vizier.[43] Although there is no evidence of this peculiar arrangement occurring in this particular case or indeed ever in Egypt's long history, the idea of "job sharing" has been repeated several times in conjunction with Nebet. In an alternate theory, Nebet acquired the titles posthumously in an attempt to elevate her status and obscure her otherwise humble background after two of her descendants married into the royal family and became mothers to kings Merenre and Pepi II.[44] However, the family's status would have been equally elevated—possibly even more effectively so—if the title of vizier had been given to her husband instead.[45] Behind the different theories, which are sometimes espoused simultaneously despite their contradictory premises,[46] is the assumption that Nebet, and by extension her descendants, came from a common or nonroyal background and that this was a situation that needed to be remedied somehow, even if posthumously. In a recent article, however, Kanawati has argued that Nebet may actually have been a member of the extended royal family, and suggested that she was the daughter of King Wenis and his wife Nebet.[47] By marrying two of her daughters, Pepi I would have married two of his own cousins, not two commoners.[48] Nebet's appointment as vizier would then have been part of a deliberate royal strategy aimed at consolidating royal power by appointing trusted members of the royal entourage, or family, into key government positions.[49] Kanawati's explanation of Nebet's exceptional position seems more plausible than a convoluted, and equally exceptional, posthumous honorific appointment. Be that as it may, there are several documented instances in Egyptian history where we find kings hailing from modest backgrounds or marrying into nonroyal families, boasting about their rise to power or the families they married into or, at the very least, not attempting to obscure their backgrounds by awarding titles, posthumously, to deceased family members.[50] Underlying these various theories is a deep-rooted belief that a woman could have never become a vizier in ancient Egypt, and if the evidence indicates otherwise, then it must be explained away, dismissed, or ignored altogether.[51] Nebet's title as vizier is indeed intriguing, as are her other epithets, but it seems that several prominent scholars are willing to consider all imaginable possibilities except that Nebet may have actually performed the duties of vizier.

On Women's Economic Independence

Egyptian women, especially of the Old Kingdom, certainly held religious and administrative titles. Several Old Kingdom women are known to have been responsible for the burials of their sons, indicating that these mothers had accumulated enough economic resources to pay for the construction and decoration of their sons' tombs.[52] Later, in the New Kingdom, the evidence suggests that women had a measure of autonomy regarding the dispensation of their resources. For example, we know from Ramesside documents that women could indeed dispose of their property as they wished, disinheriting some and bequeathing property to others.[53]

Yet evidence for women's employment and their economic independence has been regularly undermined or dismissed altogether. All too often, evidence of women's employment outside the home, as signified by their titles, is downplayed, their titles considered "honorific."[54] Women's titles in the temple and the administration are hardly, if ever, viewed as potentially income-generating.[55] For example, Fischer presents evidence of two Old Kingdom sisters, both of whom held a feminized version of the title "director of the works," but he dismisses the possibility that their titles could have entailed any supervisory duties, arguing that "the term 'director' [was] a relative one," and suggesting, once again, that their titles were honorific.[56] In this volume, Kelly presents some of the results of her doctoral research and argues that women's titles in the Old Kingdom could indeed reflect their activity in the economic domain.[57]

Noting the fragmentary nature of the evidence, Quirke points out that two of the "most splendid sets of burial equipment" belong to women, suggesting that the women, both chantresses, may have acquired their wealth not only through inheritance but possibly due to their association with the choral service in the temple, which would have allowed them a "share in the divine estates."[58]

Apart from temple service, women's involvement in income-generating activities has been downplayed by scholars. For example, the feminine title *šmst* is usually translated as "handmaiden" or "maidservant,"[59] while a masculine version of the title, *šmsw*, has been understood as "guard" or "bodyguard," depending on the context.[60] The widely varying translations obscure the fact that both the masculine and feminine versions of the title share the same root. A gender-neutral, literal translation of "follower" (or "retainer"),[61] would convey the original sense of the Egyptian title while simultaneously avoiding the denigration of the women who held this title.

In a similar manner, while several women are labeled as "female scribes" (*sšt*/*sẖ3t*) on objects dating to the Middle Kingdom,[62] the evidence for such women has been dismissed, ignored, or misinterpreted. In several instances, the argument has been that the final letter, the feminine marker "*t*," is missing or that it is a mistakenly read, superfluous blot of ink or surface damage.[63] At other times, the hieratic sign for *sš/sẖ3* itself has been called into question.[64]

The most creative dismissal of "female scribes," however, may be traced back to a short article published by Posener in 1969. In it, he rejected the possibility that the female holders of the title *sšt/sẖ3t nt r.s*, literally translated as "(female) scribe of her mouth," were scribes acting in a secretarial capacity in the service of other women, suggesting instead that they were cosmeticians, who would arguably apply lip liner to the mouths of the elite women they served.[65] Regrettably, Posener's translation of the title as "make-up artist" or "cosmetician" was uncritically accepted and included in such standard reference works as Ward's *Index to Middle Kingdom Titles* and *Essays on Feminine Titles*.[66] Although Fischer pointed out that the Egyptians did not use lip liners and that a cosmetician's title would have referred to eyes rather than lips or the mouth, the translation of the title as "beautician" or "cosmetician" persisted even after the publication of Fischer's 1976 essay.[67] One of the main reasons cited for adhering to Posener's translation is that this title occurs among a list of subordinates that include hairdressers,[68] a point that was deemed irrelevant by Bryan.[69]

I have argued elsewhere that the title should really be translated as "(female)-scribe of her utterance."[70] The possessive in the title remains enigmatic and could be taken as a reference to an elite woman in whose service a female scribe worked, possibly taking down dictation and generally acting as a secretary or personal assistant.[71] Evidence of women serving women abounds, and ranges from the Old Kingdom up to the Late Period.[72] An alternate interpretation would view the possessive after "utterance," *r.s*, as referring to the female scribe herself, not her mistress, leading to a translation of the epithet as a "scribe of her [*own*] utterance." According to this interpretation, the title would refer to some sort of a creative composition on the part of the female scribe, possibly as a lyricist. In my view, either interpretation would better resolve the issues posed by the preposition and associated pronoun than Fischer's suggestion that the title describes a "woman who was able to report on inventory and accounts as a scribe did, but orally."[73]

However that may be, it seems reasonable to link the reluctance to acknowledge female scribes with the broader discussion of female literacy in ancient Egypt and the seemingly relentless effort to dismiss evidence pointing to women's literacy.

On Female Literacy

Attitudes toward evidence pointing to female literacy have not been much different from attitudes toward females holding power and influence or being economically independent. In 1983, Baines and Eyre published an article on literacy in ancient Egypt in which they briefly discussed the issue of female literacy in ancient Egypt.[74] In that article, they narrowly defined literate persons as "those who completed their training and then exercised a literate function in adult life."[75] They then used that definition to estimate the percentage of literacy in ancient Egyptian society, which they placed at 1 percent for the general population and ranging between 5 and 7.5 percent for the community of workers at Deir al-Medina.[76] These percentages, however, have been criticized as too low for a culture as prolific as that of ancient Egypt, and the methodology and models used to arrive at these estimates have been questioned.[77] Using this narrow definition excludes not just women, but also a sizable portion of Egyptian society.

It is remarkable that, in their discussion of female literacy, the authors do not acknowledge that women bearing administrative titles would have needed to be literate in order to fulfill their official duties. Rather, they dismissively consider female administrative titles as honorific, exceptional, or unworthy of inclusion because most of these titles are attested in the service of other women. Thus, Nebet's employment as vizier is deemed "uncertain" at best, while the Middle Kingdom scarabs of female scribes are but a few that "must *naturally* be set against the thousands of known scarabs with male titles."[78] Ireteru, a Twenty-sixth Dynasty female scribe in the employ of the God's Wife Nitocris, is mentioned in this context, but the authors seem ambivalent about the evidence, writing that "the title 'female scribe' was itself striking enough to convey an important message of status."[79] Others have considered the evidence provided by her titles "too late" to be relevant for discussions of female literacy in earlier periods.[80]

The debate regarding Nebet's titles has been summarized above and does not need to be repeated here, but the evidence for Middle Kingdom female scribes extends beyond the few scarabs cited by Baines and Eyre. In addition to p.Boulaq 18, discussed above, women are identified as *sšt/sẖ3t*, or "female scribes," on several Middle Kingdom stelae.[81] Further, since the publication of their remarks on Ireteru, her tomb has been excavated by the South Asasif Project and more information regarding her status and titles has emerged.[82]

As for women working for women, it is not only conceivable but also quite probable that a queen or a princess, as well as other elite women, would need to use the services of an underling to do their accounting, correspondence, and so forth. Indeed, the God's Wives of Amun had an extensive staff of male *and* female attendants from the early Eighteenth Dynasty through the end of the Twenty-sixth Dynasty,[83] as did the queens of the Old, Middle, and New Kingdoms. In fact, the evidence suggests that Queen Ashayet employed one or more female scribes who were considered important enough to be included in the inscriptions on the queen's coffin (CG 47267).[84] On the interior of her coffin, a hieratic inscription identified a woman carrying a jar and a mirror as a (female) scribe. On the coffin's exterior, a woman leads the queen by the hand.[85] She is labeled as a "scribe." However, since the signs are not fully carved, the identification remains tenuous, leading Bryan to consider this as the "most ambiguous example."[86]

Baines and Eyre used five categories of evidence in their assessment of literacy: iconographic scenes and material objects such as scribal palettes; titles; letters (to the living and to the dead); and (auto-)biographical texts. However, in their discussion of female literacy, they fail to treat two categories that may point to female literacy: iconographic evidence and (auto-)biographical texts.

In the Sixth Dynasty tomb of Princess Seshseshet Idut in Saqqara, the princess is represented standing in a boat, sniffing a lotus flower as she inspects six registers of attendants, hunting, fishing, and snaring birds. She wears a tight sheath dress, anklets, and a sidelock of youth. Her larger-than-life scale of representation points to her importance. Behind Idut, at a much smaller scale, is a female attendant who is identified as "*mnˁt nbt*." Represented behind both women is a scribal kit depicted atop a scribal desk (fig. 1.2).[87] The Egyptian title *mnˁ*/*mnˁt* is attested for both men and women. When a woman is labeled as *mnˁt*, the title has traditionally been taken to indicate that she was a "wet nurse." However, when men hold the masculine version of the title, it is typically translated as "tutor."[88] The scribal kit and box represented behind the two standing women may then indicate that Nebet was Idut's governess, or that either or both women were proud of their ability to write. Regardless, the message is that it was acceptable for a woman to indicate her possession of such items, thus indicating her literacy visually.

Instead of contemplating the significance of depicting this scribal kit, this scene has typically been excluded from all discussion. Idut's tomb was originally intended for the use of a male official. Accordingly, the assumption has been that the writing equipment belonged to the tomb's previous owner and should not be considered as Idut's or her attendant's. Their presence in this scene is thus dismissed as a mistake or an oversight on the part of the ancient artists and scribes. In actuality, this is not the case. In her doctoral research examining female reuse of previously decorated tombs, Betbeze was able to

Fig. 1.2. Idut standing, a scribal box behind her, Hall B, West Wall (= PM III², 617 and plan LXIII (7)).

demonstrate that when women appropriated tombs originally decorated for male officials, scenes that were inappropriate for female use were recarved and repainted.[89] Those scenes that were considered suitable and acceptable for the use of females were retained. Thus, even if the scribal desk and kit had been part of the tomb's original decorative scheme, the fact that they were retained for Idut's use indicates that it was acceptable for a woman in her position, a princess and an "overseer of cloth,"[90] to possess and use writing equipment.

Further iconographic evidence of women possessing scribal kits was collected and published by Bryan in 1985.[91] In five New Kingdom Theban tombs, writing equipment appears underneath the chairs of women, where normally one might find prestige objects such as mirrors, unguent jars, or the occasional pet baboon.[92] In a few instances, the women seem to share their seat with a husband, or their separate seats overlap in the representation (e.g., fig. 1.3).

Fig. 1.3. Henuttawy and Menna seated, a scribal kit under her seat, Tomb of Menna (TT 69), Broad Hall, right

Fig. 1.4. Tomb of Amenemope (TT 148), Broad Hall, southern Statue Room, West Wall

This arrangement has led some scholars to suggest that the scribal kits actually belonged to the men and not to the women. However, this is not the case in the five tombs studied by Bryan, including TT 148, where male and female members of the deceased's family are depicted seated on separate, *non-overlapping* chairs.[93] Underneath each chair is a prestige object: an unguent jar or a scribal pouch (fig. 1.4), but the assignment of objects does not seem to be gender-specific. Several of the women have scribal pouches underneath their chairs, just as several men have unguent jars under theirs.

While it might be argued that the interpretation of such iconographic scenes is up for debate, one would think that scribal palettes, inscribed with a woman's name, would provide sufficient evidence of that woman's literacy. Yet that has not been the case, as the evidence provided by women's palettes has been deemed inconclusive. For example, a scribal palette bearing the name of Akhenaten's daughter, Princess Meketaten (MMA 26.7.1295), has been variously interpreted as a votive object, a toy, or even a painter's palette.[94] Contrary to Hayes's assessment, this ivory palette, with its four ink wells (of red, black, and yellow pigments), is reasonably sized to have been used by a royal princess.[95] Furthermore, as Bryan pointed out, the presence of a pen holder in this palette sets it apart from other known painters' palettes.[96] In Dorothea Arnold's assessment, Meketaten's is a "writing palette."[97] A pen holder is also found in another palette belonging to another Amarna princess, Meritaten, whose palette was discovered in Tutankhamun's tomb.[98] Baines and Eyre considered Meritaten's palette (but not Meketaten's) in their discussion of female literacy, suggesting that its small size made it only usable for painting a "vignette or figured ostracon."[99] Size, coupled with the atypical presence of several colored pigments (white, yellow, green, and traces of blue in addition to the more typical red and black pigments normally associated with scribal palettes) led Baines and Eyre to discount it as evidence of the literacy of its royal owner. Although a royal princess could conceivably have had access to a luxury item with luxury pigments and would not have been limited to what was commonly available to regular scribes, the lighter pigments (white and yellow) especially seem to indicate that Meritaten's palette may indeed have been used for painting rather than writing. That does not preclude, however, that a royal princess, especially of the Amarna Period, would have had access to a palace education.

Finally, by omitting from their discussion the evidence for women's (auto-)biographical texts, Baines and Eyre further assumed that women did not possess this particular marker of literacy. But (auto-)biographical texts are attested for women. An Eleventh Dynasty biographical text was discovered in Bersha and at least four different inscriptions dating from the Twenty-second to the Twenty-sixth Dynasties have been published and discussed in recent scholarship.[100]

The next category of evidence that Baines and Eyre used in their essay is "letters to the living and to the dead." Once more, they dismissed letters addressed by or to women on the assumption that they might have been written by someone else.[101] A similar opinion that has been echoed more recently as well is that "[i]t is practically impossible, however, to prove that women penned the letters themselves, and it remains a plausible possibility that they dictated the letters to a *literate person*."[102] The implication is that such a "literate person" would be some male relative or professional scribe. However, this and similar statements do not take into account that notes from and to women are frequently very brief, often abrupt, lack the florid language of more formal letters, and would not need the services of a scribe. Moreover, some of the women's notes to one another discuss very personal matters that would best remain private.[103]

By very narrowly defining literacy as a skill needed for a professional role in the administration, Baines and Eyre managed to exclude not only women but also the vast majority of ancient Egypt's population from the "literate classes." Applying those stringent criteria to women, they engaged in what has been called the "'add women and stir' approach . . . where gender issues are tacked on to existing, usually androcentric, paradigms."[104] Despite various flaws in their methodology, pointed out by Lesko and others, their suggested literacy rate of 1 percent for the general population during the Old Kingdom has now acquired the status of "fact." It is a status never originally intended by the authors, who wrote that their article was meant to generate discussion on the issue of literacy in ancient Egypt.[105] A more nuanced approach to female literacy, and literacy in general, may be found in Szpakowska's discussion of this issue, in which she acknowledges that reading and writing, while related abilities, are two different skill sets.[106]

Concluding Remarks

In ignoring the evidence for women's (auto-)biographical texts and not considering iconographic evidence showing women in possession of scribal kits, Baines and Eyre discounted two major elements from their consideration of female literacy. While they may not have been aware of the evidence at the time of their article's original publication in 1983, it is remarkable that these elements were not considered in the updated version of the article, published in 2007.

While applying their own androcentric criteria to female literacy, insisting on examining the evidence for women's literacy through the very narrow lens of administrative function, Baines and Eyre went a step further. They set about dismissing all evidence for female involvement in the administration, as seen in their discussion of the Old Kingdom vizier Nebet and Middle Kingdom female scribes, as well as downplaying the impact of women working in the service of other women and the need for at least some of them to be literate in order to carry out their duties. The tendency to downplay the impact of women's work is not limited to its potential impact on literacy rates but extends to issues pertaining to women's earning power and implications about their work outside the home.

When elite women are shown to have held titles denoting work outside the home, their titles are considered "honorific" (e.g., *šmꜥyt*, *ḥmt-nṯr*, and *ṯꜣyt*), bearing no actual responsibility, or are interpreted in an inaccurate or overly sexualized manner (e.g. *ẖkrt-nsw*, *ẖnrwt*, and *ḥmt-nṯr*).

Male and female titles sharing the same root have been translated in drastically different ways. For example, as mentioned previously, *šmsw* may be translated as "guard" when found in association with the king or his palace, but its feminine counterpart, *šmst*, is translated as "handmaiden" or "maidservant." A more gender-neutral and literal translation of this title as simply "follower" might be more prudent.

Unfounded sexualized interpretations of female titles can be seen, for instance, in the interpretation of the feminine title *ẖkrt-nsw*. That title was initially interpreted as "concubine," but careful examination of the women who held it demonstrates that the title was borne by high-ranking provincial women who were connected to the royal palace. Eventually, the revisionist translation of "lady-in-waiting" became a standard way of translating this title.[107] Conversely, *ẖnr*/*ẖnrwt* is still regularly translated as "*harim*," despite several studies showing the unsuitability of this interpretation.[108]

In spite of consistent efforts by (predominately female) Egyptologists from the late 1970s onward, titles and epithets denoting ancient Egyptian women's work outside the home still are often dismissed as honorific, or treated in an overly sexualized manner, or reduced to servant status. Considered separately, some of these arguments may appear cogent, logical, or even plausible. However, viewed collectively, they have the effect of a concerted effort—conscious or unconscious—to undermine ancient Egyptian women's agency, as seen in their ability to exercise power in influential positions, in their self-expression through written modes of communication, or in exercising economic autonomy.

The studies presented in this volume aim to help correct this skewed view of ancient Egyptian women. The volume commences with a thorough examination of the earliest written evidence of Egyptian women, both royal and nonroyal, followed by six studies dealing with Egyptian queens. Ten papers, representing the bulk of the studies presented in this volume, deal with evidence pointing to the legal status and economic role of nonroyal women from the First Dynasty through the Old, Middle, and New Kingdoms, the Late Period, the Greco-Roman Period, and up to the fifth century CE. Within this sweeping chronological range, each work is intensely focused on the evidence recovered from a particular site or a specific time period. Two studies deal with the funerary texts and funerary equipment of elite women of the New Kingdom and Third Intermediate Period, while three focus on the female body, its health and adornment. This volume concludes with a chapter that examines female bodily adornment and tattoos. Rather than following a strictly chronological arrangement in this volume, a thematic presentation enables the readers to discern diachronic patterns of continuity and change within each group of women. It is hoped that this volume will be the first among many in a series focused on current research on women in ancient Egypt resulting from meetings similar to the one held at the American University in Cairo in Fall 2019, where we can come together to compare notes and learn from one another.

Acknowledgments

Finally, I would like to express my heartfelt gratitude to Dr. Alaa Adris, Associate Provost for Research, Innovation, and Creativity, and Ms. Heba Sheta, Manager, Advancement in Humanities and Creativity, for their support and encouragement throughout the planning phase of the conference on Women in Ancient Egypt: Current Research and Historical Trends, held at AUC October 31–November 2, 2019 and for supporting the publication of its proceedings, which appear in this volume.

Special thanks go to the members of the scientific committee who vetted the dozens of abstracts received in response to our Call for Papers: my colleagues at the American University in Cairo, Professors Fayza Haikal, Salima Ikram, and Lisa Sabbahy; Professor Ola al-Aguizy of Cairo University's Faculty of Archaeology; and Professor Laila Azzam of Helwan University's Faculty of Arts, without whose dedication and expertise the conference would not have been as broad in scope or as intense in its level of scholarship.

Last, but not least, I would also like to thank Ms. Heba Amer, Senior Application Developer at AUC's Tech Solutions Department, for her technical support and for recommending and following up on the software used to organize the conference. I would be remiss not to thank Mr. Samir Kamel, Financial Director, School of Humanities and Social Sciences, without whose help none of this could have happened.

Notes

1 An earlier version of this paper was presented at the International Conference on *Women in Ancient Egypt: Current Research and Historical Trends*, held at the American University in Cairo, October 31–November 2, 2019.

2 E.g., Steffen Wenig, *Die Frau im Alten Ägypten* (Leipzig: Helmut Heyne, 1967); Wenig, *The Woman in Egyptian Art* (New York: McGraw-Hill, 1969); Barbara S. Lesko, *The Remarkable Women of Ancient Egypt* (Berkeley: B.C. Scribe Publications, 1978); and B.S. Lesko, ed., *Women's Earliest Records from Ancient Egypt and Western Asia* (Atlanta: Scholars' Press, 1989); Gay Robins, "Egyptian Queens in the Eighteenth Dynasty up to the Reign of Amenhotep III" (PhD diss.,

Oxford University, 1981); Lisa Kuchman Sabbahy, "The Development of the Titulary and Iconography of the Ancient Egyptian Queen from Dynasty One to Early Dynasty Eighteen" (PhD diss., University of Toronto, 1982); Christiane Desroches-Noblecourt, *La femme au temps des pharaons* (Paris: L. Pernoud, 1986); Barbara Watterson, *Women in Ancient Egypt* (New York: St. Martin's Press, 1991); Sylvia Falke, *Die Frau im Alten Aegypten* (Berlin: PZ, 1992); Gay Robins, *Women in Ancient Egypt* (Cambridge, MA: Harvard University Press, 1993); Joyce A. Tyldesley, *Daughters of Isis: Women of Ancient Egypt* (London and New York: Viking, 1994); Zahi H. Hawass, *Silent Images: Women in Pharaonic Egypt* (Cairo: Ministry of Culture, 1995); Anne K. Capel and Glenn E. Markoe, eds., *Mistress of the House, Mistress of Heaven: Women in Ancient Egypt* (New York: Hudson Hills Press, 1996); Henry G. Fischer, *Egyptian Women of the Old Kingdom and of the Heracleopolitan Period* (New York: The Metropolitan Museum of Art, 1989, 2000); Jaana Toivari-Viitala, *Women at Deir el-Medina: A Study of the Status and Roles of the Female Inhabitants in the Workmen's Community during the Ramesside Period.* EGU 15 (Leiden: NINO, 2001); Wolfram Grajetzki, *Ancient Egyptian Queens: A Hieroglyphic Dictionary* (London: Golden House Publications, 2005); Carolyn Graves-Brown, *Dancing for Hathor: Women in Ancient Egypt* (London: Continuum, 2010); Vivienne G. Callender, *In Hathor's Image* 1: *The Wives and Mothers of Egyptian Kings from Dynasties I–VI* (Prague: Charles University Faculty of Arts, 2011); Franziska Großmann, *Die Rolle der Frau und die Erziehung im Alten Ägypten* (Hamburg: Diplomica Verlag, 2012); Jean Li, *Women, Gender and Identity in Third Intermediate Period Egypt* (London and New York: Routledge, 2017). Due to space limitations, this list is by no means comprehensive nor does it include volumes dealing with individual queens or specific priestly titles or the hundreds of journal articles and book chapters dealing with various aspects of women's experience in ancient Egypt.

3 For women's occupations, see Henry G. Fischer, "Administrative Titles of Women in the Old and Middle Kingdom," in *Egyptian Studies. I, Varia* (New York: Metropolitan Museum of Art, 1976), 69–79; Fischer, "Women in the Old Kingdom and Heracleopolitan Period," in *Women's Earliest Records*, ed. B.S. Lesko, 5–24; Fischer, *Egyptian Women of the Old Kingdom*; Susan A. Kelly, "Women in the Economic Domain: First to Sixth Dynasties" (in this volume); Catherine H. Roehrig, "Women's Work: Some Occupations of Nonroyal Women as Depicted in Egyptian Art," in *Mistress of the House, Mistress of Heaven*, ed. A.K. Capel and G.E. Markoe, 13–24; Betsy M. Bryan, "In Women Good and Bad Fortune Are on Earth: Status and Roles of Women in Egyptian Culture," in *Mistress of the House, Mistress of Heaven*, ed. A.K. Capel and G.E. Markoe, 39–44; William A. Ward, "Non-royal Women and Their Occupations in the Middle Kingdom," in *Women's Earliest Records*, ed. B.S. Lesko, 33–43; Melinda Nelson-Hurst, "Spheres of Economic and Administrative Control in Middle Kingdom Egypt: Textual, Visual and Archaeological Evidence for Female and Male Sealers," in *Structures of Power: Law and Gender Across the Ancient Near East and Beyond*, ed. Ilan Peled (Chicago: The Oriental Institute of the University of Chicago, 2017), 131–41; and Bernadette Menu, "Women and Business Life in the First Millennium B.C." in *Women's Earliest Records*, ed. B.S. Lesko, 193–205. For women in temple ritual, see Schafik Allam, *Beiträge zum Hathorkult (bis zum Ende des Mittleren Reiches)*, MÄS 4 (Berlin: B. Hessling, 1963); M. Gavin, "The Hereditary Status of the Titles of the Cult of Hathor," *JEA* 70 (1984): 42–49; R.A. Gillam, "Priestesses of Hathor: Their Function, Decline and Disappearance," *JARCE* 32 (1995): 211–37; Saphinaz-Amal Naguib, *Le clergé féminin d'Amon thébain à la 21e Dynastie*, OLA 38 (Leuven: Peeters, 1990); Suzanne Onstine, *The Role of the Chantress (šmꜥy.t) in Ancient Egypt*, BARIS 140 (Oxford: Hadrian Books, 2005); and Onstine, "Women's Participation in the Religious Hierarchy of Ancient Egypt," in *Women in Antiquity: Real Women Across the Ancient World*, ed. S.L. Budin and J. MacIntoch Turfa (London and New York: Routledge, 2016), 218–28; Mariam Ayad, *God's Wife, God's Servant: The God's Wife of Amun (c. 740–525 BC)* (London and New York: Routledge, 2009); Carola Koch, "*Die den Amun mit ihrer Stimme zufriedenstellen.*" *Gottesgemahlinnen und Musikerinnen im thebanischen Amunstaat von der 22. bis zur 26. Dynastie*, SRaT 27 (Dettelbach: J.H. Röll Verlag GmbH, 2012); Florence

Gombert-Meurice and Frédéric Payraudeau, eds., *Servir les dieux d'Égypte: Divine adoratrice, chanteuses et prêtres d'Amon à Thèbes* (Paris: Musée de Grenoble and Somogy éditions d'art, 2018). For women's ability to inherit and own property, see S. Allam, "Women as Owners of Immovables," in *Women's Earliest Records*, ed. B.S. Lesko, 123–35; Allam, "Women as Holders of Rights in Ancient Egypt (During the Late Period)," *JESHO* 32 (1990): 1–34; Allam, "Egyptian Law Courts in Pharaonic and Hellenistic Times," *JEA* 77 (1991): 109–27, esp. 113n22 and p. 122; Kathrin Gabler, "The Women of Deir al-Medina in the Ramesside Period: Current State of Research and Future Perspectives on the Community of Workers" (in this volume); Reinert Skumsnes, "Family Contracts in New Kingdom Egypt" (in this volume); and Janet H. Johnson, "Women in Demotic (Documentary) Texts" (in this volume). For their legal and marital rights, see P.W. Pestman, *Marriage and Matrimonial Property in Ancient Egypt: A Contribution to Establishing the Legal Position of the Woman* (Leiden: Brill, 1961); S. Allam, "L'apport des documents juridiques de Deir el-Medineh," in *Le droit égyptien ancien: Colloque organisé par l'Institut des Hautes Etudes de Belgique 18 et 19 mars 1974*, ed. A. Theodorides (Brussels: Institut des Hautes Etudes de Belgique, 1974), 145–46; Janet H. Johnson, "The Legal Status of Women in Ancient Egypt," in *Mistress of the House, Mistress of Heaven*, ed. A.K. Capel and G.E. Markoe, 175–86; Brian Muhs, "Gender Relations and Inheritance in Legal Codes and Legal Practice in Ancient Egypt," in *Structures of Power*, ed. Ilan Peled, 15–25. For a summary of Egyptian women's legal testimonials, see Barbara S. Lesko, "'Listening' to the Egyptian Woman: Letters, Testimonials, and Other Expressions of Self," in *Gold of Praise: Studies on Ancient Egypt in Honor of Edward F. Wente*, ed. Emily Teeter and J.A. Larson, SAOC 58 (Chicago: Oriental Institute, 1999), 250–51. For women receiving rations as members of the *ḳnbt* in the Middle Kingdom, see P.Boulaq 18, xxix, 10, in A. Scharff, "Ein Rechnungsbuch des königlichen Hofes aus der 13. Dynastie (Papyrus Boulaq Nr. 18)," *ZÄS* 57 (1922): 51–68; and William A. Ward, *Essays on Feminine Titles of the Middle Kingdom and Related Subjects* (Beirut: American University of Beirut, 1986), 14. For women serving on the Deir al-Medina *ḳnbt*, see ostracon O. Gardiner 150, published in Jaroslav Černý and Alan H. Gardiner, *Hieratic Ostraca* (Oxford: University Press, 1957), 21 and pls. LXXI, 3–LXXIA, 3, and discussed briefly in Allam, "L'apport des documents juridiques de Deir el-Medineh," 145; and Toivari-Viitala, *Women at Deir el-Medina*, 44 and 232–33.

4 See, for example, M. Brosius, *Women in Ancient Persia, 559–331 BC* (Oxford: Clarendon Press, 1996); L.K. McClure, *Women in Classical Antiquity: From Birth to Death* (Newark: John Wiley and Sons, 2019); Sarah B. Pomeroy, *Goddesses, Whores, Wives, and Slaves: Women in Classical Antiquity* (New York: Schocken Books, 1995).

5 One of the best-contextualized overviews of Hatshepsut's life and reign may be found in C.H. Roehrig, ed., *Hatshepsut: From Queen to Pharaoh* (New York: Metropolitan Museum Press, 2005); see also Cooney's account of her reign in K. Cooney, *The Woman Who Would Be King* (New York: Crown, 2014).

6 Alan Gardiner, *Egypt of the Pharaohs: An Introduction* (Oxford: Clarendon Press, 1961), 184. Until the mid- to late 1990s, *Egypt of the Pharaohs* was a standard textbook in courses on Egyptian history.

7 N. Grimal, *A History of Ancient Egypt*, trans. I. Shaw (Oxford: Blackwell, 1992), 209.

8 P.F. Dorman, "The Career of Senenmut," in *Hatshepsut*, ed. C.H. Roehrig, 107–109.

9 Grimal, *A History of Ancient Egypt*, 211.

10 See Cooney, *The Woman Who Would Be King*, 87–88, for the availability of other potential lovers for Hatshepsut and for the argument for the erroneous identification of the woman depicted in the graffiti with Hatshepsut published in Edward F. Wente, "Some Graffiti from the Reign of Hatshepsut," *JNES* 43, no. 1 (1984): 47–54.

11 Cooney, *The Woman Who Would Be King*, 140.

12 R.A. Fazzini, "Report on the 1983 Season of Excavation at the Precinct of the Goddess Mut," *ASAE* 70 (1984–85): 287–307; K. Myśliwiec, *The Eighteenth Dynasty before the Amarna Period*, Iconography of Religions 16 (Leiden: E.J. Brill, 1985), 19–21; J.P. Allen, "The Role of Amun,"

in *Hatshepsut*, ed. C.H. Roehrig, 84; and B.M. Bryan, "The Temple of Mut: New Evidence on Hatshepsut's Building Activities," in *Hatshepsut*, ed. C.H. Roehrig, 181–83; B.M. Bryan, "Hatshepsut and Cultic Revelries in the New Kingdom," in *Creativity and Innovation in the Reign of Hatshepsut*, ed. J. Galán, B.M. Bryan, and P.F. Dorman, SAOC 69 (Chicago: Oriental Institute, 2014), 93–123, especially at 97; Z.E. Szafrański, "The Exceptional Creativity of Hatshepsut," in *Creativity and Innovation in the Reign of Hatshepsut*, ed. J. Galán, B.M. Bryan, and P.F. Dorman, 129.

13 Myśliwiec, *The Eighteenth Dynasty before the Amarna Period*, 10. For the scenes, see PM II^2, 348–49; and E. Naville, *The Temple of Deir el-Bahari*, Part 2: *The Ebony Shrine and the Middle Platform*, Expedition Memoir 14 (London: EEF, 1896), pls. 47–49. For the iconographic scenes depicting Amenhotep III's birth cycle, see A. Gayet, *Le Temple de Louxor* (Paris: Leroux, 1894), pls. lxiii–lxvii. See also Hellmut Brunner, *Die Geburt des Gottkönigs: Studien zur Überlieferung eines altägyptischen Mythos*, ÄA 10 (Wiesbaden: Harrassowitz, 1986), 22–89, and pls. 2–8, 12.

14 Urk. IV, 390; A.H. Gardiner, "Davies's Copy of the Great Speos Artemidos Inscription," *JEA* 32 (1946): 47–48; D.B. Redford, "Textual Sources for the Hyksos Period," in *The Hyksos: New Historical and Archaeological Perspectives*, ed. E. Oren (Philadelphia: University Museum, University of Pennsylvania, 1997), 17. For an alternate reading of the text, see Hans Goedicke, *The Speos Artemidos Inscription of Hatshepsut and Related Discussions* (Oakville, CT: HALGO, 2004), 91.

15 PM II^2, 344–47; Naville, *The Temple of Deir el-Bahari*, part 3: *End of Northern Half and Southern Half of Middle Platform*, Expedition Memoir 16 (London: EEF, 1898), 11–21; pls. 69–86.

16 D.B. Redford, *History and Chronology of the Eighteenth Dynasty of Egypt: Seven Studies* (Toronto: University of Toronto Press, 1967), 57–62.

17 D.B. Redford, *Egypt, Canaan and Israel in Ancient Times* (Princeton: Princeton University Press, 1992), 149.

18 Grimal, *A History of Ancient Egypt*, 207.

19 A point well articulated in D. Panagiotopoulos, "Foreigners in Egypt in the Time of Hatshepsut and Thutmose III," in *Thutmose III: A New Biography*, ed. Eric H. Cline and David O'Connor (Ann Arbor: University of Michigan Press, 2006), 406n1.

20 Marie-Ange Bonhême, *Pharaon: Les secrets du pouvoir* (Paris: Armand Colin, 1988), especially 28–40, 72–92, 245–54, and 273–80.

21 Jacquelyn Williamson, "Power, Piety, and Gender in Context: Hatshepsut and Nefertiti" (in this volume). A similar situation may be argued, for example, for the Ayyubid queen Shajar al-Durr in the thirteenth century CE, who likewise had to step up and fill a power vacuum in order to mitigate an urgent political crisis. But whereas Shajar al-Durr held power for just under three months, Hatshepsut was able to rule for two decades. For an overview of Shajar al-Durr's reign, see Taef El-Azhari, "The Ayyubids: Their Two Queens and Their Powerful Castrated Atabegs," in *Queens, Eunuchs and Concubines in Islamic History, 661–1257* (Edinburgh: University Press, 2019), 372–73, 380–81; and E. Arafa, "The Legitimacy of Shajar al-Durr Reign as Represented in Light of a Rare Dinar," *Egyptian Journal of Archaeological and Restoration Studies* 6, no. 1 (2016): 65–70.

22 M. Gitton, *L'épouse du dieu, Ahmes Néfertary* (Paris: Belles Letters, 1975).

23 For a thorough discussion of the Donation stela and references, see B.M. Bryan, "Property and the God's Wives of Amun," in *Women and Property*, ed. D. Lyons and R. Westbrook (Cambridge: Harvard University Center for Hellenic Studies, 2005), 1–7.

24 For a historical review of this period and the circumstances surrounding the appointment of each of these five GWAs, see Ayad, *God's Wife, God's Servant*, 10–28. See also M.F. Ayad, "The Transition from Libyan to Nubian Rule: The Role of the God's Wife of Amun," in *The Libyan Period in Egypt: Historical and Chronological Problems of the Third Intermediate Period*, ed. G.P.F. Broekman, R.J. Demarée, and O.E. Kaper (Leiden: NINO, 2009), 29–49.

25 K.A. Kitchen, *The Third Intermediate Period in Egypt (1100–650 BC)* (Warminster: Aris and Phillips, 1996), 201; Ayad, *God's Wife, God's Servant*, 118; M.F. Ayad, "Gender, Ritual, and the

Manipulation of Power: The God's Wife of Amun (Dynasty 23–26)," in *Prayer and Power: Proceedings of the Conference on the God's Wives of Amun in Egypt during the First Millennium* BC, ed. M. Becker, A. Blöbaum, and A. Lohwasser, ÄAT 84 (Münster: Ugarit-Verlag, 2016), 97–99.

26 Kitchen, *Third Intermediate Period*, 403–404; R.A. Caminos, "The Nitocris Adoption Stela," *JEA* 50 (1964): 71–101; Bryan, "Property and the God's Wives of Amun," 7–12; A.I. Blöbaum, "The Nitocris Adoption Stela: Representation of Royal Dominion and Regional Elite Power," in *Prayer and Power*, ed. M. Becker et al., 183–204.

27 A view also expressed in Robins, *Women in Ancient Egypt* (1993b), 153.

28 See Ayad, *God's Wife, God's Servant*, 35–51, 151–52.

29 See G. Legrain, "Le temple et les chapelles d'Osiris à Karnak I: Le temple d'Osiris, Hiq-Djeto," *RecTrav* 22 (1900): 127; and Ayad, *God's Wife, God's Servant*, 43.

30 D.B. Redford, *From Slave to Pharaoh: The Black Experience of Ancient Egypt* (Baltimore: The Johns Hopkins University Press, 2004), 114.

31 Ayad, *God's Wife, God's Servant*, 127–29 and fig. 3.6 on p. 128; Bonhême, *Pharaon: Les secrets du pouvoir*, 247–52, 274–77.

32 R.A. Fazzini, *Egypt: Dynasty XXII–XXV* (Leiden and New York: Brill, 1988), 20, for his description of pl. XVIII, 2.

33 Bonhême, *Pharaon: Les secrets du pouvoir*, 85–92, 272–73; Jean Leclant, "Le rôle du lait et l'allaitement d'après les textes des pyramides," *JNES* 10 (1951): 123–27; Leclant, "The Suckling of Pharaoh as a Part of the Coronation Rites in Ancient Egypt. Le rôle de l'allaitement dans le cérémonial pharaonique du couronnement," in *Proceedings of the IXth International Congress for the History of Religion* (Tokyo: Maruzen, 1960), 135–45; Ayad, *God's Wife, God's Servant*, 125–27.

34 Ayad, *God's Wife, God's Servant*, 124–41.

35 Ayad, *God's Wife, God's Servant*, 116–20.

36 Ayad, *God's Wife, God's Servant*, 140. For the adoption stela of Ankhnesneferibre, see A. Leahy, "The Adoption of Ankhnesneferibre at Karnak," *JEA* 82 (1996): 146 (fig. 1, lines 5, 8, and 10), 148, 155.

37 For a comprehensive list of Ankhnesneferibre's titles, see L. Troy, *Patterns of Queenship in Ancient Egyptian Myth and History*, BOREAS 14 (Uppsala and Stockholm: [Universitet]; Almquist and Wiksell International, 1986), 178. See also M. Ayad, "Some Thoughts on the Disappearance of the Office of the God's Wife of Amun," *JSSEA* 28 (2001): 1–14, for the suggestion that it was Ankhnesneferibre's exceptionally elevated status that prevented a Persian princess from replacing her as God's Wife of Amun.

38 A. Mariette, *Catalogue général des monuments d'Abydos découverts pendant les fouilles de cette ville* (Paris: L'imprimerie nationale, 1880), 87 and pl. 78; L. Borchardt, *Denkmäler des alten Reiches (ausser den Statuen) im Museum von Kairo, nr. 1295–1808 [57001–57100]*, CG (Berlin: Reichsdruckerei, 1937; reprint 1964), 59; Fischer, "Administrative Titles of Women," 74–75.

39 H. Schäfer, *Principles of Egyptian Art*, trans. John Baines (Oxford: Griffith Institute, 1986), 233–34.

40 G. Robins, "Some Principles of Compositional Dominance and Gender Hierarchy in Egyptian Art," *JARCE* 31 (1994): 33.

41 The reference to the Twenty-sixth Dynasty may be found in Fischer, "Administrative Titles of Women," 74n32, where statue Cairo CG 42205 is referred to. See also G. Legrain, *Statues et Statuettes de rois et de particuliers* III (Cairo: IFAO, 1914), 13–14, pl. XII. Fischer, however, did not provide the name of the owner of that statue, who was none other than the Saite God's Wife of Amun, Ankhnesferibre, whose titles are very similar to Nebet's. The titles are inscribed on the base of her statue, which is currently in the Nubia Museum, Aswan. There, though, the bird forming the first part of the word for vizier, *ṯꜥty*, looks more similar to the *sꜣ*-bird (Gardiner sign list #39) than the fledgling *ṯꜣ* (Gardiner sign list #47), giving rise to the suggestion that the intended word here was *sꜣt*, "daughter." Bryan also mentions the later occurrence of the title in B.M. Bryan, "In Women Good and Bad Fortune Are on Earth," 39, 190–91n109.

42 Fischer, "Administrative Titles of Women," 75; a view also expressed in N. Strudwick, *The Administration of Egypt in the Old Kingdom: The Highest Titles and Their Holders* (London: KPI, 1985), 303.

43 Fischer, "Administrative Titles of Women," 75; N. Strudwick, *Texts from the Pyramid Age* (Atlanta: SBL, 2005), 395.

44 Fischer, "Administrative Titles of Women," 75; Bryan, "In Women Good and Bad Fortune Are on Earth," 39.

45 Also noted by Kanawati in N. Kanawati, "The Vizier Nebet and the Royal Women of the Sixth Dynasty," in *Thebes and Beyond: Studies in Honor of Kent R. Weeks*, ed. Zahi A. Hawass and Salima Ikram (Cairo: Conseil Suprême des Antiquités de l'Égypte, 2010), 115.

46 E.g., Fischer, "Administrative Titles of Women," 74–75.

47 Kanawati, "The Vizier Nebet and the Royal Women of the Sixth Dynasty," 118–19.

48 Kanawati, "The Vizier Nebet and the Royal Women of the Sixth Dynasty," 119, 123.

49 Kanawati, "The Vizier Nebet and the Royal Women of the Sixth Dynasty," 116–17.

50 For Amenemhat I's nonroyal origins (famously touted in Middle Kingdom literature), see Dorothea Arnold, "Amenemhat I and the Early Twelfth Dynasty at Thebes," *MMJ* 26 (1991): 18–20; and L.M. Berman, "Amenemhat I," in *Dictionary of African Biography* 1, ed. E. Akyeampong and H.L. Gates (Oxford and New York: Oxford University Press, 2012), 203–204. For Amenhotep III's union with Tiye, "a woman of nonroyal origins," see Grimal, *A History of Ancient Egypt*, 221–22. For a discussion of Tiye's family and her provincial background, see L.M. Berman, "Overview of Amenhotep III and His Reign," in *Amenhotep III: Perspectives on His Reign*, ed. D. O'Connor and E. Cline (Ann Arbor: University of Michigan Press, 1998), 5–6; and N. Reeves, "The Royal Family," in *Pharaohs of the Sun: Akhenaton, Nefertiti, Tutankhamun*, ed. R.E. Freed, Y.J. Markowitz, and S. D'Auria (London: Thames and Hudson, 1999), 8.

51 For instance, in Grimal, *A History of Ancient Egypt*, 83, Nebet is completely edited out of the account given of her daughters' marriages to Pepi I; instead only Khui, her husband, is mentioned in this context.

52 M.F. Ayad, "Women's Self-presentation in Pharaonic Egypt," in *Living Forever: Self-representation in Ancient Egypt*, ed. H. Bassir (Cairo: American University in Cairo Press, 2019), 224; see the examples cited in H.G. Fischer, "Women in the Old Kingdom and the Heracleopolitan Period," in *Women's Earliest Records from Ancient Egypt and Western Asia*, ed. B. Leko (Atlanta: Scholars' Press, 1989), 9–10; Fischer, *Egyptian Women of the Old Kingdom*, 5–8 and figs. 2–6.

53 A.H. Gardiner, "Adoption Extraordinary," *JEA* 26 (1941): 23–29; S. Allam, "A New Look at the Adoption Papyrus (Reconsidered)," *JEA* 76 (1990): 189–91; and, more recently, Toivari-Viitala, *Women at Deir el-Medina*, 98, 100–104, 106; and J. Černý, "The Will of Naunakhte and the Related Documents," *JEA* 31 (1945): 29–53.

54 See, for example, Fischer ("Administrative Titles of Women," 69–79), who, despite enumerating the titles held by women in the Old and Middle Kingdom, does not consider whether any of these titles generated an income for the women who held them.

55 Exceptionally, but quite correctly, Onstine supports the view that women were compensated for their temple service. See S. Onstine, "Women's Participation in the Religious Hierarchy of Ancient Egypt," 225–26n10, where she cites the Tutankhamun Restoration stela (Urk. IV2030.6–8) for payments made to "temple singers and dancers."

56 Henry G. Fischer, "A Memphite High Priest and His Sisters," in *Egyptian Studies* 1: *Varia* (New York: Metropolitan Museum of Art, 1976), 62.

57 Kelly, "Women in the Economic Domain: First to Sixth Dynasties" (in this volume).

58 S. Quirke, "Women in Ancient Egypt: Temple Titles and Funerary Papyri," in *Studies on Ancient Egypt in Honour of H.S. Smith*, ed. A. Leahy and J. Tait (London: EES, 1999), 229, referring to the burial equipment of Henutmehyt and Tamutnofret, currently at the British Museum and the Louvre, respectively. For a detailed discussion of their burial equipment and bibliographic references, see K.M. Cooney, *The Cost of Death: The Social and Economic Value of Ancient Egyptian Funerary Art in the Ramesside Period* (Leiden: NINO, 2007), 398–404, 413–18.

59 *Wb.* IV, 487.1.

60 *Wb.* IV, 485.6–486.19; S. Quirke, *Titles and Bureaux of Egypt 1850–1700 BC* (London: Golden House Publications, 2004), 104–105.

61 R.O. Faulkner, *A Concise Dictionary of Middle Egypt* (Oxford: Griffith Institute, 1981), 267. For *šmsw* as "retainer" in a variety of Middle Kingdom compound titles, see W.A. Ward, *Index of Egyptian Administrative and Religious Titles of the Middle Kingdom* (Beirut: American University of Beirut, 1982), 175–77nn1515–27.

62 The hardness of the crystalline material of the scarab would render an erroneous "*t*" highly unlikely. See Fischer, "Administrative Titles of Women," 77–78; Ward, "Non-royal Women and Their Occupations in the Middle Kingdom," 35–36.

63 This, however, cannot be the case for the scarab bearing the name and title of the female scribe Idwy (Michailides Collection in Berlin, Inv. No. 42/73); see G.T. Martin, *Egyptian Administrative and Private-name Seals, Principally of the Middle Kingdom and Second Intermediate Period* (Oxford: Griffith Institute, 1971), 28, no. 301. There, the final feminine "*t*" must have been intentional because, as Fischer pointed out, the hardness of the crystalline material of the scarab would render an erroneous "*t*" highly unlikely. See Fischer, "Administrative Titles of Women," 77–78 and n. 57.

64 See A. Scharff, "Ein Rechnungsbuch des königlichen Hofes," 65 for papyrus Boulaq 18; and W.C. Hayes, *A Papyrus of the Late Middle Kingdom in the Brooklyn Museum* (New York: Brooklyn Museum, 1955), 107, for the misreading of this title on papyrus Brooklyn 35.1446. For the questionable reading of *sšt* on the sarcophagus of Aashayet, see B.M. Bryan, "Evidence for Female Literacy from Theban Tombs of the New Kingdom." *BES* 6 (1984): 17.

65 G. Posener, "Maquilleuse en Égyptien." *RdE* 21 (1969): 150–51.

66 Ward, *Index*, 167–68nn1456–1457; Ward, *Essays on Feminine Titles*, 17.

67 Fischer, "Administrative Titles of Women," 77–78.

68 Posener, "Maquilleuse en Égyptien," 150; and Quirke, "Women in Ancient Egypt: Temple Titles and Funerary Papyri," 228. See S. Quirke, *The Administration of Egypt in the Late Middle Kingdom: The Hieratic Documents* (New Malden: SIA, 1990), 101n18, for a rejection of a misconstrued interpretation of Fischer's suggestion that the title should be understood as "a female scribe taking oral orders," an interpretation that I would gladly accept but one that was not put forward by Fischer (for references, see note 72 below).

69 Bryan, "Evidence for Female Literacy from Theban Tombs," 17–18.

70 Ayad, "A Scribe of the Utterance: Author or Secretary?" (forthcoming).

71 Ayad, "A Scribe of the Utterance: Author or Secretary?" (forthcoming).

72 See, for example, Fischer, "Administrative Titles of Women," 73; Fischer, "Women in the Old Kingdom and the Heracleopolitan Period," 14–15, 20–21; Fischer, *Egyptian Women of the Old Kingdom*, 19, 26–27; Ward, "Non-royal Women and Their Occupations in the Middle Kingdom," 35–37; Robins, *Women in Ancient Egypt* (1993b), 116–18, 125. For women (and men) in the service of the GWA from the New Kingdom through the end of the Twenty-sixth Dynasty, see E. Graefe, *Untersuchungen zur Verwaltung und Geschichte der Institution der Gottesgemahlin des Amun vom Beginn des neuen Reiches bis zur Spätzeit* (Wiesbaden: Harrassowitz, 1981).

73 H.G. Fischer, *Egyptian Titles of the Middle Kingdom: A Supplement to Wm. Ward's Index*, 2nd rev. ed. (New York: Metropolitan Museum of Art, 1997), 77, nos. 1456–57.

74 J. Baines and C.J. Eyre, "Four Notes on Literacy," *GM* 61 (1983): 81–85, expanded, updated, and republished in J. Baines, *Visual and Written Culture in Ancient Egypt* (Oxford: Oxford University Press, 2007), 83–89.

75 Baines, *Visual and Written Culture*, 63.

76 Baines and Eyre, "Four Notes on Literacy," 69–70, 90–91; Baines, *Visual and Written Culture*, 73, 94.

77 L.H. Lesko, "Some Comments on Ancient Egyptian Literacy and Literati," in *Studies in Egyptology Presented to Miriam Lichtheim* 2, ed. S. Groll (Jerusalem: Magness Press, Hebrew

University, 1990), 656–59; Lesko, "Literature, Literacy, and Literati," in *Pharaoh's Workers*, ed. L.H. Lesko (Ithaca: Cornell University Press, 1994 and 2018), 134–36.

78 Baines and Eyre, "Four Notes on Literacy," 81–82; Baines, *Visual and Written Culture*, 84–85, emphasis mine.

79 Baines and Eyre, "Four Notes on Literacy," 82; Baines, *Visual and Written Culture*, 84.

80 Bryan, "Evidence for Female Literacy from Theban Tombs," 18.

81 E.g., the Middle Kingdom stelae Turin C 1534 and Ny Carlsberg AEIN 1025. For the former, see most recently *Museo Egizio* (Turin: Fondazione Museo delle Antichità Egizie di Torino, 2015), 80–81 (no. 76). For the latter, see M. Jørgensen, *Catalogue Egypt I (3000–1550 B.C.)* (Copenhagen: Ny Carlsberg Glyptotek, 1996), 187.

82 Elena Pischikova, ed., *Tombs of the South Asasif Necropolis, Thebes: Karakhamun (TT 223) and Karabasken (TT 391) in the Twenty-fifth Dynasty* (Cairo: American University in Cairo Press, 2014), 1; M.F. Ayad, "The Female Scribe Irtieru and Her Tomb (TT 390) in South Asasif," in *The South Asasif Project*, ed. E. Pischikova (Cairo: American University in Cairo Press, 2021), 273–83.

83 Meticulously documented in the two volumes of Graefe, *Untersuchungen zur Verwaltung und Geschichte der Institution der Gottesgemahlin des Amun vom Beginn des neuen Reiches bis zur Spätzeit.*

84 J.J. Clère and J. Vandier, *Textes de la Première Période Intermédiare et de la XIeme dynastie* (Brussels: Fondation Egyptologique Reine Elisabeth, 1948), 25–29.

85 Clère and Vandier, *Textes de la Première Période Intermédiare*, 26, §27 (2).

86 Clère and Vandier, *Textes de la Première Période Intermédiare*, 26, n. (a); Bryan, "Evidence for Female Literacy from Theban Tombs," 17.

87 PM III^2, 617 and plan LXIII (7); R. Macramallah, *Le Mastaba d'Idout.* Fouilles à Saqqarah (Cairo: IFAO, 1935), pl. VII.

88 C.H. Roehrig, "The Eighteenth Dynasty Titles Royal Nurse (*mnꜥt nsw*), Royal Tutor (*mnꜥ nswt*), and Foster Brother/Sister of the Lord of the Two Lands (*sn/snt mnꜥ n nb tꜣwy*)" (PhD diss., University of Berkeley, 1990), especially 1–2, 314, 322–24, 330–33.

89 Romane Betbeze, "Ostentation in Old Kingdom Female Tombs: Between Iconographic Conventions and Gendered Adaptations" (in this volume).

90 Fischer, "Administrative Titles of Women," 70.

91 Bryan, "Evidence for Female Literacy from Theban Tombs," 17–32.

92 Bryan, "Evidence for Female Literacy from Theban Tombs," 19–20.

93 Boyo Ockinga et al., *The Tomb of Amenemope at Thebes (TT 148)* (Oxford: Aris and Phillips, 2009), pls. 19 (a) and 73; evidence from TT 148 was also cited in Bryan, "Evidence for Female Literacy from the Theban Tombs," 23–24.

94 W.C. Hayes, *Scepter of Egypt: A Background for the Study of the Egyptian Antiquities in the Metropolitan Museum of Art*, vol. 2, *The Hyksos Period and the New Kingdom (1675–1080 B.C.)* (Cambridge, MA: Metropolitan Museum of Art, 1959), 281, 300, fig. 185.

95 The palette's dimensions are L. 13.3 cm, W. 2.3 cm, and Th. 0.5 cm. Details of the palette are available online through the Metropolitan Museum at https://www.metmuseum.org/art/collection/search/544694.

96 Bryan, "Evidence for Female Literacy from Theban Tombs," 18.

97 Dorothea Arnold, "Aspects of the Royal Female Image during the Amarna Period," in *The Royal Women of Amarna: Images of Beauty from Ancient Egypt*, ed. D. Arnold (New York: The Metropolitan Museum of Art, 1996), 115.

98 H. Carter, *The Tomb of Tut.Ankh.Amen* 3 (London: Cassell and Co, 1933), 45 and pl. 22.

99 Baines and Eyre, "Four Notes on Literacy," 82–83; Baines, *Visual and Written Culture*, 85.

100 H. Willems, *Historical and Archaeological Aspects of Egyptian Funerary Culture: Religious Ideas and Ritual Practice in Middle Kingdom Elite Cemeteries* (Leiden and Boston: Brill, 2014), 74–75; K. Jansen-Winkeln, "Bemerkungen zu den Frauenbiographien der Spätzeit," *AoF* 31, no. 2 (2004): 358–73; Ayad, "Women's Self-presentation in Pharaonic Egypt," 231–36.

101 Baines and Eyre, "Four Notes on Literacy," 83; Baines, *Visual and Written Culture*, 85–86, where they state: "In general, author and addressee of letters need not be literate."

102 N. Allon and H. Navratilova, *Ancient Egyptian Scribes: A Cultural Exploration* (London and New York: Bloomsbury, 2017), 72. Emphasis mine.

103 See, for example, E.F. Wente, *Letters from Ancient Egypt* (Atlanta: Scholars Press, 1990), letters nos. 34, 39, 44, 132, 200, 228, 229, 232, 290, 314, 319, 324, and 331.

104 A.B. Knapp, "Boys Will Be Boys: Masculinist Approaches to a Gendered Archaeology," in *Reader in Gender Archaeology*, ed. K. Hays-Gilpin and D.S. Whitley (London and New York: Routledge, 1998), 368.

105 Baines and Eyre, "Four Notes on Literacy," 65, title note.

106 K. Szpakowska, *Daily Life in Ancient Egypt* (Oxford: Blackwell, 2008), 102–103.

107 For the translation of this title as "concubine," see, for example, Faulkner, *Concise Dictionary*, 205. For a full discussion of that title, see especially D. Nord, "'Xkrt-nsw'= 'King's Concubine'?," *Serapis* 2 (1976): 1–16; and R. Drenkhahn, "Bemerkungen zu dem Titel *ẖkr.t Nswt*," *SAK* 4 (1976): 59–67. See also Ward, *Essays on Feminine Titles*, 14, 26–28; Ward, "Non-royal Women and Their Occupations in the Middle Kingdom," 42–43; Robins, *Women in Ancient Egypt* (1993b), 117; and, more recently, D. Stefanović, *The Non-royal Regular Feminine Titles of the Middle Kingdom and Second Intermediate Period: Dossiers* (London: Golden House Publications, 2009), 85–109.

108 See, most recently, Izold Guegan, "The *ḫnr.wt*: A Reassessment of Their Religious Roles" (in this volume). See also D. Nord, "The Term *ḫnr*: 'Harem' or 'Musical Performers'?," in *Ancient Egypt, the Aegean and the Sudan*, ed. W.K. Simpson and W.M. Davis (Boston: MFA, 1981), 137–45; Fischer, *Egyptian Women of the Old Kingdom*, 26; Ward, *Essays on Feminine Titles*, 69–80; Ward, "Non-royal Women and Their Occupations in the Middle Kingdom," 39–41. For a broader discussion of the *ḫnrt*, see M. Di Teodoro, *Labour Organisation in Middle Kingdom Egypt*, Middle Kingdom Studies 7 (London: Golden House Publications, 2018), 62–73.

2

Early Dynastic Women: The Written Evidence

Eva-Maria Engel

Old Kingdom women are attested in countless decorated *mastabas* and rock-cut tombs as well as three-dimensional images.[1] In all of these formats, queens, princesses, wives, mothers, and priestesses are depicted, in addition to women working in different positions in the households of the respective tomb owners. Due to a shortage of similar sources, the evidence for women from the preceding Early Dynastic Period is much scarcer. Although some female members of the royal family are known by name for the First and Second Dynasties—for example, Neithhotep, Merneith, and Nimaathapi—their precise status is still subject to debate:[2] Whose wife or mother were they? What impact did they have?

For historical research purposes, objects bearing the names of these women are useful in that they help date archaeological findings. In his description of the so-called Narmer mace head, Walter B. Emery exemplified how royal women were treated in Egyptological literature: "a representation of the union of Nithotep and Narmer, for there is strong evidence to show that the conqueror of the North attempted to legitimize his position by taking the Northern princess as his consort,"[3] displaying a rather romantic idea of Narmer's approach to power, especially since neither Neithhotep's origin or position nor her connection with Narmer is attested without doubt.

Nonroyal individuals are even less well attested in written records owing to the developing and not yet widespread use of writing. Still, there are two large corpora which are taken as sources for the present study on written evidence of women in the Early Dynastic Period: first, a group of 359 stelae from Abydos,[4] and second, several hundred privately owned cylinder seals (table 2.1).

Table 2.1. Comparison of Early Dynastic stelae and private cylinder seals

Stelae	Cylinder Seals
Abydos (royal tombs, enclosures)	mostly unprovenanced
359 objects	ca. 600 objects
Dyn. 1	Dyn. 1 – Old Kingdom?
Personal name	Personal name
Personal name + classifier	Personal name + classifier
Personal name + title	Personal name + title
Personal name + title + classifier	Personal name + title + classifier

Stelae

The stelae were mostly excavated by Émile Amélineau, William Matthew Flinders Petrie, and the German Institute of Archaeology at Abydos during the re-excavation of the site.[5] The stelae marked subsidiary graves that surrounded the royal tombs of the First Dynasty and, while the poor quality of limestone often renders reading of the stelae's inscriptions difficult, it is still possible to sort them into different groups. At a minimum, the stelae mention a personal name[6] that, in many cases, is complemented by a determinative or classifier (fig. 2.1);[7] the most complete ones also give a title.[8]

A single elaborate example from the end of the First Dynasty has one of the oldest sequences of titles known from Egypt, mentioning that the owner served as chief of different magazines or institutions (fig. 2.2).[9] The determinative indicates that Sabef, the owner, was of short stature.[10] Other classifiers on the stelae are crouching women and men, foreigners, and dogs (table 2.2). Still, there are many stelae without any additional information that can assist in interpreting the inscriptions. Furthermore, differentiation between genders is made difficult by the fact that the feminine marker *.t* was not yet used in writing. The stelae usually appear as one homogeneous group in the literature, where we read of "sacrificial servant burials"[11] or "members of the royal *harim*."[12] Women are mentioned in line with "dwarfs, hairdressers, other artisans, and dogs."[13] For many Egyptologists, men were professionals of some kind, while women were perceived as "concubines."[14] Depending on the findspot, information on the stelae varies.[15] The oldest examples from the burial of King Djer (Tomb O) mostly have the crouching woman as a determinative (see table 2.2), while stelae without classifiers are rare. By the middle of the

Fig. 2.1. Stela of *sṯi(?)* (Cairo JE 99602, Stela 286)

Fig. 2.2. Stela of *s3b.f* (Cairo JE 34416, Stela 48)

Table 2.2. Classifiers on stelae

Classifier	Detail
Crouching woman	
Crouching man	
Person of short stature	
Foreigner	
Dog	

First Dynasty, during the reign of King Den (Tomb T), there are female and male classifiers, sometimes combined with titles, and this pattern is maintained until the end of the dynasty (Tombs U/King Semerkhet and Q/King Qa'a). Classifiers were therefore being increasingly used, as they were the only means to distinguish between women and men.

The titles indicate that there were several high-ranking persons buried in Abydos, such as the above-mentioned Sabef, as well as chiefs of a palace[16] and queens.[17] The burials of queens and high-ranking officials in close proximity to the kings contradicts the interpretation that they served solely as "servant burials," the latter of which, nevertheless, are present in the same context.[18] Actual titles in combination with a female classifier are rare, but there is an example in which a woman might have been a weaver, although it is difficult to determine because of the condition of the object.[19] Another stela points to an individual dealing with linen,[20] while a third seems to connect its owner to spinning.[21] These examples link these persons to the production of textiles, which formed a major part of funerary equipment.[22]

The connection of these persons with the *harim* might thus be correct since in later periods the royal *harim* was connected with the production of textiles.[23] However, the Egyptological understanding of these women as solely sexually exploited individuals, as implied by the widely used term "concubine," has to be refuted since these women had professions of their own.

Cylinder Seals

The case of the cylinder seals is more difficult, as they were mostly purchased in the art market at different locations all over Egypt. Neither their findspots nor their dates are secure, and only a small number were found in situ in private tombs of the First and Second Dynasty at Naga al-Deir by George Andrew Reisner.[24] It thus seems likely that the majority were obtained by looting similar burials.

In 1963 and 1964, Peter Kaplony published about six hundred seals from museums and private collections all over the world.[25] However, since then the seals have received very little scholarly attention. Kaplony's publication serves as the principal source for the drawings presented here.[26] The inscriptions of the seals are quite similar to those of the stelae: they mention names, titles, and epithets in varying combinations. Their dates are less restricted than the stelae: some were found in a First Dynasty context, and paleographic evidence dates others to the period between the First and Third Dynasty or possibly even later.[27] It has been argued that these seals were used solely to mark the production of funerary equipment for the deceased,[28] as up until a few years ago hardly any impressions of similar objects had been found. However, recent

Fig. 2.3. Cylinder seal of *ḥtp-nb(.i)* (New York 26-2-48.)

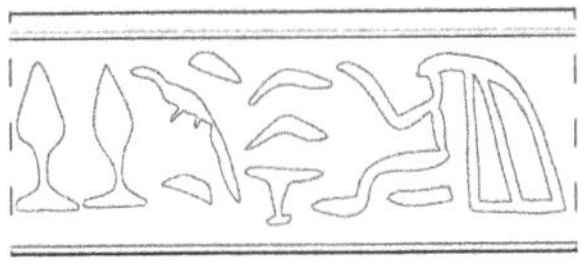

Fig. 2.4. Cylinder seal of *ḥms.t/msḥ.t* (Berlin 20333)

finds in the tomb of Khasekhemwy in Abydos,[29] at Tell al-Iswid,[30] and from the settlement on Elephantine Island,[31] prove that these seals were indeed used either for controlling different commodities during the lifetime of the owner or for purposes other than the seal-holder's private burial.

While these seals have hardly been mentioned in the literature as a group, some recurring details, such as the standard of the goddess Neith[32] (fig. 2.3) and the image of a person sitting at an offering table (fig. 2.4), have gained attention. The latter was entered as a15/a30 into the Early Dynastic Sign list,[33] and Kaplony read it as *šps,* taking it to be the title of the deceased.[34] He and others interpreted the images that mostly show figures with a large wig or headdress as "part of a traditional costume for men and women alike"[35] and, as a result, identified many of the individuals represented as men.[36] While these interpretations only dealt with the images concerned, another more recent statement claims that only the male Early Dynastic intellectual elite made use of writing as a means of communication,[37] implying that there was no need for women to employ cylinder seals.

In the case of the stelae, we have seen that while the feminine marker *.t* was not used in writing, at least figures of crouching women served to identify them. For the seals, however, the images of figures with a large wig have largely been interpreted as men, with only a few exceptions in which the feminine *.t* indicates otherwise. These latter exceptions are, however, probably of a Second or Third Dynasty date, and therefore later than the stelae. It thus seems that all "classical" techniques of interpreting grammar and image are inconclusive. How then do we read the Early Dynastic inscriptions, interpret them, and recognize women in the written record?

If we accept continuity from the Early Dynastic Period to the Old Kingdom, then we can assume that personal names are similar or even identical. It is indeed possible to relate many signs on the seals with the personal names compiled by Hermann Ranke[38] and Katrin Scheele-Schweitzer,[39] the names often spelled identically or with variations. Other elements, like the Neith-standard, do not seem to be part of the names.

Table 2.3. Female and male names on Early Dynastic cylinder seals

	Female	Probably female	?	Probably male	Male	Total
Name	9	6		4	19	38
Name + Neith	6		1		3	10
Name + "offering table"	25	4	2	2	5	38
Name + Neith + "offering table"	21	6	2	5	3	37
Name + title (including *sḫn-3ḫ*)	16	9	13	12	60	110
Name + epithet	2		1		9	12
ḥm-nṯr ḥw.t-ḥr.w			17			17
?			282			282
Excluded			58			58
Total	79	25	376	23	99	602

From a total of 602 seals,[40] fifty-eight must be excluded, as they are either only partially preserved or possibly fakes (table 2.3). It is not possible at present to read another 282 seals or to sort them into one of the following categories. Seventeen mention the title *ḥm-nṯr*, "priest of the goddess Hathor," but do not contain a personal name.[41] There are therefore only 245 seals of the 602 that contain personal names: thirty-eight seals have only personal names (fig. 2.5),[42] often repeated several times; ten have a personal name and the standard of the goddess Neith;[43] thirty-eight have a personal name and an image of a figure sitting in front of an offering table;[44] thirty-seven have all three groups of personal name, standard, and offering table scene (fig. 2.6);[45] fifty-four seals show a personal name and title;[46] forty-seven present a personal name and the title *sḫn-3ḫ* (fig. 2.7),[47] an Early Dynastic title of a funerary priest; nine have a title and an additional *sḫn-3ḫ*;[48] and there are a final twelve examples with personal names and epithets.[49]

After establishing a reading of the names that is supported by later, better-known examples, we then can attribute single seals to male or female owners. There are, however, some limitations: in many cases, an attribution is not possible and some names are attested equally for men and women alike (table 2.3). Despite these limitations, however, a tendency is recognizable: contrary to the prevailing opinion in the literature,[50] we have a percentage of women in this sample that is nearly as high as that of men.

Still, we should take a closer look at one group of inscriptions: that with the so-called offering table scene. Although the majority of recognizable names

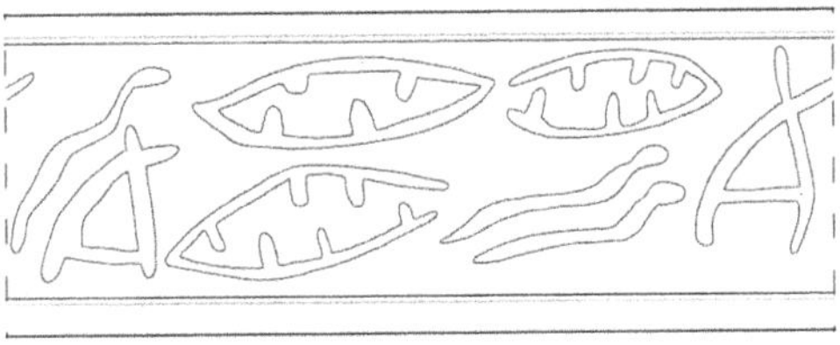

Fig. 2.5. Cylinder seal of *mr(i).f* (UC 11731).

Fig. 2.6. Cylinder seal of *ḳꜥj.s* (NY 10.130.1610.)

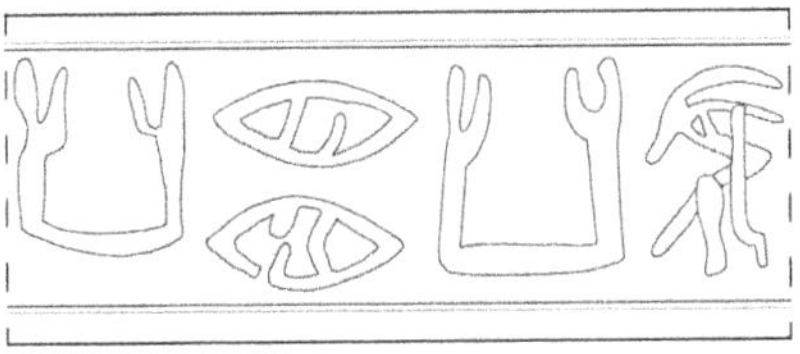

Fig. 2.7. Cylinder seal of the *sḫn-ꜣḫ k(ꜣ)r/kl* (UC 11741).

in these scenes are female, there are, indeed, a few male names. Furthermore, it is possible to differentiate gender in the accompanying offering table scene—a figure with a large headdress often accompanies female names, while male names are accompanied by bald-headed figures or figures with a beard, which, in several cases, represented writing for the name *šps* (fig. 2.8). The sitting figures in cases of the female names are not, however, a part of the name.[51] Another distinction is the presence of a small triangle or table sign that is missing on the "male" seals. The assumption that the wig is part of a male dress, as forwarded by von Bissing, Kaplony, and others, thus cannot be maintained. In fact, one can now tentatively identify all holders of seals with representations of sitting figures with a large wig as women, as many of these representations are accompanied by female names (table 2.3).

Conclusion

The treatment of Early Dynastic women works on two different levels. As far as the ancient Egyptians are concerned, the vast majority of attestations show that it was obviously necessary to use a determinative or classifier if a woman was mentioned, as seen in the crouching woman on the stelae or the woman

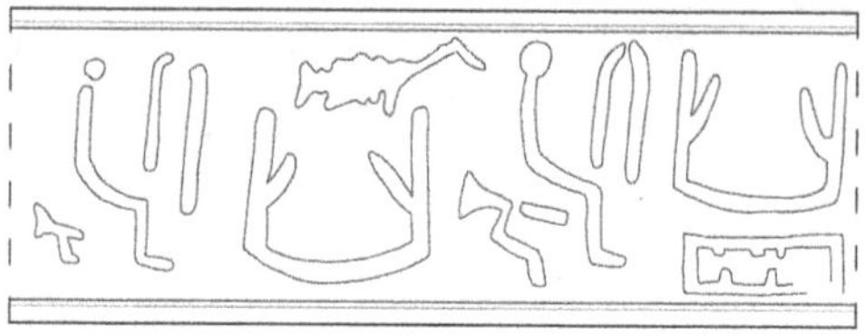

Fig. 2.8. Cylinder seal of *šps-kꜣ-nḏs* (UC 11730).

in front of the offering table on the seals. The same was true for persons of short stature, foreigners, or dogs on the stelae. Men, on the other hand, did not need an explanation. It therefore seems that men were seen as the "standard" version of human beings, deviations from which had to be marked.

Modern Egyptologists, on the other hand, have treated Early Dynastic women in two different ways. Only in cases where women were, like men, victims of ritual mass killings (as was the case in the environment of the First Dynasty tombs, documented by the Abydos stelae) are they recognized by scholars. Furthermore, these women have only been seen as objects of male desire. On the other hand, if women appear in the same elite environment as owners of cylinder seals and, therefore, as persons who controlled property and had the same responsibilities as men, Egyptologists have ignored them and turned them into men.

In summary, we can recognize from both corpora a large percentage of women being treated like men—being buried like men as parts of the royal household at Abydos after having participated in the production of grave goods; holding seals and titles like their male counterparts in other crafts or positions; and being engaged in the cult of the goddess Neith. This percentage is less than approximately 50 percent of the population, but is still far more than the close to 0 percent that Egyptologists have recognized previously. The evidence shows that women were responsible for their property and owners of estates, as in the case of two women from the royal family—Nimaathapi, the mother of the king's children,[52] and the "king's daughter of his own body," Nebtireput[53]—who contributed more to the funerary equipment of King Khasekhemwy, the last king of the Second Dynasty and predecessor of Netjerikhet (Djoser), than all other private persons put together.

During the Early Dynastic Period, orthographical rules thus developed to differentiate between women and men in writing. It seems that Egyptian men were considered the "standard," as their names were only rarely accompanied by classifiers, while women (as well as foreigners, and men and women of short stature), on the other hand, had to be differentiated. What was used by the

Early Dynastic writers to identify women (and the other groups) as being different from men has thus been subsequently ignored in research. The real problem of the study of Early Dynastic women, therefore, seems to be the gender bias of modern Egyptologists.

Notes

1 I am indebted to Sara Ahmed and Bianca van Sittert for improving my English.

2 See, for example, for Merneith, Kara Cooney, *When Women Ruled the World* (Washington, DC: National Geographic, 2018), 23–58.

3 Walter B. Emery, *Archaic Egypt* (Harmondsworth: Penguin Books, 1961), 47.

4 See also Eva-Maria Engel, "Why Can't a Woman Be More Like a Man? Frauen (und Männer) in den Nebenkammern der königlichen Grabanlagen in Umm el-Qa'ab," *ZÄS* 148 (2021):124–36; Kelly, "Women in the Economic Domain: First to Sixth Dynasties" (in this volume).

5 See the (re)publication by Geoffrey Thorndike Martin, *Umm el-Qaab VII: Private Stelae of the Early Dynastic Period from the Royal Cemetery at Abydos*, AV 123 (Wiesbaden: Harrassowitz Verlag, 2011). Martin's study extended the numbering system introduced by William Matthew Flinders Petrie.

6 E.g., *ỉn-sꜥḥ* (name): Martin, *Umm el-Qaab VII,* 192–93 (Stela 302, Ab K 6904, Tomb U); compare Hermann Ranke, *PN* 1, 35 [6]: *ỉn-nb.f.*

7 E.g., *stỉ* (name) + (classifier): Martin, *Umm el-Qaab VII*, 188–89 (Stela 286, Ab K 1645, Tomb Q); see Ranke, *PN* 1, 322 [16]: *sṯ.t*. For the discussion of this name, see Eva-Maria Engel, "The Early Dynastic Neith," *SAK* 50 (2021): 77n57.

8 For example, *sḫn-3ḫ* (title) + *šps-nṯr* (name) + (classifier): Martin, *Umm el-Qaab VII*, 130–31 (Stela 179, Cairo JdE 31858f = CG 14607, Tomb Z or T); compare Ranke, *PN* 1, 326 [1]: *šps.j-ptḥ*.

9 *ḫrp ḫnt sḥ ḥw.t s3-ḥ3-nb ḫrp sḥ ỉrp pr(.w)-dšr ḥw.t pỉ-ḥr.w-msn.w smr pr(.w)-nzw ḥri-wḏ-mdw ḥri-sšt3 špss(?) nb sḥ ḏd* (title) + *s3b.f* (name) + (classifier): Martin, *Umm el-Qaab VII*, 44–45 (Stela 48, Cairo JdE 34416, Tomb Q); for the name, see Katrin Scheele-Schweitzer, *Die Personennamen des Alten Reiches: Altägyptische Onomastik unter lexikographischen und sozio-kulturellen Aspekten*, Philippika 28 (Wiesbaden: Harrassowitz Verlag, 2014), 634 [3013].

10 Male classifiers seem to occur from the reign of Den. Sign Gardiner A1, a crouching man, accompanies the individual's name. In some cases, the inscriptions depict a standing person with proportions of persons with short stature (Gardiner A282), therefore, Sabef should also have been one of this group.

11 Kerry Muhlestein, *Violence in the Service of Order: The Religious Framework for Sanctioned Killing in Ancient Egypt*, BARIS 2299 (Oxford: Archaeopress, 2011), 11–15.

12 Bruce Trigger, "The Rise of Egyptian Civilization," in *Ancient Egypt: A Social History*, ed. B.G. Trigger, B.J. Kemp, D. O'Connor, and A.B. Lloyd (Cambridge: Cambridge University Press, 1983), 52.

13 Rainer Stadelmann, *Die ägyptischen Pyramiden. Vom Ziegelbau zum Weltwunder* (Mainz am Rhein: Philipp von Zabern, 1997), 20: "es waren sicher keine Prinzen und hohe Beamte, sondern Zwerge, Friseure, kleine Handwerker, Frauen und sogar Hunde."

14 For example, Lana Troy, *Patterns of Queenship in Ancient Egyptian Myth and History*, BOREAS 14 (Uppsala and Stockholm: Almqvist and Wiksell, 1986).

15 See, for instance, Eva-Maria Engel, "Review of Geoffrey Thorndike Martin, *Umm el-Qaab VII. Private Stelae of the Early Dynastic Period from the Royal Cemetery at Abydos*, AV 123 (Wiesbaden: Harrassowitz, 2011)," *BiOr* 70 (2013): 659–63.

16 Martin, *Umm el-Qaab VII*, 22–23 (stela 8), 28–29 (stela 18), 30–31 (stela 23), 32–33 (stela 29).

17 For the titles, see Dilwyn Jones, *An Index of Ancient Egyptian Titles, Epithets and Phrases of the Old Kingdom*, 2 vols., BARIS 866 (Oxford: Archaeopress, 2000), 684 [2500], 980 [3618], 348

[1297], 685 [2503]; Silke Roth, *Die Königsmütter des Alten Ägypten von der Frühzeit bis zum Ende der 12. Dynastie*, ÄAT 46 (Wiesbaden: Harrassowitz, 2001), 38; Troy, *Patterns of Queenship*, 189; the attestations are *ḥtm(.t)-ḥr.w skr-ḫ3s.tj* (. . . *(?)*: Martin, *Umm el-Qaab VII*, 98–99 (Stela 124, Berlin 15483, Tomb T); . . . *(?)*: Martin, *Umm el-Qaab VII*, 28–29 (Stela 21, UC 14266, Tomb T); *šd(.t)-k3*: Martin, *Umm el-Qaab VII*, 96–97 (Stela 120, Upenn E.9902, Tomb T); *sšm.t-k3*: Martin, *Umm el-Qaab VII*, 96–97 (Stela 121, UC 14272, Tomb T); *šd(.t)-k3*: Martin, *Umm el-Qaab VII*, 98–99 (Stela 122, Tomb T); *k3-n.t*: Martin, *Umm el-Qaab VII*, 98–99 (Stela 123, UC 14273, Tomb T); . . . *(?)*: Martin, *Umm el-Qaab VII*, 98–99 (Stela 124, Berlin 15483, Tomb T); *m3ʿ.t/wḏb.t*: Martin, *Umm el-Qaab VII*, 98–99 (Stela 125, Pittsburgh, Tomb T)); *wr ḥts rmn/ʿ.w ḥr.w* (*nḫ.t-n.t:* Martin, *Umm el-Qaab VII*, 82–83 (Stela 95, JE 35005, Tomb O); Roth, *Die Königsmütter*, 379 [I.3.3/4], Troy, *Patterns of Queenship*, 152 [1.10])); *m33 ḥr.w wr ḥts rmn/ʿ.w stš* (*sšm.t-k3*: Martin, *Umm el-Qaab VII*, 82–83 (Stela 96, OIM 5863, Tomb O/marked T), Roth, *Die Königsmütter*, 379 [I.3.4/4]; Troy, *Patterns of Queenship*, 152 [1.8], Jones, *Index of Ancient Egyptian Titles*, 349 [1300], 421 [1561])); *m33 ḥr.w rmn/ʿ.w stš* (. . . *(?)*: Martin, *Umm el-Qaab VII*, 100–101 (Stela 128, OIM 6433, Tomb T); Roth, *Die Königsmütter*, 382–83 [I.5.3/3]; Troy, *Patterns of Queenship*, 152 [1.12]; *wdpw*: Martin, *Umm el-Qaab VII*, 100–101 (Stela 129, Berlin 15484, Tomb T) or *sm3.t*: Roth, *Die Königsmütter*, 382 [I.5.2/3]; Troy, *Patterns of Queenship*, S. 152 [1.13]; . . . ?: Martin, *Umm el-Qaab VII*, 190–91 (Stela 288, Tomb T, SCA)).

18 E.g., butcher (*sḫn 3ḫ* (title) + *ḥtp-sḫm* (name): Martin, *Umm el-Qaab VII*, 30–31 (Stela 24, Oxford E.3939, Tomb T); *nb-ḥtp* Martin, *Umm el-Qaab VII*, 176–77 (Stela 260, London 14279, enclosure Tomb 117); *k* . . . *(?)*: Martin, *Umm el-Qaab VII*, 199 (Stela 359, SCA, enclosure, date: Merneit)); hunter (*ḥtp (?)*: Martin, *Umm el-Qaab VII*, 184–85 (Stela 277, SCA, Tomb T)); baker (in: Martin, *Umm el-Qaab VII*, 42–43 (Stela 46, Chicago 6741, between Tombs U and Q); *di.n.f*: Martin, *Umm el-Qaab VII*, 142–43 (Stela 200, Louvre E.21707, Tomb Z or T)).

19 As suggested by Martin, *Umm el-Qaab VII*, 134–35: *ḥ3b.t (?)* (Stela 189, Hannover 1935.200.36, Tomb T).

20 *imi-nḥ.f (?)*: Martin, *Umm el-Qaab VII*, 196 (Stela 323, SCA, Tomb U).

21 *di.f (?)*: Martin, *Umm el-Qaab VII*, 146–47 (Stela 207, Louvre E.21713, Tomb Z or T).

22 Jana Jones, "Pre- and Early Dynastic Textiles: Technology, Specialisation and Administration During the Process of State Formation," in *Egypt at Its Origins 2: Proceedings of the International Conference "Origin of the State: Predynastic and Early Dynastic Egypt," Toulouse (France), 5–8 September 2005*, ed. B. Midant-Reynes and Y. Tristant, OLA 172 (Leuven, Paris, and Dudley: Peeters, 2008), 99–132.

23 E.g., Elfriede Reiser, *Der königliche Harim im alten Ägypten und seine Verwaltung*, Dissertationen der Universität Wien 77 (Vienna: Verlag Notring, 1972), 57–58.

24 George A. Reisner, *The Early Dynastic Cemeteries of Naga-ed-Dêr*, pt. 1 (Leipzig: J.C. Hinrichs, 1908), 119–22, pls. 43–44.

25 Peter Kaplony, *Die Inschriften der ägyptischen Frühzeit*, ÄA 8 (Wiesbaden: Harrassowitz, 1963); Peter Kaplony, *Die Inschriften der ägyptischen Frühzeit, Suppl.* ÄA 9 (Wiesbaden: Harrassowitz, 1964); Peter Kaplony, *Kleine Beiträge zu den Inschriften der ägyptischen Frühzeit*, ÄA 15 (Wiesbaden: Harrassowitz, 1966).

26 See Eva-Maria Engel, *Private Rollsiegel der Frühzeit und des frühen Alten Reiches. Versuch einer Einordnung*, Menes 8 (Wiesbaden: Harrassowitz, 2021).

27 Ilona Regulski, "Egypt's Early Dynastic Cylinder Seals Reconsidered," *BiOr* 68 (2011): 5–32.

28 E. Christiana Köhler, "Ursprung einer langen Tradition. Grab und Totenkult in der Frühzeit," in *Grab und Totenkult im Alten Ägypten*, ed. Heike Guksch, Eva Hofmann, and Martin Bommas (Munich: C.H. Beck, 2003), 23. Reisner had previously stated that some of the examples he had unearthed showed traces of use (Reisner, *Early Dynastic Cemeteries of Naga-ed-Dêr*, 122).

29 Eva-Maria Engel, "Siegelabrollungen," in "Umm el-Qaab. Nachuntersuchungen im frühzeitlichen Königsfriedhof: 16./17./18. Vorbericht," ed. Günter Dreyer et al., *MDAIK* 62 (2006): 121.

30 Ilona Regulski, "Seal Impressions from Tell el-Iswid," in *Tell el-Iswid, 2006–2009*, ed. Ahmed Baher and Beatrix Midant-Reynes, FIFAO 73 (Cairo: IFAO, 2014), 230–42.

31 Jean-Pierre Pätznick, *Die Siegelabrollungen und Rollsiegel der Stadt Elephantine im 3. Jahrtausend v. Chr. Spurensicherung eines archäologischen Artefaktes*, BARIS 1339 (Oxford: Oxbow Books, 2005); Eva-Maria Engel, "Die Rollsiegel und Siegelabrollungen," in *Elephantine* 24. *Funde und Befunde aus der Umgebung des Satettempels*, ed. Peter Kopp, AV 104 (Wiesbaden: Harrassowitz, 2018), 127–44.

32 Ramadan el-Sayed, *La déesse Neith de Saïs: Importance et rayonnement de son culte*, BdE 86 (Cairo: IFAO, 1982); Engel, "The Early Dynastic Neith," 69–85.

33 Jochem Kahl, *Das System der ägyptischen Hieroglyphenschrift in der 0.–3. Dynastie*, GOF IV, vol. 29 (Wiesbaden: Harrassowitz, 1994), 432 [a15], 434 [a30]: "auf Siegeln mit zumeist unklaren PN(?)." They were not included in Ilona Regulski, *A Palaeographic Study of Early Writing in Egypt*, OLA 195 (Leuven: Peeters, 2010).

34 Peter Kaplony, "Toter am Opfertisch," in *LÄ* 6 (Wiesbaden: Harrassowitz, 1986), 711.

35 Kaplony, "Toter am Opfertisch," 711: "Nicht nur Frauen, sondern auch Männer tragen eine über die Schulter fallende, große Perücke (als heliopolitanische Totentracht?)"; F.W. Freiherr von Bissing, *Der Tote vor dem Opfertisch*, Sitzungsberichte der Bayerischen Akademie der Wissenschaften 1952/3 (München, 1952), 9: "In der Frühzeit bestand noch kein grundsätzlicher Unterschied zwischen männlicher und weiblicher Haartracht."

36 See also recently Regulski, "Seal Impressions from Tell el-Iswid," 236; the inclusion of the sign as a15/a30 in the group of signs for men and their activities instead of B for women and their activities indicates that this sign was also taken to refer to men by Kahl (see above, footnote 33).

37 Ludwig D. Morenz and Robert Kuhn, "Ägypten in der Vor- und Frühzeit. Vorspann oder formative Phase? Ein kurzer Überblick," in *Vorspann oder formative Phase? Ägypten und der Vordere Orient 3500–2700 v. Chr.*, ed. Ludwig D. Morenz and Robert Kuhn, Philippika 48 (Wiesbaden: Harrassowitz, 2011), 8: "Außerdem ist *bis dato* davon auszugehen, dass vorwiegend die männliche Elite sich der Schrift als Kommunikationsmittel bediente. Dies wird zumindest durch die Überlieferung von Schreibertiteln belegt, die bisher nur für Männer ab der 1. Dyn. unter Pharao Semerchet bekannt sind."

38 Ranke, *PN*.

39 Scheele-Schweitzer, *Die Personennamen des Alten Reiches*.

40 Since this research is a work in progress, the numbers presented here are subject to change. See note 26, above.

41 E.g., Kaplony, *Die Inschriften der ägyptischen Frühzeit* 3, fig. 633.

42 E.g., *mri-kꜣ*: Kaplony, *Die Inschriften der ägyptischen Frühzeit, Suppl.*, fig. 919 (Cairo JdE 72554); for the name, see Scheele-Schweitzer, *Die Personennamen des Alten Reiches*, 389 [1345]: m and Stelae 61, 126 (Martin, *Umm el-Qaab VII*, 54–55, 100–101).

43 E.g., *it.i; it.it*: Kaplony, *Die Inschriften der ägyptischen Frühzeit, Suppl.*, fig. 924; for the possible names, see Scheele-Schweitzer, *Die Personennamen des Alten Reiches*, 273 [553, 552]: m, f.

44 E.g., *ḏs.ti*: Kaplony, *Die Inschriften der ägyptischen Frühzeit, Suppl.*, fig. 939; for the name, see Scheele-Schweitzer, *Die Personennamen des Alten Reiches*, 757 [3874]: f.

45 E.g., *mr(i).t-it(i.s)*: Kaplony, *Die Inschriften der ägyptischen Frühzeit* 3, fig. 613; for the standard, see el-Sayed, *La déesse Neith de Saïs* [Doc. 33]; for the name, see Scheele-Schweitzer, *Die Personennamen des Alten Reiches*, 394–95 [1377]: f.

46 E.g., *(i)r(i)-(i)ẖ.t* (title) + *nfr.i/nfr-ꜥnḫ* (name): Kaplony, *Die Inschriften der ägyptischen Frühzeit* 3, fig. 332 (Abydos Tombs P and V); for the names, see Scheele-Schweitzer, *Die Personennamen des Alten Reiches*, 465, 488 [2027; 1860]: m.

47 E.g., *hn.t*: Kaplony, *Die Inschriften der ägyptischen Frühzeit, Suppl.*, fig. 923; for the name, see Scheele-Schweitzer, *Die Personennamen des Alten Reiches*, 525 [2300]: *hn.tw*/m.

48 E.g., *ꜣḫ, sšm* (titles) + *šps-nṯr* (name): Kaplony, *Die Inschriften der ägyptischen Frühzeit, Suppl.*, fig. 921; for the name, see Scheele-Schweitzer, *Die Personennamen des Alten Reiches*, 674 [3295]: *šps-ptḥ*.

49 E.g., *im3-ib* (epithet) + *k3-ʿpr* (name): Kaplony, *Die Inschriften der ägyptischen Frühzeit* 3, fig. 424; for the name, see Scheele-Schweitzer, *Die Personennamen des Alten Reiches*, 694 [3430]: m.

50 See above, notes 34–36.

51 By reading the offering table sign as *šps*(*t*) and taking it to refer to women, it would denote the female title of a noblewoman; see Reiser, *Der königliche Harim*, 19.

52 Kaplony, *Die Inschriften der ägyptischen Frühzeit* 3, fig. 325.

53 Günter Dreyer, "Funde," in "Umm el-Qaab. Nachuntersuchungen im frühzeitlichen Königsfriedhof. 11./12. Vorbericht," ed. Günter Dreyer et al., *MDAIK* 56 (2000): 127, Abb. 27g.

3

The Funerary Domains of Setibhor and Other Old Kingdom Queens

Hana Vymazalová

The Djedkare Project for the exploration and documentation of the pyramid complex of King Djedkare at south Saqqara has been ongoing since 2009.[1] In 2018, the team uncovered new evidence on the owner of the smaller pyramid complex, which is located to the northeast of the king's funerary temple. This smaller monument, known as the pyramid complex of an "anonymous queen," was partly explored by Ahmed Fakhry in 1952, but the results of his exploration were never fully published. Two plans of the monument have been available, including Fakhry's plan published later by Mohamed Moursi,[2] and another drawn by Vito Maragioglio and Celeste Rinaldi,[3] both of which show the same general features although they differ in many details.[4] Despite the differences in the two plans, it is clear that the precinct of the anonymous queen was an exceptional monument. A detailed study of the architectonic features by Peter Jánosi shows that this funerary precinct combined elements typical for queens with elements typical for kings, indicating that its owner played an important role at the end of the Fifth Dynasty.[5] The unusual features of this queen's monument have led to long-term discussions, and multiple hypotheses have been presented over the years to explain the special status of the owner of this anonymous pyramid complex. It has been suggested that the owner might have been the wife of Djedkare,[6] that she might have herself ruled,[7] acted as a regent,[8] or, as the king's mother, played a role in the ascension of Unas,[9] or that her monument was later reused by one of the rulers of the late Old Kingdom.[10]

During the exploration of Djedkare's pyramid complex, which in 2018 concentrated on the area to the northeast of the king's funerary temple, a part of the queen's funerary temple was newly uncovered along the south side of her pyramid. It was here that the entrance into her temple was situated, opposite the so-called northern portico of the king's funerary temple.[11] In addition to the architecture, some remains of the relief decoration of the queen's monument were also uncovered in 2018, including blocks and fragments with reliefs and inscriptions. These revealed that the exceptional pyramid complex belonged to "King's wife, Setibhor." Besides several fragmentary inscriptions from the walls of her funerary temple, the most complete inscription listing her titles survived on a column from the entrance: "The one who sees Horus and Seth, the great one of the *ḥts*-scepter, greatly praised, king's wife, his beloved, Setibhor."[12] Despite the fragmentary state of preservation of the monument and many of the reliefs, the evidence that is available at the current state of research seems to confirm that Setibhor was the owner of the until-now anonymous pyramid complex, and that she was Djedkare's wife. The precise role that she played in the late Fifth Dynasty, however, remains to be studied.[13]

Funerary Domains of Queen Setibhor

After the discovery of the inscriptions with the title and name of Queen Setibhor, which helped to identify her as the owner of the until-then anonymous pyramid complex in Saqqara, it became apparent that her name had been attested previously.[14] The name Setibhor occurs in names of several funerary domains that are listed in tombs of Old Kingdom officials,[15] Akhethotep and Ptahhotep at Saqqara.[16]

The tomb of Akhethotep (D64), dating perhaps to the late Fifth–early Sixth Dynasty,[17] contains the procession of personifications of funerary domains in two different places: in the entrance room and in the chapel (fig. 3.1). The entrance room features the personifications of funerary domains along the bottom register of the east wall.[18] The figures have the traditional form of females carrying offerings, facing right toward the interior of the tomb; the names of the domains are carved in front of each respective figure. The domains attested in this procession (see table 3.1) have names that comprise the divine names of Anubis, Re, Wadjet, and Maat as well as the names of kings, including Djedefre, Userkaf, Sahure, Raneferef (Neferefre), Nyuserre, Menkauhor, and Djedkare, in addition to one domain with the name of Akhethotep himself and two domains bearing the name of Setibhor (in the second and sixteenth positions in the list).

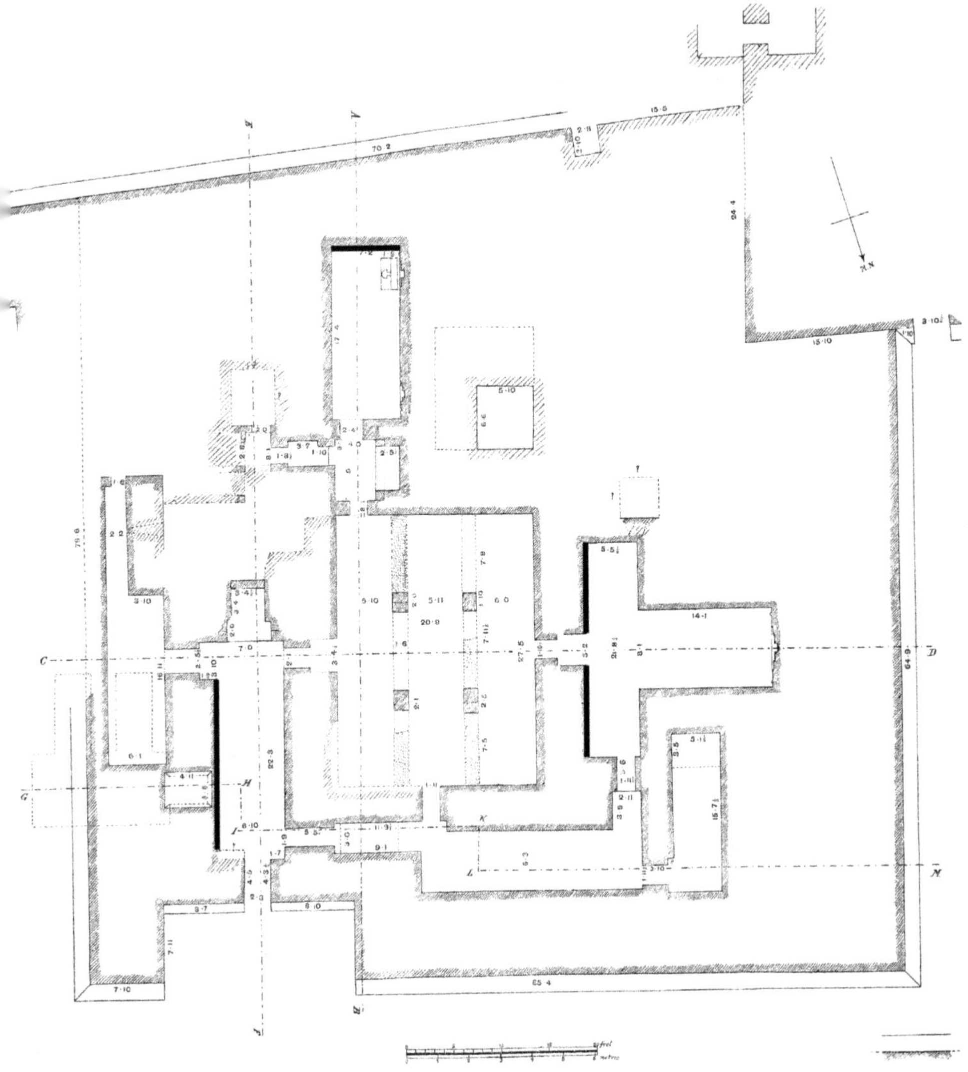

Fig. 3.1. The plan of the tomb of Akhethotep and Ptahhotep at Saqqara; the marked walls bear depictions of funerary domains

Table 3.1. Names of the personifications of funerary domains in the entrance hall of the tomb of Akhethotep

Entrance Room, East Wall	Name of the funerary domain	Location of the funerary domain
1	*ḥwt: sʿnḫ Ỉnpw* [*Ỉzz*]*i*	21st nome of Upper Egypt
2	*ḥwt-k3 St-ib-Ḥr*	20th nome of Upper Egypt
3	*ḥwt: sʿnḫ W3ḏt* [*Ỉzzi*]	11th nome of Lower Egypt
4	*mr M3ʿt* [*Ỉzzi*]	11th nome of Lower Egypt
5	*w3ḏt Ỉzzi*	11th nome of Lower Egypt
6	*mr M3ʿt Ỉzi*	7th nome of Lower Egypt
7	*ḥwt: M3ʿt Ny-*[*wsr-Rʿ*]	7th nome of Lower Egypt
8	*mr M3ʿt Ỉzzi*	7th nome of Lower Egypt
9	*ḏb3t* [*Wsr-k3.f*]	7th nome of Lower Egypt
10	*mr Rʿ ʿnḫ* [...]	11th nome of Lower Egypt
11	*sḫm Ḏd.f-Rʿ*	11th nome of Lower Egypt
12	*ḥwt: sʿnḫ Ḥr Ỉzzi*	2nd nome of Lower Egypt
13	*mnt Ỉzzi*	2nd nome of Lower Egypt
14	*grgt 3ḫt-ḥtp*	1st nome of Lower Egypt
15	*nfr hzwt Ỉ-k3w-Ḥr*	20th nome of Upper Egypt
16	*ḥwt-k3 St-ib-Ḥr*	21st nome of Upper Egypt
17	*int S3ḥw-Rʿ*	22nd nome of Upper Egypt

In the chapel of Akhethotep, the procession of the personifications of funerary domains covers the bottom registers of the east wall, which is divided by the doorway into north and south halves.[19] The domains are facing away from the entrance, as if entering the chapel, toward the figure of a standing scribe, who is identified as "his eldest son, Ptahhotep." The domains are depicted in the usual female form, carrying baskets on their heads and leading or carrying animals. Their names (see tables 3.2–3.3), which are written in front of each figure, include the divine names of Horus, Re, Anubis, and Maat; the names of kings Djedefre, Userkaf, Sahure, Raneferef, Nyuserre, Menkauhor, and Djedkare; the name of Akhethotep himself; and the name of Setibhor in three locations (in the fifth position on the north side, and in the fourth and fifth positions on the south side of the east wall). Nine of the domains bear no names.

Table 3.2. Names of the personifications of funerary domains on the north side of the east wall of the chapel of Akhethotep

Chapel entrance, north side	Name of the funerary domain	Location of the funerary domain
18	*ḥwt: sꜥnḫ Ḥr Ỉzzi*	2nd nome of Lower Egypt
19	*ḥwt: mnt Ỉzzi*	2nd nome of Lower Egypt
20	*grgt ꜣḫt-ḥtp*	1st nome of Lower Egypt
21	*nfr mnw Ỉzzi*	3rd nome of Lower Egypt
22	*ḥwt-kꜣ St-ib-Ḥr*	3rd nome of Lower Egypt
23	*mr Mꜣꜥt ꜥnḫ Ỉzzi*	11th nome of Lower Egypt
24	*mr Rꜥ ꜥnḫ* […]	11th nome of Lower Egypt
25	*sḫm Ḏd.f-Rꜥ*	11th nome of Lower Egypt
26	—	11th nome of Lower Egypt
27	*ḥwt: mr Mꜣꜥt ꜥnḫ Ny-wsr-Rꜥ*	7th nome of Lower Egypt
28	*mr Mꜣꜥt ꜥnḫ Ỉzzi*	7th nome of Lower Egypt
29	*ḏbꜣt Wsr-kꜣ.f*	7th nome of Lower Egypt
30	*mr Mꜣꜥt ꜥnḫ Ỉzi*	7th nome of Lower Egypt

Table 3.3. Names of the personifications of funerary domains on the south side of the east wall of the chapel of Akhethotep

Chapel entrance, south side	Name of the funerary domain	Location of the funerary domain
31	*ḥwt: sꜥnḫ Ỉnpw Ỉzzi*	21st nome of Upper Egypt
32	*nfr ḥswt Mn-kꜣw-Ḥr*	20th nome of Upper Egypt
33	*int Sꜣḥw-Rꜥ*	11th nome of Upper Egypt
34	*ḥwt-kꜣ St-ib-Ḥr*	20th nome of Upper Egypt
35	*grgt St-ib-Ḥr*	21st nome of Upper Egypt
36	—	—
37	—	—
38	—	—
39	—	—
40	—	—
41	—	—
42	—	—
43	—	—

Several occurrences of the name of Setibhor can be found among the funerary domains of Ptahhotep, whose chapel is situated in the southern part of his father Akhethotep's tomb.[20] It seems to be dated to the late Fifth or early Sixth Dynasty.[21] In this case, the procession of personifications of the funerary domains occupies the second and third top registers of the south wall of the chapel.[22] The personifications have the form of female offering bearers facing right—that is, toward the false door. The total number of funerary domains listed in this chapel is smaller as compared to Akhethotep's entrance room and chapel (see table 3.4). Similarly, however, it includes funerary domains with the names of the gods Anubis, Maat, Bawy (Two Souls), and Osiris; the names of kings, including Sneferu, Khufu, Userkaf, Sahure, Neferirkare, Menkauhor, and Djedkare; and the names of Setibhor and of Ptahhotep himself.

The funerary domains that are listed in the tombs of Akhethotep and Ptahhotep at Saqqara include mainly domains of kings of the Fourth and Fifth Dynasties, of which Djedkare's name occurs most frequently.[23] Moreover, several domain names occur in the lists of domains in both Akhethotep's and Ptahhotep's tombs, and these are marked by an asterisk in table 3.4. This evidence may indicate that the privilege to access offerings from these domains may have been transmitted from father to son. On the other hand, other domains are attested only in one of these tombs, and we can presume that these domains were probably assigned by the king directly to each tomb owner. These may have been associated with the various offices the tomb owners held.[24] No sources inform us directly about the principle of assignment of funerary domains to officials, and we do not have many indications concerning this aspect of the funerary cults besides the processions depicted in the tombs. In some tombs, we can find only funerary domains with the tomb owners' names, and these perhaps refer to tomb owners who could establish or were assigned their own estates (e.g., Ti or Rashepses[25]), while in other tombs, royal domains are more frequent, as here in the tombs of Akhethotep and Ptahhotep.

Besides the named kings, both Akhethotep and Ptahhotep received offerings from estates established for (or by) Setibhor. Moreover, in this tomb the specification of its location is given for each domain, which helps us with further identification.

In the tomb of Akhethotep we can find four or perhaps five funerary domains with the name of Setibhor: *ḥwt-kꜣ St-ib-Ḥr* located in the 20th and 21st nomes of Upper Egypt (nos. 2, 16, 34 in tables 3.1 and 3.2) and in the 3rd nome of Lower Egypt (no. 22 in table 3.2), and a *grgt St-ib-Ḥr* in the 21st nome of Upper Egypt (no. 35 in table 3.3). It is worth mentioning that numbers 2 and 34 bear an identical name and were situated in the same nome, and

Table 3.4. The names of the personifications of funerary domains from the chapel of Ptahhotep

Chapel South Wall	Name of the funerary domain	Location of the funerary domain
1*	*ḥwt: sʿnḫ Ỉnpw Ỉzzi*	21st nome of Upper Egypt
2	*ḥwt Ḫw.f-wi*	20th nome of Upper Egypt
3*	*ḥwt-k3 St-ib-Ḥr*	20th nome of Upper Egypt
4*	*grgt St-ib-Ḥr*	21st nome of Upper Egypt
5	*w3*	16th nome of Upper Egypt
6	*wr im3ḫ Ỉzzi*	11th nome of Lower Egypt
7	*nfr ʿnḫ Ỉ-k3w-Ḥr*	7th or 8th nome of Lower Egypt
8*	*mr M3ʿt Ỉzzi*	7th nome of Lower Egypt
9	[...] *Wsr-k3.f*	9th nome of Lower Egypt
10	*mr B3wy ʿnḫ Ỉzzi*	12th nome of Lower Egypt
11*	*ḥwt: sʿnḫ W3ḏt Ỉzzi*	11th (?) nome of Lower Egypt
12	*ḥwt: mr nfrt S3ḥw-Rʿ*	7th or 8th nome of Lower Egypt
13	*mn ḏf3 K3k3i*	12th nome of Lower Egypt
14	*nḫn Wsir*	9th nome of Lower Egypt
15	*w3ḫ Ỉzzi*	—
16	*int Snfrw*	1st (?) nome of Lower Egypt
17*	*ḥwt-k3 St-ib-Ḥr*	3rd nome of Lower Egypt
18	*rwḏ Snfrw*	10th nome of Lower Egypt
19	*Mḫrw*	2nd nome of Lower Egypt
20	*ḫnmt Ptḥ-ḥtp*	12th nome of Lower Egypt

therefore it is difficult to distinguish whether these entries refer to one and the same domain or two domains of the same names situated in the same neighborhood; the former seems more likely.

Among the domains listed in the chapel of Ptahhotep, we can find three occurrences mentioning three domains of the queen, namely a *ḥwt-k3 St-ib-Ḥr* located in the 20th nome of Upper Egypt and the 3rd nome of Lower Egypt (nos. 3 and 17 in table 3.4), and a *grgt St-ib-Ḥr* situated in the 21st nome of Upper Egypt (no. 4 in table 3.4). These three domains carry the same names and are located in the same nomes as the domains attested in the tomb of

Akhethotep. Similarly, three more domains bearing the name of Djedkare are attested in both Akhethotep's tomb and Ptahhotep's chapel (see table 3.4). It therefore seems that six domains with the names of Setibhor and Djedkare were passed from father to son, or used by both their funerary cults. This very likely points to a very close connection between the two officials to this particular king and the queen, further underlined by the suggested dating of the respective tombs to the late Fifth and possibly early Sixth Dynasty.

It is worth mentioning that the female figures that represent the funerary domains with Setibhor's name are carrying various products. In Akhethotep's entrance room, both figures carry a hemispherical basket with these products on their heads, and animals on their arms (fig. 3.2). In one of the figures, a little gazelle is placed on the domain's forearm, and in another, it is a goose along with a leash to which an antelope is tied, this time walking by the side of the domain. In Akhethotep's chapel, the figures carry baskets of conical or hemispherical shapes (fig. 3.3). The baskets are fully loaded with bread, jars, vegetables and fruits, poultry, and so forth. The domains hold the baskets with one hand on the front or back rim and in their other hand they carry a goose or duck, or a rope on which a gazelle or a calf is tied. One of the figures holds a duck and leads a gazelle with the same hand.

In Ptahhotep's chapel the depictions are similar, though not the same (fig. 3.4). One domain with Setibhor's name carries a large and heavy basket, which she holds with both hands; in addition, she has a bundle of lotuses over one of her arms. Another figure carries a closed chest on her head, while she holds a duck and a leash in her other hand, on which she leads a gazelle.

It is worth mentioning that each of the funerary domains with Setibhor's name that are depicted in the tomb of Akhethotep and the chapel of Ptahhotep is depicted differently. We can find here a general similarity of form, typical for all the funerary domains shown in the tomb, but on closer inspection, each depiction with Setibhor's name varies in such details as the shape of the basket, the variety of its products, the position of the arms, and details of the animals.

Another piece of evidence on funerary domains with Setibhor's name was uncovered recently in Djedkare's royal cemetery at south Saqqara, namely in the tomb of Khuwy.[26] The exploration of this tomb has not yet been concluded; however, it can be dated to the end of the Fifth and possibly early Sixth Dynasties;[27] thus, it seems close in date to the above-mentioned tombs of Akhethotep and Ptahhotep. The tomb contained a multi-roomed chapel, the decoration of which was almost entirely destroyed in antiquity, but many small fragments of reliefs were uncovered in the debris in front of the tomb and in the chapel.[28] Among these, we can find a few fragments of a procession of funerary domains (fig. 3.5).

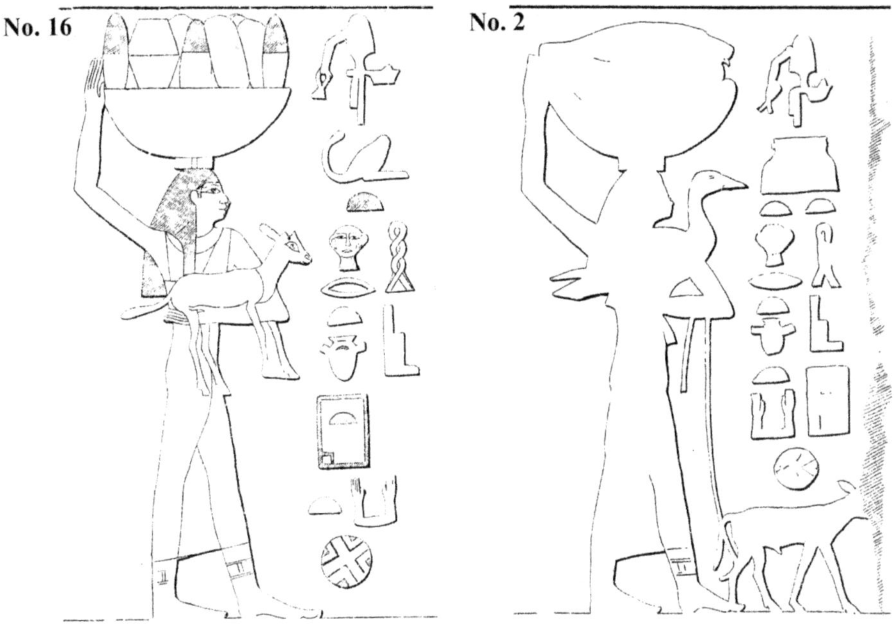

Fig. 3.2. Personifications of funerary domains with Setibhor's name in the tomb of Akhethotep

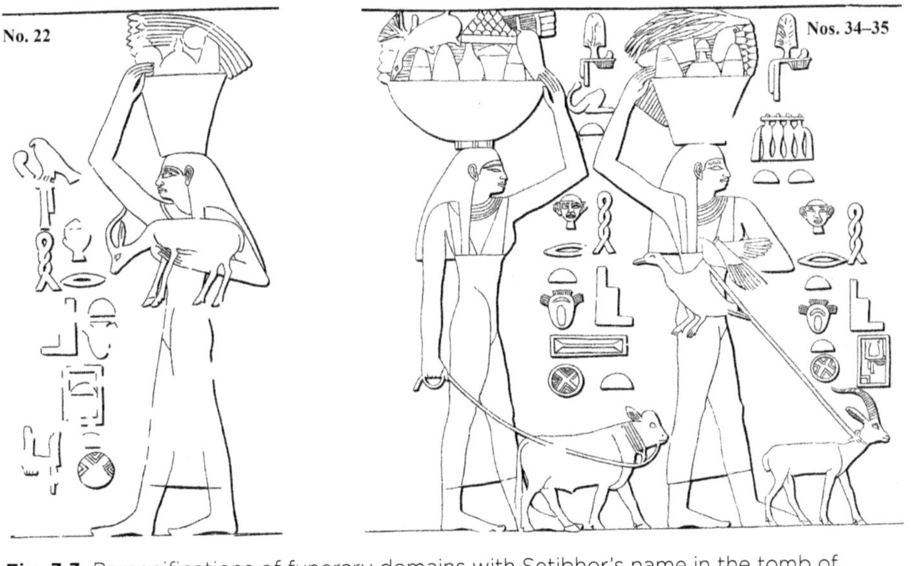

Fig. 3.3. Personifications of funerary domains with Setibhor's name in the tomb of Akhethotep

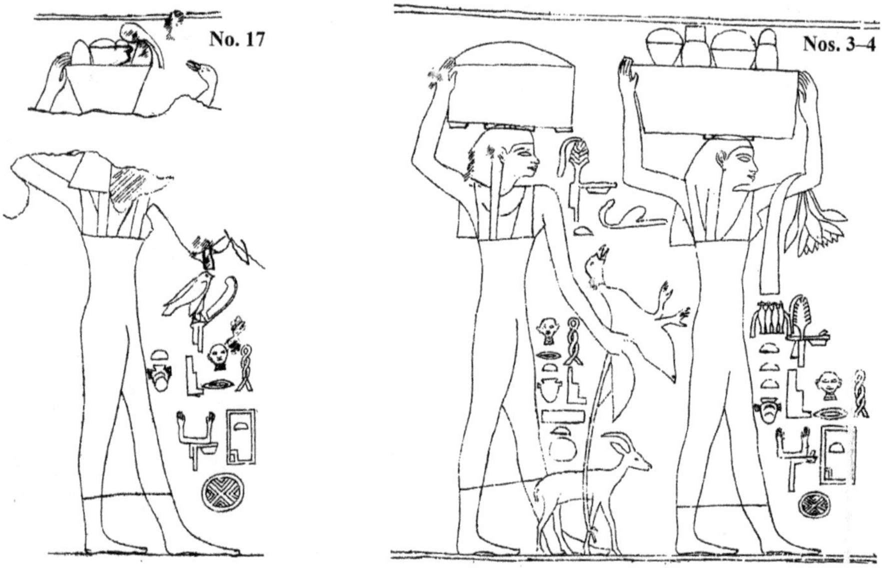

Fig. 3.4. Personifications of funerary domains with Setibhor's name in the chapel of Ptahhotep

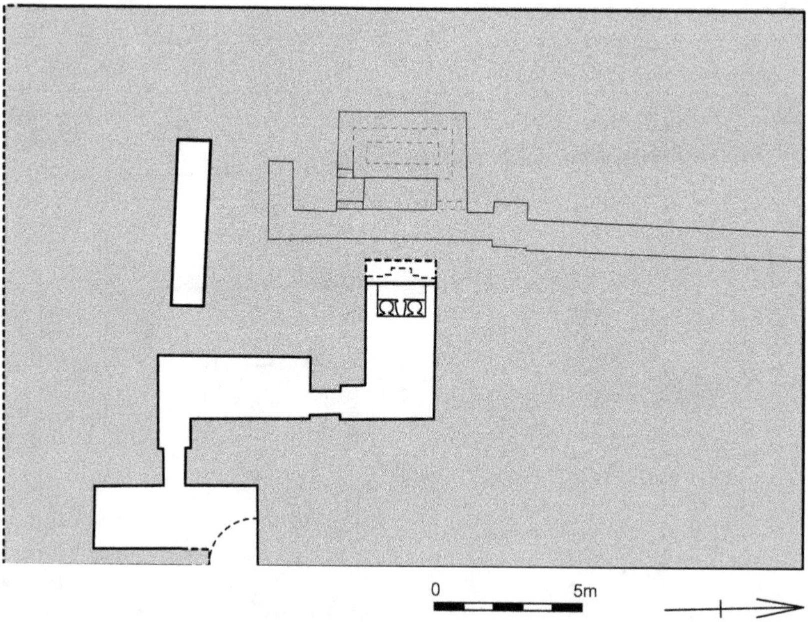

Fig. 3.5. Plan of Khuwy's tomb at south Saqqara

The preserved fragments of the depiction show several female figures representing personified funerary domains. Their names were carved in front of each figure; they are facing left, perhaps toward the interior of the chapel. The scene cannot be fully reconstructed and the total number of the depicted domains is not clear. However, on the few surviving fragments of the scene, we can recognize that one of the figures bears the name of King Djedkare while at least two fragments contain the name of Setibhor (table 3.5).[29] One of them is depicted as a female carrying a hemispherical basket loaded with bread on her head and a bird in her hand, and was probably situated in the 14th nome of Lower Egypt, the name of which is carved before the previous figure. Of the other domain with Setibhor's name, only the queen's name is preserved on a small fragment (fig. 3.6).

Table 3.5. Funerary domains on the relief fragments from the tomb of Khuwy

North wall of door thickness	Name of the funerary domain	Location of the funerary domain
1	[...]	[...]
2	*mr nfrt Ỉzzi*	16th nome of Lower Egypt
3	[...]	14th nome of Lower Egypt
4	[...] *msw St-ib-Ḥr*	
5	[...] *St-ib-Ḥr*	[...]

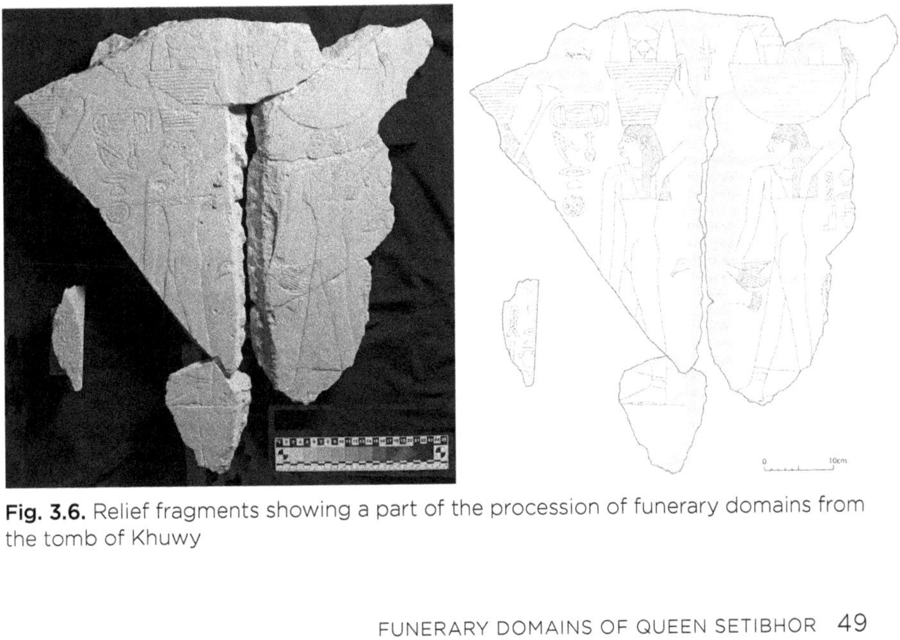

Fig. 3.6. Relief fragments showing a part of the procession of funerary domains from the tomb of Khuwy

Despite the fragmentary state of preservation of the depiction from Khuwy's tomb, we can see that the location of the funerary domain with the name of Setibhor seems to be different from the location attested for domains with her name in the tombs of Akhethotep and Ptahhotep. In addition, the preserved part of the name of the domain in Khuwy's tomb differs from the simple *ḥwt-k3* and *grgt* of Setibhor from the latter tombs. Thus, the evidence currently available from these nonroyal tombs attests to five or perhaps six different funerary domains with the name of Queen Setibhor.

The domains of Setibhor provoke interesting questions concerning the role of Old Kingdom queens in the economy of funerary cults. It is apparent that funerary domains with names of Old Kingdom queens are not often found in the evidence. It is good to remember, however, that the funerary domains of Setibhor have been known for many years, but her identification as the queen of Djedkare remained unknown until recently. We can therefore pose the question whether some more ancient Egyptian royal wives and mothers, yet unidentified as queens, may be found in the names of funerary domains from nonroyal tombs of the Old Kingdom.

Funerary Domains of Old Kingdom Queens

Besides Setibhor, the three other queens whose funerary domains are attested are Neferhetepes, the wife of King Userkaf and mother of King Sahure;[30] Khenut, the wife of Unas;[31] and Seshseshet, the mother of Teti.[32] Two of these queens played an important role at the beginning of a new dynasty.

Neferhetepes is associated with the funerary domains that were depicted in her pyramid complex, which is situated next to Userkaf's mortuary monument,[33] and also in the tomb of Persen, located nearby at Saqqara (D45).[34] In her pyramid complex, the procession includes at least two funerary domains with the name of the queen, *Ḥ3 mr Nfr-ḥtp.s* ("God of the West loves Neferhetepes"), and [...] *mr Nfr-ḥtp.s* ("God [...] loves Neferhetepes"), and yet another one bearing the name of King Khufu.[35] In Persen's tomb, *int Nfr-ḥtp.s* ("The valley of Neferhetepes") appears alongside domains with the names of Kings Sneferu and Djedefre, as well as several domains with general names.[36] In addition to the list of funerary domains, an inscription in the tomb of Persen explicitly mentions that the invocation offerings (*prt-ḫrw*) for his funerary cult were provided as a reversion of offerings (*wḏb-rd*) by Queen Neferhetepes, and that these offerings were provided by the Temple of Ptah at Memphis.[37] Naturally, one wants to know whether the inscription and the depiction of the funerary domains of Neferhetepes both express the same information in different forms or whether each refers to a certain specific aspect of Persen's cult. The latter seems more likely because the inscription only mentions offerings from the queen but not from the kings whose domains are listed in Persen's tomb, and the reference to the Temple of Ptah as the source of these products may be yet another indication of the specific nature of these offerings.[38] Therefore, the inscription seems to stress a privilege granted to Persen over and above the assignment of offerings from the funerary domains of kings and the queen, which we do not fully understand today without a wider context.

Funerary domains with the name of Queen Khenut are attested only in her tomb at Saqqara,[39] and no attestations are known from tombs of officials. The domains in Khenut's tomb include *ỉnt Ḫnwt* ("The foundation of Khenut"), *ỉrp Ḫnwt* ("The wine of Khenut"), and *tꜣ-nbs Ḫnwt* ("The *nbs*-bread of Khenut").[40] No other domains are attested in this tomb.

Funerary domains with the name of Queen Seshseshet I can be found in the tomb of Mehu at Saqqara, alongside the domains of Kings Unas and Teti. These are named *ỉrp mwt nswt Sšsšt* ("The wine of the king's mother Seshseshet") and *ḳbḥwt mwt nswt Sšsšt* ("The refreshment of the king's mother Seshseshet"),[41] clearly identifying the queen among the royal women of the same name.[42]

Yet another queen who may occur in the names of funerary domains from the Fifth Dynasty pyramid complex of King Nyuserre is Hetepheres (?).[43] However, the names of these domains as well as the names of this presumed queen are not fully preserved in all the instances, and therefore the interpretation of this evidence is rather problematic[44] and we do not include it in our discussion.

The attested names of the domains of Queens Neferhetepes, Setibhor, Khenut, and Seshseshet are not different from other examples of that period. Similar names can be found among royal funerary domains,[45] but they also correspond well to the usual names of private installations, which started to occur at Saqqara from the late Fourth and early Fifth Dynasties.[46] Names of domains with the names of private individuals[47] do not refer to the names of gods, which was an exclusive privilege of the kings. The reference to gods in the names of the domains of Queen Neferhetepes, therefore, seems to confirm that the funerary domains of queens can be understood as more "royal" than "private" establishments.

The extant evidence in the form of processions of personified estates does not inform us about the process of the establishment of the funerary domains, their precise operation, the degree of involvement of kings, or whether these domains were established and started to be used by the beneficiaries during their lifetimes or were only assigned to them for their afterlife. The lack of evidence limits our understanding of the economic operation of funerary cults, but we can suppose that the establishment and assignment of funerary domains to an individual followed a certain formal procedure which required direct approval by the ruling king. It is possible that the domains with names of private individuals were not newly created but were established by renaming already existing estates, the produce of which was then assigned exclusively to the funerary cult of these deceased individuals.[48]

The occurrence of funerary domains with the names of queens alongside those with the names of kings in nonroyal tombs further poses the question of whether the queens could independently decide about the produce of these estates or whether the estates were assigned to them only for the use of their funerary cults and otherwise were further managed by the kings. Persen's inscription states that the offerings from the cult of Queen Neferhetepes were granted to him "in the reign of Sahure,"[49] but this does not necessarily mean "by Sahure." It is not clear whether it was the queen herself or her son-king who made the order in favor of Persen. The answers to these questions will always remain rather speculative. In addition, the scarcity of attestations of funerary domains with the names of queens—at the moment, limited to Neferhetepes, Setibhor, Khenut, Seshseshet I, and possibly also Hetepheres—indicate that such a privilege may only have been given to a few important and powerful queens, and therefore it is highly likely that the king's approval of their establishment as well as management was essential.

In addition to the funerary domains of queens, however, we can find additional evidence on the donations of offerings from queens to private individuals. These come from several inscriptions from nonroyal tombs and, as with Persen's inscription mentioned above, refer to the donations of offerings from queens Nymaathap and Khamerernebty to the cults of private individuals who were undoubtedly very closely connected with them and most likely served them during their lives.[50] At the same time, however, there are no funerary domains attested for these queens. This may be simply due to the limited scale of excavation and the state of the preservation of the tombs, but a lack of evidence does not always mean a lack of existence. In his recent study of this evidence, Mohamed Ismail Khaled concluded that the queens who donated offerings to officials were kings' mothers, and that they may have gained the power to do so only during the rule of their sons.[51] His conclusion seems to underline the significant role played by these queens in the history of the Old Kingdom.

As mentioned above, it is difficult to ascertain whether the inscriptions that mention offerings from queens for private individuals refer to the same type of connection as depictions of funerary domains with queens' names in the tombs. In the latter case, it also seems likely that the lifespans of the queens and these beneficiaries overlapped because the funerary domains of the queens have thus far been found in tombs which were close in date to their own monuments.[52] Similarly, domains with the names of private individuals can be found only in their own tombs or, with some exceptions, in the tombs of their closest relatives.[53] On the other hand, royal funerary domains continued to occur in nonroyal tombs centuries after the rules of the respective kings. The small number of attestations of the queens' funerary domains together with the close date of the tombs of the private individuals in whose tombs they occur therefore seems to indicate a relatively short life of these domains.[54]

In the evidence presented above, the funerary domains of Setibhor are our main focus. Funerary domains with her name can be found in at least three tombs of high officials, who appear to have been connected to her during their lifetimes as well as in the afterlife. If we consider the hypothesis suggested above—that the donations of offerings from queens to officials were limited to mothers of kings—the case of Queen Setibhor poses a problem. At the current state of research, the only titles preserved for Setibhor in her own pyramid complex are those of the king's wife, but no evidence of a king's mother has been uncovered to date. The inscription on the granite column from the portico of the queen's funerary temple, which is undamaged, indicates that the title "king's mother" was not included among the queen's titles at this prominent part of the monument.[55] For the moment, therefore, we cannot conclude whether Setibhor was an exception to the rule, or whether there was no such rule, or whether she may have become the king's mother at a certain point not yet attested in our sources. More evidence on the queen's funerary domains as well as her status can, however, be expected to be found in the future in her pyramid complex as well as in tombs at Djedkare's royal cemetery at south Saqqara.

Notes

1 Mohamed Megahed, "Neue Forschungen im Grabbezirk des Djedkare-Isesi," *Sokar* 22 (2011): 25–35; Mohamed Megahed, "Die Wiederentdeckung des Pyramidenbezirks des Djedkare-Isesi in Sakkara-Süd," *Sokar* 28 (2014): 6–19; Mohamed Megahed and Peter Jánosi, "The Pyramid Complex of Djedkare at Saqqara South: Recent Results and Future Prospects," in *Abusir and Saqqara in the Year 2015*, ed. Miroslav Bárta, Filip Coppens, and Jaromír Krejčí (Prague: Czech Institute of Egyptology, Faculty of Arts, Charles University, 2017), 237–56; Mohamed Megahed, Peter Jánosi, and Hana Vymazalová, "Djedkare's Pyramid Complex: Preliminary Report of the 2016 Season," *PES* 19 (2017): 37–52; Mohamed Megahed, Peter Jánosi, and Hana Vymazalová, "Djedkare's Pyramid Complex: Preliminary Report of the 2017 Season," *PES* 21 (2018): 34–44; Mohamed Megahed, Peter Jánosi, and Hana Vymazalová, "Exploration of the Pyramid Complex of King Djedkare: Season 2018," *PES* 23 (2019): 12–36. See also Mohamed Megahed, Hana Vymazalová, Vladimír Brůna, and Marek Zdeněk, "Die Pyramide des Djedkare-Isesi in 3-D. Neue

Methoden zur Dokumentation der Königlichen Grabkammer," *Sokar* 32, no. 1 (2016): 40–51. For the relief decoration, see Mohamed Megahed, "The Pyramid Complex of Djedkare-Isesi at South Saqqara and Its Decorative Program" (PhD diss., Charles University in Prague, 2016).

2 Mohamed Moursi, "Die Ausgrabungen in der Gegend um die Pyramide des *Ḏd-kꜣ-Rꜥ* "*Issj*" bei Saqqara," *ASAE* 71 (1987): 185–93.

3 Vito Giuseppe Maragioglio and Celeste Ambriogio Rinaldi, *Notizie sulle piramidi di Zedefra, Zedkara Isesi, Teti* (Turin: T. Artale, 1962), 38–43, pl. 5; Vito Giuseppe Maragioglio and Celeste Ambriogio Rinaldi, *L'architettura delle piramidi menfite*, vol. 8 (Turin: Artale, 1977), pl. 15, fig. 1.

4 For more information, see Peter Jánosi, "Die Pyramidenanlage der 'Anonymen Königin' des Djedkare-Isesi," *MDAIK* 45 (1989): 187–202; Mohamed Megahed, "The Pyramid Complex of 'Djedkare's Queen' in South Saqqara Preliminary Report 2010," in *Abusir and Saqqara in the Year 2010*, ed. Miroslav Bárta, Filip Coppens, and Jaromír Krejčí (Prague: Czech Institute of Egyptology, Charles University, Faculty of Arts, 2011), 616–34.

5 Jánosi (in "Die Pyramidenanlage der 'Anonymen Königin' des Djedkare-Isesi," 191–202) compares the presumed size of the queen's pyramid, 80 cubits, to those of queens Neferhetepes and Khentkaus II, which measured only 50 cubits on their sides. The anonymous funerary temple contained, among other features, a courtyard with columns instead of pillars, as was common for Old Kingdom queens. Moreover, Jánosi noticed that the number of columns in this queen's temple was greater than the number of columns in the temple of Djedkare himself as well as those of his predecessors. The temple also contains a square antechamber, which is yet another feature known only from pyramid complexes of kings, associated with kingship and the *hebsed*; it is the largest known antechamber of the Old Kingdom. For the discussion on the queen's complex, see also Megahed, "The Pyramid Complex of 'Djedkare's Queen' in South Saqqara Preliminary Report 2010."

6 Maragioglio and Rinaldi, *L'architettura delle piramidi menfite*, vol. 8, 98.

7 Klaus Baer, *Rank and Title in the Old Kingdom: The Structure of the Egyptian Administration in the Fifth and Sixth Dynasties* (Chicago: University of Chicago Press, 1960), 299.

8 Vivienne Gae Callender, *In Hathor's Image* I: *The Wives and Mothers of Egyptian Kings from Dynasties I–VI* (Prague: Charles University in Prague, Faculty of Arts, 2011), 191.

9 Maragioglio and Rinaldi, *Notizie sulle piramidi di Zedefra, Zedkara Isesi, Teti*, 38–42.

10 Callender, In *Hathor's Image* I, 189, 191.

11 Megahed, Jánosi, and Vymazalová, "Exploration of the Pyramid Complex of King Djedkare: Season 2018," 27–29.

12 Megahed, Jánosi, and Vymazalová, "Exploration of the Pyramid Complex of King Djedkare: Season 2018," 32. For the evidence on the queen's titles, see also Mohamed Megahed and Hana Vymazalová, "Notes on the Newly Discovered Name of Djedkare's Queen," in *Guardian of Ancient Egypt: Studies in Honor of Zahi Hawass*, ed. Janice Kamrin, Miroslav Bárta, Salima Ikram, Mark Lehner, and Mohamed Megahed (Prague: Charles University, Faculty of Arts, 2020), 1034.

13 Megahed, Jánosi, and Vymazalová, "Exploration of the Pyramid Complex of King Djedkare: Season 2018," 32–33; Megahed and Vymazalová, "Notes on the Newly Discovered Name of Djedkare's Queen," 1034–37.

14 See Hermann Ranke, *PN* 1, *428;* 15; Katrin Scheele-Schweitzer, *Die Personennamen des Alten Reiches. Altägyptische Onomastik unter lexikographischen und sozio-kulturellen Aspekten*, Philippika 28 (Wiesbaden: Harrassowitz, 2014), 631 [2996].

15 It is worth mentioning that no funerary domains with the queen's name have been attested among the fragments of reliefs from her funerary monument. The study of these reliefs has not been concluded yet, but several published fragments of the theme of personifications of funerary domains from her funerary temple feature the name of King Djedkare. See Mohamed Megahed, "The Pyramid Complex of 'Djedkare's Queen' in South Saqqara Preliminary Report 2010," 629–31n361 and n435.

16 See also Megahed, Jánosi, and Vymazalová, "Exploration of the Pyramid Complex of King Djedkare: Season 2018," 32; Megahed and Vymazalová, "Notes on the Newly Discovered Name of Djedkare's Queen," 1035.

17 For the suggested dates of this tomb, see for instance: the reign of Djedkare according to Norman de Garis Davies, *The Mastaba of Ptahhetep and Akhethetep at Saqqareh*, vol. 2, ASE Memoir 9 (London: Kegan Paul and Co., 1901), 21; the reigns of Djedkare and Unas according to Yvonne Harpur, *Decoration in Egyptian Tombs of the Old Kingdom: Studies in Orientation and Scene Content*, StudEgypt 14 (London and New York: KPI, 1987), 272; the reigns of Unas and Teti according to Helen Jacquet-Gordon, *Les noms des domaines funéraires sous l'ancien empire égyptien*, BdE 34 (Cairo: IFAO, 1962), 386.

18 Davies, *The Mastaba of Ptahhetep and Akhethetep* 2, pls. 10–11; Jacquet-Gordon, *Les noms des domaines*, 387–90nn1–17.

19 Davies, *The Mastaba of Ptahhetep and Akhethetep*, vol. 2, pls. 13–14; Jacquet-Gordon, *Les noms des domaines*, 392–95nn18–35.

20 Davies, *The Mastaba of Ptahhetep and Akhethetep*; Rosalind F.E. Paget and Annie A. Pirie, *The Tomb of Ptah-hetep*, ERA 2 (London: Bernard Quaritch, 1989); Yvonne Harpur and Paolo Scremin, *The Chapel of Ptahhotep: Scene Details*, Egypt in Miniature 2 (Oxford: Oxford Expedition to Egypt, 2008).

21 For the suggestions on dating: the reign of Djedkare according to Paget and Pirie, *Tomb of Ptah-hetep*, 33; the reign of Unas according to Harpur, *Decoration in Egyptian Tombs*, 274; the reigns of Unas or Teti according to Jacquet-Gordon, *Les noms des domaines*, 398.

22 Paget and Pirie, *Tomb of Ptah-hetep*, 30–31, pls. 34–35; Harpur and Scremin, *Chapel of Ptahhotep*, 355, fig. 4. This position of the personification of funeral domains is unusual for this period; see Harpur, *Decoration in Egyptian Tombs*, 83. For the funerary domains, see Jacquet-Gordon, *Les noms des domaines*, 398–402.

23 None of the attested names of Djedkare's domains are known from this king's pyramid complex. For the available evidence on domains from Djedkare's funerary temple, see Megahed, "The Pyramid Complex of Djedkare-Isesi at South Saqqara and Its Decorative Program," 202–57.

24 See this suggestion for the vizier's office in Harpur and Scremin, *Chapel of Ptahhotep*, 284.

25 See, e.g., Jacquet-Gordon, *Les noms des domaines*, 357–65, 371–72.

26 For a preliminary report on this tomb, see Mohamed Megahed and Hana Vymazalová, "The Tomb of Khuwy at Djedkare's Royal Cemetery at South Saqqara: Preliminary Report on the 2019 Spring Season," *PES* 23 (2019): 37–48.

27 The dating of this tomb is only preliminary and will be further specified after the conclusion of the exploration and the analysis of the evidence uncovered in the tomb.

28 For this type of chapels and their decoration, see Harpur, *Decoration in Egyptian Tombs*, 106–10.

29 See also Megahed and Vymazalová, "The Tomb of Khuwy at Djedkare's Royal Cemetery," 39–40; Megahed and Vymazalová, "Notes on the Newly Discovered Name of Djedkare's Queen," 1035.

30 Miroslav Verner, *Sons of the Sun: Rise and Decline of the Fifth Dynasty* (Prague: Charles University, Faculty of Arts, 2014), 30–33, 37; Tarek El Awady, *Abusir XVI: Sahure—The Pyramid Causeway: History and Decoration Program in the Old Kingdom* (Prague: Charles University, 2009), 169, 240–44.

31 Peter Munro, *Der Unas-Friedhof Nord-West I: Topographisch-historische Einleitung. Das Doppelgrab der Königinnen Nebet und Khenut* (Mainz am Rhein: Philipp von Zabern, 1993); for titles see 85–88; Vivienne G. Callender, *In Hathor's Image*, 204–206.

32 Vivienne G. Callender, *In Hathor's Image*, 206–209.

33 Audran Labrousse and Jean-Philippe Lauer, *Les complexes funéraires d'Ouserkaf et de Néferhétepès*, BdE 130 (Cairo: IFAO, 2000).

34 Auguste Mariette, *Les mastabas de l'ancien empire* (Paris: F. Vieweg, 1885), 299–301; Hilda Flinders Petrie and Margaret A. Murray, *Seven Memphite Tomb Chapels*, BSEA 65 (London: B. Quaritch, 1952), 8–10, 20–21, pls. IX–X.

35 Labrousse and Lauer, *Les complexes funéraires d'Ouserkaf et de Néferhétepès*, 1:157–58nn272–74, 2:115, fig. 365a–b, doc. 272 A–P. A domain of Khufu is also attested, for instance, in the pyramid complex of Queen Khentkaus II in Abusir where, however, no evidence of domains with her own name have survived; see Vymazalová, "The Administration and Economy of the Pyramid Complexes and Royal Funerary Cults in the Old Kingdom" (unpublished habilitation thesis, Charles University in Prague), 202; Miroslav Verner, *Abusir III: The Pyramid Complex of Khentkaus* (Prague: Karolinum, 1995), 72–73, 88, pl. 20.

36 Jacquet-Gordon, *Les noms des domaines*, 334–36.

37 Mariette, *Les mastabas de l'Ancien empire*, 300; Urk. I, 37.10–15; Günther Roeder, *Aegyptische Inschriften aus den Königlichen Museen zu Berlin*, vol. 1: *Inschriften von der Ältesten Zeit bis zum Ende der Hyksoszeit* (Leipzig: J.C. Hinrichs, 1969), 22. Also Hratch Papazian, "The Temple of Ptah and Economic Contacts between Memphite Cult Centers in the Fifth Dynasty," in *8. Ägyptologische Tempeltagung: Interconnections between Temples*, ed. Monika Dolińska and Horst Beinlich (Wiesbaden: Harrassowitz, 2010), 137–39. See also briefly in Hana Vymazalová, "Administration and Economy," 215.

38 The Temple of Ptah at Memphis seems to have played a significant role in royal funerary cults in relation to festivals, but it is questionable whether it was involved in "ordinary" supplies of funerary cults. Therefore, Persen's inscription may have referred to specific offerings, but such information is omitted in the inscription, which refers to the everyday nature of the deliveries instead.

39 Munro, *Unas-Friedhof*, 59; the funerary domains are depicted on the north wall of Room A of Khenut's tomb in the bottom register. See also Callender, *In Hathor's Image*, 205.

40 Munro, *Unas-Friedhof*, 59, pl. 35; Jacquet-Gordon, *Les noms des domaines*, 396.

41 Jacquet-Gordon, *Les noms des domaines*, 422–23.

42 Funerary domains with the name of Seshseshet can be also found, for instance, in the tomb of Mereruka, in the chapel of his wife, Waatetkhethor Seshseshet. See Jacquet-Gordon, *Les noms des domaines*, 414–15.

43 Ludwig Borchardt, *Das Grabdenkmal des Königs Ne-User-Re*, Ausgrabungen der Deutschen Orient-Gesellschaft in Abusir 1902–1904 no. 1; WVDOG 7 (Osnabrück: Otto Zeller Verlag, 1984), 79 nos. 7, 1–9. The interpretation of the preserved names of domains from Nyuserre's pyramid complex in relation to Queen Hetepheres was suggested by Jacquet-Gordon (*Les noms des domaines*, 153), who supposed that this was probably one of the queens of the Fourth or Fifth Dynasties.

44 Borchardt's publication does not include photographs or drawings of the relief fragments in question, which complicates the collation of the evidence with the original pieces.

45 Jacquet-Gordon, *Les noms des domaines*, 125–200; Mohamed Ismail Khaled, *Abusir XXVI. The Funerary Domains in the Pyramid Complex of Sahura: An Aspect of the Economy in the Late Third Millennium BCE* (Prague: Charles University, Faculty of Arts, 2020).

46 See Jacquet-Gordon, *Les noms des domaines*, 14–20; in Giza, such domains occur even earlier than the Fourth Dynasty. For discussion on funerary domains in nonroyal tombs, see also Vymazalová, "Administration and Economy," 205–18.

47 The existence of private domains indicates that funerary cults of certain dignitaries and officials were not fully dependent on the king; see Jacquet-Gordon, *Les noms des domaines*, 17–18. In some cases, perhaps, they may have been inherited or shared with other individuals, as is indicated by the occurrence of funerary domains with private names in the tombs of other individuals; see Vymazalová, "Administration and Economy," 210.

48 Vymazalová, "Administration and Economy," 216. On the other hand, the funerary domains with general names may have been used to sustain funerary cults of more individuals and institutions. In this manner, the private domains indicate that funerary cults of certain dignitaries and officials were not fully dependent on the king, and in some cases may have been inherited or shared with other individuals.

49 See, e.g., Papazian, "The Temple of Ptah and Economic Contacts between Memphite Cult Centers in the Fifth Dynasty," 137–38.

50 Papazian, "The Temple of Ptah and Economic Contacts between Memphite Cult Centers in the Fifth Dynasty," 139n9; Mohamed Ismail Khaled, "The Donation of Royal Funerary Domains in the Old Kingdom," in *Rich and Great: Studies in Honour of Anthony J. Spalinger on the Occasion of His 70th Feast of Thoth*, ed. Renata Landgráfová and Jana Mynářová (Prague: Charles University in Prague, Faculty of Arts, 2016), 171–72.

51 Khaled, "The Donation of Royal Funerary Domains in the Old Kingdom," 171–72, 182.

52 The suggested dating of the tombs under consideration indicates that the tomb owners lived during the lifetimes of the queens, but died shortly after. Therefore, these tomb owners probably belonged to younger generations born during the queens' lives. Akhethotep and Ptahhotep represent two generations of the same family.

53 Vymazalová, "Administration and Economy," 209–11.

54 The evidence on funerary domains is very limited, but it seems likely that many domains were reused and renamed after the death of the owner in order to redirect their produce to new projects and funerary cults. See, for instance, Vymazalová, "Administration and Economy," 235–37; Khaled, *Abusir XXVI*, 190.

55 It cannot be entirely excluded that the other column from the portico, which is lost today, bore a different inscription, and that the title of a king's mother may have been included there. This possibility, however, does not seem very likely for an Old Kingdom monument. See also Megahed and Vymazalová, "Notes on the Newly Discovered Name of Djedkare's Queen," 1034–37.

4

Elevated or Diminished? Questions Regarding Middle Kingdom Royal Women

Isabel Stünkel

WITHIN ANCIENT EGYPTIAN SOCIETY, the royal women were the females with the highest status,[1] which derived from their degree of kinship to the ruler, as expressed by their highest titles: the mother of the king, the wife of the king, the daughter of the king, and the sister of the king. Among them, it was the king's mother who ranked at the top, followed by the king's wives, and then his daughters.[2] From the Thirteenth Dynasty onward, the title *ḥmt nswt wrt* was used to distinguish one among the royal wives.[3]

The generally high status of royal females is undoubted and widely recognized. Yet regarding the status of royal women in the Middle Kingdom compared to royal women of the Old Kingdom, there are differing opinions. Despite the fact that our knowledge is very incomplete, differences between these two periods can be observed—for example, in the way the women were depicted, by the titles they carried, or by the tomb structures in which they were buried. Scholars have used these differences to argue in two opposite directions. In the 2007 article "The Status of the Queen in Dynasty XII," Jack Josephson and Rita Freed talk about an "elevated status of Twelfth-Dynasty queens," a "dramatic rise in the status of the queen at this time" (meaning the reign of Senwosret II), and "a revolutionary transformation in the concept of queenship in the Middle Kingdom."[4] According to them, the queen "no longer functioned merely as a consort of the king but rose to occupy a vital position in the politics and religion of the nation."[5] This is in strong contrast to Ann Roth, who briefly mentioned in the 2005 Hatshepsut exhibition catalog that "the status of royal women declined during this period" (referring to the

Middle Kingdom).[6] These differing approaches provide us with an opportunity to discuss the topic further.[7] The present author does not agree with either of these opposing views, and a more nuanced view is presented. It will be shown that some of the arguments used to support either an elevated or a diminished status for Middle Kingdom royal women during this period cannot be upheld and that others are not secure, especially as several can be interpreted in more than one way and be used to argue for either side. What follows is not a comprehensive analysis of all the differences between Old Kingdom and Middle Kingdom royal women, or of all the aspects regarding their status, both of which would require a much more elaborate treatment. Rather, this essay intends to caution against reading certain changes in relation to status, and to offer other possible explanations for these differences.

A statue head of a royal woman with a uraeus, dating to the Twelfth Dynasty and today in the Museum of Fine Arts in Boston, was the starting point for the research of Josephson and Freed. According to them, the uraeus first appeared on depictions of royal women in the Middle Kingdom, a development which they believe indicates a raised status compared to the Old Kingdom. However, royal women in the Old Kingdom already feature the uraeus, as has been shown by Silke Roth.[8] This element is first attested for a royal woman on a *psš-kf* knife for the king's mother Khamerernebty I in the Fourth Dynasty. Other Old Kingdom king's mothers are featured with the uraeus as well, and in the Sixth Dynasty it is used for a king's wife.[9] The circle of wearers was further enlarged in the Twelfth Dynasty to include princesses,[10] and in the Thirteenth Dynasty, the uraeus became their typical iconographical element. Thus, the presence of the uraeus cannot be used as an argument for an elevated status of Middle Kingdom queens compared to Old Kingdom ones.

The head in the Museum of Fine Arts in Boston belonged to a sphinx, and several statues of royal women as sphinxes are known from the Middle Kingdom. The earliest occurrence of such a depiction of a royal woman is debated. A female sphinx was found in the complex of Djedefre in Abu Rawash and dated to the reign of Djedefre by Biri Fay.[11] Josephson and Freed, however, suggest an early New Kingdom date for that piece and believe that the depiction of a royal woman as a sphinx first occurred in the Middle Kingdom. They interpret sphinxes, in general, as an "embodiment of royal power"[12] and regard the female sphinx statues as an expression of an elevated status of Middle Kingdom queens compared to Old Kingdom ones. Yet Fay's Old Kingdom date for the Abu Rawash sphinx is convincing.[13] Even if one accepted Josephson and Freed's New Kingdom date, it is not clear if the women depicted as sphinxes were queens. The only Middle Kingdom sphinx of a royal woman with an inscription still preserved today refers only to a king's daughter—the king's daughter Ita.[14] If the sphinx statues expressed power, one would expect that this type of depiction was used first for queens and only at a later stage for princesses, who ranked lower than king's mothers and king's wives. It is, of course, possible that both princesses and queens were depicted with the body of a lion in the Middle Kingdom and that the female sphinx in the Louvre with an inscription identifying a princess had predecessors in the Old Kingdom who were queens (such as the Djedefre sphinx).[15] Another interpretation of these statues is that they were meant to express the association of these women with a goddess. Lana Troy regarded all Middle Kingdom female sphinxes as representations of princesses in their role as the daughter of the sun god, who is often associated with a lion.[16] If her interpretation of these statues as princesses is correct, they cannot be used as evidence for an increased status of queens. Unfortunately, we do not know who the owners of most of these statues were, in which context the objects were used, or what their function was. It may be the case that the sphinx statues were chosen to express the association with goddesses.[17] This type of depiction could also have been meant to underline the role of the royal women as female counterparts of the king. Alternatively, one might want to consider the likelihood that it even purposefully alluded to both aspects at the same time.

In favor of an elevated status, it was also argued that Old Kingdom queens are depicted smaller in size when accompanying their spouse, while in the Middle Kingdom they "consistently were portrayed alone."[18] This is not always the case, though, as shown by the triad statues of Senwosret III.[19] In these, the king is flanked by two royal women, who are depicted in a very small size, standing to the left and right of the king's lower legs. The triad statue with the best-preserved inscription gives the titles and names of Khenemetneferhedjet Weret I, who was Senwosret III's mother, and of Khenemetneferhedjet Weret II, his main wife. Considering the size of the royal women, one might be tempted instead to use these statues as an argument for a reduced status of royal women in the Middle Kingdom. But yet another intriguing statue of Amenemhat III from Kom al-Hisn features two royal women flanking the king, in this case in a much larger size in proportion to the king.[20] This does not need to mean that the general status of these women was different. Theoretically, there could have been an evolution of such statues. On the other hand, the context of the statues—which is not always known—and the function of the women within the statues—also often unknown—might have determined how the women were represented. The statue of Amenemhat III depicts the king in the *heb-sed* cloak. Therefore, the focus of this statue was presumably the *sed*-festival, in which the royal women played an important role in the king's rejuvenation, which might explain their large size.[21]

Ann Roth also used sculpture as evidence for her opposite view of a diminished status of royal women. She did not provide a detailed discussion, as the focus of her essay lay elsewhere, but she noted that "in the Middle Kingdom queens cease to be depicted alongside kings in statues and in the relief decoration of tombs and temples."[22] That this is not the case for statues is shown by those of Senwosret III and Amenemhat III mentioned above. It should also be remarked that over-life-size depictions of royal women are known from both the Old Kingdom and the Middle Kingdom.[23] Regarding relief decoration, one can remark that, in fact, not many such Old Kingdom representations are known, while a couple of such depictions are indeed found in the Middle Kingdom: Mentuhotep II is accompanied by his mother Iah in Shatt al-Rigal, and Amenemhat III is depicted with his mother Hetepti (and with Neferuptah) in Medinet Madi.[24]

Besides observations on Old Kingdom and Middle Kingdom sculptures of royal women, a "proliferation of royal female burials"[25] and differences in their tombs were also seen as indicators for an elevated status. Some Middle Kingdom pyramid complexes indeed feature many subsidiary pyramids.[26] Theoretically, though, one could also argue the opposite: if more royal women receive a pyramid close to the king, this is a sign of a weakened status compared to the few women who received a more exclusive treatment before. This possibility is not argued by the current author, but is only raised in order to point out that many changes in regard to the royal women can be interpreted in very different and even opposing ways. In fact, they might have nothing to do with status. In any case, the more recent excavations at the pyramid complex of Pepi I have revealed a very large cluster of pyramids for royal women at the end of the Old Kingdom.[27] The argument that the larger number of royal women burials in the Middle Kingdom compared to the Old Kingdom indicated an elevation thus cannot be upheld any more.

Another shift in burial practices was also seen as an indication for an increased importance of these women.[28] In Old Kingdom pyramid complexes, the pyramids of royal women were outside of the king's enclosure, while in the Middle Kingdom they were positioned within it.[29] Yet the move inside the king's enclosure seems to have resulted in the loss of the women's own *ka*-pyramids. Their cult buildings are also much more modest in size than those at the end of the Old Kingdom.[30] On the other hand, a prime location for a burial chamber was chosen for queens in the late Middle Kingdom pyramid complexes of Senwosret III and that of Amenemhat III at Dahshur.[31] In the complex of Senwosret III, his main wife Khenemetneferhedjet Weret I received a pyramid on the south side while her actual burial chamber was located under the southwestern corner of the king's pyramid. In the case of Amenemhat III's complex at Dahshur, there are no queens' pyramids, but the burial chambers of two queens were not only placed underneath the king's pyramid, but also connected by a corridor with the king's chamber. Even so, one should use caution interpreting these changes in relation to status. As Peter Jánosi has shown, the tombs of royal women in pyramid complexes were always dependent on the king.[32] The women were probably buried in the king's complex because they were needed for the king's regeneration. Some of the changes for the women's burials might rather have been meant to more strongly express and secure the unity of the royal women with the king for the benefit of the latter.[33]

In several burials of Middle Kingdom royal women, "substantial treasures" were found that were also used to argue for an elevated status.[34] Among this spectacular jewelry are pieces with names of kings, including several pectorals; however, except on scarabs, none of the jewelry items bear the name of the female owners.[35] The pectoral of Princess Sithathoryunet, for example, incorporates the name of Senwosret II with elements that can be read as a wish for an eternal life for this king, which suggests that the main function of such pieces was not for the women themselves, but possibly rather for the king, or kingship. As has been suggested, many of these jewelry items might have been worn in rituals, but unfortunately, we know too little about them.[36] Sithathoryunet's diadem is particularly interesting as, besides featuring the uraeus, it provides the first record of feathers in royal women's headdresses.[37] These feathers are situated on top of a papyrus umbel and together they represent the *wḫ*-emblem of the goddess Hathor. Through this iconography, the wearer of the diadem, Sithathoryunet, was associated and maybe even identified with the goddess. Twelfth Dynasty depictions of Hathoric rituals also show nonroyal women wearing a double falcon feather on a headband.[38] The first evidence of the actual double feather crown is known later, from the Thirteenth Dynasty, when the double falcon feather was connected to a modius and worn by women with the titles "King's Mother" or "King's Wife."[39] This crown was also worn by male deities and occasionally by the king; it probably connected the woman with the divine. In the New Kingdom, the feather crown became the typical headdress of royal women and was combined with the sun disk, stressing its solar connection.

Another argument brought forward for an elevated status of Middle Kingdom royal females is the fact that a royal woman, Sobekneferu, became a female pharaoh.[40] However, a female pharaoh was always an exception. It is noteworthy that two other Middle Kingdom princesses whose roles are not yet fully understood might have been considered heirs to the throne (see below). Nevertheless, these three cases do not necessarily indicate a general elevation of all Middle Kingdom royal females compared to earlier ones, and certainly female regents existed in the Early Dynastic Period and Old Kingdom.[41]

An interesting aspect that Josephson and Freed did not use as an argument, but that should be mentioned in this context, is the use of the cartouche. Princess Neferuptah of the late Twelfth Dynasty was the first royal woman known to have had her name written in a cartouche. Her case still presents many open questions. The suggestion has been made that she was possibly considered an heir to the throne before dying prematurely, which would explain why a princess and not a queen received the cartouche first.[42] The cartouche was used for Sobeknefru as a female pharaoh, and then appears again for a princess when it is featured in the Thirteenth Dynasty for Iuhetibu Fendi, who was most likely Sobekhotep III's daughter. Little is known about her but, due to the cartouche, it was suggested that she might have been regarded as a successor to her father as well.[43] The use of the cartouche for the two princesses is surprising since one would expect that within the circle of royal women (not counting a female pharaoh), queens would be granted this prestigious element first. But the first evidence for a king's wife to feature her name in a cartouche can be found only later in the Thirteenth Dynasty.[44] Theoretically, the introduction of the cartouche for royal women could indicate an elevated status. One could, on the other hand, argue that this use was at first restricted to the specific women whose status was indeed raised as heirs to the throne, and that its use was then transmitted through them to other royal females.

The title *ḥnwt t3wy* occurs first for royal women in the Twelfth Dynasty, and Josephson and Freed regarded this title as evidence for an elevation of status and as the female equivalent of the king's title *nb t3wy*.[45] However, the latter is not the case. Grammatically, it is the female title *nbt t3wy* that is the direct female equivalent, and this title occurs first at a later period, in the New Kingdom. Nevertheless, the title *ḥnwt t3wy* surely signifies a generally high status and, in theory, one might ask whether it indicates a higher status compared to the time when this title was not yet in use. It still does not need to designate a new function, but could very well have been added to the queen's title repertoire to stress her existing ideological role as the female counterpart of the king (see below).[46] In general, it is not surprising that new titles and iconographic elements were added for queens over time, especially as some titles and iconographical elements that were previously reserved for queens (like the uraeus) started to be used for the lower-ranking princesses. In any case, there is no indication that the title *ḥnwt t3wy* indicated actual political power. As Silke Roth has shown in detail for New Kingdom foreign policy, one has to differentiate between the ideological picture of queenship and actual political power.[47] Most sources represent the ideological image of royal women, and we do not know whether royal women took part in political decisions. Such actions might have been limited to personal influence on the king and probably varied greatly depending on the individuals involved.

Many of the observed differences in iconography and titles discussed above relate to the realm of goddesses and/or the king. Already in the Old Kingdom, royal women were associated with divinity.[48] This is evident, for example, in the vulture headdress, which was first worn by king's mothers in the Fourth Dynasty, and later by king's wives.[49] The headdress linked the wearer to goddesses, who are the only other women wearing it, and also associated her specifically with Nekhbet, thus clearly stressing the divine aspect of queenship. As noted previously, Old Kingdom queens had already received the uraeus, which probably refers directly to the king to show the woman as his female counterpart while also linking her with various goddesses, such as Wadjet. Depictions of the queen directly in front of a goddess demonstrate as well that she was considered the ideological female counterpart of the king already in this period: Iput I is standing in front of a goddess, and Wedjebetni is offering to Hathor.[50] The queens are shown as the same size as the goddess, in the same way that the king is depicted offering to a deity.

In this essay, some changes in the iconography and titles of royal women in the Old Kingdom and the Middle Kingdom were reviewed.[51] In the New Kingdom, we again find new elements, such as the new title *nbt t3wy*, and the sun disk and horns as well as the double uraeus. Through their appearances and titles, over time, royal women are represented as more similar to goddesses and to the king. These changes do not need to be explained as expressions of status alterations.[52] Instead, perhaps, they are meant to underline the ideological roles of the royal woman as a representative of a goddess and a female counterpart of the king. One might want to see these new titles or insignia as new expressions of existing functions and part of a gradual development to further strengthen the link of the royal women with the divine and the king.[53] Even though the royal women were not divine themselves, they had goddess-like aspects and represented the divine concept of queenship which was an integral part of Egyptian kingship.

Notes

1 For royal women in general, see, for example, Michel Baud, *Famille royale et pouvoir sous l'Ancien Empire égyptien*, 2 vols., BdE 126 (Cairo: IFAO, 1999); Vivienne Gae Callender, *In Hathor's Image*, vol. 1: *The Wives and Mothers of Egyptian Kings from Dynasties I–VI* (Prague: Charles University, Faculty of Arts in Prague, 2011); Lisa Kuchman Sabbahy, "The Development of the Titulary and Iconography of the Ancient Egyptian Queen from Dynasty One to Early Dynasty Eighteen" (PhD diss., University of Toronto, 1982); Silke Roth, *Die Königsmütter des Alten Ägypten von der Frühzeit bis zum Ende der 12. Dynastie*, ÄAT 46 (Wiesbaden: Harrassowitz, 2001); Lana Troy, *Patterns of Queenship in Ancient Egyptian Myth and History*, Acta Universitatis Upsaliensis, BOREAS 14 (Uppsala and Stockholm: Almquist and Wiksell International, 1986); Christiane Ziegler, ed., *Queens of Egypt: From Hetepheres to Cleopatra* (Monaco: Grimaldi Forum, 2008). I would like to thank Dieter Arnold, Marsha Hill, Adela Oppenheim, and Diana Craig Patch for various helpful discussions related to topics of this essay.

2 See, for example, Roth, *Königsmütter*, 303–304. The title "King's Sister" occurs first at the end of the Twelfth Dynasty to the beginning of the Thirteenth; see Julien Siesse, *La XIIIe dynastie: Histoire de la fin du Moyen Empire égyptien* (Paris: Sorbonne Université Presses, 2019), 150–51, 155–56. Females with this title seem to have ranked lowest among the royal women; see Bettina Schmitz, *Untersuchungen zum Titel S3–NJŚWT "Königssohn"* (Bonn: Rudolf Habelt, 1976), 206–207.

3 See, for example, Roth, *Königsmütter*, 247.

4 Jack A. Josephson and Rita E. Freed, "The Status of the Queen in Dynasty XII," in *Studies in Memory of James F. Romano*, ed. James P. Allen, *BES* 17 (2007): 135–43. Also see Rita E. Freed and Jack A. Josephson, "A Middle Kingdom Masterwork in Boston: MFA 2002.609," in *Archaism and Innovation: Studies in the Culture of Middle Kingdom Egypt*, ed. David P. Silverman, William Kelly Simpson, and Josef Wegner (New Haven: Department of Near Eastern Languages and Civilizations, Yale University; Philadelphia: University of Pennsylvania Museum of Archaeology and Anthropology, 2009), 1–15. They did not define their use of the term "queen." Within Egyptology, it is usually applied for either just royal wives or for royal wives and royal mothers; the latter definition is used by the current author. Also see Gay Robins (*Women in Ancient Egypt* [Cambridge, MA: Harvard University Press, 1993], 23), who focused mainly on the New Kingdom and uses the term for royal mothers and for only those royal wives who bear the title *ḥmt nswt wrt*.

5 Josephson and Freed, "The Status of the Queen in Dynasty XII," 137. Also see Sabbahy ("Development," 370–77), who discussed many of the changes highlighted by Josephson and Freed and saw them in relation to the king and as expressions of the evolving position and role of the queen.

6 Ann Macy Roth, "Models of Authority: Hatshepsut's Predecessor in Power," in Roehrig, *Hatshepsut*, 11, 14n19.

7 Also see Isabel Stünkel, "Royal Women: Ladies of the Two Lands," in *Ancient Egypt Transformed: The Middle Kingdom*, ed. Adela Oppenheim, Dorothea Arnold, Dieter Arnold, and Kei Yamamoto (New York: The Metropolitan Museum of Art, 2015), 92–95, 332.

8 Roth, *Königsmütter*, 283–88. Interestingly, Eleventh Dynasty royal women are very rarely featured with specific iconography such as the vulture headdress or the uraeus.

9 Josephson and Freed ("The Status of the Queen in Dynasty XII," 136n11) question Roth's identification of a uraeus for the king's wife Iput II. This element is small in Roth, *Königsmütter*, pl. 2a, but its shape can nevertheless be recognized as that of a uraeus and does not fit to that of a vulture head; it can also be noted that Roth was able to study the original relief work and did not need to rely on a photograph.

10 Fittingly called "Königinnen im Wartestand" by Roth, *Königsmütter*, 284.

11 Biri Fay, *The Louvre Sphinx and Royal Sculpture from the Reign of Amenemhat II* (Mainz am Rhein: Philipp von Zabern, 1996), 62, pl. 83a–d; Biri Fay, "Royal Women as Represented in Sculpture During the Old Kingdom, Part II: Uninscribed Sculptures," in *L'art de l'Ancien Empire égyptien:*

Actes du colloque organisé au Musée du Louvre par le Service culturel les 3 et 4 avril 1998, ed. Christiane Ziegler with Nadine Palayret (Paris: La Documentation Française, 1999), 106, 136, figs. 26–27; see also Hourig Sourouzian, "Les sphinx dans les allées processionelles," in *Sphinx: Les gardiens de l'Égypte* (Brussels: ING Belgique and Fonds Mercator, 2006), 101–102, fig. 4.

12 Josephson and Freed, "The Status of the Queen in Dynasty XII," 135.

13 The general plumpness of the sphinx as well as the thick shape and high position of its tail indicate an Old Kingdom date and do not fit to a period much later than that. For dating criteria with regard to sphinxes and lions, see Fay, *Louvre Sphinx*, 22; Dorothea Arnold, "Recumbent Lion," in *Recent Acquisitions. A Selection: 2001–2002, The Metropolitan Museum of Art Bulletin* 60 (Fall 2002): 6; and Hourig Sourouzian, "Lion and Sphinx Varia in the Egyptian Museum, Cairo," in *The Art and Culture of Ancient Egypt: Studies in Honor of Dorothea Arnold*, ed. Adela Oppenheim and Ogden Goelet, *BES* 19 (2015): 598–99. For more photographs of the Abu Rawash sphinx, including one that shows the tail, see Michel Valloggia, *Abou Rawash I: Le complexe funéraire royal de Rêdjedef*, FIFAO, 63 (Cairo: IFAO, 2011), 2:7, fig. 13.

14 The sphinx was found in Qatna, Syria, and is in the Louvre today; see Fay, *Louvre Sphinx*, 30–32, 44–45, pls. 58–60. In addition, a fragment of a second inscribed sphinx with unknown whereabouts should be mentioned. See Fay, *Louvre Sphinx*, 68n50; Georges Legrain, "Achats à Louqsor," *ASAE* 4 (1903): 133. Its inscription was recorded as containing the partial name of Amenemhat III and reading "for the *ka* of the king's daughter Neferuptah," which indicates that this sphinx must be a presentation of the princess herself. It is very interesting that the only other inscribed female sphinx likewise depicts a princess. However, Neferuptah might have been seen as an heir to the throne; see below. A sphinx of Sobekneferu (see Fay, *Louvre Sphinx*, 69) is not included in the above discussion, as she was a female pharaoh.

15 Another possibility might be that the inscribed statue originally was part of a pair, and that the companion piece might have featured the title "King's Wife." For splitting up the highest titles of royal women, see Isabel Stünkel, *The Decoration of the North Chapel of Khenemetneferhedjet Weret I at Dahshur*, Bonn University Doctoral and Postdoctoral Theses Online repository, https://bonndoc.ulb.uni-bonn.de/xmlui/handle/20.500.11811/7451 (Bonn: Rheinische Friedrich-Wilhelms-Universität, 2018), 398–401.

16 Troy, *Patterns of Queenship*, 64. Also see Roth (*Königsmütter*, 212–13), who doubts that the Twelfth Dynasty sphinx statues were limited to princesses, as the lion relates to both daughter and mother roles.

17 An intriguing Twelfth Dynasty statue shows another type of sphinx that connects the head of a woman with that of a bird—likely a vulture, though the possibility cannot be fully excluded that it is a falcon. See L. Keimer, "Sur un fragment de statuette en calcaire ayant la forme d'un oiseau (vautour?) à tête de reine," *ASAE* 35 (1935): 182–92, pls. 1–4. The statue can probably be seen as identification of a royal woman with a goddess, such as Nekhbet or Mut.

18 Josephson and Freed, "The Status of the Queen in Dynasty XII," 135.

19 See Isabel Stünkel, "Notes on Khenemet-nefer-hedjet Weret II," in *The Art and Culture of Ancient Egypt: Studies in Honor of Dorothea Arnold*, ed. Adela Oppenheim and Ogden Goelet, *BES* 19 (2015): 631–32n1, 638, fig. 1, with further references; also see Simon Connor and Luc Delvaux, "Ehnasya (Heracleopolis Magna) et les colosses en quartzite de Sésostris III," *CdE* 92 (2017): 247–65. Excavation work undertaken by the Metropolitan Museum (directed by Adela Oppenheim and Dieter Arnold) in the south temple of the Senwosret III pyramid complex in 2018 and 2019 resulted in the discovery of statue fragments that belong to two different triads. Several of those fragments join a large piece with part of a queen's torso found near de Morgan's house in 1992, confirming that the de Morgan statue originated from this structure.

20 Sabbahy ("Development," 210–12) pointed out that it is unclear if they are queens or princesses, although, based on their titles, she found it more likely that they are princesses. Also see Wafaa el Saddik, "A Head for Amenemhat III's *Heb-sed* Triad?," in *The Art and Culture of Ancient Egypt: Studies in Honor of Dorothea Arnold*, ed. Adela Oppenheim and Ogden Goelet, *BES* 19 (2015): 553–56.

21 For the role of the royal women in the *sed*-festival, see, for example, Troy, *Patterns of Queenship*, 56–57, fig. 34, and 89–90, fig. 62.

22 Roth, "Models of Authority," 14n19. She also saw the supposed decline of status of Middle Kingdom royal women as a parallel to an overall decline of women's power in general, following Henry Fischer. Regarding Fischer's view, however, see Betsy M. Bryan, "In Women Good and Bad Fortune Are on Earth," In *Mistress of the House, Mistress of Heaven: Women in Ancient Egypt*, ed. A.E. Capel and G.E. Markoe (New York: Hudson Hills Press, 1996), 39. More recently a diminished status of queens seems to be implied as well by Joyce Tyldesley ("Foremost of Women: The Female Pharaohs of Ancient Egypt," in *Tausret: Forgotten Queen and Pharaoh of Egypt*, ed. Richard H. Wilkinson [Oxford: Oxford University Press, 2012], 11), who writes, "While the Middle Kingdom pharaohs reestablished . . . , their consorts, denied the prominence accorded to the Old Kingdom queens, had little impact on state affairs and all but vanished from the royal monuments."

23 For the statue of Khamerernebty II, see Biri Fay, "Royal Women as Represented in Sculpture during the Old Kingdom," in *Les critères de datation stylistiques à l'Ancien Empire*, ed. Nicolas Grimal, BdE 120 (Cairo: IFAO, 1998), 164, 178, fig. 10; and for one of the two Nofret statues, see, for example, Dieter Arnold, "The Middle Kingdom and Changing Notions of Kingship," in *Egyptian Treasures from the Egyptian Museum in Cairo*, ed. Francesco Tiradritti (Vercelli: White Star Publishers, 1999), 92.

24 See Roth, *Königsmütter*, 189–94, 568, fig. 90; and Edda Bresciani and Antonio Giammarusti, *I Templi di Medinet Madi nel Fayum* (Pisa: Edizioni Plus–Pisa University Press, 2012), 85 (and 86). (It should also be noted that altogether less relief material is preserved from the Middle Kingdom than from the Old Kingdom.)

25 Josephson and Freed, "The Status of the Queen in Dynasty XII," 136.

26 In addition to the king's *ka*-pyramid, the complex of Senwosret I, for example, included nine subsidiary pyramids; however, the owners of only two of them are known. See Dieter Arnold, *The South Cemeteries of Lisht*, vol. 3, *The Pyramid Complex of Senwosret I*, Publications of The Metropolitan Museum of Art Egyptian Expedition 25 (New York: The Metropolitan Museum of Art, 1992), 19–40.

27 See, for example, Audran Labrousse with Marc Albouy, *Les pyramides des reines: Une nouvelle nécropole à Saqqâra* ([Paris:] Éditions Hazan, 1999); Audran Labrousse, "Huit épouses du roi Pépi I," in *Egyptian Culture and Society: Studies in Honour of Naguib Kanawati*, ed. Alexandra Woods, Ann McFarlane, and Susanne Binder, vol. 2, SASAE 38 (Cairo: Conseil Suprême des Antiquités de l'Égypte, 2010), 297–314.

28 Josephson and Freed, "The Status of the Queen in Dynasty XII," 136.

29 For the pyramids of royal women, see Peter Jánosi, *Die Pyramidenanlagen der Königinnen: Untersuchungen zu einem Grabtyp des Alten und Mittleren Reiches*, Österreichische Akademie der Wissenschaften: Denkschriften der Gesamtakademie 13, UÖAI 13 (Vienna: Verlag der Österreichischen Akademie der Wissenschaften, 1996); in addition, see Dieter Arnold, *The Pyramid Complex of Senwosret III at Dahshur: Architectural Studies*, Publications of The Metropolitan Museum of Art Egyptian Expedition 26 (New York: The Metropolitan Museum of Art, 2002).

30 See, for example, Jánosi, *Pyramidenanlagen der Königinnen*, 178–80, or Stünkel, *Decoration of the North Chapel of Khenemetneferhedjet Weret I*, 465–77, and note that changes in burial structures for the king occurred as well. The smaller buildings for the royal women and the thus restricted decorative program might explain why certain elements such as the papyrus scepter and the *wꜣs*-scepter are not known for Middle Kingdom royal women (for a probable, fragmentary *wꜣs*-scepter, see Roth, *Königsmütter*, 295, 434). For these and other potential status markers of Old Kingdom royal women, see Baud, *Famille royale*, 193–234, and also Roth, *Königsmütter*, 288–95.

31 See Dieter Arnold, *The Pyramid Complex of Senwosret III*, 79–80; and Dieter Arnold, *Der Pyramidenbezirk des Königs Amenemhet III. in Dahschur*, vol. 1: *Die Pyramide*, AV 53 (Mainz am Rhein: Philipp von Zabern, 1987), 37–61. In all three cases, a south tomb existed as well.

32 Jánosi, *Pyramidenanlagen der Königinnen*, 179–80.
33 See Stünkel, *Decoration of the North Chapel of Khenemetneferhedjet Weret I*, 475–77.
34 Josephson and Freed, "The Status of the Queen in Dynasty XII," 136.
35 For the jewelry finds in general, see, for example, Adela Oppenheim, "The Royal Treasures of the Twelfth Dynasty," in *Egyptian Treasures from the Egyptian Museum in Cairo*, ed. Francesco Tiradritti (Vercelli: White Star Publishers, 1999), 136–41; for the pectorals, see Diana Craig Patch, "Excursus: Considering Middle Kingdom Pectorals," in *Ancient Egypt Transformed: The Middle Kingdom*, ed. Adela Oppenheim, Dorothea Arnold, Dieter Arnold, and Kei Yamamoto (New York: The Metropolitan Museum of Art, 2015), 112–14.
36 See Kim Benzel and Diana Craig Patch, "Activating the Divine," in *Jewelry: The Body Transformed*, ed. Melanie Holcomb (New York: The Metropolitan Museum of Art, 2018), 79; Gabriella Scandone Matthiae, "La dea e il gioiello," *La parola del passato* 40 (1985): 321–37.
37 Roth, *Königsmütter*, 248n1394. For an image, see Ziegler, *Queens of Egypt*, 132.
38 See Ľubica Hudáková, *The Representations of Women in the Middle Kingdom Tombs of High Officials*, Harvard Egyptological Studies 6 (Leiden and Boston: Brill, 2019), 504–10, figs. 11.34 and 11.36, also with references to other interpretations of the feathers.
39 See Roth, *Königsmütter*, 247–48; Lana Troy, "The Queen as a Female Counterpart of the Pharaoh," in *Queens of Egypt: From Hetepheres to Cleopatra*, ed. Christiane Ziegler (Monaco: Grimaldi Forum, 2008), 158; and Robins, *Women in Ancient Egypt* (1993b), 24. For the New Kingdom crown, also see Eva Barbara Althoff, *Kronen und Kopfputz von Königsfrauen im Neuen Reich*, Hildesheimer Ägyptologische Beiträge 49 (Hildesheim: Verlag Gebrüder Gerstenberg, 2009), 12–13, 20–21, 27, 32–33, 37.
40 Josephson and Freed, "The Status of the Queen in Dynasty XII," 136. For Sobekneferu, see, for example, V.G. Callender, "Materials for the Reign of Sebekneferu," in *Proceedings of the Seventh International Congress of Egyptologists, Cambridge, 3–9 September 1995*, ed. C.J. Eyre, OLA 82 (Leuven: Peeters, 1998), 227–36; and Mélanie Lelong, "Néférousobek ou comment concevoir la royauté au féminin," *Égypte, Afrique & Orient* 69 (March–May 2013): 47–54. (The current author does not agree with the identification of the Metropolitan Museum statuette 65.59.1 as Sobeknefru.) A posthumous cult of Meretseger, the supposed wife of Senwosret III, can be disregarded as evidence for an elevated status, as she was most likely a fictional person; see Wolfram Grajetzki, "La place des reines et des princesses," in *Sésostris III: Pharaon de légende*, ed. Fleur Morfoisse and Guillemette Andreu-Lanoë (Ghent: Éditions Snoek, 2014), 55.
41 The term "regent" is used here for a person exercising ruling power on behalf of a young king. Whether Meritneith was an actual ruler in her own right is still debated; for Neithhotep, Meritneith, and Ankhenespepi II, see, for example, Callender, *In Hathor's Image*, 7–15, 30–37, 258–71; and Roth, *Königsmütter*, 18–26, 31–35, 147–53. For a new reading of the names of the first two, see Victoria Almansa-Villatoro, "Renaming the Queens: A New Reading for the Crossed Arrows Sign and a Religious Approach to the Early Dynastic Onomastics," *SAK* 48 (2019): 35–51.
42 See Aidan Dodson and Dyan Hilton, *The Complete Royal Families of Ancient Egypt* (London: Thames and Hudson, 2004), 98.
43 Dodson and Hilton, *Complete Royal Families*, 105.
44 See Siesse, *La XIIIe dynastie*, 145, table 36.
45 Josephson and Freed, "The Status of the Queen in Dynasty XII," 136–37.
46 It might also be possible that this title did not derive from the king, but from goddesses, who are known to carry it from the Eleventh Dynasty onward, although it appears rarely; see Maria Münster, *Untersuchungen zur Göttin Isis vom Alten Reich bis zum Ende des Neuen Reiches*, MÄS 11 (Berlin: Verlag Bruno Hessling, 1968), 204; and *LGG*, vol. 5, OLA 114 (Leuven, Paris, and Dudley, MA: Peeters, 2002), 212–13.
47 See Silke Roth (*Gebieterin aller Länder: Die Rolle der königlichen Frauen in der fiktiven und realen Aussenpolitik des ägyptischen Neuen Reiches*, OBO 185 [Freiburg, Switzerland: Universitätsverlag,

2002]), who points out that queens only very rarely actively participated in diplomatic correspondence (that they did so, even if rarely, is nevertheless intriguing); see Roth, *Gebieterin aller Länder*, 67–80. Also see Althoff, *Kronen*, 109–12; and Sabbahy, who mentioned a new political role for Middle Kingdom royal women, but also said: "No title actually describes the queen as an active participant in the royal court" (Sabbahy, "Development," 373).

48 See Callender, *In Hathor's Image*, 338–40. Her general view regarding the question of status is different; she says about the Old Kingdom: "What is very apparent is that the status of the queen had undergone a gradual accumulation of privileges and honours between the 1st Dynasty and the 6th and the pattern of queenship for both the royal mother and the royal wife had changed dramatically over the centuries" (Callender, *In Hathor's Image*, 340).

49 For the vulture headdress and the uraeus, see, for example, Roth, *Königsmütter*, 276–88; Gay Robins, "Ideal Beauty and Divine Attributes," in *Queens of Egypt: From Hetepheres to Cleopatra*, ed. Christiane Ziegler (Monaco: Grimaldi Forum, 2008), 118–21.

50 See Callender, *In Hathor's Image*, 227, fig. 93, and 339, fig. 121. Such a depiction is not known from the Middle Kingdom, which might be due to the poor state of preservation and/or the smaller size and thus restricted decorative program of the cult buildings of the royal women in this period.

51 It should also be noted that these changes occurred over time throughout these periods and not at a specific moment. Countering this view, see Josephson and Freed, "The Status of the Queen in Dynasty XII," 137, who talk about a "*suddenness*" and express the belief that within the Middle Kingdom many of these changes happened in the reign of Senwosret II.

52 It is important not to conflate changes in representations with changes in meaning. They can be related in various ways that need to be carefully parsed. It is the hope that this essay will encourage further discussions related to Middle Kingdom royal women.

53 Also see Robins (*Women in Ancient Egypt* [1993b], 21–23), who says about royal women in general: "The surviving evidence, which spans nearly three millennia from the First to the Thirty-First Dynasties, shows a number of changes over time relating to their titles and insignia and to the contexts in which the women were represented. It is unclear how far these represent basic changes in the way royal women were regarded, and how far they simply reflect different and developing ways of portraying the same fundamental truths."

5

Egyptianizing Female Sphinxes in Anatolia and the Levant during the Middle Bronze Age

Yasmin El Shazly

FEMALE SPHINXES WITH EGYPTIAN INFLUENCES, such as Hathoric wigs and the royal uraeus, have been found in central Anatolia, an example of which is a set of gilded ivory furniture legs (figs. 5.1a–5.1d) from the Metropolitan Museum of Art's Pratt collection, probably found at Açemhoyuk and dating approximately to the eighteenth century BCE, which is contemporary with the Egyptian Middle Kingdom.[1] The Middle Kingdom (c. 2066–1650 BCE) was a time in which representations of female royal figures as sphinxes became popular in Egypt, although the reason behind this is unclear. It has been argued that it emphasizes these women's importance as the source of royal legitimacy for their husbands,[2] or that the sphinxes represent princesses who are associated with the daughter and eye of the solar deity.[3] A major problem in understanding the meaning of these statues in the Egyptian context lies in the fact that the exact identities of most of these women and their relationship to the king of Egypt are still unknown.[4]

The fact that the Pratt sphinxes are clearly Egyptianizing and that they were produced in a time contemporary to the Egyptian Middle Kingdom, when female sphinxes were popular, suggests that the Egyptian female sphinxes were a source of inspiration. How this Egyptian iconography reached Anatolia is still unclear, but it is important to note that Egyptian royal statues, including female sphinxes, have been found outside of Egypt. This study focuses on the Pratt sphinxes and their Egyptianizing iconography, the Egyptian female royal sphinxes of the Middle Kingdom as a direct or indirect source of inspiration, and the possible methods of transfer of this iconography from Egypt to Anatolia.

Fig. 5.1a. MMA 32.161.46 Furniture support: female sphinx with Hathor-style curls

Fig. 5.1b. MMA 32.161.47 Furniture support: female sphinx with Hathor-style curls

Fig. 5.1c. MMA 36.70.1 Furniture support: female sphinx with Hathor-style curls

Fig. 5.1d. MMA 36.70.8 Furniture support: female sphinx with Hathor-style curls

The Metropolitan Museum of Art houses an important and famous collection known as the Pratt Ivories, which includes small inlay panels carved in sunk or low-raised relief, figures in high relief or carved in the round, several of which have attachment holes, and furniture legs in the shape of lion's legs or sphinxes, the latter being the focus of this paper.[5] Unfortunately, none of the ivories were excavated, but rather were purchased on the market for George D. Pratt's personal collection. The objects therefore lack a secure provenance. They were ultimately given to the museum by Mr. and Mrs. Pratt in a series of four donations between 1932 and 1937. The total number of ivory objects from the Pratt collection is sixty-nine.[6]

After the first donation was made, Winlock interpreted the ivory sphinxes as "little ivory stool legs" made by a Phoenician or Syrian craftsman for the Assyrian market. He based his interpretation on the similarities he noticed between these pieces and objects excavated in the Assyrian capital, Nimrud (9th–7th centuries BCE).[7] Therefore, the objects would have been dated to the early first millennium BCE at the time.[8] As the three subsequent donations were made, scholars debated the origins and dating of these objects until M.S. Dimand, then a curator at the Metropolitan Museum of Art, dated the collection to the thirteenth or twelfth century BCE, stating that they may have been "products of some unknown Aramaean art center in northern Syria, where Hittite and early Phoenician influences met. As further material from the same site becomes available, we hope that a more definite dating can be established."[9]

Years later, excavations at the Turkish site of Acemhöyük helped provide a more definitive date and provenance for these ivories. Nimet Özgüç, who started excavating the site in 1962, discovered two monumental buildings dating to the early second millennium BCE, one of which was designated the Sarikaya Palace.[10] The palace, which occupied the southeastern region of the mound, was a large building with approximately fifty rooms that had been destroyed by a large fire in antiquity. The palace was dated to the nineteenth and eighteenth centuries BCE, based on the clay bullae that were found in its rooms, which carried the sealings of known historical figures.[11] In 1965, excavations in a room in the western side of the palace yielded a number of luxury objects, among which were several ivory pieces.[12] The most important of these was a wing that looked very much like those on a falcon from the Pratt collection (MMA 36.70.6) (fig. 5.2). The museum had produced a replica to replace a missing wing, which turned out to be the wing found in the Sarikaya Palace. Other ivory items found in the palace were stylistically very similar to those in the Pratt collection as well. Today the Pratt collection is believed to have been produced in Anatolia sometime between the nineteenth and eighteenth

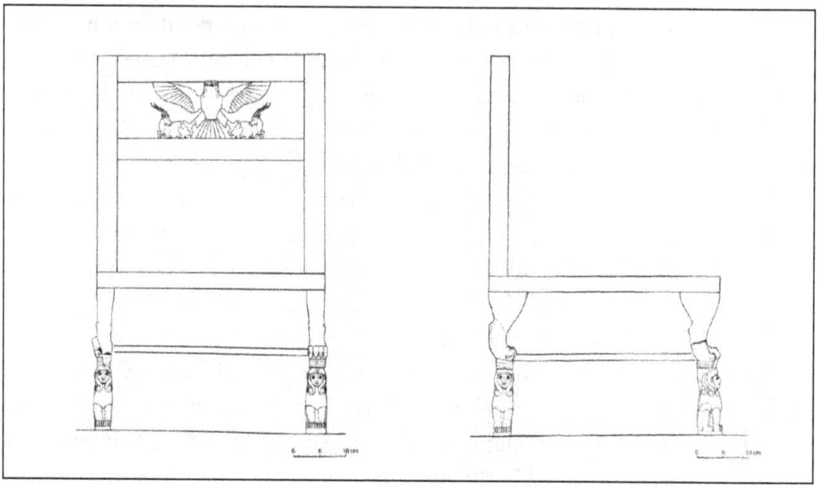

Fig. 5.2. MMA 36.70.6 Furniture plaque: hawk

centuries BCE.[13] The bullae excavated in both the Sarikaya Palace and the Hatipler Palace (located northwest of the tumulus) suggest that the inhabitants were involved in commerce with traders from Ashur in northern Mesopotamia. It is therefore probable that Acemhöyük supported an Assyrian trading colony (*karum*), as did its northeastern neighbor, Kültepe-Kanis.[14]

Pratt Sphinxes

The Pratt sphinxes are very interesting and have been the subject of much discussion among scholars[15] due to their Egyptianizing elements combined with their very Anatolian style. What is particularly intriguing is that their date seems to coincide with a time when royal female sphinxes were popular in Egypt—namely, the Egyptian Middle Kingdom (c. 2050–1710 BCE).

The sphinxes are all made of hippopotamus tusks (possibly imported from Egypt),[16] specifically from lower incisors.[17] Their maximum dimensions are H. 13.1 cm x W. 4.05 cm x L. 4.9 cm. All four sphinxes appear to be female and are represented seated on their haunches with their forelegs in a standing position, a position that is rare or nonexistent in Egyptian sphinxes. They wear the Egyptian "Hathoric wig" surmounted by a modius. On the brow of each sphinx is a rough rendition of what appears to be a royal uraeus. The sphinxes have very large eyes, the pupils of which would have been inlaid. Unfortunately, only one (MMA 32.161.46) still retains the inlay in the pupil of the left eye, which is now dark brown in color (fig. 5.1a). Traces of gold leaf survive on the hair, the headdresses, and the eyes of some of the sphinxes.[18]

Fig. 5.3. MMA 32.161.46 Furniture support: female sphinx with Hathor-style curls

One interesting characteristic of these sphinxes is their variations in color, despite the fact that they all seem to have belonged to the same object. Their colors range from gray (MMA 36.70.8) to pink (MMA 32.161.46 and 36.70.1) and red (MMA 32.161.47).[19] This is most probably due to the effects of the contact between the objects and the soil as well as exposure to the fire that took place in the Sarikaya Palace. E. Simpson also argues that all four pieces came from one impressive chair (fig. 5.2a–b).[20] She creates a reconstruction in which she shows that the four sphinxes and three lion legs (MMA 36.70.5, 36.70.7, and 36.152.1), along with other ivory pieces from the Sarikaya Palace, all belonged to that one object, the frame of which would have been made of fine wood ornamented with gilded and inlaid ivory attachments and other possible additions in precious metals. The ivory attachments were most probably colored with a red clay slip to give them the reddish color that was popular at the time.[21] The slip possibly also acted as a bole for the gilded areas. When the palace and its contents were burned during the fire, the clay slip would have been fired, probably resulting in the dark red color of MMA 32.161.47 (fig. 5.1b).[22]

Egyptian Female Sphinxes

The androsphinx seems to have originated in Egypt with the famous, colossal Giza sphinx, dating to the Egyptian Old Kingdom, most probably to the reign of Khafre (c. 2516–2493 BCE).[23] However, housed in Egypt's New Administrative Capital Museum is another sphinx of a much smaller scale that may be of earlier date. The painted limestone statuette of a recumbent sphinx (JE 35137) was discovered in the funerary temple of Djedefre (c. 2524–2516 BCE) at Abu Rawash.[24] Scholars have attributed it to Djedefre's reign due to its provenance and facial features, which were believed to resemble those of that king. Others, such as William Stevenson Smith, questioned this date. He states:

> There is no conclusive evidence to prove that it belongs to the time of Radedef [Djedefre] and its form suggests a much later date. On the other hand, it is not absolutely impossible that it may be early. The skin of the Abu Roash creature is painted yellow, an unusual feature as the face of the great Sphinx of Giza was coloured red like other male statues. The face is beardless and full, and the forms throughout plump.[25]

Biri Fay dates the Abu Rawash sphinx to the Fourth Dynasty, arguing that the statue's features are stylistically very similar to those of a quartzite head of Djedefre from a seated statue in the Louvre (Louvre E 12626). She believes the sphinx represents one of Djedefre's queens or daughters.[26]

Josephson and Freed,[27] however, prefer a New Kingdom date, arguing that "[i]ts findspot notwithstanding, we believe it does not reflect the style of the sensitive portraits of the king in whose temple it was found, and dates from a considerably later period, perhaps the early New Kingdom."[28] A more detailed stylistic analysis of the sphinx is still required, but if Josephson and Freed are right, the earliest known example of a female sphinx would date to the Middle Kingdom.

In the Middle Kingdom, the sphinx form that was previously used almost exclusively to represent the king in association with the sun god[29] was now also used to represent queens and/or princesses. The reason behind this is unclear but may be a reference to the daughter of the sun god, who could take the form of a lioness and whose role could be assumed by the royal women. The lioness could also be a symbol of the maternal role of these women.[30] Royal women were depicted in other new statue forms during the Middle Kingdom, all of which seem to emphasize their role as goddesses on earth and female counterparts of the king or to stress their regenerative powers.[31] Unfortunately, most of the Middle Kingdom female sphinxes found so far are broken and lack an inscription. Their identities can, therefore, not be confirmed, but are dated to the Middle Kingdom usually on stylistic grounds and archaeological context. One of the few Middle Kingdom female sphinxes that have been attributed to a specific royal figure is Louvre AO 13075.[32] The schist statue measures 0.58 x 1.61 x 0.26 m and was discovered in the southeastern part of the sanctuary of the temple of Ninegal in the ancient city of Qatna in Syria (modern Mishrifa). It was excavated in 1927 by R. du Mesnil du Buisson and can be firmly attributed to a Princess Ita, based on a hieroglyphic inscription between the paws of the sphinx that reads: *i͗ryt pꜥt sꜣt nsw n ẖt.f mrt.f I͗t(ꜣ) nbt i͗mꜣḫw*[33] ("The princess, daughter of the king, of his belly, his beloved, Ita, possessor of worth").[34] The fact that Amenemhat II had a daughter of the same name, who was buried within his pyramid complex in Dahshur, has led scholars to believe that the Qatna sphinx represented the daughter of that king.[35] Stylistically, the sphinx of Ita also fits in the period of Senwosret I/Amenemhat II.[36] It has been argued, however, that the Princess Ita buried in Dahshur does not date to the reign of Amenemhat II, but rather to the end of the Twelfth Dynasty, based on the style of the contents found in her burial.[37] The Louvre AO 13075 sphinx from Qatna, attributed to Princess Ita, and the documented remains of the Princess Ita in Dahshur are the only examples we have of that name, in association with the title "king's daughter," to survive from the Middle Kingdom. Unfortunately, the name and title on the Louvre sphinx do not provide sufficient information to enable us to date the sculpture to a specific reign in the Middle Kingdom. Sabbahy, however, argues convincingly that the burial of Ita in Dahshur and, in turn, the sphinx of Ita could still belong to the daughter of Amenemhat II if she had outlived her father and died at an age of over thirty-five.[38]

The Louvre sphinx of Ita was badly damaged when it was discovered and had to be reconstructed from about four hundred pieces. Many details, therefore, are sadly gone. Ita is represented in the form of an androsphinx, with the head of a woman and the body of a recumbent lion, wearing a striated tripartite wig. Unfortunately, the spot where a uraeus hood would have been is broken. We can therefore not be sure if the uraeus hood had been present and, if it was, what its shape would have been.[39] It has been argued by Freed and Josephson that female royal figures are not depicted wearing uraei prior to the Middle Kingdom.[40] Silke Roth, however, demonstrated that the uraeus appeared in the iconography of royal women during the Old Kingdom, but was restricted to the king's mother and wife.[41] In the Twelfth Dynasty princesses started to wear it too.[42] Most known Egyptian female sphinxes dating to the Middle Kingdom wear the striated tripartite wig, sometimes combined with a uraeus on the brow. Although the Hathor wig was popular with women, both royal and nonroyal, during the Middle Kingdom, there are, to my knowledge, only three known examples of female sphinxes wearing the Hathor wig attributed to that period; one is a gneiss head of a female sphinx (Bibliothèque Nationale 24 from Saqqara[43]) and a uraeus can be seen on the brow. This head was dated by Fischer to as early as the reign of Senwosret II, but Fay, Evers, Johnson, and Freed prefer a date in the reign of Amenemhat III. Vandier assigns it to the end of the Twelfth Dynasty.[44]

Another example of a female sphinx wearing a Hathor wig is ÄS 5753,[45] which is the forepart of a headless granodiorite sphinx adorned with a broad collar, flanked by the curls of what used to be a Hathor wig. The statue was found in Mit Rahina and is inscribed with the name of Amenemhat II. The third possible example is a fragmentary granite female sphinx, probably originally represented with the Hathor wig.[46] The statue was purchased in Luxor and is inscribed with the names of Amenemhat III and Neferuptah (Amenemhat III's daughter). This is probably the only firmly dated female sphinx from the Middle Kingdom that is attributed to a specific princess. Unfortunately, its current location is unknown.[47]

Other examples exist of royal female sphinxes from the Middle Kingdom not wearing the Hathor wig. One is Boston Museum 2002.609,[48] which is a quartzite head of a female sphinx, probably from Matariya, most likely dating to the reign of Senwosret II.[49] The sphinx wears a striated tripartite wig with a uraeus adorning the brow. There is also a fragment of another quartzite head of a sphinx, probably female, at the Metropolitan Museum of Art—MMA 1978.204[50]—wearing a striated head covering/wig with a uraeus. This piece is dated, based on style, to the beginning of the Twelfth Dynasty; unfortunately, the provenance is unknown.[51]

Another interesting piece is Brooklyn 56.85,[52] which is the head of a chlorite female sphinx wearing a striated tripartite wig and a rudimentary uraeus. This piece was likely from Hadrian's villa at Tivoli, Italy, but is believed to have originally come from Matariya. The sphinx is stylistically dated to the reign of either Amenemhat II or Senwosret II. It is believed that the statue's once inlaid eyes, nose, mouth, and chin were probably damaged at the same time after the head was cut from the body and the fragments used as building material. The head seems to have been restored in Rome in the eighteenth century CE, when the area of the uraeus was made to look more like a hair clip.[53]

Comparison between the Pratt Sphinxes and Egyptian Middle Kingdom Female Sphinxes

The Pratt sphinxes (fig. 5.1a–d) are described as "Egyptianizing" mainly because of the Hathor wig and uraeus. Their pose, however, is not found in contemporary Egyptian sphinxes, which are normally represented in the recumbent position (see female sphinxes discussed above). As for the Hathor wig, a glimpse at the Pratt sphinxes in profile (fig. 5.3) shows that, unlike Egyptian depictions of this hairstyle, they have multiple curls, a known Mesopotamian feature.[54] A comparison between the Pratt sphinxes and the Bibliothèque Nationale 24 sphinx,[55] however, demonstrates that the Egyptian Hathor wig was clearly being evoked, albeit with a Mesopotamian touch. The uraei on the brows of the Pratt sphinxes emphasize the Egyptian influence. Another feature that may appear to be Egyptianizing is the modius. There are, however, no known representations of Egyptian female royal figures wearing the modius prior to the Thirteenth Dynasty,[56] and all the known Middle Kingdom female sphinxes seem to date to the Twelfth Dynasty. The *polos*[57] modius crown first appears in Anatolia during the Bronze Age,[58] possibly before this cylindrical headdress appears in Egypt, indicating that the modius on the Pratt sphinxes is probably not an Egyptianizing feature. Simpson's reconstruction of the Sarikaya chair[59] shows that what appears to be a modius looks more like an Anatolian *polos*, as seen on a much later representation of Kybele, the Phrygian mother goddess.[60]

How did the Egyptianizing iconography reach Anatolia? Aruz states that there are different opinions regarding how sphinxes with Hathoric curls appeared in the arts of central Anatolia during the Middle Bronze Age, pointing out that they may have been introduced through contemporary Syrian-style cylinder seals bearing Egyptian imagery.[61]

Additionally, Aruz notes that Central Anatolia, which may seem remote due to its indirect access to the sea, and therefore unlikely to directly interact with the coastal areas of the central Mediterranean and be affected by Egypt's strong influence on the region at the time,

> was the center of a vast trading network that brought rare materials to the west through the Mesopotamian city of Ashur. By the nineteenth and eighteenth centuries B.C., central Anatolia also attracted traders from the Levant and, indirectly, from as far away as the Aegean, seeking access to these resources. In such an environment, the discovery of a Middle Kingdom plaque at Alaca Höyük and the imagery on the Pratt ivories in the Metropolitan Museum, attributed to Acemhöyük while featuring stylistic allusions to Egypt, do not come as a complete surprise.[62]

Assyrian Trading Colonies

During the first centuries of the second millennium BCE, Assyrian merchants from Ashur organized large-scale trade with central Anatolia. They settled in several areas, known as *karums*, which refers to the Assyrian merchant district and its administrative building. The Karum period, which corresponds to the Old Assyrian period, is the time when Assyrian merchants conducted trade in Anatolia, from the middle of the twentieth to the end of the eighteenth century BCE—in other words, during the Middle Bronze Age. The material culture of this period exhibits a strong mixing of native and foreign styles.[63]

There are about forty known *karums* in the region, Acemhöyük being the site of one of them.[64] The merchants of Ashur seem to have monopolized trade in Anatolia. There is, however, textual evidence for the existence of traders from Ebla[65] and possibly from other parts of Anatolia.[66] Relations between central Syria, Assyria, and Anatolia during the first two centuries of the second millennium BCE were strong. This is marked by the consistency of style apparent in the glyptic of the Old Assyrian Trading Colony period (the "Syrian style"), seen in impressions found on documents in Level II of *karum* Kanesh at Kültepe and evident in the material culture of Ebla.[67] The Pratt sphinxes are a product of the mixing of styles that characterized this period. How the Egyptian iconography reached Anatolia must remain the subject of debate until further evidence emerges. It is certainly possible that the iconography reached Anatolia through Syro-Palestinian cylinder seals, which often carried Egyptian iconography, such as images of the pharaoh, Egyptian/Egyptianizing deities, sphinxes, winged sun discs, the *ankh* sign, and other Egyptian symbols.[68] It is also possible that other types of Egyptianizing material produced by the artists of the Levant, who were inspired by the Egyptian female sphinxes that they saw in Qatna (or elsewhere), were carried by the merchants of the Old Assyrian Trading Colony period to Anatolia, where they inspired the artists over there.

Material Related to Middle Kingdom Female Royal Figures Found Outside of Egypt

Ahrens points out that it is curious that a large number of the inscribed objects found at different sites in the Levant—including royal statuary—do not belong to kings, but to princesses of the Twelfth Dynasty. He adds that this should not be regarded as evidence for the presence of these royal figures in the northern Levant or for the contact of these princesses with the rulers of the Levant at the time. He believes that these objects only reached the Levant during the Second Intermediate Period as a result of the looting of the Middle Kingdom royal tombs.[69] Examples of such pieces are, of course, the sphinx of Ita, of which I have already spoken, that was found in Qatna, and a stone vessel of princess Itakayet, that was also found in Qatna, inside Tomb VII. The vessel is a tall shouldered cylindrical jar, made of andesite porphyry (also referred to as hornblende diorite). It bears a column of inscription, running vertically through the center, reading: *iryt pꜥt sꜣt nsw nt ẖt.f Ỉtꜣ-kꜣ<y>t nbt imꜣḫw*, "the hereditary princess, the king's daughter, of his body, *Ỉtꜣ-kꜣyt* possessor of favor." The vessel is dated with certainty to the Middle Kingdom; however, a more specific date cannot be determined since there are at least two Middle Kingdom princesses with the name Itakayet, one of whom may have lived during the reigns of Amenemhat I and Senwosret I and possibly into the reign of Amenemhat II. A second Itakayet lived during the reigns of Senwosret II and Senwosret III.[70] The vessel was found inside Tomb VII, associated with a number of vessels dating to the Middle Kingdom and the Early Dynastic Period.[71] This seems to support the argument that the Middle Kingdom royal material found outside of Egypt left Egypt after the Middle Kingdom, possibly during the Second Intermediate Period. The possibility that these objects left Egypt during the Middle Kingdom through gift exchange or trade, however, remains strong. The Mit Rahina inscriptions of Amenemhat II provide a wealth of information on the extensive interaction between Egypt and the Levant at the time, indicating that the Egyptian material found in the Levant could have, indeed, left Egypt during the Middle Kingdom, and not necessarily in the Second Intermediate Period.[72]

Another example of an Egyptian piece found in the Levant and associated with a Middle Kingdom female royal figure is a basalt statue of a seated woman, missing the head and shoulders, which was excavated in Ugarit. It bears the inscription *sꜣt nsw n ẖt.f ẖnmt-nfr-ḥḏt ꜥnḫ.ti*, "King's daughter of his body, Khnumet-nefer-hedjet, may she live."[73] Lisa Sabbahy argues convincingly that *ẖnmt-nfr-ḥḏt* was a title, rather than a name, that was held by one queen or one princess at a time. This statue probably belonged to Itweret or Khnumet, both possible daughters of Amenemhat II who had held this title.[74]

Concluding Remarks

It is believed that if a Middle Kingdom princess did not marry to become a queen, she remained celibate.[75] All inscribed female sphinxes from the Middle Kingdom seem to have belonged to princesses, not queens, and seem to date to the reigns of Amenemhat II, Senwosret II, or Amenemhat III (c. 1932–1794). This does not rule out the possibility that some of the uninscribed ones may have belonged to queens. The Pratt sphinxes are believed to have been produced in Anatolia sometime between the nineteenth and eighteenth centuries BCE,[76] a time that coincides with that of the production of the Egyptian Middle Kingdom female sphinxes. It is probably not a coincidence that these Egyptianizing sphinxes were produced in a time when royal female sphinxes were popular in Egypt. It is relevant that royal female sphinxes were found in sites like Qatna and Ugarit, areas that were likely crossed by the merchants of Ashur on their way to Anatolia during the Old Assyrian Trading Colony period.[77] Therefore, while the idea that these statues left Egypt during the Second Intermediate Period is attractive, I would argue that they may have left during the Middle Kingdom through either trade or gift exchange. Their iconography could then have been transferred to Anatolia through small Egyptianizing objects or Levantine cylinder seals, the impressions of which may have been on vessels or documents transported by the traders of Ashur or the Levant. These objects would have subsequently inspired the artists who produced the Pratt sphinxes.

This paper is a work in progress. More research and archaeological evidence should shed light on the artistic exchanges that took place in the region at the time and the methods of transfer of Egyptian iconography.

Notes

1 This paper is part of ongoing research that was initiated through a collaborative project between The Johns Hopkins University and the National Hellenic Foundation in Athens and funded through the Getty Foundation's Connecting Art Histories Initiative. My project focuses on Egyptianizing representations of female sphinxes in Anatolia and other parts of the Mediterranean

and the Near East during the Middle Bronze Age. I attempt to analyze the iconography and its meaning, and investigate the possible methods of transfer, whether commercial or political.

2 Lana Troy, *Patterns of Queenship in Ancient Egyptian Myth and History*, Acta Universitatis Upsaliensis, BOREAS 14 (Uppsala and Stockholm: Almquist and Wiksell International, 1986), 64; A.K. Capel and G.E. Markoe, eds., *Mistress of the House, Mistress of Heaven: Women in Ancient Egypt* (New York: Hudson Hills Press, 1996), 108.

3 Capel and Markoe, *Mistress of the House*, 108.

4 Lisa Kuchman Sabbahy, "The Female Family of Amenemhat II: A Review of the Evidence," in *Hommages à Fayza Haikal*, ed. N. Grimal, BdE 138 (Cairo: IFAO, 2002), 439–44.

5 Joan Aruz, "Central Anatolian Ivories," in *Beyond Babylon: Art, Trade, and Diplomacy in the Second Millennium B.C.*, ed. J. Aruz, K. Benzel, and J. Evans (New York: The Metropolitan Museum of Art, 2008), 82.

6 Elizabeth Simpson, "An Early Anatolian Ivory Chair: The Pratt Ivories in the Metropolitan Museum of Art," in *AMILLA: The Quest for Excellence. Studies Presented to Guenter Kopcke in Honor of His 75th Birthday*, ed. Robert B. Koehl (Philadelphia: INSTAP Academic Press, 2013), 224; M.S. Dimand, "A Gift of Syrian Ivories," *BMMA* 31, no. 11 (1936): 221.

7 See, for example, R.D. Barnett, "The Nimrud Ivories and the Art of the Phoenicians," *Iraq* 2, no. 2 (1935): 190, fig. 3.

8 Herbert E. Winlock, "Assyria: A New Chapter in the Museum's History of Art," *BMMA* 28, no. 2 (1933): 24.

9 Dimand, *A Gift of Syrian Ivories*, 222–23.

10 Sarikaya is a town in Central Anatolia.

11 Nimet Özgüç, "New Light on the Dating of the Levels of the Karum of Kanish and of Acemhöyük near Aksaray," *AJA* 72 (1968): 319–20.

12 Nimet Özgüç, *Acemhöyük Kazilari/Excavations at Acemhöyük* (Ankara: Türk Tarih Kurumu Basimevi, 1966), 15–16.

13 Özgüç, "New Light," 319–20.

14 Simpson, "An Early Anatolian Ivory Chair," 224; Dimand, *A Gift of Syrian Ivories*, 226.

15 See, for example, Aruz, "Central Anatolian Ivories"; Simpson, "An Early Anatolian Ivory Chair"; Dimand, *A Gift of Syrian Ivories.*

16 In antiquity, hippopotamus populations could be found in Egypt and small areas of Syria–Palestine. Little research has been done on the patterns of export of hippopotamus tusk from Egypt in ancient times, but the Egyptianizing features of the Pratt sphinxes suggest that Egypt may have been the source, although Syria–Palestine is also a possibility. See O. Krzyszkowska and R. Morkot, "Ivory and Related Materials," in *Ancient Egyptian Materials and Technology*, ed. P.T. Nicholson and I. Shaw (Cambridge: Cambridge University Press, 2000), 326.

17 Simpson, "An Early Anatolian Ivory Chair," 229.

18 See https://www.metmuseum.org/art/collection/search/323527. Detailed descriptions of each of the four sphinxes can be found in Simpson, "An Early Anatolian Ivory Chair."

19 Simpson, "An Early Anatolian Ivory Chair," 224; Dimand, *A Gift of Syrian Ivories*, 225.

20 Simpson, "An Early Anatolian Ivory Chair," 224; Dimand, *A Gift of Syrian Ivories*, 221–61.

21 Simpson, "An Early Anatolian Ivory Chair," 258; Biri Fay, "Royal Women as Represented in Sculpture during the Old Kingdom," in *Les critères de datation stylistiques à l'Ancien Empire*, ed. N. Grimal, BdE 120 (Cairo: IFAO, 1998), 106.

22 Simpson, "An Early Anatolian Ivory Chair," 258; Fay, "Royal Women" (1998), 106.

23 C.M. Zivie, "Sphinx," in *LÄ* 5, ed. W. Helck and E. Otto (Wiesbaden: Harrassowitz, 1984), 1139–47; Christiane Zivie-Coche, *Sphinx: History of a Monument* (Ithaca and London: Cornell University Press, 2002), esp. ch. 4; Ancient Egypt Research Associates, "Khafre's Giza Monuments as a Unit," The Sphinx Project, Part 4, http://www.aeraweb.org/sphinx-project/khafres-monuments/, retrieved 23 October 2017. It seems to have appeared in Mesopotamian glyptic at approximately the same time. See A. Dessenne, *Le Sphinx, Étude iconographique I: Des*

origines à la fin du second millénaire, Bibliotheque des Écoles françaises d'Athènes et de Rome, fasc. 186 (Paris: E. de Broccard, 1957), 3 (§13), 4 (§17), 132–33 (§296); Nimet Özgüç, "The Composite Creatures in Anatolian Art during the Period of the Assyrian Trading Colonies," in *Near Eastern Studies: Dedicated to H.I.H. Prince Takahito Mikasa on the Occasion of His Seventy-fifth Birthday*, ed. Masao Mori et al. (Wiesbaden: Harrassowitz, 1991), 296.

24 Biri Fay, *The Louvre Sphinx and Royal Sculpture from the Reign of Amenemhat II* (Mainz am Rhein: Philipp von Zabern, 1996), 62, no. 1, pl. 83a–d.

25 William Stevenson Smith, *A History of Egyptian Sculpture and Painting in the Old Kingdom* (London: Oxford University Press, 1946), 33.

26 Biri Fay, "Royal Women as Represented in Sculpture during the Old Kingdom," in *L'art de l'Ancien Empire égyptien: Actes du colloque organisé au Musée du Louvre par le Service culturel les 3 et 4 avril 1998*, ed. C. Ziegler and N. Palayret (Paris: La Documentation Française, 1999).

27 J.A. Josephson and R.E. Freed, "The Status of the Queen in Dynasty XII," in *Studies in Memory of James F. Romano*, ed. James P. Allen, *BES* 17 (2007): 135.

28 Josephson and Freed, "The Status of the Queen in Dynasty XII," 135.

29 With the exception of one female sphinx (discussed above) that may date to the Fourth Dynasty. See Fay, *The Louvre Sphinx*, 106.

30 Isabel Stünkel, "Royal Women: Ladies of the Two Lands," in *Ancient Egypt Transformed: The Middle Kingdom*, ed. Adela Oppenheim, Dorothea Arnold, Dieter Arnold, and Kei Yamamoto (New York: The Metropolitan Museum of Art, 2015), 95; See also Silke Roth, *Die Königsmütter des Alten Ägypten von der Frühzeit bis zum Ende der 12. Dynastie*, ÄAT 46 (Wiesbaden: Harrassowitz, 2001), 212–13; and compare Lana Troy ("The Queen as a Female Counterpart of the Pharaoh," in *Queens of Egypt: From Hetepheres to Cleopatra*, ed. C. Ziegler [Monaco: Grimaldi Forum, 2008], 64–65), who regards all female Middle Kingdom sphinxes as royal daughters. For another Middle Kingdom combination of an animal body (a bird, probably a vulture) with the head of a royal woman, see L. Keimer, "Sur un fragment de statuette en calcaire ayant la forme d'un oiseau (vautour?) à tête de reine," *ASAE* 35 (1935): 182–92, pls. 1–4.

31 Stünkel, "Royal Women," 95.

32 Fay, *The Louvre Sphinx*, 64n19, cat. 4, pls. 58–60; Alexander Moret, "L'éducation d'un prince royal égyptien de la IXe dynastie," *CRAIBL* 71, no. 4 (1927): 116–17; R. du Mesnil du Buisson, "L'ancienne Qatna ou les ruines d'el-Mishrifé au N.-E. de Homs (Émèse). Deuxième campagne de fouilles (1927)," *Syria* 9 (1928): 10–11, 16–17, pls. VII (upper left), XII, and 30, 34, 73; A. Parrot, *Musée du Louvre: Le département des Antiquités orientales: Guide Sommaire* (Paris: Réunion des Musées nationaux, 1947), 57–58; William Stevenson Smith, *Interconnections in the Ancient Near East: A Study of the Relationships Between the Arts of Egypt, the Aegean, and Western Asia* (New Haven: Yale University Press, 1965), 15, fig. 25; PM VII, 392; W. Helck, "Ägyptische Statuen im Ausland, ein chronologisches Problem," *Ugarit Forschungen* 8 (1976): 104; B. Schmitz, *Untersuchungen zum Titel sä-niswt "Königssohn"* (Bonn: Rudolf Habelt, 1976), 193n2; O. Perdu, "Khenemet-nefer-hedjet: une princesse et deux reines du Moyen Empire," *RdE* 29 (1977), 82; W. Helck, "Qatna," *LÄ* 5 (1984), cols. 46–47; Troy, *Patterns of Queenship*, 158 (12.15).

33 Fay, *The Louvre Sphinx*, 32, fig. 13.

34 James P. Allen, *Middle Egyptian: An Introduction to the Language and Culture of Hieroglyphs*, 3rd ed. (Cambridge: Cambridge University Press, 2014), 341–45.

35 Fay, *The Louvre Sphinx*, 30, 44–45.

36 Fay, *The Louvre Sphinx*, 31–32, 45.

37 Fay, *The Louvre Sphinx*, 44; Aidan Dodson, "The Tombs of the Queens of the Middle Kingdom," *ZÄS* 115 (1988): 131.

38 Sabbahy, "The Female Family of Amenemhat II," 242–43.

39 Fay, *The Louvre Sphinx*, 31.

40 Rita E. Freed and Jack A. Josephson, "A Middle Kingdom Masterwork in Boston: MFA 2002.609," in *Archaism and Innovation: Studies in the Culture of Middle Kingdom Egypt*, ed.

David P. Silverman, William Kelly Simpson, and Josef Wegner (New Haven: Yale University; Philadelphia: University of Pennsylvania, 2009), 1–15; Fay "Royal Women," 103.

41 Roth, *Königsmütter*, 283–88.

42 Roth, *Königsmütter*, 284.

43 See Fay, *The Louvre Sphinx*, 68 *51, pl. 93c–d.

44 Jacques Vandier, *Manuel d'archéologie égyptienne, Tome III. Les Grandes époques: La Statuaire* (Paris: Picard, 1958), 233; Josephson and Freed, "The Status of the Queen in Dynasty XII"; H.G. Evers, *Staat aus dem Stein. Denkmäler, Geschichte und Bedeutung der ägyptischen Plastik während des mittleren Reichs* (Munich: F. Bruckmann, 1929), pl. 6; Fay, *The Louvre Sphinx*, 68n51, pl. 98c–d; Musée des beaux-arts, Lille, *Sésostris III, pharaon de légende: Exposition au Palais des beaux-arts de Lille, du 10 octobre 2014 au 26 janvier 2015* (Heule: Éditions Snoeck, 2014), 58.

45 See *The Louvre Sphinx*, 67–68n49 and pl. 93a–b; B. Jaroš-Deckert, *Kunsthistorisches Museum Wien, Lieferung 1: Statuen des Mittleren Reichs und der 18. Dynastie*, Museum Wien, Ägyptisch-Orientalische Sammlung (Mainz am Rhein: Philipp von Zabern, 1987).

46 Fay, *The Louvre Sphinx*, 68n50; M. Valloggia, "Amenemhat IV et sa corégence avec Amenemhat III," *RdE* 21 (1969), 109; N. Farag and Z. Iskander, *The Discovery of Neferuptah* (Cairo: Government Printing Office, 1971), 101.

47 Fay, *The Louvre Sphinx*, 68, no. 50.

48 See Dietrich Wildung, *Sesostris und Amenemhet: Aegypten im Mittleren Reich* (Fribourg: Hirmer, 1984), fig. 75.

49 Adela Oppenheim, Dorothea Arnold, Dieter Arnold, and Kei Yamamoto, eds., *Ancient Egypt Transformed: The Middle Kingdom* (New York: The Metropolitan Museum of Art, 2015), 108–109, cat. 50; Fay, *The Louvre Sphinx*, 64n16, pl. 84f; Freed and Josephson, "A Middle Kingdom Masterwork."

50 See https://www.metmuseum.org/art/collection/search/545504; Fay, *The Louvre Sphinx*, 64, n. 15; Sotheby's, London, July 12, 13, 1976, lot 412c; Christine Lilyquist, "Royal Head," in *The Metropolitan Museum of Art Annual Report 1977–1978* (New York: Metropolitan Museum of Art, 1978), 37; Christine Lilyquist, "Royal Head, Middle Kingdom," in *The Metropolitan Museum of Art Notable Acquisitions 1975–1979* (New York: Metropolitan Museum of Art, 1979), 12.

51 Fay, *The Louvre Sphinx*, 64, n.16

52 Fay, *The Louvre Sphinx*, 28–30, 65, n.24, cat 3, pls. 55–57; see also Cyril Aldred, *Egyptian Art in the Days of the Pharaohs 3100–320 BC* (London: Thames and Hudson, 1980), 31, figs. 93 and 133; Richard A. Fazzini, Robert S. Bianchi, and James F. Romano, *Nefrut Net Kemit: Egyptian Art from The Brooklyn Museum* (Brooklyn: Brooklyn Museum, 1983), no. 21; Eva Martin-Pardey, "Kopf einer Sphinx," in *Nofret—die Schöne II. Die Frau im Alten Ägypten. "Wahrheit" und Wirklichkeit*, ed. Arne Eggebrecht (Mainz am Rhein: Philipp von Zabern, 1985), 46, illus. p. 47; Richard A. Fazzini, Robert S. Bianchi, James F. Romano, and Donald B. Spanel, *Ancient Egyptian Art in The Brooklyn Museum* (Brooklyn: Brooklyn Museum, 1989), no. 19, illus.; Wilfried Seipel, "Sphinxkopf einer Königin oder Prinzessin," in *Gott, Mensch, Pharao. Viertausaend Jahre Menschenbild in der Skulptur des Alten Ägypten* (Vienna: Kunsthistorisches Museum, 1992), 155–57. For references prior to 1980, see Fay, *The Louvre Sphinx*, 30.

53 Adela Oppenheim et al., *Ancient Egypt Transformed*, cat. no. 49, 107.

54 Hélène Bouillon, "A New Perspective on the So-called Hathoric Curls," *Ä&L* 24 (2014): 215.

55 See Fay, *The Louvre Sphinx*, 68n51; pl. 93c–d.

56 The earliest known attestation of a modius on a queen's wig dates to the Thirteenth Dynasty, under the reign of Sobekhotep III in Sehel and Wadi al-Hol. See Labib Habachi, "Notes on the Altar of Sekhemrē'-Sewadjtowĕ Sebkhotpe from Sehēl," *JEA* 37 (1951): 17–19; H. Wild, "A Bas-relief of Sekhemrē'-Sewadjtowĕ Sebekhotpe from Sehēl," *JEA* 37 (1951): 12–16, pl. IV, 2; M.F.L. Macadam, "A Royal Family of the Thirteenth Dynasty," *JEA* 37 (1951), pl. VI. For

another Thirteenth Dynasty queen wearing a modius, see Edward R. Ayrton, Charles Trick Currelly, and Arthur Weigall, *Abydos* 3 (London: EEF, 1904), pl. XIII. In statuary, the first known instance is a queen found in Karnak North; see J. Jacquet, "Fouilles de Karnak Nord: neuvième et dixième campagnes (1975–1977)," *BIFAO* 78 (1978): 49, pl. XV. The second example is Isis, mother of Thutmose III, Cairo CG 42072. See G. Legrain, *Statues et statuettes de rois et de particuliers* 1 (Cairo: IFAO, 1906), 41, pl. XLII. I would like to thank Hourig Sourouzian for providing me with these references.

57 The *polos* is a "cylindrical headdress without a brim" and "one of the most popular headdresses worn continuously by Anatolians throughout the ages." See Tuna Şare-Ağtürk, "Headdress Fashions and Their Social Significance in Ancient Western Anatolia: The Seventh through Fourth Centuries BCE," *Anatolia* 40 (2014): 46.

58 Şare-Ağtürk, "Headdress Fashions," 46–47.

59 Simpson, "An Early Anatolian Ivory Chair," 244, fig. 16.23.

60 Şare-Ağtürk, "Headdress Fashions," fig. 1a.

61 Aruz, "Central Anatolian Ivories," 84.

62 M.T. Larsen, "The Old Assyrian Merchant Colonies," in *Beyond Babylon: Art, Trade, and Diplomacy in the Second Millennium B.C.*, ed. J. Aruz, K. Benzel, and J. Evans (New York: The Metropolitan Museum of Art, 2008), 70–73.

63 Cécile Michel, "The Kārum Period on the Plateau," in *The Oxford Handbook of Ancient Anatolia*, ed. S.R. Steadman and G. McMahon (Oxford: Oxford University Press, 2011); Larsen, "The Old Assyrian Merchant Colonies," 70–73.

64 Özgüc, "New Light," 318–20; Cécile Michel, "The Old Assyrian Trade in the Light of Recent Kültepe Archives," *Journal of the Canadian Society for Mesopotamian Studies* (2008): 78.

65 K.R. Veenhof and Jesper Eidem, *Mesopotamia: The Old Assyrian Period* (Fribourg: Academic Press; Göttingen: Vandenhoeck and Ruprecht, 2008), 59.

66 Larsen, "The Old Assyrian Merchant Colonies," 71.

67 Paolo Matthiae, "Ebla," in *Beyond Babylon: Art, Trade, and Diplomacy in the Second Millennium B.C.*, ed. J. Aruz, K. Benzel, and J. Evans (New York: The Metropolitan Museum of Art, 2008), 34.

68 Beatrice Teissier, *Egyptian Iconography on Syro-Palestinian Cylinder Seals of the Middle Bronze Age* (Fribourg: University Press, 1996).

69 Alexander Ahrens, "A Stone Vessel of Princess Itakayet of the Twelfth Dynasty from Tomb VII at Tell Misrife/Qatna (Syria)," *Ä&L* 20 (2010): 23.

70 Ahrens, "A Stone Vessel," 19.

71 Ahrens, "A Stone Vessel," 16.

72 Ezra S. Marcus, "Amenemet II and the Sea: Maritime Aspects of the Mit Rahina (Memphis) Inscription," *Ä&L* 17 (2007): 137–90.

73 C.F.A. Schaeffer, "Fouilles de Minet-el-Beida et de Ras-Shamra. Troisiéme campagne (printemps 1931). Rapport sommaire," *Syria* 13 (1932): 20.

74 Sabbahy, "Female Family of Amenemhat II," 241. For Egyptian material found in Ugarit and Qatna (with bibliographic references), see Teissier, *Egyptian Iconography*, 1–2nn2–3 (note that Teissier mistakenly refers to the lower part of a seated statue of *ḫnmt-nfr-ḥḏt* as "a sphinx." See Schaeffer, "Fouilles de Minet-el-Beida et de Ras-Shamra," pl. XIV).

75 Sabbahy, "Female Family of Amenemhat II," 243.

76 Özgüç, "New Light," 319–20.

77 For a map of the Ancient Near East showing the location of this colony, see Joan Aruz, Kim Benzel, and Jean M. Evans, *Beyond Babylon: Art, Trade, and Diplomacy in the Second Millennium B.C.* (New York: The Metropolitan Museum of Art, 2008), xviii.

6

An Intriguing Feminine Figure in the Royal Cachette Wadi: New Findings from the C2 Project

José Ramón Pérez-Accino Picatoste
and Inmaculada Vivas Sainz

Introduction

The C2 Project is a Spanish–Egyptian mission directed by José-R. Pérez-Accino (Universidad Complutense, Madrid) and Hisham El Leithy (CEDAE, Ministry of Antiquities and Tourism, Egypt), currently working at the so-called Royal Cache wadi, immediately south of Deir al-Bahari bay, on the Theban Western Bank. The project aims to survey the graffiti inscribed on the mountainside and attempts to identify and understand the human activity carried out at this location in pharaonic times.

The Royal Cache, or Royal Cachette, referring to Tomb TT 320, which gives the wadi its current name, was discovered around 1871 by the Abd al-Rasoul brothers. It was explored and emptied in 1881 by Emile Brugsch and Ahmed Kamal. Subsequent relevant archaeological investigations were carried out in 1920 by Ambrose Lansing, who made an extensive archaeological intervention, digging trenches every few meters around the contour of the surface of the wadi in the lower and upper grounds, without any tangible results.[1] Later Graefe and Belova focused on the cachette itself.[2] The only other traces of human activity in the wadi found so far were the graffiti, surveyed first by Spiegelberg,[3] then by Černý,[4] and later by Černý and Sadek.[5] Recently, during a brief survey conducted in the Deir al-Bahari area by the Polish–Egyptian Archaeological and Conservation Mission at the Temple of Hatshepsut at Deir el-Bahari, a new graffito by the scribe Butehamun was identified.[6] Rzepka has also published an interesting graffito of Nubkheperre Antef located near the entrance of the Royal Cachette.[7] The discovery was probably the result of Rzepka's occasional survey in the tomb area. Apart from the works mentioned above, no other research on the wadi has been published so far, and a comprehensive study of the whole wadi is still lacking.

The project has analyzed the graffiti in the wadi as evidence of "space appropriation," focusing on the high concentration of graffiti in specific areas, which suggests a religious or cultic use of certain locations within the wadi. For instance, many graffiti are located in Section 96[8] (including Butehamun's prayer, Graffito No. 914), or in Section 209 in the upper level, where several graffiti made by priests of the Temple of Mentuhotep are attested.[9] Many of the graffiti carry religious content and were made by people from Deir al-Medina.[10] Within the corpus of the new graffiti, textual as well as figurative, recently discovered during the fieldwork carried out at the C2 wadi, two figurative examples deserve further investigation due to their location and iconography. One of them consists of a feminine figure that will be the main topic of the present paper, as it may shed some light on the general interpretation of the site.

A Feminine Depiction, Graffito No. 8001

During the 2017 survey, a new graffito (No. 8001) was discovered in Section 94 just at the right side of the entrance of TT 320. The position of this new graffito is unusual, as it is located approximately 4.5 meters above the current ground surface. It was found in a similar position as the graffito containing the name of Nubkheperre Antef,[11] and the two graffiti form a symmetrical "entrance" to the recess where the opening to the cachette's shaft is located.

The surface of the graffito, incised on the rock surface, is partially eroded and has significant natural concretions, but a scene within a rectangular frame is still visible, with approximate dimensions of 60 cm wide and 75 cm high (fig. 6.1). A standing female human figure, facing left, is represented in the middle of the composition. The lower part of her body is clearly defined. Noteworthy are her rounded limbs and legs, as well as a rounded belly. The left arm is visible and depicted extended in a rather loose way, while the right arm seems to be bent and is close to the body. The head of the woman is not clearly visible, but it does not seem to be very well proportioned, indicating that, perhaps, it does not correspond to the original design (see below). The head features a single large frontal eye and voluminous hair (perhaps a wig). The lady might be wearing a long garment, because on the right side of her body a thin line is depicted, possibly indicating a transparent tunic typical of the Eighteenth Dynasty (fig. 6.2).

A rounded object is placed next to the right leg of the figure, an element only seen in a few New Kingdom examples—for instance, in the vignettes of *Book of the Dead* Spell 92, where it has been identified as a black sun or

Fig. 6.1. Detail of Graffito No. 8001

Fig. 6.2. Image of Graffito No. 8001 (with color contrast and sketch of the scene)

netherworld sun, connected with the concept of the shadow.[12] The closest parallels are attested in two Deir al-Medina Ramesside tombs, TT 219 and TT 290, where a black disk is represented on the ground in connection with a tomb. It is noteworthy that the black disk is depicted only when a black figure of a man is also represented, so they must be linked and have a certain meaning in the repertoire of Egyptian artists.[13] In fact, in TT 219, the black disk is represented on the ground exactly in front of the tomb entrance and the human black figure is depicted leaving the tomb (fig. 6.3), reinforcing the idea of a connection between the black disk and the funerary realm. TT 290 offers similar iconography: a black figure in a door gate, standing by a black disk with the image of the *ba* of the deceased coming in and out of the tomb. In our opinion, the rounded object in Graffito No. 8001 depicted by the image of a lady might also be tentatively identified as a shaft, possibly a tomb shaft.

Further examination of the upper part of Graffito No. 8001 showed that the disproportioned head of the lady may in fact be a later addition to the drawing, as it is displaced to the left in relation to the body. It seems probable that the original head was lost or damaged and that, at a certain point in time, a big head was drawn on top of the body. Several diagonal lines are visible emerging from the big head and running downward, simulating the slope of a

Fig. 6.3. Details of the image of shadow, TT 219, Deir al-Medina

mountain. It seems to be a depiction of a lady standing between two hills, with the one on the right drawn with more detail and including a possible representation of an entrance. The hill on the left is only represented by a straight line, with the above-mentioned rounded object next to the leg of the figure, tentatively identified as a representation of a tomb shaft. The whole scene seems to represent a landscape of hills with a main figure in the middle.

Some comments regarding practical and ergonomic considerations are worth mentioning. The graffito clearly adapts to the surface of the rock and to the available space, in which a kind of rectangular frame or tablet was made. The creator of the graffito did his or her best to create a balanced composition, with the woman standing right in the middle of the two hills. The scene was obviously made without the usual grid system drawn in red ink that is used in ancient Egyptian tombs. Therefore, it was more difficult to maintain the proportions of a human figure, especially when drawing from below. The graffito is located approximately four meters above ground surface, notably not in a place easily accessible at the present time. If the ground level in pharaonic times was the same as today, the most obvious conclusion would be that the graffito was made with the help of a structure, possibly a scaffold or even a ladder. It is also possible that the level of debris in the area was considerably higher when the graffito was made, so other explanations may be taken into account. During the visual inspection of the graffito, first using a ladder and afterward on scaffolding, it became clear that the graffito was necessarily made with the help of a makeshift secure structure. Although the use of a ladder was safe enough for our visual inspection during fieldwork, it would have not been ideal for drawing a complete scene. The graffito was probably made with the flint chips commonly found in the area.[15] In fact, we may consider that the less carefully executed strokes of the upper part of the graffito—those defining the form of a rectangular frame or tablet—may have been due to the more difficult access to the upper part of the rock.

Probable Masculine Depiction, Graffito No. 8002

The other relevant figurative graffito (No. 8002) was found during the 2017 survey campaign of the C2 Project, forty-eight meters from the origin of Section 93, but well to the east of that section. Graffito No. 8002 is located 1.45 meters from ground level, which could be considered eye level currently, but due to the concentration of debris in the area, it is not possible to determine the original ground level. The graffito's rounded upper part may indicate the upper part of a stela, a feature also attested in Graffito No. 8001 and common to many others in the C2 wadi. This graffito, with approximate dimensions of 71 cm in width and 61 cm in height, consists of a complex scene, partially eroded. On the right part, there is a high pyramid, including a depiction of a pyramidion and possibly a doorway. To the left of the pyramid, a human figure is shown, but only the face is clearly visible. On the left part of the composition, there is a quite elongated higher pyramid-like mountain. The face probably represents a male head with short hair and a symbol on his forehead, possibly a uraeus. The head is surrounded by an oval shape, which is mostly eroded. This kind of composition of a human figure in front of a pyramid is extremely rare in Egyptian art. This schematic rendering of a uraeus is attested on several graffiti, not only in the Theban area,[16] but also in the Memphite necropolis.[17] Therefore Graffito No. 8002 seems to depict a landscape (as does Graffito No. 8001) with a royal figure, maybe related to the surrounding landscape, as demonstrated below.

Style and Tentative Date of Graffito No. 8001

In order to establish a possible date for the graffito based on stylistic grounds, it is necessary to look for similar representations. As mentioned above, the composition of a human figure with a black disk and a tomb entrance has parallels in Ramesside tombs (TT 219, Nebenmaat, *tempus* Ramesses II/Merenptah, and TT 290, Irinefer, *tempus* Ramesses II), but the style of the lady depicted can be also a clue, considering that the head might not be not part of the original figure but a later addition. The artistic canon of proportion for human figures during the early and mid-Eighteenth Dynasty is remarkable for its robust bodies, especially with thick feet and legs, as can be seen, for instance, in the traditional style of the tomb of Rekhmire (TT 100). However, the huge number of Eighteenth Dynasty private Theban tombs include diverse styles (and several Theban schools of painters), and some mid-Eighteenth Dynasty paintings show feminine figures quite similar to the lady in our graffito. For instance, in the well-known tomb of Nakht (TT 52), the dancers and musicians show similar rounded limbs and legs, as does the spouse of Nakht, depicted standing on several walls. The style of the feminine figure in our graffito mainly resembles the typical Eighteenth Dynasty representations, and even some Amarna and post-Amarna representations. The specific pose of the woman depicted in Graffito No. 8001, with her bent arm, is attested in statues and seems to be a New Kingdom innovation, representing a significant departure from the static poses of earlier female statues.[18] This stylistic feature suggests a date no earlier than the Eighteenth Dynasty.

The woman's attire is possibly another distinctive feature. In New Kingdom statues, it is common to find a long dress reaching down to the feet and covering the ankles. This long attire appears in painting from the reign of Thutmose IV onward, and in sculpture from the reign of Amenhotep III onward. It remains the prevalent fashion throughout the Ramesside period.[19] However, the lady's dress in Graffito No. 8001 is shorter, corresponding to an earlier style that left the ankles exposed. During the early Eighteenth Dynasty, the feminine fashion seems to have been quite simple, as women are represented with a long dress which molds to the figure and does not cover the ankles. This style is depicted in paintings until the reign of Thutmose IV.[20] Therefore, the details of the garment the woman in Graffito No. 8001 is wearing seem to suggest an early Eighteenth Dynasty date.

Close analysis of the figure, based on the Egyptian proportions and canon, suggests the head might not correspond to the feminine representation. In ancient Egypt, the canon of the human figure was a main concern of the Egyptian artists, and a grid system was used in formal art to create proportioned figures.[21] By the Twelfth Dynasty, a canon based on eighteen squares was well established, being subsequently transformed into a twenty-square canon during the Amarna Period, and then in the Late Period into twenty-one squares.[22] Although figurative graffiti seem to present less rigid and less proportioned figures, belonging to informal art, the woman depicted in Graffito No. 8001 looks well proportioned. If we compare the image of the lady in Graffito No. 8001 to these three canons, the result points to the same interpretation: the head of the figure is absent or not visible, and the big head does not correspond to the rest of her body (fig. 6.4). It might be a later addition, or perhaps the author of the graffito considered it necessary to include the image of a big head exactly in this same scene, as the two images seem to be fighting for space.

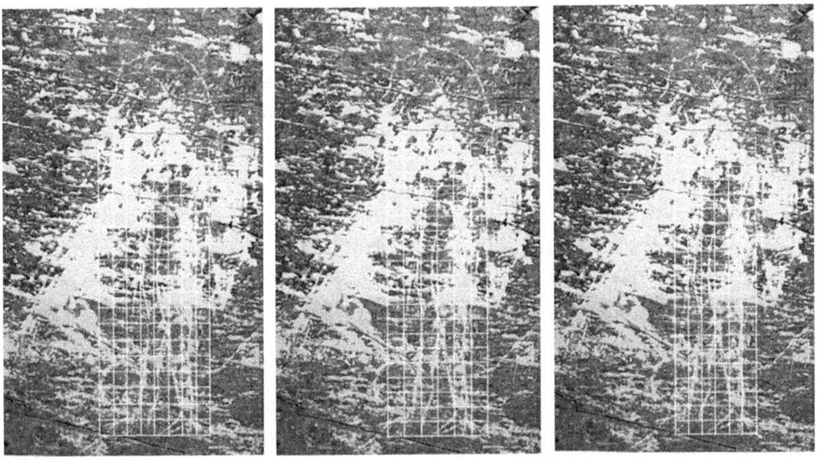

Fig. 6.4. Comparison of the proportions of the feminine figure in Graffito No. 8001 and ancient Egyptian canon. Left: 18-unit grid (Twelfth Dynasty, Pre-Amarna); Middle: 20-unit grid (Amarna canon); Right: 21-unit grid (Late Period canon, Twenty-fifth Dynasty onward)

Who Is the Lady?

As Graffito No. 8001 has no associated text, the exact identification of the woman depicted cannot be determined. However, its location just at the entrance to the Royal Cachette of TT 320 may indicate a connection with the tomb, where a group of mummies belonging to the most important kings and queens of the New Kingdom were hidden in later times, probably during the Third Intermediate Period. Of course, other explanations are possible; for instance, it may be a casual drawing of a woman made by private individuals on the site and related to the image of feminine relatives or ancestors. But the uniqueness of the graffito—being the only figurative graffito in large scale—and its location by the entrance to the Royal Cachette may suggest a royal woman's depiction. The identity of the original owner of Tomb TT 320 is debated, but it has been argued that it could have belonged to a royal woman—possibly Queen Inhapi, wife of Tao Seqnenre II. However, more recently David Aston has tentatively suggested that TT 320's former owner was Ahmose-Nefertari.[23] Comparing the graffito with images of Queen Ahmose-Nefertari may therefore prove instructive. Queen Ahmose-Nefertati had a long and lasting cult in Thebes, and therefore many of her depictions were not made in her own lifetime or era, but later in the Ramesside period.

One of the earliest depictions of Ahmose-Nefertari is the donation stela found at the Third Pylon in Karnak, showing Ahmose and Ahmose-Nefertari before the god Amun, accompanied by their son Ahmose-Ankh. The stela, dated to the end of the reign of Ahmose, shows Queen Ahmose-Nefertari behind the king, wearing a long dress, her left arm in an extended position (fig. 6.5).[24] The image of Ahmose-Nefertari is also found in several reliefs from the chapel of Amenhotep I in Karnak, linked to her title of "God's Wife"; for instance, she is depicted wearing a long dress and a short wig, and with a ribbon around her head without any royal emblems.[25]

The later depictions of Ahmose-Nefertari are much more frequent, as the queen was given a cult as the founder of Deir al-Medina along with Amenhotep I, as attested by the numerous stelae dedicated by private individuals,[26] as occasionally Egyptian artists rendered personalities from the distant past in an updated style.

There are many statues and figurines dedicated to Ahmose-Nefertari long after her death, such as the ones in the collection of the Museo Egizio in Turin.[27] For instance, the pose of the queen in the Turin Museum statuette cat. 1388, standing with one arm folded and the other extended close to the body, is very similar to the one in Graffito No. 8001. But, surprisingly, our lady is shown with her right arm folded, and her left arm extended, just the opposite

Fig. 6.5. Donation stela

Fig. 6.6. Statuette of Ahmose-Nefertari, Deir al-Medina

Fig. 6.7. Ahmose-Nefertari figurine statue. Louvre Museum (N470)

of the pose in these examples (fig. 6.6). The rounded limbs of this figurine resemble the style of the woman in our graffito as well. The Louvre Museum holds a similar figurine statue with the same pose (N740) (fig. 6.7).[28]

Interpretation

As mentioned above, the female figure of Graffito No. 8001 has no royal insignia. However, its proximity to the Royal Cachette of TT 320 may indicate that the lady depicted has some connection to this tomb in particular, or with the wadi. Many of the textual graffiti found in the C2 wadi are associated with scribes or priests—that is, men who may have come to the place for a ritual purpose. Alternatively, they may have been commissioned by the Egyptian state, possibly due to policing tasks or inspections. Local people could have freely visited the place and left their marks there. Women are neither represented elsewhere in figurative examples nor were they the authors of any graffiti in the wadi. Only a few examples specifically mention women, in which they are named as "mother of" in graffiti made by priests dating to the Middle Kingdom (Graffiti Nos. 931, 934, 952, 966, and 985). Although the lady does not wear any royal insignia, the uniqueness of this depiction within the corpus of the graffiti attested in the C2 wadi points to her status as a woman of significance. Furthermore, the doorway represented on the right hill may be tentatively identified as a tomb entrance in view of the graffito's proximity to the Royal Cachette. The presence of a rounded object, tentatively identified as a tomb shaft, could be a further connection with funerary symbolism. As mentioned above, the black disk depicted in the *Book of the Dead* Spell 92 vignette is interpreted as a black sun or a netherworld sun connected with the concept of the shadow.[29] In both interpretations—netherworld sun and tomb shaft—there is a common funerary connection. The right leg of the woman is depicted superimposed on the disk (and partially covering it), so it seems that the figures of the woman and the disk were made at the same time. Furthermore, the big head within the slope of the mountain represented in Graffito No. 8001 may be connected to the existence of a monumental rock formation in the shape of a human head at the Royal Cachette wadi, recently attested by the C2 Project. Therefore, Graffito No. 8001 may somehow represent the landscape around TT 320. This rock formation, still under study, is located in the area where a niche, a rough offering table, and the graffito of a prayer by Butehamun are located in the southwestern corner of the wadi, pointing to the existence of a cultic area there.

The royal emblem on the figure represented in Graffito No. 8002 suggests that a king or a royal figure is represented. Furthermore, the similarity between the landscape of the wadi—that is, the view of the mountain tip, the *Qurn*, and the image of a tomb with a pyramidion—and the scene depicted on the graffito lead us to believe that this scene has a connection with the view one could have had at the place where Graffito No. 8002 is located. Apart from the potential historical connections between the graffiti and TT 320, the scenes represented in them deserve further iconographic study. The authors of these figurative depictions—probably draftsmen or artists with a trained hand, in view of the proportioned figures and detailed outlines—seem to have followed a realistic approach, quite similar even to a modern linear perspective. Both scenes are unique within the corpus of graffiti (and not only Theban) and may be understood as an innovative way of representing landscape, perhaps including the symbolic or fictional representation of a tomb with a pyramidion.

In fact, the kind of landscape scenes shown in Graffiti Nos. 8001 and 8002 are unique in this medium, but a good parallel for them may be found in a small stela or tablet recovered during the 1936–37 excavation season at Giza in the vicinity of the temple built by Amemhotep II.[30] Possibly dating to the Eighteenth Dynasty, the front part of the stela is divided into two registers. The lower register shows two men standing with their hands raised in a pose of adoration. The upper register shows a seated sphinx with a small statuette placed underneath its chin. Two pyramids in the background are depicted in an unusual way, with the pyramids behind the sphinx, following the rules of modern linear perspective. According to Hassan, the scene in the stela might be a unique representation in ancient Egyptian art of the Giza pyramids, not shown in a complete fashion following Egyptian conventions, but partially represented. The stela includes two texts: a dedicatory inscription to Hor-em-akhet made by the scribe Mentu-her, and another made by the scribe KaMut-Nekhteu. As Hasssan pointed out, there is no mention of a relationship between these two men, but we may assume they were master and pupil. In Egyptian art, objects are drawn with every part visible,[31] but in the Giza stela, the statuette is depicted standing between the paws of the sphinx, and the lower part of the legs of the statuette is hidden by the near foreleg of the sphinx.[32] The Giza stela shows two pyramids in perspective, the one slightly overlapping the other, while their bases are hidden from view by the body of the sphinx. This is the view that can be seen by any person standing on the roof of the Khufu Temple and looking northwest, so it could be interpreted as a realistic rendering of the landscape, which is similar to the scene in Graffito No. 8002. In fact, this graffito seems to represent a realistic view of the surrounding landscape in which a tomb with a pyramidion, a higher peak, and a royal head are depicted, maybe representing TT 320, the *Qurn*, and even a royal head emerging from the mountain, which might be connected to the

Fig. 6.8. Stela found in Giza, reverse

monumental human head recently attested on the rock surface in the Royal Cachette wadi.

The reverse of the Giza stela shows a woman, standing, wearing a long and transparent dress, and looking to the right (fig. 6.8). As this side is uninscribed, we cannot say for certain if she is connected with the two men on the obverse of the stela, or if she is a later addition and the stela may have been reused. Yet the style of this feminine figure is very similar to the scribes depicted on the other side, especially in the way in which the hands are rendered. Surprisingly, the pose and proportions of that woman are nearly identical to the lady depicted in Graffito No. 8001, found in the C2 wadi, but on the graffito, she is oriented to the left.

To sum up, the stylistic features of Graffito No. 8001, such as dress and pose, as well as the parallel from the Giza stela, suggest a New Kingdom date, probably Eighteenth Dynasty. Ahmose-Nefertari stands as an ideal candidate in the identification of the lady depicted in Graffito No. 8001, bearing in mind her possible connections with the Royal Cachette as well as her links to Deir al-Medina as royal patron. We may even wonder if the queen's outstanding and lasting cult in the workmen's village, which indeed is located very close to the C2 wadi, was in some way reinforced by an idea rooted in the popular belief that she was connected to the Royal Cachette wadi. The Royal Cachette wadi may have been considered a sacred place where many graffiti of a religious nature were incised. Future archaeological or epigraphic evidence may confirm or dismiss this working hypothesis, but for the moment we may tentatively consider Graffito No. 8001 as a possible representation of Queen Ahmose-Nefertari.

Notes

1 Herbert Winlock, "The Egyptian Expedition 1918–1920: Excavations at Thebes 1919–20," *BMMA* 15 (1920): 12–32.

2 Erhart Graefe and Galina Belova, eds., *The Royal Cache TT 320: A Re-examination* (Cairo: Supreme Council of Antiquities Press, 2010).

3 Wilhelm Spiegelberg, *Ägyptische und andere Graffiti (Inschriften und Zeichnungen) aus der Thebanischen Nekropolis. Text und Atlas* (Heidelberg: Carl Winter, 1921).

4 Jaroslav Černý, *Graffiti hieroglyphiques et hiératiques de la nécropole thébaine. Nos. 1060 à 1405* (Cairo: IFAO, 1956).

5 Jaroslav Černý and Abdel Aziz Sadek, *Graffiti de la Montaigne Thébaine* (Cairo: Antiquities Department, 1974).

6 Andrzej Niwiński et al., "Deir El-Bahari Cliff Mission, 2000," *PAM* 12 (2001): 227–29.

7 Slawomir Rzepka, "Graffiti of Nubkheperre Intef in Deir el Bahari," *MDAIK* 60 (2004): 149–58.

8 The nomenclature used is based on the sections established in the publication *Graffiti de la Montaigne Thébaine.*

9 Alexander Peden, *The Graffiti of Pharaonic Egypt: Scope and Role of Informal Writings (c. 3100–332 BC)* (Leiden and Boston: Brill, 2001), 31.

10 Slawomir Rzepka, *Who, Where and Why: The Rock Graffiti of Members of the Deir el-Medina Community* (Warsaw: University of Warsaw Publications, 2014), 240–43.
11 Rzepka, "Graffiti of Nubkheperre," 151–52, fig. 3.
12 Teodor Lekov, "The Shadow of the Dead and Its Representation," *JES* 3 (2010): 53.
13 Lekov, "The Shadow of the Dead," 53.
14 Peden, *The Graffiti*, 31.
15 Juan Candelas Fisac, "Presence of Lithic Industry in the Wadi C2 at West Thebes," in *Proceedings of the Congress "In Thy Arms I Lost Myself"—Images, Perceptions and Productions in/of Antiquity, Lisbon 2019* (Cambridge: Cambridge Scholarly Publishers, in press).
16 Helen Jacquet-Gordon, *Graffiti on the Khonsu Temple Roof* (Chicago: OIP, 2003), 110.
17 Geoffrey Martin, *The Memphite Tomb of Horemheb, Commander-in-Chief of Tutankhamun* 1 (London: EES, 1989), 159, Graffito No. 15, pl. 149; Nico Staring, "Interpreting Figural Graffiti: Case Studies from a Funerary Context," in *Current Research in Egyptology* 11, ed. Maarten Horn et al. (Oxford: Oxbow Books, 2010), 152.
18 Edna Russmann, "Art in Transition: The Rise of the Eighteenth Dynasty and the Emergence of the Thutmoside Style in Sculpture and Relief," in Catharine Roehrig, *Hatshepsut*, 39.
19 Federico Poole, "Flawed and Fine? The Statue of Hel in the Museo Egizio, Turin (Cat. 7352)," *Rivista del Museo Egizio* 3 (2019): 9.
20 Roland Tefnin, "La date de la statuette de la dame Toui au Louvre," *CdE* 46, no. 91 (1971): 39–41.
21 Gay Robins, "Composition and the Artist's Squared Grid," *JARCE* 28 (1991): 41.
22 Gay Robins, *Proportion and Style in Ancient Egyptian Art* (London: Thames and Hudson, 1994), 70, 76.
23 David Aston, "TT 320 and the *k3y* of Queen Inhapi: A Reconsideration Based on Ceramic Evidence," *GM* 236 (2013): 7–20; David Aston, "TT 358, TT 320 and KV 39: Three Early Eighteenth Dynasty Queens' Tombs in the Vicinity of Deir-el-Bahari," *PAM* 24, no. 2 (2015): 15–42.
24 Michel Gitton, "La résiliation d'une fonction religieuse: Nouvelle interprétation de la stèle de donation d'Ahmès Néfertary," *BIFAO* 76 (1976): pl. 1.
25 Pierre Lacau and Henri Chevrier, *Une chapelle d'Hatshepsout à Karnak I* (Cairo: IFAO, 1977), 318, pl. 5.
26 For example, Brooklyn Museum 37.1485E and the stela at the Metropolitan Museum of Art, New York, Inv. No. 59.93, erected by the sculptor Qen in the Ramesside era.
27 For instance, the statuette of the deified Queen Ahmose-Nefertari, Collezione Drovetti (1824), Museo Egizio in Turin, cat. 1388.
28 The statue was dedicated to Ahmose-Nefertari by a quarryman from Deir al-Medina, Djehutyhermaketef, dated under the reign of Ramesses II. Guillemette Andreu, *La statuette d'Ahmès Néfertari* (Paris: Éditions de la Réunion des musées nationaux, 1997).
29 Lekov, "The Shadow of the Dead," 53.
30 Selim Hassan, *The Great Sphinx and Its Secrets: Historical Studies in the Light of Recent Excavations* (Cairo: Government Press, 1953), 61–62, figs. 53, 54.
31 Heinrich Schäfer, *Principles of Egyptian Art*, trans. John Baines (Oxford: Griffith Institute, 1986), 159–72.
32 Hassan, *The Great Sphinx*, 62–63.

7

The Role of Amunet during the Reign of Hatshepsut

Katarzyna Kapiec

As one of only a few female rulers of ancient Egypt, Hatshepsut had to find her own way of establishing her position as king.[1] She legitimized her reign on various levels, using methods such as male royal iconography and specific compositions of religious texts highlighting her right to the throne. Even though her iconography eventually developed into a fully traditional one (which required adoption of a seemingly male image), Hatshepsut kept full female titulary and continued to mark her female gender in texts. She emphasized the feminine side by promoting the role of goddesses, especially Hathor, which is reflected, for instance, in the goddess's shrine at the temple of Hatshepsut at Deir al-Bahari. Furthermore, in another part of the temple, namely at the Southern Room of Amun, another goddess, Amunet, embraces Hatshepsut. The most substantial occurrences of Amunet's depictions can be found in Hatshepsut's *Chapelle Rouge* at Karnak. Preliminary research, a summary of which is included here, indicates that Hatshepsut had specific ideas for the development of the cult of Amunet.

Evidence of Amunet Prior to the Reign of Hatshepsut

There is very little evidence of Amunet during the Old Kingdom. In fact, no iconographic scenes representing her are known from the Old Kingdom, although her name is mentioned several times in the *Pyramid Texts* (*PT*).[2] These *PT* occurrences may be connected to the Heliopolitan myth in which Amunet is the spouse of Amun. For example, *PT* 301 reads "Your offering of bread for you, Amun and Amunet, couple of protectors of the gods, who protect the gods as their shadow."[3]

In the Middle Kingdom, Amunet is mentioned once in the *Coffin Texts* in a similar context.[4] There are, however, attestations of Amunet at Karnak dated to this period. In Senwosret I's *Chapelle Blanche*, Amunet's name occurs on one of the pillars in a text above a scene depicting Amun giving an *ꜥnḫ* sign to Senwosret I.[5] The text states that the king is beloved by Amunet. It is the first attestation linking Amunet directly to kingship. Also dating to the reign of Senwosret I is another short inscription mentioning Amunet. On a red granite offering table found in the debris of the so-called Middle Kingdom court at Karnak (albeit of unknown original provenance),[6] the inscription is similar in character to the one from the *Chapelle Blanche*. Another offering table from Karnak bearing the name of Amunet is now at the Egyptian Museum in Cairo.[7] The name of the goddess is located on one side of the table, while the name of Khonsu is inscribed on the other side. The occurrence of the names of both Amunet and Khonsu on the same object may imply some connections with the later Theban Triad.

Amunet during the Reign of Hatshepsut: The Iconographic Evidence

Amunet appears for the first time in temple iconography during the reign of Hatshepsut. Figures of Amunet are attested only in the Theban region, where they occur only in the decorative schemes of two of Hatshepsut's monuments: the *Chapelle Rouge* in Karnak and her temple at Deir al-Bahari. The iconography of the goddess is simple: she is always depicted in the anthropomorphic form, wearing the Red Crown of Lower Egypt[8] and a simple long dress (fig. 7.1)

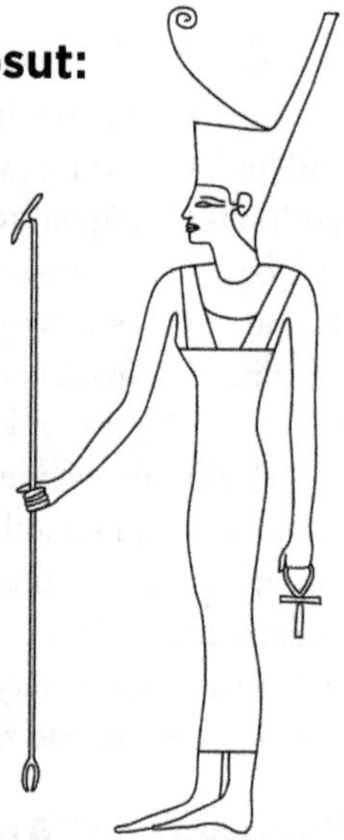

Fig. 7.1. Typical iconography of Amunet

Amunet's iconography is consistent throughout the New Kingdom. In only three scenes at the temple of Khonsu at Karnak does Amunet appear wearing the Hathoric crown.[9] When she is depicted among members of the Ennead, where all deities are represented in the same way—enthroned wearing the Osirian cloak—Amunet is similarly represented.[10]

Amunet's attributes are limited. Most often, she holds a *wꜣs*-scepter in one hand and an *ꜥnḫ* sign in the other.[11] Sometimes, however, she may be represented holding a year-staff (palm frond of millions of years).[12] In a single (albeit later) example at the temple of Luxor (Room XVIII, reign of Amenhotep III), Amunet holds a jubilee sign.[13]

Amunet's Occurrence at Deir al-Bahari

There are only three attestations of this goddess in the temple of Hatshepsut at Deir al-Bahari.

In the Hathor Shrine, on the eastern part of the south wall of the vestibule,[14] Amunet is the first goddess depicted in the lowest register on that wall showing the expanded Ennead. Her figure was destroyed during the Amarna Period and then restored in the late Eighteenth or early Nineteenth Dynasty. She features here with a restored title of *ḥryt-ib Ỉpt-swt*. Unfortunately, since the original epithet is no longer visible, it is impossible to assess the accuracy of the post-Amarna restoration of her title.

Another figure of Amunet is located in Niche J in the west wall of the Upper Courtyard.[15] Niche J is the first niche to the right of the entrance to the Main Sanctuary of Amun. The figure of Amunet is depicted in the middle register on the south wall of that niche. Amunet, similar to all the other gods depicted in these niches, faces west, being oriented toward the original Osiride statue which once stood inside the niche. Below, in the lower register of the same wall, Amun-Re is depicted. On the opposite wall, in the middle register, Atum is represented, while Montu appears in the lower register. Both deities, Atum and Montu, are listed after Amunet in the canonical list of the Ennead. All divine figures were erased during the Amarna Period before they were restored in the late Eighteenth or early Nineteenth Dynasty. The restored text accompanying Amunet reads as follows: "She gives all life and health, Amunet, the one who resides in Karnak" (*di.s ꜥnḫ snb nb Ỉmnt ḥryt-ib Ỉpt-swt*).

The third attestation of Amunet in the *Djeser-djeseru* temple is located in the eastern part of the north wall of the Southern Room of Amun (fig. 7.2).[16] The original depiction showed Amunet embracing Hatshepsut (during the reign of Thutmose III, the name of the king was changed to Thutmose II). In this instance, Amunet is depicted alone with the ruler and not as a member of the Ennead or as a partner of Amun. Amunet is represented here in a typical manner: wearing a long white sheath dress and the Red Crown. Both her figure and her name were destroyed during the Amarna Period and then restored in the late Eighteenth or early Nineteenth Dynasty on a slightly bigger scale than the original decoration. The iconography of Hatshepsut in this scene is unusual; she is represented wearing the White Crown and a corselet with two straps.[17] Her kilt is tied with a wide colorful apron, and a dagger nestled into the belt of the kilt is also visible. In her rear hand, she holds an *ꜥnḫ* sign and a *ḥḏ*-mace, while in the front hand, she carries a *mks*-staff. The details of this costume imply that it is an Upper Egyptian garment.[18] Furthermore, the selection of crowns is noteworthy: Amunet's typical iconography showing

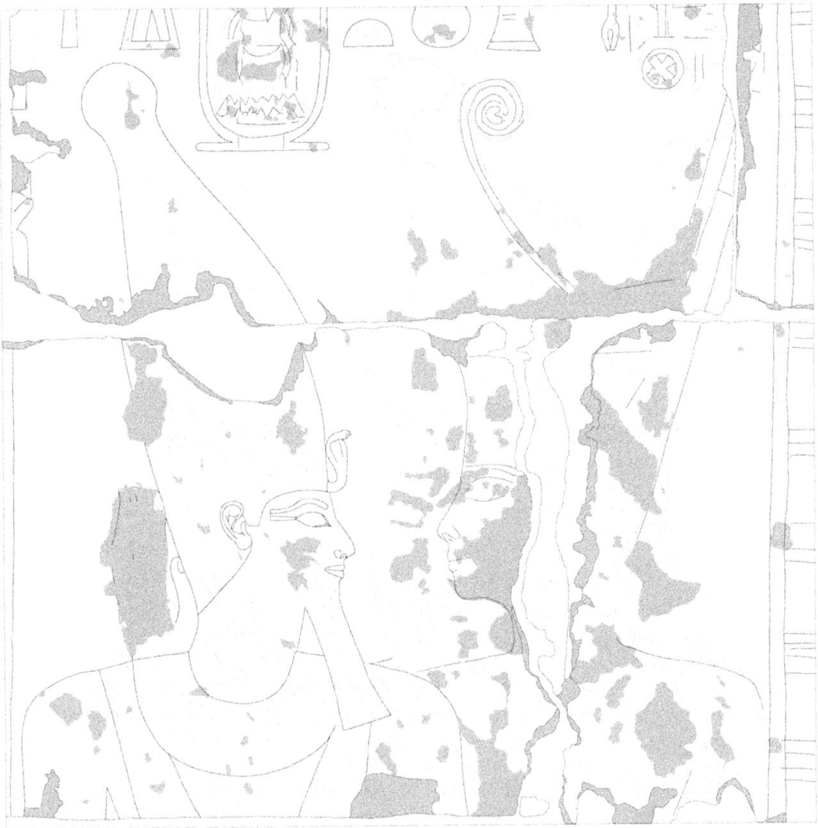

Fig. 7.2 a–b. Embracing scene of Hatshepsut and Amunet, Southern Room of Amun, temple of Hatshepsut at Deir al-Bahari

her wearing the Red Crown seems to balance Hatshepsut's White Crown. This composition may be understood as a special arrangement to create a complementarity between the goddess and the ruler. The epithets of Amunet were changed over the course of the restoration. The original expression was "Lady of the Sky" (*nbt pt*), while the restored title is "The one who resides in Karnak" (*ḥryt-ib Ꞽpt-swt*).[19] Both titles are typical for this goddess; however, the former title is attested more frequently during Hatshepsut's reign (see below), while the latter one becomes more popular from the Ramesside period onward.[20]

Amunet in the *Chapelle Rouge*

The most abundant collection of Amunet's depictions during Hatshepsut's reign comes from the *Chapelle Rouge*. There, Amunet is represented iconographically ten times,[21] while she is mentioned five more times in the text, for a total of fifteen attestations in that chapel. The representations of Amunet there can be divided into five types of scenes:

1. Embracing scenes (four examples)[22]
2. Coronation scene (one example)[23]
3. Amunet assisting the main action of the scene, while holding the year-staff (two examples)[24]
4. Adoration of Amunet (two examples)[25]
5. Amunet as a member of the Ennead (one example).[26]

Embracing Scenes

With the selection of these scenes, Hatshepsut highlights the role of Amunet in her ideology of kingship. The close and intimate relationship between deity and ruler may be observed in the embracing scenes. Those scenes are all located in the vestibule, twice on the south wall and twice on the north wall, close to the entrance to the sanctuary. In all these scenes, Amunet is labeled as *nbt pt*, the same epithet as the one originally inscribed in the Southern Room of Amun at Deir al-Bahari. Moreover, in a scene depicted on Block no. 55, the goddess occurs with two titles: *nbt pt* and *ḥryt-ib Ỉpt-swt*.

In the representations located on the south wall of the vestibule, Hatshepsut is depicted wearing a curly wig and the *shendyt* (Block no. 55) and the *nemes* (Block no. 59; other clothing not preserved). On the north wall of the vestibule, there is also a scene of Hatshepsut wearing a curly wig, but this time combined with a simple apron (Block no. 161), while the second scene shows her wearing the *nemes* and a simple apron (Block no. 153).

In all of those scenes, the gesture of embracing is slightly different from the one attested in the Southern Room of Amun at Deir al-Bahari. There, the embrace is much more intimate, as both figures stand much closer to each other than in the *Chapelle Rouge*. It might also be a question of space, which is very limited in the Southern Room of Amun. However, the front hand of Amunet is raised in a protective gesture just behind the head of Hatshepsut (fig. 7.2). With the other hand, the goddess tightly holds the arm of the queen. In the *Chapelle Rouge*, their position relative to one another is more detached. The two figures stand at some distance from each other. Hatshepsut has one arm across the chest of Amunet, her hand resting on the rear arm of the goddess. Amunet wraps her arm around Hatshepsut's rear arm, while with her other arm she supports the elbow of the ruler. It is noteworthy that this arrangement is typical for the *Chapelle Rouge*. These scenes are quite simple in their composition. In addition to the titles and epithets of Hatshepsut and

Amunet, in the accompanying texts, there is only simple inscription—for example, "She gives life and dominion" (*di.s ꜥnḫ wꜣs*) (Block nos. 55 and 153)—which corresponds to the similar text attested in the Southern Room of Amun. Most of the embracing scenes are located in the sequence of the offerings performed by Hatshepsut for the benefit of Amun-Re, shown enthroned. Two out of four of these scenes directly follow the offering scene, behind the enthroned Amun (Block nos. 55 and 153), and one directly precedes it (Block no. 59). Among the offerings to Amun-Re, there are: *mḏt* oil (Block no. 153), something kept in a vessel (Block no. 59; scene partially unpreserved), and milk (Block no. 55). As Grassart-Blésès noticed, these embracing scenes are located in the vestibule, in front of the sanctuary, providing Hatshepsut with preparation and transformation before entering the sanctuary.[27] This is a common location of embracing scenes, which may be viewed as initiating the king's access to the ritual activities. This arrangement corresponds to the one seen in the Southern Room of Amun, where the embracing scene precedes the offering scenes (as on Block no. 59, but in reverse).

The fourth scene is located in the course of the foundation ritual (Block no. 161). It is worth noting that embracing scenes do not indicate any specific ceremony. These scenes are universally used to express welcome and acceptance of the ruler, preparing him or her for the further steps of the ritual.

Coronation Scene

The next important context of Amunet's involvement in kingship ideology is most clearly seen in the coronation sequence. Amunet is attested only in one coronation scene in the *Chapelle Rouge* (Block no. 23), but most probably the goddess was depicted twice. In the coronation sequences observed on the walls of this monument, it seems that, despite the destruction of certain blocks, the same selection of various goddesses was depicted on the north and south sides, while in the western and eastern coronation scenes, only Werethekau is depicted as the accompanying goddess. This suggests that in addition to the preserved depiction of Amunet on the southern side, she was most likely depicted also on the north side. In the preserved scene, Amunet takes part in Hatshepsut's coronation with the *khepresh* crown, where she assists the main action, which is performed by Amun. As noted by Grassart-Blésès, the goddess was chosen to assist in the coronation with this particular crown most probably due to the close link between this headdress and Amun.[28] It is also a crown which seems to be the most emblematic of the coronation ritual. In the short versions of the coronation ritual (as is the case, for instance, on the east and west sides of the *Chapelle Rouge*), when only one crown is shown, it is the *khepresh* crown that is represented.[29]

The arrangement of the scene can be described as follows. Hatshepsut kneels with her back to the enthroned Amun-Re (both of them are in the *pr-wr* shrine), while Amunet stands just by the shrine, facing the ruler. In one hand, she holds the long staff ending in an *ꜥnḫ* sign, which she gives to Hatshepsut. With the other arm, she performs the protective gesture toward the female king, stretching her hand over the royal uraeus.[30] Above the figure of Amunet, her title (*nbt pt*) is inscribed, and behind her, her speech is inscribed in four columns:

1. *ḏd mdw s3t.(i) Ḥ3t-[špswt]-ḫnmt-Ỉmn šsp n.ṯ ḫꜥt m ḫprš*
2. *ḫkr ḫꜥ n Nb-r-ḏr ḥꜥꜥw psḏti*
3. *m m33 n.f sim3.f n.ṯ ibw pꜥt rtḥ.f n.ṯ*
4. *pḏwt psḏt iw n.ṯ ꜥnḫ w3s ḥwn fnḏt ḥk3yt t3wy mi Rꜥ*

1. Words spoken: "My daughter, Hat[shepsut]-united-with-Amun, receive your crown, which is *khepresh*,
2. the emblem of appearance of the Lord of All, whom the Double Ennead is delighted
3. to see, so that it softens for you the hearts of the noblemen and imprisons for you
4. the Nine Bows. Yours are the life and dominion and your nostril is invigorated, while you rule over the Two Lands, like Re."

The speech refers to the coronation only, not revealing the character of Amunet. The appearance of Amunet in the coronation sequence seems to indicate her relevance to the concept of kingship and her function in supporting the new ruler in her new role.

Scenes with a Year-staff

The next set of scenes are Amunet's depictions with a year-staff. In the *Chapelle Rouge*, only two such representations are preserved. The first one (Block no. 207), located on the north side, is fragmentary, depicting only Amunet with two year-staffs in her hands. In her front hand, the goddess holds the staff with an additional *ḥfn* sign ("one hundred thousand") in a straight position, while the rear one is supported on her chest and has no extra features. Lacau proposed the reconstruction of this scene in the following manner: Hatshepsut would be standing between two goddesses each holding a year-staff.[31] The title of Amunet here is *nbt pt*.

In another scene (Block no. 52), which belongs to the south wall of the vestibule, Amunet and Thoth look on as an enthroned Amun-Re embraces a standing figure of Hatshepsut. Amunet is the closest to the divine–royal embrace, followed by Thoth. Amunet holds a year-staff in the front hand and an *ꜥnḫ* sign in the rear hand. This time, a year-staff with *ḥfn* sign is held by Thoth, who records the event on it. Unfortunately, the titles and epithets of the goddess are lost. The speech of Amunet is arranged around the year-staff and above the goddess; it reads:

1. *ḏd mdw in Ỉm*[*n.t ... s3t*(*.i*) (a)] *mr*(*y*)*t*(*.i*) [*Ḥ3t-šps.wt-ḫnm.t*]-*Ỉmn*
2. *di.n*(*.i*) *n.t rnpwt nḥḥ*

1. Words spoken by Amun[et ...: "My daughter], my beloved, [Hatshepsut-united-with]-Amun,
2. I have given you years of eternity."

Comment: Note that preceding the (a), the word *s3t* was reconstructed on the basis of the analogous block from the north wall of the vestibule.[32]

In the context of these two scenes, Amunet is responsible for guarding and supporting Hatshepsut's kingship, sharing this role with Thoth, who is typically accompanied by Seshat.[33]

On the opposite wall of the vestibule, another scene represents the embrace between Hatshepsut and the enthroned Amun-Re, but there, Thoth is accompanied by Hathor of Thebes, not Amunet.[34] A similar scene, in which Hathor and Amunet are depicted as counterparts during the reigns of Hatshepsut and Thutmose III, is attested in the southern rooms of the *Akh-menu*.[35]

The Adoration of Amunet

Other scenes from the *Chapelle Rouge* represent the worship of Amunet. The first such scene is located on the south side (Block no. 244), where Hatshepsut is performing the ritual adoration (*dw3-nṯr*) of the goddess. According to Lacau, this scene belongs to a sequence representing the adoration of each member of the Ennead.[36] There are no parallel scenes on the north side. However, scenes with other, subsequent members of the Ennead (Montu and Atum) are preserved with a space big enough to fit a scene depicting Amunet, possibly indicating that originally the goddess was depicted on both sides of the monument in adoration scenes. The titles of Amunet (*nbt pt ḥnwt nṯrw*) are concentrated above her head, while her speech is preserved behind her in a single column, reading:[37]

1. *ḏd mdw di.n*(*.i*) *n.ṯ ḥtpt nb*(*t*) *ḏf nb ḥw nb ḫr.i*

1. Words spoken: "I have given you all the offerings, all provisions, and all food which is mine."

The next scene (Block no. 209) is located on the south wall of the vestibule and represents Thutmose III consecrating a great offering to ithyphallic Amun-Re and Amunet. The epithets of Amunet, inscribed above her head, are not fully preserved (being cropped by the block's edge). The speech of Amun is located behind him, inscribed in two columns. The speech of Amunet, if there ever was one, is lost. Only her title of *nbt pt* is still preserved. In fact, it is the only depiction from the reign of Hatshepsut where ithyphallic Amun has a companion, and it is Amunet.

Amunet as a Member of the Karnak Ennead

On the south wall of the sanctuary, Amunet is depicted among other members of the Karnak Ennead (Block no. 28). The goddess is represented here in the same manner as all other deities in the scene: enthroned, clad in an Osirian cloak (similar to her depiction in the Hathor Shrine at Deir al-Bahari). She is situated after Amun and before Min.[38] The text accompanying Amunet reads: "Amunet, in Karnak in Thebes, he gives all life, stability, and dominion" (*Ỉmnt m Ỉpt-swt m W3st di.f ꜥnḫ w3s ḏd nb*).[39]

Textual Evidence of Amunet during the Reign of Hatshepsut

The textual attestations of Amunet from the *Chapelle Rouge* come from two contexts. The first is an offering list, located on the north wall of the sanctuary, giving the name of the goddess twice among other gods of the Karnak Ennead.[40]

The second is a longer text and is the most relevant in understanding the role of Amunet and her introduction to the temple cult by Hatshepsut. Two parts of this text are preserved on separate blocks on different walls; one block is located in the north wall of the vestibule (Block no. 284),[41] and the parallel continuation of the text is located on the south wall of the vestibule (Block no. 29).[42] The first block bears only a fragment of a scene depicting the erased figure of Hatshepsut consecrating a large offering table to Amunet. The depiction of the goddess is not preserved. The speech of Hatshepsut begins between her figure and the offering table and continues in two columns behind her figure, the second of which breaks vertically in the middle by the block's edge. The text from the other block consists of ten columns, the first of which is cut vertically by the block's edge as well.

Text from Block no. 284:

1. [*nswt ḏ*]*s.s sm3ʿ ḥtp-nṯr t ḥnḳt k3 3pd ḫrp wḏḥw ʿš3 n mwt.s Ỉmnt nbt pt*
2. *ỉr.n.s m mnw.*[*s n*] *mwt.s Ỉmnt nbt pt ḥnwt nṯrw ḥryt-ib Ỉpt swt*
3. *mst n ḥmt*[*.s*] *s*[*šmw*] *šps n ḫw* (a) *mwt.s Ỉmnt m ḫ*[*m*]

1. [The king] her[self] presents the divine offering of bread, beer, ox, and fowl; consecrates numerous offering tables for her mother Amunet, Lady of the Sky.
2. She has made as [her] monument [for] her mother Amunet, Lady of the Sky, Mistress of the Gods, who resides in Karnak:
3. The creation for [her] Majesty of a noble [barque] for protection of her mother, Amunet, in the shri[ne].

Text from Block no. 29:

x+1. *n-mrt rdit wḏ3* [*ḥm*]*t* [*nṯrt*] (a) *ṯn m prt r-ḥ3 m*
2. *šmswt nṯr pn šps Ỉmn nb nswt t3wy r-ṯnw* [. . .] *ḥb nb* [*tpy-tr*] (b) *hb ʿ3*
3. *w3ḥ.n ḥmt.s m m3wt n ỉt.s Ỉmn* (c) *ḏr-ntt wnn sšm pn n ḥmt*
4. *nṯrt ṯn ʿ3t m ỉmyt-pr.s ḏr p3wt n sp pr.t.s. r-ḥ3*
5. *ḫʿ.n.s sḥḏ.n.s n nswt bỉty M3ʿt-k3-Rʿ n-3ʿt-n mrr sy r nswt*
6. *nb ḫpr ỉst ḫrp.n n.s ḥmt.s wḏḥw ʿš3 m ḥḏ nbw*
7. *ḥsmn ḫkr m ʿ3t nbt špst w3ḥ.n.s n.s ḥtpt-nṯr t3* [*ḥnḳt*] *k3 3pd ʿ3t*
8. [. . .] *n.s w*[. . .] *nn*
9. *w* [. . .] *rnp*[*wt*] *ḫ* (d) [. . .]*s t3 m*
10. [. . .] (e) *Ḥ3t-špswt-ḫnmt-Ỉmn di ʿnḫ* (f) *ḏt r nḥḥ*

x+1. In order to cause this [divine Majesty] to proceed in the (course of) going outside
2. following this noble god, Amun, Lord of the Thrones of the Two Lands, on every occasion (of) [. . .] every festival of the [beginning of the seasons] (and) great festival,
3. which Her Majesty established anew for her father Amun, since this guidance of the Majesty
4. this great goddess was in her testament since the origins of the earth. (Although) she has never gone outside,
5. (but now) she has appeared and illuminated for the King of

Upper and Lower Egypt, Maatkare, because she is more beloved than

6. any king who had existed (before). Now, Her Majesty has consecrated for her numerous offering tables of silver, gold,
7. and bronze, adorned with all precious stones. She has established for her the great divine offerings in bread, [beer], ox, and fowl
8. [. . .]
9. [. . .] year[s] [. . .] in (?)
10. [. . .] Hatshepsut-united-with-Amun, given life forever and for eternity.

Comments:

a. The textual reconstruction follows the suggestion of Lacau. However, on the drawing and photo in Burgos and Larché's publication, the preserved traces may indicate other signs, not readable due to the destructions.[43]

b. The term *ḥb n tpy-tr* refers to the well-attested festival celebrated at the beginning of the year, and was reconstructed here by Lacau; however, it is usually attested without the genitival *n*.[44] The examples with the genitival *n* were noted by Paul Barguet.[45]

c. An expression similar to the part of the clause *ḥb n tpy-tr ḥb ꜥ3 w3ḥ.n ḥmt.s m m3wt n it.s ỉmn* is attested in the southern rooms of Hatshepsut's edifices in Karnak.[46]

d. Lacau put sign D2 in his reconstruction; however, on the drawing and photo from Burgos and Larché's publication, there are no traces of this sign.[47]

e. Lacau reconstructed the title of *s3 Rꜥ* before the cartouche, which is a typical title preceding the birth name of the king. However, there are no traces of the signs forming it on the block.[48]

f. The signs in the expression *di ꜥnḫ* are reversed on the block.

This is the only known text that explains the introduction of Amunet and her role in Hatshepsut's royal ideology. Hatshepsut introduced Amunet and expanded her role beyond being merely the spouse of Amun. Still, her close connection is highlighted in the text as well. In the text, the building activity of the ruler as a duty assigned by the gods is once again mentioned. As noted by Lacau, the "testament" (*imyt-pr*) of Amunet might relate to the set of duties which the ruler was obliged to fulfill, including building of monuments for the gods.[49] It can also be inferred that only the legitimate ruler was the right person to fulfill this divine testament. To date, this text is our only source of such a monumental dedication to Amunet. It further informs us that Hatshepsut established new festivals for Amunet and provided her sanctuary (or temple) with all possible offerings. The text is illustrated with the consecration of a very impressive offering table. The other aspect hinted at in this inscription is the possibility of the construction of the portable barque for Amunet. The key signs which would indicate that indeed in this text a portable barque is mentioned are not fully preserved (*sšmw-ḫw* in the third column of the first part of the inscription is preserved only partially on the north wall of the vestibule); however, there is also no argument against Lacau's theory apart from the lack of evidence for this action from any other source. Nonetheless, further expressions in the text may prove the validity of this theory. The term "to follow" (*šms*) Amun may indicate that the barque was constructed for the festivals during which the barque of Amun was transported. Hatshepsut may have introduced Amunet to follow her divine partner. Such action may also have been connected with the New Year festival and with her association with Hathor.

Furthermore, the expression "causing Amunet to proceed" (*rdỉt wḏꜣ*) may also imply that the barque was also intended to be carried during the festival. It is noteworthy that expressions like "she has never gone outside" (*n sp prt.s r-ḥꜣ*) may suggest that Hatshepsut is emphasizing the fact that Amunet had not been involved in festival processions and that Hatshepsut is the one who provided such an opportunity for the goddess. The fact that no other sources from Hatshepsut's reign depict or mention the barque of Amunet might be connected with the change of the Theban theology and the development of the cult of Mut. For instance, the divine barques represented in the temple of Hatshepsut at Deir al-Bahari were all restored after the Amarna Period and depict the Theban Triad. The barque of Amunet is, however, attested in later sources—for instance in the Ramesseum[50] and in the temple of Khonsu at Karnak,[51] where she joins the Theban Triad.

Amunet after the Reign of Hatshepsut

It seems that Hatshepsut's efforts to expand the cult of Amunet were not upheld by her immediate successors.[52] In the Eighteenth Dynasty, the climax for Amunet's attestations occur during the reign of Hatshepsut, and then decrease significantly under Thutmose III. At Karnak, the only monument where Amunet is attested during the reign of Thutmose III is the *Akh-menu*. There, Amunet is depicted twice on the pillars in embracing scenes,[53] once in the scene of consecrating the great offering for the Ennead,[54] and as a companion to Amun in the southern rooms.[55] The goddess is also present on one of the pillars in the Eighteenth Dynasty temple at Medinet Habu.[56]

In the mid- and late Eighteenth Dynasty, the goddess occurs in the massive temple complex of Karnak only once, in the portico of Thutmose IV.[57] In the Luxor temple, Amunet is attested at least eight times during the reign of Amenhotep III and at least once under Ramesses II.[58] However, the goddess gains popularity later on, in the Nineteenth and Twentieth Dynasties[59] and especially during the reigns of Ramesses XI and Herihor, as seen in the decorative scheme of the temple of Khonsu at Karnak.[60] However, the character of Amunet and her close connection to the ruler seem to have changed. As Amun's spouse, Amunet is typically depicted with Amun-Re (in both his striding pose and his ithyphallic form).[61] Rare are the cases where she is depicted alone, but such scenes are attested as well. Since the time of Amenhotep III, she is depicted while performing the *nini*-gesture (sharing this role mainly with Hathor).[62] She is still present in the coronation scenes as well. In the texts accompanying her figure, she frequently refers to the endless years of rulership for the reigning king[63] as well as to his right to rule over Egypt and foreign lands.[64] In the Late Period, Amunet, as the female counterpart of Amun, is sometimes included among the gods of the Hermopolitan Ennead.[65] This aspect of the goddess, however, is beyond the scope of this study.

Conclusions

Analysis of the occurrences of Amunet prior to and during the reign of Hatshepsut has shown that it was Hatshepsut who most likely introduced Amunet into temple iconography and also tried to expand her cult in the Theban region. In doing so, Hatshepsut sought to put her ideology into practice and use Amunet to legitimize her rule. The embracing scenes from the *Chapelle Rouge* and the Southern Room of Amun at Deir al-Bahari indicate a desire to underscore an intimate and special relationship between Hatshepsut and Amunet. This message is emphasized in the texts accompanying the consecration of offerings to Amunet and may help explain the development and expansion of Amunet's cult under Hatshepsut.

Amunet's connection to the ruler during the reign of Hatshepsut is illustrated through her guarding and supporting the rights of kingship by maintaining intimacy with the king (as in the embracing scenes) and by highlighting royal authority over Egypt through the goddess's offerings and her gifting the sovereign with years of eternal power (as through the scenes with a year-staff). In the scenes representing the worship of Amunet, the goddess is characterized as the one who guides the ruler and invests her with royal duties, revealing the protective and supportive role of Amunet. A subtle emphasis is placed on the principal role played by Amunet in the coronation sequences at the *Chapelle Rouge* in the scene depicting Hatshepsut's investiture with the *khepresh* crown in which her role is that of the powerful goddess who supports Hatshepsut's power.

Emphasizing Amunet in Hatshepsut's royal ideology conveyed a complex meaning. It not only served as the introduction of a new form of the feminine aspect to Hatshepsut's reign, but also strengthened Hatshepsut's close connection with Amun, as Amunet was his spouse and partner in the Ennead. Highlighting the close connection with the Ennead may be understood as an attempt to forge a connection with the primeval gods, whose acceptance of the ruling king as their heir was of crucial importance. It may also be interpreted as placing an emphasis on Hatshepsut's position in the primeval order of creation.

An important element in defining the divine personality of Amunet is the cult of another female divinity: Hathor, who was conceived as the counterpart to this goddess. Both goddesses, along with Mut, share the role of Amun's consort. During the reign of Hatshepsut, the cult of Mut was already developing;[66] however, the female king had other ideas for highlighting her filial relationship with Amun. She did not use Mut to link herself to Amun as she did with Amunet and Hathor. The divine personality of Mut is different from Amunet's. Mut, the lioness goddess, is connected with the Eye of Re and has the role of the Distant Goddess, with an underlying "dangerous" aspect and a ritual need to calm her down.[67] Amunet is closely connected with kingship itself, as can be deduced from the context of the scenes in which she participates. Hathor, however, links both aspects.[68] Grassart-Blésès has suggested that the divine couples of Amun–Hathor and Amun–Mut are perceived as parents of Hatshepsut in the context of her divine parentage. The couple Amun–Amunet, on the other hand, was perceived as the primal couple who transfer power to the legitimate king from the point of view of dynastic descent.[69] Thus, Hatshepsut highlighted the connection between Amun–Amunet and herself in edifices devoted to Amun as it was the most suitable context for her royal ideology.

After Hatshepsut's reign, the role of Amunet in royal ideology and temple iconography decreased noticeably. Remarkably, after the reign of Thutmose III, Amunet is almost never shown embracing the king in iconographic scenes. This change may indicate that there was no longer a need to emphasize the intimate and close connection with the feminine counterpart of Amun. Alternatively, some other changes may have determined the limitation of Amunet's cult, such as the development of the cult of Mut, the creation of the Theban Triad, and therefore the prominence of different aspects of other feminine deities. Nevertheless, the introduction of Amunet into Hatshepsut's royal ideology may have helped consolidate the goddess's position in the Theban pantheon, as indicated by her later occurrences.

Notes

1 I would like to express my gratitude to Professor Ewa Laskowska-Kusztal and Dr. Filip Taterka for reading the manuscript and for their valuable comments.
2 *Pyr.* 446c–d, 1071b, 2282. See Kurt Sethe, *Pyr. 1*, 231–32; Luc Gabolde, *Karnak, Amon-Rê: la genèse d'un temple, la naissance d'un dieu*, BdE 167 (Cairo: IFAO, 2018), 396–98.
3 *Pyr.* 446c–d; Gabolde, *Karnak, Amon-Rê*, 397.
4 CT VII, 108r. See Adriaan de Buck, *The Egyptian Coffin Texts* 7, OIP 87 (Chicago: The Oriental Institute of the University of Chicago, 1961).
5 It is the only attestation of a female deity in this monument. See PM II², 62 [a]; Karnak Identifiant Unique (henceforth KIU), no. 1081; see http://sith.huma-num.fr/karnak). See also Pierre Lacau and Henri Chevrier, *Une chapelle de Sésostris Ier à Karnak* (Cairo: IFAO, 1956–69), 85–86, §215, 217, pl. 19.
6 Gabolde, *Karnak, Amon-Rê*, 293–95; François Larché, *L'anastylose des blocs d'Amenhotep Ier à Karnak*, Études d'égyptologie 18 (Paris: Soleb, 2019), pl. 19. Luc Gabolde found an interesting analogy to this offering table—a similar object, also found in Karnak, but now stored in the Egyptian Museum in Cairo, where the name of Amunet is replaced by those of Nephthys and Isis—CGC 23008 (Ahmed Kamal, *Tables d'offrandes. CG 23001–23256* (Cairo: IFAO, 1906–1909), 8; Gabolde, *Karnak, Amon-Rê*, 295.
7 For CGC 23040, see Kamal, *Tables d'offrandes*, 31–37.
8 The symbolism of the Red Crown worn by Amunet was discussed by Amandine Grassart-Blésès, "Les représentations des déesses dans le programme décoratif de la chapelle rouge d'Hatchepsout à Karnak: le rôle particulier d'Amonet," *CahKarn* 16 (2017): 258–59. See also Marianne Eaton-Krauss, *Post–Amarna Period Statues of Amun and His Consorts Mut and Amunet*, Harvard Egyptological Studies 9 (Leiden and Boston: Brill, 2020), 16–18.
9 PM II²; The Epigraphic Survey, *The Temple of Khonsu* 1: *Scenes of King Herihor in the Court*, OIP 100 (Chicago: The Oriental Institute of the University of Chicago, 1979), pls. 95, 98, 108.
10 As seen, for instance, in the temple of Hatshepsut (Hathor Shrine). See PM II², 351 [36]; Nathalie Beaux et al., *La chapelle d'Hathor: Temple d'Hatchepsout à Deir El-Bahari* 1. *Vestibule et sanctuaires*, MIFAO 129 (Cairo: IFAO, 2012), pl. 7.
11 For instance, in the temple of Hatshepsut at Deir al-Bahari, Niche J; see PM II², 364. See also Jadwiga Iwaszczuk, *Sacred Landscape of Thebes During the Reign of Hatshepsut: Royal Construction Projects* 2: *Topographical Bibliography of the West Bank* (Warsaw: Institut des Cultures Méditerranéennes et Orientales de l'Académie Polonaise des Sciences, 2016), 157. In the *Chapelle Rouge*, see KIU 1292; Pierre Lacau and Henri Chevrier, *Une chapelle d'Hatshepsout à Karnak* (Cairo: IFAO, 1977–79), 220, § 341–42; Franck Burgos and François Larché, *La chapelle Rouge: le sanctuaire de barque d'Hatshepsout*, 1: *Facsimilés et photographies des scènes* (Paris: Recherche sur les Civilisations, 2007), 71. In the Great Hypostyle Hall at Karnak, see PM II², 60 [179c, V]; Harold H. Nelson and William J. Murnane, *The Great Hypostyle Hall at Karnak* 1, Part 1: *The Wall Reliefs*, OIP 106 (Chicago: The Oriental Institute of the University of Chicago, 1981), l. 115; Peter J. Brand, Rosa Erika Feleg, and William J. Murnane, *The Great Hypostyle Hall in the Temple of Amun at Karnak*, vol. 1, pt. 3, OIP 142 (Chicago: The Oriental Institute of the University of Chicago, 2018), pl. 115. In the Temple of Ramesses III in Medinet Habu, see PM II², 508 [133h]; The Epigraphic Survey, *Medinet Habu* 5: *The Temple Proper*, 1: *The Portico, the Treasury and Chapels Adjoining the First Hypostyle Hall with Material from the Forecourts*, OIP 83 (Chicago: The University of Chicago Press, 1957), pl. 324.
12 For instance, in the *Chapelle Rouge*, see KIU 1516; Lacau and Chevrier, *Une chapelle d'Hatshepsout*, 215, 278; Burgos and Larché, *La chapelle Rouge*, 121, 175. In the Luxor Temple, see PM II², 322 [130, III]; Albert Gayet, *Le temple de Louxor* 1: *Construction d'Aménophis* 3 (Paris: Leroux, 1894), pl. XLVI, fig. 111; pl. LV, fig. 114. In the Temple of Ramesses III in Medinet Habu, see The Epigraphic Survey, *Medinet Habu* 6: *The Temple Proper*, Part 2: *The Re Chapel, the Royal Mortuary Complex and Adjacent Rooms with Miscellaneous Material from the Pylons, the*

Forecourts, and the First Hypostyle Hall, OIP 84 (Chicago: The University of Chicago Press, 1963), pl. 374A.

13 PM II², 331 [180, II]; Hellmut Brunner, *Die südlichen Räume des Tempels von Luxor*, AV 18 (Mainz am Rhein: Philipp von Zabern, 1977), pl. 148 (XVIII/143).

14 PM II², 351 [36]; Beaux et al., *La chapelle d'Hathor*, 30, 32, pl. 7.

15 PM II², 364; Iwaszczuk, *Sacred Landscape*, 157.

16 PM II², 361 [108]; Édouard Naville, *The Temple of Deir el-Bahari*, 5: *The Upper Court and Sanctuary*, Memoir of the Egypt Exploration Fund 27 (London: EEF, 1906), pl. CXXX; Katarzyna Kapiec, "The Southern Room of Amun in the Temple of Hatshepsut at Deir el-Bahari: Epigraphic Work Between 2014 and 2015," *PAM* 26, no. 1 (2017): 216–17; Katarzyna Kapiec, *The Southern Room of Amun. Part 1: History and Epigraphy*, Deir el-Bahari 10 (Warsaw: Institute of Mediterranean and Oriental Cultures, Polish Academy of Sciences; Wiesbaden: Harrassowitz, 2021), 65–70, figs. 37, 39, 40, pl. 3.

17 In this period, only divine figures were represented wearing clothing with two straps, while the kings wore clothes with only one strap (personal communication from Dr. Andrzej Ćwiek). Therefore, this representation emphasizes the intimate contact between the king and the goddess in the embracing scene, where the king shares the divinity of Amunet.

18 A detailed commentary on the iconography of Hatshepsut in this scene will be included in the second volume of the publication of the Southern Room of Amun, which is being prepared by the author.

19 Kapiec, "The Southern Room of Amun in the Temple of Hatshepsut at Deir el-Bahari," fig. 9.

20 For instance, PM II², 43 [148i, II], 46 [157, III.2], 47 [158, II.1], 50 [164b.II], 49 [160, III.7], 45 [155, II.5], 59–60 [177, V], 59 [176c, III], 60 [179c, V; 180, V.1], 233 [25, 3; 26, II.A; 27, II.4], 234 [30, II.2]; Nelson and Murnane, *The Great Hypostyle Hall at Karnak*, pls. 2, 23, 47, 56, 102, 106, 111, 115, 209, 243, 246; Brand, Feleg, and Murnane, *The Great Hypostyle Hall*, vol. 1, pt. 2, 33–34, 64, 97–98, 114, 167, 171–73, 287, 324, 328, 344, 347–48; Brand, Feleg, and Murnane, *The Great Hypostyle Hall*, vol. 1, pt. 3, pls. 2, 23, 47, 56, 102, 106, 111, 115, 209, 243, 246; The Epigraphic Survey, *The Temple of Khonsu* 1, pls. 35, 39, 44, 48, 50, 63, 67, 73, 80, 87, 94, 95, 98, 108; The Epigraphic Survey, *The Temple of Khonsu* 2: *Scenes and Inscriptions in the Court and the First Hypostyle Hall*, OIP 103 (Chicago: The Oriental Institute of the University of Chicago, 1981), pls. 114C, 126B, 141B, F, 158A, 165, 176, 178A, 188B.

21 Representations of Amunet in the *Chapelle Rouge* were also commented on by Grassart-Blésès, "Les représentations des déesses," 253–57.

22 Block nos. 55, 59, 153, 161; see KIU 1533, 1524, 1497, 1485 (respectively); Burgos and Larché, *La chapelle Rouge*, 162, 169, 170, 184; see also Lacau and Chevrier, *Une chapelle d'Hatshepsout*, 273–74, 291, 296; § 436, 478, 487.

23 Block no. 23; see KIU 1308; Burgos and Larché, *La chapelle Rouge*, 80; see also Lacau and Chevrier, *Une chapelle d'Hatshepsout*, 240–41; § 387–89.

24 Blocks nos. 52, 207; see KIU 1516, 1394 (respectively); Burgos and Larché, *La chapelle Rouge*, 121, 175; see also Lacau and Chevrier, *Une chapelle d'Hatshepsout*, 215, 278; § 328, 448.

25 Blocks nos. 209, 244; see KIU 1292, 1538 (respectively); Burgos and Larché, *La chapelle Rouge*, 71, 187; see also Lacau and Chevrier, *Une chapelle d'Hatshepsout*, 220, 292; § 341–42, 492. As Grassart-Blésès noticed, the scene on Block no. 209 is the only one from the *Chapelle Rouge* where Amun is accompanied by any goddess while receiving the offering. The scene was completed during the reign of Thutmose III (eighth row). See Grassart-Blésès, "Les représentations des déesses," 257.

26 Block 28; see KIU 1694; Burgos and Larché, *La chapelle Rouge*, 244. See also Lacau and Chevrier, *Une chapelle d'Hatshepsout*, 338–39, §589–90.

27 Grassart-Blésès, "Les représentations des déesses," 260.

28 Grassart-Blésès, "Les représentations des déesses," 255nn15 and 16; for the link of *khepresh* crown with Amun, see Sandra A. Collier, "The Crowns of Pharaoh: Their Development and Significance in Ancient Egyptian Kingship" (PhD diss., University of California, 1996), 118–19.

29 Lacau and Chevrier, *Une chapelle d'Hatshepsout*, 61n1, 251, 254. For instance, on the obelisks in Karnak, see *LD* 3, pl. 22–23; Labib Habachi, *The Obelisks of Egypt: Skyscrapers of the Past* (New York: Charles Scribner's Sons, 1977), pl. 14; Labib Habachi, *Die unsterblichen Obelisken Ägyptens* (Mainz am Rhein: Philipp von Zabern, 2000), pls. 45a, b. At the Luxor Temple, see PM II^2, 323 [131, I], 327 [154, II.2]; Gayet, *Le temple de Louxor* 1, pl. LIV, fig. 98; and pl. LXXIV, fig. 188. At the Great Hypostyle Hall at Karnak, see PM II^2, 44 [152, II.9], 47 [158, II.4; III.4]; Nelson and Murnane, *The Great Hypostyle Hall at Karnak*, pls. 49, 52, 150; Brand, Feleg, and Murnane, *The Great Hypostyle Hall* I.3, pls. 49, 52, 150.

30 Pierre Lacau interpreted this gesture as touching or fixing the uraeus in *Une chapelle d'Hatshepsout*, 240–41, § 387–80.

31 Lacau and Chevrier, *Une chapelle d'Hatshepsout*, 215, § 328.

32 Burgos and Larché, *La chapelle Rouge*, 163; see also Lacau and Chevrier, *Une chapelle d'Hatshepsout*, 279–80; § 451–54.

33 For instance, PM II^2, 47 [158, I.2], 347 [17, 2; 18]; Édouard Naville, *The Temple of Deir el-Bahari* 3: *End of the Northern Half and Southern Half of the Middle Platform*, Memoir of the Egypt Exploration Fund 16 (London: EEF, 1898), pls. LIX–LX, LXXIX, LXXXI; Nelson and Murnane, *The Great Hypostyle Hall at Karnak*, pl. 44; Brand, Feleg, and Murnane, *The Great Hypostyle Hall* I.2, 92–94; Brand, Feleg, and Murnane, *The Great Hypostyle Hall* I.3, pl. 44.

34 Burgos and Larché, *La chapelle Rouge*, 163; see also Lacau and Chevrier, *Une chapelle d'Hatshepsout*, 279–80; § 451–54.

35 PM II^2, 115 [363b]. Furthermore, Amunet is depicted several times more in these southern rooms of the *Akh-menu*. See PM II^2, 114 [358, c.2; 359, 3; 360, 3].

36 Lacau and Chevrier, *Une chapelle d'Hatshepsout*, 220, § 341.

37 The rest of Amunet's speech was located on the following block, which is not preserved.

38 For the comment about the appearance of Min in the Karnak Ennead, see Lacau and Chevrier, *Une chapelle d'Hatshepsout*, 338–39, §590.

39 The masculine form was wrongly applied in this inscription; see Lacau and Chevrier, *Une chapelle d'Hatshepsout*, 338, §589.

40 For Block 54, see KIU 1633; Burgos and Larché, *La chapelle Rouge*, 212; see also Lacau and Chevrier, *Une chapelle d'Hatshepsout*, 311–17, §529–36.

41 KIU 1488; Burgos and Larché, *La chapelle Rouge*, 164; see also Lacau and Chevrier, *Une chapelle d'Hatshepsout*, 273–74, §457–62.

42 Burgos and Larché, *La chapelle Rouge*, 178; see also Lacau and Chevrier, *Une chapelle d'Hatshepsout*, 283–85, §460–61.

43 Burgos and Larché, *La chapelle Rouge*, 164, 178; see all suggestions of Lacau in Lacau and Chevrier, *Une chapelle d'Hatshepsout*, 283–84, §460.

44 Lacau and Chevrier, *Une chapelle d'Hatshepsout*, 283–84, §460; Maurice Alliot, *Le culte d'Horus à Edfou au temps des Ptolémées* 1, BdE 20.1 (Cairo: IFAO, 1949), 430–33.

45 Paul Barguet, *Le temple d'Amon-Re à Karnak: Essai d'exégèse* (Cairo: IFAO, 1962), 62.

46 *Urk.* IV, 877, 14–15; Barguet, *Le temple d'Amon-Re à Karnak*, 142–43.

47 Lacau and Chevrier, *Une chapelle d'Hatshepsout*, 284, §460.

48 Burgos and Larché, *La chapelle Rouge*, 178; see also Lacau and Chevrier, *Une chapelle d'Hatshepsout*, 284, §460.

49 Lacau and Chevrier, *Une chapelle d'Hatshepsout*, 284, §460; for the *imyt-pr* in a more practical insight, see Tom Logan, "The *Jmyt-pr* Document: Form, Function, and Significance," *JARCE* 37 (2000): 49–73.

50 Jean-François Champollion, *Monuments de l'Égypte et de la Nubie: Notices descriptives conformes aux manuscrits autographes* 1(1834), 579, 897; PM II^2, 439 [22].

51 PM II^2, 230 [19, III]; The Epigraphic Survey, *The Temple of Khonsu* 1, xi, 22, pl. 44.

52 The broader comment on Amunet after Hatshepsut's reign will be given in the second volume of the publication of the Southern Room of Amun in the temple of Hatshepsut at Deir al-Bahari, which is being prepared by the author.

53 PM II^2, 110–111; KIU 2318, 2366; Jean-François Pécoil, *L'Akh-menou de Thoutmosis III à Karnak: La Heret-ib et les chapelles attenantes. Relevés épigraphiques* (Paris: Éditions Recherche sur les civilisations, 2001), pls. 41, 49.

54 Pécoil, *L'Akh-menou de Thoutmosis III*, pl. 113.

55 PM II^2, 114 [358c, 2; 359, 3; 360, 3]. Eaton-Krauss suggested that Amunet was also represented in the statue triad with Amun and Thutmose III, nowadays located in the *Akh-menu* (Room XXXVIII). The identifying marker was the lack of tripartite wig, which is characteristic for all other goddesses beside Amunet. See Eaton-Krauss, *Post–Amarna Period Statues*, 18–19.

56 PM II^2, 467; Karol Myśliwiec, "Les couronnes à plumes de Thoutmosis III," in *Mélanges Gamal Eddin Mokhtar* II, ed. Paule Posener-Kriéger, BdE 97, vol. 2 (Cairo: IFAO, 1985), 151, fig. 1. Amunet is also attested in the inner decoration of the Barque Chapel in the Eighteenth Dynasty temple at Medinet Habu; however, this part of the decoration was restored in Ptolemaic times, so it is not certain if Amunet was originally depicted there. See PM II^2, 466 [38], 469 [47, I.5]; *LD* 3, 158 (text). There is also a possibility that Amunet was depicted in the *Djeser-akhet* temple of Thutmose III at Deir al-Bahari. The figure of Amunet was reconstructed there as the goddess who performs the *nini*-gesture. Only part of the goddess's body with the *nini*-gesture is preserved (personal communication from Janina Wiercińska), but there is no evidence of her name on any of the blocks coming from this temple. Amunet performs the *nini*-gesture in the Luxor temple (PM II^2, 305 [15, d.I], 320 [122, IV.1], 323 [137, III]; Gayet, *Le temple de Louxor* I, pl. XIX, fig. 76), in the temple of Ramesses III at Medinet Habu (The Epigraphic Survey, *Medinet Habu* 5, pl. 284A), and in the temple of Khonsu at Karnak (The Epigraphic Survey, *The Temple of Khonsu* 1, pls. 48, 67, 95), but there is no evidence from Thutmose III's reign.

57 KIU 2982; Serge Sauneron and J. Vérité, "Fouilles dans la zone axiale du IIIe pylon," *Kêmi* 19 (1969): 255–56, fig. 4; Nicholas Grimal and François Larché, "Karnak 1994–1997," *CahKarn* 11 (2003): pl. Vic; Bernadette Letellier and François Larché, *La cour à portique de Thoutmosis IV*, Études d'Égyptologie 12 (Paris: Soleb, 2013), 242–43, pl. 76, dépliants 7–8. Apart from the depictions in relief, Amunet's presence in Karnak in the Eighteenth Dynasty is marked by the erection of her statues in dyad with Amun. One of them is dated for Tutankhamun's or Ay's reign and currently is located near the sixth pylon in Karnak, in the Hall of Annals of Thutmose III; see, for instance, PM II^2, 90 [253]; Barguet, *Le temple d'Amon-Re à Karnak*, 133, pl. XXIIb; Cyril Aldred, *Akhenaten: King of Egypt* (London: Thames and Hudson, 1996), pl. XVI; René Adolphe Schwaller de Lubicz, *The Temples of Karnak* (London: Thames and Hudson, 1999), pls. 142–43. Aidan Dodson and recently Eaton-Krauss noted that this statue of Amunet was erected during the reign of Ay. See Aidan Dodson, *Amarna Sunset: Nefertiti, Tutankhamun, Ay, Horemheb, and the Egyptian Counter-Reformation* (Cairo: American University in Cairo Press, 2009), 77, fig. 58; Eaton-Krauss, *Post–Amarna Period Statues*, 59–62 [cat. no. 30]).

58 For Amenhotep III, see PM II^2, 318 [102, I.2], 320 [122, IV.1], 322 [129, II; 130, I], 323 [131, I; 137, III], 324 [139, II.1], 331 [180, II]; Gayet, *Le temple de Louxor* 1, pl. XIX, fig. 76; pl. XLVI, fig. 11; pl. LV, fig. 114; pl. LVI, fig. 112; Brunner, *Die südlichen Räume des Tempels von Luxor*, pl. 145 (scene XVIII/141), TLA document DZA 20.767.190. For Ramesses II, see PM II^2, 305 [15a–b, I]; TLA, document DZA 20.767.110. There are several more depictions, which might be attributed to Amunet in the Luxor temple, but the titles and epithets are lost (Brunner, *Die südlichen Räume des Tempels von Luxor*, pls. 45 (scene XVII/12), 48 (scene XVII/15), 171 (scene XVI/178), 175 (scene XVI/183).

59 For instance, in the temple of Ramesses III: PM II^2, 30 [80, I.4], 31 [83, I.1; 84, I.1], 34 [123, I.2]; The Epigraphic Survey, *Reliefs and Inscriptions at Karnak* 1: *Ramses III's Temple within the Great Enclosure of Amon*, Part 1, OIP 25 (Chicago: University of Chicago Press, 1936), pls. 15D, 44D, 45C, 46F, 64; or in the temple of Ramesses III in the Mut precinct at Karnak; see The Epigraphic Survey, *Reliefs and Inscriptions at Karnak: Ramses III's Temple Within the Great Enclosure of Amon* 2; *and Ramses III's Temple in the Precinct of Mut*, OIP 35 (Chicago: University of Chicago Press, 1936), pl. 99A.

60 PM II², 230 [17–18, I.5, II.5; 20–21, I.6], 233 [25, I.3; 26, II.1; 27, II.4], 234 [28, II.3; 30, II.2]; The Epigraphic Survey, *The Temple of Khonsu* I, pls. 35, 39, 44, 48, 50, 63, 67, 73, 80, 87, 94, 95, 98, 108; and The Epigraphic Survey, *The Temple of Khonsu* 2, pls. 114C, 126B, 141B, F, 158A, 165, 176, 178A, 188B.

61 There are some exceptions, though. In the sequence of offerings to the Ennead, see PM II², 59–60 [177, V]; Nelson and Murnane, *The Great Hypostyle Hall at Karnak*, pls. 82, 243; Brand, Feleg, and Murnane, *The Great Hypostyle Hall* I.3, pls 82, 243.

62 See n. 56 above.

63 For instance, PM II², 47 [158, II.], 49 [160, II.7, IV.2–3], Nelson and Murnane, *The Great Hypostyle Hall at Karnak*, pls. 47, 102, 106; Brand, Feleg, and Murnane, *The Great Hypostyle Hall* I.3, pls. 47, 102, 106.

64 For instance, PM II², 50 [164b, II], 60 [179c, V]; Nelson and Murnane, *The Great Hypostyle Hall at Karnak*, pls. 56, 115; Brand, Feleg, and Murnane, *The Great Hypostyle Hall* I.3, pls. 56, 115.

65 For details, see *LGG* 1, OLA 110 (Leuven: Peeters, 2002), 357–58.

66 As suggested by Maria Michela Luiselli, Mut was introduced to the Theban region during the Seventeenth Dynasty: Maria Michela Luiselli, "Early Mut(s): On the Origins of the Theban Goddess Mut and Her Cult," *RdE* 66 (2015): 122–24.

67 Betsy Bryan, "Hatshepsut and Cultic Revelries in the New Kingdom," in *Creativity and Innovation in the Reign of Hatshepsut*, ed. José M. Galán and Betsy Bryan, SAOC 69 (Chicago: Oriental Institute of the University of Chicago, 2014), 107; Luiselli, "Early Mut(s)," 112.

68 On the link between Mut and Hathor, see for instance Betsy Bryan, "The Temple of Mut: New Evidence on Hatshepsut's Building Activity," in Catharine H. Roehrig, *Hatshepsut*, 181–83; Bryan, "Hatshepsut and Cultic Revelries," 103–11. On the link between Hathor and kingship, see for instance C.J. Bleeker, *Hathor and Thoth: Two Key Figures of the Ancient Egyptian Religion*, Studies in the History of Religions 26 (Leiden: Brill, 1973), 51–53.

69 Grassart-Blésès, "Les représentations des déesses," 262.

8

Power, Piety, and Gender in Context: Hatshepsut and Nefertiti

Jacquelyn Williamson

This chapter analyzes questions of gender and power in ancient Egypt with a specific focus on Hatshepsut and Nefertiti, two women who are often lauded as exemplars of female agency in the ancient world. Before considering gender roles in relation to religion, politics, and legitimate power, however, we must be aware that academic paradigms in studies of the past often misconstrue ancient boundaries by anachronistically judging sex and gender according to modern contexts.

The process of identifying women and restoring them to the pages of history is a valid contribution. However, the search for "women-worthies," as it is called by other disciplines, can be reductive.[1] Writings that focus on exceptional women tend to focus on their "worthy" status, and to ignore women who were not "exceptional" to the modern eye. Simply adding more numbers of women to existing categories of sex and gender[2] may not always advance our understanding of women in ancient Egyptian society as a whole. Instead, a more contextualized understanding of ancient Egyptian women requires acknowledgment that they are being placed in categories that were created for them by "moderns." Women in the public sphere, such as queens, were not de facto empowered or disempowered. Instead, their identities were mediated by complex mechanisms of politics, social issues, and religion. Unfortunately, distant time and lack of evidence have obscured those mechanisms.

At first, the study of sex and gender appears to be a simple one. Normative sex and gender approaches may assume that "every" person has a single sex and a single gender, so therefore it is also assumed that it is possible to analyze others through our own lenses. However, there are many issues to contend with that need to be considered. The most obvious of these is, of course, bias. Scholars who study sex or gender must first deconstruct and identify unavoidable biases that accompany privilege, race, social standing, class, and country of origin.

To clarify my own bias, I am a Western woman, born in the United States and raised to be a feminist. The motivation for my study along the lines discussed here is that I have found that the set of assumptions I initially brought to my work hindered it because I unconsciously wanted my evidence to fit within the social values upon which I was raised. When presented with alternative ways of understanding agency, such as those proposed by Lihi Ben Shitrit, Sarah Bracke, and Saba Mahmood, I found that my reception of evidence fundamentally changed.[3]

This focus on Hatshepsut and Nefertiti shows the hazards of applying modern Western assumptions to studies of the ancient world. In considering that Hatshepsut transgressed gender norms, we must consider that times of political or social crises often dissolve boundaries around gender roles. Hatshepsut undeniably had substantial agency, but she used her power to support tradition and actually reaffirmed pious traditional kingship.[4] In contrast, despite a lack of evidence, Nefertiti is often attributed with both violent and religious power in an iconoclastic era.

Piety and Hatshepsut

This first section examines Hatshepsut's assumption of kingship. The rule of Hatshepsut highlights the question of the dynamics of power, raising the questions: was power itself her desired goal, or was her assumption of power a necessary role that she felt obliged to take on due to the youth of Thutmose III?

Three women were crowned kings: Sobekneferu in the Twelfth Dynasty, Hatshepsut in the Eighteenth Dynasty, and Tawosret in the Nineteenth Dynasty. All were daughters or wives of kings, and came to their positions through the conventional halls of power as internal power players with vested interests in upholding the rights and identity of the royal house.

Hatshepsut was both a daughter and a wife of kings, so she enjoyed the benefits of inherited family power from birth. Her husband, Thutmose II, died early, elevating his surviving son Thutmose III to the throne, although he was only two or three years old and too young to rule. Thutmose III was the son of Isis, a secondary wife, and Hatshepsut was named his regent, a logical choice considering that she was an insider par excellence to divine/royal power. Around Thutmose III's seventh regnal year, she adopted the kingship, declaring Thutmose III her co-ruler.

In representing herself as king, Hatshepsut went several steps beyond Sobekneferu, whose female-looking statues depict her in male royal regalia.

Most notably, much of Hatshepsut's royal iconography represents her with the body of a man. The transformation from female to male representation was slow, but her inscriptions retained female pronouns and female gender markers. She also created several legitimation texts and displayed them at Deir al-Bahari and the Luxor Temple. The texts emphasized that her father had wanted her to rule because she was the child of the god Amun-Re and her father's queen, Ahmose.

Hatshepsut's rule has been viewed through various lenses. Some suggest she was a power-hungry usurper who infuriated the people by stepping outside gender boundaries. Naville suggested that her father was to blame: "In raising his daughter to his own rank, Thotmes I clearly acted against the feelings of his people. The Egyptians were averse to the throne being occupied by a woman; otherwise Hatshepsut would not have been obliged to assume the garb of a man."[5] Modern scholarship has tried to approach her reign moderately, but with underlying assumptions that she indeed tried to grab power. This article argues that she may have had genuine piety and devotion to the Egyptian religion and the divine identity of the kingship. That is, by appearing as a male, she was honoring tradition and her co-ruler.

Ancient Egyptian kingship is inherently neither male nor female, but a combination of both aspects.[6] As Roth observed, through the combination of female grammar and a male appearance, Hatshepsut invoked the androgyny of creator and fertility gods.[7] As both male and female, she embodied the full range of proper kingship.

However, queens were supposed to be manifestations of Hathor and Isis,[8] while kings were sons of Re and Amun-Re and embodiments of Horus. By performing as a male, Hatshepsut appears to have correctly embodied those religious concepts. Artistic representations that gave her the physical attributes of a man demonstrated that gender is inherently a physical manifestation of cultural sex roles. However, how was her entire rule, not just her choice of artistic representation, framed to both herself and her people?[9] There is no question that her reign would have been perceived as unusual by her people, so how then was it adopted and understood, and why was it accepted?

The issue involves power and agency. Scholars have studied Hatshepsut's assumption of power in terms of her monuments and inscriptions, but in some cases, there may be an underlying assumption that she seized power because she wanted it and she could. Her representations as a male king, her inscriptions, and her depictions of herself with Thutmose III are often called efforts at "legitimation" and "propaganda," even while acknowledging that she represented Thutmose III as a "multifaceted and powerful figure" and "did not intentionally portray Thutmose III as any less of a king than she herself."[10]

Legitimation and propaganda imply doubt, if not subterfuge, and in some cases could reveal underlying bias among modern scholars.[11] Instead of being power-hungry and intending to "sell" her rule, she may have feared her country would be imperiled if she did not assume the throne.

This last point can be illuminated by a study of religions with clearly defined complementary gender roles which often find women stepping out of those roles as a means of protecting the norm. This is most particularly the case with religious movements concerned with nationalist politics. Nationalist conservative religious movements with a rigid prescription for gender roles frame some events in terms of an existential threat to the nation. This threat requires unusual or exceptional responses by women,[12] creating a motivational framework that articulates women's actions in exceptional ways. Even if women's actions in defense of the religious nation-state are not appropriate for their sex and gender, women's actions, when motivated by a legitimate concern for national protection and the very survival of a nation, are seen as legitimate. These women also often forcefully reject the labels of feminist and feminism, even if their actions appear to a biased Western eye as the actions of an empowered feminist woman.

This "frame of exception" excuses women from their own fear of stepping outside gender and sex norms when they become activists in defense of their nation. It also serves to create acceptance of their activist positions within the patriarchal power structure. For example, Phyllis Schlafly, in the United States of America, asserted in the 1970s that her proper place was in the home, and subject to her husband's authority.[13] However, she believed that the United States was itself under threat by the introduction of the Equal Rights Amendment, which aimed to assure that women, who are not explicitly mentioned in the US Constitution, would receive equal rights to men. Her campaign against the ERA was key to its defeat.[14] Her vigorous campaign required her to leave the home and occupy public roles not occupied by traditional women.[15] She excused her campaign by claiming that the exceptional time in which she found herself required her actions. She always assured others that she had received permission from her husband for her activities. If the times were "proper," she said, then she would not "have to" step outside of her "proper" place. And once the threat was vanquished, she intended to return to that "proper" place.

In modern post-Enlightenment societies, religion and state are separate under democratic rule. To observe how exceptions to strict gender hierarchy can be uniquely framed while avoiding post-Marxist Western biases, we can study nationalist religious movements that would place religion at the helm of government. By imagining a world without church and state division, we can better understand reactions to the upending of traditional religious rules.

The tendency of the Western mind is to assume that the women of these nationalist movements only claim that they do not want to be empowered, while actually using these exceptions to gain power and escape their prescribed roles. The bias presumes that the Western model is primary and superior, and that everyone desires empowered equal status and agency.

Western thought, based on Enlightenment philosophies, celebrates individuals who act independently from tradition, in defiance of convention,[16] especially those who resist established power structures. Western scholarship and feminist thought accord women agency—the independent ability to act—only when they rebel against social norms that ban equality.[17] Thus the autonomous subject exercises free will only by acting independently from social pressure. Individuals who act within tradition are thought to be constrained or "ignorant" of a "better" way, as in the Western feminist model. An objective of the early feminist movement in 1970s America was to criticize Kant and Descartes for failing to accord women autonomous agency. As the movement grew, theorists systematically assigned agency only to rebellions against social norms assigned to sex. In many instances, they imbued agency with political and moral imperatives; women who supported existing social structures were disdained[18] as lacking the ability to make their own decisions, "brainwashed" by their culture, too "disempowered" to "properly" rebel.[19]

However, the paradigms are obfuscating. Anthropologist Saba Mahmood studied the new Islamic movements so popular among contemporary educated Arab women who reject the Western feminist model. She observed that power and agency are found beyond the Western feminist model,[20] and that the voluntary struggle to achieve Islamic values is powerfully charged and agentive. Rather than being pressured, women independently choose traditional gender norms.

Agency, the independent ability to act, can be found in the conscious, educated support of a traditional power hierarchy. For agency to have an analytical application in studying gender, it must be divorced from political notions, such as empowerment, that are irrelevant to an ancient, nonwestern culture.[21] Ben Shitrit observes in her study of religious nationalist movements that "varieties of feminism stand for a rejected Western, secular agenda. For religious-political movements across the Middle East, feminism has been a placeholder for colonial and neo-colonial Western politics. Islamists, for example, have viewed feminism as an arm of Western colonialism."[22]

Women in nationalist religious movements use their frame of exception not to seek "power" in the Western feminist sense but to voice their concerns while reinforcing traditional gender hierarchies. While campaigning on national stages, sometimes violently, they reinforce women's traditional positions in the home. Their frame of exception excuses their nationalist actions without violating the hierarchy of the domestic sphere.[23]

Hatshepsut and her court found themselves in the exceptional circumstance of trying to determine what was to be done with a young king who could not take the reins of power. Hatshepsut had wielded royal power as a member of the royal family, as a princess, and as a queen. Nevertheless, for her commands to have primary weight and authority, she needed the backing of traditional rulership. Thus, her frame of exception may have been similar to the traditional religious nationalist movements we have discussed: she identified a threat to the state and recognized that she had the most appropriate experience, but also knew that her rule had to be uncontested and integrated into the traditional religious framework of power.

Unlike Akhenaten, Hatshepsut was no activist king. Instead, she adhered to a very traditional agenda. Framing herself as a person within exceptional circumstances, she emphasized her support for tradition and promoted all the traditional religious aspects of kingship. To signal her support of tradition, she represented her rulership as the embodied Horus. Egyptian art is conceptual; it expresses ideas rather than realistic images. Hatshepsut's images show that the divine king supports and defends Maat, order, and tradition, and therefore the Egyptian nation itself.[24]

Her frame of exception within traditional Egyptian orthodoxy explains her choice of artwork and her desire to include Thutmose III as co-ruler.[25] She particularly emphasized her divine birth as the child of Amun-Re and her position as the preferred heir of her father to ensure legitimation within the boundaries of traditional divine Egyptian kingship. Her right to command thus rested on solid traditional grounds; she did not want to upend the traditional order, or Maat, as evidenced by her throne name of Maatkare. Her protective stance toward tradition is also the reason she continued to show Thutmose III in a position of authority (see fig. 8.1), always at her side while she acted as a traditional king:[26] As Davies observes: "the two kings are dressed identically . . . these visual indicators underscore their equality rather than their disparity in rank . . . The circumstances of the co-regency provided a new way to express the idea of duality that was so prevalent in ancient Egyptian thought . . . (which) suggests that the appearance of an equitable sharing of power was not objectionable to the older member of the co-regency."[27]

However, by becoming the embodiment of Horus, Hatshepsut would have insulted the proper order of divine Egyptian rule if she had left the throne before she died. Total abdication is impossible in devout religion-based monarchies, especially in Egypt, where the king is the manifestation of Horus until

Fig. 8.1. Hatshepsut followed by an identical Thutmose III from the Red Chapel at Karnak

death. To our knowledge, no ancient Egyptian king abdicated power before death. However, co-rulership was possible. Whatever his age or experience, Thutmose III could not be declared sole ruler until Hatshepsut died.

Thus, Hatshepsut's rule was framed as an exception in a moment of crisis and explained by Egyptian religious orthodoxy.[28] As Ben Shitrit notes, "frames of exception are a concrete discursive tool that settles . . . contradiction by making transgression on the one hand righteous, given the demand of the nationalist struggle, and on the other hand, temporary, as it remains a strategy for exceptional times that would and *should* be relinquished once normalcy is achieved."[29] In this way, Hatshepsut's upsetting of traditional ruling norms actually reinforced them. Rather than being an example of an activist woman whose legacy encourages women to take power, she served her country by adhering to tradition.

When we call Hatshepsut's methods "propaganda" and "legitimation," we are inadvertently suggesting cynicism, implying that she tried to dupe her people. Instead, the people embraced her rule because the circumstances of her time and her situation formed a frame of exception. In short, Hatshepsut wielded power and had complete agency, but used her position to serve the orthodox establishment of traditional Egyptian rule. Her exception to tradition is indeed the exception that proved—and reinforced—the rule.

Violence and Nefertiti

Moving from a reign that tried to protect tradition, we turn to Akhenaten's iconoclastic reign in which a king consciously upended religious tradition and used his queen, Nefertiti, to reinforce his power.

Nefertiti is a particular focus for modern biases that take nontraditional Egyptian motifs at face value without considering the context of the time.

Fig. 8.2. Nefertiti smiting a female captive

Fig. 8.3. Nefertiti shown smiting captives and as a trampling sphinx on a talatat from Luxor Temple block yard

Even more so than with Hatshepsut, modern views laud Nefertiti as a proto-feminist "woman worthy" and past scholars have identified her as a vain, power-hungry manipulator who usurped Akhenaten's power. In 1965, Cooney wrote about a scene in which Nefertiti is seen smiting foreigners: "if we are to take this scene at its face value Nefertiti must have been a forceful and energetic woman who held power at least equal to her husband's. Her striking but cold beauty and her apparent meddling in affairs of state are curiously reminiscent of the similar beauty and political interference of the last Czarina of Russia."[30] Here, Cooney diagnosed the problem with his own interpretation: he took the scene at face value, viewing it through a modern anachronistic lens.[31]

Two genres of Amarna Period images are often used to argue that Nefertiti had unusual power in Akhenaten's reign. In one, Nefertiti is depicted in smiting poses or as a trampling sphinx to violently vanquish foreigners. In the other, she is alone, piously offering to the Aten at Karnak. Both of these categories are used to construct arguments that Nefertiti had an unusual amount of power in the reign of her husband. I will first examine the category of Nefertiti smiting enemies.

There are possibly three examples of Nefertiti striking foreigners, most recently discussed by Uros Matić.[32] One example can be found on a talatat in Boston, from Hermopolis (fig. 8.2). This image is part of a larger composition made up of several additional talatat. In the original scene, Nefertiti appears in a second boat under the boat depicted in the Boston block,[33] while Akhenaten appears on yet another boat, with his sickle sword raised high, in the same smiting pose.[34]

On the second example, found in Luxor,[35] several scenes show Nefertiti violently attacking enemies. Four kiosks are represented on this block; on each kiosk, she is shown alternating between the smiting pose and a trampling sphinx (fig. 8.3). The third image with Nefertiti smiting can be found on a talatat from Abydos. Part of a kiosk is represented on the right side of this block, but only part of it is preserved. The Luxor and Hermopolis blocks will serve as the main focus for this analysis because the Abydos block is not as well preserved.[36]

Wilson describes Nefertiti's smiting scenes as "scenes of power and terror . . . elsewhere restricted to kings or gods . . . this showed her (Nefertiti's) independent power."[37] In addition, Wilson supposes that "Nefertiti followed [Akhenaten] faithfully and was herself depicted in distortion. A beautiful woman must have been devoted to the new movement to permit such a perversion of her grace."[38] In 2007, Darnell and Manassa suggested that "Nefertiti's unprecedented participation in pharaonic activities enabled her to adopt the same bellicose attributes and poses as her husband."[39] Tawfik makes similar assumptions: "She expressed her vanity and emphasized her femininity by all means in her attributes, in all her scenes, and even in both her names."[40]

Those suppositions assume that Nefertiti had total agency and was involved in creating the religion, art, and propaganda of Akhenaten's reign. But in fact Akhenaten marginalized all influence when he declared that he would listen to no counsel but his own. He dismissed Nefertiti specifically, asserting that she had no voice in his decision making.[41] He declared his sole access to the Aten with his titles "the Unique One of Re" and "Sole Prophet." His complete control is seen in the construction of his monuments, as described by the stele of the sculptor Bak, and on the Akhenaten colossi.[42]

We know nothing about Nefertiti as a person, so we certainly cannot determine whether she had agency over her appearance, let alone whether she was vain, emasculating, or power-hungry. When we look at any image of Nefertiti, we look at a concept rather than a person. Just as masculine images of Hatshepsut do not indicate a literal miraculous transformation of female to male, we must assume that Nefertiti's images were equally conceptual. Her image, like Hatshepsut's, was created to communicate ideas of rule.

Matić and I have both pointed out that assumptions about Nefertiti's vanity, beauty, potential for violence, and desire for power are deeply engrained in popular culture, where she is seen as a potentially dangerous, beautiful woman who fought against prescribed gender roles and wielded the power of the king.[43]

Most of the analyses presented above focus on images without considering where they were found or the surrounding iconographic details. However, context is essential. Like a sherd found on an unexcavated surface, any analysis of images of Nefertiti, smiting and trampling, is almost meaningless out of context.

First, the smiting images of Nefertiti are found on day-to-day kiosks and ship's cabins rather than in sacred contexts. In contrast, images of kings smiting can be found taking up a side of a temple pylon, understood as a representation of the proper scope of protective divine kingship, where he guards Maat and the cosmos.[44] Nefertiti is never shown in such a manner.

In addition, as O'Connor and Matić point out, the pharaonic smiting scene is entirely male: men harming other men. We never see the king smiting or harming female enemies.[45] In contrast, the Egyptian[46] queens Tiye[47] and Nefertiti,[48] as well as several Meroitic queens, are depicted as smiting or trampling females only. Thus, when it comes to this specific motif in Egyptian art, queens adhere to a strict gendered division of power; they reinforce the traditional gender hierarchy by complementing male power.

Often Tiye's[49] representation as a trampling sphinx is cited as inspiration for Nefertiti's representations as both a smiting queen and a trampling sphinx.[50]

Some suggest that the trampling sphinx image of Tiye on the side of her throne indicates that she usurped her husband's power, because he is not seated on a similar throne in the same scene (figs. 8.4a and 8.4b). This reading again indicates anachronistic thought patterns, assuming that any marker of significance associated with a woman must equal usurpation of male prerogative. However, Amenhotep III's throne is placed in front of Tiye's, indicating his eminence. Furthermore, the elaboration of her throne is not a marker of power; it indicates the personal allegiance of her steward, the owner of the tomb, again showing the need to study representations within iconographic and historical contexts.

We tend to adopt a black-and-white perspective when it comes to analyzing sex and gender representations, and prefer interpretations that place men and women "against" each other in a power hierarchy. But Troy notes that the office of kingship required queenship for balance, so the image of the queen in these actions would be seen as merely calling out the proper status of the queen. In other words, just because one is emphasized, that does not mean the other is destabilized, disregarded, or eclipsed.

However, Nefertiti's smiting pose is unique—except for the Meroitic queens[51]—but must first be placed in the overall context. As discussed, Egyptian art is inherently conceptual and communicates the abstract unseen, including religious ideas of Egyptian rulership and the world. An image of Nefertiti smiting prisoners is a discussion of rule, not a factual depiction. In the Amarna Period, ideas about the queenship changed with the religion.[52]

In Thutmose IV's reign, the queen was explicitly associated with Maat and Hathor. The relationship was further elaborated under Amenhotep III. Akhenaten similarly equated Nefertiti with Maat and Hathor, as well as with Isis.[53] But as he continued to nuance the Atenism philosophy, he added to the queen's traditional identities by casting himself and Nefertiti as children of the Aten, reimagining the traditional triad grouping of the creator god Atum, so that the king and queen became the twins Shu and Tefnut.[54]

Akhenaten may have been motivated by more than religious inspiration. By abandoning traditional religion, he risked accusations of illegitimacy. Unlike Hatshepsut, who supported and promoted the divine status quo of Egyptian rulers, Akhenaten discarded the status quo by abandoning the Osiris paradigm. As mentioned above, to protect his rule, he equated Nefertiti with the traditional goddesses Maat, Hathor, and Isis. By uniting those traditional qualities, he mollified issues of orthodoxy. However, to support his new religion, he established Nefertiti as the divine twin Tefnut to his Shu. He adhered to an essential part of traditional Egyptian rulership by emphasizing binaries, where "opposite similars" duplicate and support each other.[55]

Fig. 8.4a. Amenhotep III and Tiye upon their thrones, Tomb of Kheruef, southern wall

Fig. 8.4b. Detail of the side of Tiye's throne with her as a trampling sphinx on the armrest and bound female captives below

Thus, Akhenaten prevented accusations that his kingship was invalid if it excluded the traditional Horus and Son of Amun-Re identities. To placate those upset by the loss of traditional male and female royal elements,[56] Akhenaten created a divine triad by establishing himself and Nefertiti as divine twins who already existed in the solar religion. He repackaged tradition to serve his nontraditional rule.

Identical but separate images of Akhenaten and Nefertiti smiting prisoners of different genders show that they act as divine twins, one reinforcing the acts of the other, assuring the public that changes in philosophy were moderate rather than extreme, and thus acceptable. When they both thrash symbolic representations of Egypt's traditional male and female enemies, as Matić observes, the message "not only structures the dominance of Egypt over her foes but also frames the dominance of male over female gender in Egyptian decorum."[57] When Nefertiti smites or tramples only female enemies, the image signals that the queen performs a twinned, and either lower-ranked or equal-opposite, version of kingly actions.

Thus, smiting and trampling images of Nefertiti "are not scenes of real events or real power, but rather metaphorical discussions of dominance over the north and south, the whole world, of men and women, to proclaim the totality of Egyptian domination and the proper role of divine rule."[58] The differing genders of vanquishers and vanquished define a divided power hierarchy in the traditionally gendered world.[59] Akhenaten created the images as a new concept of queenship for a singular moment in Egyptian history.

In the second genre of images used to prove Nefertiti's personal agency, power, and piety, she worships the Aten by herself.[60] The images appear on a pylon gateway[61] and on the "Nefertiti Pillars."[62] My book on Kom al-Nana, Nefertiti's Sun Temple, includes detailed explanations,[63] but I will summarize my arguments and add a few points. As with the smiting images, the images of Nefertiti worshiping the Aten without the king are frequently taken out of context.

First, those images appear in the new Aten temple at Karnak only, not at Amarna where the genre appears to have been abandoned entirely. If the genre indeed represented Nefertiti's independence, its absence would imply that her independence was rescinded after the move to Tell al-Amarna. Instead, I believe that Nefertiti appears under the rays of the Aten by herself to bolster the eminence and rightness of Akhenaten's changes at the start of his switch to Atenism. Rather than indicating power, her solitary appearance indicates her secondary status to Akhenaten and her identity as Tefnut.

Both the gateway and the pillars feature unique scenes of Nefertiti under the rays of the Aten, without Akhenaten. She stands before an offering table wearing a Hathoric crown; her daughter holds up sistra. As discussed, the

Hathoric regalia show that Akhenaten connected Nefertiti's queenship with Hathor to align with tradition, despite his philosophical changes. Hathor, as the child of Re, was never discarded by Akhenaten.

As discussed previously, scholars may base conclusions on Enlightenment modes of feminist Western thought when they interpret these images as indicating that Nefertiti was an independent, powerful woman with sufficient agency to stand free from social convention and gender structure. We see that the assumptions are mistaken if we place them in context with other representations of women alone before a deity.

For example, in the tomb of Mereruka, his wife Waatetkhetthor's chapel does not have any images of her husband Mereruka.[64] His absence gives her complete formal ownership of the area and primary access to its mortuary chapel. If he were represented, he would be the primary beneficiary of its rituals. Instead, as Robins observes, "Watetkhether has her own section of the mastaba . . . but the fact that she appears alone, unaccompanied by her husband is not because of her high rank . . . but because there could be no place for him in the scenes if she was to be shown formally as the owner."[65]

A stele from Deir al-Medina in the Bankes Collection describes a woman named Bukhanefptah, who commissioned or dedicated the monument (fig. 8.5).[66] In the lunette, she is alone before the Hathoric goddess Nebethetepet.[67] Below, in a lower register, her husband Kasa precedes a procession of musicians.[68] To reinforce proper gender hierarchy, the woman directly behind him in the procession is smaller in scale and is labeled as "his wife, mistress of the house, Bukhanefptah." Bukhanefptah is thus shown twice on her stele, but in the second instance she is in the "proper" place behind her husband. However, I believe her solitary state in the lunette indicates more than gender hierarchy.[69]

In the lunette of a second stele from the Bankes Collection, a solar deity stands in a boat (fig. 8.6).[70] Below the deity, a woman kneels with her arms raised in praise.[71] Behind her, a much smaller man stands with his arms also raised in praise. The inscription indicates that the woman dedicated the stele herself. She is identified as Iyneferty, wife of the workman Sennedjem.[72] The smaller man behind her is Anhotep, her grandson.[73] Sennedjem is not represented or named on the monument. Perhaps he was dead when she commissioned the stele, but the presence of Anhotep suggests that family hierarchy rather than gender was considered in representing direct access to deities.

A male child would not usurp his mother's or grandmother's priority on a stele intended for her use, nor would his status be undermined by appearing with her. If Iyneferty's grandson overshadowed her in rank based on his gender alone, he would either be absent from the stele or be shown in front of her to

Fig. 8.5. Bankes collection number 6

Fig. 8.6. Bankes collection number 6

preserve his status. Here, gender was not the determining factor; instead, a mother is artistically represented as ranking above her descendants.[74] As Exell points out, these stele do not focus exclusively on religion, and should not be taken out of context to read them only as indicators of increased piety. They use the medium of religion to articulate social concerns, like status. None of these stele are exactly alike, which demonstrates the level of independent agency and engagement with their creation as a means to discuss the specific concerns and interests of the dedicant, including status.[75] Exell has suggested that since men usually proceed women on these stele, female access to monumentality may have been limited and female rites of passage were not as publicly marked as those of men.[76] However, there is no way to know exactly why more women did not create monuments with themselves showcased. Eyre has suggested that it was less a question of access than one of status-seeking by men who worked in the public sphere and thus needed greater visibility for their actions to impress the community.[77]

However, the evidence clearly shows that when women were represented as primary ritualists before a deity, respect for family hierarchy and decorum dictated the omission of their husbands. Therefore, images of Nefertiti acting alone before the Aten do not indicate particular piety, independence, or an independent power base. Instead, we must understand the images within the restrictions of the pervasive decorum of the time and Akhenaten's changes.

Images of Nefertiti worshiping the Aten alone may be early versions of Akhenaten's attempt to cast her as his twin Tefnut, as in the smiting images. She and Akhenaten perform similar actions when worshiping the Aten at Karnak, and by showing such similar images, Akhenaten may have been promoting the Shu and Tefnut expression of twinning ideology.

The images in which Nefertiti worshiped behind Akhenaten at Amarna, wearing similar clothes and copying his gestures, may be the next stage for establishing the "pious twin" image. Instead of separating Nefertiti from the king by more forcefully establishing her as Tefnut at Amarna, Akhenaten signaled that she supported rather than undermined him. She could be shown worshiping the Aten behind him without undermining his status because the image expressed new concepts of divine rule under Atenism.

At Kom al-Nana and several private tombs at Tell al-Amarna, Nefertiti appears behind Akhenaten and mimics his gestures in holding up objects to the Aten. She is frequently even clothed identically (fig. 8.7).[78] At Karnak, she appears passively behind him and offers to the Aten only when alone, but at Amarna she and Akhenaten both make offerings. At Amarna she takes an active role in the Window of Appearance scenes, either handing objects to Akhenaten or leaning forward with him.[79] Her position or identity in the Aten cult could have changed sometime between years 5 and 6, when the gateway and pillars were erected at Karnak, and the time she is represented at Kom al-Nana, which began around year 8,[80] when her status as the divine twin Tefnut may have been more assured. Certainly, it is more explicit at Amarna. As Akhenaten's duplicate, she would not undermine his status, so she could appear behind him, copy his actions, and wear similar clothing and regalia.

The smiting scenes and images of Nefertiti acting alone copy Akhenaten's actions. As his twin Tefnut, the identical actions signal an important element of Amarna ideology and Akhenaten's redefinition of rulership. The images convey ideas and concepts. They cannot be viewed as actual depictions of Nefertiti's historical role. No texts or letters have been found indicating for

Fig. 8.7. Akhenaten and Nefertiti dressed identically in long pleated gowns and *hem-hem* crowns. Note that their gestures are also identical. Southern thickness of the entrance to the Tomb of Panehsy, Tell al-Amarna

certain where she was born or when or where she died. Although it is possible, we have substantial reasons to doubt that she ruled after Akhenaten. Thus, Akhenaten controlled all images of Nefertiti to serve his agenda. They cannot be used to diagnose her identity as a person. Her personal inspiration and voice may never be known.

This article comprises an analysis of two women who engaged with the Egyptian power hierarchy in different ways but have been equally misunderstood. At a time when Egypt faced a crisis of succession, Hatshepsut used her substantial power and agency to support tradition and to reinforce and protect her country, not necessarily to seize power. As a former queen and member of the royal family since birth, she already had ample power. Nefertiti, on the other hand, is often used as an exemplar of power in an iconoclastic era, despite the total lack of evidence that she possessed power or agency of her own.

Pharaonic art should not be used uncritically as if they are photographs of real life. They should instead be placed in context and understood, not as representing fact, but as a form of conceptual art: politically motivated to communicate a specific agenda. Hatshepsut and Nefertiti both represent issues of power and hierarchy as they relate to culture and religion, and emphasize that anachronistic applications of modern boundaries of sex and gender to the past must be avoided.

Notes

1 N. Zemon Davis, "Women's History in Transition: The European Case," *Feminist Studies* 3, no. 3/4 (1976): 83–103; L. Rupp, "Review: Women Worthies and Women's History," *Reviews in American History* 12, no. 3 (1984): 409–13.

2 "Sex" indicates genital biological markers that signal sexual identity. However, such markers are not strictly definitive or reliable. For example, many individuals carry diverse chromosome pairs. "Gender" is the social construct of identity, often created through culturally stereotyped, nonuniversal behaviors. For example, many cultures use different values and markers for constructing gender perceptions. Thus, we cannot assume that modern Western feminine or masculine behaviors are globally applicable, especially when viewing antiquity, because such assumptions are temporally subjective.

3 Lihi Ben Shitrit, *Righteous Transgressions: Women's Activism on the Israeli and Palestinian Religious Right* (Princeton: Princeton University Press, 2016), 1–31; S. Bracke, "Conjugating the Modern/Religious: Conceptualizing Female Religious Agency: Contours of a Post-secular Conjecture," *Theory, Culture & Society* 25, no. 6 (2008): 51–67; Saba Mahmood, "Feminist Theory, Embodiment, and the Docile Agent: Some Reflections on the Egyptian Islamic Revival," *Cultural Anthropology* 16, no. 2 (2001): 202–36.

4 This examination is inspired by the work of Ben Shitrit; see, for example, Ben Shitrit, *Righteous Transgressions*, 179–80.

5 Edouard Naville, *The Temple of Deir el-Bahari*, part 3 (London: EEF, 1896), 5–6, pl. 61.

6 L. Troy, *Patterns of Queenship in Ancient Egyptian Myth and History*, BOREAS 14 (Uppsala: Almquist and Wiksell International, 1986), 11.

7 Ann Macy Roth, "Models of Authority: Hathshepsut's Predecessors in Power," in C.H. Roehrig, *Hatshepsut*, 9.

8 Hatshepsut is suckled by Hathor in the Hathor Chapel at Deir al-Bahari, but the image is not associated with queenship.

9 Regarding models of women who preceded Hatshepsut in authority roles: Roth, "Models of Authority," 10–14.

10 V. Davies, "Hatshepsut's Use of Tuthmosis III in Her Program of Legitimation," *JARCE* 41 (2004): 65–66.

11 I do not intend to point fingers here, as I am most certainly guilty of using these words myself.

12 Ben Shitrit, *Righteous Transgressions*, 13.

13 For a discussion of Schlafly's involvement in the battle against the Equal Rights Amendment and also the most recent definitive biography of her, written by a scholar sympathetic to her politics, see Donald T. Critchlow, *Phyllis Schlafly and Grassroots Conservatism: A Woman's Crusade* (Princeton: Princeton University Press, 2005), 212–42. For a more current and balanced account of the battle over the Equal Rights Amendment in the United States, see Marjorie J. Spruill, *Divided We Stand: The Battle over Women's Rights and Family Values that Polarized American Politics* (New York: Bloomsbury Publishing, 2017).

14 Schlafly's protests sprang from a desire to protect traditional American family values and gender roles. She argued that the Equal Rights Amendment would take away many of the gendered privileges of women, such as women's exemption from the draft and the "dependent wife" benefits under the American Social Security program.

15 Schlafly was criticized by many leading feminists for her assertion that she was a traditional homemaker, when in fact she was a trained lawyer, the author of multiple books, and active in the political arena.

16 Mahmood, "Feminist Theory, Embodiment, and the Docile Agent," 202–36.

17 That is why Akhenaten has also been called the "first individual."

18 Such dismissal was inherent to the comments made by Hillary Clinton during Bill Clinton's presidential campaigns in the United States of America, particularly when she suggested that having a career was more valuable than "staying home and baking cookies." This assumption reveals a bias of privilege and a negative perception of women who do not embrace orthodox feminism.

19 For a complete discussion, see Saba Mahmood's essential analysis in *Politics of Piety: The Islamic Revival and the Feminist Subject* (Princeton: Princeton University Press, 2011).

20 Mahmood, "Feminist Theory, Embodiment, and the Docile Agent," 202–36.

21 Some theorists suggest that Sheryl Sandberg, author of a popular book on women in business, lacks agency because she acts within an established patriarchal system. Such an argument shows the difficulty of judgments burdened by post-Enlightenment Western notions. Sandberg identifies herself as having power and agency. Certainly, her book is burdened by privilege and race biases, but being employed within a patriarchal system does not negate her agency or deny her the right to claim agency.

22 Ben Shitrit, *Righteous Transgressions*, 45.

23 For example, a female political activist who advocates for a traditional gender hierarchy, speaking to Ben Shitrit (in *Righteous Transgressions*, 43), asserted: "The feminist movement . . . destroys the home and people don't know why. We see that the institution of the family is almost completely shattered in the Western world . . . People cannot survive (in the Western feminist model) . . . we must clarify this, strengthen this, and give women the tools that are appropriate in our age for building a good marital relationship."

24 Several interpretations exist for the Speos Artemidos inscription of Hatshepsut. To these possibilities we can add the suggestion that this inscription is a statement regarding what Hatshepsut saw as an ongoing threat to Egyptian security that her accession to traditional kingship helped subdue. I am grateful for Mariam Ayad's productive conversations concerning this inscription. Urk. IV, 390; A.H. Gardiner, "Davies's Copy of the Great Speos Artedmidos Inscription," *JEA* 32 (1946): 47–48; D.B. Redford, "Textual Sources for the Hyksos Period," in *The Hyksos: New Historical and Archaeological Perspectives*, ed. E. Oren (Philadelphia: University Museum, University of Pennsylvania, 1997), 1–44; Hans Goedicke, *The Speos Artemidos Inscription of Hatshepsut and Related Discussions* (Oakville, CT: HALGO, 2004).

25 Davies, "Hatshepsut's Use of Tuthmosis III," 55–66.

26 Davies, "Hatshepsut's Use of Tuthmosis III," 65.

27 Davies, "Hatshepsut's Use of Tuthmosis III," 64.

28 In conservative religious nationalist movements, the frame of exception extends to all women, as they are all encouraged to forgo tradition for the greater good. Hatshepsut, however, asserts that her exceptional nature is the reason for her transgression, and does not advocate that all women should follow her example.

29 Ben Shitrit, *Righteous Transgressions*, 14.

30 J.D. Cooney, *Amarna Reliefs from Hermopolis in American Collections* (Mainz am Rhein: Philipp von Zabern 1965), 84.

31 The Oriental "other" is often visualized as cold, beautiful, and potentially violent. For the foundational discussion on Orientalism, see E. Said, *Orientalism* (London: Penguin, 1977). Also see Uroš Matić, "Her Striking but Cold Beauty: Gender and Violence in Depictions of Queen Nefertiti Smiting the Enemies," in *Archaeologies of Gender and Violence*, ed. Uroš Matić and Bo Jensen (Oxford and Philadelphia: Oxbow Books, 2017), 109–10. Matić explains that in 1955 the Soviets were financially supporting the Egyptian socialist regime. Egypt played a key role in organizing unaligned nations as an alternative to the Soviets and NATO. In addition, the 1956 Suez crisis suggested that Egypt was a "dangerous other" to the United States.

32 Matić, "Her Striking but Cold Beauty," 103–21.

33 The best-preserved image shows Nefertiti smiting a Syrian captive, but Cooney suggests that the broken kiosk scene must be Akhenaten smiting a female Nubian; thus, they were equal smiters (Cooney, *Amarna Reliefs from Hermopolis*, 84–85). However, Matić observes that the figure in question wears a long garment that does not touch the ground (Matić, "Her Striking but Cold Beauty," 115). Cooney argued that the shorter garment must indicate that the figure is Akhenaten, but many images show queens wearing dresses that do not perfectly touch the ground. G. Roeder, *Amarna-Reliefs aus Hermopolis* (Hildesheim: Gebrüder Gertenberg, 1969), Tf. 16, 406–VIIA. In addition, on the Luxor talatat, Nefertiti wears a long dress that does not touch the ground. Both images of female captives on the Hermopolis blocks are associated with Nefertiti. She must also own the two royal barges. If Akhenaten is smiting a male Syrian on one barge, he must be smiting a male Nubian on the second according to Matić ("Her Striking but Cold Beauty," 115).

34 Cooney, *Amarna Reliefs from Hermopolis*, 84–85; Matić, "Her Striking but Cold Beauty," 107, fig. 5.1.

35 Matić, "Her Striking but Cold Beauty," 163, fig. 1.

36 For the discussion surrounding the identity of this figure, also see E.S. Hall, *The Pharaoh Smites His Enemies: A Comparative Study* (Munich: Deutscher Kunstverlag, 1986), 25; Cooney, *Amarna Reliefs from Hermopolis*, 85; Matić, "Her Striking but Cold Beauty," 108.

37 J.A. Wilson, "Akh-en-aton and Nefert-iti," *JNES* 32 (1973): 239.

38 Wilson, "Akh-en-aton and Nefert-iti," 241. This obvious modernist gender bias is based on unquestioning assumptions that her famous bust is "accurate," that all women are inherently vain, and that we know enough about Nefertiti as an actual person to know her thoughts on Atenism.

39 J.C. Darnell and C. Manassa, *Tutankhamun's Armies: Battle and Conquest during Ancient Egypt's Late Eighteenth Dynasty* (Hoboken, NJ: John Wiley and Son, 2007), 34.

40 Sayed Tawfik, "Aton Studies," *MDAIK* 31 (1975): 162.

41 The early proclamation on Boundary Stelae X, M, and K. William Murnane, *Texts from the Amarna Period in Egypt* (Atlanta: SBL, 1995), 76–77; Jacquelyn Williamson, "Alone before the God: Gender, Status, and Nefertiti's Image," *JARCE* 51 (2015): 187.

42 Ägyptisches Museum und Papyrussammlung Berlin 31009. Rolf Krauss, "Der Oberbildhauer Bak und sein Denkstein in Berlin," *Jahrbuch der Berliner Museen* 28 (1986): 5–46; Rita E. Freed, Sue D'Auria, and Yvonne Markowitz, eds., *Pharaohs of the Sun: Akhenaten, Nefertiti, Tutankhamen* (Boston: MFA, 1999), 244, cat. no. 131; J. Williamson, "Evidence for Innovation and Experimentation on the Akhenaten Colossi," *JNES* 78, no. 1 (2019): 25–36.

43 Matić, "Her Striking but Cold Beauty," 111; Williamson, "Alone before the God," 190–91. Note that E.L. Ertman ("Smiting the Enemy in the Reign of Akhenaten: A Family Affair," *KMT: A Modern Journal of Ancient Egypt* 17, no. 4 [2007]: 61) suggested that she was supreme ruler before and after Akhenaten's death. No evidence definitively supports this contention. In any case, these smiting images are not evidence.

44 R.K. Ritner, *The Mechanics of Ancient Egyptian Magical Practice*, SAOC 54 (Chicago: The Oriental Institute of the University of Chicago Press, 1993), 115–16; D. O'Connor, "Egypt's View of 'Others,'" in *Never Had the Like Occurred: Egypt's View of Its Past*, ed. J. Tait (London: University College London Press, 2003), 174; L.M. Meskell, *Object Worlds in Ancient Egypt: Material Biographies Past and Present* (Oxford and New York: Berg, 2004), 121; L. Morenz, "Fremde als potentielle Feinde. Die prophylaktische Szene der Erschlagung der Fremden in Altägypten," in *Annäherung an das Fremde. XXVI. Deutscher Orientalistentag vom 25 bis 29.9.1995 in Leipzig*, ed. H. Preissler and H. Stein (Stuttgart: Franz Steiner, 1998): 101; Matić, "Her Striking but Cold Beauty," 104. For the discussion about whether these scenes represent actual violence, see Matić, "Her Striking but Cold Beauty," 105.

45 D. O'Connor, "The Eastern High Gate: Sexualized Architecture at Medinet Habu?," in *Structure and Significance: Thought on Ancient Egyptian Architecture*, ed P. Jánosi (Vienna: Verlag der Österreichischen Akademie der Wissenschaften, 2005), 439–54; Uroš Matić, "Her Striking but Cold Beauty," 105–106.

46 Hall, *The Pharaoh Smites His Enemies*, 44. These are the only scenes of women smiting foreigners in the monumental context. C. Bayer, *Die den Herrn Beider Länder mit ihrer Schönheit erfreut. Teje. Eine ikonographische Studie* (Ruhpolding: Franz Philipp Rutzen, 2014), 400–401; S. Schoske, "Das Erschlagen der Feinde. Iconographie und Stilistik der Feindvernichtung im alten Ägypten" (PhD diss., Heidelberg University, 1982), 171; Uroš Matić, "Her Striking but Cold Beauty," 104.

47 For TT 192, see A. Fakhry, "A Note on the Tomb of Kheruef at Thebes," *ASAE* 42 (1943): 469–72. She appears as a sphinx with the *sema tawy* motif on the side of her throne. The motif shows a female Nubian bound with the lily; the Syrian woman is bound with papyrus. The inscription says: "trampling all the foreign lands." As a sphinx, the queen tramples a female Syrian and a female Nubian prisoner. The throne is similar to Akhenaten's in the tomb of Amenemhat Surer, TT 48, where he is shown as a lion trampling male Syrians and Nubians. T. Säve-Söderbergh, *Four Eighteenth Dynasty Tombs: Private Tombs at Thebes* 1 (Oxford: Oxford University Press, 1957), pl. XXX; Uroš Matić, "Her Striking but Cold Beauty," 114.

48 Dorothea Arnold, "Aspects of the Royal Female Image during the Amarna Period," in *The Royal Women of Amarna: Images of Beauty from Ancient Egypt*, ed. D. Arnold (New York: Metropolitan Museum of Art, 1996), 85; C. Graves-Brown, *Dancing for Hathor: Women in Ancient Egypt* (London: Continuum, 2010), 156; Darnell and Manassa, *Tutankhamun's Armies*, 34; Matić, "Her Striking but Cold Beauty," 112.

49 D.B. Larkin, "Titles and Epithets of Kheruef," in *The Tomb of Kheruef: Theban Tomb 192*, edited by Ch. F. Nims et al., OIP 102 (Chicago: Oriental Institute of Chicago Press, 1980), 78–80, pl. 47.

50 Graves-Brown, *Dancing for Hathor*, 153; Darnell and Manassa, *Tutankhamun's Armies*, 34; Ch.F. Nims, "*Amarna Reliefs from Hermopolis in American Collections* by John D. Cooney, Review," *JAOS* 88, no. 3 (1968): 546; Schoske, "Das Erschlagen der Feinde," 170; J. Tyldesley, *Chronicle of the Queens of Egypt: From Early Dynastic Times to the Death of Cleopatra* (London: Thames and Hudson, 2006), 132.

51 Matić points out that the reign of Thutmose IV marks the first time a queen is included in a smiting scene, not as an actor but as a witness. Later, she appears on barges of queens in the Ramesside period—specifically in the reigns of Ramesses III and Herihor. But the queen is not shown smiting in the same way as her husband. As is typical iconography of the post–Amarna Period, the decorum surrounding the queen smiting or trampling was abandoned to break cleanly from Atenism and the Eighteenth Dynasty. Matić, "Her Striking but Cold Beauty," 116–17.

52 Schoske, "Das Erschlagen der Feinde," 171.

53 Williamson, "Alone before the God," 179–92.

54 Troy, *Patterns of Queenship*, 136–37; L. Van Dijk, "The Amarna Period and the Later New Kingdom (c. 1352–1069 BC)," in *Oxford History of Ancient Egypt*, ed. I. Shaw (Oxford: Oxford University Press, 2000), 269; Williamson, "Alone before the God," 189.

55 Troy, *Patterns of Queenship*, 11.

56 Neferure is used to play the female element of Hatshepsut's rule. J. Tyldesley, "The Role of Egypt's Dynastic Queens," in *Women in Antiquity: Real Women across the Ancient World*, ed. S. Budin and J. Turfa (London and New York: Routledge, 2016), 272.

57 Matić, "Her Striking but Cold Beauty," 117.

58 Matić, "Her Striking but Cold Beauty," 119.

59 With "man at the apex." Matić, "Her Striking but Cold Beauty," 118.

60 Nicolas Reeves, "The Royal Family," in *Pharaohs of the Sun: Akhenaten, Nefertiti, Tutankhamen*, ed. Rita E. Freed, Sue D'Auria, and Yvonne Markowitz (Boston: MFA, 1999), 87–91; Rita Freed, "Art in the Service of Religion and the State," in *Pharaohs of the Sun: Akhenaten, Nefertiti, Tutankhamen*, ed. Rita E. Freed, Sue D'Auria, and Yvonne Markowitz (Boston: MFA, 1999), 115–16; Gay Robins, *Women in Ancient Egypt* (London: British Museum, 1993), 53–54.

61 Henri Chevrier, "Rapport sur les travaux de Karnak 1953–1994," *ASAE* 53 (1955): 21–42, pl. 11; Ray Winfield Smith and Donald Redford, *The Akhenaten Temple Project* 1 (Warminster: Aris

and Philips Ltd., 1976), 33–36, fig. 6, pls. 19, 20 (1, 2), 23 (1, 9), 28, 29, 30, 31; M. Azim, "La structure des pylones d'Horemheb à Karnak," *CahKarn* 7 (1982): 127–34; Christian E. Loeben, "Nefertiti's Pillars: A Photo Essay of the Queen's Monument at Karnak," *Amarna Letters* 3 (1994): 41–45.

62 Many talatat that made up the Nefertiti pillars were found in the Second Pylon, built under Horemheb, and more were found under the Great Hypostyle Hall, between the Second and Third pylons. They may have been erected in the area that is now the Great Hypostyle Hall because so many of the talatat from these pillars were located in the Second Pylon and under the floor of the hall, arranged in their original square formats. However, Akhenaten's successors may have moved them there. For a good discussion in favor of placing the pillars in the Great Hypostyle Hall, see Jean-François Carlotti and Philippe Martinez, "Nouvelles observations architecturales et épigraphiques sur la grande salle hypostyle du temple d'Amon-Rê à Karnak," *CahKarn* 14 (2013): 231–77.

63 Williamson, "Alone before the God," 179–92.

64 P. Duell, *The Mastaba of Mereruka I–II* (Chicago: University of Chicago Press: 1938); PM III^2 ii, 534–35.

65 Gay Robins, "Some Principles of Compositional Dominance and Gender Hierarchy in Egyptian Art," *JARCE* 31 (1994): 38.

66 Women appear less often than men on Deir al-Medina stelae. They may have chosen other venues. Their religious practice may have been more private and less ostentatious because they were less likely to be seeking status. C. Eyre, "Women and Prayer in Pharaonic Egypt," in *Decorum and Experience: Essays in Ancient Culture for John Baines*, ed. Elizabeth Frood and Angela McDonald (Oxford: Griffith Institute, 2013), 109–16; D. Sweeney, "Women at Deir el-Medîna," in *Women in Antiquity: Real Women across the Ancient World*, ed. S. Budin and J. Turfa (London and New York: Routledge, 2016), 249–50; M. Luiselli, *Die Suche nach Gottesnähe: Die altägyptische "persönliche Frömmigkeit" von der Ersten Zwischenzeit bis zum Ende des Neuen Reiches* (Wiesbaden: Harrassowitz, 2011), 130, 141–42; K. Exell, *Soldiers, Sailors and Sandalmakers: A Social Reading of Ramesside Period Votive Stelae*, GHP Egyptology 10 (London: Golden House Publications: 2009), 58–59, 66.

67 No. 7 in the Bankes Collection, from Deir al-Medina, Nineteenth Dynasty. Jaroslav Černý, *Egyptian Stelae in the Bankes Collection* (Oxford: Griffith Institute: 1958), no. 7; Robins, *Women in Ancient Egypt* (1993a), fig. 50; Gay Robins, "Some Principles of Compositional Dominance and Gender Hierarchy in Egyptian Art," 33–40.

68 Bukhanefptah and Kasa both dedicated stelae. Kasa's is British Museum EA369. It has a comparable representation of an anthropomorphic Hathor with ritual paraphernalia and family members with musical instruments in the lower register. Unfortunately, the lunette is damaged on the side that would show the dedicant, but he is not represented in the lower register, where his wife and child are at the front of the procession. This is opposite to his wife's stele, where he heads the procession. Exell, *Soldiers, Sailors and Sandalmakers*, 67.

69 Exell noted that in rare cases when women are sole dedicators and are represented on the same monument as a man, convention dictated that the man must precede the woman, even if the woman is the primary benefactor; Exell, *Soldiers, Sailors and Sandalmakers*, 131. I would agree and caveat this statement by saying that if the man was shown with the woman directly in front of the deity, the man must be first.

70 Deities shown in the lunettes of Deir al-Medina stele are selected relative to issues in the lives of the dedicant, and may also relate to a transposition of text formulations. See, for example, K. Gabler, "Stele Turin CGT 50057 (= Cat. 1514) im ikonografischen und prosopografischen Kontext Deir el-Medines: *nbt-pr Mwt(-m-wjꜣ)* (vi) im Spannungsfeld der Mächte der Taweret und des Seth?," *Revista del Museum Egizio* 1 (2017): 1–34. DOI: 10.29353/rime.2017892.

71 Bankes collection Number 6, Nineteenth Dynasty, reign of Seti I, from Deir al-Medina. Černý, *Egyptian Stelae in the Bankes Collection*, no. 6.

72 His tomb number 1 at Deir al-Medina is well known.

73 He is called "her son" as per the usual Egyptian tendency.

74 Extended and nuclear families had internal rankings that were predicated on more than sex. Meskell observed that in family tombs, the lady of the house had more elaborate burial objects than people of both sexes outside the nuclear family. In earlier family tombs, women and men had similar, more egalitarian burial items. Women at that time may have supplemented family income equally, so that the burial reflects their allocations. Sweeney, "Women at Deir el-Medîna," 249–50; L. Meskell, "Deir el Medina in Hyperreality: Seeking the People of Pharaonic Egypt," *Journal of Mediterranean Archaeology* 7, no. 2 (1994): 193–216.

75 Exell, *Soldiers, Sailors and Sandalmakers*, 14.

76 To add nuance to this point, note that in Exell's database number 33, Irynefer's wife Mehykhati is represented in the second register offering incense, which is usually the role of the primary dedicant. However, she is shown on the lower register. Exell suggests this is because of a desire to preserve decorum and is also an indicator that she is given "indirect access to monumentality." I would propose that it goes beyond questions of access to monuments, and instead reflects access to deity and restrictions of gender norms. The main attention of Irynefer's monument, and thus the god, is directed not to her but to her husband. Exell, *Soldiers, Sailors and Sandalmakers*, 131–34.

77 Eyre, "Women and Prayer in Pharaonic Egypt," 109–16.

78 In the tomb of Panehsy, both she and Akhenaten wear floor-length draped garments and *hem-hem* crowns. He offers incense; she offers a bouquet of flowers. Norman de Garis Davies, *Rock Tombs of Amarna* 2 (London: EEF, 1905), pl. VIII. Although not a religious offering scene, in the tomb of Meryra II, Akhenaten and Nefertiti overlap and hold hands in a foreign tribute scene. She is not shown behind him or at a smaller size. Instead her identity and status seem identical to Akhenaten's; Davies, *Rock Tombs* 2, pl. XXXVIII.

79 At Karnak, Nefertiti merely stands to one side during the Window of Appearance ceremony and holds up one hand in the gesture of praise, like a courtier to the king. Robert Vergnieux, *Recherches sur les monuments thébains d'Amenhotep IV à l'aide d'outils informatiques*, CSEG 4 (Geneva: Société d'Égyptologie, 1999), fasc. 2, pl 1. At Amarna she is much more actively engaged, such as in the tomb of Ay, where she is the same size as Akhenaten and helps him distribute *shebyu* collars; Norman de Garis Davies, *Rock Tombs of Amarna* 6 (London: EEF, 1908), pl. XXIX.

80 Although Kom al-Nana was one of the first built at Tell al-Amarna, the first three daughters are shown in the North Shrine, suggesting the structure was decorated in relief around year 8. Like many of the structures at Tell al-Amarna, the buildings appear to have been erected first in mud brick that was replaced with decorated stone work as the occupation continued. One example of the late version of the Aten cartouche appears at Kom al-Nana. Thus, carving could have resumed or continued into year 11. See also Jacquelyn Williamson, "The Sunshade of Nefertiti," *EA* 33 (2008): 5–7.

9

Arsinoë II and Berenike II: Ptolemaic Vanguards of Queenly Political Power

Tara Sewell-Lasater

Kleopatra VII ranks among the most famous of all historical queens. Her legacy, which was detrimentally shaped by Roman propaganda, is often the only point of reference for Hellenistic Egypt. For many nonspecialists, she suddenly appears and as quickly vanishes from the world stage. That she was Kleopatra, the seventh of that name, is often overlooked, but it is a fact which should reflect the long process that culminated in her rule. Kleopatra VII, in wielding independent queenly power, was not an anomaly, and yet the current consensus on prior queens in Hellenistic scholarship contends that, while these women could have public roles as the insurers of dynastic continuance and stability, their power was fleeting and conditionally based on that of their husbands.[1] This generalizing of all Hellenistic queens, regardless of dynastic affiliations, is overly simplistic and negates the efforts of the women themselves.

For the Ptolemaic kingdom, specifically, although this theory can be argued somewhat for the early queens of the dynasty, it cannot apply to the queens of the second and first centuries BCE. These later Ptolemaic queens were able to carve out a public and political space for themselves which ultimately culminated in instances of female regency, co-rule, and sole rule. For that reason, the preliminary development of Ptolemaic independent queenly power is often placed with Kleopatra I and II, but even this is too short-sighted. This paper will advance a new argument: the ability of the later Ptolemaic queens to acquire political power was a result of the efforts of the earliest queens of the dynasty, specifically Arsinoë II and Berenike II. These two queens were restricted from engaging in officially acknowledged co-rulerships with their husbands, but they produced a perception of power that later queens could emulate and make a reality.

New Interpretations

A theory that the earlier queens of the dynasty ultimately contributed to the accumulation of female power has been hampered by both the ever-changing definition of what constitutes queenly power and the ongoing scholarly debate concerning the extent to which these queens had access to that power. The contention originated with historians of the late nineteenth and early twentieth centuries, who conferred a puppeteer-like influence on Arsinoë II over Ptolemy II and direct rule of Cyrene to Berenike II after her father's death.[2] The active rulership attributed to these queens by the turn-of-the-century scholars led to a split among later historians, creating two camps of scholarship. The first camp argues that Arsinoë and Berenike held active and recognized political power.[3] These arguments then led to a reaction from the second camp, which contends that these women had either fleeting or no power. Burstein was one of the first scholars to propose that a reevaluation of queenly power needed to be undertaken, and Hazzard then overcorrected by suggesting that these queens held no influence or authority whatsoever.[4] While Burstein was correct in stating that a reassessment was needed, those reevaluations should not go to the opposite extreme and strip these women of any impact.

This paper aims to stabilize the debate in two ways: first, by proposing clearer categories for discussing queenly power, and second, by interpreting the remaining evidence as it would have been at the time vis-à-vis the double cultural milieu of Ptolemaic Egypt. For terminology, I have proposed the following categories, which utilize the contemporary Hellenistic term *basilissa* (see table 9.1).[5]

The term *basilissa*-consort, which will be used for Arsinoë II and Berenike II, indicates a royal woman who was married to the reigning king and held moderate power and influence but was not acknowledged as holding official power in administrative documentation, as later co-ruling *basilissai* and *basilissai*-regnants would be.

Although early Ptolemaic queens had inherited many rights from their double Egyptian and Macedonian heritage, both Egypt and Macedon were still patriarchal societies in which men were the authoritarian figures, with women able to act in supporting roles to those men.[6] Ptolemaic Egypt itself was a new consolidation, only about thirty years old by Arsinoë's reign, and the administration was still determining how to rule a populace comprised of both Greco-Macedonian immigrants and native Egyptians.[7] While Arsinoë and Berenike unquestionably cooperated with their husbands in establishing

Table 9.1. Queenly terminology (in increasing order of power)

Term	Definition	Examples
Queen, princess, *basilissa*	General terms for any royal woman, regardless of power	All
Basilissa-consort	Married to king, little to moderate political influence/power	Berenike I, Arsinoë I, Arsinoë II, Berenike II, Kleopatra IV, Kleopatra Selene I
Basilissa-regent	Ruling power, as guardian to male heir. This is depicted as a joint rule, where the queen is the dominant partner	Kleopatra I
Co-ruler	Ruling power equal to that of male spouse or relation	Kleopatra II, Kleopatra III, Kleopatra Berenike III
Basilissa-regnant	Sole rule or female as the dominant ruling power	Kleopatra II, Kleopatra Berenike III, Berenike IV, Kleopatra VII

governing propaganda and even acted as advisors to their spouses (see section entitled "Acting in support of their husbands," below), they were restricted from engaging in officially recognized co-rulerships by the attitudes of their day. They had to act unobtrusively and in positions of support to achieve their aims. Consequently, the *prostagma* and official documents issued during the first part of the dynasty listed only the king as exercising governance, and the queen was mentioned exclusively in relation to her parentage of the current king or as one half of the deified royal couple.[8] Berenike II, for example, remained queen of Cyrene in name after her father's death, but the Cyrenaian government seems to have been ruled by a republican-style council, over which Berenike was more of a figurehead.[9] There is also no extant evidence that indicates she ruled as a regent during the Third Syrian War. No *prostagma* were issued in Berenike's name, and the dating protocols on papyri were not changed, as they would be for later queens who did hold regentships for or co-rulership with their sons and husbands.[10] It was not until Kleopatra I, II, and III that a queen's name would appear alongside her son's or husband's name, indicating officially recognized female participation in governance. This is one of the primary reasons that these three queens are often credited with the preliminary development of independent queenly power. That Arsinoë II and Berenike II were not acknowledged co-rulers, however, should not negate their efforts in expanding queenly influence. These early queens worked within the bounds placed on them by their positions as *basilissai*-consorts, queens who were expected to be one half of the public image of the monarchy but to act only in support of their husbands, to create an image of queenly, publicly wielded power that the later queens of the dynasty could then use as a precedent for their own assumptions of more independent political power.

The Policies of Ptolemy II and III

Since these early queens were working within a system that was established by their husbands, it is imperative to briefly review the relevant policies instituted by those men. The dynastic cult of the Ptolemies developed around the eponymous priesthood of Alexander the Great, which was instituted by Ptolemy I, and it would come to encompass the priest of Alexander, as founder of Alexandria, the deceased kings with their wives, the current living monarchs, and the priestesses of the individual queens, such as the *kanephoros* ("basket-bearer") of Arsinoë II and the *athlophoros* ("prize-bearer") of Berenike II.[11] Although Ptolemy I had deified Alexander, it was Ptolemy II who officially connected Alexander's divinity to the burgeoning dynasty. Ptolemy II deified his father and mother in 280 BCE, both individually and jointly, as the *Theoi Soteres* ("the Savior Gods"), and he founded the Ptolemaieia festival in 279/8 BCE.[12] He then used his incestuous marriage to associate himself and his sister with the gods, as will be argued below, and he promoted the connection to both the Greek pantheon and the new royal cult by naming himself and his sister the *Theoi Adelphoi*, the "Sibling-loving Gods," sometime in 272/1 BCE.[13] The cult of the living royal couple was added to the title of the priest of Alexander to cement the chain of deification. This was an important piece of propaganda for the newly instituted royal cult, as the connection of the Sibling-loving Gods with Alexander meant that their epithets were repeated as part of the dating protocols on all official Demotic and Greek documents.[14] Ptolemy III then followed in his father's footsteps in building the royal cult, adding himself and Berenike II as the *Theoi Euergetai*, "Benefactor Gods," in 243 BCE, and they were worshiped as such while they were both alive.[15] For the Adelphoi, their deification occurred over ten years into their reign, and Arsinoë died shortly after. With Ptolemy III and Berenike II, the royal couple was inducted into the cult from the outset of their reign (within three years of their ascension), and worshiped as living, coupled deities for the entirety of their rulership, a pattern copied by all succeeding royal couples. This basing of the royal cult on the divinity of the royal couple as a ruling unit is the initial aspect that would provide queens with a platform from which they could build personal power.

Ptolemy II and III also ended the polygamy practiced by Ptolemy I and replaced it with an official practice of incest, both real, in the case of Ptolemy

II, and symbolic, in the case of Ptolemy III, establishing royal incest as a defining policy of Ptolemaic monarchy. There is a great deal of scholarly debate surrounding why this practice was instituted by the Ptolemies. For brevity's sake here, it will simply be stated that Ptolemy II wanted to associate his reign more fully with the gods, and incestuous marriage among royalty could be equated to the relationship between the Egyptian Isis and Osiris and the Greek Zeus and Hera.[16] In combination with the religious purpose, incest was also used to solidify the Ptolemaic line around the chosen heirs of Ptolemy II and Arsinoë II and to emphasize the legitimacy of those heirs since their reign was plagued by succession issues that resulted from the polygamy of Ptolemy I.[17] Ptolemy II married his full sister, Arsinoë II, and she adopted Ptolemy's children from his first marriage, so his heir, Ptolemy III, could inherit power from his deified "parents."[18] Ptolemy III married his first cousin, Berenike II, but in Ptolemaic propaganda, she was depicted as his *ἀδελφὴ καὶ γυνή* ("sister and wife"). For the Ptolemies, marrying the king to his closest blood relative, usually his sister after Ptolemy III, would impede the dilution of the royal line and allow for the transmission of divinity from both mother and father.[19] Thus, by the death of Ptolemy III, the practice of incest (both real and symbolic) had become completely entrenched in the Ptolemaic system, and his children by Berenike II, Ptolemy IV and Arsinoë III, would return to a true, incestuous union, the first of the dynasty to produce children.

The institutionalization of the royal cult by the early Ptolemies not only emphasized the male power, legitimacy, and succession of the dynasty, but it also incorporated their wives into that power balance since their divinity was based on the royal couple as a ruling unit. The inclusion of incest as a dynastic policy in both the aspects of actual incestuous marriages and the usage of the symbolic title "sister" in the few exogamous marriages allowed these royal women to gain political power and led to an increasing pattern of co-rule as the throne came to be defined by the royal sibling-couple as a deified pair.

Arsinoë II and Berenike II as Vanguards

While Arsinoë II and Berenike II were incorporated into the dynastic image their husbands created and were thus restricted to the roles laid out for them in that propaganda, they acted efficiently within the limits their position, as *basilissai*-consorts, placed on them. They set the precedents for the public ways in which a Ptolemaic queen could act and, in doing so, they became exemplars for their succeeding queens. In support of this thesis, three instances of their public, precedent-setting actions are presented below, but it should also be noted that there are many additional examples, of which space prevents inclusion here.[20]

Personal Wealth, the Cultivation of *Philoi*, and Artistic Patronage

Ptolemaic queens, as an inheritance from both the Macedonian and Egyptian traditions out of which their rulership emerged, could gain personal wealth via owning property;[21] engage bureaucrats, known as *philoi*, "friends," to manage that property and act as consultants;[22] and receive Greek-style educations that allowed them to understand and participate in the politics of their day.[23] Pomeroy posits that Arsinoë received a similar education to her brother-husband and, as an educated and wealthy Hellenistic woman, she was able to patronize poets at her court, including her *philos* Theokritos.[24] Arsinoë was able to pay patronage expenses herself since she earned her own income, and Theokritos describes the festival to Aphrodite and Adonis that she sponsored and financed for the people of Alexandria.[25] This festival, which was presented as an act of piety and a gift to the people by Arsinoë, had the supplemental purpose of promoting affection for and loyalty to the royal couple and dynasty, which would have been important since this was around the same time Ptolemy II was instituting the dynastic cult. But, more importantly, it may have had the effect of beginning to normalize Ptolemaic queenly power for the Greek portion of the population that would have still found a woman wielding individual power in public inappropriate.[26] Royal women of the Diadochic period had set the precedent for women acting publicly, but it was always in support of their family name.[27] Arsinoë's actions here are similar in that they fit into a traditional role of female euergetism and piety that would bring renown to her family, but she is credited with financing the festival all on her own, an act of piety on a larger scale that was usually only performed by men.

Berenike would have also received a Hellenistic education, since she was a princess of the Greco-Macedonian tradition. Her father, the king of Cyrene, strove to emphasize the arts and sciences in his own court, perhaps in emulation of his fellow Hellenistic monarchs of much larger kingdoms.[28] Consequently, when Berenike became queen of Egypt, she followed in her father's footsteps and those of her predecessor queen to become a patron of the arts in her new home. She appears to have had a special interest in supporting scholars from Cyrene so, as a patroness of the arts, she included the scholars Posidippos of Pella, Apollonios of Rhodes, Kallimachos of Cyrene, and Eratosthenes of Cyrene as part of the royal court.[29]

Kallimachos was an especially important poet of the Ptolemaic Period because he wrote prolifically about the court under Ptolemy II and Ptolemy III.[30] His surviving works are one of the main sources that provide some insight into Berenike's life. For instance, his epigram 15 is an appeal to Berenike for court patronage. As shown by his petition, and much like Arsinoë II, Berenike may have been able to pay patronage expenses herself, and Clayman theorizes that Kallimachos's allusion in the epigram to Berenike's statue being "damp with perfume" is a reference to the Cyrenaian perfume industry that supplied much of her personal wealth.[31] In her role as benefactor to her *philoi*—men like Kallimachos and Eratosthenes, who served as scholars and librarians in the Alexandrian Library and Mouseion—Berenike became a patron of those great institutions and helped expand their fame and knowledge. The act of a queen becoming a patron to world-renowned institutions also continued the normalizing processes, initiated by Arsinoë, of expanding both the acceptable public actions and scale of those activities for royal women.

Acting in Support of Their Husbands

As one half of the deified, ruling couple, the Ptolemaic queen was expected to act in support of her husband's administration and policies. Arsinoë, consequently, was present at important ceremonies, both political and religious. In the political sphere, the Pithom Stele (CG 22183) describes a royal visit to the Egyptian borders during which Ptolemy II and Arsinoë II traveled to Heroonpolis/Pithom in order to inspect the border defenses, conduct irrigation repairs, and see to the return of statues taken during the Persian period.[32] This visit and Arsinoë's presence in the public duties described on the stele demonstrate that the public image of the Ptolemaic monarchy was becoming centered on the royal couple.[33] While Arsinoë did not act overtly in a military capacity, her presence on this foray would begin a regularizing process of depicting queens as taking part in the duties of rulership, including the defense of their realm.[34] Religiously, Arsinoë's earliest duties as queen would have included appearing in public to take part in rituals connected to the cults of her parents, the *Theoi Soteres*, and her sister, Philotera; and, before her own death, she perhaps had a hand in developing the rituals dedicated to herself and her husband as the *Theoi Adelphoi*.[35] This cult was important because it not only presented the current ruling couple as a divine unit, but it was the first cult in which those being worshiped were also those instituting the worship, allowing Arsinoë to emphasize the queen as an essential half of that divine, ruling unit.[36] Arsinoë may have also acted as a private advisor to Ptolemy. Mori and Carney, for example, propose that Apollonios's depiction of Arete in his *Argonautica* is an allusion to Arsinoë II. In the story, Arete is shown influencing her husband behind the scenes, where they could make joint decisions in private.[37] This arrangement would have enabled Arsinoë to have her say while also allowing Ptolemy to appear as the main decision maker in public. The allusion to their private cooperation in court poetry, however, may also demonstrate that it was a recognized arrangement within the court.

Just as the Pithom Stele (CG 22183) had helped establish the royal couple of Ptolemy II and Arsinoë II as the center of Ptolemaic public image during their reign, so too did the literature issued during Ptolemy III and Berenike II's rule strive to center the Ptolemaic public image on the new royal couple. The *Coma Berenices*, which was issued by Kallimachos in 245 BCE, said that when Ptolemy III left for the Third Syrian War, Berenike dedicated a lock of her hair at the temple of Arsinoë-Aphrodite, after which it was discovered by the court astronomer, Konon of Samos, as a new constellation.[38] This poem is the earliest issuance from the Ptolemaic court to reference Berenike as Ptolemy's sister, putting forth the concept of her as one half of the ruling couple, and it also connected her to the previous reign by both establishing a pseudo-incestuous marriage and having her dedicate her hair at Arsinoë's temple in Cape Zephyrion.[39] Subsequent pronouncements would follow suit, including the Canopus Decree (*OGIS* 56), which commemorated the actions taken by both the king and queen in protection of their people during a famine.[40] Berenike also traveled with her husband throughout their kingdom and participated in temple-building efforts. For example, Ptolemy and Berenike, accompanied by their children, visited the Temple of Isis at Philae in 243/2 to make dedications to the goddess and her son Harpocrates.[41] At Canopus, they dedicated a temple to Osiris.[42] Berenike's acts of benefaction were almost always coupled with those of her husband in an effort to show the unity of the king and queen. In this way, Berenike was able to act in a supporting political role, but just as her actions were coupled with his, so too were Ptolemy's actions coupled with those of his wife, as it says on the dedicatory plaque to Osiris (*OGIS* 60): "King Ptolemy, son of Ptolemy and Arsinoë, the Sibling Gods, and Queen Berenike, his Sister and Wife, dedicate this precinct to Osiris." Their jointly presented activities thus continued the normalizing processes started by Ptolemy II and Arsinoë II that confirmed the queen as taking part in the duties of rulership.

Similarly to Arsinoë, Berenike also acted as an advisor to Ptolemy III. Aelian writes that Ptolemy would play dice while making decisions about subjects who had been condemned to death, and Berenike reprimanded him, saying "when the lives of men were in question, it should not be so slightly considered, but seriously and not at play: for there is no comparison betwixt dice and men."[43] These words, while brief, are the only ones credited to the queen that survive.[44] They depict her as a wise and moral monarch who takes her responsibility to her people seriously. She is portrayed as a good influence on Ptolemy, and he is shown to respect her opinion. This story and Ptolemy's reliance on her for advice may also be corroborated by her title *ṯ3tj.t*, "Female Vizier."[45] Analogously to Arsinoë, Berenike is shown working somewhat behind the scenes and in conjunction with her husband. Much like the Adelphoi's relationship, Ptolemy had the final say in governmental decisions, and Berenike was there to guide and advise him, while not overstepping her role as *basilissa*-consort.

Religious Public Image

Arsinoë II became an important part of Ptolemaic ritual and the religious public image of the dynasty as she became a Greek and Egyptian goddess. She was first associated with older, well-established deities, including both Aphrodite and Isis, which paved the way for her personal deification.[46] As previously mentioned, Arsinoë was deified as one half of the *Theoi Adelphoi* sometime in 272/1 BCE.[47] Then she received individual deification as the *Thea Philadelphos* either right before or immediately following her death in 270 or 268 BCE, and she likely had a hand in planning some of the aspects of her individual cult, perhaps basing it on aspects of her worship as Aphrodite.[48] Subsequently, both the cults of the *Theoi Adelphoi* and the *Thea Philadelphos* were necessary to Ptolemy's image after his queen's death. As has been repeatedly emphasized, Ptolemy had based Ptolemaic dynastic and religious imagery on the two of them as a ruling unit, so for the remainder of his reign, which lasted until 246 BCE, another twenty-four or twenty-two years after Arsinoë's death, Ptolemy needed to continue to use her image to maintain the popularity and stability of his reign. Although he had many mistresses, Ptolemy II never married again, and Arsinoë continued to be presented as his queen in official propaganda until the end of the dynasty.[49]

Accordingly, Ptolemy II reinforced the founding of Arsinoë's cult with several augmenting actions. He established the Arsinoite nome where Arsinoë could be worshiped in both her Greek and Egyptian personae, and that worship helped to create a commonality between the native and immigrant members of the population.[50] He issued coinage bearing a portrait of the deified Arsinoë which included iconography of deification that was meaningful for both the Egyptian and Greek portions of the population.[51] Finally, Ptolemy gave Arsinoë the throne name of *nsw bỉtj*, "King of Upper and Lower Egypt." Arsinoë was the first Ptolemaic queen to receive a throne name added to her birth name.[52] There is much debate over the significance of Ptolemy's bestowing this title on his deceased queen along with depicting her with additional kingly attributes, including her distinctive crown, which, as mentioned above, has led previous scholars to argue that Arsinoë co-ruled with Ptolemy.[53] Here, it should simply be stated that the title was conferred to bolster her religious importance and that of her new cult, and not to indicate that an acknowledged co-rulership was exercised between her and her brother-husband, as it would be by later queens of the dynasty.[54]

Although Arsinoë did not co-rule with her brother-husband, that should not negate her importance as a precedent-setting queen. Ultimately, Arsinoë helped create a religious and political public image of herself that could be emulated by succeeding queens. Religiously, the cult of Arsinoë Philadelphos was extremely important, not only to Ptolemy II's plans, but also because it served as the model for many later queenly cults, including that of Berenike II. Ptolemy's efforts to propagate the cult succeeded spectacularly, and it was still attested to by the reign of Kleopatra VII.[55] This meant that Arsinoë's roles as patron, cult originator, and advising and supporting figure to her husband were well remembered and able to be utilized by succeeding queens. Thus, Arsinoë II, because of the immense popularity of her cult, held recognizable power and influence after her death, which caused subsequent kings and queens to look to her for the pattern of queenship. In the political sphere, although Arsinoë was restricted in the political power she could exercise during her lifetime, the regular representation of her with kingly attributes, which were repeatedly copied well after her death, normalized the image of a queen with political power for both the Egyptian and Greek portions of the population, so that by the second century BCE, Ptolemaic queens could begin to actively wield the power previous queens had been depicted with, but unable to act upon.

While Ptolemy II was able to use his queen's memory to great effect, Ptolemy III had a living queen by his side, allowing for a more realistic portrayal of the unity of two living monarchs. Just as it had been Arsinoë's responsibility to participate in rituals to the *Theoi Soteres*, so now it became Berenike's charge to conduct rites to both the Soteres and Adelphoi, and to take part in the public religious duties of the monarch. Ritual acts could include participating in the major festivals, such as the Arsinoeia, but also in smaller tasks performed by the king and queen, such as offering libations of myrrh, scented oils, incense, or wine to their ancestors.[56] Berenike was also assimilated to several well-established deities, with some of whom Arsinoë had also been associated, including Aphrodite and Isis, but others were more emphasized, such as Demeter and Hathor. Berenike expanded the avenues of goddess-assimilation to the greatest extent thus far, and her succeeding queens would follow suit.[57]

Berenike's true religious importance, however, lies in her monumental depictions. Berenike was shown in ceremonial dress alongside and of equal rank to her husband, and she was the first living queen to appear in scenes of the transference of power.[58] These scenes depicted the current ruling couple inheriting both their power to rule and legitimacy from the Egyptian gods and the coupled deities that ruled before them. Temple reliefs showing the pharaoh alone inheriting power from the gods and paying homage to them were commonly produced throughout the Pharaonic period. The Ptolemies, beginning with the Adelphoi, regularized the image of the pharaoh and his queen appearing together before the gods, but the Euergetai were the first living couple to participate in a transition of power scene.[59] For instance, on the Euergetes Gate in the Temple of Khonsu at Karnak the royal couple is given their formal titles by Khonsu as the deified Adelphoi and Soteres observe, an act by which the divine powers of the deceased and deified couples are passed to the new royal pair.[60] Quaegebeur additionally comments that in this scene Berenike is titled the "heir(ess) of the brother–sister gods," which indicates that she is receiving the transfer of power alongside Ptolemy; it is not just he, as pharaoh, who is ascending, but rather the royal couple is inheriting ruling power jointly.[61] These types of scenes would be repeated by many of the succeeding Ptolemaic couples.

Similarly to Arsinoë, Berenike was also conferred with titles that would have a lasting impact on Ptolemaic queenship. On the Euergetes Gate, as described above, she was titled the "female Horus" (*ḥrt*), wearing the first Ptolemaic royal consort Horus name (also called a royal titulary), *ḥrt ḥḳ3t ỉrt n ḥḳ3t*, "Daughter of a Ruler, Who Is Born of a Ruler."[62] While Arsinoë II had received a throne name after her death, generally these were given to queens to mark their position as royal consorts. Only queens who ruled in their own right during the Pharaonic period, such as Hatshepsut and Tawosret, were given a royal titulary.[63] As Berenike did not rule on her own and was instead almost always coupled with her husband in their public imagery, her presentation with a royal titulary must have been an additional way of presenting Berenike II and Ptolemy III as one ruling unit.[64] Since she was presented as equal to her husband in their monumental religious depictions, she needed a corresponding titular equality to complete the concept that they were a royal unit acting in harmony both religiously and politically.

Berenike could be shown with kingly attributes in her Egyptian-style depictions and titles because a precedent was set for it in the Egyptian tradition by powerful New Kingdom queens and by Arsinoë herself. But, as with her predecessor queen, Berenike was not yet an officially acknowledged co-ruler. It is in this instance, however, that Berenike's significance as a precedent-setting Ptolemaic queen is the clearest: conferring titles like "Female Horus" and "Female Pharaoh" on Berenike produced an image of Berenike as the equal of Ptolemy. While, in reality, Ptolemy had the final say in governance and Berenike acted in more of a supporting role, her being presented as equal to her husband in both dynastic imagery and title created a perception of equality. Just as a perception of power was created for Arsinoë, so too did Berenike present a perception of power and equality in rulership that the later queens of the dynasty would emulate, and Berenike, in the titles she was presented with, acted as the model for the later co-rulerships of the dynasty, even though she did not truly participate in one herself.

Concluding Points

Arsinoë II and Berenike II used their positions as the wives of two initial *basileus*-pharaohs—Ptolemy II and Ptolemy III—to create a public image on which subsequent queens would build. They both accumulated individual wealth, which they used to undertake public actions, including artistic patronage and religious euergetism. They cultivated *philoi* networks which allowed them to promote their own ambitions. These *philoi* were responsible for commemorating many of their queenly undertakings, such as traveling their kingdom with their husbands and acting as an advisor—actions that would be transmitted to their successors. Additionally, their public acts of euergetism, such as patronizing festivals or dedicating at temples, also had the effect of normalizing the public ruling actions of royal women. Most importantly, both Arsinoë and Berenike received titles and were depicted with kingly attributes that would create a perception of power and equality that later queens could emulate. While they did not co-rule or sole-rule, as the Ptolemaic queens of the second century would, Arsinoë II and Berenike II's contributions to the female power of the dynasty should not be underestimated. Rather, because of the prevalence of oversimplified theories on queenly power, it is imperative to identify the starting point from which Ptolemaic queens ascended to political prominence.

Notes

1 See Ivana Savalli-Lestrade, "Il ruolo pubblico delle regine ellenistiche," in *Historie: Studie offerti dagli Allievi Giuseppe Nenci in occasione del suo settantesimo compleanno*, ed. Salvatore Allessandri (Congedo: Galatina LE, 1994); Ivana Savalli-Lestrade, "La place des reines à la cour et dans le royaume à l'époque hellénistique," in *Les femmes antiques entre sphère privée et sphère publique*, ed. Regula Frei-Stolba, Anne Bielman, and Olivier Bianchi (Bern: P. Lang, 2003); Anne Bielman-Sánchez, "Régner au féminin. Réflexions sur les reines attalides et séleucides," in *L'Orient mediterranéen de la mort d'Alexandre aux campagnes de Pompé: Cités et royaumes à l'époque hellénistique*, ed. F. Prost (Paris: Rennes, 2015); Anne Bielman-Sánchez and Giuseppina Lenzo, "Deux femmes de pouvoir chez les Lagides: Cléopâtre I et Cléopâtre II (IIe siècle av. J.-C.)," in *Femmes influentes dans le monde hellénistique et à Rome: IIIe siècle av. J.-C.–Ier siècle apr. J.-C.*, ed. Anne Bielman, Isabelle Cogitore, and Anne Kolb (Grenoble: ELLUG, 2016).

2 For Arsinoë II, see Edwyn Bevan, *The House of Ptolemy: A History of Egypt under the Ptolemaic Dynasty* (Chicago: Argonaut, 1968 reprint), 60–61; Grace Harriet Macurdy, *Hellenistic Queens:*

A Study of Woman-Power in Macedonia, Seleucid Syria, and Ptolemaic Egypt (Baltimore: The Johns Hopkins Press, 1932), 118. For Berenike II, see Macurdy, *Hellenistic Queens*, 132; Auguste Bouché-Leclerq, *Histoire des Lagides* (Paris: E. Leroux, 1903), 245n4; J.P. Mahaffy, *A History of Egypt under the Ptolemaic Dynasty* (London: Methuen and Co., 1899), 99; Branko F. van Oppen de Ruiter, *Berenice II Euergetis: Essays in Early Hellenistic Queenship* (New York: Palgrave Macmillan, 2015), 39, 117, 127.

3 For example, Quaegebeur and Hauben proposed that Arsinoë exercised sovereign power and served as a co-ruler to Ptolemy II. Jan Quaegebeur, "Ptolémée II en adoration devant Arsinoé II divinisée," *BIFAO* 69 (1969): 205, 208–209; Hans Hauben, "Arsinoé II et la politique extérieure de l'Égypte," in *Egypt and the Hellenistic World: Proceedings of the International Colloquium Leuven, 24–26 May 1982*, ed. E. van't Dack and P. van Dessel (Leuven: Peeters, 1983), 110, 127; Sarah B. Pomeroy, *Women in Hellenistic Egypt: From Alexander to Cleopatra* (Detroit: Wayne State University Press, 1990), 17–18. Following the same pattern, Berenike is also often credited with ruling Egypt in 246–245 BCE while Ptolemy was away for the Third Syrian War (246–241 BCE). See Elaine Fantham et al., *Women in the Classical World: Image and Text* (New York: Oxford University Press, 1994), 148; Maria C. Caltabiano, "Berenice II: Il ruolo di una *basilissa* rivelato dalle sue monete," in *La Cirenaica in Età Antica: Atti del Convegno Internazionale di Studi*, ed. Enzo Catani and Silvia M. Marengo (Macerata: Università degli studi di Macerata, 1998), 103–104; Oppen de Ruiter, *Berenice II Euergetis*, 33n69, 37, 39.

4 Stanley Burstein, "Arsinoe II Philadelphos: A Revisionist View," in *Philip II, Alexander the Great, and the Macedonian Heritage*, ed. W. Lindsay Adams and Eugene N. Borza (Washington, DC: University Press of America, 1982), 205n42, 210, 212. On Arsinoë II, see R.A. Hazzard, *Imagination of a Monarchy: Studies in Ptolemaic Propaganda* (Toronto: University of Toronto Press, 2000), 96–99. On Berenike II, see Hazzard, *Imagination of a Monarchy*, 113.

5 See Tara Sewell-Lasater, "Becoming Kleopatra: Ptolemaic Royal Marriage, Incest, and the Path to Female Rule" (PhD diss., University of Houston, 2020), 14–19. It should also be noted that *basilissa* was a title used by many Hellenistic royal women. It is often translated as "queen" because it came into use at the same time Hellenistic royal men began using the title *basileus*, but *basilissa* was used to describe a royal wife of the king or heir, a royal daughter, a sister to the king or heir, and/or a female regent. On its own, the term is better translated as "royal woman." See Anne Bielman-Sánchez, "Régner au féminin. Réflexions sur les reines attalides et séleucides," in *L'Orient méditerranéen de la mort d'Alexandre aux campagnes de Pompé: Cités et royaumes à l'époque hellénistique*, ed. F. Prost (Paris: Rennes, 2015), 43; Elizabeth D. Carney, "What's in a Name? The Emergence of a Title for Royal Women in the Hellenistic Period," in *Women's History and Ancient History*, ed. Sarah B. Pomeroy (Chapel Hill: University of North Carolina Press, 1991), 156, 161; Elizabeth D. Carney, "Being Royal and Female in the Early Hellenistic Period," in *Creating a Hellenistic World*, ed. Andrew Erskine and Lloyd Llewellyn-Jones (Swansea: The Classical Press of Wales, 2010), 202. Subsequently, in table 9.1, *basilissa* has been hyphenated with several clarifying terms to indicate the different categories of queenly power and/or influence.

6 For an overview of the rights and influences Ptolemaic queens inherited from their Egyptian and Macedonian heritages, see Sewell-Lasater, "Becoming Kleopatra," 21–35, 90–93.

7 The span of thirty years is calculated from Ptolemy I's assumption of the titles *basileus* ("king") and "pharaoh" in 305 BCE, which heralded Egypt's transformation from a satrapy of Alexander's empire to an independent kingdom.

8 Official documents were headed by a dating protocol; see Bielman-Sánchez and Lenzo, "Deux femmes de pouvoir chez les Lagides," 158–59. The dating protocols of Ptolemy I through Ptolemy V included the name of the reigning male monarch, his parentage, and the eponymous priesthoods established up to the current date, beginning with the priest of Alexander, whose title also included all the current deified royal couples. In the listing of deified royal couples, the queen was not mentioned by name, but only by her joint spousal epithet, such as *Theoi Adelphoi* for Arsinoë II. The queenly eponymous priestesshoods were listed after the Alexander priest's titles,

however, and both Arsinoë II and Berenike II were mentioned by name with their respective priestesses. On the Alexander priest and queenly eponymous priestesshoods, see note 11, below. Including the queen in the dating protocol only vis-à-vis her role in the parentage of the current king and religious affiliations remained the norm until Kleopatra I's regency for her son from 180 to 177 BCE, after which, queens were regularly included as co-ruling monarchs in the protocols. For expanded dating protocols, see Sewell-Lasater, "Becoming Kleopatra," Appendix C.

9 Polyb. 10.22.2–3; Plut. *Vit. Phil.* 1.3–4; Gunther Hölbl, *A History of the Ptolemaic Empire*, trans. Tina Saavedra (London: Routledge, 2001), 46; Oppen de Ruiter, *Berenice II Euergetis*, 23, 26, 39.

10 During the Third Syrian War, petitions such as P.Col. 4.83, which was issued in 245/4 BCE, were addressed directly to the king, Ptolemy III (*βασιλεῖ Πτολεμαίωι*), rather than to a regent. But in later periods, when Ptolemaic kings and queens held publicly acknowledged co-rulerships, plural addresses were used that mentioned both the king and queen. See, for example, P.Freib. 3.22 from the reign of Kleopatra I and Ptolemy VI, or P.Gen. 2.87 from the reign of Ptolemy VIII and Kleopatra II. For a full analysis of the Berenike-as-regent issue, see Sewell-Lasater, "Becoming Kleopatra," 147–51.

11 Jan Quaegebeur, "The Egyptian Clergy and the Cult of the Ptolemaic Dynasty," *AncSoc* 20 (1989), 94; Jan Quaegebeur, "Cleopatra VII and the Cults of the Ptolemaic Queens," in *Cleopatra's Egypt: Age of the Ptolemies*, ed. R.S. Bianchi (Brooklyn: Brooklyn Museum, 1988), 42; P.M. Fraser, *Ptolemaic Alexandria* (Oxford: Oxford University Press, 1972), 216. By the reign of Ptolemy IV, for instance, the dating protocol for the priest of Alexander would read: "In the Priesthood of [priest's name], of Alexander, the *Theoi Soteres*, *Theoi Adelphoi*, *Theoi Euergetai*, *Theoi Philopatores*, the *athlophoros* of Berenike Euergetis, and the *kanephoros* of Arsinoë Philadelphos." The *kanephoros*, established for Arsinoë II in 267/6, and the *athlophoros*, established for Berenike II in 211/10, were both eponymous priestesshoods instituted to conduct rights to the deified, deceased queens. Ludwig Koenen, "The Ptolemaic King as a Religious Figure," in *Images and Ideologies: Self-definition in the Hellenistic World*, ed. A. Bulloch (Berkeley: University of California Press, 1993), 56; Hölbl, *A History of the Ptolemaic Empire*, 103, 170. For expanded dating protocols, see Sewell-Lasater, "Becoming Kleopatra," Appendix C.

12 Athen. 5.196A–203B; Hölbl, *A History of the Ptolemaic Empire*, 94; Koenen, "The Ptolemaic King as a Religious Figure," 50–51; Michael Goyette, "Ptolemy II Philadelphus and the Dionysiac Model of Political Authority," *JAEI* 2 (2010): 2, 7. On the Ptolemaieia, see Charlotte Wikander, "Religion, Political Power and Gender—The Building of Cult-image," in *Religion and Power in the Ancient Greek World: Proceedings of the Uppsala Symposium 1993*, ed. Pontus Hellström and Brita Alroth (Uppsala: Uppsala University, 1996), 184–85. It should also be briefly noted that although Ptolemy II deified his parents, they were not added to the Alexander priest's eponymous formula until the reign of Ptolemy IV. Fraser, *Ptolemaic Alexandria*, 217–18.

13 P.Hib. 2.199; Stefan Pfeiffer, "The God Serapis, His Cult, and the Beginnings of the Ruler Cult in Ptolemaic Egypt," in *Ptolemy II Philadelphus and His World*, ed. Paul McKechnie and Philippe Guillaume (Leiden: Brill, 2008), 398; Elizabeth D. Carney, *Arsinoë of Egypt and Macedon: A Royal Life* (Oxford: Oxford University Press, 2013), 97n104; Koenen, "The Ptolemaic King as a Religious Figure," 51n61. See also Hauben, "Arsinoé II et la politique extérieure de l'Égypte," 113.

14 On the dating protocol, see note 8, above. Elizabeth D. Carney, "The Reappearance of Royal Sibling Marriage in Ptolemaic Egypt," *Parola del Passato* 237 (1987): 430; Koenen, "The Ptolemaic King as a Religious Figure," 51–52; Hölbl, *A History of the Ptolemaic Empire*, 95, 110; Angelos Chaniotis, "The Divinity of Hellenistic Rulers," in *A Companion to the Hellenistic World*, ed. Andrew Erskine (Malden: Blackwell, 2005), 437. Hölbl and Chaniotis observe that as each coupled epithet was added to the priest of Alexander's title (Soteres, Adelphoi, Euergetai, and so on), the line of deification was continued.

15 Hölbl, *A History of the Ptolemaic Empire*, 95; Koenen, "The Ptolemaic King as a Religious Figure," 52–53.

16 For a thorough overview of the contention surrounding Ptolemaic incest and Ptolemy II's reasons for instituting the practice, see Sewell-Lasater, "Becoming Kleopatra," 64–82.

17 Carney, *Arsinoë of Egypt and Macedon,* 4–5, 22–24, 76–77. On the contention between the Eurydikean and Berenikean lines of Ptolemy I's offspring, see Sewell-Lasater, "Becoming Kleopatra," 71–72.

18 Although Arsinoë II was not Ptolemy III's biological mother, she was depicted as such in subsequent Ptolemaic inscriptions and monuments. After Ptolemy III's marriage, both he and Berenike II were depicted as the children of Ptolemy II and Arsinoë II, which provided them both with new parents that distanced them from past embarrassments, including the treason committed by Ptolemy III's biological mother (Schol. Theoc. 17.128) and the rebellion of Berenike II's biological father (Paus. 1.7.1).

19 There were a few exceptions to direct brother–sister marriages as the dynasty progressed, including Kleopatra I, who was the only other exogamous bride of the dynasty after Berenike II, and Ptolemy VIII, who married first his sister and then his niece.

20 For a thorough overview of the achievements of each of these queens and the ways in which they set a precedent for their successors, see Sewell-Lasater, "Becoming Kleopatra," Part 2, chs. 5 and 6.

21 Arsinoë II, for example, was granted income from several cities by her first husband, Lysimachos, and, as queen of Egypt, she was granted revenue from the fish in Lake Moeris: Pomeroy, *Women in Hellenistic Egypt,* 14. Similarly, Berenike II earned personal wealth from the thriving Cyrenaian perfume industry (Athen. 15.689A), and, as queen of Egypt, she owned grain transport ships (P.Ryl. 4.576; P.Lille 22, 23; P.Teb. 1034, 1035). Dee L. Clayman, *Berenice II and the Golden Age of Ptolemaic Egypt* (Oxford: Oxford University Press, 2014), 60, 85, 124; C.H. Roberts and E.G. Turner, *Catalogue of the Greek and Latin Papyri in the John Rylands Library, Manchester*, vol. 4, *Documents of the Ptolemaic, Roman, and Byzantine Periods* (Manchester: Manchester University Press, 1952), 26–27.

22 Since Ptolemaic queens cultivated networks of *philoi,* they did not have to rely solely on the support of their spouses, but through their own wealth and the networks of *philoi* they competently cultivated, they had the means to see to their own ambitions. Savalli-Lestrade, "Il ruolo pubblico delle regine ellenistiche," 426; Savalli-Lestrade, "La place des reines," 63–64. See also Sewell-Lasater, "Becoming Kleopatra," 110–11, 116, 153–54 on the *philoi* of Arsinoë II and Berenike II.

23 For the Macedonian traditions out of which the emphasis on education for Ptolemaic women emerged, see Sewell-Lasater, "Becoming Kleopatra," 26–35.

24 Pomeroy, *Women in Hellenistic Egypt,* 20. See also Carney, *Arsinoë of Egypt and Macedon,* 17, 103.

25 Theoc. *Id.* 15.22 and 106–11.

26 Carney, *Arsinoë of Egypt and Macedon,* 100–101, 103–104. It should also be noted that there is some debate surrounding whether Arsinoë paid expenses herself (Carney, *Arsinoë of Egypt and Macedon,* 101n159) and whether Ptolemy II, Arsinoë II, or both patronized the court poets (Carney, *Arsinoë of Egypt and Macedon,* 103). But, as Carney points out, at times it is "difficult to distinguish Arsinoë's actions and role from those of her brother because the royal pair was so thoroughly integrated into a joint image of monarchy" (104). Regardless of whether Arsinoë, Ptolemy, or both paid the expenses and patronized the poets, the important point is that the public image presented was of her doing these actions on her own.

27 For example, earlier Macedonian women, such as Eurydike, the mother of Philip II, earned *kleos* ("renown") through their piety and patronage of Greek women and Greek-style education; Carney, "Being Royal and Female in the Early Hellenistic Period," 197.

28 Magas was connected to the Cyrenaic school of philosophy (Diog. Laer. 2.102–103), and may have also received Buddhist missionaries from the Mauryan king, Asoka (*Major Rock Edict* 13). He was one of only five Hellenistic rulers to do so.

29 Clayman, *Berenice II,* 50–57.

30 Clayman contends that Kallimachos would have been established at the Ptolemaic court during the reign of Ptolemy II, holding an important position as court poet when Berenike arrived in 246 BCE, and he probably remained part of that court well into the 230s. Clayman, *Berenice II,* 51–54.

31 Ep. 15.2 G-P; Athen. 15.689A; Clayman, *Berenice II*, 60, 103. See note 21, above.

32 The Achaemenids ruled Egypt during the periods of 525–404 and 343–332 BCE. After the Ptolemies took over, they sought to emphasize their adherence to Pharaonic religious duties by returning removed religious artifacts *(simulacra deorum)* to temples. Ptolemy I (Satrap Stele, CG 22263), Ptolemy II (Pithom Stele, CG 22183), and Ptolemy III (Canopus Decree, *OGIS* 56) each issued decrees describing their actions to that effect. For Ptolemy II and Ptolemy III, their queens were included in the decrees as taking part in their actions, demonstrating that it was the duty of the queens as well to act in the interest of the kingdom.

33 Carney, *Arsinoë of Egypt and Macedon*, 90.

34 The Chremonides decree (*IG* II^2 686–87; *SIG*^{3} 4334–35) is another example of Arsinoë's involvement in Ptolemaic governance and foreign policy, but it is steeped in scholarly debate that there is not space to analyze here. See Sewell-Lasater, "Becoming Kleopatra," 114–15.

35 Carney, *Arsinoë of Egypt and Macedon,* 88, 97n104. There is contention surrounding whether the cult of the *Theoi Adelphoi* was established in 273 or 272/1 (see Carney, *Arsinoë of Egypt and Macedon*, 97n104), but either year is well before Arsinoë's death in c. 270 or 268 BCE, which indicates she would have been aware of and could have helped in establishing the new cult. See note 48, below.

36 Carney, *Arsinoë of Egypt and Macedon*, 97. Carney notes, for example, that previous cults for women of the Diadochic period had been instituted by their *philoi.*

37 Anatole Mori, "Personal Favor and Public Influence: Arete, Arsinoë II, and the *Argonautica*," *Oral Tradition* 16, no. 1 (2001): 85, 88–89, 91; Carney, *Arsinoë of Egypt and Macedon*, 105 n198.

38 Callim. Frg. 110; *PSI* 1092; P.Oxy. 2258C; Catull. 66. Although the poem was written by Kallimachos, it describes the actions of Berenike, and Gutzwiller indicates that the dedication of the lock and Kallimachos's subsequent poem were likely "staged with the knowledge and consent of the court." Kathryn Gutzwiller, "Callimachus' Lock of Berenice: Fantasy, Romance, and Propaganda," *AJP* 133, no. 3 (1992): 363, 372–73, 384. For a translation of Catullus's version of the poem, see Fantham et al., *Women in the Classical World*, 149–50.

39 Catull. 66.22; Oppen de Ruiter, *Berenice II Euergetis*, 36n89. The portion of the poem that describes Berenike as being mournfully parted from her "dear brother" *(fratris cari)* only survives in Catullus's reproduction of the work, but it is assumed that Catullus would not have used the term "brother" if Kallimachos had not also used the word. For Berenike's connection to Arsinoë, see Hans Hauben, "Ptolémée III et Bérénice II, divinités cosmiques," in *More than Men, Less than Gods: Studies on Royal Cult and Imperial Worship*, ed. P.P. Iossif, A.S. Chanikowski, and C.C. Lorber (Leuven: Peeters, 2011), 359. He writes that "la personnalité royale et divine de la nouvelle reine se développera sous l'égide spirituelle de sa devancière." See also Hauben, "Arsinoé II et la politique extérieure de l'Égypte," 119–24n90; Gutzwiller, "Callimachus' Lock of Berenice," 363.

40 For a translation of the Canopus Decree, see Fantham et al., *Women in the Classical World*, 151–54. On the famine, see Hölbl, *A History of the Ptolemaic Empire*, 49; Oppen de Ruiter, *Berenice II Euergetis*, 33n70, 76; Sewell-Lasater, "Becoming Kleopatra," 156–58, 160.

41 *OGIS* 61; Hölbl, *A History of the Ptolemaic Empire*, 87; Clayman, *Berenice II*, 163. *OGIS* 61 states: "King Ptolemy, son of Ptolemy and Arsinoë, the Sibling Gods, and Queen Berenike, the Sister and Wife of King Ptolemy, and their small children, dedicate this temple to Isis and Harpocrates."

42 *OGIS* 60; Macurdy, *Hellenistic Queens*, 133–34; Hölbl, *A History of the Ptolemaic Empire*, 87; Clayman, *Berenice II*, 166; Hazzard, *Imagination of a Monarchy*, 112.

43 Ael. *VH* 14.43.

44 Clayman, *Berenice II*, 123.

45 Lana Troy, *Patterns of Queenship in Ancient Egyptian Myth and History* (Sweden: Uppsala University, 1986), 179; Oppen de Ruiter, *Berenice II Euergetis*, 37. See also Sewell-Lasater, "Becoming Kleopatra," Appendix E.

46 Sewell-Lasater, "Becoming Kleopatra," 116–19. See also Carney, *Arsinoë of Egypt and Macedon*, 99; Elizabeth D. Carney, "The Initiation of Cult for Royal Macedonian Women," *CP* 95 (2000):

33n63, 64; Gutzwiller, "Callimachus' Lock of Berenice," 365nn21, 22. An example of this has already been mentioned at note 39, above, with her assimilation to Aphrodite at Cape Zephyrion.

47 P.Hib. 2.199; Pfeiffer, "The God Serapis, His Cult, and the Beginnings of the Ruler Cult in Ptolemaic Egypt," 398; Carney, *Arsinoë of Egypt and Macedon*, 97n104; Koenen, "The Ptolemaic King as a Religious Figure," 51n61. See also Hauben, "Arsinoé II et la politique extérieure de l'Égypte," 113.

48 For a thorough analysis of the debate surrounding the death date of Arsinoë, see Branko F. van Oppen de Ruiter, "The Death of Arsinoe II Philadelphus: The Evidence Reconsidered," *ZPE* 174 (2010): 139–50. For arguments that Arsinoë had a hand in shaping her cult, see Gutzwiller, "Callimachus' Lock of Berenice," 366n25; Pomeroy, *Women in Hellenistic Egypt*, 29–30; Carney, *Arsinoë of Egypt and Macedon*, 100, 107.

49 Athen. 13.576E-F; Carney, *Arsinoë of Egypt and Macedon*, 127. See also Daniel Ogden, *Polygamy, Prostitutes, and Death: The Hellenistic Dynasties* (London: Duckworth with The Classical Press of Wales, 1999), 74; Jim Roy, "The Masculinity of the Hellenistic King," in *When Men Were Men: Masculinity, Power and Identity in Classical Antiquity*, ed. Lin Foxhall and John Salmon (London: Routledge, 1998), 120. Roy emphasizes the importance of the dynastic image that was based on the royal couple, and he also observes that maintaining that royal image did not prevent Hellenistic kings from having mistresses. These mistresses were instead left out of propaganda that emphasized the royal couple, even if the mistresses were publicly acknowledged, as Bilistiche was for Ptolemy II.

50 Hölbl, *A History of the Ptolemaic Empire*, 103; Carney, *Arsinoë of Egypt and Macedon*, 108.

51 Hölbl, *A History of the Ptolemaic Empire*, 103. For the iconography on the Arsinoë coins, see Julien Olivier and Catharine Lorber, "Three Gold Coinages of Third-century Ptolemaic Egypt," *RBN* 159 (2013): 78–79; H.A. Troxell, "Arsinoe's Non-era," *ANSMN* 28 (1983): 41.

52 For arguments that the name was given to her posthumously, see Hölbl, *A History of the Ptolemaic Empire*, 85; Carney, *Arsinoë of Egypt and Macedon*, 85, 115–16; Pomeroy, *Women in Hellenistic Egypt*, 19; Quaegebeur, "Ptolémée II en adoration devant Arsinoé II divinisée," 205, 208–209; Jan Quaegebeur, "Reines ptolémaïques et traditions égyptiennes," in *Das ptolemäische Agypten*, ed. H. von Maehler and V.M. Stocka (Mainz am Rhein: Akten des Internationalen Symposions, 1978), 258. Recently Nilsson has put forth a new argument, that the title was bestowed upon her during her lifetime; see Maria Nilsson, "The Crown of Arsinoë II: The Creation and Development of an Imagery of Authority" (PhD diss., University of Gothenburg, 2010), 400, 402, 405. See also Martina Minas, "Macht und Ohnmacht. Die Repräsentation ptolemäischer Königinnen in ägyptischen Tempeln," *AfP* 51 (2005): 134n28.

53 See, for example, Quaegebeur, "Ptolémée II en adoration devant Arsinoé II divinisée," 205, 208–209; Hauben, "Arsinoé II et la politique extérieure de l'Égypte," 110, 127; Nilsson, "The Crown of Arsinoë II," 405.

54 For a full analysis of the debate surrounding this title, see Sewell-Lasater, "Becoming Kleopatra," 107–108, 125–27.

55 Stefano G. Caneva, "Queens and Ruler Cults in Early Hellenism: Festivals, Administration, and Ideology," *Kernos* 25 (2012): 87n52. Caneva cites stele *BM* 392. See also Quaegebeur, "Cleopatra VII and the Cults of the Ptolemaic Queens," 42.

56 Oppen de Ruiter, *Berenice II Euergetis*, 90; Koenen, "The Ptolemaic King as a Religious Figure," 110; Hölbl, *A History of the Ptolemaic Empire*, 110.

57 Koenen, "The Ptolemaic King as a Religious Figure," 108; Oppen de Ruiter, *Berenice II Euergetis*, 112–13; Lloyd Llewellyn-Jones and Stephanie Winder, "A Key to Berenike's Lock? The Hathoric Model of Queenship in Early Ptolemaic Egypt," in *Creating a Hellenistic World*, ed. Andrew Erskine and Lloyd Llewellyn-Jones (Swansea: The Classical Press of Wales, 2010), 263–64; Sewell-Lasater, "Becoming Kleopatra," 173–79.

58 Pomeroy, *Women in Hellenistic Egypt*, 23; Hölbl, *A History of the Ptolemaic Empire*, 85, 168; Quaegebeur, "Reines ptolémaïques et traditions égyptiennes," 247–48, 254; cf. Minas, "Macht und Ohnmacht," 133, 134–35.

59 Hölbl, *A History of the Ptolemaic Empire*, 110; Quaegebeur, "The Egyptian Clergy and the Cult of the Ptolemaic Dynasty," 96; Quaegebeur, "Reines ptolémaïques et traditions égyptiennes," 246; cf. Minas, "Macht und Ohnmacht," 129; Clayman, *Berenice II*, 163; Oppen de Ruiter, *Berenice II Euergetis*, 38.

60 Hölbl, *A History of the Ptolemaic Empire*, 110; Clayman, *Berenice II*, 162, fig. 9; Quaegebeur, "The Egyptian Clergy and the Cult of the Ptolemaic Dynasty," 96; Quaegebeur, "Reines ptolémaïques et traditions égyptiennes," 248, fig. D; cf. Minas, "Macht und Ohnmacht," 135, fig. 5; Oppen de Ruiter, *Berenice II Euergetis*, 38, pl. 3.13(a). Another transference scene is shown on the arch of the Stele of Kom al-Hisn (CG 22186), see Quaegebeur, "Reines ptolémaïques et traditions égyptiennes," 247, fig. C; cf. Minas, "Macht und Ohnmacht," 133.

61 Quaegebeur, "The Egyptian Clergy and the Cult of the Ptolemaic Dynasty," 98n27.

62 See note 60, above; Minas, "Macht und Ohnmacht," 135; Hölbl, *A History of the Ptolemaic Empire*, 85, 167; Quaegebeur, "The Egyptian Clergy and the Cult of the Ptolemaic Dynasty," 98n27; Troy, *Patterns of Queenship*, 179. See also Sewell-Lasater, "Becoming Kleopatra," Appendix E. Berenike's Horus name was also used in the Canopus Decree that is preserved on the Stele of Kom al-Hisn (CG 22186), according to Anne Bielman-Sánchez and Giuseppina Lenzo, "Réflexions à propos de la régence féminine hellénistique: l'exemple de Cléopâtre I," *Studi ellenistici* 29 (2015): 152n36.

63 Troy, *Patterns of Queenship*, 179.

64 Some demotic sources also name Berenike *tꜣ Pr-ꜥꜣt Brnigꜣ*, the "female-pharaoh Berenike." Quaegebeur, "Reines ptolémaïques et traditions égyptiennes," 255; Hölbl, *A History of the Ptolemaic Empire*, 85; Pomeroy, *Women in Hellenistic Egypt*, 23; Clayman, *Berenice II*, 163. Her being addressed as female Horus and female pharaoh has often been used as supporting evidence for the argument that Berenike ruled as regent while Ptolemy was away during the Third Syrian War. See, for example, Oppen de Ruiter, *Berenice II Euergetis*, 37; Bielman-Sánchez and Lenzo, "Réflexions à propos de la régence féminine hellénistique," 152n35. However, I argue that she did not rule as regent in either Cyrene or Egypt. See section entitled "New Interpretations," above, and Sewell-Lasater, "Becoming Kleopatra," 134–35, 147–51.

10

Women in the Economic Domain: First to Sixth Dynasties

Susan Anne Kelly

For more than a century, scholarly commentary regarding ancient Egypt's women has been impacted by an androcentric lens. Much of the gender bias encountered in historical scholarship reflects the gender assumptions existing within the authors' society.[1] Androcentrism is indicative of the cultural environment of the lives and times of late nineteenth- and early twentieth-century scholars, whose contemporary values struggled with the roles of women and their significance in society and the idea that women could belong to history.[2] Thus, early scholars perceived the ancient gender bias embedded in the archaeological record of ancient Egypt's patriarchal society as reflective of their own similar gender assumptions, and recounted Egyptian history accordingly. As a result, investigations focused on women were omitted from general inquiries while other studies stereotyped women as harem members and concubines, inferior and generally subordinate to their male counterparts.[3] Ultimately, ancient Egyptian women's history has been disadvantaged, and their participation in ancient Egyptian society undervalued. For nearly half a century now, the inclusion of women and gender subjects in historical scholarship has increased exponentially and is challenging these dominant androcentric narratives.

The Egyptological study of women has intensified since the late 1980s.[4] Now termed "gender studies," the original focus was nearly exclusively on the study of women.[5] Yet, over the next three decades, the nascent field of gender-specific studies matured into a subdiscipline that involves the scholarly investigation of all genders,[6] gender bias,[7] intersectionality,[8] and the adoption of interdisciplinary and theoretical approaches. One vital area of women's studies that remains underrepresented in modern scholarship is women's engagement in the economic structure of the ancient Egyptian state. The state's hierarchical socioeconomic structure is often investigated by studying official titles that act as barometers for the personnel's status and rank and their associated offices; however, women's public and active engagement in the state has not advanced congruently. Women have rarely been considered in the socio-politico-economic structure, as it was considered the domain of men.[9] Women's participation has generally been demarcated to the private sphere, particularly in other women's employ, or that women's titles were applied honorifically.[10] The state's economic mechanisms were composed of resource collection and redistribution; the end-to-end management of raw produce through warehouses and production centers;[11] expeditions for raw materials;[12] construction programs, mortuary and cult practices;[13] and all essential labor.[14] Thus, identifying women's participation in roles associated with any of these activities helps demonstrate female agency in ancient Egypt's economic structure. The preliminary findings presented in this paper are a part of a more extensive study that is briefly outlined below.

My PhD research aims to present a comprehensive understanding of women's engagement in the ancient Egyptian state by analyzing women's biographical data from the First to the Sixth Dynasty (3100–2181 BCE). The study evaluates women's access to the political, economic, and ideological domains of social power through the study of their titles.[15] The theoretical approach applies Mann's premise that power is exercised through the media of resources,[16] which is analogous with the factors that led to the development of social complexity in ancient Egypt. The differentiation in social ranking or class in ancient Egypt can be outlined by "access to and/or control of economic, productive and symbolic resources."[17] Thus, this methodological approach aims to refashion Mann's social power principle in order to analyze women's biographical data to gauge the extent of females' participation and agency through their access to or over resources. Women's duties, associated with their titles or social relationships, are used to situate them in the applicable (and sometimes overlapping) social power domains. While this paper features the preliminary results of examining women's agency in the economic domain, an overview of the data's scope and treatment is provided first.

To identify the extent of women's engagement in the social power domains of the state, women's names and titles were extracted from ancient source material, including rock inscriptions and papyri as well as visual and material culture from mortuary contexts from the Nile Valley and desert regions, covering the First through the Sixth Dynasties. The research collated, categorized, and indexed a cross section of 1,400 women, including a small sample of

Table. 10.1. Economic domain titles held by women in the First through Sixth Dynasties

Title No	Title	Title Translation	Title Holders
[0461]	*imy(.t)-r3 pr.w*	Steward/overseer of the house/ estate;	W151; W673.
[0464]	*imy(t)-r3 -pr-inʿwt/ḥts(w)t*	Overseer of the house of weavers;	W785; W787; W788.
[0466]	*imy(.t)-r inʿ.t/ḥts.(w).t nt ẖnw*	Overseer of the house of weavers/(weaving women) of the Residence;	W426.
[0501]	*imy(.t)-r3 pr-šnʿ*	Overseer of the storehouse/ labour establishment / department of stores;	W1381; W1392; W1397.
[0673]	*imy(t)-r3 ḥm(w)-k3*	Overseer of K3-servants/ priests;	W729.
[0675]	*imy(t)-r3 ḥm(w)-k3 mw.t nsw.t*	Overseer of K3-servant/priest of the King's Mother;	W480.
[0761]	*imy[t]-r3 swnw.t*	Overseer of physicians;	W480.
[0857]	*imyt-r3 sḫmḫ-ib*	Overseer of amusements/ entertainment;	W478.
[0859]	*imyt-r3 sḫmḫ-ib nb nfr nsw.t*	Overseer of all royal amusements;	W478.
[0864]	*imyt-r3.t sšr*	Overseer of cloth/linen/ clothing distribution;	W674; W675.
[1098]	*imyt-r3 ib3w n nsw.t*	Overseer of dancers of the king;	W478.
[1101]	*imyt-r3 is pr-nsw.t*	Overseer of the chamber of the king's house/royal domain;	W575.
[1102]	*imy(t)-r3 ir(w)-šnw*	Overseer of the chamber of wigs;	W576.
[1103]	*imy(t)-r3 m3ṯrt*	Overseer of mourners?;	W940.
[1105]	*imyt-r3 ḥs(w)t*	Overseer of singing;	W596.
[1106]	*imyt-r3 ḫnr(wt)*	Overseer of the troupe of musical performers/singers and dancers;	W596.
[1109]	*imyt-r3 ḫnr(wt) n nsw.t*	Overseer of the 'musical performers' of the king;	W478.

[1114]	*inˁ.wt*	Midwife ?;	W556.
[1131]	*ir(w) šn*	Hairdresser/hairdoer;	W202.
[1477]	*wr(.t) pr*	Great one of the house;	W1329.
[1494]	*wpd.w(.t)*	Butler, attendant, steward, cupbearer);	W192.
[1605]	*mnˁ.t?*	Wet nurse;	W1395.
[1829]	*nḏ.t*	Grinding woman, miller;	W117.
[1871]	*ḥm(.t)*	Slave, servant;	W1240.
[2377]	*ḥry-tp sšr*	Supervisor of cloth;	W194.
[2457]	*ḥkꜣ ḥw.t ˁꜣ.t*	Chief/manager of a great estate/district;	W1013.
[2530]	*ḫnty-š*	Official/attendant/land-tenant – (Bodyguard);	W051; W052; W227; W508.
[2531]	*ḫntt-š ˁḪˁ-Nfr*	Land-tenant/ *ḫnty-š* official, attendant of *ˁḪˁ-Nfr*;	W810.
[2682]	*ḫrp(.t) sḥ*	Director of the dining-hall;	W576.
[2763]	*ḫtm(w)*	Sealer;	W196; W198; W199; W200; W201; W944; W947(?); W1382; W1385; W1386; W1387; W1388; W1389; W1390; W1391; W1393; W1394; W1396; W1397; W1399; W1400; W1401; W1411.
[2807]	*ḫtm(w) ḥw.t [...] ?*	Sealer of the *ḥw.t*?;	W1354.
[2827]	*ḫr-ˁ=f*	Assistant;	W942; W943.
[3159]	*sš ḥsb ḳd.w ḥtp.w*	Accounts-scribe of the *ḳd ḥtp*;	W1365.
[3507]	*sḥḏ(.t) ḫtm(w).t*	Inspector of sealbearers;	W676.
[3628]	*sḏꜣw.t(y)*	Sealer;	W1165.

royal,[18] but predominantly nonroyal, women for analysis. In total, 777 women (55.3 percent) held at least one official title,[19] with 129 titles identified in the corpus. An unanticipated result from the analysis was that thirty-five titles, over a quarter (27.5 percent) of the current corpus, associate the women with public and active contributions in the economic sector.

Moreover, as figure 10.1 demonstrates, the higher percentage (60 percent) of the roles belong to supervisory positions, with twenty-one titles documenting female engagement in such roles of authority as *imy(t)-rꜣ*, *ḫrp(t)*, and *sḥḏ(t)*. The overview of the titles that follows demonstrates women's participation in and contribution to the economy through service in the domestic sector, administrative capacity, vital industries, and oversight of a number of the state's ideological practices. The first section considers women's engagement in the domestic service sector.

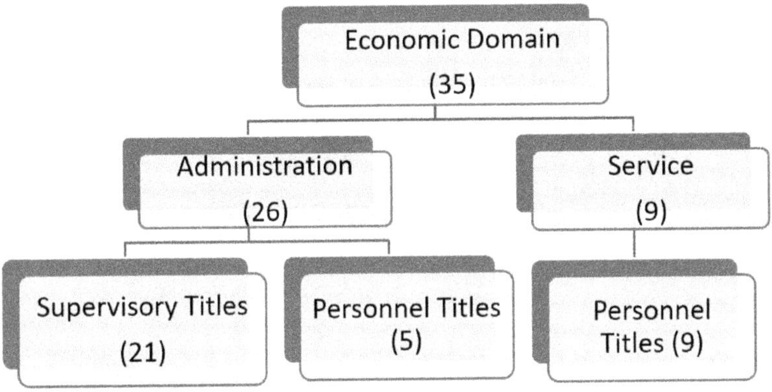

Fig. 10.1. Synopsis of women's titles in the economic domain, First through Sixth Dynasties

Domestic Service

There are eight separate titles denoting female domestic service personnel ranging from general domestic help to female overseers of the house, estate, or district, and key roles in the palace.[20] Four particular titles held by women indicate positions of domestic service: *ḥmt* ("female servant"),[21] *wrt pr* (female great one of the house),[22] *wpdwt* (female butler/attendant/steward/cupbearer),[23] and *nḏt* (female miller/grinding woman).[24] The first two titles come from stelae recovered from the royal necropolis at Abydos. No further details have been found regarding these roles, as only the names or titles were recorded on the earliest stelae. However, that the women were buried in the royal necropolis may imply that these women were engaged in the service of members of the Early Dynastic court. Previously, the First Dynasty title *wrt pr*[25] was interpreted as representing a senior head of the harem;[26] however, this interpretation remains precarious, as Ward points out that one needs to first establish that these women did constitute a harem.[27]

Contextual information on these titles can help situate women's activities in the economy. For example, the recording of Khent's name and title (*wpdwt*)[28] on the east wall of Whemeka's Giza *mastaba* places her in his employ.[29] Yet, when women hold multiple titles, it is often difficult to distinguish if the roles are distinct or if a working relationship between the duties exists. An example of this is Khenmet, who, along with her role as a miller, upheld the duties of a *ḥmt-k3*, "(female) funerary priest," which could indicate an interrelationship between her domestic and priestly duties. At other times, there is a clear distinction between the roles that demonstrate women were responsible for multiple areas. Mentions of both Khent and Khenmet are dated to the late Fifth Dynasty and, as table 10.2 shows, the majority of titles in this study date from this period onward. The opportunity for female service appears to have increased in line with the governmental reforms that commenced at the end of the Fourth Dynasty, as the state's economic model transitioned from a palace to a temple economy.[30]

Table 10.2. Chronological placement of titles, First through Sixth Dynasties

Title	Dyn I	Dyn II	Dyn IV	Dyn V	Dyn VI
imy(t)-rȝ ir(w)-šnw				W576.	
imy(.t)-rȝ pr.w					W151; W673.
imy(t)-rȝ -pr-inʿwt/ḥts(w)t				W785; W787; W788.	
imy(.t)-rȝ inʿ.t/ḥts.(w).t nt ḫnw				W426.	
imy(.t)-rȝ pr-šnʿ					W1381; W1392; W1397.
imy(t)-rȝ ḥm(w)-kȝ				W729.	
imy(t)-rȝ ḥm(w)-kȝ mw.t nsw.t				W480.	
imy[t]-rȝ swnw.t				W480.	
imyt-rȝ sḫmḫ-ib				W478.	
imyt-rȝ sḫmḫ-ib nb nfr nsw.t				W478.	
imyt-rȝ.t sšr					W674; W675.

imyt-rꜣ ibꜣw n nsw.t				W478.	
imyt-rꜣ is pr-nsw.t				W575.	
imy(t)-rꜣ mꜣṯrt				W940.	
imyt-rꜣ ḥs(w)t				W596.	
imyt-rꜣ ḫnr(wt)				W596.	
imyt-rꜣ ḫnr(wt) n nsw.t				W478.	
inʿ.wt			W556.		
ir(w) šn				W202.	
wr(.t) pr	W1329.				
wpd.w(.t)				W192.	
mnʿ.t?					W1395.
nḏ.t				W117.	
ḥm(.t)	W1240.				
ḥry-tp sšr				W194.	
ḥkꜣ ḥw.t ʿꜣ.t				W1013.	
ḫnty-š				W051; W052; W227; W508.	
ḫntt-š ʿḪʿ-Nfr					W810.
ḫrp(.t) sḥ				W576.	
ḫtm(w)				W196; W198; W199; W200; W201; W947(?).	W944; W1165.
ḫtm(w) ḥw.t [...] ?	W1354.				
ḫr-ʿ=f			W942; W943.		
sš ḥsb ḳd.w ḥtp.w		W1365.			
sḥḏ(.t) ḫtm(w).t				W676.	
sḏꜣw.t(y)					W1165.

Eight women were identified with administrative management roles in the domestic sector. Two from the Sixth Dynasty—one whose name is lost and the other called Ma'kheruy—were *imy(t)-rȝ prw*, "(female) steward/overseer of the house/estate."[31] The functionality of the role comprises the management of resources and oversight of the people connected with maintaining the house or estate. Three women,[32] shown as offering bearers in the tombs at Qubbet al-Hawa, carried out their duties as *imy(t)-rȝ pr-šnˁ*, "(female) overseer of the storehouse/labor establishment/department of stores."[33] A management title associated with the *pr-šnˁ*, a produce center,[34] places the women at the center of an economic hub with access and control over resources linked to the state.[35] Another management role involving oversight of a great estate or district is *ḥkȝ ḥwt ˁȝt*, "chief/manager of a great estate/district."[36] This title has received varying interpretations and has previously only been attributed to men.[37] However, a case is presented here for assigning the title to the woman Iufi, the wife of Kaikhenet from al-Hammamiya from the Early Fifth Dynasty.[38]

Iufi is attributed with several titles in the priesthood of Hathor, including *rḫt-nswt* and *ẖkrt-nswt*, along with evidence of the erasure of the important kinship title "king's daughter of his body" from throughout the tomb.[39] The title of "chief/manager of a great estate/district" should be attributed to Iufi based on the textual and pictorial evidence recorded on the tomb's north wall scene. The wall scene depicts Iufi in a papyrus boat performing the "pulling the papyrus" ceremony, an activity often associated with the goddess Hathor, in whose priesthood she was engaged (fig. 10.2).[40] The title's position is also vertically dissociated above the unnamed diminutive man depicted in front of Iufi. Previous excavators El-Khouli and Kanawati caution that the connection of the title with the male depicted is uncertain.[41] Since the late First Dynasty, names and titles have regularly been positioned above the head or read into the front of the person's face to whom they belong.[42] Iufi's husband Kaikhenet also held the title *ḥkȝ ḥwt ˁȝt* as well as familial affiliation titles to the king. That the title was recorded for the husband and wife could suggest that they shared or held the management role consecutively. In either case, Iufi can be recognized for her participation in managing the estate, as indicated by the title written before her face.

The following titles situate two women in the heart of the palace and in proximity and service to the monarch. The first title belongs to Niankhhathor, who was the *imyt-rȝ is pr-nswt*, "overseer of the chamber of the king's house/royal domain," in the late Old Kingdom.[43] Conversely, Jones does not record an equivalent title held by men, although male titles associated with the *is* include *imi-is*, "one who is in the council chamber,"[44] and *smsw-is*, "elder of

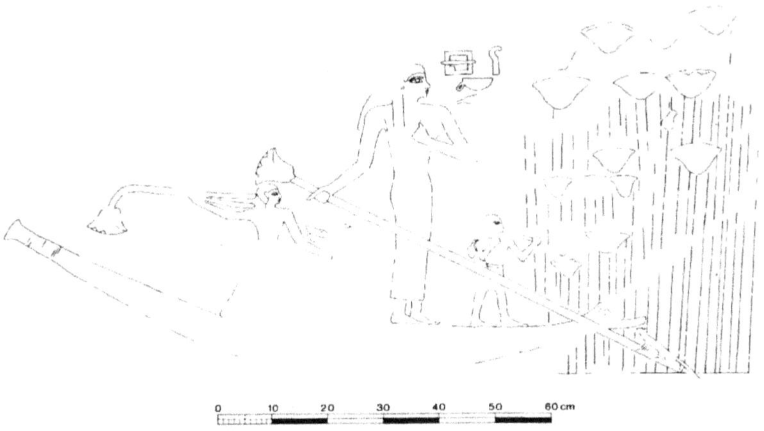

Pl. 36. Kai-khent (A2), south entrance corridor, north wall, detail

Fig. 10.2. Iufi "Pulling the Papyrus"

the council chamber."[45] Based on the identification of the *ỉs* as the council chamber, a more precise reading of this title would be "overseer of the council chamber of the Palace"; however, the role's exact functionality remains undefined. Meretites held the role of *ḫrp(t) sḥ*, "director of the dining-hall,"[46] a better-understood title held by both genders. The earliest attestation of the *ḫrp sḥ* title dates to the Early Dynastic Period.[47] It is most commonly understood to be associated with the supervision of the proper supply of food or banquet in the "dining hall" or similar readings, such as booth, tent, or pavilion.[48] An alternate translation has been suggested based on the additional meaning given to *sḥ* as "counsel" or "plan," interpreted as "director of the 'audience chamber' of the palace."[49] Speidel, however, questions whether Meretites' role should be assigned to civic or civil service due to the lack of affiliation to the *pr ꜥꜣ* or *nswt*.[50] Male holders of the same title—Merka, for example—do not have their positions questioned. Access to both the dining hall/audience chamber and the council chamber would situate both women in the heart of the palace, in the monarch's service, which would establish them as part of the state administration. Furthermore, Meretites' responsibilities extended beyond the domestic sphere, providing an opportunity to demonstrate women upholding distinctly separate roles in different industries. This discussion is continued in conjunction with the following review of the personal care roles identified in the corpus.

Personal Care Service

The personal care sector encompasses roles involved in providing products and services to the royal and elite court, such as personal grooming and medical services. In both private and state roles, the hairdressing profession is well attested in the Old Kingdom and was a specialized and significant industry in ancient Egypt.[51] Different levels of that occupation are identified in the corpus. First, with the title of *ir(w) šn*, "hairdresser/hairdoer,"[52] Hy appears to have been employed in the private sector, as her name and title were recorded in Whemeka's tomb. A second title from this industry belongs to Meretites, who, apart from her responsibilities as *ḫrp(t) sḥ*, held the role of *imy(t)-rꜣ is-šn*, "overseer of the chamber of wigs,"[53] or, alternatively, an overseer of hairdressing.[54] Wigs were an important commodity in ancient Egyptian society and were mainly worn by elite men and women to display social status.[55] While it has been determined that state hairdressers were primarily male,[56] Meretites' title attests to her high-ranking achievements in that male-dominated occupation. However, Speidel asserts that not only should her role be considered in the employ of "Privatemannes" (private man/citizen), but also that both her titles should be deleted from the rank of female state officials.[57] As an administrator, Meretites would have had access to and control over the tools of the trade and products required in the practice of hairdressing,[58] the manufacture and circulation of wigs,[59] and the management of personnel, whether in the employ of the civic or civil sector. Meretites is one example of a woman in the corpus who upheld significant responsibilities in separate roles; another is Peseshet.

Peseshet appears to have reached the pinnacle of her eminent profession as "overseer of physicians."[60] The title *imy[t]-rꜣ swnwt* is written three times on her false door,[61] once on the lintel, another time on the inner lintel, and again on the right jamb along with her other title of *imy(t)-rꜣ ḥm(w)-kꜣ mwt nswt*.[62] The inner lintel differs in that the text starts with the only attestation of the term *mwt nswt* on the false door. Excavator Hassan interpreted the script as "The Overseer of Ka-servants of the King's Mother, the Overseer of the Doctors, Peseshet."[63] In this manner, Peseshet's duties covered different industries and responsibilities, including the treatment of the living and the management of the rituals for the Ka of a queen mother. Fischer, however, extended the honorific transposition of the term "king's mother" to the overseer physician role as well, interpreting Peseshet's position as probably an overseer of doctors for a queen mother.[64] Fischer's premise suggests that Peseshet's position was to manage a team of doctors all caring for a royal mother. Moreover, he classified the role as specifically overseeing female doctors.[65] There is nothing in the writing of the title to support Fischer's interpretation of Peseshet's role as an overseer specialized in the care of a royal patient or an administrator of only other female physicians.

The next personal care role belonged to Wadjkawes, the only woman identified in the corpus as a *mnʿt*, "wet nurse."[66] Another specialized and vital service captured in the corpus comes from a title that is only attested in the Old Kingdom: Neferhetepes's role as an *inʿt*, "midwife,"[67] was recorded twice in the pyramid builders' cemetery (fig. 10.3).[68] Fischer noted further support for this profession with the identification of an "overseer of the plurality of *inʿwt*" on a libation basin belonging to Meret-ib (and possibly a second attestation to Khentkaus, but the inscription is badly damaged);[69] however, neither of these women were included in the current corpus. The second attestation of Neferhetepes's title has been written with the addition of a quail chick (G43), providing the transliteration of *inʿwt*, which excavator Hawass interprets differently from the midwife title, assigning her the additional title of "weaver and seamstress."[70] The determinative used in Neferhetepes's titles is not that of the (B87) sign that represents a woman with a weaver's shuttle. Instead, both inscriptions use a determinative that shows a seated woman holding a brick-shaped object.[71] As such, it is not a separate title, but rather, a repeat of the midwife title.

Fig. 10.3. *Nfr-ḥtp.s*, GSE 1919/LG 53

Weaving and the textile industry, however, played a significant role in the ancient Egyptian economy, and the range of titles from the corpus indicating women's involvement in that sector follows.

Textile Industry

Seven Fifth Dynasty women were identified with official titles in high-ranking roles involved in producing and distributing the vital commodity of textiles. Evidence for the production and distribution of textiles is found in inventory lists of textile offerings on funerary stelae dating to as early as the late First Dynasty, which provides much of the associated terminology for the typology of ancient fabrics. Possibly the oldest title associated with weaving comes from a First Dynasty stela from Abydos that documents Hebet, who held the title *mr*(*t*), which has been defined as "weaver" based on the determinative (V16), representing a loom.[72] Egyptologists acknowledge the participation of women in the weaving industry; however, not all have given due recognition to women's contributions to that vital industry as a part of the state's socioeconomic structure. For example, Fischer describes the occupation of an ordinary weaver as menial,[73] disregarding the economic value and utility of the commodity for all members of society and the heavy reliance on linen required in the mummification process. Several women are identified with administrative and supervisory roles in the textile industry, which contradicts Ward's premise that there were no female overseers or that no women who practiced a trade received a promotion.[74]

The women's administrative roles are involved in the different stages of the production of textiles. Henutempet is accredited with the title *ḥry-tp sšr*, which is translated as "(female) supervisor of cloth."[75] This title is also held by men, with alternate readings including "overlord of linen,"[76] "[one] who is in charge of clothing,"[77] and "head of linen."[78] These interpretations of the title suggest that the role entails the management of the finished product. Another title, *imyt-rꜣ sšr*, "overseer of cloth/linen/clothing distribution,"[79] can similarly be interpreted as being concerned with post-production activities. Two women, whose names were not recorded in the scene on the north wall of Waatetkhethor's tomb, are attributed with the title.[80] Another four women held titles that record their supervision over the manufacturing process. Rewedzawes, Mehut, and Ptahhesten all held the title of *imy(t)-rꜣ-pr-inʿwt/ḥts(w)t*, "(female) overseer of the house of weavers,"[81] while the final title is associated directly with the palace. On a false door commissioned by her son, another Rewedzawes[82] is credited with the important title *imy(t)-rꜣinʿt/ḥts(w)t nt ẖnw*, "overseer of the house of weavers/weaving women of the residence."[83] In both state and private roles, women played an integral role in the weaving and textile industry. It was not until the New Kingdom that men were employed in the role of weavers.[84]

Administrative Capacity

Not all female administrative roles identified in the corpus were in management positions. The titles of thirty-three women are documented as occupying lower-level administrative positions. The earliest attestation belongs to a female sealer from the First Dynasty, the lady Djeret-Neith, with the title *ḫtm(w) ḥwt* [. . .].[85] The stela's physical condition prevents a full translation of the title, given both the lacunae and the obscure details within the *ḥwt* sign; however, Martin offered the interpretation "sealer of the palace [. . .]?"[86] Previous scholarship had attributed the title to a male, but the present author has argued elsewhere for female ownership.[87] The case presented was based on the female determinative and the absence of males with Neith in their names in the Early Dynastic funerary stelae/slab's corpus of Abu Rawash, Helwan, and Abydos.[88] A further seventeen women held the title of "sealer,"[89] five of whom were recorded in Whemeka's tomb,[90] with an additional nine recovered from the Old Kingdom cemetery at Qubbet al-Hawa. Neferhetepes's title was recorded in Nikaiankh's tomb in Tehna, while a second possible attestation for Meresankh remains speculative due to the poorly preserved state of the title.[91] Recent excavator Elizabeth Thompson recorded *mitrt/ḫtm(t)*, "the lady-sealer Meresankh," from the tomb owner's false door.[92] An alternate translation of the sealer's role is *sḏ3wt(y)t*,[93] which De Morgan recorded for Neferankhet from Aswan.[94] Ward differentiates between the use of the Old Kingdom title *sḏ3wt(y)* for men and women. For male sealers, he identifies it as a common function performed by men from various ranks, from state treasury positions to assistants of minor officials, whereas he sees women with the title *sḏ3wt(y)* as in the employ of private households of females of varying status.[95] One unnamed woman from Waatetkhethor's tomb held the role of *sḥdt ḫtmt*, "(female) inspector of seal bearers."[96] As an inspector, the duties could consist of inspecting the little known seal-cutters' work.[97] Alternatively, we can infer that the role entailed supervising a range of things, from correct sealing practices to economic production. Seals have often been used in scholarship to gather information about the early Egyptian administrative structure. The evidence presented in this section associates a sizable number of women with the long tradition of seals and seal bearers with access and control over material resources in the ancient Egyptian economy.[98]

Turning to other administrative roles, two women from Tehna—Satmeret and Nebet-[r-int][99]—are recorded in Nikaiankh's tomb as his "assistants" (*ḫr-ꜥ.f*).[100] The generalization of the title prevents defining the role further, although both women were also Ka-priests.[101] The only evidence of a woman associated with a scribal title was a Second Dynasty female accounts scribe, although the title was previously attributed to a male. I have argued elsewhere that the funerary slab from Helwan belonged to the woman, [Men]-Hekat.[102] The original excavator Saad agreed that the hair and appearance suggested that the owner was a woman, but stated that the *sš ḥsb ḳdw ḥtpw*, "accounts-scribe of the *ḳd-ḥtp*," title[103] made it a difficult argument to accept: "The owner may have been a man as the title denotes."[104] Kaplony confirmed the title's translation, only noting that he could not determine the *ḥsb* sign, but suggested there was a small space for it.[105] Furthermore, in his onomastic analysis of the slab, Kaplony determined that the name was a female theophoric one associated with the fertility goddess Hekat.[106] In a recent re-examination, Köhler and Jones could not discern this title due to the deterioration of the slab; however, they did note that there appeared to be at least four signs to the right of her name.[107] Köhler and Jones determined the owner as female and identified her as the king's funerary priestess from the surviving title on the slab.[108] The impact of Saad's original determination is evident when later studies, such as Piacentini's volume on ancient Egyptian scribes, continue to credit the scribe as male.[109] [Men]-Hekat offers another example of a possible working relationship between her two roles. It would be easy to correlate an interdependent relationship between her work in the offering places and her duties of the funerary priest to the king, but it cannot be confirmed.

The next two titles to be discussed pertain to the roles of *ḫnty-š*, whose meaning and functions remain ambiguous. Earlier studies considered that the functions associated with the role related to the "custodial" management and maintenance of the land and its produce.[110] A more recent study on the topic defined three separate categories of *ḫnty-š*,[111] two of which have been identified in the current corpus. Four women—Seseshekh, Baru, Iupu, and Hetepet[112]—hold the title of *ḫnty-š*, translated here as "official/attendant/land-tenant."[113] The *ḫnty-š* roles are considered to have managed the local fields, which were administered in the *phyle* system, and functioned as attendants in a royal mortuary complex.[114] The other class of *ḫnty-š* were directly linked to a mortuary cult of a king (i.e., "pyramid-compounded" *ḫnty-š*) and were tenant landholders of the royal mortuary establishment, and domain administrators,[115] as was Sebutet, who was an *ḫntt-š ꜤḪꜤ-Nfr*, "land-tenant/*ḫnty-š* official, attendant of *ꜤḪꜤ-Nfr*."[116] The *ḫnty-š* connection to the royal mortuary complex could conceivably suggest that the resource access in this role involved symbolic or cultic resources. However, with the rise of the temple economy, the pyramid complexes, towns, and royal mortuary cult became economic entities, substantiating the categorization of these roles in the economic domain.

The Ideological Practices of the State

Five women held nine overseer roles in kingship, cult, and mortuary ideological practices of the early Egyptian state. However, for this research, the administrative capacity of their roles warrants including them in the economic domain. While their positions were based in the ideological domain, their contributions to the state economy, especially in terms of the mortuary cult, were immense. For example, ancient Egyptian funerary practices were instrumental for both the individuals who could afford it and the state's economy. In keeping with their religious beliefs, individuals were dedicated to preparing for their afterlife.[117] Arrangements for their burials and provisions for their perpetual mortuary cults were necessary for royal and nonroyal individuals. From an economic perspective, the mortuary cult created a market for the goods and services involved in grave construction, funerary equipment, mummification, and mortuary cult rituals.[118] The maintenance of the deceased's mortuary cult was upheld by both men and women,[119] sometimes by family members, but mainly by people employed to perpetuate the cult practices.[120]

Three titles in the corpus document female engagement in overseeing the maintenance of funeral and mortuary cult practices. Khentkaus, from Saqqara, held the role that supervised the priests employed to maintain mortuary cults in the Fifth Dynasty.[121] Her title of "overseer of *k3*-servants/priests" was the only attestation identified in the current corpus;[122] however, Fischer noted that there was at least one other case of a woman holding the title.[123] The precise functions of the role are not defined, but it is conceivable that they involved the rostering of priests, procurement of offerings, and disbursement of payments in the form of inversion offerings.[124] As mentioned in an earlier section, Peseshet held a similar, but elevated, role of "overseer of the *k3*-servant/priest of the King's Mother."[125] The final role identified in the mortuary cult is involved in the funeral procession. Nefertiri was a Fifth Dynasty *ỉmy*(*t*)-*r3 m3ṯrt*, "(female) overseer of mourners."[126] As part of the funeral procession, the deceased's kin were often joined in their lament by professional mourners.[127] Mourning was ritually enacted as part of the funerary procession.[128] Two key mourners performed the role of the chief mourners, Isis and Nephthys.[129] Nefertiri's responsibilities as "overseer of mourners" suggest the function involved ensuring the enactment of this key element of the funerary procession.

Two women held six overseer roles in the performance of ritual dancing and singing. Hemetra held the position of *ỉmyt-r3 ẖnr*(*wt*), "(female) overseer of the troupe of musical performers/singers and dancers,"[130] along with a less defined role of "(female) overseer of singing,"[131] which could have been performed in both secular and religious contexts.[132] The earlier concubine and harem-woman connotations previously attributed to the *ẖnr*(*wt*) and women performers of dancing and singing are no longer applicable in modern scholarship.[133] The women who constituted these troupes were involved in ritual performances for funerary activities and cults,[134] as well as secular institutions.[135] Guegan's recent work has determined that the *ẖnr*(*wt*) were associated with the cult of the goddess Neith through their intimate involvement with the *pr-šnd.t*, as well as with Hathoric rites, placing the *ẖnr*(*wt*) in an interdependent partnership with the priestesses.[136] Hemetra's roles appear to have included overseeing both the preparation and the production of such rituals. The generalized wording of her role as overseer of singing prevents our defining the environment of the singers. Neferesres held a similar position to

Hemetra in that she was *imyt-rȝ ḫnr(wt) n nswt*, "overseer of the musical performers of the king,"[137] but she also held several administrative roles in the performance profession, particularly associated with the palace. Her titles document that she was *imyt-rȝ sḫmḫ-ib*, "overseer of amusements/entertainment,"[138] *imyt-rȝ sḫmḫ-ib nb nfr nswt*, "overseer of all royal amusements,"[139] and *imyt-rȝ ibȝw n nswt*, "overseer of dancers of the king."[140] Both genders maintained multiple responsibilities in the performance profession.

Conclusion

The thirty-five titles discussed in this chapter are only the preliminary findings of the study, but offer a representative sample of the women's titles in the economic domain during the First through the Sixth Dynasties. This chapter documents a diverse collection of women's roles ranging from the most basic domestic services through to high-level administration, demonstrating women's engagement in ancient Egypt's economic structure. By evaluating the titles in a framework that considers the economic domain inclusive of civic and civil service, it is possible to reveal women's contributions and influence in the economy. Previous scholarly resistance to the idea of women as active members of the state's administration has been referred to throughout the discussion to demonstrate the androcentric frame of reference that has resulted in an artificial absence of reporting on women in the state. Moreover, most women featured in this paper (60 percent of the corpus) held positions of authority equal to their male counterparts, which substantiates that these women had equivalent access to and control over economic resources. It is hoped that this study can augment the current literature on early Egypt by including women's narratives of their active and public engagement in the state's economic structure.

Notes

1 J. Balme and C. Bulbeck, "Engendering Origins: Theories of Gender in Sociology and Archaeology," *Australian Archaeology* 67 (2008): 3.

2 J.H. Blok, "Sexual Asymmetry: A Historiographical Essay," in *Sexual Asymmetry in Ancient Society*, ed. J.H. Blok and P. Mason (Amsterdam: Gieben, 1987), 17.

3 "One could argue that Egyptology in the past was almost entirely a study of ancient Egyptian men"; see T.G. Wilfong, "Gender in Ancient Egypt," in *Egyptian Archaeology*, ed. W. Wendrich (Chichester and Malden: Wiley-Blackwell, 2010), 166.

4 The 1987 interdisciplinary "Conference on Women in the Ancient Near East" held at Brown University can be seen as a defining moment in the establishment of a field dedicated to the scholarship of ancient Egyptian women.

5 C. Graves-Brown, "Introduction," in *Sex and Gender in Ancient Egypt: "Don Your Wig for a Joyful Hour,"* ed. C. Graves-Brown (Swansea: Classical Press of Wales, 2008), xi.

6 C. Mack-Canty, "Third-wave Feminism and the Need to Reweave the Nature/Culture Duality," *National Women's Studies Association* 16, no. 3 (Autumn 2004): 159; U. Matić, "(De)queering

Hatshepsut: Binary Bind in Archaeology of Egypt and Kingship beyond the Corporeal," *Journal of Archaeological Method and Theory* 23, no. 3 (September 2016): 812.

7 "[T]he women indoors, private and incidental to the record, as opposed to men, outdoors and public"; see C.J. Eyre, "Women and Prayer in Pharaonic Egypt," in *Decorum and Experience: Essays in Ancient Culture for John Baines*, ed. E. Frood and A. McDonald (Oxford: Griffiths Institute, 2013), 109; Ayad, "Moving Beyond Gender Bias" (in this volume).

8 Matić, "(De)queering Hatshepsut," 812.

9 H.G. Fischer, *Egyptian Women of the Old Kingdom and of the Heracleopolitan Period*, 2nd ed. (New York: Metropolitan Museum of Art, 2000), 46; G. Robins, *Women in Ancient Egypt* (London: British Museum Press, 1993), 11.

10 For relevant discourses, see W.A. Ward, "Non-royal Women and Their Occupations in the Middle Kingdom," in *Women's Earliest Records from Ancient Egypt and Western Asia*, ed. B.S. Lesko (Atlanta: Scholars Press, 1989), 35; V.G. Callender, "Female Officials in Ancient Egypt," in *Stereotypes of Women in Power: Historical Perspectives and Revisionist Views*, ed. B. Garlick, S. Dixon, and P. Allen (Westport, CT: Greenwood Press, 1992), 14; Robins, *Women in Ancient Egypt* (1993a), 35; R.A. Gillam, "Priestesses of Hathor: Their Function, Decline and Disappearance," *JARCE* 32 (1995): 213; B.M. Bryan, "In Women Good and Bad Fortune Are on Earth: Status and Roles of Women in Egyptian Culture," in *Mistress of the House, Mistress of Heaven: Women in Ancient Egypt*, ed. A.E. Capel and G.E. Markoe (New York: Hudson Hills Press, 1996), 35.

11 H. Papazian, "Domain of Pharaoh: The Structure and Components of the Economy of Old Kingdom Egypt" (PhD diss., University of Chicago, 2005), 64; E.F. Morris, "Propaganda and Performance at the Dawn of the State," in *Experiencing Power, Generating Authority: Cosmos, Politics, and the Ideology of Kingship in Ancient Egypt and Mesopotamia*, ed. J.A. Hill, P. Jones, and A.J. Morales (Philadelphia: University of Pennsylvania, 2013), 56; J.C. Moreno García, "The Territorial Administration of the Kingdom in the 3rd Millennium," in *Ancient Egyptian Administration*, ed. J.C. Moreno García (Leiden: Brill, 2013), 90; M. Bárta, "Kings, Viziers, and Courtiers: Executive Power in the Third Millennium B.C.," in *Ancient Egyptian Administration*, ed. J.C. Moreno García (Leiden: Brill, 2013), 162; V. Dulíková et al., "Invisible History: Hidden Markov Model of Old Kingdom Administration Development and Its Trends," in *Old Kingdom Art and Archaeology 7: Proceedings of the International Conference Università degli Studi di Milano 3–7 July* 2017, ed. P. Piacentini and A. Delli Castelli (Milan: Sala Napoleonica-Palazzo Greppi, 2019), 227.

12 T.A.H. Wilkinson, "The Early Dynastic Period," in *A Companion to Ancient Egypt*, ed. A.B. Lloyd (Chichester and Malden: Wiley-Blackwell, 2010), 58.

13 Papazian, "Domain of Pharaoh," 1; H. Küllmer, "Marktfrauen, Priesterinnen und Elde des Königs: Untersuchung über die Position von Frauen in der sozialen Hierarchie den Alten Ägypten bis zum Ende der 1. Zwischenzeit" (PhD diss., University of Hamburg, 2007), 90; M. Baud, "The Old Kingdom," in *A Companion to Ancient Egypt*, ed. A.B. Lloyd (Chichester and Malden: Wiley-Blackwell, 2010), 63; H. Vymazalová, "The Administration of the Royal Funerary Complexes," in *Ancient Egyptian Administration*, ed. J.C. Moreno García (Leiden: Brill, 2013), 177.

14 P. Springborg, *Royal Persons: Patriarchal Monarchy and the Feminine Principle* (London: Unwin Hyman, 1990), 31.

15 "A general account of societies, their structure, and their history can best be given in terms of the interrelations of what I will call the four sources of social power: ideological, economic, military and political (IEMP) relationship"; see M. Mann, *The Sources of Social Power*, vol. 1, *A History of Power from the Beginning to AD 1760* (Cambridge: Cambridge University Press, 2012), 2.

16 Mann, *Sources of Social Power*, 6.

17 "To the extent that these references establish distributions of power (differential control over or access to material and symbolic resources), gender becomes implicated in the conception and construction of power itself," see J.W. Scott, "Gender: A Useful Category of Historical Analysis,"

American Historical Review 91, no. 5 (1986): 1069; J.E. Richards, *Society and Death in Ancient Egyptian Mortuary Landscapes of the Middle Kingdom* (Cambridge: Cambridge University Press, 2005), 15–17.

18 Kings' wives and mothers have already received considerable attention in scholarship, see L.K. Sabbahy, "The Development of the Titulary and Iconography of the Ancient Egyptian Queen from Dynasty One to Early Dynasty Eighteen" (PhD diss., University of Toronto, 1982); L. Troy, *Patterns of Queenship in Ancient Egyptian Myth and History* (Uppsala and Stockholm: Almquist and Wiksell International, 1986); V.G. Callender, "The Wives of the Egyptian Kings: Dynasties I–XVII" (PhD diss., Macquarie University, 1992); S. Roth, *Die Königsmütter des Alten Ägypten von der Frühzeit bis zum Ende der 12. Dynastie*, ÄAT 46 (Wiesbaden: Harrassowitz, 2001); however, a small sample of the titulary of royal women—*mwt nswt, ḥmt nswt*, and *s3t nswt/s3t nswt nt ẖt.f*—is included. Only royal affiliations providing intrinsic kinship details to the king are recorded.

19 D. Jones, *An Index of Ancient Egyptian Titles, Epithets and Phrases of the Old Kingdom*, 2 vols. (Oxford: Archaeopress, 2000) was used as the primary source to identify official titles; the title number is recorded in the relevant footnote as [xxxx].

20 For cross-referencing, women's database record numbers from the dissertation are provided in the footnotes when the woman is first introduced into the text and are indicated by the number in square brackets starting with the letter W.

21 Merys [W1240]; *Wb*., vols. 1–7 (Berlin: Akademie-Verlag, 1971), http://aaew.bbaw.de/—WB III [88,10]; Jones, *Index of Ancient Egyptian Titles*, 499– [1871]; G.T. Martin, *Umm el-Qaab VII: Private Stelae of the Early Dynastic Period from the Royal Cemetery at Abydos* (Wiesbaden: Harrassowitz, 2011), 134—Stela 35.

22 Khent/Khen-ka [W1329]; Jones, *Index of Ancient Egyptian Titles*, 401– [1477]; Martin, *Umm el-Qaab: Private Stelae,* 215—Stela 196.

23 Khent [W192]: Jones, *Index of Ancient Egyptian Titles*, 406– [1494].

24 Khenmet [W117]; Jones, *Index of Ancient Egyptian Titles*, 496– [1829].

25 Jones, *Index of Ancient Egyptian Titles*, 401.

26 "Great one of a house"; see P. Kaplony, *Die Inschriften der ägyptischen Frühzeit* (Wiesbaden: Harrassowitz, 1963), 373, 1049.

27 Ward, "Non-royal Women and Their Occupations in the Middle Kingdom," 42n45.

28 Jones, *Index of Ancient Egyptian Titles*, 406.

29 H. Kayser, *Die Mastaba des Uhemka: Ein Grab in der Wüste* (Hannover: Fackelträger, 1964), 69.

30 Papazian, "Domain of Pharaoh," xvii.

31 [W151] and [W673] respectively; Jones, *Index of Ancient Egyptian Titles*, 114– [461].

32 Semet-[. . .] [W1381]; Khenut [W1392]; Merit [W1397].

33 Jones, *Index of Ancient Egyptian Titles*, 125– [501].

34 "Such a centre was not exactly a storage facility, nor a revenue-collecting department, nor 'kitchens', but somehow a mixture of the three"; see C.J. Eyre, "Village Economy in Pharaonic Egypt," in *Agriculture in Egypt: From Pharaonic to Modern Times*, ed. A.K. Bowman and E.L. Rogan (Oxford: Oxford University Press, 1999), 40.

35 "[T]here is no clear evidence for private *per-shenas* at this time"; see D. Vischak, *Community and Identity in Ancient Egypt: The Old Kingdom Cemetery at Qubbet el-Hawa* (New York: Cambridge University Press, 2015), 198.

36 Jones, *Index of Ancient Egyptian Titles*, 671– [2457].

37 For different interpretations applied to the title, see N. Kanawati and A. McFarlane, *Deshasha: The Tombs of Inti, Shedu and Others* (Sydney: ACE, 1993), 15n37; Eyre, "Village Economy," 38; K.A. Kóthay, "Categorisation, Classification, and Social Reality: Administrative Control and Interaction with the Population," in *Ancient Egyptian Administration*, ed. J.C. Moreno García (Leiden: Brill, 2013), 488; Moreno García, "Territorial Administration," 124.

38 [W1013].

39 "[T]he titles *s3 nswt* and *s3t nswt* have been methodically chiselled out everywhere they existed"; see A. El-Khouli and N. Kanawati, *The Old Kingdom Tombs of El-Hammamiya* (Sydney: ACE, 1990), 31.
40 El-Khouli and Kanawati, *Old Kingdom Tombs*, 35.
41 El-Khouli and Kanawati, *Old Kingdom Tombs*, 31.
42 "The element of positioning the name and titles above the head and around the face appears to become the general format for recording the identification of the owner from this time forward" (i.e., Merka, c. late First Dynasty); see S.A. Kelly, "Identifying the Women of the Early Dynastic Egypt: An Analysis of the Women's Funerary Stelae/Slabs from Abu Rawash, Helwan and Abydos" (Master of Research thesis, Macquarie University, 2016), 45.
43 [W575]; Jones, *Index of Ancient Egyptian Titles*, 301– [1101].
44 Jones, *Index of Ancient Egyptian Titles*, 49– [247].
45 Jones, *Index of Ancient Egyptian Titles*, 898– [3296].
46 [W576]; for the alternate translations, see WB III 328[14]; B.S. Lesko, "Women's Monumental Mark on Ancient Egypt," *The Biblical Archaeologist* 54, no. 1 (March 1991): 5; Callender, "Female Officials," 14; H.G. Fischer, *Egyptian Studies*, 3, *Varia Nova* (New York: Metropolitan Museum of Art, 1996), 253; Jones, *Index of Ancient Egyptian Titles*, 736– [2682].
47 T.A.H. Wilkinson, *Early Dynastic Egypt* (London: Routledge, 1999), 116.
48 A.H. Gardiner, *Egyptian Grammar: Being an Introduction to the Study of Hieroglyphs* (London: Oxford University Press on behalf of the Griffith Institute, 1957), 495. This interpretation is suggested by the large number of late Old Kingdom funerary priests who held the same title and whose duties included supervision over the supply of "a rich table" for the official in both the house and tomb; see M. Bárta, *Journey to the West: The World of the Old Kingdom Tombs in Ancient Egypt* (Prague: Charles University, 2011), 256–57.
49 Wilkinson, *Early Dynastic Egypt*, 116.
50 M.A. Speidel, *Die Friseure des ägyptischen alten Reiches: eine historisch-prosopographische Untersuchung zu Amt und Titel (ỉr-šn)* (Konstanz: Hartung-Gorre, 1990), 30; Köhler identifies the *ḫrp* roles that involve "storage, supplies and logistics at the court and are most probably part of the central administration"; see E.C. Köhler, "Early Dynastic Society in Memphis," in *Streiflichter aus Ägyptens Geschichte zu Ehren von Günter Dreyer*, ed. E.-M. Engel, V. Müller, and U. Hartung (Wiesbaden: Harrassowitz, 2008), 39.
51 L. Hudáková, *The Representations of Women in the Middle Kingdom Tombs of High Officials: Studies in Iconography* (Leiden: Brill, 2019), 297.
52 [W202]; Jones, *Index of Ancient Egyptian Titles*, 309–10– [1131].
53 Jones, *Index of Ancient Egyptian Titles*, 301–302– [1102].
54 H.G. Fischer, *Egyptian Studies*, 1, *Varia* (New York: Metropolitan Museum of Art, 1976), 74.
55 G. Robins, "Some Principles of Compositional Dominance and Gender Hierarchy in Egyptian Art," *JARCE* 31 (1994): 58.
56 Speidel, *Die Friseure*, 91–95.
57 Speidel, *Die Friseure*, 30.
58 PM III^2, 727.
59 A.R. David, *Handbook to Life in Ancient Egypt* (Oxford: Oxford University Press, 2007), 366.
60 [W480]; Jones, *Index of Ancient Egyptian Titles*, 203– [761].
61 Central Field– G8942.
62 Jones, *Index of Ancient Egyptian Titles*, 177–78– [675].
63 S. Hassan, *Excavations at Giza* 1: *1929–1930* (Oxford: Oxford University Press, 1932), 81.
64 Fischer, *Egyptian Women of the Old Kingdom*, 27.
65 Fischer, *Egyptian Women of the Old Kingdom*, 27.
66 [W1395]; Jones, *Index of Ancient Egyptian Titles*, 436– [1605].
67 [W556]; Jones, *Index of Ancient Egyptian Titles*, 306– [1114]; Z.A. Hawass, *Builders of the Pyramids* (Giza: Nahdet Misr, 2008), 17.
68 GSE 1919/LG 53.

69 Fischer, *Egyptian Women of the Old Kingdom*, 27–29.
70 Hawass, *Builders of the Pyramids*, 40.
71 Fischer, *Egyptian Women of the Old Kingdom*, 27.
72 [W1326]; WB II [109, 19]: "Weberei"; as this title is not included in Jones's *Index of Ancient Egyptian Titles*, it has not been included in the corpus or statistical analysis; Martin, *Umm el-Qaab: Private Stelae*, 134–35, 215; Kelly, "Identifying the Women," 72–73.
73 Fischer, *Egyptian Studies*, 3, *Varia Nova*, 238.
74 Ward, "Non-royal Women and Their Occupations in the Middle Kingdom," 36.
75 [W194]; Jones, *Index of Ancient Egyptian Titles*, 649– [2377].
76 WB IV [296, 7].
77 H. Goedicke, "Reviewed Work(s): *Untersuchungen zur Ägyptischen Provinzialverwaltung bis zum Ende des Alten Reiches* by E. Martin-Pardy," *JARCE* 14 (1977): 122.
78 V. Vasiljevic, *Untersuchungen zum Gefolge des Grabherrn in den Gräbern des Alten Reiches* (Belgrade: Filozofski Fakultet, 1995), 24.
79 Jones, *Index of Ancient Egyptian Titles*, 234–35– [864].
80 [W674] and [W675].
81 [W785], [W787], and [W788] respectively; B.S. Lesko, *The Remarkable Women of Ancient Egypt* (Berkeley: B.C. Scribe Publications, 1978), 5; Jones, *Index of Ancient Egyptian Titles*, 114–[464].
82 The two Rewedzawes are identified as separate individuals, both mothers, with [W426] being the mother of Mersu-ankh and [W785] the mother of Khnumhotep.
83 [W426]; Jones, *Index of Ancient Egyptian Titles*, 116– [466].
84 Fischer, *Egyptian Women of the Old Kingdom*, 20.
85 [W1354]; Jones, *Index of Ancient Egyptian Titles*, 773; Martin, *Umm el-Qaab: Private Stelae*, 186.
86 Martin, *Umm el-Qaab: Private Stelae*, 186.
87 Kelly, "Identifying the Women," 74–76; S.A. Kelly, "Women's Work in the Early Dynastic Period," *PES* 23 (2019): 97.
88 Kelly, "Identifying the Women," 75.
89 Jones, *Index of Ancient Egyptian Titles*, 760– [2763].
90 Kayser, *Die Mastaba*, 69–71; Nesi [W196]; Nezet [W198]; Zenti [W199]; Sety [W200]; Persenet [W201].
91 [W947].
92 Elizabeth Thompson (in preparation): title and details are unknown due to the recent passing of the author.
93 Jones, *Index of Ancient Egyptian Titles*, 985– [3638].
94 [W1165].
95 W.A. Ward, *Essays on Feminine Titles of the Middle Kingdom and Related Subjects* (Beirut: American University of Beirut, 1986), 36.
96 [W676]; Jones, *Index of Ancient Egyptian Titles*, 950–51– [3507].
97 N.B. Millet, "Ancient Cylinder Seals" (MA thesis, University of Chicago, 1959), 11.
98 M.W.B. George, "Those Documents Are Sealed: A Study of the Evolution of the Structure and Function of the Egyptian Administration in the Late Predynastic and Early Dynastic Period, with Special Attention to Seals and Seal Impressions" (Master of Research thesis, Macquarie University, 2014), 31.
99 [W942] and [W943], respectively.
100 Jones, *Index of Ancient Egyptian Titles*, 777– [2827].
101 These inscriptions, which are now lost, were originally recorded by Edel; see E. Edel, *Hieroglyphische Inschriften des Alten Reiches* (Opladen: Westdeutscher, 1981), 40–52, Abb. 18.
102 [W1365]; Kelly, "Identifying the Women," 76–77; Kelly, "Women's Work," 97–98.
103 Jones, *Index of Ancient Egyptian Titles*, 863– [3159].
104 Z.Y. Saad, *Ceiling Stelae in Second Dynasty Tombs: From the Excavations at Helwan* (Cairo: IFAO, 1957), 8.

105 Kaplony, *Die Inschriften*, 487.
106 Kaplony, *Die Inschriften*, 230.
107 E.C. Köhler and J. Jones, *Helwan* 2: *The Early Dynastic and Old Kingdom Funerary Relief Slabs* (Rahden/Westf: Marie Leidorf, 2009), 164.
108 Köhler and Jones, *Helwan* 2, 69.
109 P. Piacentini, *Les scribes dans la société égyptienne de l'Ancien Empire*, vol. 1, *Les premières dynasties: Les nécropoles memphites* (Paris: Cybele, 2002), 61.
110 Fischer, *Egyptian Studies*, 1, *Varia*, 69.
111 M.J. Adams, "The Title *ḫnty-š* in the Old Kingdom" (MA thesis, Pennsylvania State University, 2003), iii.
112 [W051], [W052], [W227], and [W508], respectively.
113 Jones, *Index of Ancient Egyptian Titles*, 692– [2530].
114 Adams, "*ḫnty-š*," 96–97.
115 Adams, "*ḫnty-š*," 93, 98.
116 Jones, *Index of Ancient Egyptian Titles*, 692– [2531].
117 A.M. Roth, "The Social Aspects of Death," in *Mummies and Magic: The Funerary Arts of Ancient Egypt*, ed. S. D'Auria, P. Lacovara, and C.H. Roehrig (Boston: MFA, 1988), 52.
118 Küllmer, "Marktfrauen," 90.
119 Fischer, *Egyptian Women of the Old Kingdom*, 26.
120 "The funerary cult, which was formally maintained by members of the family, but in practice much more frequently organised by priests from the ranks of the lower dignitaries"; see Bárta, *Journey to the West*, 52.
121 [W729].
122 Jones, *Index of Ancient Egyptian Titles*, 176– [673].
123 Fischer, *Egyptian Women of the Old Kingdom*, 26.
124 Bárta, *Journey to the West*, 52.
125 Jones, *Index of Ancient Egyptian Titles*, 177–78– [673].
126 [W940]; Jones, *Index of Ancient Egyptian Titles*, 302– [1103].
127 D. Sweeney, "Walking Alone Forever, Following You: Gender and Mourner's Laments from Ancient Egypt," *NIN: Journal of Gender Studies in Antiquity* 2 (2001): 27.
128 C.H. Roehrig, "Women's Work: Some Occupations of Nonroyal Women as Depicted in Ancient Egyptian Art," in *Mistress of the House, Mistress of Heaven*, ed. A.K. Capel and G.E. Markoe (New York: Hudson Hills Press, 1996), 14.
129 R. Shalomi-Hen, "The Two Kites and the Osirian Revolution," in *Edal: Egyptian & Egyptological Documents Archives Libraries*, ed. P. Piacentini (Milan: Pontremoli editore, 2009), 374.
130 [W596]; Jones, *Index of Ancient Egyptian Titles*, 303– [1106].
131 Jones, *Index of Ancient Egyptian Titles*, 302–303– [1105].
132 S. Onstine, "The Role of the *Šmꜥyt* Chantress in Ancient Egypt" (PhD diss., University of Toronto, 2001), 15.
133 B.M. Bryan, "The Etymology of *ḫnr* 'Group of Musical Performers,'" *BES* 4 (1982): 36; Onstine, "Role of the *Šmꜥyt* Chantress," 16; Graves-Brown, *Sex and Gender*, xvii.
134 Fischer, *Egyptian Women of the Old Kingdom*, 26
135 Bryan, "Etymology of *ḫnr*," 35.
136 Izold Guegan, "The *ḫnrwt*: A Reassessment of Their Religious Roles" (in this volume); personal communication: "They are intimately related to the institution of the *pr-šndt* and are therefore primarily related to Neith . . . associated with the goddess Hathor and became the partners of the *ḥmwt-nṯr* and *ḥmw-nṯr* of the goddess."
137 [W478]; Jones, *Index of Ancient Egyptian Titles*, 304– [1109].
138 Jones, *Index of Ancient Egyptian Titles*, 232– [857].
139 Jones, *Index of Ancient Egyptian Titles*, 232–33– [859].
140 Jones, *Index of Ancient Egyptian Titles*, 301– [1098].

11

Ostentation in Old Kingdom Female Tombs: Between Iconographical Conventions and Gendered Adaptations

Romane Betbeze

HISTORICALLY, STUDIES ON Ancient Egyptian tomb chapels have focused on male (nonroyal) tombs, since they constitute the majority of currently known burials.[1] For this reason, we have defined Old Kingdom iconographical conventions through the analysis of tombs that belonged to *men*. These conventions have only recently been questioned with regard to a tomb belonging to a major female figure,[2] perhaps because researchers considered the context to be exceptional. Yet, during the Old Kingdom, numerous tombs and decorated chapels belonged to women, which stands in contrast to later periods. Indeed, the data from the work of Porter and Moss and other recent publications record sixty-eight monuments from the Memphite necropolis with female tomb owners.[3] To own an individual tomb implied an economic capacity to create a monument meant for self-representation containing property and some funerary personnel, which usually belonged to elite men. However, these monuments show that some women also had this capacity, although half of these cases were women from the royal family,[4] with a direct, blood connection to the king.

If female possession of goods and the notion of a female elite did not seem to be a problem in Ancient Egyptian society, women were still a subset of the elite, minor at least in their number. They were integrated into an official dominant discourse created by and for men.[5]

Since these women had resources of their own, they could not be represented in the usual female way—that is, as hierarchical subordinates, defined through their relationship to a man (as his spouse, mother, or daughter, for example).[6] Thus, female tomb owners could not use traditional iconographical norms for their funerary decoration without adapting them. Although they were still depicted through certain strictly gendered conventions, such as pale skin color and body proportions characterized by narrow shoulders and no indications of muscles,[7] two major types of adaptations[8] are analyzed in this paper, by comparing them to the data collected for male elite tombs:

- The representation of the major (feminine) figure and its attitude;
- The representation of her subordinates, their genders, and their activities.

Passivity: A "Feminine" Quality or an "Elite" Quality?

Conventions of Attitude

Traditionally, one of the first iconographic conventions associated with women is a passive attitude, in which they are depicted standing with the legs and feet joined. Even in a context with a woman at its focal point, women tend to be represented in this way, in contrast to men, who tend to be depicted in a walking attitude, with one leg forward, and usually grasping a stick. Although some exceptions are pointed out by Y. Harpur, with women sometimes depicted in this walking attitude,[9] we see an almost universal gendered distinction between female passivity and male action, even in the elite environment.

Conventions of Scenes

Except for this specific convention of a walking versus a standing attitude, it has to be noted that tomb owners, whether male or female, generally participate in the same scenes. Indeed, both are often seated behind an offering table, in a passive attitude, waiting for the offerings and the funerary cult. In other cases, the main character is supervising or inspecting numerous activities performed by subordinates (fig. 11.1): attending cattle, hunting or fishing, preparing funerary furniture, and so forth. The static major figure is highlighted in contrast to the dynamic subordinates. Indeed, this graphic contrast shows the tomb owner as monolithic, whereas the subordinates are depicted moving, with a great iconographical variation and on a much smaller scale. Additionally, the text accompanying the major figure corroborates this observation, often by beginning with the word *m33*, expressing that the tomb owner is passively observing the actions of the subordinates. A very different type of text, called *Reden und Rufe*, is associated with the attendants, artificially recreating a casual discourse between them, and often expressing their submission to their master or mistress.[10] Thus, in these decorative programs, it is not the gender of the tomb owner that is most important, but rather the fact that he or she possessed wealth in the form of property and personnel. Passivity,

Fig. 11.1. Waatetkhethor supervising her attendants, tomb of Waatetkhethor, Saqqara

therefore, is a fundamental quality of the elite, defined as a superior class benefiting from lower classes who work for it.

Some Gendered Activities: The Scenes in the Marsh

By comparing the decorative differences between male and female tombs, some gendered specificities come to light. Indeed, some rare scenes where the major figure is physically active are noteworthy, but they are only used for male figures, and seem inappropriate in a female context. The analysis of exceptional

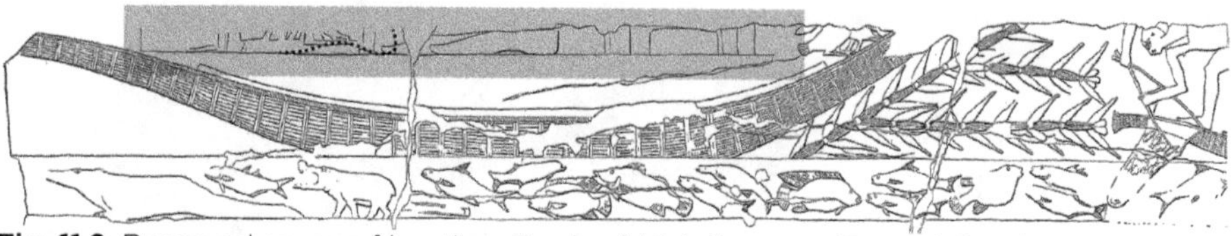

Fig. 11.2. Recarved scene of hunting, Tomb of Idut, Saqqara, Room 1, South Wall

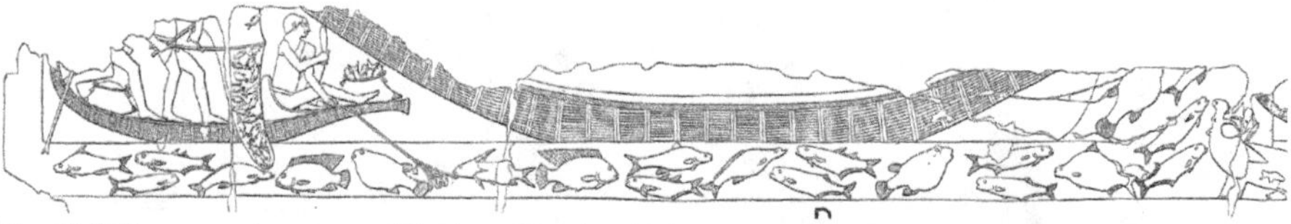

Fig. 11.3. Recarved scene of fishing, Tomb of Idut, Saqqara, Room I, North Wall

cases of some "usurped" tombs, which belonged first to men but were later reused by women, highlights this adaptation process by which a decoration was transferred from a male to a female tomb owner.

For example, at Saqqara, in the tomb of Ihy, a male vizier from the Fifth Dynasty, reused by Seshseshet Idut, a princess of the royal family, probably a daughter of King Teti,[11] some interesting modifications were made.[12] Indeed, in most such cases, changes focused on the representation of the tomb owner, and not on the nature of the scenes. For instance, almost no modifications occurred on a seated major figure, except for its clothes, its canon of proportions,[13] or the suppression of its stick, associated with masculine power, which was recarved as a column of text or an offering subaltern.[14] When the first, male, tomb owner was depicted in a walking attitude, the sculptors would modify this representation to appear like a woman with legs and feet joined.[15] However, the *types* of scenes remained unchanged, except for one, a marsh hunting scene whose nature was modified.

In Room I, on the south wall, some fragments of a scene in the marsh can be observed; they originally depicted a hunting scene (fig. 11.2), as we can deduce from the decorative program of this room. Indeed, on the north wall of this same room, symmetrically, a fishing scene in the marsh (fig. 11.3) can be identified, thanks to the surviving bit showing water with fishes located in the bottom part of the wall.[16] In Old Kingdom private tombs, depictions of the tomb owner fishing are usually mirrored by the same person hunting. In this hunting scene, a rectangular zone, marked on the drawing, is clearly recarved. The remains of a foot can still be seen at the prow of the boat (indicated by the dotted line), which proves that the previous tomb owner was depicted in a hunting attitude. Instead, this figure has been changed into a woman seated on a throne, in a "cruise in the marsh scene," according to Harpur's classification.[17]

Clearly, the original male tomb owner was depicted in action,[18] but the artists decided to change this active figure to an inactive, seated woman. In the fishing scene on the south wall, however, it is difficult to know if the representation has been transformed because the upper part is lost; yet we can assume that the original carving was changed, since no depictions of women in this attitude are known so far. So, in both scenes in the marsh, the active figure was not considered to be adaptable to the female gender.

Physically Active Scenes as Masculine Prerogatives for a Major Figure

Active scenes in the marsh—hunting birds and fishing—are not the only activities "forbidden" to elite women. Indeed, various other pastimes are also only known for male tomb owners, including writing,[19] playing the *senet*,[20] and hunting with a lasso,[21] with dogs,[22] or with nets.[23] Thus, passivity seems to be an elite quality, but inactivity is specific to elite women. First of all, iconographically, the very tight dresses shown as feminine garments during the Old Kingdom would have impeded physical movements and could not be easily adapted to scenes of hunting or fishing. Second, it is possible that such active scenes did not fit with the habitual decorum of elite women, perhaps because they reflected specific social conventions. For example, hunting was probably a masculine prerogative, linked to the notion of virility, and an outdoor physical activity where a man confronted the "uncivilized" world, according to R. Parkinson.[24] In the literature, hunting and fishing were associated with masculinity by presenting an eroticized masculine body,[25] and therefore were not suited for the depiction of elite women.[26]

The Inner Circle of Elite Women and the Convention of "Homosociality"

Additional Feminine "High Subordinates" with Names and Titles Situated around Their Mistress

Another convention associated with female elite tombs is the inclusion of various secondary women surrounding the female major figure, as is noticeable in the aforementioned tomb of Idut (fig. 11.4).

Such characters are not randomly added, but belong to the inner circle of Idut since they are represented behind rather than in front of her in the numerous registers of subordinates and workers. In fact, in most of the tombs of women, female figures are depicted carrying chests, furniture, or other objects belonging to the "personal sphere" of the tomb owner. They are not from the lower social classes, because they often own a title that links them to an administrative system and provides them with some social status. For example, in the

Fig. 11.4. Idut with male and female subordinates behind her chair, Tomb of Idut, Room V, North Wall

tomb of Idut, an *ỉmyt-r sšr*, "(female) overseer of cloth," is depicted behind the chair of her mistress.[27] Similarly, in the tomb of Waatetkhethor, an *ỉmyt-r pr*, "(female) overseer of the domain," another *ỉmyt-r sšr*, "(female) overseer of the cloth," and a *sḥḏt ḫtmt*, "(female) inspector of the treasure," are represented around the carrying chair of their mistress, the latter two holding objects of hers in their hands.[28] It is interesting to note that the attestations of an *ỉmyt-r sšr*, a *sḥḏt ḫtmt*, or a *ỉmyt-r pr*—female counterparts of traditionally masculine functions—who are not family relatives of the deceased are to be found solely in female tombs.[29]

Depictions of such female subordinates are very scarce in tombs of male officials, and the fact that these are *additions* to the tomb of Idut due to the changing of gender of the tomb owner appears to indicate that an entourage must at least partially match the tomb owner's gender. Therefore, it seems that a woman has to have a feminine entourage, whereas a man has to have a masculine one. Furthermore, when two persons of different sexes are represented together in a tomb at the same scale—usually a man and his spouse—the attendants may be divided into two groups, feminine and masculine. For instance, in the tomb of the vizier Mehu from Saqqara, in the middle room, the tomb owner is depicted with his wife.[30] Behind them, four registers of subordinates are separated into three upper registers of male attendants, associated with Mehu, and a last one at the bottom, composed of females, probably added in order to match the gender of his spouse.[31] Moreover, it seems that the subordinates of an elite man or an elite woman were represented as mirror images: they are nearly identical in their attitude or their attributes, except for their gender. Even some stereotypical characters, such as masculine people of short stature—very often depicted in the entourage of the tomb owner, or in a row of offering bearers—have been turned into female persons of short stature for a female tomb owner; for example, in the tomb of Nebet.[32]

Definition and Limits of Homosociality as an Iconographical Convention

The tendency to match the gender of the attendants to that of their master or mistress reveals the convention of *homosociality* in iconographical decorum. According to B. Lion, *homosociality* can be defined as the primacy given to relations between same-sex people in a society.[33] This iconographical rule probably reflected a social convention whereby certain areas were characterized by gender segregation, especially in the elite sphere. This segregation would have impacted the spatial organization of tomb scenes by creating separate areas for men and women, as suggested, for example, by the banquet scenes of the New Kingdom, where men and women were not mixed.[34] It would also imply, in some exceptional cases, the creation of corps of female servants surrounding a female elite figure,[35] and bearing official titles traditionally known for men (for example, *imyt-r pr*, *imyt-r sšr*, and so forth). Similarly, in the ancient Middle East,[36] B. Lion remarks that women from the royal family lived with the men in the same palace, but did also have their own separate areas and female servants.[37] According to G. Robins,[38] it may have been a way of restricting the activities of women so that they could not be part of the state bureaucracy.

Women were sometimes placed in charge of "female sectors" of the palace administration, such as the *imyt-r*, "(female) overseer," of other female personnel (singers, dancers, and so forth).[39] Very few women appear as overseers of male dignitaries in the professional environment of the elite, and, when found,

Fig. 11.5. Male "overseer of funerary priests" in front of Khentkaus, Tomb of Khentkaus, East Room, West Wall

such occurrences are much debated.[40] For instance, an *ỉmyt-r ḥmw-kꜣ*,[41] an *ỉmyt-r swnw / swnwt*,[42] and some *ỉmyt-r (pr) ḥtsw(t)*[43] are known, but some scholars think that it is a female group of workers despite the masculine spelling of the substantives *ḥmw-kꜣ*, *swnw*, and *ḥtsw*.[44] They argue that the *-t*, expressing a feminine collective, would have been omitted for scriptural reasons, as was very often done during the Old Kingdom.[45] Furthermore, the group of weavers *ḥtsw(t)*, in particular, might have been a strictly female one, according to G. Robins, after comparison with the representations of such workers in wooden models and with the Egyptian determinative of this word depicting a woman seated.[46] However, this very limited range of functions of female attendants in palace and private administration, and an assumed societal interdiction for women as overseers of male workers, may also reflect a bias due to the iconographical convention of homosociality in private tombs. Indeed, since women with some administrative titles are *never* represented in male elite tombs, or are exclusively mentioned in a very specific context, our current knowledge of their administrative roles may be very superficial.

Finally, the inner circle of the female elite seems to be mostly, but not exclusively, female since in most of the cases, a male subordinate stands out from this entourage,[47] whether by his size, his frequency of representation, or some specific identification (name and titles).

In the tombs of Khentkaus (fig. 11.5), Meresankh III,[48] Hemetra,[49] and Idut,[50] this attendant is depicted presenting a scroll to his mistress, and is identified as the *ỉmy-r ḥmw-kꜣ*, "overseer of funerary priests." Thus, the main character in the entourage of the tomb owner, and the only one to interact directly with the tomb owner, remains a male.

The So-called "Daily Life" Scenes: Selection and Gendered Conventions

Gender of Lower-class People in Female Tombs

The last classification that can be applied to elite female tombs is the type of scene where the tomb owner is observing workers from the lower social classes. First of all, in the tomb of Idut (fig. 11.4), the gender of the subordinates as well as their activities are not modified despite the changing of the gender of the tomb owner. They remain mostly men, in accordance with the decorative program of private tombs from this period which only rarely depict women working in so-called scenes of daily life. Accordingly, representations of lower-class women are comparable to representations of people with disabilities (persons of short stature, those who are lame, and so forth), because their unusualness introduces a break in the register, and therefore represents a variation in the iconographical program.[51] Moreover, the gender of the subordinates was probably not the intended focus of the scenes, which are concerned more with conveying the action they depict than with the individual and her identity.

Daily-life Activities Depicted in Female Elite Tombs

The daily-life activities represented in the funerary chapels appear not to be selected in accordance with the gender of the main figure, since they were not modified in Idut's or Hemetra's tombs. By collecting the data from the MastaBase[52] and sorting them by the gender of the tomb owner, it is possible to analyze the scenes selected (or not) according to whether the deceased is male or female.[53] It turned out that none of these activities are specific to women's tombs; they are shared by monuments owned by both genders. Contrary to Fischer,[54] for example, the representation of linen gathering in the tomb of the lady Hetepet cannot be explained by associating textile work with a specific female sphere, because this scene is also present in the tombs of males.[55] However, there are some daily-life representations that could have been reserved for male tomb owners, since they only appear in the tombs of males, but this option remains hypothetical, as there are fewer than ten occurrences of these scenes, which cannot be considered statistically representative of a phenomenon. Yet it is interesting to notice that the scene of producing jewelry might be associated with a masculine aesthetic because it is only depicted in tombs of males,[56] contrary to what could be suggested by our projection of the division of male and female social roles.[57]

Physical (In)activity, Gender, Social Class, and Relationship to Others

The depiction of people of lower social class in elite tombs introduces a paradox in the iconographical convention of activity and inactivity according to gender. Indeed, in this case, all subordinates, men and women, are depicted performing physical activities. Thus, there are not universal "feminine" qualities in Ancient Egyptian art, but rather the presentation takes into consideration the social class of the persons depicted as well as their relationship to the tomb owner. A woman of a lower social class, like a man, is acting for or serving her master or mistress. An elite woman also can be depicted as active under specific conditions. She is depicted in this way if she is not the main character of the tomb, but instead represents a secondary character, hierarchically subordinate to the tomb owner. For instance, in the tomb of Mereruka, his spouse is depicted playing the harp for him (fig. 11.6); the spouse of Ankhtify, similarly, is hunting with a boomerang in the scene of hunting birds.[58]

Besides, in the case of the so-called "servant statues" that were placed with the funerary furniture of the tomb owner, the workers represented, male and female, are actually people from the tomb owner's family, although elite people doing "housework" are never shown in two-dimensional art.[59] Even elite women, as in the case of the statues of Kakhenet's daughters[60] grinding grain, can therefore be depicted working or acting. Thus, gendered iconographical representations undergo some variations according to the media used (wall of a funerary chapel versus *serdab* statue), but also according to social class and relationship to others.

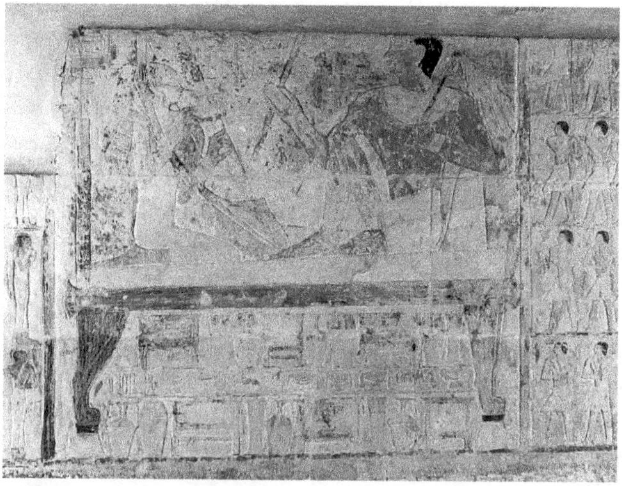

Fig. 11.6. Waatetkhethor playing the harp for her husband, Mereruka, Tomb of Mereruka, Saqqara

Conclusion

It is important to think of iconographical conventions as plural and not monolithic, especially through the notion of intersectionality. Indeed, this concept of intersectionality, which originated from gender studies,[61] invites us to examine the data linked to gender, and also to race, as a sociological category—like social class or age, for example—in order to fully understand the complexity of a system, in this case the ancient Egyptian iconographical program. For instance, in this program, the elite are passive, but elite women are, additionally, inactive, in opposition to their subordinates, whether the latter are male or female. These qualities of activity and passivity characterize a social class, and also, partially, a gender. There is not one unique feminine convention, but rather, various conventions; the same is applicable to men.

Thanks to gender studies, we can avoid a projection of our own interpretations of gendered social roles on the society we are analyzing, as such studies are very helpful in deconstructing the layers of comprehension and in considering the multiple sides of social identity that might have been taken into consideration when creating a pictorial discourse.

Appendix

Table 1: Decorated female tombs from the Old Kingdom

Giza

Name	Dating	Main titles	Main bibliography
Iabtet	Dyn 4	*s3t nswt nt ẖt.f*	PM III[1], 134; Junker, *Gîza* I: *Bericht über die von der Akademie der Wissenschaften in Wien auf gemeinsame Kosten mit Dr. Wilhelm Pelizaeus unternommenen Grabungen auf dem Friedhof des Alten Reiches bei den Pyramiden von Gîza. Die Maṣṭabas der IV. Dynastie auf dem Westfriedhof* (Vienna and Leipzig: Hölder-Pichler-Tempsky, 1929), 216–27.
Meresankh III	Dyn 4	*s3t nswt nt ẖt.f*	PM III[1], 197; Dunham and Simpson, *The Mastaba of Queen Mersyankh III. G 7530–7540*. Giza Mastabas 1 (Boston: MFA, 1974).
Khamerernebty II	Dyn 4	*s3t smswt nswt nt ẖt.f, ḥmt nswt, m33t ḥr stẖ*	PM III[1], 273–74; Callender and Jánosi, "The Tomb of Queen Khamerernebty II at Giza: A Reassessment," *MDAIK* 53 (1997): 1–22.

Wenchet	Dyn 4	*s3t nswt nt ẖt.f, ḥmt-nṯr ḥwt-ḥr, ḥmt-nṯr nt*	PM III[1], 139; Junker, *Gîza* I: *Bericht über die von der Akademie der Wissenschaften in Wien auf gemeinsame Kosten mit Dr. Wilhelm Pelizaeus unternommenen Grabungen auf dem Friedhof des Alten Reiches bei den Pyramiden von Gîza. Die Maṣṭabas der IV. Dynastie auf dem Westfriedhof* (Vienna and Leipzig: Hölder-Pichler-Tempsky, 1929), 249–56.
Meresankh II	Dyn 4(–5)	*s3t nswt nt ẖt.f, ḥmt nswt*	PM III[1], 194; Boston MFA 33.720.
Tjentet	Dyn 4–5	*s3t nswt*	PM III[1], 139; Curto, *Gli scavi italiani a El-Ghiza (1903)* (Roma: Bardi, 1963), Tav. XVI, figs. 17, 61.
Wehemneferet	Dyn 4–5	*s3t nswt*	PM III[1], 139–40; Silvio Curto, *Gli scavi italiani a El-Ghiza (1903)* (Roma: Bardi, 1963), Tav. XVII, XVIII, fig. 20.
Nensedjerkai	Dyn 4–5	*s3t nswt, ẖkrt nswt, ḥmt-nṯr ḥwt-ḥr, ḥmt-nṯr ḫwfw*	PM III[1], 72; Manuelian and Simpson, *Mastabas of Nucleus Cemetery G2100* I: *Major Mastabas G 2100–2220. Giza Mastabas* 8 (Boston: MFA, 2009).
Hemetra	Dyn 4–5	*s3t smswt nswt nt ẖt.f, ḥmt-nṯr ḥwt-ḥr*	PM III[1], 243; Hassan, *Excavations at Gîza: 1934–1935. The Mastabas of the Sixth Season and Their Description* (Cairo: Service des Antiquités de l'Égypte, 1950), 43–65.
Bunefer	Dyn 4–5	*ḥmt nswt, s3t nswt nt ẖt.f, ḥmt-nṯr špss-k3.f*	PM III[1], 256; Selim Hassan, *Excavations at Gîza*: *1931–1932* (Cairo: The Faculty of Arts, Government Press, 1941), 176–99.
Nensedjerkai	Dyn 5	*ḥmt-nṯr ḥwt-ḥr, ḥmt-nṯr nt*	PM III[1], 134; Reisner, *A History of the Giza Necropolis* I (Cambridge, MA: Harvard University Press, 1942), 495–99.
Khenit	Dyn 5	*ḥmt-nṯr ḥwt-ḥr*	PM III[1], 162; Junker, *Gîza* VII: *Bericht über die von der Akademie der Wissenschaften in Wien auf gemeinsame Kosten mit Dr. Wilhelm Pelizaeus unternommenen Grabungen auf dem Friedhof des Alten Reiches bei den Pyramiden von Gîza* (Vienna: Hölder-Pichler-Tempsky, 1944), 241–46.
Neferesres	Dyn 5	*imyt-r ib3w nswt, imyt-r ḫnrwt nswt, ẖkrt nswt wꜥtt*	PM III[1], 282; Hassan, *Excavations at Gîza: 1930–1931* (Cairo: The Faculty of Arts; Government Press, 1936), 202–25.
Hetepet	Dyn 5–6	*ḥmt-nṯr ḥwt-ḥr*	PM III[1], 298; Fischer, *Egyptian Women of the Old Kingdom*, 41.

Khentkaus	Dyn 6	*ḥmt-nṯr ḥwt-ḥr*	PM III[1], 148; Junker, *Gîza* VII: *Bericht über die von der Akademie der Wissenschaften in Wien auf gemeinsame Kosten mit Dr. Wilhelm Pelizaeus unternommenen Grabungen auf dem Friedhof des Alten Reiches bei den Pyramiden von Gîza* (Vienna: Hölder-Pichler-Tempsky, 1944), 68–85.
Hetepheres	Dyn 6	*ḥmt-nṯr nt*	PM III[1], 227; Junker, *Gîza* XI: *Bericht über die von der Akademie der Wissenschaften in Wien auf gemeinsame Kosten mit Dr. Wilhelm Pelizaeus unternommenen Grabungen auf dem Friedhof des Alten Reiches bei den Pyramiden von Gîza. Der Friedhof südlich der Cheopspyramide, Ostteil* (Vienna: Rudolf M. Rohrer, 1953), 258–63.

Saqqara

Name	Dating	Main titles	Main bibliography
Neferhotep Hathor	Dyn 3–4	*rḫt nswt*	PM III[2], 449; Murray, *Saqqara Mastabas* I (London: Bernard Quaritch, BSA, 1905).
Hemetra	Dyn 5–6	*jmyt-r3 ḥswt, jmyt-r3 ḫnrwt*	PM III[2], 450; Roth, "The Usurpation of Hem-Re: An Old Kingdom 'Sex-Change Operation,'" in *Egyptian Museum Collections Around the World* II, ed. Eldamaty and Trad, 1011–23 (Cairo: Supreme Council of Antiquities, 2002).
Meresankh	Dyn 5	*ḥmt nswt*	PM III[2], 488; Auguste Mariette, *Les mastabas de l'Ancien Empire* (Paris: Vieweg, 1889), 183.
Khenut and Nebet	Dyn 5	*ḥmt nswt*	PM III[2], 623; Munro, *Der Unas-Friedhof Nord-West* I: *Topographisch-historische Einleitung. Das Doppelgrab der Königinnen Nebet und Khenut* (Mainz am Rhein: Philipp von Zabern, 1993).
Inti	Dyn 6	*s3t nswt nt ḫt.f*	PM III[2], 508; Málek, "Princess Inti, the Companion of Horus," *JSSEA* 10 (1980): 229–41.

Seshseshet Idut	Dyn 6	*s3t nswt nt ẖt.f*	PM III², 617; Kanawati and Abdel Raziq, *The Unis Cemetery at Saqqara* II: *The Tombs of Iynefert and Ihy (reused by Idut)*, ACER 19 (Warminster: Aris and Phillips, 2003).
Waatetkhethor	Dyn 6	*s3t nswt*	PM III², 534–535; Kanawati and Abdel Raziq, *Mereruka and His Family* II: *The Tomb of Waatetkhethor*, ACER 26 (London: Aris and Phillips, 2008).
Nedjetempet	Dyn 6	*ḥmt-nṯr ḥwt-ḥr, ḥmt-nṯr nt*	Hassan and Kanawati, *The Teti Cemetery at Saqqara* I: *The Tomb of Nedjet-em-pet, Ka-aper and Others*, ACER 8 (Warminster: Aris and Phillips, 1996).
Satinteti	Dyn 6 or later	*ḥmt-nṯr ḥwt-ḥr, ẖkrt nswt wꜥtt*	PM III², 539; Firth and Gunn, *Teti Pyramid Cemeteries* I (Cairo: IFAO, 1926), 38, 185–86, 203–204.

Notes

1 As pointed out by Vivienne Gae Callender, who underscores the necessity for and interest in studying some aspects of female burials: Vivienne Gae Callender, "A Contribution to the Burial of Women in the Old Kingdom," *Archív Orientální* 70, no. 3 (2002): 301–302.

2 According to the nomenclature used by Y. Harpur in *Decoration in Egyptian Tombs of the Old Kingdom: Studies in Orientation and Scene Content* (London and New York: Routledge and Kegan Paul, 1987), 125. For iconographic studies on Old Kingdom monuments belonging to elite women, see, for example, Vera Vasiljević, "Female Owners of Carrying Chairs: *Sitzsänfte* and *Hocksänfte*," *SAK* 41 (2012): 395–406; Ann Macy Roth, "The Usurpation of Hem-Re: An Old Kingdom 'Sex-Change Operation,'" in *Egyptian Museum Collections around the World* 2, ed. Mamdouh Eldamaty and May Trad (Cairo: Supreme Council of Antiquities, 2002), 1011–23.

3 That number does not include queens' pyramids, but only private *mastaba*s and rock tombs. For the tombs selected for analysis in this paper, see appendix, table 1.

4 In total, twenty-nine females were included from the sixty-eight monuments recorded.

5 Ann Macy Roth, "The Absent Spouse: Patterns and Taboos in Egyptian Tomb Decoration," *JARCE* 36 (1999): 37; Vivienne Gae Callender, "Non-royal Women in Old Kingdom Egypt," *Archív Orientální* 68, no. 2 (2000): 228; Gay Robins, *Women in Ancient Egypt* (London: British Museum Press, 1993a), 176.

6 Vera Vasiljević, "Der Grabherr und seine Frau: zur Ikonographie der Status- und Machtverhältnisse in den Privatgräbern des Alten Reiches," *SAK* 36 (2007): 337.

7 For these traditional "feminine" conventions, see Robins, *Women in Ancient Egypt* (1993a), 180–81.

8 These adaptations will be analyzed in a corpus of twenty-four tombs from the sixty-eight mentioned before. These twenty-four tomb chapels are those still bearing some wall decoration (see appendix, table 1).

9 Harpur, *Decoration in Egyptian Tombs*, 138.

10 On the relationship between the *Reden und Rufe* and the subaltern position of the workers in elite tombs, see Pascal Vernus, "Comment l'élite se donne à voir dans le programme décoratif de ses chapelles funéraires. Stratégie d'épure, stratégie d'appogiature et le frémissement du littéraire," in *Élites et pouvoir en Égypte ancienne: actes du colloque Université Charles-de-Gaulle–Lille 3, 7 et 8 juillet 2006*, ed. Juan Carlos Moreno García (Lille: Université Charles-de-Gaulle–Lille III, 2009–10), 77–78. On the *Reden und Rufe*, see also Aurore Motte, "*Reden und Rufe*, A Neglected Genre? Towards a Definition of the Speech Captions in Private Tombs," *BIFAO* 117 (2017): 293–317.

11 Naguib Kanawati and Mahmud Abdel Raziq, *The Unis Cemetery at Saqqara* 2: *The Tombs of Iynefert and Ihy (reused by Idut)*, ACER 19 (Warminster: Aris and Phillips, 2003), 37.

12 Another tomb which could have been used as an example in this study is the tomb of Hemetra, first owned and occupied by Tiye, currently at the Cairo Museum (reliefs: JE 72137; false door: CGC 1380). For a full report on this chapel, see Roth, "The Usurpation of Hem-Re: An Old Kingdom 'Sex-change Operation,'" 1011–23.

13 Similarly, in the tomb of Hemetra, see Roth, "The Usurpation of Hem-Re: An Old Kingdom 'Sex-Change Operation,'" 1015.

14 For example, Kanawati and Abdel Raziq, *The Unis Cemetery at Saqqara* 2, pl. 62.

15 Kanawati and Abdel Raziq, *The Unis Cemetery at Saqqara* 2, pl. 54.

16 Kanawati and Abdel Raziq, *The Unis Cemetery at Saqqara* 2, pl. 53 (f).

17 Theme 1.2. Pleasure cruise in a marsh (*Oxford Expedition to Egypt: Scene-details Database* [Linacre College, Oxford, 2006; https://doi.org/10.5284/1000009]). This scene was probably similar to the complete scene found in the tomb of Meresankh II (Boston MFA 33.720).

18 The other common point—the context of these scenes, that is to say the localization in the marsh—did not seem to be a problem in gendered representations, since in Room 3 of this same tomb, on the west wall, an original scene of "cruise in the marsh" has not been modified at all, except for the gender and identification of the major figure (Kanawati and Abdel Raziq, *The Unis Cemetery at Saqqara* 2, pl. 54).

19 Naguib Kanawati, Alexandra Woods, Sameh Shafik, and Effy Alexakis, *Mereruka and His Family*, part 3.1, *The Tomb of Mereruka*, ACER 29 (Oxford: Aris and Phillips, 2010), pl. 99.

20 Naguib Kanawati, Alexandra Woods, Sameh Shafik, and Effy Alexakis, *Mereruka and His Family*, part 3.2, *The Tomb of Mereruka*, ACER 30 (Oxford: Aris and Phillips, 2011), pl. 81.

21 Tomb façade of Akhetmerutnesut (Boston MFA 13.4352).

22 W.M. Flinders Petrie, *Medum* (London: Nutt, 1892), pl. XXVII. Here, Nefermaat is depicted in the funerary chapel of his spouse hunting with dogs.

23 Petrie, *Medum*, pl. XXII.

24 Richard Parkinson, "'Boasting about Hardness': Constructions of Middle Kingdom Masculinity," in *Sex and Gender in Ancient Egypt: "Don Your Wig for a Joyful Hour,"* ed. Carolyn Graves-Brown (Swansea: Classical Press of Wales, 2008), 122.

25 Parkinson, "'Boasting about Hardness,'" 130.

26 However, elite women can be secondary participants in this type of scene (see next section).

27 See also Kanawati and Abdel Raziq, *The Unis Cemetery at Saqqara* 2, pl. 70. This woman is also a *ḥmt-kꜣ*, "funerary priest"; but *ḥmwt-kꜣ* can also be represented in a male elite tomb, attending a male master—for example, in the *mastaba* of Kapi (G 2091). See Ann Macy Roth, *A Cemetery of Palace Attendants including G 2084–2099, G 2230+2231, and G 2240*, Giza Mastabas 6 (Boston: Department of Ancient Egyptian, Nubian, and Near Eastern Art, MFA, 1995), pls. 41, 61. For other attestations of *ḥmwt-kꜣ*, see Henry George Fischer, "Administrative Titles of Women in the Old and Middle Kingdom," in *Egyptian Studies* 1: *Varia* (New York: Metropolitan Museum of Art, 1976), 70, §11, and n15.

28 Naguib Kanawati and Mahmud Abdel Raziq, *Mereruka and His Family* 2: *The Tomb of Waatetkhethor*, ACER 26 (London: Aris and Phillips, 2008), pl. 69.

29 For *ỉmyt-r sšr*, see the tomb of Idut: Kanawati and Abdel Raziq, *The Unis Cemetery at Saqqara* 2, pl. 70; and the tomb of Waatetkhethor, see Kanawati and Abdel Raziq, *Mereruka and His Family*

2: *The Tomb of Waatetkhethor*, pl. 69). For *imyt-r pr*, see the tomb of Khenut and Nebet: Peter Munro, *Der Unas-Friedhof Nord-West I: Topographisch-historische Einleitung. Das Doppelgrab der Königinnen Nebet und Khenut* (Mainz am Rhein: Philipp von Zabern, 1993), Tf. 11; and the tomb of Waatetkhethor, see Kanawati and Abdel Raziq, *Mereruka and His Family* 2: *The Tomb of Waatetkhethor*, pl. 69. In the case of a male tomb owner, his spouse or family members can bear such titles (for *imyt-r sšr*, see, for example, the stela of Iunka (CG 1501) in H.G. Fischer, *Egyptian Studies*, 1, *Varia* (New York: Metropolitan Museum of Art, 1976), 70 and n13). In the case of *sḥḏt ḫtmt*, the only occurrence of this title is in the tomb of Waatetkhethor; see Kanawati and Abdel Raziq, *Mereruka and His Family* 2: *The Tomb of Waatetkhethor*, pl. 69. However, another *sḥḏt* is attested in Mehu's tomb; see Fischer, *Egyptian Studies*, 1, *Varia*, 71 (18). Similarly, for *ḫtmt*, three occurrences are known, in the tombs of Uhemka, Hirkhuf, and Mekhu and Sabni; see Fischer, *Egyptian Studies*, 1, *Varia*, 70 (6).

30 Hartwig Altenmüller, *Die Wanddarstellungen im Grab des Mehu in Saqqara* (Mainz am Rhein: Philipp von Zabern, 1998), pl. 53.

31 For a similar disposition, see the tomb of Uhemka: Hans Kayser, *Die Mastaba des Uhemka: ein Grab in der Wüste* (Hannover: Fackelträger; Schmidt-Küster, 1964), 39; also in the tomb of Mereruka (see fig. 11.6).

32 Munro, *Der Unas-Friedhof Nord-West* I, Tf. 14.

33 "La primauté donnée, dans une société, aux relations entre personnes de même sexe, sans que celles-ci soient nécessairement d'ordre sexuel" (Brigitte Lion, "La notion de genre en assyriologie," in *Problèmes du genre en Grèce ancienne*, ed. Violaine Sebillotte Cuchet and Nathalie Ernoult (Paris: Éditions de la Sorbonne, 2007), 59).

34 Gay Robins, *Women in Ancient Egypt* (London: British Museum Press, 1993), 99.

35 Fischer, *Egyptian Studies*, 1, *Varia*, 73. Whether this elite woman is the owner of the tomb (see "Conventions of Scenes," above) or a relative of a male tomb owner—for example, the female attendants of Tepemnefret, wife of Hirkhuf, or of the wife of Niankhka (Fischer, *Egyptian Studies*, 1, *Varia*, 73); or of the wife of Uhemka (Kayser, *Die Mastaba des Uhemka*, 39).

36 The ancient Middle East is the closest context, geographically and chronologically, for comparison to Old Kingdom Egypt. However, this homosociality within the ruling elite is special neither to the Middle East nor to antiquity.

37 "Dans les palais, les femmes de la famille royale vivent dans une relative ségrégation par rapport au monde des hommes; de ce fait, elles ont à leur service des servantes qui exercent des métiers qui ailleurs sont masculins, comme cuisinières ou jardinières" (Lion, "La notion de genre en assyriologie," 61).

38 Robins, *Women in Ancient Egypt* (1993a), 113.

39 Fischer, *Egyptian Studies*, 1, *Varia*, 71. However, men could supervise such female sectors of the palace administration; see, for example, Nimaatra, *imy-r ḥsywt pr-ꜥ3*, "overseer of the female singers of the palace." See also Selim Hassan, *Excavations at Gîza* 2: *1930–1931* (Cairo: Faculty of Arts of the Egyptian University, 1936), 211.

40 According to Ghalioungui, they could not have existed in the ancient Egyptian context. See Paul Ghalioungui, "Les plus anciennes femmes-médecins de l'Histoire," *BIFAO* 75 (1975): 163, although some evidence is known.

41 Fischer, *Egyptian Studies*, 1, *Varia*, 70 (title #10).

42 Fischer, *Egyptian Studies*, 1, *Varia*, 71 (title #21).

43 Fischer, *Egyptian Studies*, 1, *Varia*, 71 (titles #22 and #23).

44 For the debate on the reading of *imyt-r swnw*, "(female) overseer of male doctors," and *imy(t)-r swnwt*, "(female) overseer of (female) doctors," see Ghalioungh, "Les plus anciennes femmes-médecins de l'Histoire," 163–64.

45 Henry George Fischer, *Egyptian Women of the Old Kingdom and of the Heracleopolitan Period* (New York: Metropolitan Museum of Art, 2000), 20–21; Robins, *Women in Ancient Egypt* (1993a), 119.

46 Robins, *Women in Ancient Egypt* (1993a), 119.
47 Fischer, *Egyptian Studies*, 1, *Varia*, 73–74.
48 Dows Dunham and William Kelly Simpson, *The Mastaba of Queen Mersyankh III (G 7530–7540)*, Giza Mastabas 1 (Boston: MFA, 1974), fig. 3b.
49 Selim Hassan, *Excavations at Gîza 6 (3): 1934–1935. The Mastabas of the Sixth Season and Their Description* (Cairo: Service des Antiquités de l'Égypte, 1950), 53, fig. 39; 56, fig. 40.
50 Kanawati and Abdel Raziq, *The Unis Cemetery at Saqqara* 2, pl. 62.
51 Defined by Pascal Vernus as a "stratégie d'appogiature" in Vernus, "Comment l'élite se donne à voir," 95–101.
52 René van Walsem, *MastaBase: The Leiden Mastaba Project* (Leuven: Peeters, 2008).
53 Without taking into account rare scenes where the tomb owner is active, as we discussed before with the scenes in the marsh.
54 Fischer, *Egyptian Women of the Old Kingdom*, 41: "It is true that we may not have a complete picture of the decoration of the chapel, but it seems to be devoted to feminine preoccupations to an unusual degree."
55 This theme is depicted in thirty male tombs.
56 As well as other activities, such as offering the lotus, playing the *senet*, or in market scenes.
57 For a study of this gender bias toward jewelry in archaeology, see Ulrike Dubiel, "'Dude Looks Like a Lady': Der zurechtgemachte Mann," in *Sozialisationen: Individuum—Gruppe—Gesellschaft: Beiträge des ersten Münchner Arbeitskreises Junge Aegyptologie*, ed. Gregor Neunert, Kathrin Gabler, and Alexandra Verbovsek, MAJA 1 (Wiesbaden: Harrassowitz, 2012), 61–78.
58 Harpur, *Decoration in Egyptian Tombs of the Old Kingdom*, fig. 60.
59 Ann Macy Roth, "The Meaning of Menial Labor: 'Servant Statues' in Old Kingdom Serdabs," *JARCE* 39 (2002): 109–15.
60 Roth, "The Meaning of Menial Labor," 111–13.
61 A notion first highlighted in feminist studies by Kimberlé Crenshaw in "Demarginalizing the Intersection of Race and Sex: A Black Feminist Critique of Antidiscrimination Doctrine, Feminist Theory and Antiracist Politics," in *University of Chicago Legal Forum* (Chicago: University of Chicago Law School, 1989), 139–68. For some thoughts about using this concept in sociological studies, see Hae Yeon Choo and Myra Marx Ferree, "Practicing Intersectionality in Sociological Research: A Critical Analysis of Inclusions, Interactions, and Institutions in the Study of Inequalities," *Sociological Theory* 28, no. 2 (2010): 129–49.

12

The *ḫnrwt*: A Reassessment of Their Religious Roles

Izold Guegan

The *ḫnrwt* represent a religious group, mostly female, attested for three millennia. Its longevity, along with the diversity of its textual and iconographical representations, sheds new light on the female religious experience in ancient Egypt.[1] Women's role in religion has often been minimized because of the greater focus given to textual evidence and the observed rarity of feminine priestly titles in the New Kingdom. In addition, most of the iconographic data showing women in a religious context present them performing musical activities.[2] The clear association of women with music, notably through iconography, ends up constituting a pitfall for Egyptologists, who have tended to underestimate women's roles inside and outside the temple. Although the sacred nature of music is recognized, researchers easily forget that it is an essential vector in the relationship with the divine and not an end in itself.[3]

The *ḫnrwt*, Their Name, and Its Meaning

The word *ḫnr* is a title carried by a group mostly composed of female members. The spelling varies throughout Egyptian history, but is often written as 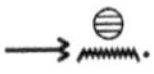. During the Old and Middle Kingdoms, examples show the use of both feminine and masculine determinatives.[4] Although the majority of New Kingdom examples do not include any determinatives, when there is one, it is the feminine one.[5]

The  (U31) Sign

One of the keys to understanding the meaning of the term *ḫnrwt* is based on its spelling, which can vary. The sign that raises the most questions is the determinant U31 , sometimes written with the two lateral branches extending in either direction. It is a logogram, used in particular for the word *rtḥ*, "bread,"[6] and in the Old Kingdom, it was also read *itḥ* when referring to the verb evoking the notion of restricting or imprisoning as well as its derivatives. From the Old Kingdom onward, sign U31 was also used for words whose radical is *ḫnr*, such as the word for "fortress." Furthermore, the horizontal line of sign U31 tends to split, probably under the influence of sign D19 , as pointed out by Ph. Collombert[7] and S. Quirke.[8] This influence manifests itself exclusively in hieratic writing. In the case of words formed on the root *ḫnr*, F. Relats-Montserrat has shown that sign D19 replaces sign U31 exclusively in hieratic Coffin Texts.[9] Conversely, the replacement of sign D19 by sign U31 occurs only once in hieroglyphs, in the chapel of Imeny-Yout in the sanctuary of Heqaib.[10] However, with the two signs having the same hieratic form, the distinction proves difficult. The use of sign D19 instead of sign U31 would therefore only be the fruit of a graphic confusion, which would find its origin in the transition from hieroglyphic to hieratic.[11]

Although sign U31 does not appear to transcribe the term *ḫnr* and its derivatives systematically, it nevertheless remains widely used, and several researchers have attempted to identify its reference in the real world.

B. Bryan recognizes two clappers used by rhythmists in the symbol, and suggests that the root *ḫnr* refers to the idea of keeping the rhythm.[12] This original meaning would therefore precede the derived terms appearing only from the Middle Kingdom onward, which would be associated with the concept of "prison."[13] However, it is surprising that sign U31 is never used to transcribe the terms *m3ḥt* or *ḥst*, which were used precisely to evoke rhythm and the associated click.[14] Roth proposes that we see in it the representation of the knife used to cut the umbilical cord, and conceives of the activities of the members of the *ḫnr* as being mainly related to childbirth and maternity.[15] She interprets the scene from the chapel of Waatetkhethor in Saqqara[16] in this sense.

In reality, sign U31 may not be the key to understanding the meaning of *ḫnr*. Nevertheless, it is still likely that all the terms derived from *ḫnr* have the same connotation. The identification of the term is often ambiguous according to its many graphic variations. Indeed, Bryan considers that the terms *ḫni* or *ḫnr* have the same meaning, the *i* and the *r* being interchangeable, bringing the terms *ḫni*/*ḫnwt* closer to *ḫnr*. It is, indeed, true that the term *ḫnwt*, translated as "musician," is often used in relation to activities in common with those of the *ḫnr* members.

The "Harem"

Before distinguishing the *ḫnr* as a group distinct from the royal "harem," it is necessary to define the reality of the latter. If the pharaonic harem is different in many respects from the Ottoman one—notably, by the fact that the women and children living there were not separated from public life[17]—there nevertheless existed a place dedicated to the women attached to the person of the king. The two terms that cover this pharaonic "harem," both as a building and as an institution, are *ỉpt nswt* and *pr-ḫnr*. According to Marine Yoyotte, this palace institution existed de facto in the Old Kingdom due to the practice of royal polygamy, and developed further during the New Kingdom due to the increase in diplomatic marriages.[18] The very nature of this institution is not always obvious, the term *ỉpt-nswt* not being used, for example, to designate the living quarters of the multiple wives of Montuhotep II.[19] In the New Kingdom, a new word appears to designate the royal harem: *pr-ḫnty*, sometimes written *pr-ḫnr*. M. Yoyotte understands the *pr-ḫnty* as designating the whole institution, while *ỉpt-nswt* was used to refer to the living quarters of its members.[20] The emergence of the title *wrt ḫnr* in the Eighteenth Dynasty, borne by women of the royal family, reinforces this fusion of terms.[21]

Some documents enable us to make the distinction between the harem and the religious group. The tomb of Ihy, dating from the Middle Kingdom,[22] is inscribed with the titles of its owner. Ihy was *ỉmy-r(ȝ) ỉpt-nswt*, "director of the harem," as well as *ỉmy-t-rʿ ḫnr.w(t) n nsw*, "director of the *ḫnr.wt* of the king." This is the first *ḫnr* association with the royal harem. It is important to note that the term *nswt* here is determined by the sign of the god . The sovereign is here designated as a deity. He was therefore surrounded by both a harem and a religious group dedicated to his worship.

The distinction between a purely royal *ḫnr*, evolving around the person of the king, and a purely religious *ḫnr* is very delicate. Indeed, the terms often have identical spellings and the nature of each group is ambiguous.[23] It would be problematic, however, to completely disconnect the two realities. Indeed, both the presence of members of the so-called religious *ḫnr* in the palace and the association of some of them with the *ỉpt-nswt*, as well as the progressive superposition of the two terms, prove the intrinsic ambiguity of what the word *ḫnr* covers. It is unlikely that the fusion of the two terms is the result of a simple confusion: rather, it is more probably due to a shift between two very close realities.[24] As the king was also considered a deity, it is legitimate that a group devoted to his worship existed in parallel with an earthly "harem."

The Origins of the *ḫnrwt*

The *pr-šnḏt*

The *pr-šnḏt*, or the "Acacia House," appeared during the Predynastic period as an institution mainly associated with funeral and mortuary rites, notably involving butchery activities. Many representations of the *pr-šndt* associate them with dance in mortuary and funerary contexts in connection to the *ḫnr*,[25] who are subsequently labeled as the "*ḫnrwt* of the *pr-šndt*." The members of the Acacia House probably also included royal women, as six queens were identified by Kinney as bearing the title *ḫprt sšmtyw šnḏt*, "supervisor of the butchers of the Acacia House."[26] The main outfit of the officiants common to the institutions of *pr-šndt* and *ḫnr* are the bands crossed on the torso. In the Egyptological literature, these bands are often labeled as "Libyan bands." Indeed, different representations of Libyan women, especially in the Temple of Sahure, represent them thus dressed.[27] However, during the Old Kingdom and the Middle Kingdom, the crossed bands were also part of the traditional clothing of hunters.[28] These bands are found throughout the period and, in particular, on the various female figurines who probably represented the *ḫnr*.[29]

The *ḫnrwt* and the Royal Family

What is striking regarding the early developments of the *ḫnr* is their equal involvement in royal and nonroyal contexts. At the same time, we can also observe the involvement of female members of the *ḫnr* close to the king, such as Neferesres, having important charges within the institution.[30] There were also powerful men in the service of the king connected to the *ḫnr* of Hathor through their female relatives, and who had members of the *ḫnr* group represented in their tombs, such as Mereruka or Tiye.[31] The worship of the king, both during his lifetime and after his death, is well attested, and the involvement of the *ḫnrwt* in this royal postmortem worship from the Old Kingdom onward is recorded in scenes from the Temple of Sahure.[32] The link between the *ḫnrwt* and the king also exists through the female cult of Hathor, which was closely related to the *ḫnrwt*. This was particularly important at the beginning of the Middle Kingdom under the reign of Mentuhotep II, who bolstered the Hathoric priesthood.[33] In the Eleventh Dynasty, another character makes the link between the king, the harem, and the *ḫnr*: namely Iha,[34] who bore the titles of *sṯꜣ ḫnrwt*, "ushering the *ḫnrwt*," and *imi-r(ꜣ) ipt-nswt*, "supervisor of the *ipt-nswt*." The rest of his titles indicate other charges, including *mꜣꜣ ḫstm ḫkrwt* and that he "saw dancing in sacred spaces" (*ḏsrw*). During the reign of Tutankhamun, Temwadjesi,[35] who was most probably married to the general Amenhotep, was responsible for the Faras *ḫnr* and bore, in particular, the title of *wrt ḫnr n pr nb ḫprw-rʿ* as well as *wrt ḫnr n pr n imn nb nsw*. The *ḫnr* is directly connected to a temple dedicated to other deities. It is therefore necessary to see these various documents as evidence that a part of the group was dedicated to the worship of the king, who, like any deity, was to receive daily worship.

The queen is the first royal person associated with the *ḫnrwt* group. Both Queen Meresankh III[36] and princess Waatetkhethor[37] have representations of the *ḫnrwt* in their respective tombs. Princesses and queens also retained a prominent influence vis-à-vis the Hathoric priesthood during the Middle Kingdom. This involvement is all the stronger in that we know of six queens who bore the title of *ḫprt sšmtyw šndt*, "directress of butchers of the Acacia House,"[38] which confirms the links between the *ḫnr* and the queen indirectly. In the New Kingdom, other royal women, such as Bentanat,[39] Uya,[40] and Tawosret,[41] bore priestly titles indicating responsibilities within the institution.

The *ḫnr* seems to have long been an integral part of private religious practices, designating the institution as the privileged intermediary between the temple, the palace, and the outside world.

Private people and royals had contact with deities through the rituals performed by the *ḫnr*. At the head of these deities, we find Hathor.

The Rites and Rituals of the *ḫnrwt*

It is possible to identify seven types of rites, each corresponding to a specific realm, for which certain rituals are identified. These seven realms are: the realm of the dead, the realm of the living, the sacrificial rites, the realm of the living king, the realm of the dead king, the realm of the deities, and the other forms of rites.

The Mythological Backdrop

It appears that each rite and ritual was performed with reference to at least one particular mythological event. These mythological references seem to have always revolved around Hathor. One of them is the union of the goddess with the sun god, echoing the creation through her union with the sun god, and evoking the appeasement of the goddess in the story of the "Destruction of Mankind." Certain scenes from the Old Kingdom clearly illustrate this celebration of the creation of the world. They were labeled the "mirror dance" by Hickman[42] and their choreography also normally entailed the use of clappers. According to Hickmann, the clappers are the representation of Hathor as "hand of the god." Kinney, relying on Hickmann's theory on the clappers, proposed that, if the dances were performed outdoors, the mirrors would have captured the sunlight and thus resembled miniature solar disks. The

Fig. 12.1. Mirror dance in the tomb of Mereruka

performance, therefore, would have been a reenactment of the moment of Creation by the solar god, helped by his hand, Hathor, in the form of the dancer holding the mirror embodying the goddess.[43] This officiant would, therefore, embody the goddess and, playing the role of Atum's hand, would have seen her clapper transformed into flesh.[44] Another form of the union of Hathor with the sun god would have been the emphasis placed on the genitals of the female officiants. Morris, who identified the *ḫnrwt* in the paddle doll figurines, believes the exposure of the pubis triangle on the figurines represents the culminant point of the ritual, during which the officiant removed her skirt to offer her genitals to the sun god in order to enable him to exercise his power again. Therefore, the dancer's pose, labeled "layout" by Kinney, would have represented the two-dimensional form of this ritual step.

According to the myth, the sun god Re decided to punish humanity for plotting against him, sending his daughter Hathor, as the violent Eye of Re, to destroy mankind. A rite called the "Festival of Drunkenness" recreated this myth in which religious officiants re-enacted what the humans did to appease the ferocious goddess—namely, get her drunk with red beer, imitating the color of blood.[45] Dance and music would have been fundamental to the realization of this festival since, according to the myth of the Eye of Re, the eye, personified by Hathor, had fled to Nubia, and Thoth had to persuade the goddess to return to Egypt, using music and dance in particular to carry this out.[46] The appeasement of the goddess would have been the backdrop for several different rites and rituals performed by the *ḫnr* in either royal or nonroyal contexts.[47] While some scenes placed more emphasis on the union of the goddess with the sun god, and others placed more on the need to appease her, the two references were often intertwined. For Horvath, the reason that the "Festival of Drunkenness" can be represented both for private individuals and for royal persons lies in the fact that it has a strong regenerative connotation because of the symbolic union between the deceased (or the living king) and the goddess.[48] According to Lesko, it was for private persons to participate in and personally benefit from the worship of the goddess Hathor, the most important goddess invoked during mortuary and funeral rites.[49] The association of the Hathoric festival with the funeral rite would have served to ask the goddess to ensure the survival of the *ka*.[50] The ritual would have involved song, music, and dance in order to welcome the funeral procession as it entered the necropolis on the west bank of the Nile, the domain of the Lady of the West, Hathor.[51]

The Realm of the Dead

Mortuary rites

These rites are among the earliest represented, since they appeared during the Fourth Dynasty and survived into the New Kingdom within the nonroyal sphere. They included the whole series of rituals performed at the beginning, end, and middle of the mortuary procession. The corpus indicates that the *ḫnrwt* were most often represented at the beginning[52] or at the end,[53] and rarely in the middle[54] of a rite.

Rites of maintenance

These were intended to maintain contact between the two dimensions, the tangible world and the sacred, non-perceivable one. For the *ḫnr*, only the rituals intended for deceased nonroyal individuals are documented. The offerings made it possible to feed the *ka* of the individual, and, therefore, to perpetuate his rebirth in the hereafter. The space and time devoted to these rites were characterized by joy. The offerings were part of the ritual stage of "reintegration," since the deceased had obtained new status.[55] The sacrifice was represented through the killing of cattle,[56] as well as by the curved sticks sometimes held by the officiants.[57] The rebirth of the deceased was achieved through their repeated union with Hathor, further symbolized by the motifs of gazelles and flowers. These scenes are particularly found in Old Kingdom tombs.[58]

Fig. 12.2. Rite of maintenance in the tomb of Mehu, Saqqara

The Realm of the Living

Rites of passage

This rite entailed bringing a living individual from one state to another during his lifetime by symbolically killing him so that he might be reborn. Within the framework of this study, the rites relating to circumcision, royal jubilees, and initiations of novices are documented.[59] The use of violence by means of weapons, such as knives, was, therefore, justified to allow the destruction of one state and the birth of another. This violence also corresponded to the chaotic forces of the universe, which the ritualistic agents controlled and directed toward the initiates. Several scenes, often labeled by scholars as "circumcision scenes," are most likely rites of passage, but the act that is perpetrated there is more uncertain.[60] These scenes include young boys, one of whom is kept on the ground, most often in a sort of hut, the members of the *ḫnr* being outside the hut.[61] Among the officiants, there is a character in a lion mask who is common to most of the rites of passage. He is actually seen in tombs until at least the New Kingdom, since we find a similar scene in the tomb of Kheruef in Thebes, in a composition representing the *sed* feast of Amenhotep III.[62] The lion mask would, therefore, belong with the equipment of a member of the *ḫnr*, used for private or royal rites. For Horvath, all of these scenes[63] are reminiscent of the Hathoric Festival of Drunkenness.

Fig. 12.3. Detail of the wall in the chapel of princess Waatetkhethor in Saqqara

Inside the chapel of Princess Waatetkhethor in Saqqara, an entire wall is dedicated to the *ḫnrwt*, showing the princess seated in front of them. This scene is the only long and detailed text regarding the *ḫnrwt* that dates to the Sixth Dynasty and is, paradoxically, the most difficult one to understand. The scene presents five registers of dancers and singers performing different dance steps and acrobatic moves in front of the deceased, who sits on a lion-footed seat. On the right, a column of text says *irrw n.s*, "what is done for her."[64] On all the registers, the dancers are dressed in short loincloths, are shirtless, and have long braided hair that ends in a ball. Unfortunately, the poor state of conservation of the wall prevents us from seeing the entire composition, which could originally have contained more registers than we currently see. Reading the signs is indeed made difficult at several places on the wall.[65] The inscriptions mention "the secret of the *ḫnrt*," *mk sštꜣ n ḫnrt*. Roth,[66] Kinney,[67] and many others[68] generally have concluded that it was a ritual to celebrate birth and rebirth. S. Grunert asserted instead that it was a funerary dance.[69] Although these interpretations may be accurate, we can suggest another. One word that might shed more light on the activity taking place is "*nfrt*." In the context of the *ḫnr*, the word appears often in the documentation and should be translated as "novice" rather than "beautiful."[70] Death and rebirth would only be one aspect of this combination of text and images.

Sacrificial Rites

The sacrificial rites correspond to all the rituals associated with animal and plant sacrifices.[71] They are part of the hunting,[72] fishing,[73] and harvesting activities,[74] and are of two types. First, there are those which seem to directly entail animal sacrifice as well as, in a secondary way, the sacrifice of plants. Second, we find the same sacrificial ritual, but overlapping with another ritual action. In the Middle Kingdom, for example, the rites of sacrifice were often included in scenes showing the procession of the statue of the deceased.[75] In general, we observe that the rites and rituals of the *ḫnr* are always performed near a butchery scene. In the Middle Kingdom, the sacrifice is more often illustrated by hunting. The erotic dimension of these rites is indicated by the proximity of the marshes, which provide an echo of Hathor.[76] The marsh is the place of creation, and thus of fertility and regeneration in the hereafter. The ritual character of these scenes may be confirmed by a hieratic text whose narration takes place at the time of Amenemhat II, and which describes the hunting and fishing parties of the king in the marshes in which the women and children of his entourage participate.[77] Hendrickx and his colleagues see, in this text, the evocation of a ritual feast.[78]

Realm of the Living King

Uncertain rituals

The *ḫnrwt* also served the living and dead king, which has led to confusion regarding the "harem." Indeed, some *ḫnrwt* were dedicated to the living king. Documents dating from the reign of Tutankhamun, found in Faras[79] and Kawa,[80] mention married ladies who were also *ḫnrwt* of the king. These documents were found in temples, indicating that we are dealing with a religious institution worshiping the living king.

During the jubilee

The jubilee of King Amenhotep III depicted in the tomb of Kheruef[81] shows a great variety of representations of *ḫnrwt* performing rituals and fulfilling different roles. We can note the diversity of their garments, many of them wearing the long wig, which had become common by the New Kingdom, and others the archaistic style, with the short hair and the crossed bands typical of the Old Kingdom. The inscriptions[82] give us the names of some territories (the oases) from which many of these *ḫnrwt* originated, as well as ethnic groups.[83] They indicate that the institution was indeed present in many different parts of Egypt's territories and could gather its members for certain events, such as the king's jubilee.

Many different funerary temples[84] of the Old Kingdom show representations of the *ḫnrwt*. There is no doubt that the officiants served the king within his sanctuary.

Realm of the Deities

The festivals included all the rites and their ritual sequences performed during the New Kingdom. Unfortunately, only the processions of the Opet festival[85] and the Beautiful Feast of the Valley[86] are documented for the *ḫnr*. What is shown are the rituals taking place at the start of the procession, and those that took place at its arrival. The nature and the function of the *ḫnr* fit the situation, since the role of the officiants was to first open and then close the sanctification of space and time to allow the visit of the divinity and his or her departure. The union of Hathor with Amun, similar to the union of Hathor with Re, is particularly explicit within the framework of the Beautiful Feast of the Valley.

Other Forms of Rites

Among the other forms of rites were those involving the types of female figurines that appeared at the end of the Old Kingdom and seem to have vanished during the Second Intermediate Period.[87] These figurines are the so-called paddle dolls and the truncated figurines. The two are often decorated with

Fig. 12.4. *ḫnrt* performing the "diamond" dance in the tomb of Tiye, Saqqara. The diamond pattern evokes the shape of the tattoos found on the priestesses of Hathor and the feminine figurines

various motifs, including checkered patterns and cowry belts, and with their pubic area emphasized. These two types were identified by Morris as being embodiments of the *ḫnrwt*.[88] According to Donnat, the explicit votive character of these figurines suggests that they not only represented officiants of the *ḫnr*, but also, perhaps, were evocations of the (grand-)daughters of the deceased.[89] Indeed, as that author rightly points out, the *ḫnr* officiants are often mingled with the children of the deceased in the tombs.[90] The sources remain silent, however, as to the technical modalities of the rites involving these objects.

Organization of the *ḫnrwt*

Hierarchy

Most of the titles seem to be attributed to the leaders of the group, and the differences between them are not always clear. In the upper ranks, we find:

- *sḥḏt ḫnr(wt)*: inspector of the *ḫnr(wt)*[91]
- *ỉmy(.t)-r ḫnrwt* (these two titles become "*wr.t ḫnrt/wrt ḫnrwt* (+ name of a deity)" in the New Kingdom): director of the *ḫnrwt*[92]
- *ỉmy-t-r ḫnr(wt) n nsw*: director of the *ḫnrwt* of the king[93]
- *ỉmy-r r ḫnr nswt mỉ-ḳd.f*: director of the entire *ḫnr* of the king[94]
- *sṯ3 ḫnrwt*: who ushers/ushering the *ḫnrwt*[95]

Ranks concerning the novices and their supervisors include:

- *ỉmy-r ḫnrwt nfrwt*:[96] director of the *ḫnrwt* (and) the *nfrwt*
- *sb3*: instructor. This title is related to the *ḫnr*, but specifically to novices.[97]

We also have titles referring to the sacred cattle of the group, especially in the Middle Kingdom:

- *ỉmy-r km(y)t ḫnrw(t)*:[98] overseer of the black cattle of the *ḫnrw(t)*

Gender

If we look at the range of rites and rituals performed by the *ḫnrwt*, we see that they can be of mixed gender. Men perform the same choreographies as women and accompany them in the orchestra or act as instructors. However, when present, men are always in smaller numbers than their female partners.

From the Sixth Dynasty onward, we see both genders performing rites together on the same register, which seems to reflect an equality of roles. It was also at this time that the orchestras became increasingly female and the men and women were less segregated.

During the Middle Kingdom, the relationship between men and women evolved. While the iconography presents rites performed by both genders, it also shows the first recorded bodily contacts between men and women.[99] The leaders of the group were mostly men. It would be tempting to compare this predominance of males in the Middle Kingdom with the announced decline of female priestly titles. However, we can see that in the New Kingdom, those performing the rites remained mixed in gender, and most of the titles related to the *ḫnr* were borne by women (over sixty of them recorded). Therefore, the situation is not comparable to that of the near disappearance of the female priestly title of *ḥmt-nṯr*. It is more reasonable to consider this state of affairs as a reflection of the changes in the priesthood and the political framework in the Middle Kingdom. The same theological and political developments led to the reorganization of feminine priesthood in the New Kingdom, with the great importance placed on the role of the God's Wife. The influence of the God's Wife is probably responsible for the supremacy of women over the *ḫnr*.

Ethnicity

There is very little reference to ethnicity or geography in the collected corpus. The discovered materials all come from the Nile Valley, with only a few from Nubia; few references to other geographical areas are to be found. Only the jubilee of Amenhotep III specifies that the *ḫnr* had gathered members from the oases.[100] There is evidence which may indicate that the *ḫnr* had some connection with Nubia, since some of its members are recorded in Faras and Kawa.[101] The appearance of diamond patterns on the feminine figurines[102] (the truncated and paddle dolls discussed above) and two-dimensional representations of the *ḫnrwt* evoke the tattoos[103] of the priestesses of Hathor who lived at the beginning of the Middle Kingdom. S. Ashby is one of the authors who considers that the priestesses buried in the Deir al-Bahari complex, and whose diamond-shaped tattoos made it possible to establish a connection with the female figurines, are of Nubian origin and not Egyptian.[104] There is no evidence that the officiants of the *ḫnr* portrayed in two- and three-dimensional iconography had Nubian features. However, it may be necessary to recall that Egypt was a multiethnic society.[105] Instead of talking about an influence of Nubia on the Egyptian *ḫnrwt* (or the reverse), we should keep in mind that Nubia played an important role in the mythological background of the rites they performed. In the myth of the Distant Goddess, for example, Hathor, after the Destruction of Mankind, fled to Nubia, from where she was brought back to Egypt by Thoth and Shu, playing music. We might, then, suggest that the iconography of the *ḫnr* expresses a particular idea of Nubia related to that myth.

Finally, in the tomb of Kheruef, the officiants are stated to originate from different territories and ethnic groups. The oases are mentioned, as well as various ethnic groups, such as the *s3t Mntiw*.[106] Darnell identifies the *s3t Mntiw* as belonging to the Libyo-Nubian tribe of *Mntiw*,[107] and they also appear in the Hathoric hymns of the Temple of Medamud.[108]

Deities

Although the *ḫnrwt* were primarily related to Hathor, they worshiped a wide range of deities throughout the period, among whom were Re, Osiris, Wadjet, Bat, Amenhotep I, Montu, and Bastet. Despite the rarity of the feminine priestly titles at the beginning of the New Kingdom, their own institution did not suffer any decline. After the beginning of the Eighteenth Dynasty, the two major deities they worshiped were Amun and Hathor. The two major religious feminine figures of the New Kingdom were indeed the God's Wife and the chief of the *ḫnrwt*, the *wrt ḫnr(w)t*.[109] Considering their power and influence, we cannot speak of a decline of the role of the Egyptian priestesses, but rather a kind of essentialization of the female religious role.

Disappearance of the *ḫnrwt*

The disappearance of the *ḫnrwt* remains unclear. They may have survived until late antiquity and might have been evoked in the Temple of Edfu as the priestesses "who shake the sistrum before the face of the deities"[110] and the "concubines of Amun" mentioned by Diodorus during the last century BCE.

Conclusion

The *ḫnr* is primarily a female religious group. Men gradually entered the group, but appear to have never been more numerous than the women.

If most of the members are anonymous and the iconography does not generally highlight individual peculiarities, it is because the *ḫnr* functioned as a united and coherent whole. The *ḫnr* is the generic name given to several different groups officiating in different places and contexts. They possessed sacred cattle, at least from the First Intermediate Period, and therefore had a local anchorage with a sanctuary that provided them with income.

In addition to being attached to the services of several deities and operating over a very large territory, ranging from Nubia to Lower Egypt and through the oases, the members of the *ḫnr* put themselves at the service of various people.

The troops of *ḫnr* were charged with carrying out various ritual activities for both the living and the dead, as well as for both private individuals and royalty.

Part of the *ḫnr* revolved around the king. Evidence of the worship of the king during his lifetime and after his death indicates that some members of the xnr devoted themselves to the ruler. Due to the proximity to the royal harem as well as through the priestesses of Hathor, who were closely linked to the *ḫnr*, it is possible that some *ḫnrw*(*t*) may have formed part of the royal harem.

The *ḫnr* was, from its appearance in the documentation of the Old Kingdom, a structured group with leaders, instructors, novices, and ordinary members. There is no document that indicates, however, how these different titles of authority were obtained. It also remains difficult to know the reasons for and the methods of entry of novices into the group. We can suppose that entry into the group had to take place at a young age, at least for the dancers, because of the flexibility that the dances and acrobatics required. It is possible that the terms of entry and development within the group evolved over time, especially in the New Kingdom, a period during which the *ḫnr* became feminized.

A study of the documentation from the Old to the New Kingdom identified at least six main rites to which were added various secondary rituals. To these six identifiable rites, we must add the rites of responding to requests made directly by individuals to a deity through objects in the image of members of *ḫnr*.

If the *ḫnr* had relationships with different deities, Hathor clearly appears to have been the most important deity for the group. The members of the *ḫnr* ensured the success of their rites and rituals through appeasement and union with the divinity. Its members acted as intermediaries between the divinity and the subject of the ritual, deceased or living.

The ritual action of the members of the *ḫnr* went beyond simple devotion to the divinity and the capacity to make him or her manifest. It was a question of manifesting the presence of the divinity through music and dance, activities which could potentially lead to a form of trance. Most of the *ḫnrw*(*t*) practiced singing and music, always in a very rhythmic way. Were the orchestras accompanying them composed of permanent members of the *ḫnr*, or independent groups occasionally joining *ḫnr* activities? Either way, they worked closely together. The orchestra needed to know the tunes to which the dancers performed their choreographies.

The members of the *ḫnr* were definitely kept apart from other members of society, and were distinct from the traditional clergy. Their relationship to the divine and their ritual skills made them special religious officiants. This singularity is reinforced by the space–time framework in which they officiated and which extended beyond temples, palaces, and private houses, in addition to the episodes punctuating life and death.

The *ḫnr* is obviously a term that refers to the idea of separation. Its meanings vary according to contexts and periods. However, there is nothing to convincingly suggest a definition for the term when it refers to officiants most often involved in activities combining dance and music. We have to go back to our first idea and translate *ḫnrwt* and *ḫnrw* as "those who are apart."

The accepted understanding of one who performs rituals, such as the *ḫnr*, may have been influenced by the imagery of the Ottoman harem and a vision perhaps too compartmentalized in Egyptian society. Here was a group responsible for various ritual activities, able to intervene in different contexts, both for deities and for the living and the dead. This polymorphic character makes the group elusive to anyone who wants to confine its definition to a single type of activity or sphere of competence.

The study of the *ḫnr* allows us to return to the place of women in the pharaonic world and, more broadly, to the perception of the feminine. While at first considered as inferior to men in religious practices, and specifically confined to the sphere of entertainment, the understanding of ancient Egyptian women has benefited from a radically different treatment from the 1980s onward. From then on, a will to rehabilitate women in history was perceptible in many scientific productions, freeing women from the harem and allowing them an active role independent of that of men. If the feminist wave has made it possible to highlight the fundamental role of women in the ancient Egyptian religion, it is now necessary to reassess the question of gender and the female in ancient Egypt from an emic point of view, far from the taboos of our contemporary societies.

Notes

1 This chapter is the result of a PhD thesis, supervised by Pierre Tallet and Kasia Szpakowska and defended in 2020. I thank Kasia Szpakowska for her critical review of this chapter and her valuable advice. I alone am responsible for any possible errors and shortcomings. My gratitude also goes to Jérôme Rizzo, who kindly agreed to take the photographs presented in this article and authorized me to publish them.

2 See, for instance, Lise Manniche, *Music and Musicians in Ancient Egypt* (London: British Museum, 1991); Lesley Kinney, *Dance, Dancers and the Performance Cohort in the Old Kingdom* (Oxford: Archaeopress, 2008).

3 Onstine rightly underlines this by citing the papyrus of Ani (3. 3–10), in which song, dance, and incense are presented as the food of the deities. See Suzanne Onstine, "Gender and the Religion of Ancient Egypt," *Religion Compass* 4, no. 2 (2010): 7.

4 See the inscriptions in the tomb of Hemetra, who was a member of the court and held the titles of *ẖkrt nswt wꜥt.t*, "director of *ḫnrwt*, song director," *ẖkrt nswt wꜥtt im* (*y*) *-t-r* (*ꜣ*) *ḫnrw* (*t*), and *imyt r*(*ꜣ*) *ḥst*. See Dilwyn Jones, *An Index of Ancient Egyptian Titles, Epithets and Phrases of the*

Old Kingdom (Oxford: Archaeopress, 2000), 303n1106; William Ward, *Essays on Feminine Titles of the Middle Kingdom and Related Subjects* (Beirut: American University of Beirut, 1986), 72; here the word is written ←. Another example is to be found in the chapel of Waatetkhehor. See Naguib Kanawati and Mahmud Abdel Raziq, *Mereruka and His Family* 2: *The Tomb of Waatetkhethor* (Sydney: ACE, 2008), 6–28, fig. 58. The spelling here is . See also the inscription in the tomb of Kheni in Ali el-Khouli and Naguib Kanawati, *Quseir el-Amarna: The Tombs of Pepyankh and Khewen-wekh* (Sydney: ACE, 1989), 1, fig. 37a. The inscription shows both female and male performers of the *ḫnr* with the spellings of their names, including both masculine and feminine determinants. See in particular the stelae of Meru in the Egyptian Museum in Turin, inv. C. 1447, in Lilian Postel, "Un homme de cour de Sésostris Ier: le préposé au diadème royal Emhat" (Louvre C 46 et Leyde AP 67), in *Ex Aegypto lux et sapientia: homenatge al professor Josep Padró Parcerisa*, ed. Núria Castellano et al. (Barcelona: Universitat de Barcelona, 2015), 489–99. This makes a distinction between the genders: *ḫnrw* and *ḫnrwt*. See also the stela of Emhat in Detlef Franke, "Middle Kingdom Hymns, and Other Sundry Religious Texts—An Inventory," in *Egypt—Temple of the Whole World: Studies in Honor of Jan Assmann*, ed. Sibylle Meyer (Leiden: E.J. Brill, 2003), 47n45.

5 For the spelling of the word during the Twenty-first Dynasty, see Saphinaz-Amal Naguib, *Le clergé féminin d'Amon thébain à la 21e dynastie*, OLA 38 (Leuven: Peeters, 1990), 194.

6 Vivienne Callender, *El-Hawawish: Tombs, Sarcophagi, Stelae. Palaeography* (Cairo: IFAO, 2019), 384–86.

7 Philippe Collombert, *Le tombeau de Mérérouka: paléographie* (Cairo: IFAO, 2010), 149n282.

8 Stephen Quirke, "State and Labour in the Middle Kingdom: A Reconsideration of the Term *ḫnrt*," *RdE* 39 (1988): 83–106.

9 Félix Relats Montserrat, "Le signe D19, à la recherche des sens d'un déterminatif (II): Les usages d'un signe," *NeHeT* 4 (2016): 77–121.

10 Félix Relats Montserrat, "Le signe D19, à la recherche des sens d'un déterminatif (I): La forme d'un signe," *NeHeT* 1 (2014): 129–67.

11 Relats-Montserrat, "Le signe D19, II," 93. Furthermore, the differences in spelling also seem to be linked to the geographical origin of the documents, at least during certain periods. Ilin-Tomich, for example, has shown that at the end of the Middle Kingdom, sign U31 was exclusively used in Upper Egypt, while sign D19 was exclusively used in Lower Egypt. See Alexander Illin-Tomich, "Theban Administration in the Late Middle Kingdom," *ZÄS* 142 (2015): 120–53.

12 Betsy Bryan, "The Etymology of *ḫnr* 'Group of Musical Performers,'" *BES* 4 (1982): 35–53.

13 According to Quirke ("State and Labour," 83–106), during the Middle Kingdom, the word *ḫnr* often conveyed the idea of restricting. Other scholars have translated the term as "prison." See Bernadette Menu, "Considérations sur le droit pénal au Moyen Empire égyptien dans le P. Brooklyn 35.1446 (texte principal du recto): Responsables et dépendants," *BIFAO* 81 (1981): 57–76. But Di Teodoro recently argued that no such enclosure could be identified with certainty. See Micòl Di Teodoro, *Labour Organisation in Middle Kingdom Egypt* (London: Golden House Publications, 2018), 65. The term *ḫnr*, in the Middle Kingdom only, would imply the notion of restricting people, specifically in the context of forced labor.

14 Also noted in Ann Macy Roth, "The *psš-kf* and the 'Opening of the Mouth' Ceremony: A Ritual of Birth and Rebirth," *JEA* 78 (1992): 140.

15 Roth, "The *psš-kf*," 140.

16 The chapel is located in Mereruka's tomb in Saqqara. See Kanawati and Abdel Raziq, *Mereruka and His Family* 2, 26–28, fig. 58.

17 Silke Roth, "Harem," in *UEE*, ed. Elizabeth Frood and Willeke Wendrich (Los Angeles: 2010), accessed November 19, 2020, https://escholarship.org/uc/item/1k3663r3.

18 Marine Yoyotte, "Le 'harem' dans l'Égypte ancienne," in *Reines d'Égypte: d'Hétephérès à Cléopâtre*, ed. Christiane Ziegler (Monaco and Paris: Grimaldi Forum, 2008), 76–90.

19 Vivienne Callender, "The Nature of the Egyptian 'Harim': Dynasties 1–20," *BACE* 5 (1994): 11–12.

20 Marine Yoyotte, "Le harem, les femmes de l'entourage royal et leurs lieux de résidence aux époques tardives: espace social ou espace clos?," *Topoi Orient-Occident* 20, no. 1 (2015): 27–28.
21 Michel Gitton, *Les divines épouses de la XVIIIe dynastie* (Paris: Les Belles Lettres, 1984), 97–110.
22 Ward, *Feminine Titles*, 74.
23 Nord, who first refuted the identification of the *ḫnr* with the harem, translates the title *wrt ḫnrwt* as "Chief of the Harem-women." See Del Nord, "The Term *ḫnr*: 'Harem' or 'Musical Performers'?," in *Ancient Egypt, the Aegean and the Sudan: Essays in Honor of Dows Dunham on the Occasion of His 90th Birthday, June 1, 1980*, ed. William Kelly Simpson and Whitney Davis (Boston: MFA, 1981), 140.
24 Gitton, *Les divines épouses*, 97–110.
25 See, for example, the tomb of Debeheni (Giza, LG 90, Central Field), the tomb of Ptahhotep (Saqqara, LS 31), and the tomb of Qar and Idu (Giza G 7101).
26 Lesley Kinney, "Butcher Queens of the Fourth and Fifth Dynasties: Their Association with the Acacia House and the Role of Butchers as Ritual Performers," in *Ancient Memphis: "Enduring Is the Perfection": Proceedings of the International Conference Held at Macquarie University, Sydney on August 14–15, 2008*, ed. Linda Evans (Leuven: Peeters, 2012), 253–66.
27 Andrejz Cwiek, "Relief Decoration in the Royal Funerary Complexes of the Old Kingdom" (PhD diss., Warsaw University, 2003), fig. 63, 200–201.
28 See, for instance, the hunters in Baket III's tomb at Beni Hasan. See P.E. Newberry and F.Ll. Griffith, *Beni Hasan*, vols. 1–4, ASE 1–2, 5, 7 (London: EEF, 1893–1900), 41–50, pl. IV.
29 See, for instance, the figurine Louvre E 10942.
30 Giza, CG, G 8900.
31 Saqqara, D-22.
32 Ludwig Borchhardt, *Das Grabdenkmal des Königs S3ḥu-Rʿ*, Ausgrabungen der Deutschen Orient-Gesellschaft in Abusir 1902–1908 (Osnabrück: Otto Zeller Verlag, 1982; first published 1913 by Hinrichs), 6–7 and pls. 22, 54.
33 Ellen Morris, "Paddle Dolls and Performance," *JARCE* 47 (2011): 71–103.
34 Tomb no. 8 in Bershah. See Newberry and Griffith, *Beni Hasan*, 189, pl. 21.
35 Miles Frederick Laming Macadam, *The Temples of Kawa* 1: *The Inscriptions* (Oxford: Oxford University Press, 1949), 3, pl. 4.
36 Dows Dunham and William Kelly Simpson, *The Mastaba of Queen Mersyankh III* (Boston: MFA, 1974).
37 Kanawati and Abdel Raziq, *Mereruka and His Family* 2, 2008.
38 Kinney, "Butcher Queens," 253–66.
39 *Wrt ḫnrwt n Ỉmn*. See Gitton, *Les divines épouses*, 107.
40 Labib Habachi, "La reine Touy, femme de Séthi I, et ses proches parents inconnus," *RdE* 21 (1969): 27–47.
41 *Wrt ḫnrwt n ḫnsw* (KRI III, 301: 15).
42 Hans Hickmann, "La danse aux miroirs: essai de reconstitution d'une danse pharaonique de l'Ancien empire," *BIE* 37, no. 1 (1954–55): 183.
43 Kinney, *Dance, Dancers and the Performance Cohort*, 166–67; Ellen Morris, "Sacred and Obscene Laughter in 'The Contendings of Horus and Seth,' in Egyptian Inversions of Everyday Life, and in the Context of Cultic Competition," in *Egyptian Stories: A British Egyptological Tribute to Alan B. Lloyd on the Occasion of His Retirement*, ed. Thomas Schneider and Kasia Szpakowska, AOAT 347 (Münster: Ugarit-Verlag, 2017), 309.
44 Morris, "Sacred and Obscene Laughter," 308–309.
45 Z. Horvath, "Hathor and Her Festivals at Lahun," in *The World of Middle Kingdom Egypt (2000–1550 BC)*, vol. 1, ed. Gianluca Miniaci (London: Golden House Publications, 2015), 125–44; Edward Wente, "Hathor at the Jubilee," in *Studies in Honor of John A. Wilson*, SAOC 35 (Chicago: University of Chicago Press, 1969), 83–91.
46 The myth of the "Return of the Eye of Re" is mainly known from sources of the New Kingdom and later, but attestations dating from the Old Kingdom (Pyramid Texts 705a) and the Middle

Kingdom (CT IV, 174 f–i; CT I, 378 c, 376; CT II, 5 a–b) associating Hathor with the eye and the daughter of Re already evoke the need to appease him; see Horvath, "Hathor and Her Festivals," 134. See also John Darnell, "Hathor Returns to Medamûd," *SAK* 22 (1995): 47–94, 129–38.

47 For Wente, these rites are of royal origin, but were quickly adopted by private individuals. See Wente, "Hathor at the Jubilee," 89. On the other hand, Altenmüller suggests that the private rites, and in particular the funerary ones calling upon the goddess, preceded the royal jubilees and later gave birth to the festival of the Beautiful Feast of the Valley. See Hartwig Altenmüller, "Zur Bedeutung der Harfnerlieder des Alten Reiches," *SAK* 6 (1978): 1–24. If the Festival of Drunkenness does indeed have a private origin, as Altenmüller claims, then the festivals of Amun in the New Kingdom are partly due to Hathor. All of these phenomena explain the implication of the *ḫnrwt* group in the worship of Amun during the New Kingdom. The mythological reference behind Amun would also have included Hathor, who once again had to unite with the god.

48 Horvath, "Hathor and Her Festivals," 139.

49 Barbara S. Lesko, *The Great Goddesses of Egypt* (Norman: University of Oklahoma Press, 1999), 92.

50 L'ubica Hudáková, *The Representations of Women in the Middle Kingdom Tombs of High Officials*, Harvard Egyptological Studies 6 (Leiden and Boston: Brill, 2019), 499.

51 Lesko, *The Great Goddesses*, 104.

52 See, for instance, the tomb of Djau, Sixth Dynasty, Deir al-Gebrawi, tomb no. 12, east wall.

53 See, for instance, the tomb of Isihemrê, Sixth Dynasty, Deir al-Gebrawi, tomb no. 72.

54 The tomb of Qar (Sixth Dynasty, north wall, room c) shows the members of the *pr-šnḏt* and probably also those of the *ḫnr*, although their name is not written, arriving and entering the House of Embalming (*wꜥbt*). It is interesting to note the reduplication of the determinative of Acacia, which could be an evocation of the double institution of *pr-šnḏt* and *ḫnr*. See William Kelly Simpson, *The Mastabas of Qar and Idu, G 7101 and 7102*, Giza Mastabas 2 (Boston: MFA, 1976), fig. 84A. See also the tomb of Qenamun, Eighteenth Dynasty, TT 93, showing *ḫnrwt*.

55 For the different ritual steps in general, see Victor Turner, *The Ritual Process: Structure and Anti-structure* (Chicago: Aldine Publishing Company, 1969), 94–113; within the Egyptian context, see, in particular, Christopher Eyre, "Funerals, Initiation and Rituals of Life in Pharaonic Egypt," in *Life, Death and Coming of Age in Antiquity: Individual Rites of Passage in the Ancient Near East and Adjacent Regions*, ed. Alice Mouton and Julie Patrier (Leiden: NINO, 2014), 287–309; Sylvie Donnat and Juan Carlos Moreno Garcia, "Intégration du mort dans la vie sociale égyptienne à la fin du troisième millénaire," in *Life, Death and Coming of Age in Antiquity: Individual Rites of Passage in the Ancient Near East and Adjacent Regions*, 179–87.

56 For this kind of rite in the Old Kingdom, these butchery scenes are almost always depicted either above or below the register showing the dancers of the *ḫnr*. See, for instance, the tomb of Ninutjer, Dynasty VI, Giza "GIS Cemetery."

57 Examples of these short and curved sticks were found in predynastic tombs. For a discussion on the use of these sticks in dance scenes, see Aurélie Roche, "Des scènes de danse dans l'iconographie prédynastique? Essai d'identification et d'interprétation à la lumière de la documentation pharaonique," *Archéo-Nil* 24 (2014): 176–77.

58 See, for instance, the tomb of Merefnebef, Fifth Dynasty, Saqqara, "West of Step Pyramid," and the tomb of Mehu, Sixth Dynasty, Saqqara, "Unis Cemetery." For the Middle Kingdom, see, for instance, the tomb of Ahanakht I, Eleventh Dynasty, al-Bersheh. For the New Kingdom, see, for instance, the tomb of Amenemhat, Eighteenth Dynasty, TT 82, and the tomb of Menkheperraseneb, Eighteenth Dynasty.

59 See the chapel of Waatetkhethor, as discussed below.

60 For circumcision outside royalty, see, in particular, Joachim Quack, *Menschenbilder und Körperkonzepte im Alten Israel, in Ägypten und im Alten Orient* (Tübingen: Mohr Siebeck, 2012), 589–91.

61 See the relief dating from the Fifth to the Sixth Dynasty, no. EA 994, now in the British Museum. See also Jean Capart, "Note sur un fragment de bas-relief au British Museum," *BIFAO* 30 (1931): 73–75; Edna Russmann, *Eternal Egypt: Masterworks of Ancient Art from the British*

Museum (Berkeley: University of California Press, 2001), 73–74, and the tomb of Idu, Sixth Dynasty, Giza "Eastern Field," G 7102, south wall.

62 Romano suggested that representations of this hybrid creature would not refer to an officiant wearing a mask, but perhaps rather to a statue of this deity, probably Aha; James Romano, "The Bes-image in Pharaonic Egypt" (PhD diss., New York University, 1989, pp. 12–13). However, Petrie discovered in Lahun what Horvath considers to be a female figurine with a leonid mask. In the same building, visibly a domestic habitat, Petrie also found a pair of wooden clappers and a cartonnage mask in the shape of a lion's head. He noted that the mask had traces of wear and repair marks, and it was perfectly adapted to a large human face; see Flinders Petrie, *Kahun, Gurob and Hawara* (London: K. Paul, Trench, Trübner, 1890), pl. 8. Horvath (in "Hathor and Her Festivals," 136) brings these discoveries closer to the two wooden statuettes in Sedment, one, found in a tomb of the Thirteenth Dynasty near the Ramesseum, representing a woman wearing a lion mask and holding a bronze snake in each hand, and the other, a male statuette in ivory, also wearing a lion-headed mask and originally holding metal snakes in his hands, dating from the end of the Middle Kingdom. The mastery of the snake by a magician or a protective genius symbolizes that person's ability to neutralize the reptile's venom and turn it against negative forces. See Robert Ritner, "'And Each Staff Transformed into a Snake': The Serpent Wand in Ancient Egypt," in *Through a Glass Darkly: Magic, Dreams and Prophecy in Ancient Egypt*, ed. Kasia Szpakowska (Swansea: Classical Press of Wales, 2006), 205–26. It has been suggested, with regard to the Lahun objects, that they were used in rituals linked to the local worship of Bes; see Kate Bosse-Griffiths, "A Beset-amulet from the Amarna Period," *JEA* 63 (1997): 98–106. But as Horvath points out, such a worship has never been demonstrated with regard to Lahun. In addition, the places of discovery of the figurine and the mask are near the funerary temple of Sesostris II, suggesting that they could have been used for the members performing rituals within the temple.

63 The other representations of the performer with the lion mask are to be found in the funerary temple of Sahure. See Borchardt, *Das Grabdenkmal des Königs S3ḥu-Rʿ*, pl. 54. The relief EA 994 in the British Museum: see above.

64 It should be *irrwt*.

65 See Kanawati and Abdel Raziq, *Mereruka and His Family* 2, fig. 58, and Stefan Grunert, "Danse macabre. Ein altägyptischer 'Totentanz' aus Saqqara," *SAK* 40 (2011): 113–36.

66 Roth, "The *psš-kf*," 141.

67 Kinney, *Dance, Dancers and the Performance Cohort*, 192.

68 Etienne Drioton, "A. Hermann, *Altägyptische Liebesdichtung* (compte-rendu)," *RdE* 13 (1961): 140; Kanawati and Abdel Raziq, *Mereruka and His Family* 2, 26–28, fig. 58; Walter Wreszinski, *Atlas zur altaegyptischen Kulturgeschichte*, 2 vols. (Geneva and Paris: Slatkine Reprints, 1988), 28.

69 Grunert, "Danse macabre," 113–36.

70 "*nfr(t)*" as "beautiful" or "novice" clearly has the same etymology, and evokes the idea of newness and freshness. The word "*nfrw*," which designated a freshly enrolled soldier, evokes the same idea. For the representations of the novices, see Morris, "Paddle Dolls," 95.

71 We also see a form of sacrifice in the butchery scenes of the other types of rites, such as the rite of maintenance.

72 See the tomb of Amenemhat, discussed above, and the tomb of Baket III in Beni Hasan, Eleventh Dynasty (see above).

73 See, for instance, the tomb of Kheni, Sixth Dynasty, al-Hawawish, tomb H 24, and the tomb of Kaaihep-Tjeti-Iqer, Sixth Dynasty, al-Hawawish, tomb M 8, north wall.

74 See the block (relief EA 994) in the British Museum, discussed above.

75 See, for instance, the tomb of Amenemhat, discussed above.

76 See, for instance, the tomb of Nefer and Kahai, Fifth Dynasty, Unas Pyramid Cemetery, west room, north wall; the tomb of Kheni, Fifth Dynasty, al-Hawawish M 24; and the tomb of Kaaihep-Tjeti-Iqer, Sixth Dynasty, al-Hawawish H26.

77 Luc Camino, *Literary Fragments in the Hieratic Script* (Oxford: Griffith Institute, 1956).

78 Stan Hendrickx et al., "Late Predynastic/Early Dynastic Rock Art Scenes of Barbary Sheep Hunting in Egypt's Western Desert: From Capturing Wild Animals to the Women of the 'Acacia House,'" in *Desert Animals in the Eastern Sahara: Status, Economic Significance, and Cultural Reflection in Antiquity. Proceedings of an Interdisciplinary ACACIA Workshop Held at the University of Cologne, December 14–15, 2007*, ed. Heiko Riemer et al. (Cologne: Heinrich-Barth-Institut, 2009), 216.

79 Urk. IV, 2075. The inscriptions read: *wr.t ḫnrt n nb-ḫprw-rʿ*, "Overseer of the *ḫnrt* of Nebkheperoura," and *wrt ḫnr/ḫnr(w)t (n) pr n nb-ḫprw-rʿ nb ḥry-ib sḥtpnṯrw*, "Overseer of the *ḫnr/ḫnr(w)t* of the domain of Nebkheperoura, in the middle of the Sehetepnetjerou."

80 MacAdam, *The Temples of Kawa*, pl. 4. The inscription reads: *wrt ḫnr (n) pr n nb-ḫprw-rʿ*, "Overseer of the *ḫnr* of the domain of Nebkhereroura," and *wrt ḫnr n pr imn nb ns.w* [. . .], "Overseer of the domain of Amun, lord of the thrones [. . .]."

81 Eighteenth Dynasty, TT 192.

82 Epigraphic Survey, *The Tomb of Kheruef: Theban Tomb 192*, OIP 102 (Chicago: Oriental Institute of the University of Chicago, 1980), pls. 34, 38, 40.

83 See below, "Ethnicity."

84 For the funerary temple of Sahure, Fifth Dynasty, Abusir, see Borchardt, *Das Grabdenkmal des Königs S3ḥu-Rʿ*, pl. 54; for the funerary temple of Niuserre, Fifth Dynasty, Abusir, see H. Kees, *Das Re-Heiligtum des Königs Ne-woser-re (Rathures)*, 3: *Die grosse Festdarstellung* (Leipzig: J.C. Hinrichs, 1928), 18–19, pls. V, IX; for the funerary temple of Pepy I, Sixth Dynasty, Saqqara, see Audran Labrousse, *Le temple funéraire du roi Pépy Ier: le temps de la construction*, 2 vols. (Cairo: IFAO, 2019), 40, 251.

85 See the reliefs from the Red Chapel in Pierre Lacau and Henri Chevrier, *Une chapelle d'Hatshepsout à Karnak* 1 (Cairo: Service des Antiquités de l'Égypte, 1977); Franck Burgos and François Larché, *La chapelle Rouge: le sanctuaire de barque d'Hatshepsout* (Paris: Soleb, 2006–2008); and illustrations nos. KIU 128; KIU 1284 on the CFEETK website (http://www.cfeetk.cnrs.fr).

86 See the reliefs from the Red Chapel in Burgos and Larché, *La chapelle Rouge*, and illustration no. KIU 1367 on the CFEETK website (http://www.cfeetk.cnrs.fr).

87 Geraldine Pinch, *Votive Offerings to Hathor* (Oxford: Griffith Institute, 1993); Morris, "Paddle Dolls," 71–103.

88 Morris, "Paddle Dolls," 71–103.

89 Sylvie Donnat and Johan Beha, "Du référent au signifié: réflexions autour de deux figurines (*paddle doll* et apode) de l'Institut d'Égyptologie de Strasbourg," in *Figurines féminines nues: Proche Orient, Egypte, Nubie, Méditerranée orientale, Asie centrale (VIIIe millénaire av. J.-C–IVe siécle av. J.-C.)*, ed. Sylvie Donnat, Régine Hunziker-Rodewald, and Isabell Weygand (Strasbourg: Collection Etudes d'archéologie et d'histoire ancienne, 2020), 66.

90 Sylvie Donnat Beauquier, *Écrire à ses morts. Enquête sur un usage rituel de l'écrit dans l'Égypte pharaonique* (Grenoble: Éditions Jérôme Million, 2014), 62.

91 Sixth Dynasty, tomb of Mehu, Saqqara, Unis Cemetery, intermediary room, east wall. This title should be compared with that of *sḥḏt ib3 (w)*; see Jones, *Index of Ancient Egyptian Titles*, 910n3338.

92 When used by women, it appears during the Fifth Dynasty with Lady Hemetra (see above). It is borne by men from the Sixth Dynasty, according to various graffiti found in the Wadi Hilâl, once with the word *ḫnri* written instead of *ḫnr(wt)*. See Hans Vandekerckhove and Renate Müller-Wollermann, *Die Felsinschriften des Wadi Hilâl: Elkab Series* (Brussels: Fondation Égyptologique Reine Élisabeth, 2001), N 147, 170, O 51, 215, O 154, O 221. For the New Kingdom feminine title of *wrt ḫnrt/wrt ḫnrwt*, see Abdel-Rahman El-Ayedi, *Index of Egyptian Administrative, Religious and Military Titles of the New Kingdom* (Ismailia: Obelisk Publications, 2006), 247–54.

93 Only one attestation is known for the Old Kingdom; it is born by Neferesres. See Selim Hassan, *Excavations at Giza 2, 1930–1931* (Cairo: Government Press, 1936), 205. The lady held other titles that placed her in the environment of the king, such as that of *(i)m(y)t-r (3) ib3. wt n nsw*. The title *imyt-r (3) ḫnrw(t) n nsw* testifies, perhaps, to the existence of a group specifically linked to the service of the king.

94 Dating from the Middle Kingdom (tomb of Ihy, TT 186; see Ward, *Feminine Titles*, 74) and held by Ihy, who is also *imy-r(ꜣ) ipt-nswt*, "director of the harem."

95 This new official title appears early in the Middle Kingdom. Only one occurrence is listed, in the tomb of Iha, Eleventh Dynasty, al-Bershah tomb no. 8. See Ward, *Feminine Titles*, 74.

96 The title is held by Khesu-wr. See David Silverman, *The Tomb Chamber of ḫsw the Elder: The Inscribed Material at Kom El-Hisn 1: Illustrations* (Winona Lake, IN: Eisenbrauns, 1988). Khesu-wr is also shown in his capacity of instructing young female performers. See Campbell Cowan Edgar, "Recent Discoveries at Kom el Hisn," in *Le Musée Égyptien: Recueil de monuments et de notices sur les fouilles d'Égypte*, ed. M.G. Maspero, vol. 3 (Cairo: IFAO, 1890–1915), 54.

97 On the tomb of Nebkauhor, see Selim Hassan, *The Mastaba of Neb-Kaw-Her: Excavations at Saqqara 1937–1938*, 1 (Cairo: U.S. Government Printing Office, 1975), figs. 2–3. Khesu-wr (see above), in the Middle Kingdom, also held this title.

98 The title appears during the Tenth Dynasty on the stela of Sipet. See Dows Dunham, *Naga-ed-Dêr Stelae of the First Intermediate Period* (London and Boston: Oxford University Press for the MFA, 1937), 24–25, pl. VII.1. It is found again during the Middle Kingdom on the stela of Antef. See Donald B. Spanel, "Palaeographic and Epigraphic Distinctions between Texts of the So-called First Intermediate Period and the Early Twelfth Dynasty," in *Studies in Honor of William Kelly Simpson* 2, ed. Peter Der Manuelian (Boston: MFA, 1996), 783, and on the stela of Sankhy and Ankhu. See *Echoes of Eternity: The Egyptian Mummy and the Afterlife*, exhibition, The Nelson-Atkins Museum of Art, Kansas City, MO, June 4, 1999–May 7, 2000. It testifies to the existence of herds, making it possible to maintain the *ḫnr* financially, at least in part. If the *ḫnr* already had sanctuaries, estates, and herds before, the appearance of the title made manifest the administrative organization that presided over the maintenance of these goods.

99 Tomb of Baket III, Eleventh Dynasty, Beni Hasan. See Newberry and Griffith, *Beni Hasan*, 41–50, pl. IV.

100 See the tomb of Kheruef, above.

101 Macadam, *The Temples of Kawa* 1, pl. 4.

102 Nubia also produced feminine figurines with similar patterns. See Solange Ashby, "Dancing for Hathor: Nubian Women in Egyptian Cultic Life," *Dotawo: A Journal of Nubian Studies* 5 (2018): 72.

103 For the tattooing practice in Egypt and Nubia, see Anne Austin and Cédric Gobeil, "Embodying the Divine: A Tattooed Female Mummy from Deir el-Medina," *BIFAO* 116 (2016): 23–46; Robert Steven Bianchi, "Tattoo in Ancient Egypt," in *Marks of Civilization: Artistic Transformations of the Human Body*, ed. Arnold Rubin (Los Angeles: Museum of Cultural History, University of California, 1998), 21–28; Geoffrey Tassie, "Identifying the Practice of Tattooing in Ancient Egypt and Nubia," *Papers from the Institute of Archaeology* 14 (2003): 85–101.

104 Ashby, "Dancing for Hathor," 72.

105 Doris Pemler, "Nubian Women in New Kingdom Tomb and Temple Scenes and the Case of TT 40 (Amenemhet Huy)," *Dotawo: A Journal of Nubian Studies* (2018): 26.

106 Collectively called *msw-wrw* in the scene.

107 Darnell, "Hathor Returns to Medamûd," 72.

108 Horvath, "Hathor and Her Festivals," 140.

109 Meike Becker, "Female Influence, Aside from That of the God's Wives of Amun, during the Third Intermediate Period," in *Prayer and Power: Proceedings of the Conference on the God's Wives of Amun in Egypt during the First Millennium BC*, ed. Meike Becker et al. (Münster: Ugarit-Verlag, 2016), 21–47.

110 Frédéric Collin, "Les prêtresses indigènes dans l'Égypte hellénistique et romaine: une question à la croisée des sources grecques et égyptiennes," in *Actes du Colloque International "Le rôle et le statut de la femme en Egypte hellénistique, romaine et byzantine,"* 27–29 novembre 1997, Studia Hellenistica 37, ed. Henri Melaerts and Leon Mooren (Leuven: Peeters, 2002), 41–122.

13

Family Contracts in New Kingdom Egypt

Reinert Skumsnes

Throughout ancient Egyptian history, from the Old Kingdom to the Ptolemaic Period, the succession from father to eldest son seems to have prevailed as a normative practice. Paternal and maternal properties were kept separate, and the eldest son inherited and maintained the main share of the paternal household.[1] Yet we also see that the picture painted of nonliterary ostraca and papyri of the New Kingdom is fragmentary, and that actual practice did not always coincide with normative practice. In fact, Jaana Toivari-Viitala claims that pragmatic considerations usually took precedence over ideological ones (such as ideal sex/gender roles),[2] and according to Brian Muhs, there existed two different legal practices in New Kingdom Egypt. One practice was normative, which largely favored men, the father–son relationship, and biological kin. Yet there also existed a second, non-normative practice that was more egalitarian.[3]

Another reason to suggest a division between normative and non-normative practice is the evidence from a demotic legal code from Hermopolis. Although dated to the Late Period,[4] this legal code states that the eldest son succeeded his father as head of the undivided household if the father had not written or ascribed specific shares to the different children when he was still alive. This normative baseline is modified on three points: 1. If a younger brother claimed his individual right in court, the household should be divided into equal shares. The eldest son would then get two shares; 2. He who acted as eldest brother should be rewarded for it; 3. An eldest daughter could act in the place of an eldest son.[5]

In this contribution, I will try to broaden this understanding to include considerations of family and gender in New Kingdom Egypt from the perspective of what I call *family contracts*, which worked as a kind of welfare system—a fixed point that structured relations between men and women, young and old.

Family Contracts as an Inalienable Possession

In the New Kingdom, the married couple not only formed a link in a wider network of exchange within the village, but also formed an economic unit with internal distinct matrimonial property rights.[6] The available documents focus on "the matched and balanced investment—the recognised individual share—in the joint matrimonial property."[7] For example, the family property is suggested to have comprised different shares: the private property of the husband (goods inherited from his parents), the private property of his wife (goods inherited from her parents), and their joint property (goods acquired by both of them together). Regarding the latter, if death or divorce occurred, it seems that two-thirds would go to the husband (or his heirs) and one-third would go to the wife (or her heirs).[8] More recently, O. DeM 764 suggests that the joint property was actually the property of the whole family: one-third belonged to the father, one-third belonged to the mother, and one-third belonged to the children. The father could safeguard the children's share until they were old enough, making his share only temporarily two-thirds of the total.[9] But Christopher Eyre notes that "the key social unit was not the individual but a larger family grouping, whose head needed to marshal the resources of an essentially communal property to promote the socially necessary family solidarity, to make social alliances, especially through marriages, and to ensure provision for individual family members."[10] In fact, the

> Egyptian custom involved so full a commitment of resources to the line of inheritance, that the concept of the will and testament, central to Anglo-American legal traditions, is inappropriate; a man's ability freely to bequeath his property was so limited by custom that the concept of the will is largely irrelevant. The process associated with the *imyt-pr* is more like that of a formal endowment, made at a time when, for whatever reason, the head of the household needed to define specific shares due to individual members. In that sense an *imyt-pr* can be particularly valuable to a woman; not simply a marriage contract, nor a property settlement, nor a will, but a mixture of all three. It clarified her rights to property in the joint enterprise of a marriage.[11]

Janet Johnson suggests that, in contrast to sons, who had to wait until their parents' death, "daughters received their share of the family wealth at the time of their marriage" as some sort of dowry. She explains that "women may have been more independent and judged capable of making major decisions affecting themselves, their property, and their families; men were not."[12] Yet Johnson also notes that "real property was not really divided, but, rather, each of the children received a share in the undivided real property. It is assumed that this was done to maintain property intact and to avoid the division and subdivision of land (or buildings) which would lead to ownership of plots of land too small to work productively."[13]

This is where "family contracts" come in. The idea behind this term is inspired by philosophical theories of a social or political contract that describes the relationship among individuals, groups, and the larger society, but also anthropological theories of generational contracts within the family. Rosalind Janssen introduced the term "generational contract" to Egyptology back in 2006, arguing that "there was a clear system of reciprocity, or . . . 'generational contract': parents were expected to provide for their sons and daughters. Adult children, in their turn, had the filial duty to care and provide for elderly parents."[14] I have, however, chosen "family contract" because I find this term more befitting the Egyptian context. The system of reciprocity worked not only between generations, but also within generations, between spouses and members of the larger household. For this discussion, it seems important to distinguish between the biological eldest son, and those who actually acted *as* the eldest son: The one who acted as eldest son, be it a younger son, daughter, or someone else, could be made heir in the place of the biological eldest son. Family contracts were not only about blood, or being next of kin, but were also something that could be actively sought and constructed.[15] This is important because to be part of family contracts can be argued an *inalienable possession*, proving "one's difference, making all other exchanges resonate this difference."[16] It is my claim that family contracts based on reciprocal bonds of mutual support had significant ramifications for women's ability to network, but also to inherit, acquire, own, and dispose of property. At issue is Jac Janssens's argument that things were written down for a reason. They were socially obligatory,[17] and only balanced in the long run, or never fully paid off—the point being that "the maintenance of good relations was more important than any short-term gain."[18] As such, to be a testator or an heir was surely a source of power for women, as for men, and is likely to have impacted their position both within and beyond the household. This can be exemplified by records referring specifically to the relation between providing a burial and receiving an inheritance, on the one hand, and support in old age and receiving an inheritance, on the other.

S/he Who Buries Shall Inherit

Death was considered a transitional phase (rather than the end of existence) dependent on the contribution of the living. As such, the reciprocal bonds to one's family did not end with someone's death, but rather continued through burial and commemorative practice (or the lack thereof) on the one side, and intervention by the dead in the life of the living on the other.

The Oxford bowl (= PRM, No. 1887.27.1) is of unknown provenance and dated to the late Seventeenth or early Eighteenth Dynasty. It is a complete pottery bowl with text, with a resemblance to letters to the dead, carrying a simple statement by Tetiaa, son of Neny.

(1) *ḏd ỉn tti-ꜥꜣ sꜣ nny*	Said by Tetiaa, son of Neny:
mnỉw-pw ỉw wꜥr sꜥnḫ sw	Meniupu came (as a) fugitive, and he was nourished by
ỉt [mwt . . .] ḥmt.f (2) tti	the father [of my mother(?). . .] and his wife Teti.
mt.f ḳrs sw tꜣy.i mwt in	When he died, my mother buried him, because
h(ꜣ)y.s nny ḏd n.s ḳrs sw	her husband Neny had said to her, **"bury him**
(3) *ỉwꜥ sw*	**and inherit him."**[19]

The relationship between Meniupu, Tetiaa, and the latter's family is unclear. It is possible that Meniupu had become part of the family as adopted brother or brother-in-law of Tetiaa or Neny. There is little doubt that the importance of the text lies in the last sentence: "bury him and inherit him" (*ḳrs sw ỉwꜥ sw*). Battiscombe Gunn holds that "if Meniupu has to live and die at other people's expense there can hardly be anything to inherit from him."[20] Yet the existence of this text implies otherwise. Although it is true that Meniupu had come as a fugitive, probably carrying few or no possessions with him, it seems fair to argue that his situation must have changed for the better. After all, the bowl stands as a reminder, to ensure the good will of the deceased and substantiate the claim of a promised inheritance.

P.Cairo CG 58092 = P.Bulaq 10 probably originates from Deir al-Medina and is dated to the Twentieth Dynasty. It is a legal document that records a dispute over inheritance that had occurred after the death of the *ꜥnḫt nt niwt*

Tagemyt. The case is brought before the juridical oracle, and a son is claimed to have acted as eldest son to his mother, providing her with a proper burial in exchange for inheritance. Conflict seems to have risen after the passing of the one who had acted as eldest son. It is the grandson of Tagemyt who approaches the oracle (the deified Amenhotep I) for help. He points out why his father had inherited the property in the first place, and as such why he (as his son) was the legitimate heir to the property.

. . . *ḫr i͗.di͗.tw ꜣḫwt* (rt. 11) *n ḳrs*	Look, **you shall give the property to (him who) buries,**
ḫr (i͗w?) pꜣ hp n pr-ꜥꜣ ꜥnḫ wḏꜣ snb	so is the law of Pharaoh, LPH,
pꜣy.i͗ nb nfr ꜥnḫ wḏꜣ snb (12) *ptr*	my good lord, LPH! Look,
tw.i͗ m-bꜣḥ nꜣ srw i͗mi͗	I am in the presence of the officials to cause them
i͗rwy.w pꜣ nfrw (13) *ḫr ptri͗*	to do what is right. Now look,
di͗.tw tꜣ st n tꜣy-nḥsy n sꜣ-wꜣḏyt	one gave the place of Taynehesy to Sawadjyt
m-di͗ ḳrs.st (14) *i͗w.f di͗t n.st*	because of her burial, when he gave to her
pꜣy.f wt i͗(w.tw) di͗t n.f tꜣy.st pš	his coffin. One gave to him her share
m-bꜣḥ nꜣ srw (15) *ḫr i͗w m nswt*	in the presence of the officials. Look, it was the king
i͗mn-ḥtpw ꜥnḫ wḏꜣ snb r-di͗t st	Amenhotep, LPH, who gave it
n.f m tꜣ ḳnbt	to him in the court.[21]

The verso side of the document holds the deposition of Hay, the grandson of Tagemyt. We learn that the property was in the form of buildings and burial grounds, that it had been handed down over generations from Tagemyt, via Huy and Hay, and now Hay's children. The verso side (like the recto) stresses that the property came to belong to this line of the family because Huy had acted as the eldest son for Tagemyt and Huynefer.

This document is interesting not only because it refers to the law of Pharaoh (*pꜣ hp n pr-ꜥꜣ*), saying that you shall give the property to him who buries, but also because it refers to juridical precedent. In fact, an important part of the argument in P.Cairo CG 58092 is related to the outcome of an earlier oracular consultation, oUC 39617 = oPetrie 16. The connection between these two documents is important not only because it implies that archives were available for consultation, but also because these archives actually include cases where women are said to give or receive a burial, and therefore receive or give an inheritance.

S/he Who Supports in Old Age Shall Inherit

Children were expected to provide an extra set of hands around the house but could also help their parents to perform their tasks in the village and society at large. It seems that the various factions of a family were expected to support each other on a regular basis and, perhaps more importantly, they were security in case of acute situations, such as sickness and old age.

P.Ashmolean Museum 1945.96 = P.Adoption originates from Spermeru (Middle Egypt) and is dated to the late Twentieth Dynasty (Ramesses VII–Ramesses XI). It is a legal document that consists of two parts, both framed by different dates and lists of witnesses, but written by one scribe at one sitting.[22] In the first part, the *šmꜥyt nt stš* Naunefer (occasionally called Rennefer) seems to reproduce key parts of the original deposition of her late husband, the "stable-master" Nebnefer.[23]

(rt. 3) . . .	. . . (Then)
ꜥḥꜥ.n iryw nb-nfr pꜣy.i hꜣy	my husband, Nebnefer, came forth and
sšw n.i šmꜥ(yt) (4) *n(t) stš*	made a writing for me, the chantress of Seth,
nꜣw-nfr iw.f irt n.f n šri(t)	Naunefer. He made (me) a daughter of his, and
iw.f sšw n.i n pꜣ sꜣwt nb iw	wrote down for me all of the property, because
bn n.f šri (5) *šri(t) r-ḥr-r ink*	there was no son or daughter of him apart from me.
m	Namely (he said):
mꜥḏꜣ nb i.irw.i irm.st	"All profit that I have made together with her,
iw.i swꜣḏ.w (6) *nꜣw-nfr tꜣy.i ḥmt*	I bequeath it (to) Naunefer, my wife.
m nꜣy snw r ink ꜥḥꜥ	If (any of) these siblings of mine come forth and
rḳw n.st m pꜣy.i mt n dwꜣ(yt)	confront her after my death of tomorrow or
(7) *r-s(ꜣ) dwꜣ(yt) mtw.f ḏd*	after tomorrow, he shall say:
imi.tw.(i) dni(t) n pꜣy.i sn	'I shall give up this portion of my brother!'"
m-bꜣḥ mtryw ḳnw (8) *ꜥšꜣt* . . .	Before many and numerous witnesses: . . .

Nebnefer and Naunefer had no biological children of their own. In the second part, we learn how they had bought a servant woman, who later gave birth to three children, and that Naunefer had brought them up as if they were her own.

. . . *hrw* (15) *pn ḏdt n*	(On) this day, statement of the
ḥry-iḥ nb-nfr ḥnꜥ ḥmt.f	stable master Nebnefer and his wife,
šmꜥy(t) n(t) stš sprw-mry rn-nfr	the chantress of Seth of Spermeru, <Naunefer>,
(16) *r-nty*	quote:
in.nn ḥm(t) diw-n.i-ḥwt-tiry	"We bought the servant girl Diunihutiry
r swnw iw.st ms pꜣy (17) *3 ḫrdw*	for a price, and she gave birth to 3 children,
wꜥ ꜥḥꜣ st-ḥmwt 2 dmḏwt 3 iw.i	1 boy and 2 girls, total 3. **I**
iṯꜣy.w iw.i (18) *sꜥnḫ.w iw.i dit*	**took them, nourished them, and caused that**
iry.w pꜣ ꜥꜣ.w iw.i pḥ pꜣ hrw irm.w	**they grow up. I have reached this day with them.**
iw.w (19) *tmt irt bin ḥr.i*	**They have not caused (any) evil toward me, (but**
iw.w irt n.i nfr iw mn	**rather) they were good to me.** There is no (other)
šri šri(t) (20) *inn mntw*	brother or sister, except them."

Naunefer not only made the three children "free people of the land of Pharaoh," but also accepted the union between her own brother and the eldest of the three children. She made the four of them sole heirs to her property because they had been good to her.

iw ḥry-iḥ pn-diw ꜥḳw r pꜣy.i pr	The stable-master Pendiu entered into my house,
iw.f irt tꜣ-imn-niwt (21) *tꜣy.w*	and he made Taamenniut, their
sn(t) ꜥꜣ(t) m ḥmt iw ink sw iw	elder sister, as wife. He is (one of) mine,
pꜣy.i sn šriw iw.i šsptw.f	my younger brother, (and therefore) I accepted him
(22) *n.st sw m-di.st m pꜣ hrw*	for her, and he is with her at this day.
ḫr ptri iry.(i) st m rmṯ-nmḥy(t)	Now see, I have made her into a freewoman

n (23) *pꜣ tꜣ n pr-ꜥꜣ ꜥnḫ wḏꜣ snb*	of the land of Pharaoh, LPH, and
inn iw.st ms bn šri bn šri(t)	if she gives birth to either son or daughter,
iw.w m (24) *rmṯ-nmḥyw(t) n pꜣ tꜣ*	they shall be free people of the land
n pr-ꜥꜣ ꜥnḫ wḏꜣ snb (r)-mitt-ꜥḳꜣ	of Pharaoh, LPH, in exactly the same manner,
sp-sn iw.w irm ḥry-iḥ	repeatedly. They are together with the stable-master
pn-diw (25) *pꜣy sn šri ink iw nꜣ*	Pendiu, this younger brother of mine. The
šriw irm tꜣy.w sn(t) ꜥꜣt m pꜣ	children shall be with their elder sister in the
(26) *pr n pꜣ-diw pꜣy ḥry-iḥ pꜣy*	house of <Pendiu>, this stable-master, this
sn šri ink tw.i i.iri.f	younger brother of mine. I shall make him
n.i (vs. 1) *m šriw m pꜣ hrw*	into a son of me, on this day,
mi-ḳd.w ꜥḳꜣ sp-sn	just like them, exactly, repeatedly.
ḏd.st wꜣḥ imn wꜣḥ pꜣ (2) *ḥḳꜣ*	She said: "As Amen endures, as the ruler,
ꜥnḫ wḏꜣ snb tw.i irt nꜣ rmṯ [. . .]	LPH, endures, I make the people [. . .],
i.irw.i spḫr.w m rmṯ-nmḥyw	I make them recorded as free people
(3) *n pꜣ tꜣ n pr-ꜥꜣ ꜥnḫ wḏꜣ snb*	of the land of Pharaoh, LPH.
mtw šri šri(t) sn sn(t) n tꜣy.w	If any son, daughter, brother, or sister of their
mwt (4) *pꜣy.w it mdwt im.w wpw*	mother or their father shall quarrel with them—except
pn-diw pꜣ(y) šriw ink iw (5) *bn st*	Pendiu, this son of mine—they are not
m-di.f m bꜣkw m-r-ꜥ iwnꜣ iw.w	with him as servants, in any way at all. They
m-di.f m snw šriw (6) *iw.w m*	are with him as siblings and children. They are
rmṯ-nmḥyw n pꜣ tꜣ (n pr-ꜥꜣ	free people of the land <of Pharaoh,
ꜥnḫ wḏꜣ snb) nk sw ꜥꜣwt	LPH>, may the donkey copulate with him,
nk ꜥꜣwt ḥmt.f	may the donkey copulate with his wife,

p3 nty ỉw.f (7) *ḏd b3kw r wʿ ỉm.w*	whoever it be who speaks to any one of them as servants.
ỉnn wnw m-dỉw.ỉ 3ḥwt m sḫt	If I have at my disposal property consisting of fields,
ỉnn (8) *wnw m-dỉw.ỉ ḫt nb n p3 t3*	if I have at my disposal anything of this land,
ỉnn wnw m-dỉw.ỉ šwtyw	or if I have at my disposal (any) merchandise(?),
ỉw.w pš.w n (9) *p3y.ỉ 4 ẖrdw*	<it> shall be assigned to my 4 children,
ỉw p3-dỉw m wʿ ỉm.w	<Pendiu> being one of them.
ỉr n3 mdwt ỉ.ḏd.ỉ	As for these matters (of which) I have spoken,
(10) *r-ḏr.w sp-sn st sw3ḏ n p3-dỉw*	they are entirely, repeatedly, entrusted to <Pendiu>,
p3y šrỉ ỉnk ỉrt n.ỉ nfr	this younger (brother) of mine, **who was good to me,**
(11) *ỉw.ỉ m ḫ3rt ỉw p3y.ỉ h3y mtw*	**when I became a widow (after) my husband died**."
m-b3ḥ mtrtyw ḳnw (12) *ʿš3 . . .*	Before many and numerous witnesses: . . .[24]

The most striking feature of this document is what Koenraad Donker van Heel has called a trade-off,[25] or what I argue to be part of family contracts: Naunefer stresses that the children of the servant-woman, as well as Pendiu, had been good to her (*ỉrt n.ỉ nfr*), and she in return rewarded their goodness by adopting all four of them. She made them "free people of the land of Pharaoh" and rightful heirs to her property, which consisted of fields, land, and merchandise(?). Thus, this document not only illustrates that women could dispose of their own as well as family property, but, perhaps more importantly, that social mobility was possible through adoption and marriage. We see adoption and consanguineous marriages (in name, but not necessarily in blood) as a repeated strategy for barren couples. It was a strategy that made sure that property was kept in the hands of certain chosen individuals within the family: David agrees with Eyre that the purpose of this document was "to organize the succession of the testatrix,"[26] but Eyre importantly continues that "the very existence of the document probably implies that the arrangement falls outside the self-evident line of succession."[27] In this specific case, the most obvious irregularity is the lack of biological children. Children were probably what cemented a marriage union and, in effect, put the legal rules of property between spouses in motion.[28] This document was not only intended as security in her old age, but, more than anything, to safeguard her children and chosen heirs.

P.Turin 2021 + P.Geneva D 409 possibly originates from Medinet Habu (Thebes) and is dated to the late Twentieth Dynasty (Ramesses VII– Ramesses XI). It is fragmented and incomplete, but carries clear characteristics of a legal document. The content of the document seems clear enough. The "god's father," Amenkhau, has approached the court of the temple in order to have his dispositions formalized and put into writing.[29] He has brought with him his second wife, the *ꜥnḫt nt niwt* Ineksunedjemet, and his children by his first wife. In the opening lines of page two, Amenkhau claims to have finalized the first marriage settlement before entering into the second, and that he had done so in accordance with the laws, or sayings, of Pharaoh (*ḫr ḏd pr-ꜥꜣ*).

(II,1) . . . [*iw.ỉ ꜥr*]*ḳwi ḥr.st m*	. . . [I swo]re an oath concerning her in
tꜣ ḳnbt tꜣ ḥwt iw.ỉ irt rwy r r-3	the court of the temple: I set apart 2/3 from 1/3,
m pꜣ ỉryw.ỉ nb (2) *irm.st ỉ*[*w.ỉ ꜥḳ*]	from all that I had acquired with her. [I entered]
r pꜣ pr n ꜥnḫ(*t nt*) *niwt*	into the house of the woman of the city
ink-sw-nḏm(*t*) *tꜣy st-ḥmt nty*	Ineksunedjemet, this woman who is
ꜥḥꜥti m-bꜣḥ ṯꜣt (3) *iw.ỉ in 4 bꜣk*[*w*	standing before the vizier. I acquired 4 servants
irm]*.st iw.st nfr n.ỉ iw.st šmswy*	[with] her. **She was good to me, suited**
biꜣt.ỉ iw.st iry n.ỉ i.iryt	**my character, and did for me what a**
(4) *šr*[*i . . . šrit*] *iw.ỉ dit n.st ḥmt*	**son [or daughter] does.** I gave to her the female servant
nw-mwt-rꜥ ḥmt bwpy-mwt-ḫꜣꜥnw	Numutre, the female servant Bupymutkhaanu,
ḥnꜥ (5) *n*[*ꜣy*]*.w ms*[*w r pꜣy*]*.s r-3*	together with their children, [as] her 1/3.
iw.ỉ dwny.st m ḥm sꜣ-ptri-ḏḥwty	I also presented her with the male servant Sapetridjehuty
ḥm gm-imn-[*pꜣ*]*-ꜥš* (6) [*pꜣy*	and the male servant Gemamenpaash, these
bꜣk]*w 2 nty m-di.ỉ m dni m*	[these two servants] who (originally) were in my possession, as

pꜣy.i pš [pꜣ] iry.i nb irm.st (7) [*r*]	my share of all that I had acquired with her, [in order to]
iry.st m šri[t mi]-ḳd nꜣ ẖrdw n	treat her as a daughter, like the children of
tꜣy.i ḥmt ḥꜣw[ty]w ʿḳꜣ sp-sn	my first wife, exactly, repeatedly,
i.wnw m pꜣ[y].i (8) *pr*	who lived in my house.
iw bw-pwy.[i] smn [r] wʿ mr ky	[I] did not place one (of my) beloved above the other.
ḫr ptri tw.i iw.k m-bꜣḥ ṯꜣt	Behold, I have come before the vizier
(9) [*ḥnʿ*] *srw n tꜣ ḳnbt m pꜣ hrw*	and the officials of the court on this day
r-rdit-rḫ wʿ nb dnitw.f m nꜣy.i	in order to inform everyone of my
ẖrdw [. . .] (10) *pꜣy sḫrw nt[y i]w.i*	children about his share [. . .] these decisions which I
irw.f n ʿnḫ(t nt) niwt	have made for the woman of the city
ink-sw-nḏm(t) tꜣy st-ḥmt nty m	Ineksunedjemet, this woman who is in
pꜣ[y.i pr] m pꜣ (*11*) *hrw ḫr ḏd*	[my house] on this day. (The law of)
[*pr*]*-ʿꜣ ʿnḫ wḏꜣ snb imi iry s nb*	Pharaoh, LPH, says: "Let every man do
ꜣbwtw.f m ꜣḫttw.f tw.i dit [*pꜣ*]	what he wants with his assets!" I (thus) give
iryw.[i] (*12*) *nb irm ʿnḫ(t nt) niwt*	all that [I] have acquired with the woman of the city
ink-sw-nḏm(t) tꜣ st-ḥmt nty m	Ineksunedjemet, the woman who is in
pꜣy.i pr n.st m pꜣ h[rw] m pꜣ	my house, to her, on this day, consisting of the
(III,1) *bꜣkw 2 ʿ[ḥꜣ]wtyw*	2 male servants and
bꜣkw(t) 2 *ḥmwt dmḏ 4 ḥnʿ*	2 female servants, total 4, together with
msw.w iw pꜣ rwy ḥr pꜣy.st r-3	their children, the 2/3 upon her 1/3.
mtw.i (2) *dit pꜣy 9 bꜣkw i.hꜣy r.i*	I shall give these (other) 9 servants, who fell to me
m pꜣy.i rwy irm ʿnḫ(t nt) niwt	as my 2/3 with the woman of the city
tꜣ-ṯꜣriꜣ n tꜣy.i (3) *ẖrdw ḥnʿ*	Tatjaria, to my children, together with
pꜣ pr it mwt	the house of the father of (their) mother, (which is)
m-di.w m-r-ʿ bn st [*ꜣty*]	in their possession anyway. They are not [lacking]
pꜣ in.(i) nb irm tꜣy.w mwt	anything of what I acquired with their mother.

(4) *iw wnw iw.i dit n.w m pꜣ m*	I would have given to them from that which
inw.i irm ꜥnḫ(t nt) niwt	I acquired with the woman of the city
ink-sw-nḏm(t) ḫr pr-ꜥꜣ ꜥnḫ wḏꜣ snb	Ineksunedjemet, but (the law of) Pharaoh, LPH,
ḏd imi sfr (5) *n s*[*t nb*] *n.st*	says: "Give every woman's dowry(?) to her!"

Then follow questions by the vizier, who leads the court, and answers by Amenkhau's two eldest sons. The text shows no sign of dispute or hard feelings. The two sons simply confirm and conclude that their father can do as he pleases with his property.[30]

. . . *ḏdt.n ṯꜣt ir iw bn ḥmt sꜣwt iwnꜣ*	(Then) the vizier said: "What if there was no wife at all,
iw ḫꜣ[*ryt*] *nḥsy*(*t*) *iw mr.f sw*	that it was a Syrian or Nubian (woman) that he loved,
[*i*]*w.f dit n.s* (12) *ꜣḫwttw.f*	and to whom he had bequeathed his property?
[*nym i.*]*irw.f wsf pꜣ iry.f*	[Who] is it that would nullify what he has done?
imi [*n.s pꜣ*] *4 bꜣkw i.*[*in.f i*]*rm*	Give [to her the] 4 servants that [he acquired] with
ꜥnḫ(*t nt*) *niwt ink-sw-nḏm*(*t*)	the woman of the city, Ineksunedjemet,
(13) *ḥnꜥ pꜣ* [*in.f nb*] *irm.st i.ḏd.f*	together with all that he acquired with her, (as) he said:
tw.i dit n.st pꜣy.i rwy [*ḥr pꜣ*]*y.st*	'I give to her my 2/3, [upon] her
r-3 iw bn ir šri šri(*t*) (IV,1) *mdt*	1/3, and no son or daughter shall speak against
m pꜣy sḫrw i.ir.i n.st m pꜣ hrw	this arrangement that I have made for her on this day.'"[31]

The two-thirds of the husband and the one-third of the wife is a recurring theme and suggests a practice of shared property. Perhaps the laws and sayings of Pharaoh could be understood as measures that at some point had been taken to secure the rights of the individual, indeed a woman's legal rights? Given the context of these laws and sayings, it seems reasonable that the time for returning her dowry or her share of mutual property was when the union was dissolved.[32] There are several ways to understand this. Either the husband acted as a caretaker for the property during their marriage, or the property became common property, administered by the couple together.

It is relevant here to refer to the vizier's question. What if there was no wife at all, and it was a Syrian or Nubian woman that he loved to whom he had bequeathed his property? Although this question indicates that women were differentiated based on their ethnic background, it seems clear that it made no difference for the validity of the deposition. Women had property rights, no matter their social standing or ethnic background.

It is also interesting that the second wife was rewarded with additional property, equal to his children by his first wife. The text stresses that this is because the second wife had been good to him and suited his character. But of greatest importance is that he states she had done what was expected from a son or daughter. We see that there is an expectation toward children, but also that nonbiological children could fulfill the very same expectations and be rewarded for it.

Conclusion

The existence of family contracts and female rights(?) to property is probably a reason why few women are found interacting together with and alongside both men and women. Family, in New Kingdom Egypt, was not only about biology or being next of kin, but, more importantly, was about who actually acted *as* family. Through family contracts, individuals negotiated their position in society through their relations and encounters with others, living and dead, human and nonhuman. We are left with the impression that to be an heir was not a matter of fact; it was not a given, but rather was something you had to earn through support on a regular basis, and specifically in cases of acute situations, such as sickness, old age, and death. Inheritance thus seems to have been used as a security mechanism, a kind of leverage that was subject to constant negotiation. In fact, patterns in phrasing (*ỉrt n.ỉ nfr*) suggest that these examples were more than exceptions, and that women had a role to play in these negotiations. Family contracts based on reciprocal bonds of mutual support had significant ramifications for the relationship between generations, but also for the relationship between men and women more generally. They functioned as a kind of welfare system, and the level of ranking achieved—indeed, where power and authority came from—can be argued as directly related to the circulation and guardianship of the family's joint property.[33]

Notes

1 Detlef Franke, *Altägyptische Verwandtschaftsbezeichnungen im Mittleren Reich* (Hamburg: Borg, 1983), 257–76; Christopher J. Eyre, "Feudal Tenure and Absentee Landlords," in *Grund und Boden (Rechtliche und socio-ökonomische Verhältnisse)*, ed. Schafik Allam (Tübingen: Im Selbstverlag des Herausgebers, 1994), 112–13; Leire Olabarria, "Formulating Relations: An Approach to the *smyt*-formula," *ZÄS* 145, no. 1 (2018): 10–19.

2 Jaana Toivari-Viitala, *Women at Deir el-Medina: A Study of the Status and Roles of the Female Inhabitants in the Workmen's Community during the Ramesside Period* (Leiden: NINO, 2001), 237–38.

3 Brian P. Muhs, "Gender Relations and Inheritance in Legal Codes and Legal Practices in Ancient Egypt," in *Structures of Power: Law and Gender across the Ancient Near East and Beyond*, ed. Ilan Peled (Chicago: Oriental Institute of the University of Chicago, 2017), 15–25. See also Richard Jasnow, "New Kingdom," in *A History of Ancient Near Eastern Law*, ed. Raymond Westbrook (Leiden: Brill, 2003), 289–359; Sandra Lippert, "Inheritance," in *UEE*, ed. Elizabeth Frood and Willeke Wendrich (Los Angeles, 2013), 1–20.

4 The majority of evidence for "family law" appears in demotic and Greek documents from the Late Period, and according to Janet Johnson, these reflect a more fully spelled-out form of the social and legal practices of earlier periods. She comments that even though scholars treat later stages of Egyptian history as "so much 'polluted' by foreign contacts as to be no longer 'really' Egyptian, Egyptian culture remained vital and vibrant" and actually became more visible through post–New Kingdom documents. See J.H. Johnson, "The Legal Status of Women in Ancient Egypt," in *Mistress of the House, Mistress of Heaven: Women in Ancient Egypt*, ed. A.K. Capel and G. Markoe (New York: Hudson Hills Press, 1996), 180.

5 P.Cairo JdE 89127–30 + 89137–43. Girgis Mattha and George R. Hughes, *The Demotic Legal Code of Hermopolis West* (Cairo: IFAO, 1975).

6 Jaana Toivari-Viitala, "Marriage at Deir el-Medina," in *Proceedings of the Seventh International Congress of Egyptologists*, ed. Christopher J. Eyre (Leuven: Peeters, 1995), 1160–61. See also Christopher J. Eyre, "The Evil Stepmother and the Rights of a Second Wife," *JEA* 93 (2007): 243.

7 Eyre, "The Evil Stepmother and the Rights of a Second Wife," 230. See also Toivari-Viitala, *Women at Deir el-Medina*, 61–67, 72.

8 Jac J. Janssen and P.W. Pestman, "Burial and Inheritance in the Community of the Necropolis of Workmen at Thebes," *JESHO* 11 (1968): 165. See also Toivari-Viitala, *Women at Deir el-Medina*, 96–138; Eyre, "The Evil Stepmother and the Rights of a Second Wife," 242.

9 Jaana Toivari-Viitala, "O. DeM 764: A Note Concerning Property Rights," *GM* 195 (2003): 87–96.

10 Eyre, "Feudal Tenure and Absentee Landlords," 113.

11 Eyre, "The Evil Stepmother and the Rights of a Second Wife," 233.

12 Johnson, "The Legal Status of Women in Ancient Egypt," 184–85.

13 J.H. Johnson, "The Social, Economic and Legal Status of Women in Ancient Egypt," in *The Life of Meresamun: A Templesinger in Ancient Egypt*, ed. Emily Teeter and Janet H. Johnson (Chicago: OIP, 2009), 88.

14 Rosalind M. Janssen, "The Old Women of Deir el-Medina," *Buried History* 42 (2006), 7.

15 Leire Olabarria, *Kinship and Family in Ancient Egypt: Archaeology and Anthropology in Dialogue* (Cambridge: Cambridge University Press, 2020), 201.

16 Annette B. Weiner, *Inalienable Possessions: The Paradox of Keeping While Giving* (Berkeley: University of California Press, 1992), 63. See also Polly Weissner, who argues that "when everything else appears alienable and negotiable, (maternal) kinship provides the inalienable to tide people over and channel alliance and descent while new structures emerge." See P. Weissner, "Alienating the Inalienable: Marriage and Money in a Big Man Society," in *The Scope of Anthropology: Maurice Godelier's Work in Context*, ed. Laurent Dousset and S. Tcherkézoff (New York: Berghahn Books, 2012), 83. In Egyptology, Christina Riggs has argued that the textiles employed in wrapping rituals were inalienable possessions. They were "material goods (usually made by women) whose symbolic

significance makes them 'transcendent treasures' to be guarded against loss, for instance by restricting their exchange." See Christina Riggs. *Unwrapping Ancient Egypt* (London: Bloomsbury, 2014), 110.

17 Jac J. Janssen, "Gift-giving in Ancient Egypt as an Economic Feature," *JEA* 68 (1982): 256–57.

18 Jac J. Janssen, "Debt and Credit in the New Kingdom," *JEA* 80 (1994): 136. See also Jac J. Janssen, "Foreword: Earning a Living in a New Kingdom Village," in *Commerce and Economy in Ancient Egypt: Proceedings of the Third International Congress of Young Egyptologists 25–27 September 2009, Budapest*, ed. A. Hudecz and M. Petrik (Oxford: Archaeopress, 2010), 3.

19 The transliterations and translations are those of the author. See also Alan H. Gardiner and Kurt Sethe, *Egyptian Letters to the Dead: Mainly from the Old and Middle Kingdoms* (London: EES, 1928), 26, pl. 9; Edward F. Wente, *Letters from Ancient Egypt*, ed. Edmund S. Meltzer (Atlanta: Scholars Press, 1990), 216n351; The Pitt River Museum Online Collection, accessed 27 August 2021, https://www.prm.ox.ac.uk/collections-online. For more references, see Reinert Skumsnes, "Patterns of Change and Disclosures of Difference: Family and Gender in New Kingdom Egypt: Titles of Non-royal Women" (PhD diss., University of Oslo: Oslo 07-Media, 2018), 238n907.

20 Battiscombe Gunn, "Review of *Egyptian Letters to the Dead, Mainly from the Old and Middle Kingdoms* by Alan H. Gardiner and Kurt Sethe," *JEA* 16, no. 1/2 (1930): 154.

21 The transliterations and translations are those of the author. See also Janssen and Pestman, "Burial and Inheritance in the Community of the Necropolis of Workmen at Thebes"; Shafik Allam, *Hieratische Ostraka und Papyri aus der Ramessidenzeit* (Tübingen: Selbstverlag des Herausgebers, 1973), 1:289–93, 2:pls. 88–91; Kenneth A. Kitchen, KRI V (Oxford: B.H. Blackwell, 1983), 449–51; Kenneth A. Kitchen, *Ramesside Inscriptions: Translated & Annotated* 5 (Oxford: Blackwell, 2008), 368–69. For more references, see Skumsnes, "Patterns of Change and Disclosures of Difference," 239n909, 241n911.

22 Shafik Allam, "A New Look at the Adoption Papyrus (Reconsidered)," *JEA* 76 (1990): 189; Alan Gardiner, "Adoption Extraordinary," *JEA* 26 (1941): 27.

23 Christopher Eyre, "The Adoption Papyrus in Social Context," *JEA* 78 (1992): 207–208. See also Gardiner, "Adoption Extraordinary," 25.

24 The transliterations and translations are those of the author. See also Alan Gardiner, "Adoption Extraordinary," 23–29; Allam, *Hieratische Ostraka und Papyri* 1, 258–67; Kenneth A. Kitchen, KRI VI (Oxford: B.H. Blackwell, 1983), 735–38; Kenneth A. Kitchen, *Ramesside Inscriptions: Translated & Annotated* 6 (Oxford: Blackwell, 2012), 524–26. For more references, see Skumsnes, "Patterns of Change and Disclosures of Difference," 258n936.

25 Koenraad Donker van Heel, *Mrs. Tsenhor: A Female Entrepreneur in Ancient Egypt* (Cairo: American University in Cairo Press, 2014), 83.

26 Arlette David, *The Legal Register of Ramesside Private Law Instruments* (Wiesbaden: Harrassowitz, 2010), 119.

27 Eyre, "The Adoption Papyrus in Social Context," 209.

28 Shafik Allam, "Quelques aspects du mariage dans l'Égypte ancienne," *JEA* 67 (1981): 116–35.

29 Scholars disagree on the exact nature of the dispositions: will and/or gift—see Aristide Théodoridès, "Le testament d'Imenkhâou," *JEA* 54 (1968): 149–54; Allam, *Hieratische Ostraka und Papyri*; and David, *The Legal Register of Ramesside Private Law Instruments*, 144–45; marriage settlement—see Jaroslav Černý and Eric T. Peet, "A Marriage Settlement of the Twentieth Dynasty: An Unpublished Document from Turin," *JEA* 13, no. 1/2 (1927): 30–39; and Eyre, "The Evil Stepmother and the Rights of a Second Wife," 231; fictitious lawsuit—see Peter W. Pestman, *Marriage and Matrimonial Property in Ancient Egypt: A Contribution to Establishing the Legal Position of the Woman* (Leiden: Brill, 1961), 127, 132n5, 138–39; or divorce settlement—see Andrea G. McDowell, *Jurisdiction in the Workmen's Community of Deir El-Medîna* (Leiden: NINO, 1990), 35–36, 145n14.

30 Černý and Peet, "A Marriage Settlement of the Twentieth Dynasty," 37; Schafik Allam, "Les obligations et la famille dans la société égyptienne ancienne," *Oriens Antiquus* 16 (1977): 93–96; David, *The Legal Register of Ramesside Private Law Instruments*, 150–51.

31 The transliterations and translations are those of the author. See also Černý and Peet, "A Marriage Settlement of the Twentieth Dynasty," 30–39; Schafik Allam, "Papyrus Turin 2021: Another Adoption Extraordinary," in *Individu, société et spiritualité dans l'Égypte pharaonique et copte: mélanges égyptologiques offerts au Professeur Aristide Théodoridès*, ed. Christian Cannuyer (Brussels: Association Montoise d'Égyptologie, 1993), 23–28; Allam, *Hieratische Ostraka und Papyri* 1, 320–27, vol. 2, pls. 113–19; Kitchen, KRI 6, 738–42; Kitchen, *Ramesside Inscriptions: Translated and Annotated* 6, 526–28. For more references, see Skumsnes, "Patterns of Change and Disclosures of Difference," 263n952.

32 Černý and Peet suggest that the one-third is a "contribution made by the husband to the wife at the time of marriage, but which does not become her undivided property except in the case of his dying or divorcing her." See Černý and Peet, "A Marriage Settlement of the Twentieth Dynasty," 37.

33 I would like to thank the editors and reviewers for their generous feedback.

14

The Women of Deir al-Medina in the Ramesside Period: Current State of Research and Future Perspectives on the Community of Workers

Kathrin Gabler

THE SUBJECT OF WOMEN in Deir al-Medina has resulted in several publications over the years.[1] Some of these studies convey information from administrative texts while others take different materials into account. This contribution presents an overview of these studies before turning to examine how we can make use of the surviving evidence to gain further information about the women of Deir al-Medina. As part of this methodological discussion, I refer to two examples from my research and examine several possible avenues for future research within this subfield of Deir al-Medina studies. Ultimately, I argue for a better contextualized approach to the evidence.

History and the Current State of Research: What Do We Know about the Female Inhabitants of Ramesside Deir al-Medina?

In his well-known book, *A Community of Workmen* (1973/2001), Jaroslav Černý discussed the workmen of Deir al-Medina, as well as their jobs and tasks,[2] but not the women of Deir al-Medina. Of course, the main purpose of this special settlement was the construction of the royal tombs in the Valleys of the Kings and Queens, in which no women were directly involved. Černý thus deals only with female slaves/servants (?),[3] though women are referred to in the family trees of certain chief workmen and scribes.[4] Černý also includes many women in his recordkeeping system of card boxes (stored in the Griffith Institute Archive in Oxford) wherein the attestations of every individual named in our sources are noted.[5] According to Černý, the word *ḥm* ("slaves/

servants") is used with a feminine determinative (*ḥmt*) in the majority of surviving instances in our texts, though workmen are also referred to as servants (of the Place of the Truth). Nonetheless, Černý "safely assumed that all these slaves were women"[6] on the basis that, where male determinatives are encountered, these reflect an error of the (male) scribe. However, Tobias Hofmann's study of the terms *ḥm* and *b3k* shows that there were indeed male slaves/servants in Ramesside Egypt.[7] The gender-neutral term "slaves," referring to either males or females, is thus to be preferred. According to Černý, these (female) servants were responsible for grinding corn, making flour, and assisting in the households of the families.

Dominique Valbelle was the first scholar to draw explicit attention to the women of Deir al-Medina in *Les ouvriers de la tombe* (1982), in a chapter dedicated to aspects of family life in the village.[8] Valbelle traces certain women using letters, transactions, legal texts, gift lists, stelae, and tombs of the early Ramesside period, though most of the known sources from Deir al-Medina describe the working life of men at the royal tombs. Terms for married women include *snt* (used on private monuments), *ḥmt* (in official and legal documents), and *ʿnḫ n niwt* (used of married women),[9] while the role of women appears to have been confined to housework and raising children. In her discussion, Valbelle assumes that many of the female children born to workers' families married outside of the village, while some of the males would have gotten a job on the crew.[10]

In the same year (1982), Morris Bierbrier furnished a realistic picture of the women of Deir al-Medina in a chapter of his study on the tomb builders called "Village Life."

> The life in the village was presumably carried on during the week by the women, while their menfolk worked away at the royal tombs. Of course, there were always some men about—retired workers, invalids, men on special duty in the village, men excused work and servants bringing up goods from the river. The prime duty of the wife of a workman would be to look after his home. Unlike the wives of ordinary workers, her workload would have been lightened by the government provision of female slaves to grind her corn, though if the lady of the house chose to sell these services, she would naturally be obliged to do the work herself. She would also be responsible for the preparation of the staple diet of bread. Her duties would include the provision of clothing for the family, day weaving and sewing . . . The wife also had to tend the young children, which was not a simple task, as Deir el-Medina families were

large, often numbering as many as fifteen. Of course, many children must have died in childhood. Like most ordinary Egyptians, a workman would have only one wife at a time, but death or divorce could set him free to remarry. It is unlikely that any but elderly adults remained single for long, as marriage was regarded as the normal state in the ancient world. The important role of the wife and mother was recognized by her place in Egyptian society. The wife was equal with her husband under Egyptian law (own property, inheritance).[11]

Writing shortly thereafter, and focusing on matters related to work on the royal tombs in his book "Masters of Deir el-Medina,"[12] Eugenij Bogoslovskij (1983) examined the job titles and professions attested in and around the village, from the chief workmen to the job groups for deliveries. With respect to female job titles, Bogoslovskij records only two professions, both part of the *smdt*: the *mnˁt*, "wet nurses," and female slaves. Both positions can be excluded from the *smdt* staff, however, as the terms never appear in the context of the service personnel.[13] Women are usually cited by Bogoslovskij when their husbands are described, but some of his comments are misleading. For example, he concludes that the small sandals delivered to the village must have been for female slaves—the only women working in the royal necropolis—thus agreeing with Černý that the servants at Deir al-Medina must all have been female.[14] This conclusion ignores the fact that many women lived in the village (and naturally could wear sandals) though they played no direct role on the construction sites.

The fact that women could own huts in the Valley of the Queens led Bogoslovskij to reflect on the role of women in Deir al-Medina. He thought these huts must have belonged to single women, such as *Tȝ-skt* (i) and her sister *Tȝ-mkt* (ii), who, according to O. DeM 112 and 964, received such huts.[15] Both these women were daughters of the foreman of the right side, *Nḫ-m-Mwt* (i), during the time of Ramesses III. But even if no families or husbands are attested for these women, they certainly did not live alone in the Valley of the Queens, though they were probably married, especially because the daughters of foremen did particularly well on the marriage market, as shown below. That said, the Valley of the Queens was most likely a female-centric space in the Ramesside period—a ritual and funerary landscape dominated by the burials of royal women and children—though the area, like the Valley of the Kings, would have been dominated by male workers.[16]

In his study of Deir al-Medina, Manfred Gutgesell (1983) includes a list of all the women attested in the sources that he investigates.[17] He further discusses their names and attestations as dating criteria for the ostraca of the Twentieth Dynasty.

Benedict G. Davies (1999) discusses 150 women, as well as families whose members include some two hundred daughters, known from many ostraca, papyri, stelae, and tombs.[18] These are certainly our most valuable source for Deir al-Medina, but Davies' work, like many prosopographic studies, seldom reflects the nature and the situation of the preserved documents. It neglects possible chronological orderings within the sources, as well as the fact that a stela, for instance, furnishes a different context and provides different information about a person than an administrative or literary ostracon.

Gregor Neunert (2010) structures his work much like Černý and Valbelle, though this work includes a section about women and the wise woman.[19] His study follows Jaana Toivari-Viitala, who wrote that

> The women who came to live at Deir el-Medina were in the first instance spouses of the workmen who were being employed for the construction of the royal tombs. As time passed, there would also be an increasing number of daughters, sisters, and mothers, as well as other female relatives of the workmen, stemming from reproduction and intermarriages in the community.[20]

As Neunert's study shows, the influence of these women would certainly have belied their "traditional" role "home at the oven." They raised children and were the ladies of the household, assisted by servants and the service personnel. They traded, performed (professional) tasks in religious, legal, and business life, and sometimes even replaced their husbands on duty in the guard/watch lists, for instance. Some of them were also able to read and to write.[21]

In 2018, Benedict Davies published *A Handbook to Deir el-Medina*, which included entries for many (male) professions, work-related matters, objects, installations, and locations. Aside from the wise woman, however, no entry is dedicated to women.[22] Even the famous *Niwt-nḫt.ti* (i) goes without an entry, though her husband *Ḳni-ḥr-ḫps.f* (i) and several other men are specifically included. Women are referred to only in a couple of other entries, such as under "adultery" and "marriage," as well as in the index of personal names.[23] The entry "slaves" still builds largely on the problematic assumption that these servants were almost exclusively female. The discussion of the aforementioned O. Ashmolean Museum 90 even refers to the four daughters of the slave *Nḏmt-ḥmsi*, though the text refers to her sons (see above).[24]

In concluding this survey, I discuss the three main titles available to us when it comes to the women of Deir al-Medina. The first of these, the PhD study by Jaana Toivari-Viitala (2001), outlines the large body of previous research into women in ancient Egypt, including those studies that have influenced Deir al-Medina research, before engaging with the status and roles of women at Deir al-Medina based on five hundred ostraca and papyri and occasionally other objects.[25] Toivari-Viitala estimates that about 10 percent of the preserved (administrative) documentation relates to women; for a discussion of this estimate, see below. She reconstructs the daily existence of these women across their lifespans, moving from marriage to the marital household, through to property, motherhood, and children. Marriage is described as the key event in female life in antiquity, a cycle which begins again with the marriage of any children, who also took care of their elderly parents. Toivari-Viitala's study includes 170 women, though she does not number them according to Davies (1999) or afford them any proper prosopographic discussion. From a textual point of view, her work is very revealing and furnishes strong results. It does, however, skimp on those sources (stelae, tombs, domestic objects, etc.) that provide the best insight into questions about the female lifespan.

In 2016, Koen Donker van Heel published *Mrs. Naunakhte and Family*, a popularizing book about "the Women of Ramesside Deir el-Medina."[26] *Niwt-nḫt.ti* and her family form a case study of the "average" village woman. Marriage is presented by Donker van Heel as the final step in a woman's life. The book recounts different "stories" from the village, based on Donker van Heel's enormous knowledge of the texts from Deir al-Medina. In these stories, however, he focuses more on the men (the husbands of *Niwt-nḫt.ti*, *Ḳni-ḥr-ḫps.f*, and *Ḫʿ-m-Nwn*, as well as other relatives) than the women. He acknowledges the reason behind this focus: the only source of information we have for *Niwt-nḫt.ti* is her will.[27] At the same time, the fame of this will has meant that other women from Deir al-Medina have vanished into the background: existing research is prone to use the same case studies over and over, even though other examples are available and different stories are worth telling.[28] That said, Donker van Heel does point in his acknowledgments to the work of Deborah Sweeney, noting that she will probably publish another—and better—book on women at Deir al-Medina. I can happily confirm the existence of such a book, which—with thanks to Sweeney—I now briefly highlight.

In this forthcoming book, *Gender and Religious Activities at Deir el-Medina*, Sweeney provides an extensive overview of religious practices attested for both women and men in the village. She investigates individual activities attested for both genders as well as the relationships of the genders to different deities. She deals with textual, material, and archaeological evidence, from chapels, houses, and tombs to objects distributed in museums around the world.[29] Building on her extensive prior research,[30] her approach represents the way forward. But what remains to be done with regard to the women of Deir al-Medina, and—with respect to Sweeney's research—how should we approach this topic in future research?

In answering these questions, we have to examine the objects available for the study of women at Deir al-Medina, as well as several methodological issues. The surviving evidence from this extraordinary village provides us with a vast amount of information and includes objects from domestic, funerary, and religious spaces; anthropological evidence, such as human remains; and masses of textual evidence, including thousands of ostraca and papyri. Our biggest challenge thus remains the overwhelming amount of material from the site, though the state of the preserved material also has to be carefully considered before we begin our work.[31]

Deir al-Medina is especially famous for its wealth of texts. Estimates run up to approximately 20,000 ostraca (roughly half administrative and half literary), 500 papyri, 4,000 graffiti, and 400 stelae, not including many other inscribed artifacts.[32] With the beginning of the Nineteenth Dynasty, the number of inscribed documents that have been preserved increases exponentially. And though only a quarter of the known administrative texts have been published, their number (roughly 5,000) is large enough for statistical purposes.[33] The publication of further texts will probably only increase the number of texts dating to particular periods, but will not change our general picture of the preserved texts: most of the textual evidence dates to the period from Ramesses III to VI. This mass of written evidence does not seem to be accidental and can be explained by two factors. After the Amarna Period, people with scribal abilities increasingly lived permanently with the workmen in the small village, meaning that, after several generations, more and more people gained some skill in reading and writing. Further to this, the inhabitants of the village increasingly took advantage of their (new) skills to document their (private) affairs instead of relying on oral agreements or messages.[34]

In addition to the texts, it is important to pay attention to a variety of other objects. Deir al-Medina consisted of sixty-eight houses, many chapels, and over seven hundred tombs—often with a great deal of funerary equipment—though only fifty-two of the 480 tombs in the western necropolis are decorated. The majority of these tombs date to the reigns of Seti I and Ramesses II, while most of the stelae and statues also originated in the early Nineteenth Dynasty; there are thousands of ostraca that belong to the mid-Twentieth Dynasty and many papyri that belong to the mid- and late Ramesside period. After the abandonment of the village and the departure of the community to Medinet Habu, many objects were left in place—in chapels and tombs, for instance—and rediscovered in the nineteenth century.[35] Yet where do we find the women in these sources?

Women are usually recorded on objects originating in houses and tombs—in pictorial representations and inscriptions (often on architectural elements) as well as related domestic, religious, and funerary equipment—and most often during the short reign of Seti I (though many objects may, significantly, be dated to this period) and the much longer, sixty-six-year reign of Ramesses II. Most of our genealogical information for women derives from these sources and periods. Women are recorded in five hundred administrative texts (representing 2.5 percent of the estimated number of administrative texts and 5 percent of the estimated total of all texts); on 107 stelae (27 percent); and on all houses and decorated tombs.[36] Within these contexts, women are referred to as *nbt-pr*, "the lady of the house." This is equivalent to the male title *sḏm-ʿš m st mꜣʿt*, "servant at the Place of the Truth." *Nbt-pr* was also widely used in the domestic sphere, alongside *snt* (sister) or *ḥmt* (wife).

In the administrative texts, women are referred to as *ʿnḫ n nỉwt*, usually "married woman," which is probably equivalent to *rmṯ-ỉst*, "workman." These texts date mainly to the Twentieth Dynasty and are largely business and legal notes, though letters sometimes mention women.[37] There are also anepigraphic objects from domestic and funerary spaces that refer to women: clothes, vessels, jewelry, and so forth that cannot be qualified as to their precise date. Many of these objects were produced by men, and the references to women are thus presented to us from a male perspective. It is in light of all of these texts and objects and the circumstances of their production and use that the women of Deir al-Medina should be studied. They can be only understood when we properly comprehend the surviving evidence, its genres, uses, and the contexts of specific records. This is a challenge, in light of both the sheer number of objects (beyond any one researcher) and the need to ask the right questions about the right material. Administrative texts, for instance, will not answer (many) questions about childbirth, child rearing, or household management.[38] But they will answer questions about female business activities, or shed potential light on the activities of women in the male-dominated working sphere. The following two examples reflect the challenge that faces us in greater detail.

A Combined Approach for Future Research: How We Can Use the Available Information to Gain More Insight into the Women of Deir al-Medina

Example 1: Stela Turin Museo Egizio CGT 50057 depicts an unusual combination of gods: a triad consisting of Amun-Re, Taweret, and Seth (fig. 14.1). Seth

Fig. 14.1. Stela Turin CGT 50057. A color image is available at https://collezioni.museoegizio.it/en-GB/material/Cat_1514/?description=&inventoryNumber=&title=&cgt=50057&yearFrom=&yearTo=&materials=&provenance=&acquisition=&epoch=&dynasty=&pharaoh=

is depicted twice as a small red hippopotamus, referred to as *Stí* (*nṯr*) *nfr* and *s3 Nwt*. This limestone stela also depicts an unusually large number of women. Of the fifteen individuals depicted, twelve are female, and eleven of these are designated as kin to *Mwt*, the mistress of the house, who is shown in the center. This woman-centric stela is unparalleled among stelae from Deir al-Medina, and though it reflects many traditional aspects of ancient Egyptian images, depictions, and texts, its focus on one particular woman is exceptional.[39] An iconographic and prosopographic examination of the three registers of the stela and its figures suggests a relation to the foreman on the left side, *Ḳ3ḥ3* (i), whose sister *Mwt*(*-m-wí3*) (vi) appears to be the focus of the stela. She is accompanied by her parents-in-law, *Ípwí* and *Ḫ3wí*, and other female relatives and friends. The layout of the object suggests that *Mwt*(*-m-wí3*)'s name was abbreviated to *Mwt*. She appears to have been the first wife of the owner of the stela, *Nfr-rnpt* (i).[40] The father of *Ḳ3ḥ3* and of *Mwt*(*-m-wí3*)—who was the *ḥmw wr Ḥwí* (ii)—is visible in the third register; it is possible that he donated the stela to or for his daughter and son-in-law in the reign of Seti I or the early reign of Ramesses II. The women on the stela are all designated as *s3t.s* of the donor *Ḥwí*, to whom the women were daughters, granddaughters, nieces, and daughters-in-law.[41] The terminus *s3t* refers to later generations, as opposed to the more common *snt*. At least eight of the ten "daughters" attested on the stela had relations to the family of *Ḥwí* (ii) and *Ḳ3ḥ3* (ii). In combination with the goddess Taweret, the addition of many female relatives to the stela suggests a fertility context—pregnancy or birth—and the wish for healthy offspring.

Taweret and Seth also appear in hieratic texts from the community wherein the wise woman is consulted. According to these texts, the *b3w*-powers of both gods played a role in unsuccessful pregnancies and the deaths of infants.[42] The presence of this constellation of deities in the first register of the stela suggests that such misfortune befell *Nfr-rnpt* and *Mwt*, while the scene on the stela may represent a pictorial transposition of certain formulae from the hieratic texts that were designed to ward off the *b3w* of Seth and Taweret.

Mwt-m-wí3 only appears in the textual record for a brief period; any children born to her and *Nfr-rnpt* are unknown, and it is possible that they died (at an early age) and that *Mwt* perished in childbirth.[43] The stela may have originated in a chapel (for Taweret and Seth) on the northern side of the village. Various other objects related to these deities (fragments of stelae, statues, etc.) found in the chapels C.V. 1213, 1190, 1218, and 1193 permit us to hypothesize the stela's original location there, allowing us to better contextualize the stela via content, iconography, and prosopography. We also know of other cases in which women had no children and made some effort to change

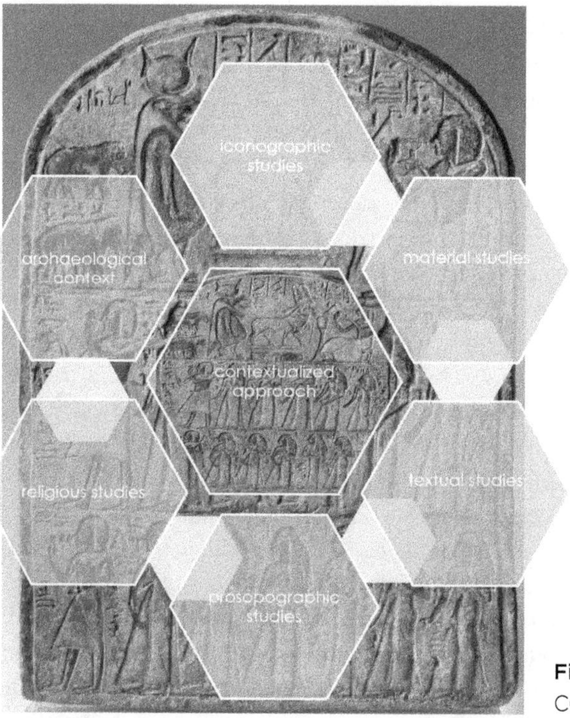

Fig. 14.2. Stela Turin CGT 50057

this: *Mwt-m-wiꜣ* (i), the wife of the scribe *Rꜥ-ms* (i), does not share only a name with the *Mwt-m-wiꜣ* but a similar fate.[44]

As the discussion above has shown, one object can provide a lot of information about ancient women if you look at it in detail. I was able to formulate the picture of *Mwt-m-wiꜣ* presented above by combining and building upon various other studies (fig. 14.2), including art historical and iconographic research by Gay Robins as well as Sweeney's research on women and Deir al-Medina, in particular; material studies by Karen Exell, Jan Moje, and Sweeney; studies of terminology like *snt*, *sꜣt*, and the like by Černý and Bierbrier; prosopographic research by Davies, Černý, Bierbrier, and Toivari-Viitala; religious studies by Joris Borghouts and Sweeney; and the archaeological context provided by Bernard Bruyère and Anne Bomann.[45]

My next example builds on various objects in order to demonstrate what kinds of conclusions one can draw with respect to ancient Egyptian women when contextualizing a larger number of artefacts. I cannot provide details and methodologies here for all of the objects because this would require a more elaborate discussion, which will appear in a separate publication.[46]

Example 2: Building on information and archival material from the excavations directed by Ernesto Schiaparelli, Georg Möller, Bernard Bruyère, and the IFAO, we can reinvestigate the assignment of houses in Deir al-Medina to their former inhabitants. The sixty-eight houses in the village are located in five different sectors or quarters. The four sectors surrounding the central quarter are named after the cardinal directions. According to fieldwork, the southern and partly central quarters (IV to VII) were built during the reign of Seti I.[47] These dwellings were built over storage facilities dating to the Eighteenth Dynasty.[48] I have revisited and verified the assignment of the houses, using different criteria to check how secure the identification of their inhabitants is, and assigning the homes to different categories.[49] Given different excavators over the last couple of centuries, as well as lost documentation, we need to reassess the available information carefully. That said, thirty-five houses (or 51 percent) can so far be assigned to a specific inhabitant at one point in time, while the remainder permit no identification; these thirty-three houses are mostly located in the N.E. and N.O sectors. Only twenty-one houses had previously been assigned.[50]

Preliminary results already demonstrate that particular families usually stayed in the same house for longer periods of time. At least thirteen different "house biographies" can be traced thus far.[51] These sometimes extend across several generations, while certain patterns reveal how houses were passed on within families. It appears that some women played an important role in the long-term family occupation of certain houses: at least five women feature in the thirteen house biographies that can be reconstructed, and at least seven of the thirty-five assigned houses reveal that the property was passed on via the female line of the family. These patterns are visible because we are dealing with a limited number of houses, a result of the lack of space in the wadi in which the village was built. The construction of new houses for new families was simply not possible. For 250 years of the Ramesside period, the inhabitants of the village occupied the sixty-eight available houses (and possibly several more in the surroundings). This forced scarcity of homes served to structure the pattern of family house occupancy that developed and allowed people to keep a particular house within the family and to remain in the community.[52]

It has been suggested that people's social status may have had a hand to play in some village marriages, but the state of preservation of our documentation (both ancient and modern) makes this assertion difficult to demonstrate.[53] Nevertheless, if we combine archaeological, prosopographic, and textual perspectives, and adopt a diachronic point of view with respect to the objects found in (or assigned to) a house, aspects of the social background of certain wives, mothers, daughters, and granddaughters (especially of the Nineteenth Dynasty) become visible. During the time of Seti I and Ramesses II, we can observe that elite village families (those of scribes, foremen, draftsmen, and sculptors) encouraged their children to marry partners of similar social standing, if not outright arranging marriages and subsequently occupying certain houses.

- Daughters of foremen, artisans, and scribes can be better traced than the daughters of ordinary workmen; they also did well on the marriage market.[54] Thus *Wbḫt* (i/iv), a daughter of the foreman of the left side, *B3ki* (i), married the workman and possible *ʿ3-n-ʿ* ritualist *Ḥri-nfr* (i). She subsequently took the foreman of the right side, *Nfr-ḥtp* (ii), for a second husband.[55] As part of her first marriage, she kept her family home. For her second marriage, she moved into the larger dwelling of her partner in the newly built southern area; her former husband kept their smaller shared house in the "old" Eighteenth Dynasty area.
- Granddaughters and great-granddaughters could inherit the homes of their great-/grandparents in a fashion akin to the principle of name-giving. A future husband thus moved to live with his wife in her parental house. Alternatively, the couple might move from their respective homes into a grandparent's home. This was the case with *Mr.s-gr* (v), the granddaughter of *Ḥwi* (ii) (the *ḥmw wr* from the Turin stela in Example 1) and *T3-Nḥsi* (i). She and her husband, *Nb-M3ʿt* (ii), probably inherited house C. V, belonging to her grandparents, when they got married.[56]
- A father without male heirs or whose son(s) moved to live with their wives might pass his house on to his daughters; this is also observable among normal workmen. The houses N.O. IX and X can be assigned to the brothers-in-law *Wn-nḫw* (i) and *Ỉri-nfr* (i) *s3 S3-W3ḏt* (i), whose wives—*Mwt-ʿ3t* (i) and *Mḥit-ḫʿti* (i)—were sisters. Unfortunately, we do not know the name of the father of the two women, but it is likely that this man split his house into two smaller units for his daughters, who then occupied them with their husbands.[57]

In the above instances, we can truly speak of a "lady of the house" (*nbt-pr*). However, the unevenly preserved nature of the evidence—which stems largely from the (early) Nineteenth Dynasty and the influential families—means that we can only speculate about the inheritance of houses in the Twentieth Dynasty and within workmen's families. Comparing documents from the two periods, it certainly appears that marriages among villagers became more flexible over the course of the Nineteenth Dynasty and that professions became more mixed. This was probably a result of constant movement within the village and permanent kinship relations. Nevertheless, the attested cases do follow certain patterns, as outlined above. An increasing literacy rate and a more firmly entrenched community (established at the time of Horemheb and in existence for over ninety years) also led to relationships among individuals from different (family) backgrounds, perhaps with little or no regard to their origins or the social status of their families—at least as far as the documents allow us to judge the situation in the later Nineteenth Dynasty and the rest of the Ramesside period.

In the case of Deir al-Medina, it is clear that future research on the women of this extraordinary community will be a group task, a shared and interdisciplinary endeavor that takes a diachronic perspective and builds on the knowledge of many researchers. As the discussion above has demonstrated, further results can be achieved only if we continue to work together on individual and/or group studies, publishing the available materials, cooperating, exchanging results, and taking into consideration various aspects of others' research.

Conclusion

In conclusion, I would like to emphasize three areas that are relevant to ongoing and future research, all of which use modern technologies and draw upon theoretical models from neighboring fields such as anthropology and sociology.[58]

- Material culture: There is still a great deal to be done with the materials preserved from Deir al-Medina—both on-site and in magazines and museums—especially with respect to the women of the community. In this volume, for instance, see the work by Rahel Glanzmann on female *shabtis*, with special attention to Deir al-Medina.[59]
- Anthropological studies: The surviving data for anthropological investigation is vast, as evidenced by Suzanne Onstine's and Anne Austin's contributions to this volume concerning women's health issues in TT 16.[60] Elsewhere, recent research by archaeologists working on Bronze Age Europe has shown that changes to the sacrum in female skeletons start at adolescence and may indicate when childbirth and motherhood began (this is evident at least from the age of sixteen onward, though motherhood may also have begun at an earlier age). The change to the sacrum occurs when a woman has many children, and is caused by the compressional forces of traumatic birth events, especially when giving birth at a young age.[61] Dental analysis of the remains of medieval women from the graveyards of monasteries evidences the role of women in early

book production: a middle-aged woman in Germany (1000–1200 CE) demonstrates ultramarine ink pigments in her mouth. As she licked the end of the brush while painting and writing, the pigments became stuck between the teeth.[62] Such investigations may be possible with respect to Deir al-Medina, and similar results could have a huge impact on our understanding of the role of women there.[63]

- Textual and prosopographic studies: The investigation of texts with new techniques, such as the ongoing analysis of the Ramesside papyri from Deir al-Medina in the collection of the Museo Egizio Turin, has the potential to make massive contributions to our knowledge.[64] Textual and prosopographic research combined with material studies and modern techniques of analysis make it possible to reconstruct lives on the micro-level, and allow us, for instance, to answer questions about the number of literate persons living in the village. Such studies may provide more details about the literacy of women at Deir al-Medina. In all cases, the evidence for women has to be weighed carefully and compared with the evidence for men in order to arrive at secure results.

All of these examples (and there are many more) require research that emphasizes teamwork and the exchange of results, a mode of cooperation for which we find a model within the ancient community of male and female workers at Deir al-Medina. This shared scholarly endeavor will facilitate a more thoroughly contextualized approach to the village. Rethinking our terminology, we should also use the gender-neutral "community of workers" in the future. The current designation "community of workmen" excludes women by its sole focus on (the work and duties of) the village's male inhabitants. But women played major roles in the village in all periods.[65] And even if, as the discussion above has shown, information about the women of Deir al-Medina is more difficult to generate and to interpret, details of these women can be discovered if we take a close(r) look at the available data,[66] thereby offering many insights into their lives some three thousand years ago.

Notes

1 I would like to thank Mariam Ayad for giving me the opportunity to present at the conference "Women in Ancient Egypt," Deborah Sweeney for feedback on the content, and Daniel Waller for improving the English of this article.

2 Jaroslav Černý, *A Community of Workmen at Thebes in the Ramesside Period*, 2nd ed., BdE 50 (Cairo: IFAO, 2001), 113–20, including the (male) youth who later became workmen.

3 Černý, *Community of Workmen*, 175–81, ch. 15, "Women Slaves."

4 The names of women were also added to the index of private personal names subsequently attached by Rob Demarée. Černý's interest apparently did not extend to women, at least not in

his planned volumes, though he did focus on them in other publications, such as Jaroslav Černy, *Egyptian Stelae in the Bankes Collection* (Oxford: Oxford University Press, 1958).

5 Černy MSS 25, as examined by the present author at the Griffith Institute Archive in Oxford in 2011.

6 Černý, *Community of Workmen*, 175n1, referring to Abd el-Mohsen Bakir, *Slavery in Pharaonic Egypt*, *SASAE* 18 (Cairo: IFAO, 1952): "On p. 102 is stated [sic] correctly that they were all women."

7 Tobias Hofmann, *Zur sozialen Bedeutung zweier Begriffe für "Diener": b3k und ḥm. Untersucht an Quellen vom Alten Reich bis zur Ramessidenzeit*, Aegyptiaca Helvetica 18 (Basel: Schwabe, 2005), 235–42, 332–33 (with missing parts of the text in lines rt. I, 1 and II, 1). O. Ashmolean Museum 90 (time of Ramesses II) includes the names of the male servants of the *ṯ3i-md̲3t Ḳn* (ii): the *ḥmw* *ʿn-ḥtp, Nfr-sẖrw, Ḥsi-ḥr-imntt, Ỉri.f, P3-rhni, Nẖi*, as well as a female servant, *Nd̲mt-ḥmsi*, and at least three (of her) children. Members of the same group are also mentioned on O. Glasgow D. 1925.83, which shows that *Ỉri.f, P3-rhni, Nẖi*, and *Wẖri3* were children of *Nd̲mt-ḥmsi*, cf. "The Deir el-Medina Database Leiden" accessed 24 March 2020, https://dmd.wepwawet.nl/. O. Turin N. 57068 records a gardener, *Ṯrj* (I), who received the monthly *b3kw*-workload of a male *b3k* from the workman *Ks s3 ʿ3-pḥti*, and a woman in a certain year 7, probably of Tawosret, cf. Kathrin Gabler, *Who's Who around Deir el-Medina. Untersuchungen zur Organisation, Prosopographie und Entwicklung des Versorgungspersonals für die Arbeitersiedlung und das Tal der Könige*, EGU 31 (Leiden and Leuven: Peeters, 2018), 279, 288, 673.

8 Dominique Valbelle, *Les ouvriers de la tombe: Deir el-Médineh à l'époque ramesside*, BdE 96 (Cairo: IFAO, 1985), 229–47.

9 Valbelle, *Ouvriers de la tombe*, 232.

10 Valbelle, *Ouvriers de la tombe*, 231–38, 242.

11 Morris L. Bierbrier, *The Tomb-builders of the Pharaohs* (London: American University in Cairo Press, 1982), 70–71.

12 Eugenij Bogoslovskij, *Drevneegipetskie mastera: Po materialam iz Der èl'-Medina. Altägyptische Meister anhand Materialien aus Deir el-Medina*, trans. Tatjana Waimer and Kathrin Gabler (Moscow: Springer, 1983).

13 Gabler, *Who's Who around Deir el-Medina*, 403–404, 436. There are few references to women in relation to the *smdt* personnel: O. Berlin P 12654 refers to forty-six women, but the interpretation of this passage is debated, cf. 584, 587. We know of six female deliverers of vegetables (O. DeM 52 and 294, cf. 276, 676). These tasks may have been undertaken as part of a family business. However, it is generally men who are represented in the texts, and women only in a few cases (464).

14 Bogoslovskij, *Drevneegipetskie mastera*, 101, 230. For a general discussion about sandals in Deir al-Medina for all age groups and genders, see Fredrik Hagen, "New Kingdom Sandals: A Philological Perspective," in *Tutankhamun's Footwear: Studies of Ancient Egyptian Footwear*, ed. Andre Veldmeijer (Norg: DrukWare; Sidestone Press, 2010), 193–97.

15 Bogoslovskij, *Drevneegipetskie mastera*, 259; Kathrin Gabler and Daniel Soliman, "P. Turin Provv. 3581: An Eighteenth Dynasty Letter from the Valley of the Queens in Context," *Rivista del Museo Egizio* 2 (2018): 15, 22, https://rivista.museoegizio.it/article/p-turin-provv-3581-an-eighteenth-dynasty-letter-from-the-valley-of-the-queens-in-context/, DOI: https://doi.org/10.29353/rime.2018.1671.

16 A possible reference to a woman in the Valley of the Kings (KV) is *Ḥnwt-nfrt* on O. Cairo CG 25598 (time of Ramesses V/VI), cf. Gabler, *Who's Who around Deir el-Medina*, 276. Setting aside texts found in the workmen's huts (which mention some women, usually among notes taken by men for private business and deliveries), only Meretseger is attested in the KV. There is no real evidence for the presence of women in this valley; cf. Andreas Dorn, *Arbeiterhütten im Tal der Könige. Ein Beitrag zur altägyptischen Sozialgeschichte aufgrund von neuem Quellenmaterial aus der Mitte der 20. Dynastie (ca. 1150 v. Chr.)*, Aegyptiaca Helvetica 23 (Basel: Schwabe, 2011).

17 Manfred Gutgesell, *Die Datierung der Ostraka und Papyri aus Deir el-Medineh und ihre ökonomische Interpretation. Teil I. Die 20. Dynastie* 1. Hildesheimer ägyptologische Beiträge 19 (Hildesheim: Gerstenberg, 1983), 624–27.

18 Benedict G. Davies, *Who's Who at Deir el-Medina: A Prosopographic Study of the Royal Workmen's Community*, EGU 13 (Leiden: NINO, 1999), 285–308. There are 1,234 people attested by name in Davies' study, usually numbered. The index includes three hundred workmen, 250 sons, seventy scribes, thirty-three chief workmen, twenty-eight deputies, forty-nine draftsmen, fifteen guardians, ten *medjay*, five doorkeepers, nine woodcutters, seven water carriers, four fishermen, three potters, two plasterers, and one laundryman. For comparison, I know of six hundred named deliverers in the service personnel, of which thirty-one are numbered by Davies. The proportion of community to *smdt*-suppliers is 2:1 in the Ramesside period, cf. Gabler, *Who's Who around Deir el-Medina*, 13, 52–54.

19 Gregor Neunert, *Mein Grab, mein Esel, mein Platz in der Gesellschaft: Prestige im Alten Ägypten am Beispiel Deir el-Medine*, Manetho 1 (Berlin: Manetho, 2010), 105–108.

20 Jaana Toivari-Viitala, *Women at Deir el-Medina: A Study of the Status and Roles of the Female Inhabitants in the Workmen's Community during the Ramesside Period*, EGU 15 (Leiden: NINO, 2001), 5.

21 Neunert, *Mein Grab, mein Esel*, 108; Toivari-Viitala, *Women at Deir el-Medina*, 189, 192–93; Deborah Sweeney, "Women and Language in the Ramesside Period or, Why Women Don't Say Please," in *Proceedings of the Seventh International Congress of Egyptologists, Cambridge, 3–9 September 1995*, ed. Christopher J. Eyre (Leuven: Peeters, 1998), 1116.

22 Benedict G. Davies, *Life within the Five Walls: A Handbook to Deir el-Medina* (Wallasey: Abercromby Press, 2018). The entry for "marriage" mentions the terms *snt, ḥmt, nbt-pr* (181), and *t3 rḫit* for women (375–76). Among the queens, only Ahmose-Nefertari merits an entry; among the goddesses, only Hathor and Meretseger.

23 Davies, *Life within the Five Walls*, 475–79.

24 Davies, *Life within the Five Walls*, 313–15. Reviewed by the present author in "Rezension Davies, Benedict G.: *Life within the Five Walls. A Handbook to Deir el-Medina* (Wallasey: Abercromby Press, 2018 . . .)," *OLZ* 115, no. 3 (2020): 210–14.

25 Toivari-Viitala, *Women at Deir el-Medina*, 11–12.

26 Koen Donker van Heel, *Mrs. Naunakhte and Family: The Women of Ramesside Deir al-Medina* (Cairo: American University in Cairo Press, 2016).

27 From this document, P. Ashmolean Museum 1945.97, we know that *Niwt-nḫt.ti* was first married to a famous scribe, *Ḳni-ḥr-ḫpš.f*. Related texts do not mention her by name, but can nevertheless be collated on the basis of their content. These texts include P. Ashmolean Museum 1945.95 and P. DeM 23 and 25; they record the children of *Ḳni-ḥr-ḫpš.f* and "their mother." For details, consult the DMD Leiden. Further evidence may be found on a double-seated statue from tomb 1126 (flanking the doorway to the inner room). This records the name of a certain *Ḳni-ḥr-ḫpš.f* and his wife, though her name is either not preserved or was not even given; the statue may record the famous scribe and his wife *Niwt-nḫt.ti*, as most of their namesakes lived in the Twentieth Dynasty, cf. Davies, *Who's Who at Deir el-Medina*, 85; PM I^2, 687; Neunert, *Mein Grab, mein Esel*, 172. A discussion of the four attested men called *Ḳni-ḥr-ḫpš.f* will appear in the present author's forthcoming study of the stone block UBKVP 526.

28 For example, the story of *Ỉi-nfrt* (iii), the wife of *Sn-nḏm* (i), is certainly one to tell: she lived to be roughly seventy years old, had at least ten children, a broken right arm, no teeth, and apparently became blind, as she recorded on Bankes Stela no. 6. She believed her blindness was a result of gossiping about other women. The same expression for blindness is used by *Nfr-3bw* (stela BM EA 589, attributed to a false vow by the name of Ptah); by *Ỉmn-nḫt* (stela BM EA 374); and by *Ḥri3* (stela ME 50050). Adel Mahmoud, "Ii-neferti, a Poor Woman," *MDAIK* 55 (1999): 315–23; Renate Germer and Claudia Näser, "Sie wurden in alle Winde verstreut. Das Schicksal der Mumien aus dem Grab des Sennedjem," in *Ägyptische Mumien. Unsterblichkeit im Land der Pharaonen* (Mainz am Rhein: Philipp von Zabern; Stuttgart: Landesmuseum Württemberg, 2007), 94–105. Many objects belonging to *Ỉi-nfrt* are attested.

29 Deborah Sweeney, *Gender and Religious Activities at Deir el-Medina*, OBO (Leuven: Peeters, forthcoming). Women could act as professional singers, priestesses, mourners, in ritual

performances, as members in court, as business partners, and as representatives of their husbands at work (on duty in watch lists, for instance).

30 Deborah Sweeney, "Women at Worship on Deir el-Medina Stelae," in *Deir el-Medina Studies: Helsinki June 24–26, 2009 Proceedings*, ed. Jaana Toivari-Viitala, Turo Vartiainen, and Saara Uvanto, The Finnish Egyptological Society—Occasional Publications 2 (Vantaa: Multiprint, 2014), 179–90; Deborah Sweeney, "Women at Deir el-Medîna," in *Women in Antiquity: Real Women across the Ancient World*, ed. Stephanie L. Budin and Jean M. Turfa (London: Routledge, 2016), 243–54; Deborah Sweeney, "Women Growing Older in Deir el-Medina," in *Living and Writing in Deir el-Medine: Socio-historical Embodiment of Deir el-Medine Texts*, ed. Andreas Dorn and Tobias Hofmann, Aegyptiaca Helvetica 19 (Basel: Schwabe, 2006), 135–53; Deborah Sweeney, "Gender and Language in Ramesside Egyptian," *LingAeg* 14 (2006): 433–50.

31 The nature of many of these remains is fragmentary, though this is the case for most ancient objects. Egyptologists are generally provisioned with well-preserved evidence, especially at Deir al-Medina.

32 A summary and discussion are provided in Susanne Beck and Kathrin Gabler, "Die Überlieferung von Text und Befund in Deir el-Medine am Beispiel des Wächters Khawy/*Ḫ3wj* (ii)," in *En détail—Philologie und Archäologie im Diskurs: Festschrift für Hans-Werner Fischer-Elfert*, ed. Marc Brose, Peter Dils, Franziska Naether, Lutz Popko, and Dietrich Raue, *ZÄS* Beihefte 7 (Berlin and Boston: De Gruyter, 2019), 29–35.

33 The literary texts are more difficult to date and are set aside here.

34 Ben J.J. Haring, "From Oral Practice to Written Record in Ramesside Deir el-Medina," *JESHO* 46, no. 3 (2003): 249–72; Ben J.J. Haring, "Workmen's Marks and the Early History of the Theban Royal Necropolis," in *Deir el-Medina Studies: Helsinki June 24–26, 2009 Proceedings*, ed. Jaana Toivari-Viitala, Turo Vartiainen, and Saara Uvanto, The Finnish Egyptological Society—Occasional Publications 2 (Vantaa: Multiprint, 2014), 87–100; Gabler, *Who's Who around Deir el-Medina*, 440–42; Abb. 12.

35 Beck and Gabler, "Die Überlieferung von Text," 29–35.

36 Valbelle, *Ouvriers de la tombe*, 232; Morris L. Bierbrier, "Geneaology and Chronology: Theory and Practice," in *Village Voices: Proceedings of the Symposium "Texts from Deir el-Medîna and Their Interpretation," Leiden, 31.05.–01.06.1991*, ed. Robert J. Demarée and Arno Egberts (Leiden: CNWS, 1992), 1–7; Davies, *Life within the Five Walls*, 181; Sweeney, "Women at Worship," 179.

37 Neunert, *Mein Grab, mein Esel*, 106; Toivari-Viitala, *Women at Deir el-Medina*, 47–48. Jacobus J. Janssen (*Donkeys at Deir el-Medîna*, EGU 19 [Leiden: NINO, 2005], table VII) records only one woman in his summary. However, several texts record women involved in donkey business: O. Berlin P 14214 (hire of a donkey), O. DeM 569 (a woman obtains a donkey and hires it out), and O. DeM 10099 (letter written by *T3i.sn* mentions a donkey).

38 Several journals, usually in absence-lists of men, record that a wife or daughter gave birth, or mention menstruation, but without further information; see, for example, O. Ashmolean Museum 679 or O. BM EA 5634. Wolfgang Helck, *Die datierten und datierbaren Ostraka, Papyri und Graffiti von Deir el-Medineh, bearbeitet von Adelheid Schlott*, ÄA 63 (Wiesbaden: Harrassowitz, 2002), 33, reason r and z (i.e., workman absent from work because his wife/daughter gave birth, etc.); Terry G. Wilfong, "Menstrual Synchrony and the 'Place of Women' in Ancient Egypt (Oriental Institute Museum Hieratic Ostracon 13512)," in *Gold of Praise: Studies on Ancient Egypt in Honor of Edward F. Wente*, ed. Emily Teeter and John A. Larson (Chicago: Oriental Institute of the University of Chicago, 1999), 419–34.

39 The complete details of this object can be found in Kathrin Gabler, "Stele Turin CGT 50057 (= cat. 1514) im ikonografischen und prosopografischen Kontext Deir el-Medines. *Nbt-pr Mwt/-m-w3* (vi) im Spannungsfeld der Mächte der Taweret und des Seth?," *Rivista del Museo Egizio* 1 (2017): 1–39, https://rivista.museoegizio.it/article/stele-turin-cgt-50057-cat-1514-im-ikonografischen-und-prosopografischen-kontext-deir-el-medines-nb-t-pr-mw-t-m-wja-vi-im-spannungsfeld-der-machte-der-taweret-und-des-seth/.

40 *Nfr-rnpt* (iii), (iv), and (VII) are unlikely candidates. See Gabler, "Stele Turin CGT 50057," 11–12. The second wife of *Nfr-rnpt* (i) was *M3ḥi* (i). Gabler, "Stele Turin CGT 50057," 11–12, 20.

41 The suffix *s* connects the women to *Mwt* from a male perspective. Gabler, "Stele Turin CGT 50057," 18–20.

42 Gabler, "Stele Turin CGT 50057," 11–12.

43 The inclusion of many female relatives was possibly intended to extend the effectiveness of the object.

44 Valbelle, *Ouvriers de la tombe*, 246; Gabler, "Stele Turin CGT 50057," 31–32.

45 The most relevant publications for the investigation of the stela are Gay Robins, "The Relationships Specified by Egyptian Kinship Terms of the Middle and New Kingdoms," *CdE* 54 (1979): 197–209; Gay Robins, "Some Principles of Compositional Dominance and Gender Hierarchy in Egyptian Art," *JARCE* 31 (1994): 33–40; Karen Exell, *Soldiers, Sailors and Sandalmakers: A Social Reading of Ramesside Period Votive Stelae*, GHP 10 (London: Golden House, 2009); Jan Moje, *Untersuchungen zur hieroglyphischen Paläographie und Klassifizierung der Privatstelen der 19. Dynastie*, ÄAT 67 (Wiesbaden: Harrassowitz, 2007); Morris L. Bierbrier, "Terms of Relationship at Deir el-Medina," *JEA* 66 (1980): 100–107; Jaroslav Černý, "Consanguineous Marriages in Pharaonic Egypt," *JEA* 40 (1954): 23–29; Bierbrier, "Geneaology and Chronology," 1–7; Joris F. Borghouts, "Divine Intervention in Ancient Egypt and Its Manifestation (*b3w*)," in *Gleanings from Deir el-Medina*, ed. Robert J. Demarée and Jacobus J. Janssen, EGU 1 (Leiden: NINO, 1982), 1–70; Bernard Bruyère, "Journal de fouilles: Deir el Médineh," archives de l'IFAO, *Archives de Bernard Bruyère (1879–1971)*, http://www.ifao.egnet.net/bases/archives/bruyere/; Anne H. Bomann, *The Private Chapel in Ancient Egypt* (London and New York: Kegan Paul International, 1991).

46 For the methodology and case study for Sennedjem, see Kathrin Gabler and Anne-Claire Salmas, "'Make Yourself at Home': Some 'House Biographies' from Deir el-Medina, with a Special Focus on the Domestic (and Funerary) Spaces of Sennedjem's Family," in *"Deir el-Medina Through the Kaleidoscope," Proceedings of the Turin International Workshop*, ed. Paolo del Vesco, Christian Greco, Federico Poole, and Susanne Töpfer (Turin: Rivista del Museo Egizio, forthcoming); Kathrin Gabler, *Homes through Time: The Inhabitants of Deir el-Medina and Their Houses Revisited* (in preparation).

47 Guillemette Andreu, *Les artistes de Pharaon. Deir el-Médineh et la Vallée des Rois, Paris, Musée du Louvre, 15 avril–5 août 2002, Bruxelles, Musées royaux d'art et d'histoire, 11 septembre 2002–12 janvier 2003, Turin, Fondation Bricherasio, 11 février–18 mai 2003* (Paris, Turnhout, Belgium: Réunion des musées nationaux, 2002), 25, fig. 5; Andreas Dorn, "Ostraka aus der Regierungszeit Sethos' I. aus Deir el-Medineh und dem Tal der Könige. Zur Mannschaft und zur Struktur des Arbeiterdorfes vor dem Bau des Ramesseums," *MDAIK* 67 (2011): 31–52.

48 The Ramesside houses were standardized to a certain degree, depending on whether they were rebuilt or modified in the northern sectors or newly constructed in the southern sectors at the beginning of the Nineteenth Dynasty. Sections S.E. and S.O. were added in the early Ramesside period and follow the shape of the wadi. Their floor plan thus differs from the houses in the north. Andreu, *Les artistes de Pharaon*, 24–28; Lara Weiss, *Religious Practice at Deir el-Medina*, EGU 29 (Leiden: NINO, 2015), 26–31.

49 Gabler and Salmas, "'Make Yourself at Home.'" Category A: assigned via inscriptions on (fixed) architectural elements or cultic installations; Category B: assigned via inscriptions on walls, discovered either in situ or (well-)documented in excavations reports; Category C: assigned via inscriptions on movable objects, such as (fragments of) stelae, statues, doors, ostraca, and so forth; Category D: a negative category of evidence, used to indicate a lack of inscriptions attributable to previous inhabitants. In these instances, uninscribed domestic artifacts only occasionally offer small clues about the daily activities of the inhabitants of the house.

50 Fourteen of these meet the criteria of Category A and are usually dated to the early Ramesside period (when the entire settlement was restructured and the houses were decorated, often for the last time in the next 250 years). The criteria of Category B pertain to only two houses; they date

from the middle to the end of the Twentieth Dynasty. Nineteen buildings meet the criteria for Category C; they feature movable inscribed objects which date from the entirety of the Ramesside period, though the surviving stelae and statues tend to date to the first half of the Nineteenth Dynasty and the ostraca to the Twentieth Dynasty. See above and Gabler, *Homes through Time.*

51 Gabler and Salmas, "'Make Yourself at Home'": at least eight of these houses appear to have been occupied by relatives of the first attested inhabitants from the reign of Seti I onward. In at least a further five buildings, a particular family can be traced over an even longer period, though this happens later than the time of Ramesses II.

52 Whether these patterns repeated elsewhere cannot be known due to a lack of information, especially written sources.

53 Davies, *Life within the Five Walls*, 181. For instance, marriages between professional artisans in the early Nineteenth Dynasty are hard to prove.

54 An initial survey shows that at least sixteen daughters of influential families of foremen, scribes, and draftsmen married within the village in the reigns of Seti I and Ramesses II: three daughters of *B3ki* (i), four from the *Ḥwi* (ii) and *Ḳ3ḥ3* (i) family, three from the *Nfr-ḥtp* (i) family, four from the *Ipwi* (v) and *Nfr-rnpt* (i) family, and two from the *Pi3i* (ii) family. With respect to the daughters of ordinary workmen, we lose track of these women due to a lack of documention. Valbelle (*Ouvriers de la tombe*, 231) argues that most of these women must have married outside the village and left.

55 Details will be provided in Gabler and Salmas, "'Make Yourself at Home'" (forthcoming). *Nb-ḏf3w* (i) and his son *Ḥri-nfr* (i) occupied house S.E. II, while *Ḥri-nfr* (i) moved to live with his first wife *Wbḫt* (i/iv) in house N.E. XII. But the marriage between *Ḥri-nfr* and *Wbḫt* did not last for long; they appear to have divorced. *Ḥri-nfr* (i) then married *Ḥmt-nṯr* (i), with whom he may have had two children; the family kept house N.E. XII. *Wbḫt* (i/iv = ii) also married again and moved into house S.E. III which belonged to *Nfr-ḥtp* (ii). There she was the neighbor of her first father-in-law (*Nb-ḏf3w*). See Davies, *Who's Who at Deir el-Medina*, Charts 6 and 20.

56 Bernard Bruyère, *Rapport sur les fouilles de Deir el Médineh (1934–1935). Troisième partie. Le village, les décharges publiques, la station de repos du col de la Vallée des Rois*, FIFAO 16 (Cairo: IFAO, 1939), 69 (referring to it accidentally as C. VII), 304–308. Diverse objects have been found in C. V that refer to various persons. Following Weiss, *Religious Practice at Deir el-Medina*, 86, it appears that the family of *Nb-n-M3ʿt* (ii) are the most likely candidates for occupancy of this home in the early Ramesside period; this is according to the criteria for Category C objects. These can be linked with the base of a column that is inscribed with the name *Ḥwi*, who was probably *Ḥwi* (ii). See Davies, *Who's Who at Deir el-Medina*, charts 21 and 27; Gabler, *Homes through Time*, in preparation. *Mri.s-gr* (v) was a niece of *Ḳ3ḥ3* (i).

57 According to Bruyère, the two buildings derive from the division of an Eighteenth Dynasty house at the beginning of the Nineteenth Dynasty. See Bruyère, *Rapport sur les fouilles de Deir el Médineh (1934–1935)*, 283–85; Gabler and Salmas, "'Make Yourself at Home.'"

58 For example, Hana Navrátilová, "Gender and Historiography (in Deir el-Medina)?," in *Sozialisationen: Individuum—Gruppe—Gesellschaft. Beiträge des ersten Münchner Arbeitskreises Junge Aegyptologie (MAJA 1), 3.–5.12.2010*, ed. Gregor Neunert, Kathrin Gabler, and Alexandra Verbovsek, GOF IV, vol. 51 (Wiesbaden: Harrassowitz, 2012), 149–67.

59 Rahel Glanzmann, "Some Remarks on the *Shabti* Corpus of Iyneferty," in this volume.

60 Suzanne Onstine et al., "Women's Health Issues as Seen in Theban Tomb 16," in this volume.

61 Doris Pany-Kucera et al., "Sacral Preauricular Extensions, Notches and Corresponding Iliac Changes: New Terms and the Proposal of a Recording System," *International Journal of Osteoarchaeology* 29 (2019): 1013–21, accessed 28 August 2021, https://onlinelibrary.wiley.com/doi/10.1002/oa.2814; on a project on "Unlocking the Secrets of Cremated Human Remains," see Katharina Rebay-Salisbury, "Doctor, Is There Still Something You Can Do? CT-scanning Bronze Age Urns," Motherhood in Prehistory (blog), 17 May 2021, https://motherhoodinprehistory.wordpress.com/, accessed 28 March 2020.

62 Anita Radini et al., "Medieval Women's Early Involvement in Manuscript Production Suggested by Lapis Lazuli Identification in Dental Calculus," *Science Advances* 5, no. 1 (2019): 1–8, https://advances.sciencemag.org/content/5/1/eaau7126, accessed 28 March 2020.

63 Initial results are to be found in the work by Anne Austin, who has already investigated five hundred human remains from Deir al-Medina found in TT 6, TT 217, and TT 291, http://www.anneeaustin.com/bioarchaeology-at-deir-el-medina/, accessed 28 March 2020.

64 "Crossing Boundaries: Understanding Complex Scribal Practices in Ancient Egypt," http://web.philo.ulg.ac.be/x-bound/, accessed 28 March 2020; Robert J. Demarée, Kathrin Gabler, and Stéphane Polis, "A Family Affair in the Community of Deir el-Medina. Gossip Girls in Two 19th Dynasty Letters," in *Ägyptologische "Binsen"-Weisheiten IV. Hieratisch des Neuen Reiches: Akteure, Formen und Funktionen. Akten der internationalen Tagung in der Akademie der Wissenschaften und der Literatur, Mainz im Dezember 2019*, ed. Svenja Gülden, Tobias Konrad, and Ursula Verhoeven, Abhandlungen der Geistes- und sozialwissenschaftlichen Klasse. Einzelveröffentlichung (Stuttgart: Steiner, 2022, forthcoming), 43–126.

65 Already in the Eighteenth Dynasty, women and children were buried alongside men in the necropoleis around the village. These women and children must have been related to the men involved in tomb construction. Ostraca showing identity marks belonging to specific workmen were found in the Valley of the Kings during the excavation of different structures from the Thutmosid period. The same marks appear on funerary equipment found in the tombs of children in the eastern and western necropoleis. There seems to be a relation between the men working in the valley (as represented by such marks) and some of the burials along the hills of the village. These tombs are undecorated and the oldest date to the reigns of Hatshepsut/Thutmose III. Families may already have been living in the village for longer periods, even permanently. Haring, "Workmen's Marks," 87–100; Daniel Soliman, "Workmen's Marks in Pre-Amarna Tombs at Deir el-Medina," in *Non-textual Marking Systems in Ancient Egypt (and Elsewhere)*, ed. Julia Budka, Frank Kammerzell, and Slawomir Rzepka, LingAegSM 16 (Berlin: Widmaier, 2015), 109–32.

66 The extent to which any of this information about the women of Deir al-Medina can be used to draw wider conclusions about women in Ancient Egypt remains an open question, however. Cf. Navrátilová, "Gender and Historiography," 153–56, 164.

15

Some Remarks on the *Shabti* Corpus of Iyneferty

Rahel Glanzmann

THIS PAPER PRESENTS THOUGHTS on the *shabtis* of Iyneferty, the wife of Sennedjem, who was a servant in the Place of Truth at Deir al-Medina in the Nineteenth Dynasty. Although her *shabtis* have all been published and well documented, they have not been closely studied as a whole, coherent ensemble. The aim of this paper is to demonstrate the great variety in form, iconography, text, and material that can occur within a group of *shabtis* for an individual owner. Such diversity among *shabtis* was not unusual, but Iyneferty's case is unique because her *shabti* corpus contains statuettes that display both the conventional androgynous form and female iconography. In addition to this discussion, a brief excursus outlines aspects of the general *shabti* practice used in female burials.

Bickel[1] has argued that the presence of men and women in the depictions on tomb walls illustrates that both sexes could expect the same conditions in the afterlife. While in real life the social status of men and women differed, there was no difference in their status at the ideological, ontological, or religious levels. Men and women had identical expectations for the hereafter, and both could meet deities in the same way.[2] Thus, they had to face the same challenges, undergo the same journey through the netherworld, and be confronted with the same judgment in the Hall of Two Truths. Eventually, both sexes were integrated into the community of Osiris and were equally summoned to work in the fields of the Sechet-Iaru.

Women thus received burials that were similar to those of men,[3] and from their first occurrence, *shabtis* were associated with both male and female burials. The precursors of the *shabti* statuette were probably wax or mud funerary figurines that were modeled after the naked human body and placed in miniature coffins.[4] They were found in burials of the Ninth through Tenth Dynasties in Saqqara and Deir al-Bahari.[5] These small, crude objects were often inscribed with personal names and served most likely as a substitute body for the deceased. Over the course of the Twelfth Dynasty, *shabti*s developed into the typical male or rather gender-neutral, androgynous Osirian mummiform figures while still representing an image of the owner. Additionally, with the introduction of agricultural implements as part of their iconography in the New Kingdom, *shabti*s acted as stand-ins for the deceased when he was summoned to perform field work in the afterlife.

In the Eighteenth Dynasty, the range of materials, sizes, forms, and individual iconographical features for *shabti*s increased considerably. Based on the example of the *shabti*s belonging to Iyneferty, this paper aims to demonstrate how this diversity could be manifested within a complete *shabti* set for a deceased.

The *Shabti* Corpus of Iyneferty

Iyneferty, "Mistress of the House" and wife of the workman Sennedjem, was buried in tomb TT 1 at Deir al-Medina beside her husband and other family members—twenty individuals in total. The tomb dates to the Ramesside period under the reign of Pharaoh Seti I and the early years of Ramesses II. It was discovered by workmen from Qurna and cleared by Gaston Maspero in 1886. The first publication of the tomb was by Bernard Bruyère in 1959.[6] TT 1 represents the only undisturbed Ramesside tomb of this site. More than 180 artefacts have been found in the funerary chamber, among them seventy-four *shabti*s.[7]

The New Kingdom *shabti*s from the workmen from Deir al-Medina are often attributed to this site because they exhibit typical characteristics. Their polychrome decoration on a white background characterizes the most representative and homogenous *shabti* corpus known today. However, this group of funerary statuettes has to date not been the subject of systematic study.[8] Most of the *shabti*s from Deir al-Medina are dispersed among different collections, not only at the Cairo Museum, but also in Europe, at the British Museum in London, at the Louvre in Paris, and at the Egyptian Museum in Turin. Yet many of them remain unpublished or poorly published.

All the *shabti*s found in TT 1 were published in 2011 by Mahmoud Abd el-Qader,[9] who illustrated and described them in a well-compiled catalogue. However, no deeper analysis was provided. Eight *shabti*s that are known today can be attributed to Iyneferty. Two further statuettes originating from TT 1 name both Iyneferty and her son, Khabekhnet II, and can thus be considered shared items. Table 15.1 presents an overview of all the *shabti*s of Iyneferty. Her *shabti*s display a striking variety, not only in their stylistic, iconographic, and textual details, but also in their sizes and materials.

Table 15.1: The *shabti* corpus of Iyneferty

ID	Form	Wig type	Implements	Text and text position	Material	Height (cm)
Cairo-CM-1[10]	Conventional mummy	Tripartite	No	BoD Ch. 6 across body in horizontal lines	Painted limestone	20.5
Cairo-CM-2[11]	Conventional mummy	Tripartite	Two hoes, one bag	BoD Ch. 6 across body in horizontal lines	Painted limestone	16.5
NY-CM-1[12]	Conventional mummy	Tripartite	Two hoes	Short text (*Wsjr NN*) Single vertical text line in front of body	Limestone (unfinished)	16.0
NY-CM-2[13]	Conventional mummy	Tripartite	No hoes, two bags	BoD Ch. 6 across body in horizontal lines	Painted wood	20.5
TUR-CM-1[14]	Conventional mummy	Tripartite	No hoes, two bags	BoD Ch. 6 across body in horizontal lines	Painted limestone	23.0
NY-CM-3[15]	Conventional mummy	Tripartite	No hoes, two bags	BoD Ch. 6 across body in horizontal lines	Painted limestone	15.0
Cairo-FM-1[16]	Female mummy	Enveloping female	No	BoD Ch. 6 across body in vertical lines	Painted wood	20.0
SB-FM-1[17]	Female mummy	Tripartite	No	Short text (*Wsjr ṯ NN*) Single vertical text line in front of body	Painted limestone	19.0
Lyon-FM-1[18]	Female mummy	Enveloping female	No	BoD Ch. 6 across body in vertical lines	Painted wood	21.5
NY-DoL-1[19]	*Shabti* in dress of daily life	Tripartite	Two hoes	Short text (*Wsjr NN*) Vertical text line in front of body	Painted limestone	16.7

Shaded row = shared shabti

Variety in Form and Iconography

While the *shabtis* of Iyneferty take various forms, all but one are mummiform. One *shabti*, inscribed with both Iyneferty's and also her son's (Kabekhnet II) names, wears the dress of daily life—but not yet the common pleated version. This is expressed by the visible feet and a hem of the sheath dress delicately indicated above the ankles.[20]

Most of Iyneferty's mummiform *shabtis* exhibit conventional androgynous attire: a mummiform figure wearing a tripartite wig. This standard coiffure for *shabtis* divides the hair into three parts: two lappets on the chest and one at the back, with the hair ends held in place by a horizontal band.[21] This hairstyle is the same for *shabtis* throughout their history. As the traditional headdress of the gods, the tripartite wig clearly associates the wearer of this headdress with the divine sphere.

Three of Iyneferty's mummiform *shabtis* are clearly differentiated by their female appearance.[22] One mummiform *shabti* displays somewhat softer facial traits.[23] Two examples wear an elaborate female wig, the so-called enveloping wig, a hairstyle that is undivided and covers the shoulders.[24] The enveloping wig is the female counterpart of the male duplex wig. The duplex wig is generally associated with the dress of daily life that was first introduced on mummiform *shabtis* during the reign of Amenhotep III,[25] before being associated with *shabtis* in the complete dress of daily life.[26]

Thus, the female enveloping hairstyle can be considered an element of daily life, contrasting with the still mummiform shape of the body. The "enveloping wig" was first introduced on *shabtis* in the late Eighteenth Dynasty and became popular in the Ramesside period. It was abandoned with the increase in the number of *shabtis* provided per person and the associated mass production of *shabtis* during the Third Intermediate Period. The tendency to render *shabtis* with a female physiognomy developed during the reign of Thutmose III[27] and is evident in a few *shabtis* for women in the New Kingdom.[28]

Jewelry, such as the *wsḫ*-collar, was common on *shabtis* during the New Kingdom.[29] Every *shabti* belonging to Iyneferty has one, which in most cases extends over the hands; in two cases, it ends above the crossed hands.[30] On one *shabti*, finely carved armlets are present.[31]

Without exception, Iyneferty's *shabtis* take the common position with the arms and hands crossed over the chest. Five are posed with crossed hands and no arms indicated,[32] and the other five have modeled arms and elbows. The majority are not equipped with either implements or attributes. Three *shabtis* hold a hoe[33] in each hand, with one of the three having a single bag hanging behind the right shoulder.[34] Two empty-handed *shabtis* are equipped with two square bags hanging over the back of each shoulder.[35]

Material and Color

Iyneferty's *shabtis* are made of either limestone[36] or wood.[37] In the New Kingdom, the majority of *shabtis* were manufactured out of wood or stone. Limestone, in particular, became highly popular during the Eighteenth and Nineteenth Dynasties. The *shabtis* differ in size, ranging from 15 cm to 23 cm.

The decoration and inscriptions are painted and/or carved. No differences are observable in the background painting, which is invariably white with the inscription in black. The skin color, without exception, is a dark reddish tone.[38] The typical polychrome painting is missing on only one unfinished limestone *shabti*.[39]

Text Position and Variations

The paleography of the hieroglyphs on Iyneferty's *shabtis* is highly characteristic for the *shabti* corpus from Deir al-Medina. The inscriptions are variably shorter or longer hieroglyphic texts. The shorter text variant is present on three *shabtis* and consists of a single vertical line of text, which includes epithets, title, and the name of the deceased.[40] The content of the short text can vary: *Wsir NN* and *Wsir* T *NN* with or without the locution *mꜣꜥ ḫrw*.[41] It is worth noting that the *shabtis* bearing the shorter text do not comprise an iconographically homogenous group. In addition to a common androgynous item, the *shabti* with female facial features[42] and the statuette Iyneferty shared with her son[43] are inscribed with this text version.

The longer text, chapter 6 of the *Book of the Dead*—known as the "*shabti* spell"[44]—is present on seven figurines. The *shabti* spell expounds the basis for understanding the purpose and function of the *shabti*: it substitutes for the deceased in the field work that the deceased is called on to perform in the afterlife. This inscription is attested in vertical lines on the two mummiform *shabtis* with female headdress.[45] On five specimens, the text is structured in horizontal bands.[46] The hieroglyphic text of both variations extends over six to eight lines, intersected by red lines. With the exception of one *shabti*,[47] all bear an incomplete version of the *shabti* spell, possibly due to lack of space.

Whereas in the shorter texts only the name and title may reveal the sex of the *shabti*'s owner, the longer texts can display adaptions in the grammatical indicative of gender. Only three *shabtis* of Iyneferty's corpus display gender indications, which are mainly observed in a kind of introductory clause. This so-called "Preliminary" usually contains the epithet *Wsir*, the title, and the name of the deceased, and is preceded—in the New Kingdom—by the *sḥḏ*-notion.[48] The Preliminary is followed by the phrase *ḏd.f* ("he says"), meaning that the deceased speaks the text that follows to the *shabti* on which the spell appears. In the subsequent direct speech, the *shabti* is summoned to take over the owner's work in the afterlife.

The three aforementioned *shabtis* use the feminine personal pronoun *.s* (*ḏd.s*) to open the direct speech. Two among these are those with female wigs.[49] In these cases, it was apparent to the craftsman that the statuette was intended for a woman. Nevertheless, one of the *shabtis* displaying the same textual gender adaptions is of a common androgynous mummiform type.[50]

On one of the two *shabtis* with female wigs,[51] the inscription displays a further gender adaption. The direct speech of the *shabti* spell starts with the invocation "*ỉ šbti*." The *šbti* is usually followed by the determinative of a standing (𓀾 Gardiner A53) or reclining mummy (𓀿 Gardiner A54). Exclusively on this *shabti*, the determinative of the sitting woman (𓁐 Gardiner B1) is present.[52]

Excursus on the Use of *Shabtis* in Female Burials

Women were typically buried in their husbands' tombs; only in rare cases did a woman possess her own tomb chapel.[53] Furthermore, some scholars have noted that the funerary equipment for men was often richer and of better quality.[54] These observations apply, at least partially, to *shabtis*.

Women were frequently provided with fewer *shabtis* compared to their male counterparts. For example, in KV 46 of Yuya and Tuya, a total of twenty *shabtis* are known, fourteen of which belong to Yuya and only four to Tuya.[55] Moreover, burials in Deir al-Medina clearly contained fewer *shabtis* for women compared to their male relatives. In some tombs, while the deceased male owned *shabtis*, none could be found for the female deceased.[56] An example is TT 8 in Deir al-Medina, which was an intact burial assemblage.[57] No *shabtis* for Merit could be found, whereas her husband, Kha, possessed two.[58] This practice can also be attested for later periods. In Qurna (Theban Necropolis) Petrie unearthed four *shabti* boxes in a tomb for a man and a woman of the later Third Intermediate Period. The two larger boxes, holding 200 and 203 pottery *shabtis* respectively, were attributed to the male individual. The two smaller boxes, which contained 185 and 183 *shabti* figurines respectively, all smaller than the first set, had been placed on the woman's coffin.[59]

Generally, female individuals were more likely to have *shabtis* included in their burials if their husbands or male relatives were provided with such items. Commonly, if the male tomb owner did not have any *shabtis*, neither did the female partner. This practice is illustrated not only by evidence from Deir al-Medina,[60] but can also be seen in the New Kingdom burials of the Nubian necropolis of Aniba.[61] In Iyneferty's case, the pattern was confirmed. Eight *shabtis*, plus two shared *shabtis*, can be assigned to Iyneferty, whereas sixteen were found for her husband, Sennedjem. Furthermore, the *shabtis* ascribed to other female family members buried in TT 1 are outnumbered by *shabtis* belonging to male relatives.[62]

Differences in the quality of workmanship of *shabtis* for men and women can be observed in some cases.[63] However, for *shabtis*, this is not a general rule; many examples exhibit equal or comparable quality. Iyneferty's *shabtis* are of the same quality as her husband's.

Interpretation

The fact that a statuette within a *shabti* set for one person could display a broad range in terms of iconography, style, material, and size is not unusual. This diversity could occur for elite individuals,[64] as well as for kings.[65] Iyneferty's case is exceptional for the New Kingdom, as her *shabti* corpus contains both androgynous and female statuettes. This is noteworthy because the notion that a deceased person could own both female and conventional *shabti* statuettes at once developed only in the Third Intermediate Period, with a further increase in the number of *shabtis* provided per person. In the Middle Kingdom, the number of *shabtis* provided per person varied, but never exceeded five.[66] In the New Kingdom, the number increased gradually and continually, and reached as many as a dozen to several hundred *shabtis* in the Twentieth Dynasty. The number continued to increase, with the role of the *shabti* as servant or worker being emphasized.

Over the course of this development, *shabtis* wearing the dress of daily life took over the role as overseers. A *shabti* "gang" was thus hierarchically organized and divided into worker and overseer statuettes. The large increase in number led to mass production, and *shabtis* became more uniform; the differences between male and female features tended to diminish. Nevertheless, worker *shabtis* could comprise a combined workforce of both male and female *shabtis*, regardless of the owner's sex, with the female *shabti* being distinguishable only by her accentuated breasts. These developments led to a gradual dissociation between the identity of the *shabti* and its owner; scholars often speak of a "depersonalization" of the *shabtis*.[67]

Although these conceptual changes had already started to develop in the late New Kingdom, they are not yet observable in Iyneferty's case. Evidence appears in several aspects. In the gender adaptions in the inscriptions, the feminine determinative is particularly crucial on one of her statuettes, confirming that the statuette was still intended to equate to Iyneferty herself. Moreover, the presence of female *shabtis* in her corpus shows an obvious desire to focus on her personal identity.

The impulse for incorporating female *shabtis* within a *shabti* corpus of commonly androgynous statuettes may imply a deeper meaning that may have been related to the general trend toward innovation that began in the New Kingdom under Thutmose III and culminated during the reign of Amenhotep III. This was a period of new innovations in art.[68] The *shabti* figurines were duly affected, resulting in the introduction of new types and diverse individual iconographical features.[69] Moreover, the appearance of the first *shabti* for a king—namely, that of Ahmose, the first ruler of the Eighteenth Dynasty[70]—may have influenced the further development away from gender-neutral statuettes. The king defined his social identity through his status, as implied by the royal regalia on his *shabtis*. However, private persons demonstrated their social identity by the differentiation of their gender, mainly marked by either the male or female hairstyle worn in daily life.[71]

Another crucial factor for the occurrence of female *shabtis* might be the introduction of the double *shabti*. This *shabti* form depicts double mummiform statuettes leaning against a stela or lying on a bier.[72] This unconventional *shabti* form typically represents husband and wife, but can also depict mother and son, father and son, or brother and brother. In the oldest known example,[73] mother and son appear physically quite similar except for their slightly different facial traits. Later examples of this *shabti* type distinguish the male and female figurines more clearly by adding the respective wigs of daily life to the statuettes.[74]

It is known that, in general, funerary objects for women seem to be adaptations of the objects made for men.[75] In the Ramesside period, there was a tendency to feminize funerary equipment for women, a practice evident, for example, in coffins.[76] This period seems to have marked a transitional time for elite women, who, especially in the funerary context, became less closely identified with their husbands or male relatives. The reasons for this trend remain largely unclear.

The sharing of funerary equipment between individuals,[77] as observed for Iyneferty and her son, was not uncommon in the New Kingdom.[78] In the course of the Ramesside period, the amount of shared goods increased notably. The fact that *shabtis* could also be shared is rather striking since the typically single mummiform statuette acted not only as a servant or substitute for the deceased in the afterlife, but also as an image or "double" of the owner. In the New Kingdom, the attribution of a *shabti* to its owner was ensured by mentioning the name in the inscription and by individualizing iconographic details—such as the female headgear or other female features in *shabtis* for women.[79] The king's *shabtis*, similarly, included the uraeus, *nemes* headdress, and other royal accoutrements. In the above-mentioned double *shabti*, the aspect of this item that was shared between two individuals was expressed in the outer appearance. The double *shabti* seems to have coexisted with the shared single mummy statuette[80] before the former was abandoned at the end of the Nineteenth Dynasty.

An interesting observation concerns one of the *shabti*s that Iyneferty shared with her son, Kabekhnet.[81] The execution of the dress of daily life on this statuette is somewhat singular, as it does not include the pleated dress observed on many Ramesside *shabti*s, but rather a sheath dress. However, the emerged feet on the statuettes are often combined with elements of daily life, such as a male or female wig. This combination indicates a clear relation to the later *shabti*s with the complete dress of daily life that first appeared in the course of the Nineteenth Dynasty.[82] Either the pleated dress of daily life was not yet fully established, or this was simply another variation in the execution of the same notion in the iconography.

Notably, Iyneferty's other son, Khonsu, was provided with *shabti*s in both the sheath dress[83] and the pleated dress of daily life.[84] He was the only person buried in TT 1 who was provided with this type of *shabti*.

A person could be given *shabti*s that bore both chapter 6 of the *Book of the Dead* and shorter texts.[85] The reasons for this apparently deliberate use of different text variants in a group of *shabti*s intended for the same owner may be manifold. Olson suggests that the *shabti* spell served to "activate" the *shabti*.[86] This implies that statuettes bearing the *shabti* spell were directly linked with their function as stand-ins and servants for the deceased in the afterlife. The New Kingdom is noteworthy not only for its variety of *shabti* forms, but also for the multiplicity of their functions.[87] In this period, the original concept of the *shabti* as a double of its owner—or more precisely, the identification of the *shabti* with its owner—was still inherent and was supplemented by the agricultural function emphasized by the *shabti* spell. The agricultural tools started to be applied on the *shabti* statuettes made during the reign of Thutmose IV. Whereas the agricultural function of *shabti*s bearing the text of chapter 6 of the *Book of the Dead* was highlighted, the focus among *shabti*s with the short text was likely the "identity" between the statuette and the owner. The occurrence of *shabti*s that bear no text at all in a *shabti* group for one owner should also be further studied in this respect.

*Shabti*s with either text could occur with agricultural tools and/or other attributes that marked the identity of the owner, such as female wigs for women's *shabti*s or royal accoutrements and uraeus for the king's *shabti*s. This point illustrates that all *shabti*s incorporated the full functions of a contemporary *shabti*, although expressed differently and perhaps with slight shifts in focus.

Concluding Remarks

The diversity of *shabtis* within a complete set for a deceased person may simply have been the result of manufacture by different workmen, maybe even at different stages in time. Considering the consistency with which this phenomenon occurs, one might assume that the trend to render *shabtis* diverse was done on purpose. It might have been a way to reflect the multiplicity in function of the New Kingdom *shabtis*. The desire of a person to own *shabtis* that display a great variety may also indicate an underlying structure within that set. However, one must not assume that a *shabti* group was already organized in a hierarchical way with a *shabti* workforce tiered in workers and overseers, as in the Third Intermediate Period. Nevertheless, there is no evidence of possible differences in status, or of whether they assumed different functions within the corpus. It remains unclear which specific meaning, if any, a particular variation might convey.

Iyneferty's *shabti* corpus is unique in that it consists of both conventional *shabtis* and *shabtis* with female features. The female *shabtis* may have served primarily as her images or "doubles." They emphasize the owner's social identity and individuality, indicative of the self-esteem of women during that period.

Future research should further consider New Kingdom *shabti* sets for individuals and as a whole coherent entirety. A comparative study across sets of *shabtis* for different owners might help to further illuminate the potential structures and/or functions that *shabtis* had within a group. Such work could shed new light on the complexity of the *shabti* statuettes.

Notes

1 Susanne Bickel, "Individuum und Rollen: Frauen in den thebanischen Gräbern des Neuen Reiches," in *Images and Gender: Contributions to the Hermeneutics of Reading Ancient Art*, ed. Silvia Schroer (Fribourg: Academic Press; Göttingen: Vandenhoeck and Ruprecht, 2006), 83–105.

2 Bickel, "Individuum und Rollen," 103.

3 Gay Robins, *Women in Ancient Egypt* (London: British Museum Press, 1993), 164–69.

4 William C. Hayes, *The Scepter of Egypt: A Background for the Study of the Egyptian Antiquities in the Metropolitan Museum of Art*, vol. 1, *From the Earliest Times to the End of the Middle Kingdom* (New York: Metropolitan Museum of Art, 1953), 327, fig. 215.

5 Harry M. Stewart, *Egyptian Shabtis*, Shire Egyptology 23 (Princes Risborough: Shire Publications, 1995), 14.

6 Bernard Bruyère, *La Tombe no. 1 de Sen-nedjem à Deir el Médineh*, MIFAO 88 (Cairo: IFAO, 1959).

7 The lack of a relevant inventory at the time of the discovery means that it is difficult to trace all the items. Dominique Valbelle, *Les Ouvriers de la Tombe: Deir el-Médineh à l'époque Ramesside*, BdE 96 (Cairo: IFAO, 1985).

8 The *shabtis* published by Valbelle belong mainly to the Third Intermediate Period; see Dominique Valbelle, *Ouchebtis de Deir el-Médineh* (Cairo: IFAO, 1972).

9 Adel Mahmoud Abd el-Qader and Sylvie Donnat, *Catalogue of Funerary Objects from the Tomb of the Servant in the Place of Truth Sennedjem (TT1): Ushabtis, Ushabtis in Coffins, Ushabti Boxes, Canopic Coffins, Canopic Chests, Cosmetic Chests, Furniture, Dummy Vases, Pottery Jars, and Walking Sticks, Mainly from the Egyptian Museum in Cairo and the Metropolitan Museum of Art of New York* (Cairo: IFAO, 2011), 294.

10 Object No. 13 in Abd el-Qader and Donnat, *Catalogue of Funerary Objects* = Inv. No. Cairo JE 27237/CG 47759 SR 4149

11 Object No. 14 in Abd el-Qader and Donnat, *Catalogue of Funerary Objects* = Inv. No. Cairo JE 27239/CG 47760 SR 4157

12 Object No. 16 in Abd el-Qader and Donnat, *Catalogue of Funerary Objects* = Inv. No. NY MMA 86.1.24

13 Object No. 17 in Abd el-Qader and Donnat, *Catalogue of Funerary Objects* = Inv. No. NY MMA 86.1.19

14 Object No. 20 in Abd el-Qader and Donnat, *Catalogue of Funerary Objects* = Inv. No. Turin M Egizio 2588

15 Object No. 24 in Abd el-Qader and Donnat, *Catalogue of Funerary Objects* = Inv. No. NY MMA 86.1.17

16 Object No. 15 in Abd el-Qader and Donnat, *Catalogue of Funerary Objects* = Inv. No. Cairo JE 27238/CG 47734 SR 4156

17 Object No. 18 in Abd el-Qader and Donnat, *Catalogue of Funerary Objects* = Inv. No. SB RFAM EL01.016.1996

18 Object No. 19 in Abd el-Qader and Donnat, *Catalogue of Funerary Objects*=Inv. No. Lyon MBA G 1722

19 Object No. 25 in Abd el-Qader and Donnat, *Catalogue of Funerary Objects* = Inv. No. NY MMA 86.1.18

20 NY-DoL-1. Similar clues to the dress of daily life are observed on other *shabtis* originating from TT 1, showing a finely carved hem above the emerging feet in combination with the duplex wig. These are evident on a *shabti* for Khons (Cairo JE 27228/CG 47749) and a *shabti* for Ramose (Cairo JE 27232/CG 47765). A *shabti* for Mose (Metropolitan Museum, New York, Accession No 86.1.27) wears a tripartite wig. Other examples with different origins include a *shabti* with a duplex wig housed at the Walters Art Museum in Baltimore (22.143), and a wooden *shabti* with a tripartite wig in the archaeological collection of the Bristol Museum (H39). Both of these display the same rare feature of the visible feet.

21 Schneider's wig type W7. See Hans D. Schneider, *Shabtis: An Introduction to the History of Ancient Egyptian Funerary Statuettes with a Catalogue of the Collection of Shabtis in the National Museum of Antiquities at Leiden* 1 (Leiden: Rijksmuseum van Oudheden, 1977), 165–67.

22 A manuscript by this author on the occurrence and development of *shabtis* with female features in the New Kingdom has been accepted for publication in a forthcoming issue of *ZÄS*.

23 SB-FM-1.

24 Cairo-FM-1; Lyon-FM-1. Schneider divides the female wigs on *shabtis* into W9—"NK elaborate female wig with headband"—and W10—"NK elaborate female wig with headband and supporting band." However, Iyneferty's *shabtis* exhibit a further variation of the female hairstyle—namely, the enveloping wig without any hair accessories. The enveloping wig, in different variations, became most popular during the Ramesside period, as shown on contemporary sculpture in the round and in relief.

25 One of the first examples is the *shabti* of Merymery, a high official during the reign of Amenhotep III. See Schneider, *Shabtis* 3, pl. 21, no. 3.2.1.23.

26 It is generally acknowledged that the first *shabtis* in the (full) dress of daily life appeared after the Amarna Period; Schneider, *Shabtis* 1, 161–62, 206–11.

27 One of the first *shabti* statuettes showing female facial features was a double *shabti* for Benermerut and his mother, Ikhem (Metropolitan Museum of Art, New York, Access No. 44.4.73). One can clearly see the distinction in the execution of Ikhem's face.

28 Another *shabti* originating from TT 1, made for Hotepi, shows clear female facial features (Metropolitan Museum of Art, Access No. 86.19.1 = Abd el-Qader and Donnat, *Catalogue of Funerary Objects*, Object No. 56).

29 See Schneider, *Shabtis* 1, 175–76.

30 NY-DoL-1, TUR-CM-1.

31 NY-CM-1.

32 Cairo-FM-1, NY-CM-2, SB-FM-1, Lyon-FM-1, TUR-CM-1.

33 NY-DoL-1, NY-CM-1, Cairo-CM-2.

34 Cairo-CM-2.

35 NY-CM-2, NY-CM-3.

36 Cairo-CM-1, Cairo-CM-2, NY-CM-1, TUR-CM-1, NY-CM-3, SB-FM-1, NY-DoL-1.

37 NY-CM-2, Cairo-FM-1, Lyon-FM-1.

38 It is well known that in Ancient Egyptian art, men's skin color is noticeably darker than women's, which is usually rendered in a light yellow-brown tone. Interestingly, most *shabti*s created for women exhibit a red tone.

39 NY-CM-1.

40 An exception is the *shabti* shared by Iyneferty and her son on which the epithets, names, and titles of both people are written on two individual lines.

41 Without "justified": NY-DoL-1 and NY-CM-1; with "justified" and title *nbt pr*: SB-FM-1.

42 SB-FM-1.

43 NY-DoL-1.

44 Schneider divides the *shabti* spell into "clauses" and classifies the different editions into seven versions (I–VII with subgroups); see also Schneider, *Shabtis* 1, 45–158.

45 Cairo-FM-1; Lyon-FM-1.

46 Cairo-CM-1; Cairo-CM-2; NY-CM-2; TUR-CM-1; NY-CM-3.

47 Cairo-FM-1.

48 Literally meaning "to make bright," which likely meant "to glorify" or something similar. See also Schneider, *Shabtis* 1, 131–33.

49 Cairo-FM-1 and Lyon-FM-1.

50 NY-CM-2.

51 Cairo-FM-1.

52 The full inscription on this *shabti* is published in Abd el-Qader and Donnat, *Catalogue of Funerary Objects*, 29–30.

53 Robins, *Women in Ancient Egypt* (1993a), 165.

54 Robins, *Women in Ancient Egypt* (1993a), 168. See also Lynn Meskell, *Archaeologies of Social Life: Age, Sex, Class et cetera in Ancient Egypt*, Social Archaeology (Oxford: Blackwell, 1999), and Lynn Meskell, "Intimate Archaeologies: The Case of Kha and Merit," *World Archaeology* 29, no. 3 (1998): 363–79.

55 Two *shabtis* could not be assigned to either of the two. Theodore M. Davis, ed., *The Tomb of Iouiya and Touiyou* (London: Constable, 1907).

56 For example, Tomb 1159A. See Meskell, *Archaeologies of Social Life*, 186–87.

57 Stuart Tyson Smith, "Intact Tombs of the 17th and 18th Dynasties from Thebes and the New Kingdom Burial System," *MDAIK* 48 (1992): 193–231.

58 Meskell, "Intimate Archaeologies," 374, table 1. For further examples, see Meskell, *Archaeologies of Social Life*, 186–87, Box 5.1 = Tomb 1159 A; 190–91; Box 5.2 = Tomb 1352. The fact that burials completely lacked *shabti*s may also point to destruction or robbery in ancient or modern times. However, the discovery of tombs with intact burial assemblages shows that *shabti*s were in no way universal goods, even for wealthier classes of society; see also Smith, "Intact Tombs," 199–200.

59 W.M. Flinders Petrie and J.H. Walker, *Qurneh* (London: BSA, 1909), 15 and pl. LIII.

60 For examples in Deir al-Medina, see Meskell, *Archaeologies of Social Life*, 194–95, Box 5.3 = Tomb 1370; 197–98, Box 5.4 = Tomb 1382; 200–201, Box 5.5 = Tomb 1388. An example from

the Memphite necropolis in Saqqara can be found in Maarten J. Raven, *The Tomb of Iurudef: A Memphite Official in the Reign of Ramesses II*, EES Excavation Memoir 57 (London: EES, 1991). The tomb owner, Iurudef, had nine *shabtis*, whereas only six could be attributed to his wife, Akhes, and eight to another female individual buried in the same tomb. These numbers are considered under reserve, as the tomb was found in a looted condition.

61 Stacie Lynn Olson, "New Kingdom Funerary Figurines in Context: An Analysis of the Cemeteries of Aniba, Gurob, and Soleb" (PhD diss., University of Pennsylvania, 1997; Ann Arbor, MI: UMI, 1997), 160–61.

62 Abd el-Qader and Donnat, *Catalogue of Funerary Objects*, 14; Meskell, *Archaeologies of Social Life*, 206–208.

63 For example, Rocío Delechuk Campello, "Tumba de Mentuemhat, ushebtis," in *Novos trabalhos de Egiptologia Ibérica: IV Congreso Ibérico de Egiptología*, vol. 1, ed. Luís Manuel de Araújo and José das Candeias Sales (Lisbon: Instituto Oriental e Centro de História da Facultade de Letras da Universidade de Lisboa, 2012), 345–55.

64 For example, the *shabti* corpus of Iyneferty's son Khons consists of sixteen *shabtis* of various materials (terracotta, limestone, and wood) and different iconographical details. Her husband Sennedjem's *shabtis* exhibit variety in size and iconography, including three *shabtis* in coffins.

65 More than four hundred *shabtis* of varying iconography and materials are known from the tomb of Tutankhamun. The quality ranges from finely carved statuettes of wood with gilded details to small faience examples in different colors. Those of his predecessor, Akhenaten, also exhibit iconographic and textual variation. See also Richard H. Wilkinson and Kent R. Weeks, eds., *The Oxford Handbook of the Valley of the Kings* (Oxford: Oxford University Press, 2016), 278–80.

66 Schneider, *Shabtis* 1, 266–67.

67 Schneider, *Shabtis* 1, 320.

68 Edith Bernhauer, *Innovationen in der Privatplastik: Die 18. Dynastie und ihre Entwicklung*, Philippika 27 (Wiesbaden: Harrassowitz, 2010). Bernhauer suggests that the reasons behind this innovative push, which started in the early New Kingdom, were linked to changes in foreign and domestic politics. These developments led to a mental shift in the self-image of the elite. See particularly Bernhauer, *Innovationen in der Privatplastik*, 159–66.

69 Schneider, *Shabtis* 1, 260–62.

70 See, for example, Stewart, *Egyptian Shabtis*, 16–18.

71 Further possible gender markers for female *shabtis* are discussed in R. Glanzmann, "The Shabti of the Lady of the House Iahhetep and the Emergence of Female Shabtis in the New Kingdom," *ZÄS* (forthcoming).

72 In Schneider, *Shabtis* 1, 162–64, these are mentioned as "Pair of mummies with back slab" and "Pair of mummies on a bier." See also FN 14 for one of the first examples of this *shabti* type known today.

73 See object mentioned in note 17 above.

74 Examples appear in the Egyptian Museum in Cairo, Inv. No. JE 21858, and in the Musée du Louvre in Paris, N 2657.

75 Robins, *Women in Ancient Egypt* (1993a), 175.

76 John H. Taylor, *Egyptian Coffins*, Shire Egyptology 11 (Princes Risborough: Shire Publications, 1989), 35–39.

77 Husband and wife, or between several family members.

78 For example, Meskell, "Intimate Archaeologies," 372. There were 196 funerary objects that belonged to Kha and thirty-nine to Merit individually, whereas six items were shared, bearing both names. In TT 1, several *shabti* boxes are shared among husbands and wives. See Abd el-Qader and Donnat, *Catalogue of Funerary Objects*, table 9, 47–48. One *shabti* box of Iyneferty, today housed in the Egyptian Museum in Cairo (JE 27277/ SR 4189), mentions the name of her son, Khons. With regard to the content of the inscription, this box was probably made by Khons for his mother, rather than shared. See also Object No. 78 in Abd el-Qader and Donnat, *Catalogue of Funerary Objects*, 118.

79 See note 12 above.

80 The fact that the sharing of a *shabti* could be expressed in different ways—either by inscription only, or by both inscription and iconography—again indicates the great variety of forms that existed among these funerary objects in the New Kingdom.

81 NY-DoL-1.

82 Schneider, *Shabtis* 1, 260. This fashion is also observed on Ramesside mummy boards and occasionally on coffins and sarcophagi. See Taylor, *Egyptian Coffins*, 38–39.

83 Abd el-Qader and Donnat, *Catalogue of Funerary Objects*, Object No. 43.

84 Abd el-Qader and Donnat, *Catalogue of Funerary Objects*, Object Nos. 31–35.

85 See Schneider, *Shabtis* 1, 300. Schneider elaborates on the examples of the *shabti*s provided for Kenamun, who was a high official under Amenhotep II. Another well-known example is the *shabti* corpus of the Chantress of Amun Henutmehyt, today housed in the British Museum (EA 41549). Five *shabti*s bear the shorter text variation, whereas three are inscribed with the *shabti* spell.

86 Olson, *New Kingdom Funerary Figurines in Context*, 195.

87 See also Schneider, *Shabtis* 1, 260–62.

16

Some Notes on the Question of Feminine Identity at the Beginning of the Twenty-first Dynasty in the Funerary Literature

Annik Wüthrich

One of the peculiarities of the Third Intermediate Period, and especially of the Twenty-first Dynasty, is the number of sources dealing with women, even when limiting the scope to funerary literature.[1] Whereas during the entire New Kingdom, the female owners of Books of the Dead represent a tiny minority,[2] the number of papyri owned by women dramatically increases at the beginning of the Third Intermediate Period. In the New Kingdom *Book of the Dead* corpus, women's destiny in the afterlife seems to have been closely connected to that of their husbands; in other words, they were associated with their husbands not as co-owners, but as dependents.[3] The vocabulary used to describe their relationship is indeed always unilaterally focused on the men ("his wife" (*ḥmt.f*), "his beloved" (*mrt.f*), "his female companion" (*snt.f*)).[4]

Nevertheless, it is difficult to trace precisely the diachronic evolution of the funerary status of women during the New Kingdom, especially for its latter part, due to the scarcity of sources dating to the Twentieth Dynasty.[5] The same type of documentation from the beginning of the Twenty-first Dynasty, at least in Thebes,[6] however, leads to a completely different picture. The papyri owned by women are almost as numerous as those owned by men while, at the same time, manuscripts which associate a wife with her husband's fate are exceptional, although not entirely nonexistent.[7] It is, therefore, of major importance to understand how women expressed their identity and orchestrated their self-presentation during the first part of the Third Intermediate Period.[8]

This contribution focuses specifically on the restricted circle of the ruling family during the Twenty-first Dynasty in Thebes. We know of approximately thirty women who can be linked to the family of the High Priests of Amun in Thebes.[9] Some of them are well known, others are attested only indirectly.[10] The funerary equipment of most of these women was discovered in the Royal Cache TT 320 and represents an incomparable source of information for the understanding of the chronology and the sociology of this period, particularly for its beginning.[11] The chronological position of each of these women within the Twenty-first Dynasty is almost certain, even if some of their filiations are still (and will probably remain) a matter of discussion.[12]

The first thing we must not neglect are the differences in the kinds of media on which any of this information is found. As noted by Eyre:

> the target audience for self-presentation is never clear, because neither the social context of text, nor the monumental display—size, location, and visual effect—is itself unitary, in purpose or effect. Nor was the location of the text uniformly accessible, even for the limited number of people able to read it.[13]

As already mentioned, the majority of the information we have for the beginning of the Twenty-first Dynasty comes from a funerary context, particularly from papyri containing the *Book of the Dead* or from coffins. What function can a funerary papyrus therefore have in the matter of self-presentation? Can we really speak of social legitimation through an indication of filiation or titles in this very particular context?

The texts written on papyrus are intended, foremost, to ensure the survival of its owner in the underworld. Moreover, in the development of this funerary literature, we observe a tendency to select—and therefore to reduce—the number of titles held by the owner, mostly in an attempt to demonstrate their devotion in connection with personal piety.[14] The relation to the god is based on the personal identity of the papyrus's owner, and it seems that social identity is of less and less importance over time. In other words, titles and filiation are often to be found on other types of sources rather than funerary papyri of the Twenty-first dynasty, whereas this information was contained regularly in the New Kingdom Books of the Dead.

For the beginning of the Twenty-first Dynasty, other types of media are attested that are directly connected with the women of the high Theban elite. Hereret, chronologically the first woman of this line, is known from only two kinds of documents: two late Ramesside Letters (LRL) and the Book of the Dead of her daughter, Nodjmet.[15] Hereret's religious title is expressed in LRL 38 and 39,[16] where it is stated that she is *wr(t) ḫnrt Ỉmn*[*-Rꜥ nswt*] *nṯrw*,

"Great one of the sacred musical troupe of Amun-Re, King of the gods."[17] This title, with variants, is transmitted from Hereret to Nodjmet according to a pattern of mother to daughter or mother-in-law to daughter-in-law, attested in the ruling family until the beginning of the Twenty-second Dynasty.[18] Its exact mode of transmission is still unclear, but some Egyptologists suggest that these women were married to the High Priest of Amun, as a feminine counterpart to this title, and gave birth to the next High Priest of Amun. They should have acquired the higher title of *ḥryt wrt ḫnrwt n(t) Ỉmn-Rᶜ nswt nṯrw* once these two conditions were fulfilled.[19] At least fifteen women of the Twenty-first Dynasty had the title of "Great one of the sacred musical troupe of Amun-Re"; eight of them are qualified as "Great Superior" (*ḥryt wrt ḫnrwt*).[20] The identity of the spouse for a number of these women can be established only by deduction. Interestingly enough, none of these women explicitly express their marital ties. The name and title of Isetemkheb (A), for instance, appears only on a number of bricks associated with the name of the High Priest of Amun, Pinudjem I.[21] No other documents can be attributed to her, and we presume that she was the mother of some of Pinudjem I's children who cannot be attributed to his other wife, Henuttawy (A).[22] If the theory of the maternity of the High Priest of Amun proves to be correct, then Isetemkheb (A) could be the mother of one (or two) of Pinudjem I's sons, whose maternal lineage is unclear.[23]

The women presented thus far, unfortunately, are attested on only a few documents or referred to indirectly on others, and the question of their self-presentation is, in this case, irrelevant. However, at least four women belonging to this high elite are of interest for this topic.

Henuttawy (A) is known in the Egyptological literature as the wife of the High Priest of Amun and King Pinudjem I, as well as the mother of several of his children. Her rich funerary equipment was found in the royal cache TT 320,[24] and includes, notably, two poorly preserved coffins, four canopic jars, and two funerary papyri, all with inscriptions.[25] While these inscriptions establish the identity of this woman, they do not distinctly identify her marital affiliation. Indeed, if we exclude the monuments on which she is represented by his side,[26] we have no precise indication that she was the wife of Pinudjem I.[27] We can deduce this information from iconographical association and because of the (at least) four children they have in common. Nevertheless, once more, the filial relationships are sometimes imprecise and need deductive work. On the basis of the inscriptions on two bracelets found in Tanis A543 and 547, on which the name of Henuttawy (A) with the title of "royal mother" faces the one of King Psusennes I, we can surmise that she is his mother.[28] Then, if we cross-reference this with the fact that Queen Mutnodjmet and Psusennes I shared a sibling relationship,[29] we can infer that these latter are two of Henuttawy (A)'s children.[30] The identification of Pinudjem I as their father must be extrapolated from the fact that Henuttawy (A) is his wife. Indeed, unlike another son of Pinudjem I, the High Priest of Amun Menkheperre, who claims his paternal ascendance on several documents,[31] Psusennes I did not associate his name with that of his father. His wife-sister Mutnodjmet is also defined as a royal daughter, but she does not name her father either. A secondary inscription on the wall of the court of Ramesses II in the Temple of Luxor presents three daughters of the High Priest of Amun Pinudjem I,[32] one of whom bears the name of Nodjmetmut. If the two other women seem to be clearly identified with the Divine Adoratrix Maatkare and the wind instrument player (*wḏnt*) Henuttawy (B), the question of the identity of the third woman has been hardly discussed. It seems quite justified to see in this third woman another daughter of Pinudjem I, otherwise undocumented, and not an early representation of the queen Mutnodjmet.[33]

The God's Wife of Amun, Maatkare (A), sister of both Psusennes I and Mutnodjmet, is also identified as a "royal daughter," but the name of her father is not included after her title. For instance, on the façade south of the pylon in the Temple of Khonsu, Maatkare (A) is called *iryt-pꜥt wr(t) ḥsyw ḥmt-nṯr n(t) Ỉmn m Ỉpt-swt sꜣt nswt n ẖt.f nbt tꜣwy*, "princess, great of praises, divine wife of Amun in Karnak, king's daughter of his body and mistress of the two lands."[34] Nevertheless, their close iconographic association[35] leaves no doubt about the identification of Maatkare (A)'s father as Pinudjem I. In the same way, Maatkare (A) also defined herself as the "daughter of the mistress of the two lands,"[36] but, once more, without naming her mother. Yet, in an inscription on the window of an otherwise anepigraphic chapel from the Temple of Karnak,[37] there are two cartouches facing outward, one with the name of Maatkare and the other with the title of royal daughter, followed by the name of Henuttawy (*sꜣt nswt Ḥnwt-tꜣwy*). The unresolved question is whether to recognize in this association a title and a name (the royal daughter Henuttawy)—Henuttawy (A) does in fact bear the title of royal daughter—or a title and a direct genitive (the royal daughter of Henuttawy). Nevertheless, at the same time, Maatkare (A) is also described on other documents as the "mistress of the two lands" (*nbt tꜣwy*).[38] It is also possible that the second part of the cartouche is again a title, meaning "mistress of the two lands," and does not present her filiation. However, the title *ḥnwt tꜣwy* does not appear linked to this woman in the rest of the documentation.[39] Even if it is quite clear that these three persons are Henuttawy (A)'s children, I would like to point out that this genealogical information has to be deduced from circumstantial evidence and is not stated explicitly. Contrary to their father and spouse Pinudjem I, who systematically and specifically emphasizes his paternal filiation even when he bears his royal title, thus adopting the usual way of indicating personal identity outside of the royal court, female members of his entourage resort to the royal practice of using the genealogical expressions not to state their personal identity or relation to an explicitly mentioned king, but rather as a title.

The two funerary manuscripts of Henuttawy (A) are of particular interest for the matter of her self-presentation. The first holds an initial vignette representing the deceased adoring Osiris and Isis, followed by a series of images belonging to the *Litany to the Sun*, separated by columns of text containing various titles and the name of Henuttawy (A).[40] The second papyrus has a layout reminiscent of the Book of the Dead of the New Kingdom Theban recension.[41] The format of this papyrus is the same as those of that period: the text is written in retrograde cursive hieroglyphs, and the vignettes are finely and colorfully executed. The deceased is represented four times in human shape and once as a *ba*-bird. Henuttawy (A) is depicted executing ritual gestures: praying, shaking the sistra, and fumigating with incense; in another vignette, she is sailing. On her head, she wears the vulture crown with the cobra or a diadem with cobras, two very common symbols of royalty, although unparalleled for *Book of the Dead* papyri, except for the beginning of the Twenty-first Dynasty.[42] This is a very important document for the reconstitution of the genealogical tree of the Theban High Priest's family, because the legend of the vignette of *BD* 66 includes the names of Henuttawy (A)'s mother and maternal grandfather.[43] The inscription in the initial vignette, however, contains a long string of descriptions and titles that can be seen as her entire titulary.[44] When analyzing it, one can observe that it follows this pattern:

- Her royal origin and her ancestry: *sꜣt nswt/sꜣt ḥmt nswt*—she is royal daughter and daughter of the king's wife.
- Descendants: *mwt nswt*[45] / *mwt n(t) pꜣ ḥm-nṯr tpy n Ỉmn/mwt n(t) dwꜣt-nṯr n(t) Ỉmn*[46]/*mwt n(t) ḥmt nswt wrt*—she is a royal mother/mother of the High Priest/mother of the God's wife of Amun/mother of the great royal wife.[47]
- Religious functions: *ḥmt-nṯr n(t) Mwt wrt nbt Ỉšrw / ꜥꜣt n(t) pr n Ḫnsw-m-Wꜣst-Nfr-ḥtp / ḥmt-nṯr n(t) Ỉn-ḥrt-Šw sꜣ Rꜥ / mwt nṯr n(t) Ḫnsw-pꜣ-ẖrd*—priestess of Mut the great, the mistress of Isheru/Great of the Temple of Khonsu in Thebes-Neferhotep/priestess of Onuphris-Shu son of Re/divine mother of Khonsu the child.

- Royal functions: *ḥmt nswt wrt tp(yt) n(t) ḥm.f / nbt tꜣwy*—main great royal wife of his majesty/mistress of the two lands.
- Identity: (*Dwꜣt Ḥwt-Ḥrw Ḥnwt-tꜣwy*)| *ms.n* (*Tꜣ-nt-Ỉmn*)|—(Adoratrix of Hathor Henuttawy)| born of (Tanutamon)|.

This long titulary holds all the information on the most important aspects of her life, but without naming any of the persons concerned, except for her mother. The model for this string of titles can be found already in the Eighteenth Dynasty, which L. Troy described as "a litany of female roles."[48] What actually differs from these earlier constructions, which were based mostly on the relation to the king—these queens are king's daughter, king's mother, and king's wife, as well as king's sister—is that the roles mentioned here are connected with her entire nuclear family as an ensemble, as well as her other religious and royal titles. As for the construction of Henuttawy (A)'s identity, it revolves around several aspects which H. Bassir calls the three spheres of manifestation and interaction:[49] origin, family (these two levels remain particularly imprecise), and social status (religious and royal); and, finally, her personal identity as revealed through her name and her mother's name. This long titulary appears to me to be some kind of an "idealized biography." It does not focus on the affirmation of the social or ideological status of this woman in relation with the king.[50] Moreover, it does not need to tie her to specific persons to legitimize her function or her rank, but it is the constellation of this information, the royal ancestry and descent, the high religious and royal functions, that constitutes her identity independently from the people involved. As noted by Troy, "the roles of daughter, sister, wife and mother, which play such important roles in the mythological expression of the generation of cosmic powers, are actualized in the kingship on the status of the royal women, adding yet another level to the pattern of queenship."[51] It means that while Henuttawy (A), as well as her direct predecessors and successors, integrated the old codes of queenship, they also used them to legitimize their royal functions, with a deep integration into their family. Henuttawy (A) is, of course, not an exception, as the women of the highest lineage of the Third Intermediate Period used this form of varying long strings of titles or epithets regularly; what is exceptional is the diversity of Henuttawy (A)'s designations and titles.

Within the scope of this study, another woman has captured my attention due to the singularity of the documentation attributed to her. Queen Nodjmet was very probably the owner of two funerary papyri.[52] On the first one, P.London BM EA 10490,[53] she appears as the "mistress of the two lands" (*nbt tꜣwy*) and "daughter of the royal mother Hereret" (*sꜣt* (*nt*) *mwt nswt Ḥrrt*) as well as "the one Hereret gave birth to" (*ms.n Ḥrrt*). She is also "royal mother" (*mwt nswt*); this title is written regularly in the cartouche before her name. Furthermore, she is defined as the "royal mother of the lord of the two lands" (*mwt nswt n(t) nb t3wy*) and "the one who gave birth to the mighty bull, lord of the two lands" (*mst k3-nḫt nb t3wy*). As in the case of Henuttawy (A), Nodjmet never names her relatives, either ascendant or descendant, other than by their titles, except for her maternal lineage.

In contrast, her second funerary papyrus[54] contains two representations of her with a man who is gesturing in adoration at her side. In addition to her title of "royal mother," Nodjmet bears her main religious titles.[55] The man is identified as Herihor, King and High Priest of Amun.[56] In both cases, Herihor precedes Nodjmet. These kinds of scenes mirror the vignettes of the deceased couple during the New Kingdom and before. Nevertheless, the presence of the couple, independently from their relationship, remains exceptional for the Twenty-first Dynasty.[57] The identification of Herihor as her husband is totally missing from the text. He is named and identified by his titles, but the relation of dependence connecting these two persons is never expressed, as it had been for New Kingdom *Book of the Dead* manuscripts. This precedent is actually the basis for interpreting this representation as one of a married couple.[58] This is also based on her representation and identification as *ḥmt nswt* in the so-called "procession of the princes and princesses" in the Temple of Khonsu in Karnak, although she is not qualified as the wife of Herihor, but only as great royal wife.[59] "Uncertainty" concerning her identity is a very complicated (even unsolvable) problem for the historian. However, in the case of Nodjmet, it seems that the construction of her identity did not require making the exact nature of her relationship with this man clear. In the first place, we should consider the rules of decorum for feminine burials, established, among others, by G. Robins and A.-M. Roth:[60] the absence of the husband is explained by the fact that the woman should be the most important person, as owner and recipient of the funerary monument. That is why she has to be the most prominent figure in the iconography. On the other hand, to conform to the rules of ancient Egyptian iconography, she should be represented on a smaller scale than her husband. To avoid this paradoxical situation, her husband must, for reasons related to gender hierarchy in two-dimensional representations, be excluded from the decoration of the tomb.

How then can we explain the presence of Nodjmet's husband in her most important passport for eternity? Whether we should see a connection with the new theocratic system remains very hypothetical, but is not to be excluded. I would like to underscore the fact that, by including her husband in her funerary papyrus, Nodjmet's *Book of the Dead* manuscript is unique, although it does not allow us to draw any definitive conclusions. However, if we compare the association of Nodjmet and Herihor in her Book of the Dead with the representation of Nodjmet in the secondary inscription in the Luxor Temple,[61] we observe that in the Luxor secondary inscription, she occupies a peculiar position. She is indeed placed behind the god Amun in the same position as that of the consorts of male divinities—in this case as Mut.[62] Therefore, I would like to tentatively suggest that the presence of Herihor, the High Priest of Amun, in the Book of the Dead of his wife Nodjmet could have the function of symbolizing the Theban divine couple Amun–Mut and not that of connecting her to someone in particular.

It seems then that the female members of the governing family in Thebes at the beginning of the Twenty-first Dynasty established new conventions in the matter of self-presentation in funerary literature. While familial relationships obviously played a key role, these women did not justify their position by mentioning the name of the person(s) through whom they obtained their religious, social, and even political status. The relationship itself and the resulting function are, therefore, more important than the person.[63]

Notes

1 The number of publications dealing with women of the Third Intermediate Period has significantly increased over the last few decades; for example, the pioneer study from Saphinaz Naguib, *Le clergé féminin d'Amon thébain à la 21e dynastie*, OLA 38 (Leuven: Peeters, 1990), and more recently, Karl Jansen-Winkeln, "Bemerkungen zu den Frauenbiographien der Spätzeit," *AoF* 31, no. 2 (2004): 358–73; Mariam Ayad, *God's Wife, God's Servant: The God's Wife of Amun (c. 740–525 BC)* (London: Routledge, 2009); Carola Koch, *"Die den Amun mit ihrer Stimme zufriedenstellen": Gottesgemahlinnen und Musikerinnen im thebanischen Amunstaat von der 22. bis zur 26. Dynastie*, SRaT 27 (Dettelbach: J.H. Röll, 2012); Jean Li, *Women, Gender and Identity in the Third Intermediate Period*, Routledge StudEgypt 4 (New York: Routledge, 2017). For a general study of the Theban society of the Twenty-first Dynasty, see the unpublished doctoral dissertation of France Jamen, "La société thébaine sous la XXIe dynastie (1069–945 av. J.-C.)" (PhD diss., Université Lumière Lyon 2, 2012).

2 Stephen Quirke, "Women in Ancient Egypt: Temple Titles and Funerary Papyri," in *Studies on Ancient Egypt in Honour of H.S. Smith*, ed. Anthony Leahy and John Tait, Occasional Publications 13 (London: EES, 1999), 227–35; Karl Jansen-Winkeln, "Die Entwicklung der genealogischen Informationen nach dem Neuen Reich," in *Genealogie—Realität und Fiktion von Identität*, ed. Martin Fitzenreiter, Steffen Kirchner, and Olaf Kriseleit, IBAES 5 (London: Golden House Publications, 2005), 137–45; Marissa Stevens, "Illustrations of Temple Rank on 21st Dynasty Funerary Papyri," in *Current Research in Egyptology 2018*, ed. Marie Peterková Hlouchová, Dana Bělohoubková, Jiří Honzl, and Věra Nováková (Oxford: Archaeopress Archaeology, 2019), 162–228; Marissa Stevens, "Family Associations Reflected in the Materiality of the 21st Dynasty Funerary Papyri," in *Invisible Archaeologies: Hidden Aspects of Daily Life in Ancient Egypt and Nubia*, ed. Loretta Kilroe (Oxford: Archaeopress, 2019), 26–56; Annik Wüthrich, "L'expression de la filiation à la XXIe dynastie: reflet d'une réalité historique ou simple effet de mode? L'exemple du Livre des Morts," *BSFE* 204 (2021): 114–40.

3 Wüthrich, "L'expression de la filiation," 121–22.

4 Gay Robins, "The Relationships Specified by Egyptian Kinship Terms of the Middle and New Kingdoms," *CdE* 54, no. 108 (1979): 197–207.

5 See Quirke, "Women in Ancient Egypt," 231–33.

6 There is indeed no evidence of female owners of the *Book of the Dead* during the Third Intermediate Period outside of Thebes.

7 Rita Lucarelli, "L'uso dei papiri funerari presso il clero femminile di Amon a Tebe nella XXI dinastia," in *Sacerdozio e società civile nell'Egitto antico: Atti del terzo Colloquio di Egittologia e di Antichita Copte. Bologna—30/31 maggio 2007*, ed. Silvio Pernigotti and Marco Zecchi (Pisa: La Mandragora, 2008), 105–13; Wüthrich, "L'expression de la filiation."

8 On self-presentation in the Third Intermediate Period, see Roberto Gozzoli, "Self-presentation in the Third Intermediate Period," in *Living Forever: Self-presentation in Ancient Egypt*, ed. Hussein Bassir (Cairo: American University in Cairo Press, 2019), 177–90; and, in the same book, with a special focus on women, see Mariam Ayad, "Women's Self-presentation in Pharaonic Egypt," 221–46. For a short definition of self-presentation, see also Mark Smith, "Egyptian Elite Self-presentation in the Context of Ptolemaic Rule," in *Ancient Alexandria between Egypt and Greece*, ed. W.V. Harris and Giovanni Ruffini (Boston: Brill, 2004), 34–35.

9 For an overview of these women and their titles for the beginning of the Twenty-first Dynasty, see Meike Becker, "Female Influence, Aside from That of the God's Wives of Amun, during the Third Intermediate Period," in *Prayer and Power: Proceedings of the Conference on the God's Wives of Amun in Egypt during the First Millenium* BC, ed. Meike Becker, Anke Ilona Blöbaum, and Angelika Lohwasser, ÄAT 84 (Münster: Ugarit Verlag, 2016), 21–37; and Lana Troy, *Patterns of Queenship in Ancient Egyptian Myth and History* (Uppsala: Uppsala University, 1986), 172–74. The main feminine protagonists are also discussed by Kenneth Kitchen in *The Third Intermediate Period in Egypt (1100–650* BC*)*, 3rd ed. (Warminster: Aris and Phillips, 1996), 40–68.

10 For instance, the mother of Nesikhons, Tahenutdjehuty, is only known from the decree in favor of her daughter. We do not know any title for her, since the people in this document are only identified by their names and possibly by their family relationships. We deduce from this document that Tahenutdjehuty was one of the spouses of the High Priest of Amun Smendes II, because he is named as the father of Nesikhons in this same document. See Jean Winand, "Les décrets oraculaires pris en l'honneur d'Henouttaouy et de Maâtkarê (Xe et VIIe pylônes)," *CahKarn* 11 (2003): 603–710.

11 The material found in the Royal Cache TT 320 can be consulted in the database of the University of Münster, https://www1.ivv1.uni-muenster.de/litw3/Aegyptologie/index04.htm. See also David A. Aston, *Burial Assemblages of Dynasty 21–25*, DÖAW 56 (Vienna: Verlag der Österreichischen Akademie der Wissenschaften, 2009); and Erhart Graefe and Galina Belova, eds., *The Royal Cache TT 320: A Re-examination* (Cairo: Supreme Council of Antiquities Press, 2010).

12 See, among others, the discussion about the existence of one or two women named Hereret at the beginning of the Twenty-first Dynasty as well as the question of the number of women called Nodjmet. For the current state of the question, see, most recently, Jennifer Palmer, "The High Priests of Amun at the End of the Twentieth Dynasty," *BEJ* 2, no. 1 (2014): 13–17.

13 Christopher Eyre, "Egyptian Self-presentation Dynamics and Strategies," in Bassir, *Living Forever: Self-presentation in Ancient Egypt*, 13.

14 Florence Albert, "Quelques observations sur les titulatures attestées dans les Livres des Morts," in *Herausgehen am Tage: Gesammelte Schriften zum altägyptischen Totenbuch*, ed. Rita Lucarelli, Marcus Müller-Roth, and Annik Wüthrich, SAT 17 (Wiesbaden: Harrassowitz, 2012), 1–66.

15 The following argument is based on the assumption that both attestations refer to the same individual, as suggested by Karl Jansen-Winkeln, "Das Ende des Neuen Reiches," *ZÄS* 119 (1992): 25. For a résumé of the arguments pro and contra this hypothesis, see Peter James and Robert Morkot, "Herihor's Kingship and the High Priest of Amun Piankh," *JEGH* 3, no. 2 (2010): 238–41; and Palmer, "The High Priests of Amun at the End of the Twentieth Dynasty," 13–17.

16 Jaroslav Černý, *Late Ramesside Letters*, BAe 9 (Brussels: Fondation égyptologique Reine Élisabeth, 1939), 60–61.

17 LRL 39 contains the variant *wr(t) ḫnrwt šmꜤyt n(t) Ỉmn-RꜤ nswt nṯrw*, which can be translated as "Great of the sacred musical troupe and singer of Amun-Re, King of the gods." This variant is unique. The title appears at the beginning of the New Kingdom as a title of women involved in the clergy of Amun, mostly, but not exclusively, from the royal family. It seems that the title disappears during the second part of the Twentieth Dynasty before it reappears in the documentation of the Twenty-first Dynasty. See Suzanne Onstine, *The Role of the Chantress (šmꜤyt) in Ancient Egypt*, BARIS 140 (Oxford: Hadrian Books, 2005), 7–8.

18 The last member of the family who bore this title seems to have been Nesikhonspakhered, probable daughter of Nestanebetisheru, who inherited the title from her mother Nesikhons (A). The latter is the last woman we can connect with a High Priest of Amun. In the Twenty-second Dynasty, the title is attested only two times. See Koch, *"Die den Amun mit ihrer Stimme zufriedenstellen,"* 201, 221. The first woman is a member of the family of Djedbastetiuefankh under the reign of Osorkon I. He was a prominent personality from the Theban elite since he was at the head of the administration of the Ramesseum. See Frédéric Payraudeau, *Administration, société et pouvoir à Thèbes sous la XXIIe dynastie bubastite*, BdE 160 (Cairo: IFAO, 2014), 274. The administration of the Ramesseum can be the link between the women of the Twenty-second Dynasty who bear this title. A second woman, whose name is probably mentioned two times on a statue (Karnak South magazine no. 180, ll. 5, 8) published by Claude Traunecker, "Un document inédit sur une famille de contemporains de la XXIIe dynastie," *BIFAO* 69 [1971]: 219–37) dating to the Twenty-second Dynasty, also has the title of *wrt ḫnrwt n(t) Ỉmn ḥr s3 3-nw*. The state of conservation of the object does not allow us to identify beyond a doubt the relationship between this woman and its dedicatee. She can be either his mother or his great-great-grandmother. However, the title "Great one of the sacred musical troupe of Amun in her third phyle" pleads for an identification with the mother of the dedicatee, since its other attestations for the Twenty-first Dynasty are all in relation to the family of the High Priest. However, the compilation of the title shows that the partition in phyles could be placed at the end of the Twenty-first Dynasty, so that this woman lived either at the end of the Twenty-first or at the beginning of the Twenty-second Dynasty. Her father (or husband) bears the same title as Djedbastetouefankh and could be his ancestor.

19 Naguib, *Le clergé féminin d'Amon*, 181–82.

20 In chronological order: Nodjmet, Isetemkheb (A), the queen Mutnodjmet, Isetemkheb (C), Djedmutiuesankh, Isetemkheb (D), Nesikhons (A), and Nestanebetisheru.

21 A.J. Spencer, *Brick Architecture in Ancient Egypt* (Warminster: Aris and Phillips, 1979), pl. 33. It is worth noting that her title is only *ḥr(yt) wrt ḫnrwt*, without the name of the deity, undoubtedly for lack of space. The counterpart effect of the male title and female title of the high clergy of Amun is very clear here.

22 On Henuttawy (A), see the discussion below.

23 If the identity of the father of the High Priests of Amun, Masaharta and Djedkhonsiuefankh, is certain, the identity of their mother(s) remains impossible to establish with certainty. For Pinudjem I as father of Masaharta, see, for instance Karl Jansen-Winkeln, *IdS* 1 (Wiesbaden: Harrassowitz, 2007), 28 (no. 3.49); for Djedkhonsiuefankh, see Kitchen, *Third Intermediate Period*, 424–25, §392.

24 The previous location of her burial place remains unknown. See Edward Loring, "The Dynasty of Piankh and the Royal Cache," in *The Royal Cache TT 320: A Re-examination*, ed. Erhart Graefe and Galina Belova (Cairo: Supreme Council of Antiquities Press, 2010), 63, 67.

25 For the complete assemblage, see Aston, *Burial Assemblages*, 224–25.

26 For instance, on Stela Cairo JE 71902 from Coptos, published by Aly O.A. Abdallah, "An Unusual Private Stela of the Twenty-first Dynasty from Coptos," *JEA* 70 (1984): 65–72. On this document, Henuttawy (A) plays the sistrum and accompanies Pinudjem I in offering incense to the god Osiris. Pinudjem I is identified as king—his two names are written in a

cartouche—whereas she is qualified as *sꜣt nswt*, "king's daughter," *wrt ḫnrwt n*(*t*) *Ỉmn-Rꜥ nswt nṯrw*, "Great one of the sacred musical troupe of Amun-Re, King of the gods," *ḥryt špswt nswt*, "Superior of the royal noble dames," *mwt nswt*, "royal mother," and *nbt tꜣwy*, "mistress of the two lands." Her name is also in a cartouche on a fragment of a door frame from Medinet Habu; see Georges Daressy, "Remarques et notes," *RecTrav* 19 (1897): 20; and Negative 3123 on the website of the Epigraphic Survey of the Oriental Institute of the University of Chicago at https://oi-idb.uchicago.edu/id/4810c8b3–39b3–4f73–93c9–1847065ac99b. Here, she bears the titles of *iryt-pꜥt*, "princess," *ḥnwt Šmꜥw-Mḥ.w*, "mistress of Upper and Lower Egypt," and *wr*(*t*) *ḫnrwt n*(*t*) *Ỉmn nb tꜣwy*, "Great one of the sacred musical troupe of Amun, Lord of the two lands." Pinudjem I is "only" identified as a High Priest of Amun and does not have any royal titles.

27 This observation is, however, not specific to her or to this period. Most of the expressions of filiation, such as "royal mother" or "royal wife," are not accompanied by the name of the corresponding king.

28 Here Henuttawy (A) bears the title of *mwt nswt*, "royal mother," and Psusennes I is qualified as *nswt-bỉti*, "king of Lower and Upper Egypt." See Pierre Montet, *Les constructions et le tombeau de Psousennès à Tanis*, La nécropole de Tanis 2 (Paris: n.p., 1951), 151, 152, fig. 56.

29 For example, on two dovetail joints from Tanis, Mutnodjmet is labeled as *ḥmt nswt snt nswt nbt tꜣwy*, "royal wife, royal sister, mistress of the two lands," whereas Psusennes I's name stands before hers. See Jean Yoyotte, *Tanis. L'or des pharaons* (Paris: Association française d'action artistique, 1987), 190–91 (object no. 53). On her coffin, reused by Amenemope, in Tanis, she is furthermore described as *sꜣt nswt*, "royal daughter," and some other religious titles—*wrt ḫnrt tpyt n*(*t*) *Ỉmn-Rꜥ nswt nṯrw*, among others. See Montet, *Les constructions et le tombeau de Psousennès à Tanis 2*, 164–66, and fig. 60.

30 This assumption is reinforced by the titles of Henuttawy (A), who is the mother of a great royal wife. For a detailed discussion of Henuttawy (A)'s titles, see below.

31 Menkheperre is the only child of Pinudjem I who clearly claims his paternal filiation—for instance, on the stela Cairo TN 3/12/24/2 from Karnak Temple; see Christophe Thiers, "Civils et militaires dans les temples: Occupation illicite et expulsion," *BIFAO* 105 (2005): 495–97.

32 Jansen-Winkeln, *IdS* 1, 17 (no. 3.22).

33 The reading of her title as *ḥryt ḫnrt n*(*t*) *Ỉmn* is questionable, and the actual state of preservation of the wall does not allow us to confirm what Daressy saw ("Notes et remarques," *RecTrav* 14 [1893]: 32–33). See, on this topic and for the older bibliography, Luc Gosselin, *Les divines épouses d'Amon dans l'Égypte de la XIXe à la XXIe dynastie*, EME 6 (Paris: Cybèle, 2007), 218–19.

34 Oriental Institute of the University of Chicago, Epigraphic Survey Negative #7367, https://oi-idb.uchicago.edu/id/74c87247–7891–41be-ad73–e1471094c4bc.

35 Besides the secondary inscription in the Temple of Luxor, Maatkare (A) accompanied her father in a representation in the pathway of the pylon in the Temple of Khonsu (Oriental Institute of the University of Chicago, Epigraphic Survey Negative #3123, https://oi-idb.uchicago.edu/id/da808037-08ad-4b5b-a8d9-edca38afc901).

36 On the pylon of the façade of the Temple of Khonsu (Oriental Institute of the University of Chicago, Epigraphic Survey Negative #7367) Maatkare (A) is *sꜣt nswt n*(*t*) *nbt tꜣwy* (royal daughter of the mistress of the two lands). We cannot, however, exclude the possibility that the scribe mistakenly wrote *nbt* instead of *nb* or that the *n* of the genitive is a mistake for *nbt tꜣwy*, since this title is frequently used to qualify Maatkare (A).

37 Originally published by Henri Chevrier, "Rapport sur les travaux de Karnak 1950–1951," *ASAE* 51 (1951): 554–55, pl. II. This architectural element is now kept in the Cheikh Labib magazine in Karnak, http://sith.huma-num.fr/karnak/231.

38 See note 29.

39 Troy (*Patterns of Queenship*, 114) suggests that the association of the two names shows the "association of the presentation of mother-daughter pairs in the context of the royal monuments"—that is to say, the duality of queenship that is embodied by these two generations of women.

40 P.Cairo J.E. 95887 (S.R. IV 992), published by Auguste Mariette, *Les papyrus égyptiens du Musée de Boulaq III, Papyrus Nos 21 & 22* (Paris: F. Vieweg, 1876), pls. 19–21. See also the information collected on TM 134663 by the Book of the Dead Project/Das Altägyptische Totenbuch: ein digitales Textzeugenarchiv, University of Bonn, totenbuch.awk.nrw.de/objekt/tm134663.

41 P.Cairo CG 40005, also published by Mariette, *Les papyrus égyptiens du Musée de Boulaq* III, pls. 12–18. Totenbuchprojekt Bonn, TM 134430. See the Book of the Dead Project/Das Altägyptische Totenbuch: ein digitales Textzeugenarchiv, University of Bonn, totenbuch.awk.nrw.de/objekt/tm134430.

42 No papyri belonging to a king or any member of the royal family are known prior to the Twenty-first Dynasty. However, vignettes of several spells of the *Book of the Dead* are attested on the walls of the tombs of the Valley of the Kings. For instance, in the vignette of *BD* 59 in KV 34, Thutmose III is represented with a royal serpent on his forehead; see Nils Billing, *Nut: The Goddess of Life*, USE 5 (Uppsala: Uppsala Universitet, 2002), 357 fig. C1. Moreover, a close examination of the funerary material in the tomb of Tutankhamun leads Horst Beinlich ("Das Totenbuch bei Tutanchamun," *GM* 102 [1988]: 7–18) to the conclusion that the absence of a papyrus with *BD* spells might be explained by the fact that the spells are in fact written on other supports. More precisely, the object on which the spell had to be written followed the instruction of the rubrics. (I would like to thank Rita Lucarelli for this reference.)

43 She bears the title of royal daughter, although without naming the royal father in question, and this is one of the main issues for the reconstruction of the beginning of the Twenty-first Dynasty genealogies. He could be either Ramesses XI or Smendes.

44 The same titulary is partially on the lid of her inner coffin (CG 61026). See Georges Daressy, *Cercueils des cachettes royales*, CGC (Cairo: IFAO, 1909), 65.

45 Besides the bracelet already mentioned (see note 28), this title is also attested on other media, such as a stela—Coptos JE 71902, published by Abdallah ("An Unusual Private Stela of the Twenty-first Dynasty from Coptos," 65–72)—on which she is represented next to Pinudjem I. It is the most frequently used title in connection with her descent.

46 On one of her canopic jars (London BM EA 51815), she is *mwt n(t) ḥmt nswt n(t) ỉmn*; see Jansen-Winkeln, *IdS* 1, 262 (Nachtrag). A statue of Sachmet also bears the title of *mwt n(t) dwꜣt-nṯr*; see Jean Yoyotte, "Une monumentale litanie de granit: Les Sekhmet d'Amenophis III et la conjuration permanente de la Déesse dangereuse," *BSFE* 87–88 (1980): 50n12.

47 By cross-referencing other sources, the first child has to be Psusennes I (maternal lineage certain; see note 28), the second Menkheperre, the third Maatkare (A), and the last Mutnodjmet (maternal lineage unclear).

48 Troy, *Patterns of Queenship*, 108.

49 Hussein Bassir, "The Self-presentation of Payeftjauemawyneith on Naophorous Statue BM EA 83," in *Decorum and Experience: Essays in Ancient Culture for John Baines*, ed. Elizabeth Frood and Angela McDonald (Oxford: Griffith Institute, 2013), 9.

50 For instance, the titles used on the coffin of her daughter (see Montet, *Les constructions et le tombeau de Psousennès à Tanis* 2, 164, fig. 60), the queen Mutnodjmet, are all connected to the royal family. First, she is the main great royal wife of his majesty (*ḥmt nswt wrt tpyt n(t) ḥm.f*), followed by her religious functions ("Great one of the sacred musical troupe of Amun-Re," "divine mother of Khonsu the child," "the Very Great one and firstborn of Amun"), and, finally, "royal daughter," "royal sister," and "royal wife," following the pattern of the New Kingdom. See Troy, *Patterns of Queenship*, 107.

51 Troy, *Patterns of Queenship*, 103.

52 On the question of the owner(s) of these two papyri, see Giuseppina Lenzo, "The Two Funerary Papyri of Queen Nedjmet (P.BM EA 10490 and P.BM EA 10541 + Louvre E. 6258)," *BMSAES* 15 (2010): 63–83.

53 P.London BM EA 10490 published by Ernest A.W. Budge, *The Book of the Dead: Facsimiles of the Papyri of Hunefer, Anhai, Kerâsher and Netchemet with Supplementary Text from the Papyrus of Nu* (London: British Museum, 1899), 44–62, pls. 1–12.

54 P.London BM EA 10541 + Louvre E. 6258 + Munich ÄS 825. The papyrus is still not completely published. For pictures and bibliography, see TM 133525 in the Book of the Dead Project/Das Altägyptische Totenbuch: ein digitales Textzeugenarchiv, University of Bonn, totenbuch.awk.nrw.de/objekt/tm133525.

55 *mwt nṯr n(t) Ḫnsw-pꜣ-ẖrd/ wrt ḫnrwt n(t) Ỉmn-Rꜥ nswt nṯrw*. She is also *ḥryt špswt* and *nbt tꜣwy*.

56 *nb tꜣwy (ḥm-nṯr tpy n Ỉmn)*| *sꜣ Rꜥ nb ḫꜥw (Ḥri-Ḥrw sꜣ Ỉmn)*|.

57 Even for the New Kingdom, in the few papyri belonging to a woman we do not have any representation of another family member. For the Twenty-first Dynasty, only a few other examples are known, such as the papyrus of Tjainefer, husband of Gatseshen (A) (P.Cairo JE 33997); see Rita Lucarelli, *The Book of the Dead of Gatseshen: Ancient Egyptian Funerary Religion in the 10th Century BC*, EGU 21 (Leiden: NINO, 2006), 33. All these papyri have a layout very similar to the New Kingdom Books of the Dead.

58 For a divergent analysis making Herihor a son of Nodjmet, see Ad Thijs, "Two Books for One Lady: The Mother of Herihor Rediscovered," *GM* 163 (1998): 101–10; and Thijs, "Nodjmet A, Daughter of Amenhotep, Wife of Piankh and Mother of Herihor," *ZÄS* 140 (2013): 54–69.

59 Epigraphic Survey, *The Temple of Khonsu I: Plates 1–110; Scenes of King Herihor in the Court, with Translations of Texts*, OIP 100 (Chicago: Oriental Institute of the University of Chicago, 1979), pl. 26, 1–2 [*iry(t)-pꜥt wrt*] *ḥswt ḥnwt Šmꜥw-Mḥw nbt <iꜣmt> bnrt mrwt wrt ḫnrwt n(t) Ỉmn-Rꜥ nswt nṯrw ḥmt nswt wrt mrt.f*.

60 Gay Robins, "Some Principles of Compositional Dominance and Gender Hierarchy in Egyptian Art," *JARCE* 31 (1994): 33–40; Ann Macy Roth, "The Absent Spouse: Patterns and Taboos in Egyptian Tomb Decoration," *JARCE* 36 (1999): 45–52. For the Old Kingdom, see Vera Vasiljevic, "Hierarchy of Women within Elite Families: Iconographic Data from the Old Kingdom," in *Art and Society: Ancient and Modern Contexts of Egyptian Art. Proceedings of the International Conference Held at the Museum of Fine Arts, Budapest, 13–15 May 2010*, ed. Katalin A. Kóthay (Budapest: Museum of Fine Arts Budapest, 2012), 139–49.

61 https://oi-idb-static.uchicago.edu/multimedia/110112/9216.1920x1200.jpg.

62 Here, however, she is not yet the wife of Herihor, but of the High Priest of Amun, Piankh.

63 This contribution is based on data collected as part of the ERC Starting Grant "Challenging Time(s)—A New Approach to Written Sources for Ancient Egyptian Chronology" (GA No. 757951), which has received funding from the European Research Council under the European Union's Horizon 2020 research and innovation program at the Institute for Oriental and European Archaeology of the Austrian Academy of Sciences. The results published are solely the responsibility of the author and do not necessarily reflect the opinion of the funding agencies or host institution, which must not be held responsible for either contents or their further use. I would like to thank Carlo Salzani and Charlotte Dietrich for editing my text and Anke Blöbaum, Delphine Driaux, Roman Gundacker, and Vera Müller for prolific discussions, valuable suggestions, and comments.

17

The Role and Status of Women in Elite Family Networks of Late Period Thebes: The Wives of Montuemhat

Anke Ilona Blöbaum

Research on the role of women in ancient Egyptian society has increased during the last few years. This is especially apparent with regard to women in the first millennium BCE, shedding light, for example, on the influence and impact of the institution of the God's Wife of Amun on (female) society in the region of Thebes and beyond,[1] and on women's cultic functions[2] as well as their status and self-identity according to female burial practices.[3] The research so far focuses mainly on different groups of women, contrasting them with the evidence concerning the male spheres of activity. It would, therefore, be of further interest to concentrate on the interface where the female and male spheres meet: the family. Is there any evidence shedding light on the interactions of female and male family members? And if so, what conclusions can be drawn about women's relationships with each other, with the male members of the family, and with other clans? How does affiliation to a special family affect women's status in the elite society of Thebes? And does affiliation to a special woman affect the status of a family? These and other questions lead to the key objective of this research—namely, to detect and to collect any evidence shedding light on the position and the influence of women within Theban society and in their families in particular.[4]

The present contribution provides an insight into the current issues based on the example of the family of the famous Montuemhat,[5] Fourth Priest of Amun and Governor of Thebes,[6] who was one of the leading figures during the time of transition between the Twenty-fifth and the Twenty-sixth Dynasties. He had been married three times and had several children.[7] But what do we know about the women in his family? Is there any evidence proving more than simply their existence?

The Wives of Montuemhat

Montuemhat is one of the most powerful individuals of his time, known through his building activities in the Mut precinct.[8] There is a long inscription in the so-called Taharqo crypt in the temple of Mut,[9] referring to his efforts, and more than twenty statues attributed to him.[10] Last but not least, there is his marvelous tomb in the Asasif.[11]

Montuemhat married three times. His first wife, Nesikhons,[12] was the mother of his firstborn son and heir, Nesptah (B),[13] the latter of whom was named after his paternal grandfather.[14] His second wife, Wedjarenes,[15] also known as his "Kushite wife," was a granddaughter of Piankhy (Piye).[16] Due to her royal descent, she seemed to have had an important function for both her husband and the whole family network. Further examination of that function shall be carried out with regard to the following questions: Do we have any evidence that clarifies her position within the family? Does her status differ from that of the two other wives?

Evidence of Montuemhat's third wife, Shepenmut,[17] is sparse. The principal source of information about these three women is the tomb of Montuemhat (TT 34). There is evidence for all of them, focusing on their role as mother (of sons, most importantly) and wife of Montuemhat.

The Three Women in Their Role as Mother

A scene on the southern wall of the pillared hall in the tomb of Montuemhat is especially significant for understanding the roles of these women as mothers (fig. 17.1).[18]

Montuemhat, who is depicted inspecting a group of craftsmen, is accompanied by six male figures who are arranged in three small registers behind him. According to the accompanying inscriptions, at least five of these figures can be identified as sons of Montuemhat. The second figure (on the right) in the third register (above) remains questionable, as his height and costume differ from the other figures. Preservation of the wall is bad, with the upper part of the third register entirely lost.[19] Each son is identified by an inscription placed in front of the figure, which records his name and titles, and by a line above referring to his mother. In each case the genealogical reference is introduced by *ir(i).n*.

Fig. 17.1. Tomb TT 34 (pillar hall, southern wall, detail): sons of Montuemhat

First register (below):

(1) ↓ [. . .] *n ḫt.f* [. . .] *Ns-Ptḥ* (2) → [. . .]
(1) [son] of his body, [. . .] Nesptah (2) [. . .]
(3) ↓ [. . .] *Ỉmn Ḏd-Ḫnsw-ỉ*[*w*]*.f-*[*ʿnḫ*] (4) → *ỉr(ỉ).n Ns-Ḫnsw*
(3) [. . .] Amun, Djedkhonsuiuefankh, (4) whom Nesikhons had borne.

Second register (middle):

(1) ↓ *s3.f ḥm nṯr Ỉmn rḫ nsw m3ʿ P3-šrỉ-n-Mwt* (2) → *ỉr(ỉ).n Wḏ3-rn.s*
(1) His son, Priest of Amun, the King's Real Acquaintance, Pasherienmut,
(2) whom Wedjarenes had borne
(3) ↓ [. . .] *rḫ nsw Ns-Ptḥ* (4) → *ỉr(ỉ).n Wḏ3-rn.s*
(3) [. . .] the King's Acquaintance, Nesptah, (4) whom Wedjarenes had borne

Third register (above):

(1) ↓ [. . .] *m W3st rḫ nsw Ns-Ptḥ* (2) → [. . .]
(1) [. . .] in Thebes, the King's Acquaintance, Nesptah (2) [. . .]

Apparently, each register refers to one of Montuemhat's wives, as we have two sons of Nesikhons in the first register—the firstborn son, Nesptah, and another son, Djedkhonsuiuefankh;[20] two sons of Wedjarenes in the second register—Pasherienmut[21] and another Nesptah; and another son with the name Nesptah in the third register, where the name of the mother is not preserved. According to the layout of the whole scene, the third register must have been reserved for Shepenmut.[22] This assumption is confirmed by the fact that a son of Shepenmut, named Nesptah, is attested as witness (no. 49) in the Saitic Oracular Papyrus (P.Brooklyn 47.218.3).[23] Nesikhons's firstborn son was also named Nesptah (B), as attested on several other monuments as well.[24] According to this evidence, all the wives of Montuemhat shared one privilege—namely, a son named after their paternal grandfather, Nesptah (A).

However, the scene, and in particular the layout and sequence of the registers, offers another important detail regarding these women: Wedjarenes follows the first wife, Nesikhons. Edna Russmann theorized that Shepenmut was the second wife of Montuemhat, followed by Wedjarenes as last wife.[25] This would best explain the strong presence of Wedjarenes in the tomb of Montuemhat as well as the fact that she was probably buried in the tomb.[26] However, the layout of the scene suggests the reversed order of the second and third wives.[27] Edna Russmann's idea that both marriages probably took place during the reign of Taharqo[28] now must be put into perspective. Nesptah (B3) is recorded as a witness (no. 49) in the Saitic Oracle Papyrus (P.Brooklyn 47.218.3).[29] This document is firmly dated to year 14 of Psamtik I, indicating that Nesptah (B3) must have been of a certain age at this time. As he bears the title of "God's Father of Amun," he could still have been a relatively young man at the time, so that the third marriage could well have taken place toward the end of the Twenty-fifth Dynasty or even at an early stage during the time of transition.

The inscriptions do not provide any titles of the women. This differs from indications of the mother on other monuments of their sons—for example, on statuary where, partly according to the space available, more comprehensive titles are used to introduce and identify the mother. We have knowledge of several sons and grandsons of Montuemhat, but only one daughter is known. Table 17.1 gives an overview of attestations that explicitly mention the mother's name.

Table 17.1. Attestations of the three women in genealogical references

Mother	Children	Source
Nesikhons	Nesptah B	N-N1: TT 34: Gamer-Wallert, *Wandreliefs*, 49–50, 123 [15], 156 [17]. N-N2: CG 42240 and TN 12/3/36/1 and Mahsan el-Makina el-Nûr no. 110: Jansen-Winkeln, *IdS* 3, 452–53 [195]. N-N3: CG 42241 (B-CK/155): Jansen-Winkeln, *IdS* 3, 457–59 [202]. N-N4: BM EA 133: Jansen-Winkeln, *IdS* 3, 490 [253]. N-N5: precinct of Mut, crypt of Taharqo, eastern wall, inscription: Jansen-Winkeln, *IdS* 3, 203. N-N6: Sarcophagus (TT 34): Awadallah and El-Sawy, "Un sarcophage de Nsi-Ptah," 33–34. N-N7: cone type 3: Jansen-Winkeln, *IdS* 3, 479.
	Djedkhonsu-iuefankh	N-D1: TT 34: Gamer-Wallert, *Wandreliefs*, 49–50, 123 [15], 156 [17].
Wedjarenes	Pasherienmut	W-P1: TT 34: Gamer-Wallert, *Wandreliefs*, 49–50, 123 [15], 156 [17]. W-P2: CG 42240 and TN 12/3/36/1 and Mahsan el-Makina el-Nûr no. 110: Jansen-Winkeln, *IdS* 3, 452–53 [195]. W-P3: cone type 5: Jansen-Winkeln, *IdS* 3, 479.
	Nesptah (B2)	W-N1: TT 34: Gamer-Wallert, *Wandreliefs*, 49–50, 123 [15], 156 [17].
Shepenmut	Nesptah (B3)	S-N1: TT 34: Gamer-Wallert, *Wandreliefs*, 49–50, 123 [15], 156 [17]. S-N2: P.Brooklyn 47.218.3, col. N, 5: Parker, *A Saite Oracle Papyrus*, 28–29, pl. 15.

With the exception of two attestations on the sarcophagus of Nesptah (B), where the verb *ms*(*i*) is used, the genealogical reference is generally introduced by the verb *ir*(*i*).

Furthermore, there is evidence of two other sons of Montuemhat, named Djedhor[30] and Montuemhat (B),[31] as well as a daughter with the name Diasehebsed.[32] However, in these attestations there is no reference to their mother. The next generation is known by at least three grandsons: Montuemhat (B) had a son with the name Djedkhonsuiuefankh,[33] Nesptah (B) had a son with the name Montuemhati,[34] and Pascherienmut had a son with the name Montuemhat[35] as well.

All but one of the genealogical references show a similar structure, with only small differences, mostly in length according to the space available. They do not provide any significant information on the central question concerning the status of each particular woman within the family. The one exception—namely, the signature of the witness no. 49, Nesptah (B2)—will be discussed in more detail within the concluding remarks at the end of the chapter.

To summarize, as display of the mother role depends on representations of a male child, differences in representation are associated with the monument and the status of the son. The information about the mother is more or less reduced to the pure genealogical relationship, oftentimes complemented with titles or the epithet *mꜣꜥ ḫrw*.

The Three Women in Their Role as Wife

Attestations of the three women in the role of wife are strictly connected to representations—be they visual or inscriptional—of the husband, Montuemhat. The main source is the tomb of Montuemhat (TT 34). Hitherto, no depiction of Nesikhons has been discovered, and she was most likely not depicted in the tomb. Her appearance in the inscriptional record of the tomb seems to be restricted to the mother role, in particular as mother of the first-born son and heir, Nesptah (B).[36]

In contrast, visual representations of Wedjarenes and Montuemhat as a couple are preserved in the tomb in several places.[37] Wedjarenes is mostly, but not exclusively, depicted within the decoration of the First and Second Courts, in areas where the decoration has been dated to the Twenty-fifth Dynasty. In the niche in the south side of the east wall, rock-cut statues depict Montuemhat and Wedjarenes.[38]

In contrast, only one visual attestation of Shepenmut has been preserved. A fragment of a relief with a depiction of Shepenmut and Montuemhat as a couple is on display in the Seattle Art Museum. It can be assigned to the tomb in general, but has not (yet) been assigned an exact position.[39]

Unlike the differences in the visual representations of the three women, all three names are preserved in funerary cones:

Cone type 7:[40]
(1) *imȝḫy ḫr Wsir* (2) *ḥm-nṯr-4.nw-Ỉmn Mnṯw-m-ḥȝt mȝʿ-ḫrw*
(3) *ḥmt.f mr(i).f rḫt-nsw nbt-pr* (4) *Ns-Ḫnsw mȝʿt-ḫrw*
(1) Honored by Osiris, (2) Fourth Priest of Amun, Montuemhat, justified,
(3) His beloved wife, the King's Acquaintance, Lady of the House,
(4) Nesikhons, justified.

Cone type 9:[41]
(1) *imȝḫy ḫr Wsir* (2) *ḥm-nṯr-4.nw-Ỉmn Mnṯw-m-ḥȝt mȝʿ-ḫrw*
(3) *ḥmt.f mr(i).f rḫt-nsw nbt-pr* (4) *Wḏȝ-rn.st mȝʿt-ḫrw*
(1) Honored by Osiris, (2) Fourth Priest of Amun, Montuemhat, justified,
(3) His beloved wife, the King's Acquaintance, Lady of the House,
(4) Wedjarenes, justified.

Cone type 8:[42]
(1) *imȝḫy ḫr Wsir* (2) *ḥm-nṯr-4.nw-Ỉmn Mnṯw-m-ḥȝt mȝʿ-ḫrw*
(3) *ḥmt.f mr(i).f rḫt-nsw nbt-pr* (4) *Špt-n-Mwt mȝʿt-ḫrw*
(1) Honored by Osiris, (2) Fourth Priest of Amun, Montuemhat, justified,
(3) His beloved wife, the King's Acquaintance, Lady of the House,
(4) Shepenmut, justified.

The structure, form, and layout of the inscriptions are very much the same, with the exception of the wife's name. They all bear the same sequence of titles referring to their position as wife of Montuemhat as well as their position within the family, the household, and the Theban elite. Edna Russmann has interpreted the similarity of these three cone types as reference to "the stability and permanence of the Egyptian institution of marriage."[43] However, in my opinion, it has to be seen in a more functional way as a manifestation of coherence and consistency in categories of display. Consequently, the structure and layout of the funerary cones of Nesptah (B) and Pasherienmut with reference to their mothers are very similar:

Cone type 3:[44]
(1) *ḥm-nṯr-4.nw-Ỉmn im(i)-rʾ Šmʿw* (2) *Mnṯw-m-ḥȝt mȝʿ-ḫrw sȝ.f wr n ẖt.f*
(3) *ḥm-nṯr-Ỉmn rḫ-nsw Ns-Ptḥ ir(i){t}.n*
(4) *nbt-pr Ns-Ḫnsw mȝʿt-ḫrw*

(1) Fourth Priest of Amun, Overseer of Upper Egypt, Montuemhat, justified, his eldest son of his body,
(3) The Priest of Amun, the King's Acquaintance, Nesptah, whom
(4) the Lady of the House, Nesikhons, justified, had borne.

Cone type 5:[45]
(1) *Wsỉr ḥm-nṯr-4.nw-Ỉmn* (2) *Mnṯw-m-ḥ3t m3ʿ-ḫrw s3.f n ẖt.f*
(3) *ḥm-nṯr-Ỉmn rḫ-nsw P3-šri-n-Mwt ỉr(ỉ).n*
(4) *nbt-pr Wḏ3-rn.st m3ʿt-ḫrw*
(1) Osiris of the Fourth Priest of Amun, Overseer of Upper Egypt, Montuemhat, justified, his son of his body,
(3) The Priest of Amun, the King's Acquaintance, Pasherienmut, whom
(4) the Lady of the House, Wedjarenes, justified, had borne.

According to the funerary cones of Montuemhat, all three wives seem to have had the same status in the family. However, the visual representation is clearly focused on Wedjarenes. This could be related to the course of construction works at the tomb or could be indicative of a superior status within the family.

The Three Women as Individuals

Is it possible to learn something about these women beyond their roles as mother and wife? According to Jean Li, "there is a potential disjunction between the ways Egyptian institutions represented gender roles and status and how women conceived of themselves as manifested in actual quotidian practices, such as preparations for death."[46] Accordingly, she focused her analysis of female identity on elite female funerary evidence.

Unfortunately, this approach does not work for the wives of Montuemhat. While some *shabti*s of Wedjarenes are preserved,[47] indicating that she was indeed buried in the tomb of Montuemhat, evidence of *shabti*s or any other funeral equipment of the two other wives is lacking. Accordingly, we do not know whether Nesikhons and Shepenmut were buried in the tomb of their husband or elsewhere.[48]

On the other hand, Wedjarenes left an offering table, which was found in the tomb of Montuemhat.[49] The inscription delivers the genealogy of Wedjarenes, mentioning her father, the *s3-nsw* Piankhy-Har. The name of Montuemhat is not mentioned in the inscription. Obviously her self-presentation in this case was focused on her royal descent and not on her actual status within the family. Nevertheless, Wedjarenes was a granddaughter of the Kushite king Piankhy (Piye), and the family had, presumably, benefited from this marriage.

The Titles of the Three Women

Following the assumption of Jean Li, that "titles are identity markers that reveal some of the axes of identity that were most relevant to elite Theban women,"[50] a comparison of the women's titles may be worthwhile. Table 17.2 provides an overview.

Table 17.2. The titles of the three women

Nesikhons	
nbt-pr	N-N5 N-N7 (cone type 3)
nbt-pr špst	N-N2
ḥmt.f mr(i͗).f rḫt-nsw nbt-pr	cone type 7
ḥmt-nṯr Ḥwt-Ḥrw nbt-pr	N-N4
Wedjarenes	
nbt-pr	W-P1 (cone type 5)
nbt-pr špst	W-P2
ḥmt.f mr(i͗).f nbt-pr	TT 34, 1. court
ḥmt.f mr(i͗).f rḫt-nsw nbt-pr	cone type 9
špst-nsw-wˁtt nbt-pr *ẖkrt-nsw-wˁtt ḥmt-nṯr Ḥw.t-Ḥr.w nbt-pr*	offering table
ḥmt.f mr[t].f špst-nsw-wˁtt ḥmt-nṯr Ḥw.t-Ḥr.w rḫt-nsw nbt-pr	TT 34, 1. court[51]
Shepenmut	
ḥmt.f mr(i͗).f rḫt-nsw nbt-pr	cone type 8

All three women are described as a wife of Montuemhat, *ḥmt.f mr(i͗).f*, "his beloved wife" (meaning Montuemhat), a standard formula that had not been changed since the Old Kingdom.[52] It is not a title in a strict sense, but simply the term for "wife." Accordingly, it is used within the tomb of Montuemhat and in the inscription of the funerary cones.

The title *nbt-pr*, "Lady of the House,"[53] which is attested for all three women, is connected, first, with her position as a person responsible for the household.[54] Whether the title reflects the marital status of a woman is still under discussion. There are late attestations (Third Intermediate Period) that are indicative of a shift in its use and function, signaling socioeconomic status rather than marital status.[55] Indeed, concerning its use in the Middle Kingdom Danijela Stefanović and Helmut Satzinger note: "Still, what seems to be undisputable is that the title *nbt-pr* emphasizes an adult, independent person, i.e. a woman who was able to manage the economics of a household—with, or without a male owner, or to be enrolled in some other business enterprise."[56]

Furthermore, all three women bear the title *rḫt-nsw*, "King's Acquaintance."[57] This title particularly needs further explanation, as its meaning has been widely discussed.[58] The male variant *rḫ-nsw* could be understood as either *ỉr(ỉ)-ỉḫt-nsw*, "Custodian of the King's Property," or *rḫ-nsw*, "King's Acquaintance." It is generally thought that the title originally described a special department in the court administration, and from the late Old Kingdom onward, it developed into a courtesy title.[59] This may lead to a reinterpretation of the title's hieroglyphic expression. The earliest evidence for the female title has been preserved from the Fifth Dynasty, indicating that it probably was already used as a courtesy title at that time.[60] The title is frequently attested until the beginning of the Middle Kingdom; afterward it apparently fell out of use and was revived in the course of the archaistic tendencies of the Twenty-fifth and Twenty-sixth Dynasties.[61] Of course, the way the male and female variants of the title are used in Late Period Thebes may have been further developed. As Christopher Naunton recently pointed out on behalf of the male variant: "The title may simply be an extension of the notion that these individuals were part of the king's circle, but also suggests that they acted as representatives of the king, perhaps as part of a network of trusted individuals with a brief to monitor the local situation on behalf of the pharaoh."[62] It is attested for very few male individuals of the highest Theban elite, including Montuemhat. Accordingly, the female variant is sparsely attested as well. Apart from the wives of Montuemhat, there is little evidence of its use. Jean Li has compiled a list of 219 Theban women for a case study of women's identity in Third Intermediate Period Thebes; with only one exception—namely, Mutirdis,[63] the "Chief Attendant of the God's Wife of Amun"—none of them bear the title.[64] Apparently, the titles identify these women as members of a very small group of the highest elite within Thebes. As regards the wives of Montuemhat, it might be worth considering Montuemhat as the main titleholder, transferring the privilege to the whole family. Indeed, the title is attested for the sons of Montuemhat as well (cf. fig. 17.1).[65]

Lastly, Nesikhons and Wedjarenes are designated as *špst*, "Noblewoman,"[66] both in connection with the title *nbt-pr*, "Lady of the House." This connection seems to be specific for its use from the Third Intermediate Period onward, while its use in earlier times reflects a stronger connection to the royal sphere.[67] Nevertheless, it designates a woman of high status and rank. However, the title *špst* has to be distinguished from *špst-nsw*, "Noblewoman of the King,"[68] a title specific in content and evidence. The latter is preserved for Wedjarenes only. While *špst* and the male variant *šps(s)* are attested up to the Roman Period, the use of the title *špst-nsw* is limited to the end of the Old Kingdom and the Heracleopolitan period.[69]

The title is attested in the tomb of Montuemhat and on the offering table of Wedjarenes found in the first court. The inscriptions of this monument especially focus on Wedjarenes's royal descent, enhanced by the choice of titles. It should be kept in mind that the variant *špst-nsw-wꜥtt*, as it is recorded on the offering table, did not exist in the Old Kingdom. This constitutes a current neologism influenced by the Old Kingdom title *ḫkrt nsw wꜥtt*, "Sole Ornament of the King,"[70] which occurs in a parallel inscription on the offering table. According to Henry George Fischer, the title *ḫkrt nsw wꜥtt* was an exclusively feminine designation that was applied only occasionally to women from the Fifth Dynasty onward and did not become very frequent until the end of the Old Kingdom both in the Memphite cemeteries and in the provinces. It was commonly in use in the Heracleopolitan Period and continued through the Middle Kingdom and into the New Kingdom, as well as nearly the whole of the Eighteenth Dynasty.[71] The interpretation of the title remains problematic:[72]

> The bottom line of the ongoing discussion is that while in some periods the title was held by few women who could have been directly connected to the royal household, be it in the king's or the queen's service or as a member of the extended royal family, in other periods the number of title-holders was so great and their connection to the royal court so unlikely that it can testify at best to brief encounters with the royal court or just denote a high social standing.[73]

However, it is interesting that in the Eleventh Dynasty the title *ḫkrt-nsw-(wꜥtt)* is connected to the title *ḥmt-nṯr Ḥw.t-Ḥrw*, "Priestess of Hathor,"[74] which is attested on the offering table of Wedjarenes as well. The sequence of both titles is attested for two groups of women buried in the funerary complex of the Eleventh Dynasty king Nephetepre Mentuhotep II in Deir al-Bahari, one consisting of royal wives, the other probably of Nubian origin, and both seemingly with a strong connection to cultic and ritual dance.[75]

The composition of Wedjarenes' titular sequence, therefore, clearly has to be seen in the context of archaizing tendencies throughout the Theban elite,[76] but likewise it reveals a specific composition perfectly adapted for Wedjarenes in her role as a Kushite royal descendant. The sequence of titles is also attested in the tomb of Montuemhat, where Wedjarenes, in the corresponding picture, is depicted with her hair shortened and styled in Kushite manner, visually resembling Old Kingdom women of high rank.[77] Therefore, the sequence of titles preserved on the offering table and in tomb TT 34 focuses on the royal descent of Wedjarenes, most likely on her Nubian roots, as well as on exclusivity intensified by the venerability of the former times.

Conclusions

While we only have very few attestations of Nesikhons and Shepenmut, Wedjarenes is depicted in the tomb of Montuemhat several times; she left *shabtis* and an offering table as monuments of her own. The results may have been compromised by the state of preservation, but the evidence indicates a superior position for Wedjarenes in the representations of Montuemhat's wives.

With this in mind, there is another exceptional attestation for Wedjarenes: she is mentioned on the Nitocris Adoption stela[78] together with her husband and his firstborn son Nesptah (B), offspring of the first wife Nesikhons. The stela commemorates the adoption of Psamtik's daughter Nitocris as heir of the reigning God's Wife Shepenwepet II and the contemporaneous Divine Votaress Amenirdis II, and therefore represents the most important document concerning the legitimation of Psamtik I as king of Egypt. The second half of the text delivers a list of provisions in order to maintain the future God's Wife, Nitocris. Parts of the provisions are guaranteed by the family of Montuemhat, as well as by the High Priest and the Third Priest of Amun. This group of men represented the highest clergy of the temple of Amun at that time, and Wedjarenes is named together with them. Montuemhat is mentioned first, followed by Nesptah (B), the son, and Wedjarenes, his wife. After the family, the High Priest and the Third Priest of Amun are mentioned. Yet an interesting detail is how Wedjarenes is described.[79] She is referred to as:

JE 36327, Z. 22:
ḥmt ḥm nṯr 4nw Ỉmn Mnṯ(w)-m-ḥ3t Wḏ3-rn.s m3ˁ(t) ḫrw
Wife (of) the Fourth Priest of Amun, Montuemhat, Wedjarenes, justified.

Where, in general, a simple *ḥmt.f* would have been utilized, this expression possibly results from the fact that Montuemhat does not occur directly before Wedjarenes in the text, as the son is second after Montuemhat. Nevertheless, this type of denotation of a wife is very uncommon and rarely attested. While I am unaware of any other example of *ḥmt* in combination with the full title and name of the husband included in the titulary of a private woman, three attestations of the royal wife Kiya are similar: *ḥmt mrrti(t) ꜥ3t n* [king's name] *Ki3*.[80]

As Wedjarenes was already deceased at this point, her funerary estate was probably responsible for her share of provisions and might well explain why she is reduced to her position as wife of Montuemhat. However, her connection to the Kushite royal family served Montuemhat and his household and is surely the reason behind the mention of her name in this text. The High Priest Horkhebi, grandson of the Kushite king Shabaqo, and Wedjarenes, the granddaughter of the Kushite king Piankhy (Piye), are mentioned as representative of the Kushite royal house. The connection to the royal family was thus important for Montuemhat and his household, and as a result, the position and status of Wedjarenes were presumably superior to those of the other wives. This is reflected in the preserved evidence.[81]

The adoption stela describes the events of the ninth year of Psamtik I. At that time, Montuemhat must have already been married to his third wife, Shepenmut, for a number of years. Unfortunately, we do not know much about her. As has been mentioned previously, her son, Nesptah (B3), known from TT 34 (cf. fig. 17.1), is attested in the Saite Oracle papyrus (P.Brooklyn 47.218.3) of year 14 of Psamtik I. He signed the Oracle petition in the penultimate position (no. 49). Among the witnesses are his father, Montuemhat, his eldest half-brother Nesptah (B), and another possible brother or half-brother Djedhor, as well as a grandson of Montuemhat, a son of Pasherienmut, the firstborn son of Wedjarenes. He signs by his own hand as:

P.Brooklyn 47.2183, col. N, 5:[82]
iti-nṯr n 'Imn-Rꜥw nsw-nṯrw s3 ḥm-nṯr-4.nw n 'Imn mwt.f Š[p-n]-mwt Ns-ptḥ,
The God's Father of Amunrasonther, son of the Fourth Priest of Amun, whose mother is She[pen]mut, Nesptah.

All other members of the family honored Montuemhat by using Gardiner A52 (the squatting noble with flagellum) instead of A1 (the sitting man) as classifier after his name.[83] Why the son of Shepenmut did not even name his famous father when, in general, the paternal line is preferred in a sacerdotal context[84] remains unclear. Although he makes reference to his mother for an unambiguous identification, it is remarkable, albeit not exceptional,[85] that he reduced his father to this position. Whether this might point to a conflict or frustrations on behalf of his mother's position within the family is left to our imagination.

Notes

1 Mariam Ayad, *God's Wife, God's Servant: The God's Wife of Amun (c. 740–525 BC)* (London and New York: Routledge, 2009); Carola Koch, *"Die den Amun mit ihrer Stimme zufriedenstellen": Gottesgemahlinnen und Musikerinnen im thebanischen Amunstaat von der 22. bis zur 26. Dynastie*, SRaT 27 (Dettelbach: J.H. Röll, 2012); Mariam Ayad, "Gender, Ritual, and Manipulation of Power: The God's Wife of Amun (Dynasty 23–26)," in *Prayer and Power: Proceedings of the Conference on the God's Wives of Amun in Egypt during the First Millennium BC*, ed. Meike Becker, Anke Ilona Blöbaum, and Angelika Lohwasser, ÄAT 84 (Münster: Ugarit-Verlag, 2016), 89–106.

2 Saphinaz-Amal Naguib, *Le clergé féminin d'Amon thébain à la 21e Dynastie*, OLA 38 (Leuven: Peeters, 1990); Suzanne Lynn Onstine, *The Role of the Chantress (šmʿy.t) in Ancient Egypt*, BARIS 140 (Oxford: Hadrian Books, 2005); Koch, *"Die den Amun mit ihrer Stimme zufriedenstellen."*

3 Jean Li, *Women, Gender and Identity in Third Intermediate Period Egypt: The Theban Case Study* (London and New York: Routledge, 2017).

4 This work is part of ongoing research that is far from complete. The following considerations must be seen as a first approach to the subject and as work in progress.

5 *Mnṯw-m-ḥꜣt*: Hermann Ranke, *PN* 1, 154 [7]; Jean Leclant, *Montouemhat, quatrième prophète d'Amon*, BdE 35 (Cairo: IFAO, 1961); Morris L. Bierbrier, "More Light on the Family of Montemhat," in *Orbis Aegyptiorum Speculum: Glimpses of Ancient Egypt. Studies in Honor of H.W. Fairman*, ed. John Ruffle, G.A. Gaballa, and Kenneth A. Kitchen (Warminster: Aris and Phillips, 1979), 116–18; John H. Taylor, "A Note on the Family of Montemhat," *JEA* 73 (1987): 229–30.

6 *Ḥm nṯr 4.nw (n) Ỉmn*: Christopher H. Naunton, "Regime Change and the Administration of Thebes during the Twenty-fifth Dynasty" (PhD diss., Swansea University, 2011), 60–65; *ḥꜣtj-ʿ n nt*: *Wb* III, 25.21; Naunton, *Regime Change*, 17–38.

7 Information about a fourth wife named Asetemchebis (*ꜣst-m-ꜣḫ-bit*: Ranke, *PN*, 4 [3]; Jansen-Winkeln, *IdS* 3, 480 [6a–b]), like information about the mother of Montuemhat, is not reliable, as Jean Leclant and Edna Russmann have already pointed out; see Leclant, *Montouemhat*, 163; Russmann, "Mentuemhat's Kushite Wife: Further Remarks on the Decoration of the Tomb of Mentuemhat 2," *JARCE* 34 (1997): 21.

8 Richard A. Fazzini and William H. Peck, "The Precinct of Mut during Dynasty XXV and Early Dynasty XXVI: A Growing Picture," *JSSEA* 11 (1981): 115–26; Richard A. Fazzini and Paul O'Rourke, "Aspects of the Mut Temple's Contra-Temple at South Karnak, Part I," in *Hommages à Jean-Claude Goyon offerts pour son 70e anniversaire*, ed. Luc Gabolde, BdE 143 (Cairo: IFAO, 2008), 139–50; Richard A. Fazzini, "Aspects of the Mut Temple's Contra-Temple at South Karnak, Part II," in *Offerings to the Discerning Eye: An Egyptological Medley in Honor of Jack A. Josephson*, ed. Sue H. D'Auria, CHANE 38 (Leiden: Brill, 2010), 83–101; Neal Spencer, "Sustaining Egyptian Culture? Non-royal Initiatives in Late Period Temple Building," in *Egypt in Transition: Social and Religious Development of Egypt in the First Millennium BCE*, ed. Ladislav Bareš, Filip Coppens, and Kveta Smoláriková (Prague: Oxbow Books, 2010), 441–90; Richard A. Fazzini, "More Montuemhat at South Karnak," in *The 62nd Annual Meeting of the American Research Center in Egypt—April 1–3, 2011, Chicago Marriott Downtown Chicago, Illinois (Book of Abstracts)*, 45, (http://archive.arce.org/files/user/page157/2011_AM_booklet_.pdf 15.02.2020); Anke Ilona Blöbaum, "Monthemhet—Priester des Amun und Gouverneur von Theben: Die Selbstpräsentation eines Lokalherrschers im sakralen Raum," ch. III.2.2, in *Inszenierung von Herrschaft und Macht im ägyptischen Tempel: Religion und Politik im Theben des frühen 1. Jahrtausends v. Chr.*, ed. Meike Becker, Anke Ilona Blöbaum, and Angelika Lohwasser, ÄAT 95 (Münster: Zaphon-Verlag, 2020).

9 Karl Jansen-Winkeln, *IdS* 3, 197–202 [142], 495–96 [260]; Jens Heise, *Erinnern und Gedenken: Aspekte der biographischen Inschriften der ägyptischen Spätzeit*, OBO 226 (Fribourg: Vandenhoeck and Ruprecht, 2007), 80–89; Silke Grallert, *Bauen—Stiften—Weihen: Ägyptische Bau- und Restaurierungsinschriften von den Anfängen bis zur 30. Dynastie*, ADAIK 18 (Berlin: Achet, 2001),

357–59; Fazzini and O'Rourke, "Aspects of the Mut Temple's Contra-Temple, Part I," 144–46; Blöbaum, "Monthemhet," ch. III.2.2.1.2.

10 Leclant, *Montouemhat*, 3–170, with the exception of Doc. 8 (Brooklyn 16.580.185), which has to be attributed to the firstborn son, Nesptah; see Herman de Meulenaere, "Nesptah: Fils et successeur de Montouemhat," *CdE* 83 (2008): 98–108, 102 [3]; Jürgen von Beckerath, "Ein Torso des Mentemḥēt in München," in *ZÄS* 87 (1962): 1–8; Biri Fay, "Another Statue of Montuemhat," *GM* 189 (2002): 23–31; Fazzini, "More Montuemhat at South Karnak," 96 with n44; for a new edition of the inscriptions, see Jansen-Winkeln, *IdS* 3, 204, 451–56, 475–77; for specific aspects of individual statues or groups thereof, see Wolfgang Müller, "Der 'Stadtfürst' von Theben, Monthemhêt," in *Münchener Jahrbuch für Bildende Kunst* 26 (1975): 7–12; Jaques Jean Clère, *Les Chauves d'Hathor*, OLA 63 (Leuven: Peeters, 1995), 153–57; Jack A. Josephson, "Sacred and Profane: The Two Faces of Mentuemhat," in *Egyptian Museum Collections around the World*, ed. Mamdouh Eldamaty and May Trad (Cairo: American University in Cairo Press, 2001), 619–27; Jack A. Josephson, "La période de transition à Thebes 663–648 avant J.-C.," *EAO* 28 (2003): 39–46; Olivier Perdu, "Statue assise sur un siège de Montouemhat," in *Le crépuscule des Pharaons. Chefs-d'œuvre des dernières dynasties égyptiennes* (Brussels: Fonts Mercator, 2012), 44–45; Laurent Coulon, "Padiaménopé et Montouemhat: L'apport d'une statue inédite à l'analyse des relations entre les deux personnages," in *Aere Perennius. Mélanges égyptologiques en l'honneur de Pascal Vernus*, ed. Philippe Collombert, Dominique Lefèvre, Stéphane Polis, and Jean Winand, OLA 242 (Leuven: Peeters, 2016), 91–119; Patrizia Heindl, "Monumentale Feindvernichtung: die Felidenfellträgerstatuen des Monthemhat," in *Funktion/en: Materielle Kultur—Sprache—Religion. Beiträge des siebten Berliner Arbeitskreises Junge Aegyptologie (BAJA 7) 2.12.–4.12.2016*, ed. Alexandra Verbovsek, Burkhard Backes, and Jan Aschmoneit, GOF IV, vol. 64 (Wiesbaden: Harrassowitz, 2018), 45–64; Blöbaum, "Monthemhet," ch. III.2.1.

11 TT 34: PM I,12, 56–61; Leclant, *Montouemhat*, 171–86; Müller, "Der 'Stadtfürst' von Theben, Monthemhêt," 7–36, 12–34; Klaus-Peter Kuhlmann and Wolfgang Schenkel, *Das Grab des Ibi, Obergutsverwalters der Gottesgemahlin des Amun (Thebanisches Grab Nr. 36)*, vol. 1, *Beschreibung der unterirdischen Kult- und Bestattungsanlage*, AV 15 (Mainz am Rhein: Philipp von Zabern, 1983), pls. 159–60, 162–63; Diethelm Eigner, *Die monumentalen Grabbauten der Spätzeit in der thebanischen Nekropole*, UÖAI 6 (Vienna: Verlag der Österreichischen Akademie der Wissenschaften, 1984), 44–46 [36k]; Mohammed Nasr, "The Excavation of the Tomb of Montuemhat at Thebes," *Memnonia* 8 (1997): 211–23; Sabine Herrmann, "Monthemhat, der Stadtgraf von Theben," *Sokar* 23 (2011): 90–95; Ingrid Gamer-Wallert, *Die Wandreliefs des zweiten Lichthofs im Grab des Monthemhat (TT 34): Versuch einer zeichnerischen Rekonstruktion*, CAENL 2/DÖAW 75 (Vienna: Verlag der Österreichischen Akademie der Wissenschaften, 2013); Louise Gestermann and Farouk Gomaà, "The Tomb of Montuemhat (TT 34) in the Theban Necropolis: A New Approach," in *Thebes in the First Millenium* BC, ed. Elena Pischikova, Julia Budka, and Kenneth Griffin (Cambridge: Cambridge Scholars Publishing, 2014), 201–203; Louise Gestermann and Farouk Gomaà, "Remarks on the Decoration and Conception of the Theban Tomb of Montuemhat (TT 34)," in *Thebes in the First Millennium* BC*: Art and Archaeology of the Kushite Period and Beyond*, ed. Elena Pischikova, Julia Budka, and Kenneth Griffin, GHPE 27 (London: Golden House Publishing, 2018), 152–61. Concerning the decoration of the tomb, see Peter Der Manuelian, "A Fragment of Relief from the Tomb of Mentuemhat Attributed to the Fifth Dynasty," *JSSEA* 12 (1982): 185–88; Manuelian, "An Essay in Reconstruction: Two Registers from the Tomb of Mentuemhat at Thebes (no. 34)," *MDAIK* 39 (1984): 131–50; Manuelian, "Two Fragments of Relief and a New Model for the Tomb of Mentemhēt," *JEA* 71 (1985): 98–121; Edna R. Russmann, "Relief Decoration in the Tomb of Mentuemhat (TT 34)," *JARCE* 31 (1994), 1–19; Russmann, "The Motif of Bound Papyrus Plants and the Decorative Program in Mentuemhat's First Court: Further Remarks on the Decoration of the Tomb of Mentuemhat, 1," *JARCE* 32 (1995): 117–26; Russmann, "Mentuemhat's Kushite Wife," 21–39; Louise Gestermann, Carolina Teotino, and Mareike Wagner, *Die Grabanlage des Monthemhet (TT 34) I.*

Der Weg zur Sargkammer (R 44.1 bis R 53), mit einem Beitrag von Farouk Gomaà† und Zeichnungen von Natalie Schmidt, SSR 31 (Wiesbaden: Harrassowitz, 2020).

12 *Ns-Ḫnsw: Rˁnke, PN*, 178 [20].

13 *Ns-Ptḥ: Rˁnke, PN*, 176 [5]; cf. Atef Awadallah and Ahmed El-Sawy, "Un sarcophage de Nsi-Ptah dans la tombe de Montouemhat," *BIFAO* 90 (1990): 29–39; de Meulenaere, "Nesptah"; Sherif El-Sabban, "Nesptah: The Heir to Power," *DE* 62 (2005): 33–41.

14 On Nesptah A: cf. Frédéric Payraudeau, "Nesptah, père de Montouemhat, à Karnak-Nord," in *A True Scribe of Abydos: Essays on First Millennium Egypt in Honour of Anthony Leahy*, ed. Claus Jurman, Bettina Bader, and D. Aston, OLA 265 (Leuven: Peeters, 2017), 319–26.

15 *Wḏ3-rn.s*: Ranke, *PN*, 88 [23].

16 She was a daughter of the prince (*s3 nsw*) Piankhy-Har; see Russmann, "Mentuemhat's Kushite Wife," 24; Angelika Lohwasser, *Die königlichen Frauen im antiken Reich von Kusch. 25. Dynastie bis zur Zeit des Nastasen*, Meroitica 19 (Wiesbaden: Harrassowitz, 2001), 42–45, 190–91; cf. Leclant, *Montouemhat*, 156–65, 264–65; Philippe Collombert, "Hout-sekhem et le septième nome de Haute-Égypte: la divine Oudjarenes," *RdE* 46 (1995): 55–79, esp. 76; Jansen-Winkeln, *IdS* 3, 483; Angelika Lohwasser, "'Nubianess' and the God's Wives of the 25th Dynasty: Office Holders, the Institution, Reception and Reaction," in *Prayer and Power*, 121–36, esp. 130.

17 *Šp-n-Mwt*: Ranke, *PN*, 325 [22].

18 This study reflects the subject within the framework of the published material. As examination and publication of the tomb is still an ongoing project—cf. Gestermann and Gomaà, "The Tomb of Montuemhat"; Gestermann and Gomaà, "Remarks on the Decoration and Conception"; Gestermann, Teotino, and Wagner, *Die Grabanlage des Monthemhet (TT 34) I*—any conclusion based on the data should be considered preliminary. For a drawing of the scene, see Gamer-Wallert, *Wandreliefs*, 123, fig. 15; for further information, see Farouk Gomaà, "Die Darstellungen an der Südwand des Zweiten Hofes," in Gestermann, Teotino, and Wagner, *Die Grabanlage des Monthemhet (TT 34) I*, 20–22. I especially thank Louise Gestermann for providing the photo of the scene in fig. 17.1 and permission to use it here.

19 See the photographic documentation in Gamer-Wallert, *Wandreliefs*, 156 [17].

20 *Ḏd-Ḫnsw-iw.f-ˁnḫ*: Ranke, *PN*, 412 [4]; other attestations: CG 42239 (B-CK/526), Jansen-Winkeln, *IdS* 3, 456–57 [201]; Blöbaum, "Monthemhet," ch. III.2.1.2.4.

21 *P3-šri-n-Mw.t*: Ranke, *PN*, 118 [19]; also attested, among others, by CG 42239 (B-CK/526), Jansen-Winkeln, *IdS* 3, 456–57 [201]; Blöbaum, "Monthemhet," ch. III.2.1.2.4; P.Brooklyn 47.218.3, col. M, 18: Richard A. Parker, *A Saite Oracle Papyrus from Thebes*, BEStud 4 (Providence: Brown University Press, 1962), 27 [47a], pl. 14.

22 Gamer-Wallert, *Wandreliefs*, 50.

23 Parker, *A Saite Oracle Papyrus*, 28–29; the signature is difficult to read and shows some peculiarities. Hence, Parker's interpretation was not left undisputed; see Hermann de Meulenaere, "Le papyrus de Brooklyn, trente ans après," in *Essays on Ancient Egypt in Honour of Herman Te Velde*, ed. Jan van Dijk, EM 1 (Groningen: STYX, 1997), 243–49. Nevertheless, Parker's interpretation gained broader acceptance; see Russmann, "Mentuemhat's Kushite Wife," 22n9; Blöbaum, "Monthemhet," ch. III.3.3.2.

24 Cf. Awadallah and El-Sawy, "Un sarcophage de Nsi-Ptah"; de Meulenaere, "Nesptah"; El-Sabban, "Nesptah."

25 Russmann, "Mentuemhat's Kushite Wife," 24.

26 Russmann, "Mentuemhat's Kushite Wife," 24: "She was certainly Mentuemhat's last wife, and there is reason to think that she was buried in his tomb. She is named in the interior of the tomb, and represented in both the First and Second Courts; she appears to be the only wife whose image is still in situ."

27 Although Ingrid Gamer-Wallert identified Nesptah B(2) as son of Shepenmut as well, she adhered to the traditional order of the wives, cf. Gamer-Wallert, *Wandreliefs*, 110.

28 Russmann, "Mentuemhat's Kushite Wife," 21.

29 Parker, *A Saite Oracle Papyrus*, 28–29, pl. 15; see above, note 23.
30 *Ḏd-Ḥrw*: Ranke, *PN*, 411 [12]; P.Brooklyn 47.218.3, col. G, 6: witness no. 22, Parker, *A Saite Oracle Papyrus*, 28 [22].
31 Gamer-Wallert, *Wandreliefs*, 50.
32 *Ḏ(i)-3st-ḥ3b-sd*: Ranke, *PN*, 396 [9]; Leclant, *Montuemhat*, 265.
33 Gamer-Wallert, *Wandreliefs*, 50, 121, fig. 13.
34 Gamer-Wallert, *Wandreliefs*, 50, 121, fig. 13.
35 P.Brooklyn 47.218.3, col. M, 17: witness no. 47; Parker, *A Saite Oracle Papyrus*, 27 [47].
36 Russmann, "Mentuemhat's Kushite Wife," 21.
37 For an analysis of these representations, see Russmann, "Mentuemhat's Kushite Wife," 24–39.
38 Russmann, "Mentuemhat's Kushite Wife," 34, fig. 10.
39 Seattle Art Museum 53.80: Russmann, "Mentuemhat's Kushite Wife," 22–24, fig. 1.
40 Jansen-Winkeln, *IdS* 3, 480; Kento Zenihiro, *The Complete Funerary Cones* (Toyko: Maruzen, 2009), 174; Bron Lipkin and Gary Dibley, *A Compendium of Egyptian Funerary Cones* (London: Bron Lipkin and Gary Dibley, 2009), 136.
41 Jansen-Winkeln, *IdS* 3, 480; Zenihiro, *Funerary Cones*, 174; Lipkin and Dibley, *Funerary Cones*, 136.
42 Jansen-Winkeln, *IdS* 3, 480; Zenihiro, *Funerary Cones*, 174; Lipkin and Dibley, *Funerary Cones*, 136.
43 Russmann, "Montemhat's Kushite Wife," 21.
44 Jansen-Winkeln, *IdS* 3, 479; Zenihiro, *Funerary Cones*, 192; Lipkin and Dibley, *Funerary Cones*, 153.
45 Jansen-Winkeln, *IdS* 3, 479; Zenihiro, *Funerary Cones*, 192; Lipkin and Dibley, *Funerary Cones*, 149.
46 Li, *Women, Gender and Identity*, 6–7.
47 For example, BM EA 68986 and BM EA 24715; cf. Morris L. Bierbrier, "Udjarenes Rediscovered," *JEA* 79 (1993): 274–75.
48 There is evidence for a family tomb in Deir al-Bahari where the father of Montuemhat, Nesptah (A), and his wife had been buried; see Payraudeau, "Nesptah, père de Montouemhat," 323, with reference to PM I², 645. Funerary cones of the wives of Montuemhat were found among other material in the refilling of the shafts found there: "The tombs were all violated in antiquity and once again during the 19th century. The shafts were backfilled evidently with little care for various small and broken objects of no use to the early excavators. The material coming from this backfill proved to be mixed but datable, containing numerous coffin and cartonnage fragments, grave goods in the form of pottery, faience, *shabti* figures and boxes, wooden sculptures, canopy jars, cones of Mentuemhat's wives and inscribed fragments of shrouds." See Zbigniew E. Szafrański, "Tombs of the Third Intermediate Period on the Upper Terrace of the Temple of Hatshepsut," *PAM* 24, no. 2 (2015): 183–201, esp. 185. Probably these are the cones of TT 34, which were spread widely in the Theban area; see Eberhard Dziobek, *Die Gräber des Vezirs User-Amun: Theben Nr. 61 und 131*, AV 84 (Mainz am Rhein: von Zabern, 1994), 42.
49 PM I², 56; G. Vittmann. "A Question of Names, Titles, and Iconography: Kushites in Priestly, Administrative and Other Positions from Dynasties 25 to 26," *MittSAG* 18 (2007): 139–61; Jansen-Winkeln, *IdS* 3, 483 [238].
50 Li, *Women, Gender and Identity*, 24.
51 Russmann, "Mentuemhat's Kushite Wife," 26n39, fig. 3.
52 *Wb* III, 76.16–77.19 (*ḥm*); *Wb* II, 98.12–100.11 (*mr(i)*); Dilwyn Jones, *An Index of Ancient Egyptian Titles, Epithets and Phrases of the Old Kingdom*, BARIS 866 (Oxford: Archaeopress, 2000), 596 [2186].
53 *Wb* II, 232; 1, 512.9–13; William A. Ward, *Essays on Feminine Titles of the Middle Kingdom and Related Subjects* (Beirut: American University of Beirut Press, 1986), 8.
54 Li, *Women, Gender and Identity*, 28–31.

55 Li, *Women, Gender and Identity*, 30.

56 Danijela Stefanović and Helmut Satzinger, "I Am a *Nbt-pr*, and I Am Independent," in *The World of Middle Kingdom Egypt (2000–1550 BC): Contributions on Archaeology, Art, Religion, and Written Sources* 1, ed. Gianluca Miniaci and Wolfram Grajetzki, Middle Kingdom Studies 1 (London: Golden House Publications, 2015), 333–38, esp. 337.

57 *Wb* II, 447.4–5; Jones, *Index of Ancient Egyptian Titles*, 327–28 [1206].

58 The major bibliography can be supplemented by references to Michel Baud, *Famille royale et pouvoir sous l'Ancien Empire égyptien*, BdE 126 (Cairo: IFAO, 1999), 108–18; Miroslav Bárta, "The Title 'Property Custodian of the King' during the Old Kingdom Egypt," *ZÄS* 126 (1999): 79–89; Jones, *Index of Ancient Egyptian Titles*, 327–28 [1206]; Christopher H. Naunton, "Titles of Karakhamun and the Kushite Administration of Thebes," in *Tombs of the South Asasif Necropolis: Thebes, Karakhamun (TT 223), and Karabasken (TT 391) in the Twenty-fifth Dynasty*, ed. Elena Pischikova (Cairo: American University in Cairo Press, 2014), 103–107; for the use of the title in the Ptolemaic Period, see Gilles Gorre, "*Rḫ-nswt*: titre aulique ou titre sacerdotal 'spécifique'?," *ZÄS* 136 (2009): 8–18.

59 For a detailed study of this development, see Bárta, "Property Custodian of the King," 81–89. He showed that the title *rḫt-nsw* was first associated with high-ranking officials at the royal court and later, during the Fifth and Sixth Dynasties, with lower-ranking officials employed in the funerary temples of the kings (p. 89).

60 Henry George Fischer, *Egyptian Women of the Old Kingdom and of the Heracleopolitan Period* (New York: Metropolitan Museum of Art, 2000), 71–72.

61 Christopher H. Naunton, "Titles of Karakhamun," 103.

62 Naunton, "Titles of Karakhamun," 104.

63 *Mwt-ir-d(i)-s(t)*: Ranke, *PN*, 147 [10]; Jan Assmann, *Grabung im Asasif 1963–1970*, 6: *Das Grab der Mutirdis*, AV 13 (Mainz am Rhein: Philip von Zabern, 1977).

64 Jean Li, "Elite Theban Women of the Eighth–Sixth Centuries BCE in Egypt: Identity, Status and Mortuary Practice" (PhD diss., University of California, Berkeley, 2010), 124.

65 It might be worth investigating whether the privilege of the title, in general, is limited to a specific person or transferable to the family.

66 *Wb* IV, 449.10–450.14; Ward, *Feminine Titles*, 22.

67 Li, *Women, Gender and Identity*, 31.

68 *Wb* IV, 450.1; Jones, *Index of Ancient Egyptian Titles*, 990–91 [3664]; Ward, *Feminine Titles*, 18.

69 Fischer, *Egyptian Women*, 30.

70 *Wb* I, 278.13; 3, 401.11; Jones, *Index of Ancient Egyptian Titles*, 795–96 [2900].

71 Fischer, *Egyptian Women*, 31 with nn180–81.

72 For a summary of interpretations in the Egyptological literature, see Danijela Stefanović, "The *ḫkrt-nswt* on the Monuments of the *ꜣṯw n tt ḥqꜣ*," in *Proceedings of the Tenth International Congress of Egyptologists, University of the Aegean, Rhodes, 22–29 May 2008*, ed. P. Kousoulis and N. Lazardis, OLA 241 (Leuven: Peeters, 2015), 861–73, esp. 866–67.

73 Alexander Illin-Tomich, "Female Titles Specific to Southern Upper Egypt in the Late Middle Kingdom and the Second Intermediate Period," *BACE* 26 (2016–18): 19–36, esp. 24.

74 *Wb* III, 90.10; Jones, *Index of Ancient Egyptian Titles*, 541–42 [2012]; Robyn A. Gillam, "Priestesses of Hathor: Their Function, Decline and Disappearance," *JARCE* 32 (1995): 211–37. During the First Intermediate Period, sequences of women's titles combined the titles *rḫt-nsw*, *špst-nsw*, and *ḫkrt-nsw-(wꜥtt)* with the title *ḥmt-nṯr Ḥw.t-Ḥrw*; see Li, *Elite Theban Women*, 51.

75 Gillam, "Priestesses of Hathor," 231–33; Ellen F. Morris, "Paddle Dolls and Performance," *JARCE* 47 (2011): 71–103; Solange Ashby, "Dancing for Hathor: Nubian Women in Egyptian Cultic Life," *Dotawo: A Journal of Nubian Studies* 5 (2018), accessed 17 January 2020, https://digitalcommons.fairfield.edu/djns/vol5/iss1/2/.

76 The sequence is not exclusively attested in the documents of Wedjarenes, but for other high-ranking women in Late Period Thebes, see Russmann, "Mentuemhat's Kushite Wife," 26.

77 Russmann, "Mentuemhat's Kushite Wife," 26–29.

78 JE 36327; PM II^2, 27; Ricardo A. Caminos, "The Nitocris Adoption Stela," *JEA* 50 (1964): 71–101; for further references, see Anke Ilona Blöbaum, "The Nitocris Adoption Stela: Representation of Royal Dominion and Regional Elite Power," in *Prayer and Power: Proceedings of the Conference about the God's Wives of Amun in Egypt during the First Millennium* BC, ed. Meike Becker, Anke Ilona Blöbaum, and Angelika Lohwasser, ÄAT 84 (Münster: Ugarit-Verlag, 2016), 183–204.

79 An analysis of the second part of the Nitocris Adoption Stela, including this observation, has already been published; see Blöbaum, "Nitocris Adoption Stela."

80 Fragment of a writing palette/pen case (UC 24382); see William J. Murnane, *Texts from the Amarna Period in Egypt*, WAW 5 (Atlanta: SBL, 1995), 90 [45A–B]; there are similar inscriptions on two stone vases (BM EA 64901, MMA 20.2.11).

81 Whether a similar conclusion could be drawn regarding two other female members of the family of Montuemhat will be the subject of further research.

82 Parker, *A Saite Oracle Papyrus*, 28–29.

83 Blöbaum, *Monthemhet*, ch. 3.3.2.1.

84 Karl Jansen-Winkeln, "Die Entwicklung der genealogischen Informationen nach dem Neuen Reich," in *Genealogie—Realität und Fiktion von Identität*, ed. Martin Fitzenreiter, Steffen Kirchner, and Olaf Kriseleit, IBAES 5 (London: Golden House Publications, 2005), 137–46, esp. 138.

85 Padiamenope, for example, never mentioned his father; see Karl Jansen-Winkeln, "Bemerkungen zu den Frauenbiographien der Spätzeit," *AfO* 31, no. 2 (2004): 358–78, esp. 359, Anm. 11; Claude Traunecker and Isabelle Régen, "La tombe d'un intellectuel dans la Thèbes des divines adoratrices," in *Servir les dieux d'Égypte: Divines adoratrices, chanteuses et prêtres d'Amon à Thebes*, ed. Florence Gombert-Meurice and Frédéric Payraudeau (Paris: Somogy, 2018), 60–63, esp. 60.

18

Women's Participation as Contracting Parties as Recorded in Demotic Documents for Money from Ptolemaic Upper Egypt: A Case Study of Change?

Renate Fellinger

> Under the influence of Greek law the Egyptian woman loses gradually, but inexorable certainly, her prominent position. *Sic transit gloria Aegypti.*[1]

After Alexander the Great's conquest of Egypt in 332 BCE, the Ptolemies[2] ruled over and, with the assistance of a minority of Greeks,[3] governed a multicultural society composed of a majority of native Egyptians as well as Greeks who migrated on a larger scale than during the Late Period.[4] These were the two largest ethnic groups,[5] with the Ptolemies introducing new reforms and customs but also following Egyptian practices.[6] Egyptians and Greeks, with different sets of cultural beliefs, traditions, and practices, lived alongside each other[7] and intermarried in some locations.[8] With respect to the legal sphere, both the Egyptian and Greek legal systems were used alongside each other,[9] despite their contrasting approaches to women's rights. For example, a woman using Greek documents had to be represented by a male guardian, while women recorded in Egyptian contracts could represent themselves.[10] However, some changes were made in the legal sphere with respect to legal instruments (such as *Doppelurkunden* being composed in demotic alongside Greek)[11] and to the institutional landscape (for example, the reorganization of the judiciary of ancient Egypt)[12] in addition to changes of an administrative nature—for example, the introduction of a requirement for demotic contracts to be registered with the Greek authorities.[13] It has been suggested in the scholarly literature that these political, social, and legal developments during the Ptolemaic Period were the reason for a change in the role of women in the

Egyptian legal landscape. Such observations have mostly been based on qualitative evidence,[14] except for those of Alexandra O'Brien,[15] who has provided some quantitative analysis.

This contribution aims to provide a novel quantitative perspective on the changes in the role of women during the Ptolemaic Period as recorded in Egyptian legal documents in the form of a case study of women's participation as contracting parties in documents for money. It also demonstrates how such a quantitative analysis may provide a different perspective on the well-established but mostly qualitative scholarly discourse on the subject.

The following research questions are investigated:

1. Did women's participation as contracting parties in documents for money from Upper Egypt change over time during the Ptolemaic Period?
2. Did developments arising in this cross-cultural environment influence women's behavior?

Literature Overview

The legal role of women,[16] as recorded in Egyptian legal records, deteriorated toward the end of the Ptolemaic Period or during the Roman Period at the latest.[17] The reasons for this change in status have mostly been attributed to the cross-cultural environment: the influence of Greek law and Greek practices, the changing administrative and legal landscapes, and the social status of Greeks in Egypt.

Greek and Egyptian laws were used alongside each other in the Ptolemaic Period, but Greek law assigned different rights to women in comparison to Egyptian legal practices, which may have had a detrimental effect on the position of Egyptian women over time.[18] For example, Pestman[19] cites P.Mich. 5 253, from 30 CE, in which a woman sold her property, but appeared with a legal guardian, although the contract was composed in demotic. The decline in the use of demotic legal documents and the increased use of Greek documents, culminating in the predominant use of Greek for any administrative and legal documentation for most of the Roman Period, may have, ultimately, led to a decline in the role of women.[20] For example, a quantitative analysis of Theban documents pertaining to real estate across the centuries during the Ptolemaic Period shows that women were mentioned in only half as many documents as men, who were present in all the documents, in the second century BCE. In contrast, women and men appeared as parties in more equal numbers of documents dating to the fourth and third centuries BCE.[21] This decreasing participation by women as parties in the later centuries coincided with a decline in the use of Egyptian documents.[22] Egyptian women also may have followed some Greek behaviors because they wanted to adapt to Greek culture for social advancement—for example, by appointing legal guardians, a Greek tradition, even though they were independent according to Egyptian legal traditions.[23] The changes in the administrative and legal landscapes from an Egyptian-oriented to a Greek, or Hellenized, focus may have also affected women's rights and visibility in the material record. As the administrative landscape became more Hellenized, women's independence may have shifted to a need for the male head of the household to be responsible for them, limiting women's capacity to act in their own right.[24] Previous quantitative analysis has shown this by considering the number of documents in which women and men appeared as contracting parties and taxpayers from before and after year 22 of the reign of Ptolemy II,[25] during which administrative reforms were introduced, presumably to align the existing administration with the Hellenistic framework.[26] For example, the number of female taxpayers, already low before the reform, decreased even further compared to the men after the initiative by Ptolemy II.[27] The number of documents in which women participated as contracting parties, both in general and in documents pertaining to real estate only, also registered a decrease after this particular reform.[28]

Data Set and Methodology

Undertaking a detailed and extensive quantitative study of the change of the legal role of women in the cross-cultural environment of Ptolemaic Egypt would require an appropriate theoretical framework and the examination of all available demotic documentary texts, but this is beyond the scope of this paper. Instead, a case study was conducted, focusing on changes in women's participation as contracting parties in one particular contract type, followed by a discussion of three possible reasons for change, which may have been connected to the cross-cultural setting.

It is crucial to use a data set sufficient in size to perform a statistical analysis. To be considered for analysis, the documents need to be in good condition so that the contract type can be identified based on specific legal clauses, the date must be legible, and the gender of the contracting parties must be clear. The data set is limited to Upper Egypt and transactions of real estate, rather than studying data from all of Egypt, because the Greek presence and thus its potential influence varied across areas, which would have resulted in regional differences and could have created biases for analyses. The focus is on real-estate transactions rather than intangible property, such as days in the temple or funerary obligations, because the latter may not have been cross-culturally accessible, which might also have biased the statistical outcome. Real estate, on the other hand, constitutes a type of property which was familiar to Greek law and society and may have been susceptible to change because Greek law had different attitudes to women owning real estate compared to Egyptian law. For example, under Athenian law, women generally could not own real estate.[29]

Documents for money[30] have been preserved in large numbers[31] across Egypt, dating from the Late to the Roman Period.[32] Such contracts were made between at least two parties: a transferor (the person who transferred interest in the property) and a transferee[33] (the person who received interest in the property). The contracts mostly transferred freehold interest and served a variety of functions.[34] The online reference database "Demotic and Abnormal Hieratic Texts,"[35] run by Trismegistos,[36] was used to search for published documents matching these criteria. In total, one hundred[37] documents, originating from various sites across Upper Egypt but with the majority stemming from the Theban area, match the above criteria and are used as the data set for this case study.

The first stage was to quantify the proportion of women appearing in these documents. All appearances of women and men as parties were counted and compared to the total number of individuals.[38] As it is important to understand the extent of the overall participation, all appearances are preferred over those of individual women and men. However, it is also important to take into account the possibility that individuals who appeared multiple times might bias the results if their behavior was not the norm. Hypothesis testing[39] was then performed on the descriptive statistics. A statistical hypothesis is an assumption about a population, an assumption that may or may not be true. Hypothesis testing provides a formal procedure to accept or reject assumptions. Therefore, hypothesis testing of the quantitative measurements was used to check whether certain trends, especially differences in behavior, were statistically significant; that is, that a certain trend is not the result of chance. In this paper, the chi-square test[40] and the Fisher's exact test[41] (in the case of at least one value in the contingency table being lower than 5) were used to assess whether two trends were dissimilar. Calculations were performed in R,[42] a programming language designed for statistical testing. There are two types of statistical hypotheses. The null hypothesis is a default assumption that there is no relationship between two measured phenomena, meaning that the sample observation occurred by chance. The alternative hypothesis is the supposition that the sample observations are indeed influenced by some nonrandom cause(s).

In order to reject the default null hypothesis and accept the alternative hypothesis, the statistical test needed to yield results above the predefined confidence level of 0.95 (or 95 percent), which is an accepted, appropriate value for most archaeological analyses.[43]

The principal limitation of this examination is the bias of preservation, which could result in an uneven distribution of documents across locations and time, and could skew regional or temporal patterns of behavior. For example, Depauw[44] has noted that the majority of demotic documents came from the first half of the Ptolemaic Period, and Hobson[45] has raised the issue of whether quantitative results can be accurate when there are gaps in the data across time. The observed and tested trends based on a few documents are not as representative as those recorded in a large number of contracts. Furthermore, the bias of preservation can lead to an arbitrary selection of special cases of women's behavior rather than representing the norm. Finally, it is important to be aware that the documents probably recorded those individuals who were part of a wealthier class of society, who owned real estate and had the means to afford the drafting of a document. This data set includes all published documents which adhere to the chosen parameters of this study and is therefore suitable for statistical analysis.

Trends of Participation

Whether women's participation as contracting parties changed over time was examined by dividing the data set into specific time intervals and observing the participation trends for each interval. When dividing a data set according to time intervals to examine a change in behavior, it is important to minimize the possibility of introducing biases which could affect the observed trends. For a change in behavior influenced by a cross-cultural environment to become a general trend across society is a long, dynamic, and fluctuating process. The objective of this paper is to investigate this change in behavior over the Ptolemaic Period rather than to investigate the influence of a specific event, such as the rule of a certain king or the introduction of a new law or a reform. Dividing the data according to specific events carries the risk of introducing biases because assumptions are made that a change in behavior may be expected. Hence, instead of choosing a specific event to classify the time interval, the data set was divided into three discrete equal time intervals of one hundred years. The one-hundred-year time intervals are sufficiently long to minimize local variations in the behavior, triggered by an event, and to capture the overall behavioral change. If only two intervals are considered—for example, by dividing the Ptolemaic Period in half—it might not provide enough contrasting data to test whether women's behavior as parties changed throughout the Ptolemaic Period, especially toward the end of the period, which has been suggested as the time when women's legal role started to change, as previously noted.

The chi-square test is used to evaluate whether the participation proportions varied between the intervals considered in this case study. This statistical analysis was performed by splitting the Ptolemaic Period into three equal time intervals of one hundred[46] years. In total, one hundred documents recorded 166 male and 78 female contracting parties. During the first one hundred years of the Ptolemaic Period, 42 men and 23 women were recorded as parties in thirty-one documents, resulting in participation proportions of approximately 65 percent and approximately 35 percent, respectively (fig. 18.1). Men's and women's participation proportions during the second interval appeared similar to the previous interval, with approximately 66 percent and approximately 34 percent, respectively, but their absolute numbers almost doubled to 82 men and 43 women in forty-nine documents. During the third interval, 42 men and 12 women participated in twenty documents, resulting in approximately 78 percent and approximately 22 percent of respective participation.

A chi-square test to check whether women's participation in the documents differed across these three intervals yielded a *p*-value of 5.52E-11. As this *p*-value is lower than the predefined threshold of significance of 0.05, it indicates a statistically significant result, and the null hypothesis is rejected. Therefore, women's participation is statistically different across the intervals.

The chi-square test proves that when the data set is divided according to three discrete time intervals of equal length, there is a difference between the proportions across intervals. Statistical tests, such as the chi-square, are not designed to identify in which interval a difference in behavior is observed, as in the interval where women and men participated differently compared to the other intervals. In order to understand the overall trends in general behavior during each time interval, the median numbers of women and men

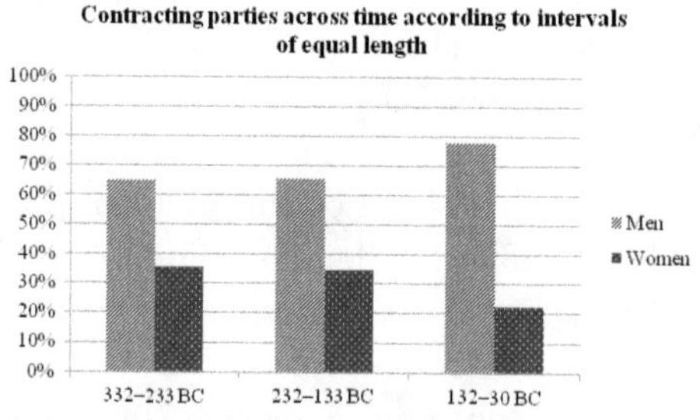

Fig. 18.1. The participation proportions of men and women as contracting parties across time according to time intervals of equal length as recorded in 100 documents for money from Upper Egypt

participating in each document during a time interval were calculated. The median value represents how many women or men are observed as parties in at least half of the documents found in an interval. Therefore, the median eliminates any influence from outliers and represents the overall behavior.[47] The median number of women and men observed in the first and second time intervals is one.[48] This means that at least half of the documents in the first and second intervals, respectively, featured at least one woman or man as parties. In the third interval, the median number of men participating in the documents increased to two while the median number of women decreased to zero. The increase in the median number of men from one to two in the third time interval shows that at least half of the twenty documents recorded at least two men, compared to at least one man in half the documents in the preceding intervals. In contrast, the decrease from one to zero in women's participation shows that at least half of the twenty documents for money did not feature any women as parties, while the preceding intervals had at least one woman in half the documents. Figure 18.2 illustrates that the documents without any female contracting parties increased from the first and second intervals to the third interval. For example, during the first interval, 55 percent of documents featured one woman and 35 percent recorded zero women, but in the third interval, these numbers were reversed: 35 percent recorded one woman and 55 percent had zero women. Men's participation also shifted from the first two intervals, where some contracts did not record any male parties, to 100 percent of documents featuring men during the third interval. In contrast, the same interval features more documents without women than with, because fewer than half of the documents recorded female parties.

The differences in the medians and in the proportion of the women participating in the documents between the intervals show that the overall behavior of women's and men's participation changed in the third interval in comparison to the other intervals. As the median represents overall behavior, the observed change in behavior can be seen as a general trend, unaffected by a few outliers. However,

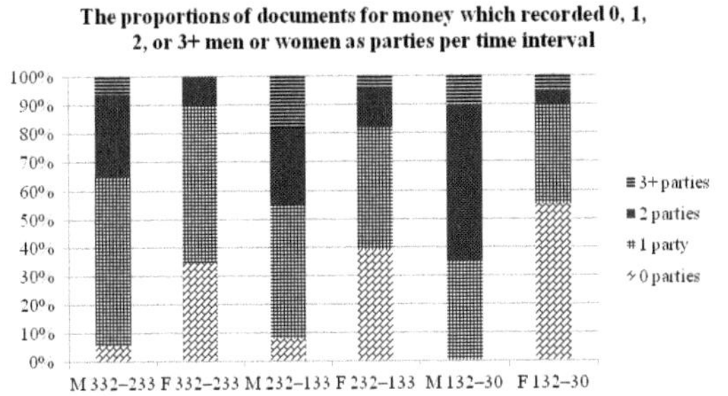

Fig. 18.2. The proportions of documents recording 0, 1, 2, or 3+ men or women as contracting parties for each time interval

the change in the median value does not identify any associated causes for this difference. This will be discussed further in the following section.

It is important to recognize that the bias of preservation could skew the number of documents preserved in certain time intervals. In order to minimize the impact of this bias, a control table was constructed, where the documents were divided into three equal sections of thirty-three or thirty-four[49] documents each, to check whether the observed trends and results from the statistical tests are consistent regardless of how the data are arranged. Although the time intervals fluctuated with this process, it guaranteed that the trends of participation would not be hampered by an uneven distribution of documents due to the bias of preservation. These two methods of dividing the data aimed to reduce the risk of introducing additional biases.

The alternate classification was used to test whether the trends of participation encountered in intervals of equal numbers of documents supported the degrees of participation observed in the examination of time intervals of equal length. Women's behavior seemed comparable with the trends observed above because women's participation, in relation to men's, seemed to remain constant between the first two intervals, but decreased in the third interval while the proportion of men's participation increased (fig. 18.3).

The difference in behavior across intervals is confirmed by another chi-square test yielding a statistically significant result with a low *p*-value of 3.10E-06. The median here followed the pattern seen above. The median number of women and men observed in the first and second intervals was one. But in the third interval, the median number of men participating in the documents increased to two while the median number of women decreased to zero. The difference in median between the intervals shows that women and men participated differently in the third interval in comparison to the other intervals. As both ways of dividing the data show similar trends regarding women's participation, this highlights that a general change in the participation trend occurred toward the end of the Ptolemaic Period.

In order to check whether recurring individuals biased the observed behavior, as presented in figure 18.1 and backed up by figure 18.2, chi-square tests were used to check whether all appearances differed from unique occurrences for each interval. They yielded high *p*-values; therefore, recurring individuals were found not to have biased the observed behavior.

Many factors arising from the cross-cultural environment of Ptolemaic Egypt could have influenced changes in women's participatory behavior, as recorded in the documents for money over time. Due to the scope of this paper, three hypotheses are discussed in more detail.

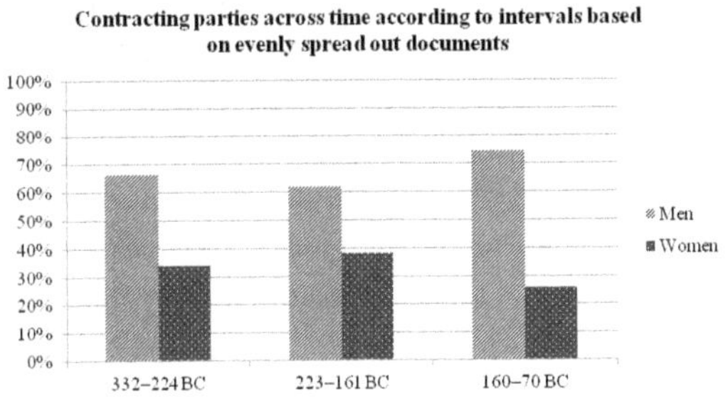

Fig. 18.3. The participation proportions of men and women as contracting parties across time according to time intervals based on evenly spread-out documents per time period as recorded in 100 documents for money from Upper Egypt

The Decrease in Demotic Legal Instruments

O'Brien[50] has suggested that a decline in women's participation, and in the role of women in general, may have coincided with a decrease in the use of demotic documents and the subsequent focus on Greek law. The division of the data by time intervals of equal length (fig. 18.1) resulted in the number of documents increasing from the first to the second interval, reaching a peak during the second interval (forty-nine documents for money in the second interval, compared to thirty-one for the first), and then decreasing to twenty documents in the third interval. As the third interval featured the least number of documents, it seemed to concur with the current literature,[51] which has suggested that the number of demotic documents generally declined toward the end of the Ptolemaic Period, as Greek was increasingly used as the main administrative language, until demotic ceased to be used for legal documents during the Roman Period. As observed in the previous section, there is a statistically significant difference in women's behavior across the time intervals. The median values suggest that during the third time interval, which represents the last 102 years of Ptolemaic rule, women's behavior overall may have been different compared to the preceding intervals.

However, women were still recorded as contracting parties in their own name or together with a male relative or husband in Greek evidence during the Roman Period, such as that from the Fayyum. For example, 20–25 percent of documents registered at the *grapheion* in Tebtunis between 42 and 46 CE recorded women, mostly in transactions pertaining to real estate—predominantly in relation to family inheritance—as well as to maintenance contracts.[52] With respect to sales of houses, women and men seem to have participated equally in Greek sales from Soknopaiu Nesos, with one-third of house registrations undertaken by a female party.[53] The number of one-third of female ownership is further confirmed by the gender of the owners of the neighboring properties, as recorded in Greek real-estate sales.[54]

These participation patterns suggest that women were present in the legal landscape, even if they had to operate within the Greek system, adhering to Greek law, during the Roman Period. The decline in the use of demotic legal documents and the increased use of Greek law may not be the sole reasons for the change in women's behavior observed in the demotic material. Further study is needed, including examination of the Greek material, to better understand women's participation as contracting parties in both the Egyptian and Greek legal systems during the Ptolemaic Period, but is beyond the scope of this paper.

The Function of Documents for Money as Inheritance-related Transfers

As previously mentioned, documents for money could serve various functions. One of these was to transfer inheritance between contracting parties.[55] Out of one hundred documents, eight[56] served such a purpose with certainty. They featured approximately equal numbers of women and men—nine and seven, respectively—resulting in a higher proportion of women participating—approximately 56 percent of women compared to approximately 44 percent of men. This stands in stark contrast to the remaining ninety-two documents for money which recorded, on average, one-third of women and two-thirds of men. But the inheritance-related transfers are only preserved from the first one hundred years of the Ptolemaic Period. This section tests whether the higher proportion of women observed in the inheritance-related transfers influenced the behavioral change in the later interval due to the lack of inheritance-related transfers during that time period.

To test this, the contracting parties of these eight documents are excluded from the count of contracting parties across time. Including these transfers, the first interval featured twenty-three women and forty-two men with participation proportions of approximately 35 percent and approximately 65 percent, respectively. Without the transfers, the absolute numbers of women and men dropped to fourteen and thirty-five, respectively, as recorded in twenty-three documents (fig. 18.4). This results in lower proportions for women, with approximately 29 percent, and a higher participation of men, with approximately 71 percent, compared to their participation in the sample set including the eight transfers.

To see whether women's behavior differed between the eight inheritance-related transfers, which were then removed, and the amended first interval excluding these documents, a chi-square test was performed, yielding a high p-value of 0.09. Therefore, the null hypothesis was not rejected, meaning that

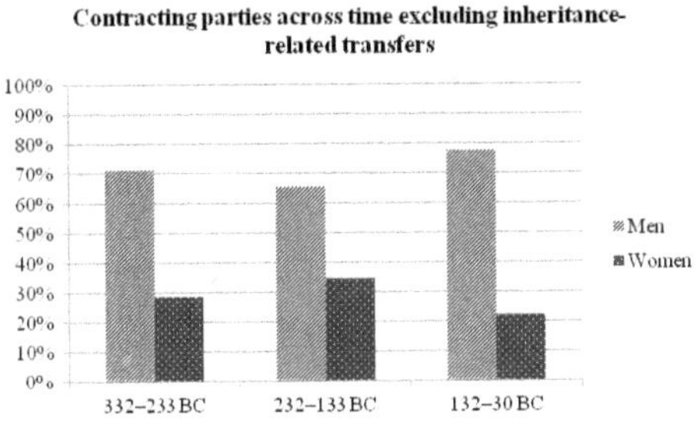

Fig. 18.4. The participation proportions of men and women as contracting parties across time according to time intervals of equal length as recorded in 92 documents for money from Upper Egypt, excluding inheritance-related transfers

women's behavior was not statistically different. This suggests that women's behavior may not have changed in the first interval when the eight transfers are not considered.

The eight inheritance-related transfers featured an almost equal participation of nine women and seven men. The median of women's and men's participation in absolute numbers in the amended first interval remained the same as in the original first interval, with one for women and one for men, although roughly 26 percent of the documents were removed in this interval. Women's participation between the inheritance-related transfers and other contracts in the first time period remained unchanged.

Having removed the eight inheritance-related documents from the first interval, it was tested whether the intervals in figure 18.4 exhibited a statistical difference. A chi-square test to check whether the participation proportions of women differed across the three intervals yielded a significant *p*-value of 1.81E-14. The rejection of the null hypothesis may suggest that the participation proportions are not the same. A statistical difference in women's proportions across time intervals still exists, even with the removal of the eight transfers. The median in the first interval remained unaffected by the exclusion of the inheritance-related transfers, and as the numbers for the second and third intervals are unchanged, their median remained the same. The exclusion of inheritance-related transfers did not change the observed difference in the median values toward the end of the Ptolemaic Period, as discussed in the previous section.

The above tests may show that the change in women's behavior across time may not be caused by moving away from this specific contract function where women participated in higher proportion. As the inheritance-related transfers all dated to the early Ptolemaic Period, their absence during later times was probably not biased by the issue of survival by chance. Instead, it may have marked a change in the nature of the legal documentation used to express such a purpose. Contract types could fall in and out of use for specific purposes—

for example, donations became increasingly important as a means to bequeath property during the New Kingdom, but seem to have been replaced by "fictitious sales" (which is one of the various functions that documents for money could serve[57]) from the Late Period onward.[58] Perhaps a move from clearly marked inheritance-related transfers to non-clearly distinguished documents for money—which could have served as such "fictitious sales" to pass on inheritance, as well as other documents, which could have been used to pass on inheritance—took place during the Ptolemaic Period.

The Multicultural Setting in Gebelein

Based on the difference in median value, the third interval was observed to indicate a change in the participation behavior of women. This section examines the influence of Hellenization during this time period on the difference in the observed participation behavior.

In Gebelein—comprised of Pathyris and Crocodilopolis[59]—the Hellenization efforts undertaken by the Ptolemies were limited to a specific time period and were well documented due to a plethora of demotic and Greek documentation preserved from this area dating to the period when the towns were important.[60] Hence, Gebelein is chosen as a reference site to study the influence of the multicultural setting on the participation behavior.

Gebelein gained importance during the second half of the Ptolemaic Period, when garrisons were built at Crocodilopolis and Pathyris as security measures after a number of events destabilized the area, such as the twenty-year rule of indigenous kings in the south from 206 to 186 BCE.[61] Greek and Egyptian soldiers moved to the area and lived alongside the local populations of these towns, creating a multicultural society.[62] Greek soldiers intermarried with women from Egyptian families, resulting in bilingual families and bilingual archives of the families' affairs. For example, Senmonthis, also known as Apollonia, from an Egyptian family, married a Greek soldier named Dryton.[63] From that point onward, Gebelein experienced the start, peak, and decline of Hellenization until the end of its habitation (88 BCE for Pathyris, at which point the documentation was discontinued).[64] Official Hellenization efforts may, for example, be represented by the introduction of Greek institutions, which were based on Egyptian ones, to facilitate their use by the population, replace Egyptian ones, or be used alongside Egyptian ones, such as Greek banks, granaries, and notarial offices.[65] At the peak of the Hellenization process encountered at Pathyris (136–110 BCE), two-thirds of the preserved documentation was composed in Greek.[66] Thereafter, Hellenization seems to have declined and the local population returned to Egyptian practices.[67]

The individuals in this community lived and operated in a multicultural society and may have experienced greater levels of exposure to Greek culture. This exposure could have been through, but not limited to, the Greek-Egyptian social profile and the establishment of Greek institutions in the towns. The period when Gebelein gained importance falls within the second half of the second interval and the third interval. Only five[68] out of forty-nine documents originated from Gebelein for the second interval (232–133 BCE). But 70 percent[69] of the twenty documents dating to the final interval (132–30 BCE) came from this area. If the difference in behavior observed in the third interval is due to the influence of the multicultural setting, then the observed participation behavior must be reflected, if not more pronounced, in the documents from Gebelein. Therefore, it was investigated whether the participation behavior, as recorded in documents from the multicultural setting in Gebelein, is different from other sites.

First, it was tested whether women's participation proportions in the fourteen documents from Gebelein falling within the third interval are different from the documents originating from other sites, predominantly Thebes and Hermonthis. The fourteen documents featured thirty men and eight women, resulting in participation proportions of approximately 79 percent of men and approximately 21 percent of women (fig. 18.5). The proportions, as found in the six documents which originated from other locations in Upper Egypt, are 75 percent of men and 25 percent of women, based on twelve men and four women. The Fisher's exact test was used to check whether the participation proportions of women in Gebelein were different in comparison to the other sites during the third interval. It yielded a high p-value of 0.73, therefore the null hypothesis was not rejected; the proportions of women's and men's participation, as recorded in documents from Gebelein compared to those from other locations, may not have been different. Therefore, at Gebelein, the multicultural society may not have influenced women's behavior with respect to their participation in these documents for money.

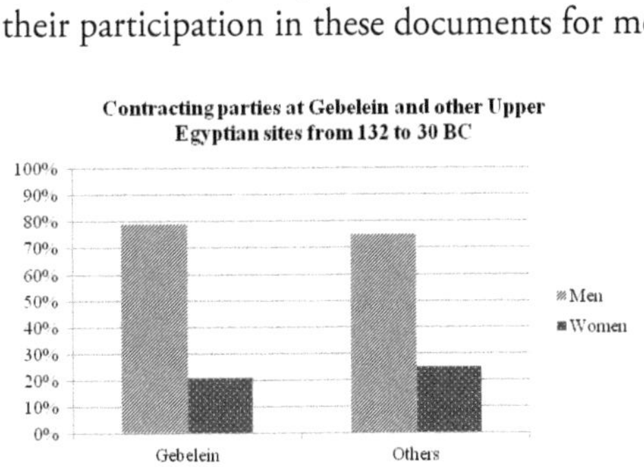

Fig. 18.5. A comparison of the participation proportions of men and women as contracting parties as recorded in documents for money from Gebelein and other Upper Egyptian sites during the third time interval (132–30 BCE)

Second, as the time frame of the data from Gebelein is longer than the third interval, the dates of the oldest and youngest documents, respectively, were considered as the endpoints for another test to ensure that no other biases had been introduced. This timeline starts in 176 BCE and ends in 88 BCE, and covers the prominence of the site including the start, peak, and decline of its Hellenization. Women's behavior, as recorded therein, was compared to that found in documents from other sites which fall within the same time frame to see whether their proportions of participation differed across sites. The nineteen documents from Gebelein feature forty-one men and nine women, resulting in participation proportions of 82 percent and 18 percent, respectively (fig. 18.6). But at other Upper Egyptian locations during this time span, forty-six men and twenty-two women were recorded in twenty-two documents, so with proportions of approximately 68 percent and approximately 32 percent, respectively. The chi-square test yielded a high *p*-value of 0.12; the null hypothesis was not rejected. Although the absolute numbers and participation proportions seem different between Gebelein and other Upper Egyptian sites, the chi-square test, which is designed to account for the overall change with respect to the total number of participants, does not show a statistical difference in the observed change. Women's behavior in documents from Gebelein may not have been different from that in documents from other sites during the second half of the Ptolemaic Period. More data or a qualitative pursuit would shed more light on this behavior, but that is beyond the scope of this chapter.

When the entire lifespan of Gebelein during the second half of the Ptolemaic Period is considered, the test shows no significant statistical difference between the sites because the total number of women participating is relatively small in comparison to the number of men in these documents. Although the number of women in the documents found at other sites is more than double the number of women participating in documents from Gebelein, the women's proportional participation remains relatively small. The difference in the participation of

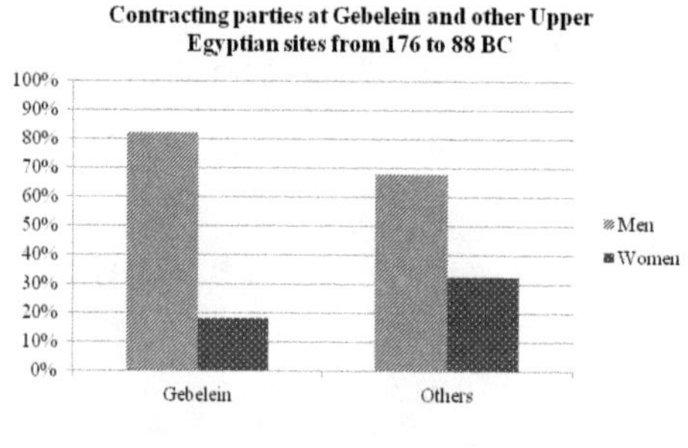

Fig. 18.6. A comparison of the participation proportions of men and women as contracting parties as recorded in documents for money from Gebelein and other Upper Egyptian sites from 176 to 88 BCE

women in the documents for money observed in the third interval may not be due to the influence of the multicultural nature of the society, for example, as found in Gebelein. Perhaps a decline in their participation may have been experienced at various sites in Upper Egypt—for example, as a general development during this time period, rather than being influenced by this specific multicultural setting. Some of the other Upper Egyptian sites also could have experienced a similar cycle of Hellenization, but because of the lack of evidence (perhaps due to the bias of preservation), this may not be well documented.

Conclusion

The results of this case study suggest that women's participation as contracting parties, as recorded in documents for money from Upper Egypt, changed toward the end of the Ptolemaic Period. Based on the statistical results, individual factors arising from the cross-cultural environment of Ptolemaic Egypt may not have been the sole reason for the observed changes in women's participation behavior. Perhaps it is not as straightforward to suggest that this cross-cultural environment is the specific reason that caused a change regarding women's behavior or changes to their role in the legal sphere and society overall.

A number of other reasons, related or unrelated to the cross-cultural environment of Ptolemaic Egypt, and the interplay between different factors could have influenced women's behavior, such as environmental or political circumstances—for example, evidence from Roman-period Greek documents shows that women's participation with their husbands in relation to debt increased during an economic crisis.[70] Although statistical tests contradict the expected change in behavior in certain contexts, even though the numbers seem to present a difference, statistical tests provide an objective view of the general behavior. Statistical tests can provide a useful frame of reference for further investigation with more data, if available, and for qualitative analysis. These can provide more insight into the multitude of factors potentially affecting the participation of women in the legal sphere, especially in cases with a dearth of data.

These results reveal the insights that quantitative analysis, and especially statistical testing, offer to further examination and testing of established hypotheses about changes in women's roles and the reasons for those changes. Interpretations of women's roles and limitations have often been influenced by scholars' frames of reference with respect to societal and cultural norms at particular points in time (as highlighted by Ayad[71]) as well as the assumptions underlying their interpretations (as showcased by Williamson[72]). Assumptions about women in ancient Egypt have long been colored by biases and subjective interpretations. Alongside qualitative analyses and discussions, quantitative methodologies, including statistical testing, offer a more objective approach to understanding and expanding our knowledge of women's roles in the legal sphere and in ancient society overall. These types of methods are useful for areas of research that may be prone to being affected by conscious or subconscious biases shaping interpretations of the evidence, such as investigations into the lives of women in ancient Egypt.

Future research will focus on a systematic and extensive study of changes in the roles of women and possible reasons for them—not exclusive to the cross-cultural environment—based on quantitative methodologies and qualitative analysis of areas where the data set is too small for statistical testing. The roles of women in the cross-cultural environment form a complex topic, and a comprehensive study will shed more light and contribute to a discussion otherwise mostly conducted with qualitative evidence.

Acknowledgments

This chapter has evolved from a chapter included in my doctoral thesis. I wish to express my gratitude to my supervisor, Professor John D. Ray, for his support and advice. I also wish to thank Dr. Krishna Kumar for his invaluable feedback on the statistical analysis. I also extend my utmost gratitude to Dr. Siân Thomas for kindly allowing me to include in the data set for my doctoral thesis the unpublished documents for money from Gebelein, which she edited and discussed in her doctoral thesis, "Ptolemaic Gebelein: An Exploration of Legal, Social and Topographical Themes Based on Unpublished Documents for Money and Cessions in the British Museum" (University of Cambridge, 2009). Furthermore, I wish to thank the organizers and attendees of the conference "Women in Ancient Egypt: Current Research and Historical Trends," held at the American University in Cairo from 31 October to 2 November 2019, for stimulating discussions on the state of research on women in ancient Egypt.

Notes

1 Pieter Willem Pestman, *Marriage and Matrimonial Property in Ancient Egypt: A Contribution to Establishing the Legal Position of the Woman*, Papyrologica Lugduno-Batava 9 (Leiden: Brill, 1961), 184.

2 For an overview of the history of the period, see, for example, Jean Bingen, *Hellenistic Egypt: Monarchy, Society, Economy, Culture*, ed. Roger S. Bagnall (Edinburgh: Edinburgh University Press, 2007); Alan B. Lloyd, "The Ptolemaic Period (332–30 BC)," in *The Oxford History of Ancient Egypt*, ed. Ian Shaw, 2nd ed. (Oxford and New York: Oxford University Press, 2003), 388–413; Joseph G. Manning, "The Ptolemaic Period (332–30 BC)," in *Law and Legal Practice in Egypt from Alexander to the Arab Conquest: A Selection of Papyrological Sources in Translation, with Introductions and Commentary*, ed. James G. Keenan, Joseph G. Manning, and Uri Yiftach-Firanko (Cambridge: Cambridge University Press, 2014), 5–6; Katelijn Vandorpe, "The Ptolemaic Period," in *A Companion to Ancient Egypt*, ed. Alan B. Lloyd (Chichester, West Sussex, and Malden, MA: Wiley-Blackwell, 2010), 159–79.

3 The term "Greek(s)" acts as a substitute here to describe individuals from various *poleis* rather than listing all their respective city-states.

4 Sandra L. Lippert, "Begegnungen und Kollisionen: Das Recht in Ägypten von der Spätzeit bis in die römische Zeit," *ZAR* 16 (2010): 158.

5 Vandorpe, "The Ptolemaic Period," 171.

6 Bingen, *Hellenistic Egypt*, 240–55; Manning, "The Ptolemaic Period (332–30 BC)"; Vandorpe, "The Ptolemaic Period," 176–78.

7 Bingen, *Hellenistic Egypt*, 104–13, 240–55.

8 Willy Clarysse, "Some Greeks in Egypt," in *Life in a Multi-cultural Society: Egypt from Cambyses to Constantine and Beyond*, ed. Janet H. Johnson, SAOC 51 (Chicago: Oriental Institute of the University of Chicago, 1992), 51–52; Vandorpe, "The Ptolemaic Period," 173.

9 Lippert, "Begegnungen und Kollisionen," 167; Joseph Mélèze-Modrzejewski, "Law and Justice in Ptolemaic Egypt," in *Legal Documents of the Hellenistic World*, ed. Markham J. Geller and Herwig Maehler (London: The Warburg Institute, in cooperation with the Institute of Jewish Studies, University College London, 1995), 6–7; Vandorpe, "The Ptolemaic Period," 172.

10 Sandra L. Lippert, *Einführung in die altägyptische Rechtsgeschichte*, Einführungen und Quellentexte zur Ägyptologie 5, 2nd ed. (Münster: LIT Verlag, 2012), 116.

11 Lippert, "Begegnungen und Kollisionen," 167.

12 Lippert, "Begegnungen und Kollisionen," 164–67.

13 Mark Depauw, *A Companion to Demotic Studies*, Papyrologica Bruxellensia 28 (Brussels: Fondation égyptologique Reine Élisabeth, 1997), 124; Lippert, *Einführung in die altägyptische Rechtsgeschichte*, 139; Joseph G. Manning, "Demotic Law," in *A History of Ancient Near Eastern Law*, ed. Raymond Westbrook, Handbook of Oriental Studies/Handbuch der Orientalistik, Section 1: The Near and Middle East, 72, 2 vols. (Leiden and Boston: Brill, 2003), 824; Manning, *Land and Power in Ptolemaic Egypt: The Structure of Land Tenure* (Cambridge: Cambridge University Press, 2003), 238.

14 Pestman, *Marriage and Matrimonial Property*, 184; Joyce A. Tyldesley, *Daughters of Isis: Women of Ancient Egypt* (Harmondsworth: Penguin Books, 1995), 44.

15 Alexandra A. O'Brien, "Private Tradition, Public State: Women in Demotic Business and Administrative Texts from Ptolemaic and Roman Thebes" (PhD diss., University of Chicago, 1999), 160–61; O'Brien, "Women in Ptolemaic and Roman Thebes," in *Acts of the Seventh International Conference of Demotic Studies, Copenhagen, 23–27 August 1999*, ed. Kim Ryholt, CNI Publications 27 (Copenhagen: Carsten Niebuhr Institute of Near Eastern Studies, University of Copenhagen, Museum of Tusculanum Press, 2002), 277.

16 For an overview, see, for example, Janet H. Johnson, "The Legal Status of Women in Ancient Egypt," in *Mistress of the House, Mistress of Heaven: Women in Ancient Egypt*, ed. Anne K. Capel and Glenn E. Markoe (New York: Hudson Hills Press in association with Cincinnati Art Museum, 1996), 175–86.

17 O'Brien, "Private Tradition, Public State," 139, 198, 202; Pestman, *Marriage and Matrimonial Property*, 184; Tyldesley, *Daughters of Isis*, 44.

18 Pestman, *Marriage and Matrimonial Property*, 184.

19 Pestman, *Marriage and Matrimonial Property*, 184n3.

20 O'Brien, "Private Tradition, Public State," 139, 198.

21 O'Brien, "Private Tradition, Public State," 161, table XV; O'Brien, "Women in Ptolemaic and Roman Thebes," 277, table III.

22 O'Brien, "Private Tradition, Public State," 139.

23 Tyldesley, *Daughters of Isis*, 44.

24 O'Brien, "Private Tradition, Public State," 163, 165, 202.

25 O'Brien, "Private Tradition, Public State," 160, table XIV; O'Brien, "Women in Ptolemaic and Roman Thebes," 277, table II.

26 O'Brien, "Private Tradition, Public State," 165, 202.

27 O'Brien, "Private Tradition, Public State," 142, table VII, 154–55, 162–65, 202; O'Brien, "Women in Ptolemaic and Roman Thebes," 276, table II.

28 O'Brien, "Private Tradition, Public State," 160, table XIV; O'Brien, "Women in Ptolemaic and Roman Thebes," 277, table II.

29 Raphael Sealey, *Women and Law in Classical Greece* (Chapel Hill and London: University of North Carolina Press, 1990), 37–38.

30 For an overview of the form of this contract type, its characteristics, and structural elements as well as contractual boilerplate, see, for example, Depauw, *A Companion to Demotic Studies*, 123–25, 141; Lippert, *Einführung in die altägyptische Rechtsgeschichte*, 138–39, 147–50; Sandra L. Lippert, Maren Schentuleit, and Karl-Theodor Zauzich, *Dokumente aus Dime* 3: *Urkunden. Mit Beiträgen von Fabian Reiter* (Wiesbaden: Harrassowitz, 2010), 5–10, 13–37; Manning, "Demotic Law," 823–25, 845–46; Karl-Theodor Zauzich, *Die ägyptische Schreibertradition in Aufbau, Sprache und Schrift der demotischen Kaufverträge aus ptolemäischer Zeit*, vol. 1: *Text*, ÄA 19 (Wiesbaden: Harrassowitz, 1968), 113–49; Zauzich, "Akten II," *LÄ* 1, ed. W. Helck and E. Otto (Wiesbaden: Harrassowitz, 1975), 126–29.

31 Karl-Theodor Zauzich, "Kaufurkunden, demotische," *LÄ* 3, ed. W. Helck and W. Westendorf (Wiesbaden: Harrassowitz, 1980), 370.

32 Depauw, *A Companion to Demotic Studies*, 142.

33 The labeling of the contracting parties as participating in a transaction may be questioned with respect to the transferees. Documents for money seemed to be unilateral agreements because the transferors addressed the transferees in the contract. However, the transferees had the option to agree to or reject the terms laid out in the documents for money, thereby rendering the seemingly unilateral contract bilateral (Johnson, "The Legal Status of Women in Ancient Egypt," 177). Most likely, both parties were present at the notary; the label "participation" is justified.

34 For detailed overviews, see Depauw, *A Companion to Demotic Studies*, 140–42; Lippert, *Einführung in die altägyptische Rechtsgeschichte*, 147–51, 172; Manning, "Demotic Law," 844–47; Zauzich, "Kaufurkunden, demotische."

35 "Demotic and Abnormal Hieratic Texts: An Online Database of Metadata," accessed 8 January 2020, https://www.trismegistos.org/daht/.

36 "Trismegistos," accessed 8 January 2020, https://www.trismegistos.org; Mark Depauw and Tom Gheldof, "Trismegistos: An Interdisciplinary Platform for Ancient World Texts and Related Information," in *Theory and Practice of Digital Libraries—TPDL 2013 Selected Workshops: LCPD 2013, SUEDL 2013, DataCur 2013, Held in Valletta, Malta, September 22–26, 2013. Revised Selected Papers*, ed. Łukasz Bolikowski et al., Communications in Computer and Information Science 416 (Cham: Springer, 2014), 40–52.

37 In-depth information on the data set can be provided on request but had to be omitted due to space constraints.

38 For the importance of studying women's rights in the context of what men could do, see Jane Rowlandson, ed., *Women and Society in Greek and Roman Egypt: A Sourcebook* (Cambridge and New York: Cambridge University Press, 1998), 2.

39 Todd L. VanPool and Robert D. Leonard, *Quantitative Analysis in Archaeology* (Chichester: Wiley-Blackwell, 2011), 97–152.

40 Karl Pearson, "On the Criterion That a Given System of Deviations from the Probable in the Case of a Correlated System of Variables Is Such That It Can Be Reasonably Supposed to Have Arisen from Random Sampling," in *Breakthroughs in Statistics*, vol. 2: *Methodology and Distribution*, ed. Samuel Kotz and Norman L. Johnson, Springer Series in Statistics (New York: Springer, [1900] 1992), 11–28; Donald Sharpe, "Your Chi-square Test Is Statistically Significant: Now What?," *Practical Assessment, Research & Evaluation* 20, no. 8 (2015): 2–10; VanPool and Leonard, *Quantitative Analysis in Archaeology*, 238–43, 248–50.

41 Graham J.G. Upton, "Fisher's Exact Test," *Journal of the Royal Statistical Society Series A (Statistics in Society)* 155, no. 3 (1992): 395–402, https://doi.org/10.2307/2982890; VanPool and Leonard, *Quantitative Analysis in Archaeology*, 250–53.

42 "The R Project for Statistical Computing," accessed 4 March 2019, https://www.r-project.org/.
43 VanPool and Leonard, *Quantitative Analysis in Archaeology*, 120.
44 Depauw, *A Companion to Demotic Studies*, 66.
45 Deborah Hobson, "Women as Property Owners in Roman Egypt," *TAPA* 113 (1983): 314–15.
46 The third interval lasts 102 years because the entire Ptolemaic Period, if considered from the time of Alexander's conquest of Egypt, was 302 years long. No documents for money included in the data set date to the last forty years of the Ptolemaic Period. Therefore, the additional two years added to the last interval do not falsify the numbers.
47 On the contrary, the mean can be biased by an outlier, such as a document featuring more contracting parties than most others. For the median to change, at least half of the documents need to record a certain behavior.
48 As an example, to see how the median works regarding this data set, thirty-one documents were included in the first time interval. The median number of women in this interval is one. This means that at least half of these thirty-one documents recorded at least one woman as a contracting party.
49 One interval needed to contain thirty-four documents so that all intervals would add up to one hundred documents. The first interval was chosen because the documents that were the thirty-third and thirty-fourth out of the one hundred in chronological order shared the same date.
50 O'Brien, "Private Tradition, Public State," 139.
51 Naphtali Lewis, "The Demise of the Demotic Document: When and Why," *JEA* 79 (1993): 276–81; Lippert, *Einführung in die altägyptische Rechtsgeschichte*, 139; O'Brien, "Private Tradition, Public State," 139.
52 Deborah Hobson, "The Role of Women in the Economic Life of Roman Egypt: A Case Study from First Century Tebtunis," *Echos du Monde Classique/Classical Views* 28, no. 3 (1984): 373–90.
53 Hobson, "Woman as Property Owners in Roman Egypt," 314–15.
54 Hobson, "Woman as Property Owners in Roman Egypt," 315.
55 Depauw, *A Companion to Demotic Studies*, 141; Lippert, *Einführung in die altägyptische Rechtsgeschichte*, 172; Manning, "Demotic Law," 845.
56 P.Schreibertrad. 1 (330 BCE); P.Phil.Dem. 2 (314 BCE); P.Ryl.Dem. 11 (284 BCE); P.Phil.Dem. 13 (273 BCE); P.Schreibertrad. 11 (267 BCE); P.BM Andrews 1 (265 BCE); P.Phil.Dem. 16 (251 BCE); P.Marseille 299 (235 BCE).
57 Depauw, *A Companion to Demotic Studies*, 141; Lippert, *Einführung in die altägyptische Rechtsgeschichte*, 172.
58 Sandra L. Lippert, "Inheritance," in *UEE*, ed. Elizabeth Frood and Willeke Wendrich (Los Angeles: University of California, 2013), 7, http://digital2.library.ucla.edu/viewItem.do?ark=21198/zz002hg0w1.
59 Ursula Kaplony-Heckel, "Die demotischen Gebelên-Papyri der Berliner Papyrussammlung," *FuB* 8 (1967): 70.
60 Francis Ll. Griffith, "Greek Papyri from Gebelên," in *The Adler Papyri*, ed. Elkan Nathan Adler et al. (London: Humphrey Milford, Oxford University Press, 1939), 63; Kaplony-Heckel, "Die demotischen Gebelên-Papyri der Berliner Papyrussammlung," 70; Kaplony-Heckel, "Das Getreide-Darlehn P. Haun. Inv. Demot. 2 in Kopenhagen," in *Acts of the Seventh International Conference of Demotic Studies, Copenhagen, 23–27 August 1999*, ed. Kim Ryholt, CNI Publications 27 (Copenhagen: Carsten Niebuhr Institute of Near Eastern Studies, University of Copenhagen, Museum of Tusculanum Press, 2002), 229n1; Katelijn Vandorpe, "A Successful, but Fragile Biculturalism: The Hellenization Process in the Upper Egyptian Town of Pathyris under Ptolemy VI and VIII," in *Ägypten zwischen innerem Zwist und äußerem Druck: Die Zeit Ptolemaios' VI. bis VIII. Internationales Symposium Heidelberg 16.–19.9.2007*, ed. Andrea Jördens and Joachim F. Quack (Wiesbaden: Harrassowitz, 2011), 292, 296.
61 Griffith, "Greek Papyri from Gebelên," 63; Kaplony-Heckel, "Die demotischen Gebelên-Papyri der Berliner Papyrussammlung," 70; Siân E. Thomas, "Ptolemaic Gebelein: An Exploration of

Legal, Social and Topographical Themes Based on Unpublished Documents for Money and Cessions in the British Museum. Vol. I" (PhD diss., University of Cambridge, 2009), 3; Katelijn Vandorpe, "City of Many a Gate, Harbour for Many a Rebel: Historical and Topographical Outline of Greco-Roman Thebes," in *Hundred-gated Thebes: Acts of a Colloquium on Thebes and the Theban Area in the Graeco-Roman Period*, ed. Sven P. Vleeming, P.L. Bat. 27 (Leiden, New York, and Cologne: Brill, 1995), 233; Vandorpe, "A Successful, but Fragile Biculturalism," 295–96.

62 Thomas, "Ptolemaic Gebelein," 3; Katelijn Vandorpe, "Apollonia, a Businesswoman in a Multicultural Society (Pathyris, 2nd–1st Centuries B.C.)," in *Le rôle et le statut de la femme en Égypte hellénistique, romaine et byzantine: Actes du colloque international, Bruxelles–Leuven 27–29 novembre 1997*, ed. Henri Melaerts and Leon Mooren, Studia Hellenistica 37 (Paris, Leuven, and Sterling, VA: Peeters, 2002), 325.

63 For Apollonia, see Vandorpe, "Apollonia, a Businesswoman in a Multicultural Society." For the archive of Dryton, see Katelijn Vandorpe, *The Bilingual Family Archive of Dryton, His Wife Apollonia and Their Daughter Senmouthis (P.Dryton), Collectanea Hellenistica 4 (Brussels: Comite Klassieke Studies, Subcomité Hellenisme,* KVAB, 2002).

64 Kaplony-Heckel, "Das Getreide-Darlehn P. Haun. Inv. Demot. 2 in Kopenhagen," 229n1; Vandorpe, "City of Many a Gate, Harbour for Many a Rebel," 235; Vandorpe, "Apollonia, a Businesswoman in a Multicultural Society," 336.

65 Vandorpe, "A Successful, but Fragile Biculturalism," 295–308.

66 Vandorpe, "A Successful, but Fragile Biculturalism," 297.

67 Vandorpe, "Apollonia, a Businesswoman in a Multicultural Society," 336; Vandorpe, "A Successful, but Fragile Biculturalism," 302–303, 308.

68 P.BM 10518 (176 BCE); P.BM 10517 (171 BCE); P.Ryl.Dem. 15A (163 BCE); P.Stras.Dem. 21 (145 BCE); P.Strasbourg, Bibliothèque Nationale Wiss. Ges. dem. 15 (138 BCE).

69 P.Adl.Dem. 2 (124 BCE); Dublin, Chester Beatty Library P.Dem. 1 + Dublin, Chester Beatty Library P.Dem. 2 (118 BCE); P.Ryl.Dem. 18 (117 BCE); P.BM 10570A (112 BCE); P.Stras.Dem. 7 (111 BCE); P.BM 10521 (106 BCE); P.Adl.Dem. 7 (103 BCE); P.Adl.Dem. 13 (98 BCE); P.BM 10504 (98 BCE); P.Stras.Dem. 6 (95 BCE); P.Stras.Dem. 44 (94 BCE); P.Ryl.Dem. 29 (91 BCE); P.Adl.Dem. 23 (89 BCE); P.Stras.Dem. 8 (88 BCE).

70 Hobson, "The Role of Women in the Economic Life of Roman Egypt," 389–90.

71 Mariam F. Ayad, "Moving Beyond Gender Bias" (in this volume).

72 Jacquelyn G. Williamson, "Power, Piety, and Gender in Context: Hatshepsut and Nefertiti" (in this volume).

19

Women in Demotic (Documentary) Texts

Janet H. Johnson

In this chapter, I concentrate on women in Demotic documentary texts, but also sneak in some non-documentary texts and even some contemporary Greek material. Demotic texts date from the seventh and sixth centuries BCE into the Roman Period, all of which is here labeled the Late Period, so although much of what is mentioned can be classified as Ptolemaic, some interesting women from the Persian and Roman periods will also appear. It is hoped those readers with little interest in the Late Period will find some interesting comparisons and contrasts with the evidence from other periods of specialization, which might lead to fruitful, if careful, discussions of both data and approaches.

Our data force us to look mostly at elite women, but this essay specifically considers nonroyal women since royal women, due to their royal status, can "get away" with doing things other women can't. Aspects of this presentation—for example, women as part of (elite) family networks, especially well documented in Thebes, and women as participants in formal, documented property sales—have been addressed (in greater detail) by colleagues in this volume. Indeed, women's roles as owners and transmitters of property, wealth, and income and as "cogs" in family networks, and the importance each of these elements may have in transforming a woman into a "force," or empowered individual, play a central role in this discussion. This is as it should be for a conference organized by Mariam Ayad, who has already pointed out the importance of women in more traditional Pharaonic Egypt in her article on "Women's Self-presentation in Pharaonic Egypt."[1]

Women and Family

As the role of women as "homemakers" remained important for women during the Late Period, I begin with a short analysis of what have been called "marriage contracts," but what are here called "marriage documents." They can be understood as legal documents with economic import confirming the husband's responsibility as a member of the "establishment" to support his wife and children, who, following social customs, were not members of the workforce. First, however, I shall summarize a short portion of a long Demotic text known as the "Petition of Petiese."[2] Despite the fact that this text concentrates almost exclusively on men and their machinations to acquire and keep property, positions, and power, it provides a fine example of the role of women, and specifically daughters, in helping preserve and extend a family's power. Sons might get jobs in the power structure, but women married men who got jobs in the power structure; thus women were expected to act in the best interests of the family as a whole. In this interesting section, Petiese identifies a potential husband for his daughter Nytemhat, brings him home to meet his own wife and this daughter, and encourages the young man to come and visit (so the "young people" can get to know one another and develop the appropriate bond). In the meantime, Petiese was checking out the young man's "credentials"—his family's (that is, male relatives') positions in the Temple of Amun in Thebes. When the young man's background checks out, and when the daughter is "old enough" (so stated, never clarified) to marry, they are married and the new son-in-law is given one share of income in the local temple while being expected to manage the rest for his father-in-law and the family. Soon the young couple are left in charge of the family concerns in the "smallish" city (modern al-Hiba) in Middle Egypt while Petiese takes the rest of the family back to Thebes.[3] Although the daughter begs to go to Thebes with the family, Petiese points out the importance to the family of their Middle Egyptian connections, and the couple are told to stay there and help the family in that way.

Petiese gave his daughter a house and income; this could have been her share of the family fortune, given at marriage rather than inherited at death. For the next decade, the daughter and son-in-law were left to handle family affairs in Middle Egypt, the man doing the work, a job that he holds through his relationship with Petiese's daughter. When the young couple's two sons were killed by locals trying to prevent the family from collecting their fair share of the wealth of the local temple, Petiese returned and used his district-wide connections to sort things out. But then, without grandsons to carry on the family position, the son-in-law was removed from local power and replaced by one of Petiese's sons. Overall, this is basically a unique description not only of an (orchestrated) courtship, but also of the intentional use of a woman and her specifically chosen spouse as an important cog in a family's power structure.

To return to the so-called marriage documents—these legal and economic documents between husband and wife—there are numerous actual Demotic contracts preserved from the Late Period, the vast majority made by a man to a woman, indicating that a man of any affluence gave (the woman to be) his wife a marriage document. But the function of these documents was not to stipulate proper female behavior within a marriage, as with the almost contemporary Greek marriage contracts, but rather to guarantee the woman that the man would take care of her and her children economically and that it was her children who would become his heirs. Such documents "protect the rights of the wife and future children, . . . provide a maintenance for the wife during the marriage, . . . provide for the disposal of property upon divorce and . . . endow any children produced during the marriage with the property of the husband."[4] In some such documents, the man made a (usually) nominal monetary gift to the wife accompanied by a promise of annual maintenance (grain, oil, money for clothing); in others, the wife made the nominal monetary gift to the husband while the husband (again) promised annual maintenance to the wife. The first type, especially, was likely to include a list of the woman's possessions which she brought with her to the marriage and their monetary value. In both forms, the wife received annual maintenance (called *sʿnḫ*—literally, "causing to live"—in the second type of document) backed up and guaranteed by the man's wealth (all his possessions, whether real or movable); women who had such documents were frequently referred to as *sḥmt n sʿnḫ*, "endowed woman." If a man divorced his wife, the documents say he will pay her a certain amount of money and return all her goods (or the value thereof). It is also important to note, a man could not unilaterally divorce. The documents frequently specified that the man was liable to pay this annual maintenance whether the woman was still living in his house or not; as long as the woman had the marriage document, he was liable and she was legally entitled to what he had promised, plus any arrears. Many marriage documents also indicate that, at divorce, the couple divided property acquired during marriage. Divorce documents make clear that the husband can no longer claim any "marital rights" from the ex-wife, and stress that she is now legally free and clear to marry a new husband. It has been suggested that a woman with a marriage document whose marriage went sour might hang on to it until she found a new man to marry and support her.[5]

So-called Demotic marriage documents were, then, economic and legal documents of importance to women but also to succeeding generations, reflecting long-standing mores that a man, who was expected to interact in public and hold a good job, was also expected to support his wife, who stayed home, ran the house, raised the children, and didn't have a major outside source of income. But these documents also committed the man to supporting his children and passing along his wealth to his children by this wife. Even after divorce, the financial and legal obligations to their children remained. If a man wished to remarry, it was incumbent upon him to get the approval of his children by the first wife, whether divorced or deceased, to any financial arrangement he made for the second wife.[6] Because of the economic and legal value of the marriage documents, with bearing on legitimate inheritance of property from both father and mother, they were frequently saved in family archives of important legal and economic documents. It should be noted that marriage was considered important, socially and practically, for men as well as women, as stressed in an early Ptolemaic letter (P.Berlin 13538)[7] in which the sender recounts people commenting that there is no woman in his house, so he asks the oracle whether he should marry woman A or woman B. He describes this as a very important matter, or he would not bother to write about it.

There are several examples of a man selling all his property to a woman in return for support in old age.[8] In one example, a man says he belongs to a woman "alive and dead"[9] and she has authority over his burial, which could suggest he had no children. It has been suggested that in many, or most, such cases, the pair are husband and wife.[10] These sales frequently take the form of (fictitious[11]) sales, serving as a will in favor of the woman/wife, just as the form of fictitious sale is found commonly when transferring property to children. In some cases, such documents may reflect a younger wife caring for her aging husband. For instance, a woman acquired[12] from her husband the occupation of mortuary priest[13] and various real properties in return for supporting him in old age and burying him after death; more than ten years later, she sold half of this property to each of her two sons.[14] The sale to the elder son specifically states that it is made in return for her own subsistence while alive and proper burial when dead; the mother continues to receive half the income (rations) from tombs, but the sons are to carry out the mortuary work. Indeed, it was regularly to her children (not her spouse) that a woman transferred property with the proviso that she be taken care of in old age and buried properly.

As in any society, women (and families) faced medical problems. Among the medical texts preserved in Demotic is one badly broken text dealing with women's gynecological problems, continuing the medical tradition known since the Middle Kingdom.[15] As in earlier times in Egypt, when medicine didn't work, individuals might turn to the gods. In year 24 of Augustus (i.e., 5 BCE), a woman left a Demotic letter[16] in a sanctuary, asking Sobek, lord of Tebtunis in the Fayum, to get rid of the disease afflicting her. She seems confident that Sobek will help her if he gets the message and she threatens that the "abomination/curse of Sobek lord of Tebtunis" will follow any person who removes the document from the sanctuary. This letter has been compared to oracular requests to cure disease and to healing statues.[17] By contrast, in so-called "sales as a servant (e.g., *bȝk*)" a person would sell him- or herself to a deity in return for protection. In one example[18] among several, a woman pays Soknopaios, the god, and Isis Neferses, the great goddess (both Fayum deities), 1 deben per month to protect herself and her children. Perhaps these self-dedications were like insurance contracts, with the owner paying monthly for divine protection. This takes us from women and the family to women and religion.

Women and Religion

In daily-life religion, women generally played a restricted role as singers/musicians in the temples.[19] An apparent major exception to the general rule that women had no formal positions in daily-life religion is found in three early Ptolemaic Demotic texts from the Fayum which seem to include lists of women members of a religious association. They include women with titles comparable to titles of contemporary leaders of men's religious associations.[20] One[21] such document is a list of *nȝ wrwt* ("the (female) great ones/leaders") then individual women's names and titles, including *tȝ wrt Bȝstt* ("the great one of Bastet") and *tȝ wrt Ỉmn* ("the great one of Amun"),[22] *tȝ mn-ỉryt tȝ mỉt* ("the nurse(-maid) of the cat"), *tȝ ḥm-nṯr nȝ nṯrw* ("the prophetess of the gods"), *tȝ mr-mšꜥ* ("the (female) general"), and *tȝ mḥ-2* ("the (female) second in command"). Each name is followed by a small amount of money,[23] perhaps their (monthly) dues? Two other early Ptolemaic Fayum documents[24] also include such lists of names of women with these and additional titles, such as *tȝ ꜥȝ.t n* 29 ("the great one of 29")[25] and *tȝ ḥȝt.t* [*ḥȝwtyt*] *n pȝ ꜥ.wy* ("the chieftainess of the house"), the latter (*ꜥ.wy*, "house") the term used to refer to religious associations or the temple they serve.[26]

Another possible role for women in formal religion was participation in public productions of religious plays containing female roles. We have, for example, references to twin sisters at Saqqara playing Isis and Nephthys in a local production.[27] Similarly, from the Roman Period we have Demotic texts[28] recording women participating in bawdy rituals, the so-called "orgiastic cult behavior" noted already by Herodotus, which have New Kingdom parallels at the Temple of Mut in Thebes—singing, dancing, feasting, drinking to drunkenness, having sex in front of the goddess—all of this going on in the temple, and specifically the Temple of Mut according to the Roman texts (but with Herodotus attributing them to the Temple of Bastet).[29] On the level of informal religion, there is also clear evidence of women turning to the gods, by letter—oracle, for example—when things went wrong, as already mentioned.

When we turn to funerary/mortuary religion, we find a number of funerary stelae dedicated for women, occasionally in Demotic, but more frequently in more formal hieroglyphs, on stone or wood. The large numbers of such funerary stelae show a wide range of quality, probably reflecting the relative wealth of these women or their families. Interestingly, although men's funerary monuments may give a wide range of titles (including very high ones), usually religious, women's monuments basically give no titles or at most *sḥmt wꜥbt DN* (name of) deity, "woman, wab-priest of deity" (in Demotic) or *nbt pr i͗ḥyt nfrt*, "lady of the house, beautiful singer" (on hieroglyphic monuments). The family of the High Priest of Ptah at Memphis at the end of the Ptolemaic Period dedicated a number of stelae, some in Demotic, some in hieroglyphs; those for his wife, Taimhotep, make it clear that her accomplishments in life were her marriage and her production of offspring, especially a son to succeed his father. For her, no public behavior which might directly accrue status was recorded; her status came through the men in her life; that is, women's roles were private, not public.[30]

Although much funerary equipment for women has been preserved, indicating women were fully integrated into Egyptian funerary culture, very little of it incorporates Demotic (which came to be used for religious texts only relatively late); but there are significant exceptions, including major Demotic liturgical texts,[31] each of which contains a distinct collection of funerary literature.

Women and the Economy

From religion, we turn now to areas where Demotic documents flourish: economy and law. It should be noted from the beginning that it is hard to separate the two, since an economic document has legal implications, and legal documents have economic implications, as already seen with the marriage documents discussed at the beginning of this chapter. Let me stress there are hundreds of documents made by and for women; I can't pretend even to mention the full range of documents. Other scholars might select a different set of categories to discuss, but what is important is the wide, and significant, range of texts where women are active and act on their own and in their own name. What must be kept in mind, too, is the sharp contrast between the public world of work/administration/the temples/skilled professions, where women are basically excluded, and the economic/legal realm, where women seem to have had (nearly) equal rights. It is possible, though, that some or many women may have been hesitant to push too far in the economic and legal realms because of their lack of experience or standing in the "public world" of work.[32] The connection of titles to (public) status may carry over into economic and legal texts: When men make a contract, they are frequently given titles[33]—religious, administrative, military, and so forth—but women are simply called *sḥmt*, even when they are selling property, such as temple liturgies, in concert with men who are given the appropriate titles.

We can look first at women and taxes. Some taxes were general and applied to everyone, such as the salt[34] tax and the oil tax; for others—various poll taxes, for example—only men were responsible; some reflect women carrying out normal business, including grain/harvest taxes, the tax on pigeon houses, and the shawl(?)/wool tax, the last paid mostly by women. Women also are recorded paying the necropolis tax, a tax paid by the person (including women) who was responsible for carrying out a burial in the necropolis. Some taxes probably reflect taxes on craft jobs, where performance bonds were needed to guarantee that the craftsman would carry out the contracted duties. Among these craft jobs is that of brewer of beer, which included female brewers.[35]

The agency of women is suggested by women serving as middlemen, paying taxes for others[36] or holding security which had been put up by a person taking out a loan: in the records of a moneylender,[37] 33–40 percent of borrowers are women, but 90 percent or more of people who hold security are women. Women were active loaners of money and grain to other women and to men, as we will see later.[38] Such behavior also indicates that (some) women were wealthy enough to make such loans.

Perhaps the agency of women is most obvious in the impressively wide range of contracts by which women act *on their own* to acquire, dispose of, or manipulate (for example, lease out, borrow against, and so forth) a wide range of valuable property. I stress here that the Egyptian women act on their own, in their own names, when making a contract or when carrying out other legal business. Unlike contemporary Greek women, who had to have a male relative (such as a father, husband, or son) act as their "lord" *(kurios)* and carry out business for them, Egyptian women not only could but did act in their own name consistently.

What kind of property did women buy and sell and lease? Among the most frequent are land, both agricultural land and building plots, with or without buildings;[39] temple income;[40] and tombs and bodies of deceased individuals to be serviced by mortuary priests;[41] occasionally animals;[42] and, presumably, lots of things not valuable enough to warrant the expense of going to the notary office and paying to have a formal contract written.

It should not surprise us that many transactions involving women, just as those involving men, seem to have been aimed at keeping property in the family, just as in Pharaonic times.[43] Since all the children in a family were eligible to inherit from both their father and their mother,[44] real property had a tendency to be split up over generations, and many recorded transactions have the effect, and presumably the intent, of restoring property, especially fields and houses, to unified ownership. This seems to become even more of a problem among families in the mortuary business since their sources of revenue (tombs and their inhabitants) were treated as private property and could, therefore, like other real property, be divided with daughters and sisters as well as sons and brothers, unlike priestly positions (and, indeed, most jobs in the public sector or government). If a woman married outside the family business, she would take her share of the family wealth with her, which could, in the long run, impoverish the family. But if the women intermarried with other families of mortuary priests, the property continued to circulate within the wider family from generation to generation. We have already seen the role of the daughter and her marriage in the Persian-period family of Petiese. The role of women, specifically daughters and sisters, in securing ownership of property[45] is made especially clear in Muhs's study, "The Girls Next Door,"[46] in which he shows how mortuary priests not only married the daughters or sisters of their colleagues, but they also frequently lived in the same neighborhood or even next door. And living close to your parents and grown siblings could be advantageous for a woman if she had problems with her husband or in-laws. Thus, it seems reasonable to suggest that this pattern, and the role of women in inheritance attested in the documents, may have been fairly widespread among families concerned with maintaining their wealth.

Thus, one general concern seen in the documents is keeping property in the family and rebuilding family holdings which have been split through the generations, both exemplified by an archive of documents[47] from Edfu, south of Thebes, which includes numerous texts where family members are reacquiring property which had become dispersed,[48] and an interesting example[49] of a woman inheriting land, but with restrictions: a woman's father gave her a gift of land with structures; if anyone, including her relatives, try to take the land from her, they will have to pay a fine; but if she wants to sell the property, she must give the first opportunity to her siblings, and may only sell outside the family if they do not want it.

Some types of property came with job responsibilities. When men deal with such property, they are given the appropriate titles reflecting the job responsibilities, but women are not. Did the women carry out the jobs without using or being accorded the titles, or did they have to or sometimes decide to hire a man to do the associated work? In some cases, the latter seems to be the situation. In a very long document from the Memphite area,[50] a man divided property with his sister. Toward the end of the document, the man mentions dealing with the woman's husband, son, or agent if there are any questions or problems with the division of the property. Are we to assume that she did not handle the property (real or movable) herself, but had a man do it for her?

A series of Theban documents[51] from Deir al-Medina seems to indicate that although a woman owned various kinds of property, she hired a man—here her brother—to carry out the associated work. In the first document, a man with the title "shrine-opener of Amun of Djeme" leases days of *sʿnḫ* ("endowment") in the Temple of Isis and the Temple of Hathor from a woman, elsewhere[52] described as his younger sister. He agrees to do all the work for the year, pays her 12 deben, and says: "The responsibility to do the work is mine and my children's." He uses all he owns as security. In the second document, from the same year, the same man takes responsibility to watch over, or guard, his sister's one-third share of a house of which he owns the other two-thirds. He pays her rent and uses all he possesses as security. In the third document in that same year, she leased high land—that is, good agricultural land—to him; he agreed to cultivate it, providing seed, cattle, workmen, and tools. He also agreed to pay to her the harvest tax and the rent[53] so that she could pay the harvest tax to the treasury of Pharaoh and get the necessary receipts. Again, all responsibility for working the land is stated to be on him and his children, and all his possessions serve as security.

This same situation is found when women own and deal with property supporting mortuary priests, both the ongoing funerary offerings the priests make to deceased individuals as their work and their own "wages" for such work. Men are regularly given the appropriate titles, but women are normally just identified as *sḥmt*.[54] Thus, there is little direct evidence[55] for women as mortuary priests or temple liturgists.[56] There are, however, some contracts where the seller of tombs or mortuary priest duties and income tells a female buyer, "Yours is the title" or "Yours is the responsibility for carrying out the work" associated with the title.[57] And in some contracts, it is not so clear that the woman is not doing the work herself. In another document from Deir al-Medina,[58] a woman acknowledges a loan of 7 *artaba*s of wheat from a man and tells him he has the right to recoup the loan directly on the threshing floor. Does this imply she worked the land or only that she would be there for the threshing and see that he was paid?

As property owners, women were also involved in borrowing both money and grain; such loans[59] note that if the borrower does not repay the loan on time, they may pay a 50 percent surcharge or lose whatever they gave the lender as their guarantee or security. Thus, if borrowers used real property as security and defaulted, they lost ownership of the property to the lender; for example, P.Hauswaldt 18,[60] where a woman used five plots of high (agricultural) land as security for a loan, then she defaulted, and so she lost ownership of the property.

As mentioned at the beginning of this chapter, men of means gave their wives a marriage document, frequently of the form called called *sẖ n sʿnḫ* ("(document of) endowment"). Among other things, such documents gave the husband the right to sell property the wife had brought to the marriage "for the benefit of the family."[61] But if a couple divorced, the husband had to return to the wife either the actual property she had brought with her to the marriage or property of equal value. These "endowment" documents are economically and legally important, giving a woman input on legal and economic actions by her husband having an impact on their family. For example, in P.OI 25258[62] a man's sale of a portion of a house has to be subscribed by his wife, saying, "He gave me a document of endowment and a transfer document transferring this property to me, but I am in agreement with this sale: 'Do everything; I am agreed.'" And it was necessary for a woman to sign off on divorce. We don't know the background, what social dynamics forced the following settlement when a couple divorced, but we can see the legal and economic impact: In P.Hamburg 3,[63] a woman releases a man from an endowment document (i.e., marriage document) of 21 pieces of silver and a sale and cession, by which he had transferred his possessions[64] to her as guarantee of that marriage document. She says, "I have given all the documents back to you. You have paid me in full and made me satisfied; I have received money."

The individual documents mentioned above, and many, many more, provide interesting and important information about women (and men) in Late Period Egypt. In addition, the Deir al-Medina documents referred to above about a man's dealings with his younger sister are an example of what modern scholars call archives, collections of contracts and other important documents consciously gathered and kept together for their value to the family; they were frequently passed along to younger generations. They include documents proving ownership of goods/property, marriage contracts through which children inherit from both parents, and so forth.

Women usually did not have their own archive, but they did not want to put their marriage document in their husband's archive (in case the marriage went sour), so her marriage document and perhaps the rest of her documents were frequently in the archive of her father or brother. These collections allow us to develop extensive family trees of wealthy and influential families but also allow us to see the same individuals or groups of individuals in several different settings so we get a more "rounded" view than from individual documents. Since all marriages solidify contacts with other important families, and since sisters' documents frequently end up in the same archive as those of their brothers, archives can provide extensive information on families through generations and on interactions between families.[65] Unfortunately, there is not space here to illustrate further examples of such archives.

Women and Law

Instead, we turn to a brief look at women and law. We have very little evidence about women and criminal law, so we must concentrate on civil law, including contract law. One of the main things to note about women and contract law is the same as with the economy: women acted on their own, could take the initiative, and were not dependent on the men in the family to take care of them.[66] But since this basically involves looking at the same range of documents as in the section on women and the economy, but from a different point of view, I won't repeat that material here. What I will note, however, is that there are no records of women who served as witnesses to legal contracts although, as we have seen, women frequently made or received such documents, and even though there were normally sixteen witnesses to each document. Why? Perhaps because the witnesses had to sign their name and patronymic, and most women apparently could not read and write.[67] This suggestion forces me to address the question of women's literacy during the Late Period. There is very little direct evidence on the subject. Certainly, some women were literate in Greek; not only do we have the mummy and mummy portrait of a (Greek) schoolteacher labeled Hermione *Grammatike*—Hermione the (Greek) language teacher[68]—but there are occasional other indications of women literate in Greek.[69] In addition, we have some, mostly indirect, evidence that some women might have been literate in Demotic,[70] but the general question of literacy cannot be resolved here. Whatever the reason women did not serve as witnesses to contracts, we must conclude that women were involved in the legal system, but not in all aspects of it.

What I will consider instead is an interesting and somewhat informative type of legal document not yet mentioned: oaths.[71] Approximately one in five of the people involved in oaths (the person swearing the oath or the person to whom the oath is sworn) is a woman (in our preserved documents, that amounts to over one hundred women making or receiving an oath). It is plausible that some women would have hesitated to go to the temple to force an oath since they were discouraged from participation in public life; but that so many did suggests, perhaps, that women were more comfortable making use of the legal system than we might have thought. What social, rather than legal, implications there might have been to swearing an oath are unknown.

About what did people swear an oath? Sometimes the topics are quite personal. Among the latter are a number in which a woman is asked to swear she has not committed adultery.[72] This apparent concern with sexual promiscuity is reinforced by P.Cairo 95205, a letter found at Qasr Ibrim, in Nubia, in which a woman asks a man to make an oracle for her, claiming that "since the moment she came from the place (*m3ʿ*) of her "beginning husband(?)" (*š3ʿ hy*) . . . she has not slept with nor had relations with any man except (Personal Name).[73] It should be noted that oaths also could be required of a man accused of adultery, but they are less common.

Very different concerns arose in one case (O. Stras 282) in which a husband and wife may have charged a man with killing a second man (perhaps their son?); the accused man is required to swear an oath to them that he didn't kill the man and doesn't know who did. If he so swears, and if his wife swears that his oath is a true oath, the couple must cease and desist from accusing him.[74]

More frequently, oaths are on economic topics. We have examples of women swearing oaths about typical business or personal affairs: debts,[75] ownership of goods (especially grain,[76] various kinds of cloth, and so forth[77]); many involve accusations of theft. Several involve squabbles over money or questions about missing goods. In one example (O. Berlin 14828),[78] a woman says to a man, "I already gave you the 1 talent concerning your document." If she takes the oath and another woman verifies her oath, the man must pay her five hundred pieces of silver; if she does not take the oath, the man pays only for expenses she can document. One thing a woman was not forced to swear an oath about was the amount and value of her "property of a woman" that she brought with her to marriage—the marriage documents say a man can't force a woman to swear about that question, and the descriptions and values are frequently listed in the marriage document.

In addition to taking oaths, women were also the recipients of oaths about ownership of movable property as well as perishable goods, payment for farmland, and various aspects of debts. [79] With oaths, we have no explanation of the background or the circumstances which led to the demand for the oath, and so we are frequently left trying to imagine exactly what might have happened. In one such example, we seem to see the difficult situation a woman might be in when she doesn't have a man to protect her: two men made oaths to the same woman, saying that since her husband had been away, they had not stolen fruit from her, they had not seen anyone else do so, nor had either man's cow eaten her fruit.[80]

How did oaths work? In general, if the person of whom an oath is demanded swears the oath before the named deity, the complainant cedes his/her case; if the person does not swear the oath, in some cases the complainant (or someone else) is made to swear a counter oath. In other cases, the complainant has the right to search for and confiscate the item in question. As in Egyptian law in general, the aim was frequently an amicable resolution to a dispute (not the determination of absolute right and wrong), and so there was room for negotiation.[81]

This seems, in a way, a fitting summary of the roles of women seen in Demotic documents: although there were some activities which were seen as normal or standard behavior for women, women who had the opportunity, interest, desire, and any special knowledge necessary to do something could do it. Men were supposed to take care of their wives and children, but this need not restrict any given woman from taking care of things herself. As in earlier Egyptian society, and despite the presence of Greeks and Greek attitudes toward the roles of women, individual women could "make themselves known,"[82] whether it involved stepping in to handle things when her husband was away or taking on roles for which she was, or felt, well equipped. To understand ancient Egyptian society, one needs to recognize and understand both the norms and the ability and tendency for individuals to go beyond the norm.

Notes

1 Mariam Ayad, "Women's Self-presentation in Pharaonic Egypt," in *Living Forever: Self-presentation in Ancient Egypt*, ed. Hussein Bassir (Cairo: American University in Cairo Press, 2019), 221–46.

2 P.Rylands 9, Persian period, al-Hiba; see the recent re-edition by Günter Vittmann in *Der demotische Papyrus Rylands 9*, ÄAT 38 (Wiesbaden: Harrassowitz, 1998), which claims to provide copies of petitions to the "Finance Minister" under the Persian king Darius. Some scholars claim this text is actually a literary text using the form of a documentary text (petition), similar to, e.g., Sinuhe, with its relation to autobiography and incorporation of hymns to the king, or Wenamun, with its ties to administrative reports. But if so, the literary value of the Petition of Petiese is far inferior to that of Sinuhe or Wenamun since the petitions are long, boring, repetitive, and even tedious. See the discussion in Jacqueline E. Jay, "The *Petition of Petiese* Reconsidered," in *Mélanges offerts à Ola el-Aguizy*, ed. Fayza Haikal, BdE 164 (Cairo: IFAO, 2015), 229–47.

3 To get his sons (back) into power positions there, especially in the Temple of Amun. Throughout the narrative, there is a basic assumption that Petiese and his (male) descendants were responsible for taking care of the family by keeping jobs within the family, getting sons the best jobs possible, marrying daughters to men who join the "family business" or are already in related businesses, and helping the family get and maintain power, prestige, and wealth.

4 J.G. Manning, "Ptolemaic Demotic Marriage Contract," in *Law and Legal Practice in Egypt from Alexander to the Arab Conquest: A Selection of Papyrological Sources in Translation with Introductions and Commentary*, ed. J.G. Keenan et al. (Cambridge: Cambridge University Press, 2014), 150–51, referencing H.S. Smith, "Marriage and Family Law," in *Legal Documents of the Hellenistic World*, ed. M.J. Geller and H. Maehler (London: Warburg Institute, University of London, 1995), 48.

5 Unless, perhaps, she was financially independent.

6 And any future half-siblings got part of their inheritance only with approval by the children of the first wife. Interestingly, there are occasional examples of marriage documents which are

replacing an earlier marriage document between the same couple. Since, as has been seen, the marriage documents are actually economic documents and have bearing on legitimate inheritance of property from both parents, it has been suggested these "renewals" reflect the birth of children (heirs). See Koenraad Donker van Heel, "Abnormal Hieratic and Early Demotic Texts Collected by the Theban Choachytes in the Reign of Amasis" (PhD diss., Leiden University, 1995), 125–32, #9, for his discussion of P.Louvre 7846.

7 Karl-Theodor Zauzich, *Papyri von der Insel Elephantine* (Berlin: Akademie, 1978).

8 See, for example, P.Marseille 298 and 299, dating to 235 BCE, in Günther Vittmann, "Ein thebanischer Verpfrundungsvertrag aus der Zeit Ptolemaios' III, Euergetes, P. Marseille 298 + 299," *Enchoria* 10 (1980): 127–40; and P.Philadelphia 13, dating to 273 BCE, which is the sale of an entire estate to a woman (probably the man's wife) to take care of the seller. See Mustafa el-Amir, *A Family Archive from Thebes* (Cairo: Government Printing Offices, 1959), 56–60; and Brian P. Muhs, *Tax Receipts, Taxpayers, and Taxes in Early Ptolemaic Thebes*, OIP 126 (Chicago: Oriental Institute of the University of Chicago 2005), 108–109, taxpayer #6.

9 P.Rylands XI, dating to 284 BCE. See F.Ll. Griffith, *Catalogue of the Demotic Papyri in the Rylands Library Manchester* (Manchester and London: University Press, 1909), 122–23 and 257–60, specifically line l. 5 on pp. 123 and 259.

10 Although without additional information, one cannot be certain since contracts do not identify marital relations.

11 That is, a sale (*sẖ ḏbꜣ ḥḏ*, "document for money") without cession (*sẖ n wy*, "document of being far"), often seen as transferring use without transferring title (which, in this case, would come with the death of the original owner).

12 P.Louvre 2429bis, dating to 292 BCE. See Karl-Theodor Zauzich, *Die ägyptische Schreibertradition in Aufbau, Sprache und Schrift der demotischen Kaufverträge aus ptolemäischer Zeit*, ÄA 19 (Wiesbaden: Harrassowitz, 1968), 14–15, #5; and P.Louvre 2428, dating to 277 BCE in Zauzich, *Die ägyptische Schreibertradition*, 79–81, #108.

13 Frequently called "choachyte" after the Greek term.

14 P Louvre 2424, dating to 267 BCE, in Zauzich, *Die ägyptische Schreibertradition*, 17–21, #11; and P.BM 10026, dating to 265/64 BCE, in Carol A. Andrews, *Catalogue of Demotic Papyri in the British Museum*, vol. 4, *Ptolemaic Legal Texts from the Theban Area* (London: British Museum Press, 1990), 16–22, #1. See also Willy Clarysse, "Deeds of Last Will: Demotic, Greek, and Latin," in *Law and Legal Practice in Egypt from Alexander to the Arab Conquest*, ed. J.G. Keenan, J.G. Manning, and U. Yiftach-Firanko (Cambridge: Cambridge University Press, 2014), 203–205, where Clarysse uses the term "will" to describe the woman's transfer to her son by "money document" without cession, transferring to the son houses in Thebes, in Djeme (West Bank/ Medinet Habu), and revenue from duties as choachyte in Hermonthis and in various tombs in the necropolis of Djeme. For more on the archive of this woman, Nesikhons, which is part of the family archive of Pachytes, son of Pchorchonsis, see Andrews, *Ptolemaic Legal Texts*, 16–37; and Muhs, *Tax Receipts*, 113–15, taxpayer #16.

15 See the Kahun Medical/Gynecological Papyrus, P.UC 32057, published by Mark Collier and Stephen Quirke in *The UCL Lahun Papyri: Religious, Literary, Legal, Mathematical, and Medical*, BARIS 1209 (Oxford: Archaeopress, 2004), 58–64.

16 P.Carlsberg 67 from Tebtunis, in the Fayum region. See J.D. Ray, "Papyrus Carlsberg 67 B: A Healing Prayer from the Fayûm," *JEA* 61 (1975): 181–88.

17 Covered with healing spells over which water was poured; the water would absorb the magic, the patient would drink the water, and the spells should cure the patient.

18 P.Ox Griff 57, dating to 138 BCE. See Edda Bresciani, *L'Archivio demotico del tempio di Soknopaiu Neso nel Griffith Institute di Oxford*, Testi e Documenti per lo Studio dell'Antichità 49 (Milan: Istituto Editoriale Cisalpino, 1975), 78–79.

19 Positions as musicians, although not a major part of the religious hierarchy or administrative structure, provided some status and probably some income, both of which could have been

important to these women in their daily lives. In one puzzling text (P.Ox. Griff. 40, a Ptolemaic text dating to the second century BCE from the Temple of Soknopaiu Nesos, in the Fayum region), a woman writes a *mḳmḳ* ("petition") to the *lesonis* ("chief economic officer"), and the inspector and *wꜥb*-priests of the temple, claiming she had been (on duty) in the temple with some men, collected money due, and put it in the appropriate collections box, but later found the collections box short; her petition demands that officials carry out interrogations. This situation is not unique, but it is unusual for a woman to be involved, much less writing the formal complaint. For the text, see Bresciani, *L'Archivio demotico*, 46–49.

20 Françoise de Cenival, *Les associations religieuses en Égypte d'après les documents demotiques*, BdE 46 (Cairo: IFAO, 1972).

21 P.Lille 31, dating to the third century BCE. See Françoise de Cenival, "Deux papyrus inédits de Lille avec une révision du P.dém.Lille 31," *Enchoria* 7 (1977): 21–23.

22 Also attested for Haremakhet, Thoth, and Horus, as well as *tꜢ ꜥšy Ꜣst wrt tꜢ bikt*, "the reciter of Isis and superior of the falcon."

23 6 *qite* down to 3/4 (2/3 + 1/12 = 9/12) of a *qite.*

24 P.Lille 97 and 98, (early) Ptolemaic; see de Cenival, "Deux papyrus inédits de Lille," 21–49.

25 Which has been compared to "the great one of the association (e.g., *swnt*)," the title of the leader of men's religious associations.

26 Note also the military-style titles: *tꜢ mr-mšꜥ Ḥt-Ḥr*, "the general of Hathor" (P.Lille 97, 2/6), and *tꜢ mr-mšꜥ n Sbk*, "the general of Sobek" (P.Lille 98, 2/5). De Cenival, who published these texts (and who suggested that they may reflect royal/government support in the early Ptolemaic Period for the growth of new and enlarged cults, and especially animal cults, and especially in the Fayum, as both Greek- and Egyptian-speaking populations moved or were moved into that oasis), suggested that women may have been chosen to fill some of the new local cult positions to keep from increasing too greatly the number of men with tax exemptions resulting from priestly status (since women didn't have to pay the taxes for which male priests were given exemptions). Such a suggestion would have social implications which have not been studied and for which I don't know whether we even have the necessary information. What are the implications, if any, of the lack of evidence of women priests in these cults later in the Ptolemaic Period?

27 Similarly, it has been suggested that women also may have played roles (again, especially, Isis/Nephthys to a male priest's Horus) in the enactment of private funerary rituals (such as P.Vienna 3865). See also Koenraad Donker van Heel, "P. Louvre E 7858: Another Abnormal Hieratic Puzzle," in *The Workman's Progress: Studies in the Village of Deir el-Medina and Other Documents from Western Thebes in Honor of Rob Demarée*, ed. B.J.J. Haring, O.E. Kaper, and R. van Walsem (Leiden: NINO, 2014), 54n4.

28 Mark Smith and Richard Jasnow, "'As for Those Who Have Called Me Evil, Mut Will Call Them Evil': Orgiastic Cultic Behavior and Its Critics in Ancient Egypt (PSI Inv. [provv.] D114a + PSI Inv. 3056 verso)," *Enchoria* 32 (2010/2011): 9–53; Richard Jasnow and Mark Smith, "New Fragments of the Demotic Mut Text in Copenhagen and Florence," in *Joyful in Thebes: Egyptological Studies in Honor of Betsy M. Bryan*, ed. K.M. Cooney and R. Jasnow (Atlanta: Lockwood Press, 2015), 239–82. For discussion of earlier festivals of drunkenness, including Mut, see Betsy M. Bryan, "Hatshepsut and Cultic Revelries in the New Kingdom," in *Creativity and Innovation in the Reign of Hatshepsut: Papers from the Theban Workshop 2010*, ed. José M. Galán and Betsy Morrell Bryan, Occasional Proceedings of the Theban Workshop, SAOC 69 (Chicago: Oriental Institute of the University of Chicago, 2014), 93–123.

29 There was harsh criticism of such practices by nondevotees, even calling the practices evil. Some statements by devotees could be interpreted as authored by practitioners cultivating solidarity, especially against antagonists. There has been speculation by Klotz that priests of Anubis had sex with women inside the temple, perhaps women who couldn't conceive with their husbands, an idea rejected by Smith and Jasnow in their publications (see preceding note) of the Mut texts.

30 Although in the case of Taimhotep, we know that her stele was commissioned by her husband, in most cases we have no idea who commissioned women's stele—the woman or her husband or son (proving what a good husband/son the dedicator was). The same is true of other funerary/mortuary equipment, including the many copies of the *Book of the Dead* made for women (the Totenbuch Project [http://totenbuch.awk.nrw.de/] has identified Ptolemaic owners of Books of the Dead: 242 women; 543 men).

31 Including P.Rhind 2, written for Tanous (the wife of the owner of P Rhind 1) published in Georg Möller, *Die beiden Totenpapyrus Rhind des Museums zu Edinburg*, Demotische Studien 6 (Leipzig: J.C. Hinrichs, 1913); P.Harkness written for Tanawerouaw and published by Mark Smith, "Papyrus Harkness," *Enchoria* 18 (1991): 95–105); and P.Louvre E 10607 made for Tatarepyt the daughter of Kludj (Mark Smith, *The Liturgy of Opening the Mouth for Breathing* (Oxford: Griffith Institute, Ashmolean Museum, 1993), all dating to the early Roman Period. Slightly earlier is the Artemis liturgical text written in hieratic and Demotic for a woman with a Greek name and matronymic. For the latter, see Jacco Dieleman, "The Artemis Liturgical Papyrus," in *Ägyptische Rituale der griechisch-römischen Zeit*, ed. J.F. Quack (Tübingen: Mohr Siebeck, 2014), 171–83.

32 One clear example of a woman owning real property which she leased out but which her husband also leased out (in different years) in his own name led Pestman to suggest it is possible that many women might let their husbands handle this rather public aspect of property ownership (and thus, women might have owned an even larger percent of real property and other assets than we see in the documents). See P.W. Pestman, "Appearance and Reality in Written Contracts: Evidence from Bilingual Family Archives," in *Legal Documents of the Hellenistic World*, ed. M.J. Geller and H. Maehler (London: Warburg Institute, University of London, 1995), 84–85.

33 Although, normally, the titles are lower ranking than those on funerary monuments.

34 Receipts were usually made to a man, to a woman, or to a man and wife; a man was usually identified by his name and patronymic, a woman by her name and patronymic or by her name and the name of her husband.

35 P.Lille 6, Ptolemaic Period/third century. See Françoise de Cenival, *Cautionnements démotiques du début de l'époque ptolémaïque (P. Dém. Lille 34 à 96)* (Paris: Éditions Klincksieck, 1973), 16–17.

36 For example, the early Roman woman paying the grain tax for her brother in Girgis Mattha, *Demotic Ostraca* (Cairo: IFAO, 1945), 181–82, #246; or the situation where a man and woman cultivated land, but the receipt for taxes shows she paid her half, noting that his half is still not paid (O. MH 520, year 14), published in Miriam Lichtheim, *Demotic Ostraca from Medinet Habu*, OIP 80 (Chicago: University of Chicago Press, 1957), 57, #129.

37 Brian P. Muhs, forthcoming.

38 Below, this section.

39 E.g., P.Berlin 3096, dating to 222 BCE, from Thebes, a sale from mother to daughter of part of a house which the mother had inherited from her mother + sale tombs, including her own tomb and half of the tombs belonging to her daughter's father—that is, the woman's husband; the other half were transferred to the couple's son, the daughter's brother. See Stefan Grunert, *Thebanische Kaufverträge des 3. und 2. Jahrhunderts V. u. Z.*, Demotische Papyri aus den Staatlichen Museen zu Berlin 2 (Berlin: Akademie, 1981).

40 E.g., P.DelM 3 = P.Turin 6072, dating to 104 BCE, from Thebes, a sale and cession (transfer of use and of ownership) from a *sḥmt* ("woman") to a man with the title "shrine-opener of Amun of Djeme and Prophet of Hathor, Mistress of the West" (*wn n ỉmn n Ḏmꜣ ḥm-nṯr n Ḥ.t-Ḥr. ḥnwt ỉmnt*), saying, "You have paid me for my days of support in the Temple of Hathor and my shares of the festival days and my shares of the cult association and all pertaining thereto, brought to/derived from/added to from field, temple, town, everyplace, and their cult duties and cult functions. It's now yours. . . . It is yours together with its legal authority." See Giuseppe Botti, *L'Archivio demotico da Deir el-Medineh*, Catalogo del Museo Egizio di Torino, Serie prima, Monumenti e Testi 1 (Florence: Le Monnier, 1967), 158–64.

41 E.g., P.Amherst dem 46 + 55 and 53 + 54, dating to 150 BCE, in P.W. Pestman, *The Archive of the Theban Choachytes (Second Century B.C.): A Survey of the Demotic and Greek Papyri Contained in the Archive*, Studia Demotica 2 (Leuven: Peeters, 1993), 66–68, #10. A woman transfers to her stepson a quarter of his father's liturgies (mummies/tombs), to be shared with his two sisters. It is mentioned that the woman had a *sẖ n sʿnḫ* from her husband/their father and he had made a *sẖ ḏbꜣ ḥḏ* ("money document") to convey his liturgies to her to comply with the *sẖ n sʿnḫ*. This is summarized in Pestman, *Archive of the Theban Choachytes*, 229: a man "sold" some property, including some liturgies, to his second wife; a month later she sold her shares to her stepson.

42 P.DelM 18 = P.Turin Suppl 6113, dating to 112 BCE, from Thebes (Botti, *L'Archivio demotico da Deir el-Medineh*, 115–17), in which a woman cedes a cow and a donkey foal to a man in exchange for a she-ass he ceded to her.

43 Just as jobs (and wealth) passed from father to son or nephew to keep wealth and power in the family.

44 And most did, unless they specifically "opted out," as in the clear example of a son in a family of choachytes, who accepted the equivalent of his inheritance while his father was still alive and separated from the financial and business activities of his family; his children were subsequently disallowed from the family inheritance; see P.BM Dem 10413 and P.Leiden Dem 375, dating to 124 BCE (Pestman, *Archive of the Theban Choachytes*, 120–22, #31), being a receipt of a share of inheritance, where one brother acknowledges to his eldest brother his receipt of his share of the family inheritance, meaning he has no further claim on his father's estate; he left the family business and was bought off.

45 Land, houses, tombs/bodies (for mortuary priests to service), and so forth.

46 B.P. Muhs, "The Girls Next Door: Marriage Patterns among the Mortuary Priests in Early Ptolemaic Thebes," *Journal of Juristic Papyrology* 35 (2005): 169–94.

47 P.Hauswaldt, most recently republished by Joseph G. Manning, *The Hauswaldt Papyri: A Third Century B.C. Family Dossier from Edfu*, Demotische Studien 12 (Sommerhausen: Gisela Zauzich, 1997).

48 Pab(eḫt), the son of Parehu, was the buyer in six of the Hauswaldt documents and part of the group which purchased land at public auction in a seventh. Manning (p. 2), in his re-edition of the texts, says, "intra-family transfer of small plots of land" (including plots growing fruit trees) is the theme of these texts.

49 P.Hauswaldt 13 (= P.Berlin 11335), dating to 243–222 BCE, from Edfu, in Manning, *Hauswaldt Papyri*, 117–20.

50 P.Louvre 3266, dating to 197 BCE. See Françoise de Cenival, "Un acte de renonciation consécutif à un partage de revenus liturgiques memphites (P. Louvre E 3266)," *BIFAO* 71 (1972): 11–65.

51 P.DelM 25a-c = P.Turin 6077, 108 BCE, in Botti, *L'Archivio demotico da Deir el-Medineh*, 135–44.

52 P.DelM 28 = P.Turin Suppl 6104, dating to 109 BCE; see Botti, *L'Archivio demotico da Deir el-Medineh*, 151–52. In this document, the brother notes that both agree to the division of land their father gave them. In P.DelM 29 = P.Turin Suppl 6083, dating to 105 BCE, the two acknowledge her payment for her one-third share of the burial (expenses) of their father. See Botti, *L'Archivio demotico da Deir el-Medineh*, 153–54.

53 "Surplus of cultivation."

54 And women were never included as members in choachytes' guild associations [because it was formal/public?]. See Donker van Heel, "P. Louvre E 7858," 54n4; Muhs, *Tax Receipts*, 127, §6.1.B.2.

55 But see Muhs, *Tax Receipts*, 127, §6.1.B.1: "6. Prosopography and Provenance."

56 That women were never included in the formal associations contrasts with the very rare examples of women in religious guilds in the early Ptolemaic Fayum, as mentioned above, in the section "Women and Religion."

57 See, for example, P.Louvre 2429bis and P.Louvre 2428, cited in note 12, above, where the terminology *wpy(t) (n) wꜣḥ-mw* ("occupation of waterpourer") is used. There is also at least one document in which a woman is told not merely that she now owns choachytal (mortuary priest)

property, but "you will go to them [the tombs and mummies] [to do the work]." See Brian Muhs, "A Demotic Donation Contract from Early Ptolemaic Thebes (P. Louvre N. 3263)," in *Millions of Jubilees: Studies in Honor of David P. Silverman*, ed. Zahi A. Hawass and Jennifer Houser (Cairo: Supreme Council of Antiquities, 2010), 444.

58 P.DelM 15 = P.Turin Suppl 6095, dating to 114 BCE, in Botti, *L'Archivio demotico da Deir el-Medineh*, 107–108.

59 For example, P.Brooklyn 37.1802, dating to 108 BCE, from Memphis; see P.W. Pestman, *Recueil de textes démotiques et bilingues*, 3 vols. (Leiden: E.J. Brill, 1977), 1:31–43, and 2:42–49, #4), where a *sḥmt* says to a man entitled "merchant" (*šwt rmṯ Pr-hn-Ꞽnp nt ḥr nꜣ sḥn.w n Mn-nfr*): "You (m.) have given me the money equivalent of 3 1/2 *artaba*s of grain; I will give you that amount of grain at your house by" + a specific date. She can't claim she has paid without a receipt, and all she owns is set as security for her future (re)payment. P.DelM 14 = P.Turin Suppl 6108, dating to 114 BCE, from the Theban region: loan of 15 *artaba*s of wheat to a woman by a man. She says, "I will pay using the same measure you used and I will deliver to your house. If the loan is not repaid on time, I cede guarantees/security which are in your possession. If I pay on time, I get back my guarantees/security." See Botti, *L'Archivio demotico da Deir el-Medineh*, 105–106. Ostraca also frequently mention women owing or owed money; for example, Mattha, *Demotic Ostraca*, 175–76, #235, a grain loan from one woman to another. See M.A.A. Nur el-Din, *The Demotic Ostraca in the National Museum of Antiquities at Leiden* 1 (Leiden: Brill, 1974), 181–82, for an example of women owing money (#214); 85, for money received from women (#99); and 89–90, for a woman owed money (#105), and so forth.

60 P.Hauswaldt 18 dates to 212–211 BCE, and is from Edfu. See Manning, *Hauswaldt Papyri*, 140–49.

61 See note 32, above, for an example of a man handling his wife's property.

62 George R. Hughes and Richard Jasnow, *Oriental Institute Hawara Papyri: Demotic and Greek Texts from an Egyptian Family Archive in the Fayum (Fourth to Third Century B.C.)*, OIP 113 (Chicago: Oriental Institute of the University of Chicago, 1997, 27–32, text #5, dating to 259 BCE, from Hawara, Fayum.

63 Dating to 67 BCE, from Hawara. See Erich Lüddeckens, *Demotische Urkunden aus Hawara: Umschrift, Übersetzung, und Kommentar*, Verzeichnis der orientalischen Handschriften in Deutschland, Supplementband 28 (Stuttgart: F. Steiner, 1998), 237–43, #23.

64 His income as mortuary priest (*sꜥnḫ mr ḫtmw wyt*).

65 Both marriages reflected in marriage documents and in names and patronymics and joint business dealings where members of different families carry out joint business, purchase land and buildings together, and so forth.

66 Although it remained incumbent upon men to do so.

67 In addition, sometimes witnesses were relatives or colleagues of the people who made the contracts, but otherwise they may have been conscripted from among the people present in the venue where the contract was written—frequently a temple space but, in any case, a public place where women were not encouraged to gather.

68 Her mummy and mummy portrait are in the collections of Girton College, Cambridge; see, among others, https://www.bbc.com/news/uk-england-cambridgeshire-50757933.

69 For example, reading and writing letters, and so forth; see Jane Rowlandson, *Women and Society in Greek and Roman Egypt: A Sourcebook* (Cambridge and New York: Cambridge University Press, 1998), 284–304.

70 For example, between 160–134 BCE, scribes writing documents in two locations of the notarial office in Jeme (that is, Medinet Habu, West Bank, Thebes, and environs) signed their contracts with their official titles and stated that they wrote in the name of an individual with a feminine name and the title *tꜣ sẖ ḳnbt mḏꜣw* [*n*] *ḏḥwty ꜥꜣ ꜥꜣ ꜥꜣ nb Ḫmnw pꜣ nṯr ꜥꜣ* ("the (female) scribe of legal documents and divine books [of] Thoth, the triply great, the lord of Hermopolis, the great god"). That is, a male scribe was writing in the name of a "female head of office." The actual

name of only one of these two women is preserved: Tasherenkhonsu/(T)senchonsis, who bears the title *tꜣ ḥmt-nṯr n ḏmꜣ* ("the prophetess of the (temple of) Djeme") and was described as a *sḥmt n sꜥnḫ* ("endowed woman") and *šrt wꜥb Ꞽmn* ("daughter of a *wꜥb*-priest of Amun"). See Pestman, *Archive of the Theban Choachytes*, 64–68 (#9, #10), 85–86 (#15), 89–91 (#17). See also note 19, above, for the woman who apparently wrote a *mḳmḳ* ("petition") to the head of the Temple of Soknopaiu Nesos, in the Fayum.

71 Oaths were taken in the temple in the presence of and in the name of a deity, and they gained their effectiveness by the population's belief in the intervention of the gods in the world and in the lives of individuals.

72 Or stolen from her husband's house, although an "endowed woman" had a right to maintenance and some of her husband's or their joint property by virtue of her marriage document. One somewhat unusual document, O. Berlin 6170, has a woman swearing to a man not that she hasn't stolen from his house but "since you (m) came to my home, I have stolen nothing from you more than 1/12 *artaba* of grain for me and my children." She mentions the man's wife and claims she owes him no grain. If she takes the oath, he must leave her alone. See Ursula Kaplony-Heckel, *Die demotischen Tempeleide*, ÄA 6.1 (Wiesbaden: Harrassowitz, 1963), 206–207, #113.

73 J.D. Ray, *Demotic Papyri and Ostraca from Qasr Ibrim*, Texts from Excavations 13 (London: EES, 2005), 1–14. The text dates to the late Ptolemaic/early Roman period.

74 Kaplony-Heckel, *Die demotischen Tempeleide*, 340–41, #211. There are other instances where a man's wife is forced to subscribe to the man's oath or swear a related oath that the man's oath is true (e.g., P.Adler 28, dating to ca. 100 BCE, from Gebelein, in Kaplony-Heckel, *Die demotischen Tempeleide*, 74–76, #30).

75 Including debts owed from a deceased individual (e.g., O. Cairo MH 4249 dating to the Ptolemaic Period, from western Thebes/Medinet Habu). See Kaplony-Heckel, *Die demotischen Tempeleide*, 151.

76 On whether someone paid for grain, or sold grain they didn't own, or repaid too little, or claimed more of a crop than was their share, and so forth.

77 For example, "this door about which you (m.) fought with me, I guaranteed your brother for 23 deben and they brought me this door. There is no *ḳnbt*-document [i.e., contract] which he made for me for the 23 deben." If she takes the oath, they will give her the door. If not, then he will give her the 23 deben she swore about and he will own the door. See O. BMH 156 in Kaplony-Heckel, *Die demotischen Tempeleide*, 281–83, #1700.

78 Dating to the early Roman period, from Armant. See Kaplony-Heckel, "Die demotischen Tempeleide der Berliner Papyrussammlung," *FuB* 10 (1968), 175, #34.

79 Not infrequently, a woman received an oath about a relative—for example, a man must swear to a woman whether he had already paid her son for work done. See, for example, O. Cambridge (originally O. Gardiner), Ptolemaic, western Thebes/Djeme, in Kaplony-Heckel, *Die demotischen Tempeleide*, 122–24, #55.

80 O. TTO 104 and O. Bodl 1066+1067, Ptolemaic, first century BCE, from western Thebes/Djeme; see Kaplony-Heckel, *Die demotischen Tempeleide*, 211–12, #117A, B.

81 P.Rylands XXXVI (written on papyrus rather than the normal ostracon) is a very complicated situation involving a woman, monies, securities, and a mirror. A man demanded the woman make an oath to him about money. If the woman so swears, the man will give her a mirror. But he withdrew his demand for an oath after(?) she gave less money, and he gave her the mirror. See Kaplony-Heckel, *Die demotischen Tempeleide* 1, 284–90, #172.

82 And, plausibly, individual men could recede into the shadows if they were so inclined.

20

Shoes, Sickness, and Sisters: The (In)visibility of Christian Women from Late Antique Oxyrhynchus

AnneMarie Luijendijk

The aim of this contribution is to determine where and how women become visible in papyrus sources relating to Christians from the Middle Egyptian city of Oxyrhynchus, modern-day al-Bahnasa.[1] The half million papyri accidentally preserved on its ancient trash heaps make Oxyrhynchus the best-documented city from antiquity. Working at the intersection of papyrology, early Christian studies, and feminist historiography, I am particularly interested in Oxyrhynchus in the third and fourth centuries of our era, a turbulent time that witnessed impactful changes. This is the period when the people inhabiting the regions of the Roman Empire gradually shifted to favor Christianity. For this paper, I have selected documents that provide a glimpse into the lives of women.

Ever since their rediscovery in the nineteenth century, papyrus documents have greatly expanded our historical sources, proving a veritable treasure trove for scholars in multiple historical disciplines, including social history, economic history, religious history, and also women's history.[2] The papyri provide different perspectives from the grand narratives of the past narrated by elite historians—more a mishmash of often fragmentary documents that pertain to the minutiae of everyday life, such as tax records, census declarations, and private letters—and in these documents, women and nonelites turn up.

Yet overall, papyrus documentation is greatly biased toward males. Although women made up roughly half of the population in antiquity—demographers calculate perhaps 100 females to 108 males[3]—they are grossly underrepresented in the documentary record. A constellation of factors has rendered women largely invisible to us. The invisibility of women and those of lower status in literary texts and papyrus documents is a function of patriarchal society. This is exacerbated by the particularities of the written record: personal identification happens often through the patronymic in official documents; business, when documented, is often conducted between men, and so forth. In regard to the biases within papyrological texts, Roger Bagnall has noted that because papyrus documents require writing, they also favor the elite whose lifestyles involved business transactions and travel, leaving behind traces in the written record. The rich had both country estates and city residences, and thus reasons for back-and-forth communication between spouses or between owners and managers.[4] Lastly, the content of documentary papyri tends to be distorted toward the grotesque, such as petitions regarding theft or violence, and matters of great interest, such as someone falling ill.

In order to detect Christian women in papyrus documents, I rely on Melanie Johnson-DeBaufre's work on rendering invisible women visible in ancient sources. Then I zoom in on three instances where women feature in Christian papyri from Oxyrhynchus. In the first section, women remain anonymous or even unmentioned, but reading against the grain, we can sense their presence. The second section analyzes why women become disproportionately visible in instances of sickness. In the third section, I discuss three small archives of Christian papyri, where women appear in more than a single snapshot.

Visibility and Invisibility

In her essay "Gazing upon the Invisible," Johnson-DeBaufre points out the discrepancy between the presence of women in the archaeological record and the absence of women in literary texts. She notes:

> Observing these tensions between material visibility and discursive invisibility opens a valuable space for examining the relationship between archaeological research and early Christian historiography. Does research into the material culture of the ancient world mitigate, exacerbate, or ignore the routine erasure of wo/men's historical presence within the texts and histories of early Christianity?[5]

She concludes that "archaeological remains, ancient texts, and our own historiographies all require . . . looking around and away, in order to identify what has been rendered visible and invisible."[6] Johnson-DeBaufre exhorts scholars to study texts from the perspective of women. In this regard, the papyrological record itself occupies an interesting position: papyri are both archaeological artifacts and texts. Nevertheless, women are materially less visible here, too. Moreover, they have been less visible in the scholarship about Oxyrhynchus.

In this paper, I apply Johnson-DeBaufre's suggestions about "material visibility and discursive invisibility" to papyrus letters from Christians found at Oxyrhynchus dating to the third and fourth centuries. To this end, I analyze the instances in these select Oxyrhynchus papyri in which we see this dynamic interplay between the presence and invisibility of women.

Christian Oxyrhynchus

In recent years, multiple studies have appeared on the topic of Christian Oxyrhynchus:[7] Eldon Epp has published on multiple aspects of Christian Oxyrhynchus papyri, both literary and documentary, including text critical studies and larger social historical studies.[8] In *Greetings in the Lord: Early Christians and the Oxyrhynchus Papyri*, I analyzed Christians in documentary papyri in three spheres of life: the marketplace, the church, and the courtroom.[9] Lincoln Blumell, in his *Lettered Christians: Christians, Letters, and Late Antique Oxyrhynchus*, examined Christian letters from Oxyrhynchus from the third through the seventh centuries.[10] Finally, Blumell and Thomas Wayment collected all available evidence for Christians at Oxyrhynchus in their volume *Christian Oxyrhynchus: Texts, Documents, and Sources*.[11] Erica Mathieson's study on *Christian Women in the Greek Papyri of Egypt to 400 CE* also deserves mention here (she does not limit her discussion to Oxyrhynchus).[12]

Although the precise number of documents written by Christians is difficult to determine,[13] at least 107 documentary texts from Oxyrhynchus relate to persons identifiable as Christians in the period until roughly 400 CE.[14] Admittedly, this is a small and selective sample: these documents are from Oxyrhynchus, from a particular period, and with a certain Christian bias. Nevertheless, the figures are relevant. In seventy-eight of these 107 documents from Christian Oxyrhynchus, the names mentioned are exclusively male; women are not featured at all, remaining entirely invisible. Despite the reasons provided above for women's exclusion, and given that women make up roughly half of the population, this underrepresentation is quite shocking. There is, for instance, Leonides, the protagonist of an archive containing thirteen texts. We know his father's name, Theon, through the customary use of a patronymic, but nothing about women in their circles.[15] However, as Johnson-DeBaufre reminds us, the apparent invisibility of women does not mean that they were not there. And in twenty-nine documents from Christian Oxyrhynchus, women do become visible, some in sharper focus than others. Their appearances vary, from vague glimpses to letters written by women to women.

For those of us interested in women's history, this data set represents both bad and good news. Evidently, these women form only a tiny fraction of the total number of women that populated the city of Oxyrhynchus. In these ancient documents that were never intended for our eyes (and not even for preservation: they were discarded), a range of women appears, from young to old, sick to recently healthy, both named and unnamed, often in terms of familial relationship, whether these terms are used to indicate actual family members or other relatives or close friends.[16]

Our documents feature *mothers*, such as Maria, the mother of Papnuthis and Dorotheus (P.Oxy. XLVIII 3403); Zenobia, the mother of Maximus; another mother called Rufina (P.Oxy. XXXIV 2731);[17] and Hanou, the mother of Helene (P.Oxy. XXXIV 2729); *wives*, such as Maximus's wife Salamai (P.Oxy. XXXIV 2731); *sisters*, such as "our sister Taion," traveling from Herakleopolis to Oxyrhynchus (P.Oxy. XXXVI 2785), as well as Syras and her sister Theodora (P.Oxy. LIX 3998); and several sisters who are not mentioned by name: Ammonius's sisters (P.Oxy. XVII 2156), and Didyme and the sisters (P.Oxy. XIV 1774 and SB VIII 9746). There is also a *daughter*: "our daughter Germania," a traveler in need of assistance (P.Oxy. LVI 3857). Several women are listed with their professional titles: Theodora and Tauris are apotactic nuns (P.Oxy. XLIV 3203), Annis is a nun (PSI VI 698), Helene an embroideress (P.Oxy. LIX 4001), and Clematia a landlord (P.Oxy. XLVIII 3406, 3407).

Regularly, women of higher status appear: the nun Annis owns a house (PSI VI 698); the landlord Clematia communicates with subordinates (P.Oxy. XLVIII 3406, 3407); Aurelia Ptolemais comes from the ruling class (P.Oxy. XVI 1690),[18] and another high-status woman is referred to by a subordinate only as "our lady" (P.Oxy. VI 939). In none of these letters are enslaved women identified as such. This is part of the genre of letters; their writers have no reason to identify people by their legal status. This identification happens in census declarations and contracts. For instance, in a will belonging to the archive of Aurelia Ptolemais, an enslaved woman comes into view: Eunoia (P.Oxy. VI 907). Likewise, children and men of lower status equally remain mostly invisible to us in letters.

Many papyrus documents offer only a snapshot.[19] For most of the women mentioned above, their names are the main thing we know about them.[20] The context of the document can provide additional clues for their identities. Sometimes we know the names of one or more of a woman's relatives and a general indication of where and when she lived. In some cases, we may determine whether she is free or enslaved, from a high social status or a low one. In most cases, though, we have to make do with very little information about these women.

Invisible and Anonymous Women

Girly Slippers

A request for a specific pair of slippers near the end of a business exchange between two men suggests the presence of a woman or girl.[21] Although she remains invisible in this letter, reading against the grain renders her, or at least her special slippers, visible. The letter reads:

> Ptolemaeus to Thonius, his beloved brother, greetings in the Lord. Before all things I pray that you are well in soul and body. I want you to know that if you have not yet bought the linen yarn and the other things, do not buy (them). For the man gave up on it, as I said to you: "I do not want." And do not neglect to send the writing-tablet[22] immediately, and let me know to whom you want me to pay its price. Remember to buy me one pair of girlish, high quality shoes made of hair[23] and one Canopic (cake).[24] Greet my beloved Tithoes from me.
>
> (Verso) To Thonius his brother, from Ptolemaeus. (P.Oxy. LXI 4127).[25]

This is an example of a letter that features only men by name, in this case Ptolemaeus, Thonius, and Tithoes. This letter may belong to the Archive of Papnuthis and Dorotheus, to which I will return below in the section "Archive of Papnuthis and Dorotheus."[26] The sender, Ptolemaeus, bears a prevalent name that harkens back to the Macedonian past in Egypt. Thonius is an Egyptian, even local Oxyrhynchite name.[27] The name Thoonis/Thonius is associated with the god Horus, who was worshiped at Oxyrhynchus.[28] Yet the fact that Ptolemaeus calls Thonius a "beloved brother" suggests that he is not a Horus devotee but a Christian,[29] just as Ptolemaeus himself signals that he is a Christian by writing "greetings in the Lord" with a *nomen sacrum*. Thonius, "his beloved brother," may be a friend, business associate, employee, or slave; their connection to the Christian community remains unclear from this short exchange.

To call this "a Christian letter," as it is classified in the *editio princeps* in the Oxyrhynchus Papyri, is slightly misleading: the content does not deal with Christian matters but with business and goods. More accurately, it is a letter from a person who identifies as Christian about purchasing and sending goods.[30] Ptolemaeus tasks Thonius with several business transactions, including the cancellation of a business deal and the purchase of a writing tablet.

Just before he signs off, Ptolemaeus requests a pair of slippers that he describes in great detail with three adjectives: παρθενικὸν τέλειον σόλιον τρίχινον. Despite the specific description Ptolemaeus sent to Thonius, it is difficult for us to determine exactly what shoes he ordered, though presumably Thonius would have known. What kind of slippers are they and for whose feet are they intended? As we will see next, they offer a glimpse, a tiny footprint of an anonymous woman's identity: her pair of shoes.

The word σόλιον means "slipper," from the Latin *solea* (sole).[31] Writers of documents from Greco-Roman Egypt frequently mention shoes, often describing them with great specificity, including intended use and financial concerns.[32] Some distinguish between men's and women's shoes. A second-century list of goods, for instance, includes: "Eight pairs of male shoes and six pairs of women's."[33] And a woman called Thaisarion requests multiple pairs of sandals for different people: "4 pairs of sandals for Herais, 2 for Serenus, 1 (pair) for Ammonius, and 1 for Ch . . . ."[34] Mentioning these recipients by name probably serves to indicate their approximate shoe size. Other descriptions of shoes include the material with which they are made. This may indicate their style and intended use, cost, or provenance. One fourth-century list of goods mentions "four pairs of women's sandals made from papyrus."[35] Footwear is also described according to geographical region; a fifth-century document refers to "Armenian boots."[36]

In addition to mentions of shoes in papyrus documents, numerous examples of ancient shoes from all periods have been preserved in the archaeological record. For instance, in Egypt, papyrus shoes appear frequently and must have been relatively cheap. Elegant leather slippers with gold embossment must have been considerably more expensive.[37]

With this information on ancient shoes, we return to our papyrus letter: what kind of slippers did Ptolemaeus order and for whom? The interpretation hinges upon the meaning of the adjectives παρθενικός and τέλειος. Παρθενικός, -ή, -όν means "of or for a maiden"; it does not occur in other papyri. Τέλειος, -η, -ον ranges in meaning from size ("full-grown, adult") to quality ("complete," "perfect"); for the ancients, full grown, complete, perfect belong conceptually together, versus younger, inferior.[38] In papyrus documents, τέλειος occurs commonly as indication of size, either for a human adult, particularly regarding clothing,[39] or for a mature, full-grown animal.[40] But it can also signify quality; in several cases, τέλειος specifies a quality of leather, contrasted with ὑποδεέστερος, "inferior," and thus cheaper.[41] So did Ptolemaeus order maidenly (that is, monastic), adult-sized slippers or high-quality ones for a girl?

Simona Russo proposed that the slippers in this letter were for a nun about to enter the monastery, because of the sender's Christian identity.[42] According to Russo, the material, τρίχινος, "hair," would fit her monastic garb: "a pair of adult-sized nun-slippers made of hair."[43] A nun would not be out of place at Oxyrhynchus. In fact, Oxyrhynchus was renowned for its nuns; according to the author of the *Historia Monarchorum in Aegypto*, there were twenty thousand nuns in the city. While this number is certainly exaggerated, it still signals a large presence of female monastics in the city.[44] Multiple nuns appear in the papyrological record from Oxyrhynchus: for instance, the nun Annis, named as the owner of a property (PSI VI 698), and the sisters Theodora and Tauris, identified as "world-renouncing nuns" in a lease contract.[45] However, as far as I know, nuns did not receive special monastic shoes upon beginning their ascetic lives.[46] Moreover, the fact that the sender identifies as Christian in the greeting of the letter does not necessarily mean that we should view all the business directions through a Christian lens, despite the presence of nuns at Oxyrhynchus.[47]

I argue that the slippers were intended for a girl or young, adolescent woman. I take παρθενικός as the indication of size and perhaps style, and τέλειος as a quality of leather. This interpretation fits with the specifications about female and male shoes in papyri discussed above. Plutarch, for instance, describes a mantle for a girl as a παρθενικὸς χιτών.[48] Ptolemaeus thus asked for "girlish high-quality slippers made of hair."[49] Shoes have turned up frequently in the archaeological record in a range of sizes and quality, including smaller ones for children and adolescents.[50]

What "shoes made of hair" are is more difficult to determine.[51] The Louvre Museum has a worn slipper with a fur inside sole, where the foot would have rested on the animal hair.[52] Ptolemaeus may have ordered a particularly warm or soft slipper for this young woman.

When scholars turn to women, they focus often on women leaders or elite women. If women often remain invisible in the papyrological record (and in the archaeological or literary record for that matter), then how much more so children, especially girls or female adolescents![53] As feminist historians have long emphasized, the historical record is largely distorted in favor of elite men, minimizing women, children, and those of marginal status.[54] This is all the more striking when one considers that the ancient population was rather young.[55]

Children occasionally appear in the greetings sections of letters. For instance, a man named Dionysius writes: "Greet the children and the people in the house. Chaeremon and the children greet you" (and so forth) (P.Oxy. XXXVI 2787, second century). Moreover, the rare discovery of a toy reminds us of the ubiquitous and vibrant presence of children. A well-worn rag doll from Oxyrhynchus evokes images of a girl clutching her toy as she plays with a friend in a dusty courtyard, or comforting her as she goes to bed.[56]

On our quest toward visibility, let's notice that the girl for whom the shoes are requested is not explicitly mentioned. Ptolemaeus does not write: "Remember to buy me a pair of really nice slippers for my daughter so-and-so"; instead he names only the materials. We do not see the full person, we do not know the woman's name or age; we only see her feet or, more accurately, her shoes. It is not the case that Ptolemaeus did not appreciate this young woman, perhaps his daughter—at least, he seems to purchase shoes for her, and specific, high-quality ones at that. Letters are often reductionistic, insistent upon goods, measures, money, and delivery. Nevertheless, we do not hear her asking for shoes for herself; her needs are mediated through her father, who does not refer to her directly. When we ponder the visibility or invisibility of women, this line near the end of a business communication confronts us with the embeddedness of women and girls in households, a position that renders them marginal in letters such as these. In this letter, the girl or young woman is reduced to a shoe style.

Ammonius's Anonymous Sisters

In other cases, women appear as if in the background of a picture, at times barely visible. For instance, women remain anonymous in a communication between two men, Amyntas and Seras (P.Oxy. XVII 2156; late fourth or early fifth century).[57] Amyntas sends his greetings: "Salute Ammonius and his sisters" and continues: "Aurelius sends many greetings to you and to my lord brother Herminus and to Leon and to all ours (our relatives) in peace." This letter serves as an example of how women remain, if not entirely invisible, then still anonymous: all the males featured in this letter are mentioned by name, but the sisters remain anonymous; we catch only a glimpse of them.[58]

In Sickness and in Health

While women and girls often remain invisible or just barely visible in papyrus documents, in certain situations they become disproportionately visible, such as in matters related to illness and health.[59] Women appear at the extremities of matters of the body and emotion. Health is a prevalent topic in papyrus letters. Most letters open and close with wishes for health and well-being,[60] phrased as prayers (with the verb εὔχομαι).[61] These phrases are so customary that ancient epistolary theorists barely reflected upon them.[62] Even if they belong to ancient epistolary clichés, these greetings express a deep truth about the importance of health. This becomes especially evident when we contextualize the customary well wishes with the topic of sickness.[63]

The small corpus of Christian texts from Oxyrhynchus contains multiple references to women who are sick or have just recovered. In some cases, these women dealing with health issues are the main subject of the letters; in one case, we even encounter a woman narrating her illness in her own voice.[64]

In contrast to the low levels of visibility of women in the entire documentary record, sick women and children are relatively prominent in papyrus letters. In these documents, the content is quite sensitive: it is heartbreaking to read about an illness that has affected a loved one, or to feel the worry and desperation of the letter writer.

In one example from our sources, a certain Eudaimon writes to his mother, grandmothers, and Kyra: "Heraklammon really upset us when he came, as he said, 'Our sister Kyra has fallen ill,' but we give thanks to the divine providence that helps us everywhere and in everything that she too has recovered" (P.Oxy. LIX 4001).[65] Eudaimon names Kyra twice in the letter, in the address (line 2) and again in the body of the letter (line 9), when he refers to her sudden health scare—namely, that he had learned from Heraklammon that Kyra had been sick and recovered. Other than this, the letter offers us virtually no clues about who she is (but again, this was abundantly clear to the people corresponding). She may have been Eudaimon's sister or another female relative or friend. After expressing gratefulness for Kyra's healing, Eudaimon seamlessly continues with a list of business matters, including sending shoes (ὑποδήματα) among other clothing items (a purple cloak, no less). These items offer a glimpse into the lifestyle of an affluent family. In addition to expensive clothing and footwear, they also count at least five books among their possessions. Because these business matters feature so prominently in the document, it is unclear what prompted Eudaimon to send the letter—the business or Kyra's sickness; probably both. The remainder of the letter indicates that Eudaimon was a physician.[66] Even so, he attributes Kyra's recovery to God's providence, appealing to divine providence twice.[67] The example of Kyra in this letter (P.Oxy. LIX 4001) is representative of the many women in letters whose visibility, in a reductionistic fashion, is increased because of health issues.[68]

In another letter, a man named Demetrius reports to his lord Flavianus that "our lady has recovered from the sickness that overtook her" and urges his "lord" to come visit her, a visit that the lady eagerly anticipates (P.Oxy. VI 939).[69] We catch a relatable glimpse of a gravely ill woman anticipating her husband's arrival. Demetrius's emphasis on her impatience functions rhetorically to press Flavianus to come soon. This letter is among the very few private letters that contain a date: Pharmouthi 6 (April 1). The mention of the day and month signals Demetrius's professionalism as a writer. In addition, the date subtly underscores the urgency, how much the gravely ill woman anticipates Flavianus's arrival. Moreover, in case something happens to her in the meanwhile, Demetrius is covered by having specified when he composed the letter, especially since this was apparently not the first communication that went out to Flavianus.

In this educated and professional letter, Demetrius does not mention the woman's name. In this instance, it is not because he did not deem her important. On the contrary, Demetrius, who from the tone appears to be a subordinate, writes about her with a combination of respect and familiarity, addressing her by her title, "my lady."[70] Both Flavianus and Demetrius, of course, knew her name.[71] Here, it is not her marginality that causes her to remain anonymous, but her status as elite woman. She becomes a subject in the letter because of her ill health.

In yet another case, after reporting on business matters, a certain Copres urges his wife Sarapias to send one of their children, probably their daughter Maximina, to travel from Oxyrhynchus to Alexandria with her grandmother to seek a cure for an eye disease, writing:

> write us about the well-being of you all and how Maximina has been, and Asena. And if it is possible, let her/him come with your mother so that her/his leucoma may be healed. For I have seen other people (that had been) healed. I pray for your (sgl.) health. (P.Oxy. XXXI 2601)

Once more, the information about these women is primarily health related, in both wishes for health and dealing with illness. So far, the letters we examined all had male senders. Now, we turn to a letter that features a woman's first-person account.

"I Am Terribly Ill": A First-person Account from a Woman Regarding Her Illness

"I write this to you in sickness, being terribly ill, unable even to rise from my bed because I am terribly ill" (P.Oxy. VIII 1161).[72] Although the feminine participles throughout the letter indicate that the sender is a woman, in an ironic turn of events, this woman remains nameless through an accident of material preservation: the top part of her letter has broken off, so that we lack the address with the names of the sender and addressees. The first preserved lines, ". . . (to our God) and gracious savior and to his beloved Son, that they all may succor our body, soul, and spirit," establish this as a Christian letter, not just a business letter with *nomina sacra* (as we encountered above). As in the case with Eudaimon, the sender appeals to the deity, in this case the Trinity, for help in her illness.[73]

Letters written by women are perhaps the closest we can get to women's voices. Roger Bagnall and Raffaela Cribiore have collected and analyzed Greek and Coptic letters from Egypt written or sent by women. As they note, "the letters are the one genre in which women are definitely expressing themselves on their own behalf and not through a male who controls the representation of their thought. . . . this is true even where a woman has used dictation in order to have her words recorded on papyrus."[74] Among the Oxyrhynchite letters from Christians, it is relatively rare to have a letter sent by a woman; in addition to P.Oxy. VIII 1161, there are only five others.[75] How do we reconstruct the writing scene of this document? Since our sender emphasizes that she feels too sick to get up from her bed,[76] I assume that she did not write the letter herself, but that she dictated these sentences from her bed to a scribe.[77] While the end of the letter is damaged, a clear reference to her illness appears again ("before I became ill"). As with the other letters we have examined so far in this section, in P.Oxy. VIII 1161, a woman, this time in her own voice, rises to visibility because of her body. It is striking that these women are only rendered visible on the brink of death.

Context of Health

In our modern context, the wellness dichotomy is between health and sickness; in antiquity, according to Helen King, the dichotomy was between health and death: "When the focus is on *disease*, the outcome of the case can only be one of two options; either health, or death."[78] Falling ill in antiquity meant facing the real possibility of death. We can feel this life-threatening aspect of illness lurking in the background of many of these messages: Demetrius urges Flavianus in multiple messages to visit his sick wife, something that she eagerly anticipates (P.Oxy. VI 939); Eudaimon expresses grave concern upon hearing about Kyra's illness and great relief when she recovers (P.Oxy. LIX 4001); and the anonymous woman emphasizes in her letter the severity of her illness, such that she cannot get up from bed (P.Oxy. VIII 1161).

This general paradigm for health and sickness also explains the association with religion and the divine that we encounter in these letters. Even a physician, Eudaimon, attributes Kyra's recovery not to medicine, but to divine providence. In the fragmented opening of the letter, the anonymous woman refers to the Trinity (P.Oxy. 1161). Other letters refer to health by the word σωτηρία (P.Oxy. XXXI 2609; P.Oxy. VI 939), a term frequently translated as "salvation" in other contexts.[79] In other words, health is so crucial that the word used for it also has the theological meaning of salvation.

According to Ric Barrett-Lennard, in the third and fourth centuries the Egyptian church developed special attention to care for the sick. His argument is based on a comparison between church orders and plays out both on the level of the community and also the bishop and specially appointed charismatic healers.[80] In contrast, in these few Christian letters, women's health appears from a personal perspective: Demetrius, writing to Flavianus, expects the visit of the relatives, not of the bishop or other church members (P.Oxy. VI 939). The letters thus offer a different, complementary side to this story of early Christianity in Egypt.[81]

Women's visibility with regard to health issues does not imply that women or Christians were more prone to illness than others. But given that so few women appear in papyrus documents, why do so many of the visible women in our papyri suffer illnesses? To answer this question, we have to examine the distortion of our evidence—distortion due to both genre and gender assumptions.

The first distortion of evidence involves the genre of letter writing: our documentation is distorted because health-related information is newsworthy. Papyrus letters, as a mode of communication between two distant parties, largely concern the sending of goods and business or personal information. The visibility of women in instances of poor health signals that women are left out of the epistolary conversation unless a significant life event occurs. In these cases, mostly men report about sick women, and often embed this information within correspondence relating to business matters. However, as in P.Oxy. VIII 1161, some women write themselves. In this letter, we hear one Christian woman, who unfortunately remains anonymous, describe how her own health has taken a turn for the worse. Given the relation of health and death in antiquity, her emphasis on her poor health reads like an emergency.

The second way that evidence is distorted toward sick women involves sociocultural assumptions about women, notions still operative today. Helen King reminds us that "in pharmaceutical research, there is a long tradition of seeing men as the norm, and women as a variation of that norm."[82] Taken together, these relatively frequent mentions of sick women in papyrus letters are partly due to the fact that women are rarely mentioned when healthy because health is the norm.

Sisters

Thus far, we have examined glimpses of women in individual letters. In many cases these women remain entirely anonymous and the accompanying details of their lives myopic, as in the case of the pair of slippers and reports of illness.

For this final portion of my paper, I expand our scope by examining three small Oxyrhynchite archives that feature Christian women: the Archive of Papnuthis and Dorotheus, the Archive of Didyme and the Sisters, and the Archive of Aurelia Ptolemais. Archives—that is, several documents preserved together—offer clearer visibility because they allow us to see beyond a single moment in time.[83] As Katelijn Vandorpe remarks: "Documentary papyri lead us into the living rooms of ancient people. Where unrelated texts are like instant snapshots, archives present a coherent film of a person, a family, or a community and may span several months, years, or decades."[84] In these three instances, we encounter multiple women by name.

Archive of Papnuthis and Dorotheus

The substantial archive of Papnuthis and Dorotheus consists of fifty-three documents from roughly the second half of the fourth century, centering around its two protagonists. The texts therein feature at least eleven women, including Maria, their mother.[85] In a letter addressed to his parents, Aphynchis and Maria, Papnuthis greets a host of people, including numerous women and also children:

> I greet my lady wife Apias, I greet my lady sister Tereous, I greet my lord brother Gerontius, I greet my master brother Dorotheus, I greet my sister Euethis, I greet my lady sister Mikke, I greet Choüs and his wife Herakleia and her children, may the evil eye not touch them. I greet my father Ammonius (*or* Ammonion), I greet Tasilbanis and her children, may the evil eye not touch them. I greet my father Petemounius and my mother Taësis and her children, may the evil eye not touch them. I greet my lady and sister Palladia, I greet all those who love us by name. (P.Oxy. XLVIII 3396)

This letter stands out among other letters in the fact that it mentions more women by name than men. All in all, Papnuthis mentions by name in this letter nine women, including his mother, and five men, including his father. Three times he includes children with their mother's name (not their own names), and a protecting vow: "may the evil eye not touch them." His social circle included at least twenty persons. Papnuthis addresses most of them in familial terms, but it remains unclear to us how these people relate to each other. Presumably Aphynchis and Maria are his parents, indeed, but for the other brothers, sisters, fathers, and mothers listed here, the relationship is unknown, beyond that they belong to the larger familial and social circle.

Of particular interest in the archive of Papnuthis and Dorotheus are two letters from a landlady named Clematia, because, in this case, the woman is the sender. In this correspondence, the class distinction is clear: Clematia orders Papnuthis, and elsewhere, Papnuthis and another man, Hatres, to do several jobs. She writes:

> From Clematia, landlady, to Papnuthis, caretaker at Sadalu, greeting. Measure out six *artabas* of wheat and lentils into Pagas's skiff so that we may have it here, and assist Pagas so that we may have the extra payments of the vintage here, and try also to bring wool up with the boat, and do not delay because of the baked brick. And collect from Paymis the two *ceramia* of honey for the festival as well as the honey cakes (*or* -combs), and from Pagas the wool. (P.Oxy. XLVIII 3406)

In the second letter, the landlady (presumably Clematia again) refers to Sunday, as she urges Papnuthis and Hatres to execute a job "today" (P.Oxy. XLVIII 3407). This is the first reference to Sunday in papyrus documents.[86]

Besides Clematia's matter-of-fact reference to Sunday, the Christian character of these letters is not so obvious. The writers do not use *nomina sacra*, but Papnuthis does refer to Divine Providence. Also included within this archive is a letter from Thonius to his wife Thecla, and possibly the one from Ptolemaeus to Thonius, discussed above, regarding the slippers.[87] The Christian names for women, Maria and Thecla, are noteworthy, indicating that they came from Christian families, with parents who bestowed these names upon them.[88]

Didyme and the Sisters

The second archive is a small dossier of two letters, dated around the year 340,[89] from Didyme and the sisters.[90] Both letters are written and sent by a woman called Didyme, who also includes in both letters "sisters" as senders (Διδύμη καὶ αἱ ἀδελφαί, P.Oxy. XIV 1774 and SB VIII 9746).[91] From the evidence, we may conclude that Didyme is a literate woman who communicates with a large network of women and men about goods and business transactions.

Didyme writes to Atienatia:

> To my lady sister Atienatia, Didyme and the sisters (send) greetings in the Lord. First of all it is necessary to greet you, praying that you are well. Write to us, my lady, concerning your health and whatever orders you need, with full liberty. Let us know if you received your orders. There is a balance with us from the money of your orders, I believe, of

1,300 denarii. Canopic cakes received for you from them will be dispatched. Greet my blessed lady sister Asous and her mother and . . .

(Address): To my lady sister Atienatia, Didyme with the sisters.[92]

The second letter from Didyme and the sisters is longer, mentioning more women and also men, and numerous goods including "2 pairs of sandals which were bought directly from the weavers," "a large ostrich egg and a small basket containing Syrian palm dates," "a head cover," and again, "2 canopic cakes."[93]

In comparison to the majority of papyrus letters in which women are absent or are only featured anonymously, the letters from Didyme and the sisters are refreshingly different. They introduce us to Didyme in her own voice and her own handwriting. Her letters also mention many women by name: Atienatia, lady sister Asous and her mother, Sophias, another Didyme, Valeriane, Bikentia, Loukila, Bikeutia, Italia, and Theodora. Didyme does not exclusively mention women either; the greetings contain a mix of women and men. That these women are mentioned by name in these letters alongside men indicates something about social situations and networks. Yet how precisely we should situate this circle of women is debated. Some scholars claim that Didyme and the sisters are ascetics, while others argue that the letters can be read as regular business communications. Again, as we saw above, Oxyrhynchus is renowned for its female ascetics in the *Historia Monachorum*. If Didyme and her companions are ascetic sisters, then these letters form the earliest evidence for nuns at Oxyrhynchus; however, the current evidence is inconclusive. These kinds of communications involving goods are common, as we already noticed in the small sample of letters quoted here. The only uncommon element in this correspondence is the inclusion of sisters in the address.[94] This raises larger questions about how we read women when they do emerge with their own network or business.

Aurelia Ptolemais

The final Oxyrhynchus archive we will examine features a third Christian woman named Aurelia Ptolemais.[95] As Bagnall has shown, her archive comprises several literary and documentary papyri, including a bookroll of the *Kestoi* by the Christian author Julius Africanus and the will of her parents.[96] The possession of a text from a Christian author and the phraseology of Ptolemais's parents hint that the family may have been Christian.[97]

Ptolemais signed her name at the bottom of the land lease (P.Oxy. XVI 1690: Αὐρηλία Πτολεμαῒς καὶ ὡς χρηματ[ίζω] ἔσχον τούτου τὸ ἴσον). She was a wealthy, literate woman, from one of the leading families of

Oxyrhynchus,[98] and she lived in a wealthy neighborhood in Oxyrhynchus.[99] Women from this socioeconomic milieu could often read and write.[100]

Ptolemais is not the only Christian woman in our papyri who owned books. A short letter asking a woman to lend out a book indicates at least a second female book owner. In fact, of the three known owners of Christian books from Oxyrhynchus that I was able to identify, two are women.[101]

Finally, it is important that the documentation from this elite family also brings into view an enslaved woman called Eunoia. Her name, εὔνοια, means "goodwill, favor," a term often taken as an equivalent of "loyalty." The name expresses the owner's wish for the slave, signaling the insidiousness of the slave system. Eunoia is bequeathed to Ptolemais by the latter's father. She becomes visible to us because the will lists her as property.

Conclusions

Let us return to the question posed at the beginning of this paper, about how examining these papyrus letters, representing at the same time written and material evidence from ancient Egypt, contributes to our understanding of Christian Egyptian women, and what additional challenges and questions emerge to complicate this question further.[102] This piece has honed in on letters from Oxyrhynchus written by Christians that feature women in some way. This subsection of letters, although narrow and specific, provided ample evidence to sift through. I organized them into three parts: anonymous women (sisters, nuns, women with professions, women of higher statuses, the girl or woman who will receive the shoes), sick women (mentioned by men or even writing themselves), and women from small archives within the Oxyrhynchus collection (a literate woman, a landlady).

Many Christian documents from Oxyrhynchus are exchanges between men exclusively and do not feature women. In numerous ways, the papyrological evidence is distorted or, perhaps, all too faithful a representation of the society. The visibility or invisibility of women is a consequence of a combination of factors, including the genre of papyrus letters, focused primarily on goods, the general marginalization of women, and the fact that these letters are exchanged between familiar people. In these papyrological texts, we encounter a constellation of features that affected women in their everyday lives that rendered them invisible and/or anonymous to us. In all these instances, we should realize that even the men who do not refer to women at all or by name knew many women by name. The methodological principle that women were present applies even if they are not directly visible in the material record.

For other women, we know only their names, sometimes the names of one or more of their relatives, and a general indication of where and when they lived. Even so, enough women do appear that we can begin to construct the contours of their lives.

In our first example, Ptolemaeus insists on a very specific pair of slippers for a girl, possibly his daughter. The detailed description of the slippers, receiving three adjectives, stands in sharp contrast to the anonymity of the intended recipient of the shoes. Feminist scholars have long pointed out the absence of women in written sources and monumental archaeology. Here, the request for special slippers offers only a brief glimpse of a girl's presence. We can assume her existence but we do not know her name or age. Nevertheless, her—probably elite—father orders high-quality, warm shoes. We discover her presence at the margins of the letter itself, appearing near the end. And so the request for the slippers symbolizes her status: taken care of, but marginalized. Her not-to-be-forgotten slippers leave us a hint of the feet that once filled them.

In the evidence examined, we have witnessed snapshots of the lives of women, some distant and out of focus, others up close. We have discovered that women owned and read literature; they were nuns; they traveled alone; they had children and husbands, and purchased and sold goods. Women owned houses and stables. We learned that one woman is a landlady, and that several of the women suffer illness.[103] The images of these women, both sharp and blurred, consist of nuns, mothers, wives, girls, sisters, landladies, ladies, travelers, and entrepreneurs.

In many cases, the appearance of the women should be understood as significant life events, not accidents or everyday things. Often, women are defined in relation to men and/or in terms of the state of their bodies. Women can remain invisible and nameless because they are not part of the conversation, deemed unimportant or irrelevant. Multiple women also remain nameless because they are referred to by their titles: Eudaimon to his mother and grandmothers (and Kyra) (P.Oxy. LIX 4001); Demetrius's "our lady," (P.Oxy. VI 939). In other cases, the material preservation of the papyri has rendered women anonymous. Even where women are the senders of their letters, in the preservation of the texts as material artifacts, their names have been lost.[104]

From an onomastic point of view, most of the women mentioned explicitly in these texts have Greek or Roman names; few have Egyptian names. In the Archive of Papnuthis and Dorotheus, women appear with Christian names, including Maria and Thecla. Other Christian women have pagan names (Didyme, Sarapias), as do the men.

The rise of Christianity in Egypt had a recognizable impact on the lives of women. For instance, several nuns appear in papyri. These ascetics have a profession that causes them to stand out: they are adopted into the bureaucracy of the documentary record. In two instances, nuns are mentioned in relation to their property: Annis, and Theodora and Tauris, the daughters of Silvanus.[105] But compared to the women of previous generations, Christian women suffered a loss of representation by not being able to function as priestesses.[106]

Needless to say, the nature of how we encounter women in our sources is complex and limited. For instance, beyond Eunoia in Aurelia Ptolemais's archive, I could not identify an enslaved woman in these private letters, although a significant portion of the population was enslaved in this period and the type of families that corresponded through letters—that is, educated, literate Oxyrhynchites—in all likelihood owned other people. Possibly, these enslaved women and men are grouped together anonymously under the phrases "all those in your house." In the shades of invisibility, this is particularly striking. The only enslaved woman in evidence, Eunoia, appeared in the will of Aurelia Ptolemais' parents, who willed her as a piece of property to their daughter.

Our papyri offer us glimpses into the lives of Egyptian Christian women from long ago: in one case, a girl eagerly awaits a nice pair of slippers; in another, a woman is so sick she cannot leave her bed. Elite and educated women penned their own letters, corresponded about luxury goods, instructed subordinate men to do jobs, and owned and read books. Although multiple historical and societal forces combined to render them invisible, several women have become briefly visible to us in the papyrus documents from ancient Oxyrhynchus.

Appendix: Documents from Oxyrhynchus with Christian Affiliation Featuring Women (until ca. 400)

1. P.Laur. II 42 Letter about a request for help on reused papyrus
2. P.Oxy. VI 903 Affidavit against a husband
3. P.Oxy. VI 907 Will of Hermogenes
4. P.Oxy. VI 939 Demetrius to Flavianus
5. P.Oxy. VIII 1151 Amulet for Joannia
6. P.Oxy. VIII 1161 Letter from a sick woman
7. P.Oxy. XII 1592 Woman to her father
8. P.Oxy. XIV 1690 Lease of land
9. P.Oxy. XIV 1774 Didyme and the sisters to Atienateia
10. P.Oxy. XVII 2156 Amyntas to Seras
11. P.Oxy. XVIII 2193 Theon to Pascentius

12. P.Oxy. XXXI 2601 Copres to Sarapias
13. P.Oxy. XXXI 2609 Membrion (?) to his sister
14. P.Oxy. XXXIV 2729 Akyleus to Dioscourides
15. P.Oxy. XXXIV 2731 Maximus to his mother Zenobia
16. P.Oxy. XXXVI 2785 Presbyters of Heracleopolis to Papa Sotas
17. P.Oxy. XLIV 3203 Lease mentioning apotactic nuns
18. P.Oxy. XLVIII 3396 Letter from Papnuthis to his parents
19. P.Oxy. XLVIII 3403 Letter from Maria to Papnuthis
20. P.Oxy. XLVIII 3406 Letter from Clematia to Papnuthis
21. P.Oxy. XLVIII 3407 Letter from the landlady to Papnuthis and Hatres
22. P.Oxy. LVI 3857 Letter of recommendation for Germania
23. P.Oxy. LIX 3998 Thoonis to Syras and Callinicus
24. P.Oxy. LIX 4001 Eudaimon to his mother, grandmothers, and Cyra
25. P.Oxy. LXI 4127 Christian letter: Ptolemaeus to Thonis
26. P.Oxy. LXIII 4365 Christian book exchange
27. PSI VI 698 Division of property mentioning a nun
28. SB VIII 9746 Didyme and the sisters to Sophias
29. SB XXII 15359 = P.Oxy. I 182 descr. Thonius to Thecla

Notes

1 My warm thanks to Mariam Ayad for organizing a great conference and for her care and hospitality toward me, including a wonderful visit to the site of Oxyrhynchus. I also presented this paper at Oxford University, and thank Hindy Najman, Constanze Guethenke, and other participants for the discussion. Roger Bagnall and Melanie Johnson-DeBaufre, whose work has been important for me in crafting this piece, gave me helpful feedback for which I am very grateful. I thank Elizabeth Bolton and Suzanne Churchill for their warm and wise support, and my research assistants Esther Levy, JP O'Connor, and Andrea Peecher for their help in multiple ways. Shortcomings obviously remain my own. Papyrological databases Papyri.info and Trismegistos have been instrumental in conducting my research. I sincerely thank the scholars who compile and maintain them. On Trismegistos, see M. Depauw and T. Gheldof, "Trismegistos: An Interdisciplinary Platform for Ancient World Texts and Related Information," in *Theory and Practice of Digital Libraries—TPDL 2013 Selected Workshops*, ed. Ł. Bolikowski, V. Casarosa, P. Goodale, N. Houssos, P. Manghi, and J. Schirrwagen, Communications in Computer and Information Science 416 (Cham: Springer, 2014), 40–52.

2 Important studies on women in papyrus documents include Jane Rowlandson, ed., *Women and Society in Greek and Roman Egypt: A Sourcebook* (Cambridge and New York: Cambridge University Press, 1998); and Roger Bagnall and Raffaella Cribiore, *Women's Letters from Ancient Egypt, 300 BC–AD 800* (Ann Arbor: University of Michigan Press, 2006). See also Katelijn Vandorpe and Sofie Waebens, "Women and Gender in Roman Egypt: The Impact of Roman Rule," in *Tradition and Transformation: Egypt under Roman Rule*, ed. K. Lembke, M. Minas-Nerpel, and S. Pfeiffer (Leiden: Brill, 2010), 415–35.

3 Determining the sex ratio in Roman Egypt is quite complex. Roger Bagnall and Bruce Frier cautiously conclude that "the overall Egyptian sex ratio was . . . probably between 100 and 120," and "the overall sex ratio . . . around 108, similar to that of present-day India"; Roger S. Bagnall and Bruce W. Frier, *The Demography of Roman Egypt*, Cambridge Studies in Population, Economy, and Society in Past Time 23 (Cambridge: Cambridge University Press, 1994), 95.

4 Roger S. Bagnall, *Reading Papyri, Writing Ancient History* (London: Routledge, 1995), 13–16; Roger S. Bagnall, *Reading Papyri, Writing Ancient History* (London: Routledge, 2019), 12–13; AnneMarie Luijendijk, *Greetings in the Lord: Early Christians and the Oxyrhynchus Papyri*, Harvard Theological Studies 60 (Cambridge, MA: Harvard University Press, 2008), 3.

5 Melanie Johnson-DeBaufre, "'Gazing upon the Invisible': Archaeology, Historiography, and the Elusive Wo/Men of I Thessalonians," in *From Roman to Early Christian Thessalonike: Studies in Religion and Archaeology*, ed. L. Nasrallah, C. Bakirtzis, and S.J. Friesen (Cambridge, MA: Harvard University Press, 2010), 74.

6 Johnson-DeBaufre, "Gazing upon the Invisible," 103.

7 Other studies focusing on different aspects of the Oxyrhynchus papyri include, for instance, Alan K. Bowman, Revel A. Coles, Nicolaos Gonis, Dirk Obbink, and Peter J. Parsons, *Oxyrhynchus: A City and Its Texts*, Graeco-Roman Memoirs 93 (London: EES, 2007); Peter J. Parsons, *City of the Sharp-nosed Fish: Greek Lives in Roman Egypt* (London: Weidenfeld and Nicolson, 2007); Peter Sarris, *Economy and Society in the Age of Justinian* (Cambridge: Cambridge University Press, 2006); T.M. Hickey, *Wine, Wealth, and the State in Late Antique Egypt: The House of Apion at Oxyrhynchus*, New Texts from Ancient Cultures (Ann Arbor: University of Michigan Press, 2012); Giovanni Roberto Ruffini, *Social Networks in Byzantine Egypt* (Cambridge: Cambridge University Press, 2008); Jane Rowlandson, *Landowners and Tenants in Roman Egypt: The Social Relations of Agriculture in the Oxyrhynchite Nome*, Oxford Classical Monographs (Oxford: Clarendon Press; New York: Oxford University Press, 1996).

8 See his collected essays: Eldon Jay Epp, *Perspectives on New Testament Textual Criticism: Collected Essays, 1962–2004* (Leiden and Boston: Brill, 2005); also Eldon Jay Epp, "The Oxyrhynchus New Testament Papyri: 'Not Without Honor Except in Their Hometown'?," *JBL* 123, no. 1 (2004): 5–55; Eldon Jay Epp, "The Jews and the Jewish Community in Oxyrhynchus: Socio-religious Context for the New Testament Papyri," in *New Testament Manuscripts: Their Texts and Their World*, ed. T.J. Kraus and T. Nicklas, Texts and Editions for New Testament Study 2 (Leiden and Boston: Brill, 2006), 13–52.

9 Luijendijk, *Greetings in the Lord.*

10 Lincoln H. Blumell, *Lettered Christians: Christians, Letters, and Late Antique Oxyrhynchus*, New Testament Tools, Studies, and Documents 39 (Leiden and Boston: Brill, 2012).

11 Lincoln H. Blumell and Thomas A. Wayment, eds., *Christian Oxyrhynchus: Texts, Documents, and Sources* (Waco, TX: Baylor University Press, 2015). On Christian literary papyri from Oxyrhynchus, see also Brent Nongbri, *God's Library: The Archaeology of the Earliest Christian Manuscripts* (New Haven: Yale University Press, 2018), 216–46, ch. 6: "Excavating Christian Litter and Literature at Oxyrhynchus."

12 Erica A. Mathieson, *Christian Women in the Greek Papyri of Egypt to 400 CE*, SAA 6 (Turnhout: Brepols, 2014). Specific studies on Oxyrhynchite women include AnneMarie Luijendijk, "A Gospel Amulet for Joannia (P. Oxy. VIII 1151)," in *Daughters of Hecate: Women and Magic in the Ancient World*, ed. K.B. Stratton and D.S. Kalleres (Oxford: Oxford University Press, 2014), 418–43; AnneMarie Luijendijk, "'Twenty Thousand Nuns': The Domestic Virgins of Oxyrhynchos," in *Christianity and Monasticism in Middle Egypt: Al-Minya and Asyut*, ed. G. Gabra and H. Takla (Cairo: American University in Cairo Press, 2015), 57–68.

13 Multiple scholars have discussed criteria for determining what counts as a Christian document, a topic I will not rehearse here. On this, in addition to the studies by Epp, Luijendijk, Blumell, and Blumell and Wayment cited above, see also Malcolm Choat, *Belief and Cult in Fourth-century Papyri*, SAA 1 (Sydney: Ancient History Documentary Research Centre, 2006); Giuseppe Ghedini, *Lettere cristiane dai papiri greci del III e IV secolo*, Pubblicazioni della Università catt. s. cuore. [ser. 4] Sez. Filologica 1 (Milan: Aegyptus, 1923); Giuseppe Tibiletti, *Le lettere private nei papiri greci del III e IV secolo d.C.: tra paganesimo e cristianesimo*, Scienze Filologiche e Letteratura 15 (Milan: Vita e Pensiero, 1979). On issues of Christian identity more generally, see also Éric Rebillard, *Christians and Their Many Identities in Late Antiquity, North Africa, 200–450 CE*

(Ithaca and London: Cornell University Press, 2012); Éric Rebillard, "Conversion and Burial in the Late Roman Empire," in *Conversion in Late Antiquity and the Early Middle Ages: Seeing and Believing*, ed. K. Mills and A. Grafton, Studies in Comparative History, Essays from the Shelby Cullom Davis Center for Historical Studies (Rochester, NY: University of Rochester Press, 2003), 61–83; Éric Rebillard, "Everyday Christianity in Carthage at the Time of Tertullian," *Religion in the Roman Empire* 2 (2016): 91–102.

14 Using Lincoln Blumell and Thomas Wayment's collection on *Christian Oxyrhynchus* (excluding the libelli since they do not feature Christians) gives fifty-three documents. There are no Coptic texts from Oxyrhynchus featuring women from this period. I have added the entire archive of Papnuthis and Dorotheus, consisting of fifty-three papyri (including four that probably belong to the archive), published chiefly in P.Oxy. XLVIII. I discuss the archive in more detail at the end of this chapter. Blumell and Wayment included one of the documents from this archive in their collection. The names of the protagonists (Papnuthis, Dorotheus, and their mother Maria) indicate that they are a Christian family, and two of the papyri in that archive contain more explicit references. On the content of the archive, see also Trismegistos Archives. I have also included two documents from the Archive of Aurelia Ptolemais.

15 AnneMarie Luijendijk, "A New Testament Papyrus and Its Documentary Context: An Early Christian Writing Exercise from the Archive of Leonides (P. Oxy. II 209/P10)," *JBL* 129 (2010): 575–96.

16 On the use of familial forms of address for nonrelatives, see Eleanor Dickey, "Literal and Extended Use of Kinship Terms in Documentary Papyri," *Mnemosyne* 57, no. 2 (2004): 131–76.

17 P.Oxy. XXXIV 2731, Maximus to his Mother Zenobia; see also Blumell and Wayment, *Christian Oxyrhynchus*, 605–608. This is a fascinating letter. It reads in translation: "To my lady mother Zenobia, Maximus (sends) greetings in the Lord God. Now at last I have found the opportunity which I have prayed of finding someone who is visiting you and of greeting your inimitable disposition. Greet my wife Salamai for me. My mother Rufina sends her best wishes to you. Greet my brothers for me, each by name. Once, twice, three times I have told you to send my wife and you have refused. Well now, exert yourself night and day to send my wife for she is my pride and joy! As for my visiting you (pl.), you (pl.) have known for a long time that my lord the *praepositus* is not releasing anyone. I implore you, write back to me about your health so that being unburdened I may be of good cheer. I greet all those who love you, each by name. Farewell, I pray for you (pl.) often." Maximus mentions his mother Zenobia, his wife Salamai, another mother Rufina. He admonishes Zenobia to send him his wife. It is remarkable that he does not write this to his wife herself. Did he also write to her in another letter? Why is Zenobia not sending the wife? Are there children? If so, Maximus does not mention them. The mother seems to be the head of the family since he addresses her. No matter how much he longs for his wife, he deals with his mother on matters concerning her.

18 See discussion below.

19 Also, for instance, Katelijn Vandorpe, "Archives and Dossiers," in *The Oxford Handbook of Papyrology*, ed. Roger S. Bagnall (Oxford and New York: Oxford University Press, 2009), 216.

20 Again, with Johnson-DeBaufre, regarding the documents without female names: that absence does not mean that women also were absent.

21 P.Oxy. LXI 4127, "Christian letter: Ptolemaeus to Thonius," ed. Traianos Gagos; TM no. 33609. Blumell and Wayment, *Christian Oxyrhynchus*, 497–500n138. I accept the dating of the *editio princeps* as "first half of the fourth century"; Blumell and Wayment propose a slightly earlier date ("third century and the first quarter of the fourth century"), Blumell and Wayment, *Christian Oxyrhynchus*, 497. If the document indeed belongs to the Archive of Papnuthis and Dorotheus (on which, see below), then the fourth-century date fits better.

22 The word **πίναξ** signifies a "board, plank," hence a "drawing or writing tablet," or a "trencher, platter" or "plate with anything drawn or engraved on it" (LJS). Gagos renders it as "dish"; Reinard proposes "writing tablet?" ("Schreibtafel?"); Gagos, P.Oxy. LXI 4129, 126; Patrick

Reinard, *Kommunikation und Ökonomie: Untersuchungen zu den privaten Papyrusbriefen aus dem kaiserzeitlichen Ägypten*, Pharos Studien zur griechisch-römischen Antike 32 (Rahden: Marie Leidorf, 2016), 254.

23 For the translation, see discussion below.

24 The adjective κανωπικός refers to the city Canopus in the Nile Delta, not far from Alexandria. For its substantivized use as a kind of cake, see LSJ. According to Gagos, the "context may imply that the word here denotes an item of clothing," for which he then provides examples; Gagos, P.Oxy. LXI 4127, 127nn35–36. Reinard lists different uses of this adjective for specific goods; Reinard, *Kommunikation und Ökonomie*, 254. See also Blumell and Wayment, *Christian Oxyrhynchus*, 526n143, and Simona Russo, *Le calzature nei papiri di età greco-romana*, Studi e testi di papirologia; nuova ser., 2 (Florence: Istituto papirologico G. Vitelli, 2004), 115 ("pasticcino," re P.Oxy. IV 738).

25 Πτολεμαῖος Θωνίῳ τῷ ἀγαπητῷ ἀδελφῷ ἐν κ(υρί)ῳ χαίρειν. π̣ρ̣[ὸ] μ̣ὲ̣ν̣ π̣[άν]των εὔχο[μαί] σε ὁλοκληρεῖ̣ν̣ ψυχῇ καὶ σώμα[τι]. γεινώσκε̣ι̣[ν] σ̣ε θ̣έλω ὅτ̣ι̣ εἰ οὔπω [ἠ]γόρασας τὸ̣ λ̣ι̣γ̣α̣ρίδιον κ̣α̣ὶ τὰ ἄλλα, μὴ ἀγοράσῃς. ὁ γὰρ ἄνθρωπος ἀπετάξατο περὶ α̣ὐ̣τ̣ο̣ῦ̣, ὡς ε̣ἶ̣ό̣ν σοι, ὅτι· οὐκ ἐγὼ θέλω. τὸν δὲ πίνακα ἐξαυτῆ̣ς μὴ ἀμελή̣σῃς πέμψαι, καὶ δήλωσόν μοι τίνι θ̣έ̣λεις μεταβ̣α̣λεῖ̣ν̣ τὴν τιμὴν αὐτοῦ. μνήσθητι ἀγοράσαι μοι π̣α̣ρθενικὸν τέλειον σόλιον τρίχινον καὶ Κανωπικὸν α. Τὸν ἀγαπητὸν Τιθ̣οῆν ἀπ' ἐμοῦ π̣ρ̣οσα̣γ̣ό̣ρ̣ε̣υ̣ε̣. ν Θωνίῳ ἀ̣[δελ]φ(ῷ) π(αρὰ) Πτολ̣ε̣μ̣α̣ί̣[ου]. l.10. γεινώσκε̣ι̣[ν] l. γινώσκειν

26 The Archive of Papnuthis and Dorotheus (TM Arch id: 172) came mainly from excavation box 45 5B.60; this papyrus, P.Oxy. LXI 4127, came from box 45 5B.57/C(4–7)a, therefore these documents probably all were found roughly at the same time and place. If this is the case, this Thonius may feature in another document: a letter from Thonius to Thecla (SB XXII 15359 = P.Oxy. I 182 descr.), which would give us slightly more information about him, including that he had a spouse named Thecla. Here the woman is mentioned by name, a Christian name at that. On the box numbers and excavation techniques at Oxyrhynchus, see Luijendijk, "A New Testament Papyrus and Its Documentary Context," esp. 578–79; Nongbri, *God's Library*, esp. 221–24. See also a forthcoming publication by Michael Zellmann-Rohrer on excavation numbers.

27 Trismegistos People lists 609 attestations of the name Θῶνις (of which Thonius is a variant), 96 percent of which come from Oxyrhynchus (17 February 2020). At Oxyrhynchus there was a cult for Horus with a Thoonieion and priests; see Blumell and Wayment, *Christian Oxyrhynchus*, 499; John Whitehorne, "The Pagan Cults of Roman Oxyrhynchus," in *Aufstieg und Niedergang der Römischen Welt*, ed. W. Haase and H. Temporini, vol. 18.5 (Berlin: Walter de Gruyter, 1995), 3083.

28 Blumell and Wayment, *Christian Oxyrhynchus*, 499.

29 On this expression, see, for instance, Luijendijk, *Greetings in the Lord*, 35–37; Blumell and Wayment, *Christian Oxyrhynchus*, 462.

30 As Eldon Epp puts it, this and several other Christian letters, "after a quick Christian greeting and the customary wish for good health (though here "in soul and body"), move directly to business"; Epp, "The Oxyrhynchus New Testament Papyri," 44. That the sender of this "Christian" letter engaged with quotidian matters exemplifies Éric Rebillard's argument, namely, that people activate different parts of their identity in different situations; Rebillard, *Christians and Their Many Identities*; Rebillard, "Everyday Christianity in Carthage at the Time of Tertullian"; Rebillard, "Expressing Christianness in Carthage in the Second and Third Centuries," *Religion in the Roman Empire* 3, no. 1 (2017): 119–34.

31 "σόλιον, τό, slipper, Lat. solea"; see LSJ; F. Preisigke and E. Kiessling, eds., *Wörterbuch der griechischen Papyrusurkunden: mit Einschluss der griechischen Inschriften, Aufschriften, Ostraka, Mumienschilder usw. aus Ägypten* (Berlin: Selbstverlag der Erben, 1925), 473a; Reinard, *Kommunikation und Ökonomie*, 278. For a full discussion of all occurrences of the term in papyri, see Russo, *Le calzature nei papiri di età greco-romana*, 56–77. In Greek, this word is attested only in papyri in the meaning of "shoe"; a search on the Thesaurus Linguae Graecae database gave four references to the word in the meaning of "seat, throne" in the sixth century CE

by the author John Lydus; see A.C. Bandy, *Ioannes Lydus: On Powers or the Magistracies of the Roman State* (Philadelphia: American Philosophical Society, 1983).

32 Russo, *Le calzature nei papiri di età greco-romana*. Ancient letter writers also often mention items of clothing in their letters. Different kinds of linen, fur coats, veils, and materials are requested in, and often shipped with, letters; Reinard, *Kommunikation und Ökonomie*, 278, 350–52.

33 σϙλια ἀρσενικὰ ζεύγ(η) η, [γυ]ναικεῖα ζεύγ(η) ς; P.Oxy. IV 741, ll. 8–9.

34 P.Mich VIII 508, second to third centuries; Bagnall and Cribiore, *Women's Letters from Ancient Egypt*, 398–99. Herais, a female, and Serenus, a male, will receive multiple pairs.

35 σόλια γυναικῖα παπύρ(ινα) δ; P.Oxy. XIV 1742, l. 6. See also Soc 206, 9 [III]: σόλια γυναικῖα δύο.

36 καλίκια ἀρμενικά; P.Harraurer 51. See also Reinard, *Kommunikation und Ökonomie*, 185.

37 Véronique Montembault and Christiane Ziegler, eds., *Catalogue des chaussures de l'antiquité égyptienne* (Paris: Réunion des Musées Nationaux, 2000). See also the work of André Veldmeijer: A.J. Veldmeijer, *Sandals, Shoes and Other Leatherwork from the Coptic Monastery Deir El-Bachit: Analysis and Catalogue* (Leiden: Sidestone Press, 2011); Veldmeijer, *Excavations of Gebel Adda (Lower Nubia): Ancient Nubian Leatherwork*, part 1: *Sandals and Shoes* (Leiden: Sidestone Press, 2016); Veldmeijer, *The Ancient Egyptian Footwear Project: Final Archaeological Analysis* (Leiden: Sidestone Press, 2019); André J. Veldmeijer and Salima Ikram, *Catalogue of the Footwear in the Coptic Museum (Cairo)* (Leiden: Sidestone Press, 2014).

38 LSJ sv.; τέλειος, -η, -ον: "was sein Ziel oder Ende erreicht hat . . . 1. vollständig, vollkommen, tadellos, richtig; 2. ausgewachsen; 3. vollzählig, restlos; 4. fertiggestellt, gebrauchsfertig"; Preisigke and Kiessling, *Wörterbuch der griechischen Papyrusurkunden aus Ägypten*, 585–87.

39 A clear example is P.Oxy. Hels. 40, a lengthy list of textiles from Oxyrhynchus that juxtaposes pieces of clothing labeled as τέλ(ειοι) with others labeled as παιδ(ικοὶ), "child-sized": for instance, χι(τῶνες) τέλ(ειοι) ιθ (δραχμαὶ) ς (διώβολον); χι(τῶνες) παιδ(ικοὶ) οβ (δραχμαὶ) ιβ, and so forth, P.Oxy. Hels. 40, l. 1–2. In this context, τέλειος can only mean "adult." On this papyrus, see Peter van Minnen, "The Volume of the Oxyrhynchite Textile Trade," *Münstersche Beiträge zur antiken Handelsgeschichte* 5 (1986): 88–95; and Bagnall, *Reading Papyri, Writing Ancient History*, 68–69. Also in P.Hamb. I 10.14, the adjective must indicate size: thirteen adult white suits (not, as LSJ renders it, "thirteen complete white suits"). Blumell and Wayment refer to P.Oxy. LVI 3869.3 τρία σανδάλεια καλὰ τέλεια π̣[υ]κ̣νὰ *πάνυ*, "three pairs of nice, well-finished, very solid [?] sandals;" Blumell and Wayment, *Christian Oxyrhynchus*, 500. This rendering doesn't take account of shoe size, which seems necessary when ordering footwear: therefore, "three pairs of nice, adult size, very solid sandals" is also an option.

40 E.g., P.Oxy. XLIII 3144, 7 (23 July 313): "a male full-grown dappled Cappadocian horse" (ἵππον ἄρενα ψαρὸν τέλιον Καμπάδοκα); P.Oxy. XLIII 3145, 7–8 (early fourth century): "a male, mouse-colored, full-grown donkey" (ὄ̣νον ἄρρενον μοιόχρωμον τέλιον).

41 That τέλειος in such cases must mean "high quality" instead of "adult, full grown" is clear from P.Oxy. LX 4081, which lists the hide of a calf, high quality versus inferior: βυρσα μοσχίου τελ (είας(?)) vac. ? ταλ(αντ)[-ca.?-]; ὑποδεεστέρ(ας) vac. ? [τα]λ̣[(αντ) -ca.?-] (βυρσα l: βύρσης).

42 Russo, *Le calzature nei papiri di età greco-romana*, 72–73.

43 Monastic clothing was made of hair; in the case of their forerunner, John the Baptist, camel hair (τὸ ἔνδυμα αὐτοῦ ἀπὸ τριχῶν καμήλου, Matt 3:4). The adjective τρίχινος appears in Rev. 6:12 where it indicates sackcloth: Καὶ εἶδον ὅτε ἤνοιξεν τὴν σφραγῖδα τὴν ἕκτην, καὶ σεισμὸς μέγας ἐγένετο, καὶ ὁ ἥλιος ἐγένετο μέλας ὡς σάκκος τρίχινος, καὶ ἡ σελήνη ὅλη ἐγένετο ὡς αἷμα ("When he opened the sixth seal, I looked, and there came a great earthquake; the sun became black as sackcloth, the full moon became like blood").

44 See Luijendijk, "'Twenty Thousand Nuns,'" 57–67.

45 μ̣οναχαὶ ἀποτακτικαί, P.Oxy. XLIV 3203; see also Luijendijk, "'Twenty Thousand Nuns,'" 60–62.

46 In Veldmeijer's description and catalogue of footwear from the Monastery of Deir al-Bachit, there does not appear to be a distinct monastic type of footwear; what is striking is that the

footwear was repaired often, indicating the frugality of the monks; Veldmeijer, *Sandals, Shoes and Other Leatherwork from the Coptic Monastery Deir El-Bachit.*

47 See, again, the work of Éric Rebillard, cited above.

48 τῷ γὰρ ὄντι τοῦ παρθενικοῦ χιτῶνος αἱ πτέρυγες οὐκ ἦσαν συνερραμμέναι κάτωθεν; "For in fact the tunic worn by their maidens were not sewn together below the waist," B. Perrin, trans., *Plutarch's Lives*, vol. 1, *Lycurgus and Numa* 3.4 (Cambridge, MA: Harvard University Press, 1914; repr. 1967): 392–93. The fourth- or fifth-century Egyptian epic poet Nonnus of Panopolis uses this adjective παρθενικός in the sense of an unmarried, chaste girl or young woman; R. Keydell, *Nonni Panopolitani Dionysiaca*, 2 vols. (Berlin: Weidmann, 1959), 1:1–500; 2:1–509; for example, in book 42, line 70 and book 45, line 44.

49 Blumell and Wayment similarly interpret this as "a girl's pair of well-finished slippers made of hair;" Blumell and Wayment, *Christian Oxyrhynchus*, 499–500.

50 For instance, Montembault and Ziegler, *Catalogue des chaussures de l'antiquité égyptienne*, nos. 105 and 125. For a discussion on children's shoes, see Annika Backe-Dahmen, "Sandals for the Living, Sandals for the Dead: Roman Children and Their Footwear," in *Shoes, Slippers, and Sandals: Feet and Footwear in Classical Antiquity*, ed. S. Pickup and S. Waite (New York: Routledge, 2018), 263–82. On distinguishing male, female, and children's shoes, see Elizabeth M. Greene, "If the Shoe Fits: Style and Status in the Assemblage of Children's Shoes from Vindolanda," in *Life in the Limes: Studies of the People and Objects of the Roman Frontiers*, ed. R. Collins and F. McIntosh (Oxford: Oxbow Books, 2014), 30–31. Children's and adolescents' shoes from Vindolanda are often smaller versions of adult shoes and signal the social status of the wearer; Greene, "If the Shoe Fits," 31–32.

51 LSJ: "τρί̈χῐνος, η, ον, of hair." In his edition of the papyrus, Traianos Gagos notes that "the exact implication of τρίχινον is hard to grasp." *Ed. princ.* P.Oxy. LXI 4127, p. 127. According to Russo, these were either shoes lined with fur, or shoes made of felt. Shoes with wool are perhaps attested in an early third-century text from Oxyrhynchus (SB III 7181) as "woolen women's slippers and woolen children's slipper; σόλια μα(λλωτὰ) γυ(ναικεῖα) and σόλιον παιδ(ικὸν) μα(λλωτόν). This is a Greek–Latin military account from Oxyrhynchus dating to the year 220. The solving of the abbreviation μα() is not entirely obvious; see Russo here. τρίχινος in the meaning of μάλλινος LBG "aus Wolle, hären," or even made of rope (taking τρίχινον as τριχίαι); Russo, *Le calzature nei papiri di età greco-romana*, 73. Blumell and Wayment render this as a "pair of well-finished slippers made of hair." For their explanation, see Blumell and Wayment, *Christian Oxyrhynchus*, 500nn31–34.

52 Montembault and Ziegler, *Catalogue des chaussures de l'antiquité égyptienne*, 84–85n25.

53 In contrast, for elite boys in the gymnasial class, the papyrological record contains multiple so-called epikrisis documents, or requests for civic status; see, for instance, Giovanni Ruffini, "Genealogy and the Gymnasium," *BASP* 43 (2006): 71–99.

54 For instance, Laura Salah Nasrallah, *Archaeology and the Letters of Paul* (Oxford: Oxford University Press, 2018).

55 Bagnall and Frier, *The Demography of Roman Egypt.*

56 British Museum 1905,1021.13; image and brief description at https://www.britishmuseum.org/collection/object/G_1905-1021-13. On ancient dolls, including this one, see Fanny Dolansky, "Playing with Gender: Girls, Dolls, and Adult Ideals in the Roman World," *Classical Antiquity* 31, no. 2 (2012): 256–92.

57 P.Oxy. XVII 2156, "Letter of Amyntas," ed. Arthur Hunt (1927; the papyrus is lost); TM no. 32837. See also the literature mentioned in Blumell and Wayment, *Christian Oxyrhynchus*, no. 160, 600–605. The letter is classified as "Christian" because the sender, Amyntas, references "the divine providence of God" ("Having now been afforded a favorable opportunity by a man who is going to you, I thought it necessary to greet you, praying at the same time to the divine providence of God that it may always protect you for us"). The content, however, deals with worldly matters: a delivery of parchment together with the letter; and business matters, such as multiple men involved with cloaks and cleaning.

58 Presumably the phrase "all our (relatives)" (τοὺς ἡμῶν πάντας) also includes women. Maximus, the sender of another letter, addresses women by name, but refers to his "brothers" generically: "Greet my brothers for me each by name" (P.Oxy. XXXIV 2731, "Maximus to his Mother Zenobia").

59 On sickness, see also examples in Reinard, *Kommunikation und Ökonomie*, 408–10.

60 "Because good health was such a fickle state in Antiquity, it was constantly on people's minds. Among the most common elements of private letters are information on the writer's health and inquiries about the health of the addressee and other acquaintances. . . . 'I pray for your health' is also a normal closing formula in imperial-period letters." Similar phrases occur already in Demotic letters; Amin Benaissa and Sofie Remijsen, "A Sound Body and Mind," in *A Companion to Greco-Roman and Late Antique Egypt*, ed. Katelijn Vandorpe (Hoboken, NJ: Wiley Blackwell, 2019), 392.

61 Writers express wishes for good health with verbs such as ὁλοκληρέω, ὑγιαίνω, and ῥώννυμι. Stanley Stowers comments: "Often the greeting was followed by a prayer for the recipient, sometimes by a wish for the recipient's health, and occasionally by a statement of thanksgiving to a god or gods. . . . Sometimes the farewell is preceded by a wish for the health of the recipient or a request for the recipient to greet family members, friends, or others named by the sender"; Stanley K. Stowers, *Letter Writing in Greco-Roman Antiquity*, Library of Early Christianity 5 (Philadelphia: Westminster Press, 1986), 20. The absence of well-wishes is rhetorically significant; see, for instance, Paul's Letter to the Galatians (Gal. 1:6) and Theon to his Father, P.Oxy. I 119 "A Boy's Letter" (second or third century).

62 "These opening and closing formulas seem to have been of little interest to the ancients when they reflected on letter writing. Discussion of openings and closings is virtually absent from extant ancient epistolary theory"; Stowers, *Letter Writing in Greco-Roman Antiquity*, 20.

63 As Peter Parsons noted: "Illness was a fact of life: all the more so in a society in which the average life expectancy at birth could be estimated at 22–25 years"; Parsons, *City of the Sharp-nosed Fish*, 180.

64 Though this is not always the case. For instance, in the case of Copres inquiring about his mother-in-law's eye problem, the subject of illness appears almost as an afterthought (P.Oxy. XXXI 2601).

65 The sender identifies multiple women by familial association (his mother and grandmothers, whose names we do not know), and by name (Kyra, Kyrilla, and Elena). He also mentions by name two men (Heraklammon and Theodoros). Receiving information that a loved one had fallen ill was upsetting and worrisome. In another letter (not belonging to our small sample of Christian letters from Oxyrhynchus), a woman called Soeris, upon learning that "her daughter Aline" was sick, wrote back: "you make me so awfully worried"; P.Brem. 64, Soeris to Aline, first quarter of the second century, Bagnall and Cribiore, *Women's Letters from Ancient Egypt*, 146.

66 On physicians at Oxyrhynchus, see Parsons, *City of the Sharp-nosed Fish*, 177–82: "Doctors and Diseases." Parsons mentions that "the choice of a doctor" was "a difficult and potentially dangerous matter"; Parsons, *City of the Sharp-nosed Fish*, 177. At Oxyrhynchus there were "public physicians, whose duty it was to visit the victims of accident and assault and report their condition to the authorities"; Parsons, *City of the Sharp-nosed Fish*, 178. There was, for instance, a surgery in the Western Stoa (P.Oxy. LXIV 4441, 316 CE).

67 If this is indeed a fourth-century text, then there is a serious possibility that it is a Christian letter or, otherwise, it indicates that Christians and pagans used the same vocabulary about divine providence. In their discussion of the expression ἡ θεία πρόνοια in P.Oxy. XII 1492, Blumell and Wayment mention five other Christian letters from Oxyrhynchus with this phrase: P.Congr. XV 20; SB XXII 15359; P.Oxy. XVII 2156; PSI I 71; SB XX 14987; and eight letters "whose religious provenance cannot be determined conclusively"; Blumell and Wayment, *Christian Oxyrhynchus*, 485–86 (no. 134).

68 In certain cases, people wore amulets as metaphysical protection against illness. Women are visible here as well. The corpus of Christian documents from Oxyrhynchus contains a reference to

an amulet for a girl or woman named Joannia, the daughter of Anastasia, also known as Euphemia, for protection against fevers. The amulet cites biblical phrases, exhorts evil spirits to flee, and calls on a host of saints for help, including local Oxyrhynchite saints (P.Oxy. VIII 1151); see AnneMarie Luijendijk, "A Gospel Amulet for Joannia," 418–43.

69 This is probably a letter written by a Christian. According to Grenfell and Hunt, "The style, which shows the influence of the New Testament, is more polished than that of the average letter of the period, and the document ranks high as a specimen of epistolary composition"; Bernard P. Grenfell and Arthur S. Hunt, *The Oxyrhynchus Papyri*, vol. 6 (London: EEF, 1908), 939, 307. Blumell and Wayment write: "we have included P.Oxy. VI 939 . . . , a fourth-century letter, which contains no single decisive Christian marker, but a cluster of markers that in our opinion decisively points toward Christian authorship"; Blumell and Wayment, *Christian Oxyrhynchus*, 15–16, see also 552. The professional, elegant, careful handwriting of the letter matches the educated, elevated tone of the content. In addition to his use of language and New Testament allusions, the writer also uses dieresis.

70 Demetrius addresses Flavianus and the sick woman reverently as **κύριέ μου** ("my lord," ll. 10, 20) and **ἡ ἡμῶν κυρία** ("our lady"). Grenfell and Hunt summarize: "An affectionately worded Christian letter, apparently from a dependent to his master, concerning the illness of his mistress"; P.Oxy. VI 939, 307. In addition to Demetrius, Flavianus, and the sick lady, the other persons mentioned by name are males: Euphrosynus, Ploutarchus, and Demetrius's "son Athanasius." Regarding illness and health, it is of interest that Athanasius was also ill.

71 Just as from our previous examples, Ptolemaeus, and probably Thonius also, will have known the identity of the slipper wearer, and Eudaimon and Kyra are intimately acquainted.

72 P.Oxy. VIII 1161, ed. A.S. Hunt (1911), 265–66, fourth century; TM no. 33632. See also Blumell and Wayment, *Christian Oxyrhynchus*, 555–59 (no. 148). "The content of the letter is also fascinating since the author was apparently very ill when she sent the letter and on numerous occasions reminds the addressee of her poor condition"; Blumell and Wayment, *Christian Oxyrhynchus*, 556.

73 Another example of a sick woman in her own voice occurs in a letter from a certain Paul and his wife Tapiam to Nepheros, a presbyteros in the Hathor monastery, near the Herakleopolite village of Nesoi (P.Neph. 1, mid-fourth century, *Das Archiv des Nepheros und verwandte Texte*, ed. B. Kramer, J.C. Shelton, and G.M. Browne, Aegyptiaca Treverensia 4 (Mainz am Rhein: Philipp von Zabern, 1987). At one point in the letter, Tapiam speaks: "For I, Tapiam, have become sick, and I still cannot get up. We beseech you to pray for our health. For before this our children have become sick and through your prayers they stopped (being sick). For we believe that our Lord will listen to you, who are righteous. For we also pray to have our end in our own house (with our own family) and we want to be delivered from the suffering of the world nearest to our own, if indeed the master deems us worthy to be saved in our living abroad." Yet another instance of a sick woman writing herself (not from Christian Oxyrhynchus) is P.Brem. 64, Soeris to Aline, first quarter of the second century. In this letter we observe two women dealing with health issues, one scolding the other that she exaggerates her illness. The relevant part of the letter reads in translation: "Soeris to her daughter Aline, greetings. Before all I pray that you are well along with your brother Apollonius and your children free from the evil eye. Why are you writing to me 'I am sick'? I was told that you are not ill; you make me so awfully worried. But see, I have been sick in my eyes for four months!"; Bagnall and Cribiore, *Women's Letters from Ancient Egypt*, 146.

74 Bagnall and Cribiore, *Women's Letters from Ancient Egypt*, 10. They add: "the letters allow us to get closer than any other category of document to a significant part of the ancient female population." See also Bagnall and Cribiore, *Women's Letters from Ancient Egypt*, "Whose Voices," 6–8. On women in petitions from Egypt, see, for instance, Joëlle Beaucamp, *Le statut de la femme à Byzance, 4e–7e siècle* (Paris: De Boccard, 1990).

75 These are: two letters from a landlord named Clematia (P.Oxy. XLVIII 3406, 3407) and two letters from Didyme and the sisters (P.Oxy. XIV 1774 and SB VIII 9746)—letters that we will turn

to shortly—and a letter from a woman to what is probably a high-ranking clergyman (P.Oxy. XII 1592). Moreover, it is possible that the anonymous sender of P.Oxy. LXIII 4365, a letter addressed to an anonymous woman, was also a woman; Epp, "The Oxyrhynchus New Testament Papyri," 28–29; Blumell and Wayment, *Christian Oxyrhynchus*, 556.

76 Indicating that you cannot get up is a way to describe a terrible illness. For example: Titianus writes: "I cannot stagger" (PSI IV 299).

77 On dictation, see also Bagnall and Cribiore: "We do not know a priori if those who wrote from dictation cleaned up what they heard as they turned it into written form. Most people, even educated ones, do not normally speak in complete paragraphs or even in complete grammatical sentences . . . . But if we can proceed with some degree of confidence that we are in identifiable cases hearing the actual voice of the author, even if not witnessing her handwriting very often (other than in signatures), there may be more nuances to be picked up"; Bagnall and Cribiore, *Women's Letters from Ancient Egypt*, 31–32.

78 "The normal opposition here is not health/disease but health/death"; Helen King, "Women's Health and Recovery in the Hippocratic Corpus," in *Health in Antiquity*, ed. H. King (London and New York: Routledge, 2005), 156. While generally true, this dichotomy may be a bit too stark, since in antiquity, as also today, chronic illness and debility are by no means an uncommon outcome.

79 For example, in the Gospel of Luke especially, this term is used to refer to good health after healing (cf. Luke 8:36, 48, 50; 17:19; 18:42). Contra Blumell and Wayment, "This is not a theologically loaded phrase as σωτηρία, which can mean 'salvation,' here simply has the meaning of 'health'"; Blumell and Wayment, *Christian Oxyrhynchus*, 573.

80 R.J.S. Barrett-Lennard, *Christian Healing after the New Testament: Some Approaches to Illness in the Second, Third, and Fourth Centuries* (Lanham, MD: University Press of America, 1994), 23–25.

81 Other Christian papyrus letters do request the intervention of a clergyman; see, for instance, P.Oxy. XVIII 2193, Theon to Pascentius, regarding an old woman (Blumell and Wayment, *Christian Oxyrhynchus*, 585–89).

82 King, "Women's Health and Recovery," 151.

83 On archives, see, for instance, Katelijn Vandorpe, W. Clarysse, and Herbert Verreth, *Graeco-Roman Archives from the Fayum*, Collectanea Hellenistica, KVAB 6 (Leuven: Peeters, 2015). In archival studies, I also find inspiring: Arlette Farge, *The Allure of the Archives* (New Haven, CT: Yale University Press, 2013); Saidiya Hartman, "Venus in Two Acts," *Small Axe* 12, no. 2 (2008): 1–14. French historian Arlette Farge, for instance, describes how she discovered, to her surprise, that the old police archives of Paris were filled with the voices of women.

84 Katelijn Vandorpe, "Archives and Dossiers," 216.

85 P.Oxy. XLVIII 3403, 3406, 3407.

86 P.Oxy. XLVIII 3407, 110.

87 SB XXII 15359 = P.Oxy. I 182 descr.; B&W no. 154, 578–81, from Thoonius to Thecla. It might belong to the archive of Papnuthis and Dorotheus.

88 About Christian names as indication of the parents' religious affiliation at the time of child's birth, see Roger S. Bagnall, "Religious Conversion and Onomastic Change in Early Byzantine Egypt," *BASP* 19, no. 3/4 (1982): 108–109.

89 In the *editio princeps* (P.Oxy. XIV 1777, 187), this letter is dated to the "early fourth century." Wipszycka dates it to ca. 340; see Ewa Wipszycka, "Del buon uso delle lettere private. Commento a *SB* III, 7243 e *P. Oxy.* XIV, 1774," in *"Humana sapit": Études d'antiquité tardive offertes à Lellia Cracco Ruggini*, ed. Jean-Michel Carrié and Rita Lizzi Testa, Bibliothèque de l'antiquité tardive 3 (Turnhout: Brepols, 2002), 469–73, esp. 470.

90 P.Oxy. XIV 1774, "Didyme and the sisters to Atienateia," and SB VIII 9746 "Didyme and the sisters to Sophias"; Bagnall and Cribiore, *Women's Letters from Ancient Egypt*, 193–97.

91 As Bagnall and Cribiore note: "The sender is the same Didyme who wrote P.Oxy. 14. 1774. The addressee, however, is different, and none of the people mentioned is common to both letters.

The letter mostly concerns the sending and receiving of supplies of various kinds (note the large ostrich egg) and the provisions for the trip of some woman. The numerous names mentioned are Greek, Roman, and Egyptian. It is clear the letters went back and forth from sender and addressee"; Bagnall and Cribiore, *Women's Letters from Ancient Egypt*, 197.

92 Translation Bagnall and Cribiore, *Women's Letters from Ancient Egypt*, 194.

93 "[To] my beloved [lady] sister, [Didyme and] the sisters, greetings in the Lord. First of all we think it necessary to salute you. We received from brother Piperas (or the brother of Piperas) the provisions for the voyage . . . her until she comes home to us. But they are being made. We also received from other people for her 7 double knidia and a coarse sack of sour grapes. If we find (someone) we will also send you through this person both the sack and the knidia we have found. We have not yet received the rest. And be eager (to tell us) what you want so that we may send it through acquaintances. I wish you to know about the cloth that you sent to Loukilos that I sent you 2 pairs of sandals of the same value, which were bought directly from the weavers for 4 talents (?) but that you did not mention to me in writing, and through the sailor Sipharos son of Plou . . . (?) for the bride of Pansophios (? or daughter-in-law of Pansophion) a large ostrich egg and a small basket containing Syrian palm dates, but you did not write about them. Salute the most beloved Didyme and the dearest Favorinus. The implements of the most beloved Didyme were found in the sack of the wool of Severus. The lady and the other lady Valeriane salute you and those of the circle of Philosophos, Loukila and Pansophion. Salute the excellent Bikeutia (and ask whether) she received from Aionios the head cover and the 2 canopic cakes. And salute everyone, Italia, Theodora. Farewell in the Lord, may the Lord preserve you for us. (Address on back): To the lady sister Sophias, Didyme and the sisters." Translation from Bagnall and Cribiore, *Women's Letters from Ancient Egypt*, 196.

94 See Luijendijk, "'Twenty Thousand Nuns,'" 59–60.

95 For a fuller discussion of this archive, see Roger S. Bagnall, "An Owner of Literary Papyri," *CP* (1992): 137–40; AnneMarie Luijendijk, "Books and Private Readers in Early Christian Oxyrhynchus: 'A Spiritual Meadow and a Garden of Delight,'" in *Books and Readers in the Pre-modern World*, ed. Karl Shuve, WGRWSup Series 12 (Atlanta: SBL, 2018), 113–15.

96 Bagnall, "An Owner of Literary Papyri." The archive contains the following documents:

- P.Oxy. III 412: Julius Africanus, Kestoi book 18 (with end title);
- P.Oxy. VI 907: "Will of Hermogenes," dated June 25–July 24, 276;
- P.Oxy. XI 1365: History of Sicyon;
- P.Oxy. XI 1386: Homer, Iliad 4.257–272 (The recto is a document with two cursive lines; see also J.-L. Fournet, "Homère et les papyrus non littéraires: Le Poète dans le contexte de ses lecteurs," in *I papiri omerici: Atti del Convegno Internazionale di Studi, Firenze, 9–10 giugno 2011*, ed. G. Bastianini and A. Casanova, Studi et Testi di Papirologia NS 14 (Florence: Instituto papirologico G. Vitelli, 2012), 126);
- P.Oxy. XI 1392: Homer, Iliad 15.303–325 (Verso: cursive writing);
- P.Oxy. XIV 1690: "Lease of Land," 19 September 287.

97 Edwin A. Judge and Stewart R. Pickering argued that the parents are Christians, based on a phrase in Hermogenes's will that commends his wife Aurelia Isidora, alias Prisca, for "fitting conduct in married life" (πρεπόντως περὶ τὴν συμβίωσιν ἀναστραφείσῃ; Edwin A. Judge and Stewart R. Pickering, "Papyrus Documentation of Church and Community in Egypt to the Mid-fourth Century," *JAC* 20 (1997): 65: "his wife Isidora, also known as Prisca (the name of a prominent collaborator of St. Paul), a *matrona stolata*, who is praised for 'fitting conduct in married life,' not a direct New Testament echo but an idea familiar to its readers." Bagnall comments: "That suggestion assumes . . . that the text of Africanus belonged to Hermogenes or one of his children (and was not acquired already as scrap); it also, less compellingly, assumes that the owner of a work written by a Christian, even a work without specifically Christian character, is likely to have been a Christian;" Bagnall, "An Owner of Literary Papyri," 139n16.

98 Her father was an *exegetes, prytanis,* and councilor of Oxyrhynchus; her mother, Aurelia Isidora, alias Prisca, a *matrona stolata* (line 4), and her grandfather Athenaius, alias Heracleides, had served as *bouleutes, kosmetes,* and *tamias* of city funds. See Bagnall, "An Owner of Literary Papyri," 139.

99 Bagnall, "An Owner of Literary Papyri," 139n13.

100 See especially Rafaella Cribiore, *Gymnastics of the Mind: Greek Education in Hellenistic and Roman Egypt* (Princeton: Princeton University Press, 2005), ch. 3: "Women and Education," 74–101; Bagnall and Cribiore, *Women's Letters from Ancient Egypt*, 48–49.

101 Luijendijk, "Books and Private Readers," 101–35. Sarit Kattan Gribetz has written an excellent piece on Christian women as readers, with an important methodological section; Sarit Kattan Gribetz, "Women as Readers of the Nag Hammadi Codices," *Journal of Early Christian Studies* 26, no. 3 (2018): 463–94.

102 Johnson-DeBaufre, "Gazing upon the Invisible," 74.

103 In one case, a woman has to deal with a husband who presses his mother to send her (his wife) to him; P.Oxy. XXXIV 2731, quoted above.

104 E.g., P.Oxy. VIII 1161, and also P.Oxy. XII 1592.

105 Luijendijk, "'Twenty Thousand Nuns.'"

106 AnneMarie Luijendijk, "On and beyond Duty: Christian Clergy at Oxyrhynchus (c. 250–400)," in *Beyond Priesthood: Religious Entrepreneurs and Innovators in the Roman Empire*, ed. R.L. Gordon, G. Petridou, and J. Rüpke (Berlin and Boston: De Gruyter, 2017), 103–26; Sabine Hübner, *Der Klerus in der Gesellschaft des spätantiken Kleinasiens*, Altertumswissenschaftliches Kolloquium 15 (Stuttgart: Franz Steiner, 2005).

21

Women's Intimacy: Blood, Milk, and Women's Conditions in the Gynecological Papyri of Ancient Egypt

Clémentine Audouit

The focus of this chapter is the women of ancient Egypt as seen through the prism of anatomy and physiology. Indeed, although the concept of "gender" is a social construction dependent on place, time, and culture, the male/female division is primarily defined by observing and interpreting physical bodies and their differences.[1] The corporal shape and sexual organs differ, of course, but the fluids that are produced by them are also distinct, as are their functions in the reproductive process. Likewise, pathology, pain, and state of health can constitute gendered data based on a dual perception of physiology: one masculine and the other feminine.

The physiology of women differs from that of men in ancient Egyptian thought in very specific ways: the female body has its own internal functioning and therefore its own issues. This perception is clearly associated with the woman's role in the generation of life, which consists of the formation of the fetus in the womb, feeding it in utero, and then giving birth and breastfeeding. Some studies have already mentioned this general idea,[2] but it will be useful to focus in more detail on the circulation and movement of feminine bodily fluids, especially blood and milk, and on some specific uterine "substances and conditions." Moreover, as we shall see, this way of considering women's physiology can also be found in other civilizations: there seems to be a clear parallel between the Near Eastern, Egyptian, and Greco-Roman worlds on this topic. To determine how the ancient Egyptians perceived the functioning of the female body, it is necessary to explore the gynecological documents[3] that focus on and describe its specificities and roles. Therefore, this paper proposes to delve into intimate female issues by studying female health problems, especially those relating to the flow of bodily fluids.

Several Egyptian papyri include a gynecology and/or obstetrics section. First, there are the Kahun papyrus (also known as the Lahun papyrus)[4] and the Ramesseum papyri nos. III and IV,[5] dating from the Middle Kingdom. From the New Kingdom, the famous papyrus Ebers[6] contains sixty-two gynecological formulas. Only one case in the Edwin Smith "surgical" papyrus relates to menstrual blood issues.[7] Magical incantations for the safety of women during pregnancy have been preserved in the London papyrus [BM 10059][8] and also in the Berlin 3027 papyrus entitled "Book of Mother and Child."[9] The Carlsberg papyrus no. VIII (badly damaged) also contains some cases relating to female fertility,[10] and finally, the same subject appears in a group of fifteen formulas in the Berlin 3038 papyrus.[11] Of course, these texts are copies of copies of copies of copies, and the Egyptians' gynecological knowledge probably dates back to much earlier times, quite likely right back to the Old Kingdom.[12] In sum, more than 150 medical recipes relating to women and children have been preserved.[13]

The purpose of these formulae is to identify women's illnesses by scrupulously describing their symptoms and, subsequently, to propose a treatment for each specific case. The most frequent topic concerns diseases affecting genital organs, for which the most commonly cited symptoms are pain or infection in different parts of the body.[14] The papyri also contain several recipes to assist conception, or, alternatively, to prevent it. Egyptians often used fertility tests to determine whether a woman was capable of becoming pregnant. Some texts cover urological or rectal issues,[15] while other formulas are dedicated to breast diseases and milk production complications. Finally, numerous formulas mention childbirth and its consequences, as well as miscarriages, which were very common in ancient Egypt.

In many of these texts, inadequate movements of typically feminine substances—menstrual blood, milk, or the results of pathological uterine manifestations—are involved in the development of diseases. Ulrike Steinert[16] discusses a disease called "locked fluids" ("*me turru*") found in many gynecological texts from ancient Mesopotamia. In that study, the author underlined the importance of "the right route for fluids" for women's health in the ancient Near Eastern conception of female anatomy. To discover how substances travel inside a woman's body, according to ancient Egyptian concepts, three major scenarios are discussed here, following the same reasoning chosen by Steinert in her paper. They are: the overabundant leakage of fluids from the body, the "blocked fluids" within the womb, and the "misplaced" uterine substances (those that "go the wrong way"). These three situations are abnormal and pathological; however, they provide the opportunity to think about the normal way in which these fluids, essential for procreation, should function. As with the early Near Eastern perspective on the subject, these concepts are interrelated with the perception of the uterus as an organic receptacle that opens and closes continually—opening to expel menstrual blood, opening to receive sperm, closing for fecundation, and reopening, of course, for birth—and is also in contact with other parts of a woman's body through a highly developed network of channels.[17]

The Route of Blood: Flow and Retention

A lot of medical treatments are performed to stop gynecological hemorrhages, especially in the case of miscarriage. Indeed, after fertilization, the womb must be sealed during pregnancy to avoid the escape of blood, which must now work within the womb.[18] Indeed, the role of the womb is to bind the masculine and feminine elements together and to maintain warmth so as to give the embryo its final shape.[19]

Several formulas from the London papyrus use the metaphor of a "massive flood" to describe the irrepressible leakage of blood when the womb opens prematurely. For example, "*Another incantation to repel bleeding*:[20] Anubis will come out to repel the inundation *(Ḥ'py)* from flowing over what is pure, the land of Tait. What is in it is protected (i.e., the fetus). This incantation is to be spoken over linen *r3-j33t* weave made into an amulet knot and placed inside her flesh (vagina)."[21] When the situation is normal or, in other words, in conformity with Maat—the embodiment of the cosmic order—both blood and flood-*Ḥ*ʿ*py* are beneficial and have a function in fertility, creation, and growth. However, when the wave is brutal and uncontrolled, it becomes dangerous and damaging to life, devastating everything in its path, an abnormal situation that can lead to chaos.[22] The Egyptians often used hydrological metaphors to compare the path of bodily fluids with the Nile, especially blood in traumatic surgery contexts, which could also be called *3gb* ("flood").[23] Thus, our text refers to deities that would save the woman and her child by helping to close the orifice using a linen blockage: Taït, the goddess of fabrics, whose "pure land" corresponds to the linen tampon, placed in the vagina to stop the hemorrhage, and Anubis, in charge of protecting corpses by bandaging them (to avoid the release of putrid fluids), also assisted the physician.

The method is different in another formula: "*Incantation for repelling blood* (. . .) Let the red blood, that just came out, be repelled. Are you unaware of the dam? *This incantation is to be recited over a carnelian bead placed inside a woman.*"[24] Here, a red amulet is put into the vagina to stop the blood from overflowing and to seal the womb artificially. This magic mineral functions like a dam for an inundation, the protective role of a dike being so fundamental in Egypt to prevent flooding that the motif is often reinterpreted to evoke the protective function of the king himself.[25] The menstrual blood, like the river, is always intended to perpetuate the same movement: from the top (the source) down (the exit), and the fertilized womb, whose function is to be a receptacle and a protective space for gestation, will therefore close itself and act as a barrier. It holds back the flow while it works on the development of the child. However, in the case of malfunction, the container organ can open up, becoming a gaping vessel, allowing once again the continuous flow of blood to escape freely down its usual course, even if this results in the death of the fetus it has fashioned.

In contrast to the purpose of stopping gynecological hemorrhages, medical texts often highlight problems of menstrual blood retention within the uterus of fertile but nonpregnant women. Here the diagnosis is reversed: the womb has sealed up or is clogged; it seems unable to open normally, and the evacuation of menstrual blood is impossible. Such flow abnormalities are monitored by the physician and, in the case of dysmenorrhea or amenorrhea, he will attempt to "extract the blood"[26] and to assist the uterus to reopen. In this situation, trapped blood, as a corporeal living and dynamic substance, needs to be in continual motion and will thus try another way to get out. This can cause deterioration of the patient's health, as described in a formula from the Smith papyrus: "*If you examine a woman suffering from pain in her jb, whose menstruation has not come, and that you find something on the upper side of her navel, you should conclude: there is a blood obstruction in her womb.*"[27] Here, blood has clogged and sealed (*šnꜤ*) the uterine orifice and accumulated within the woman's body, possibly in the navel area, causing pain to be felt right up to the ventral/thoracic zone (the *jb*). This is mentioned in the Hippocratic texts, which say that the menstrual blood, when it cannot find a way out, can rise to the heart and to the diaphragm.[28]

Another formula from the Ebers papyrus describes a woman who has not had a menstrual period for several years: "*When you examine a woman for whom many years have passed without her menstruation coming. She vomits something like ḥbb.t-water; her belly is like one afflicted with fever; it stops after she vomits. You should conclude: it is an increase of the level of blood in her uterus due to a spell.*"[29] She seems to suffer from amenorrhea caused by long-term intrauterine blood retention. Symptoms such as vomiting or hot flashes are like those generated by the beginning of menopause. However, the physician considers the pathology curable. He can reverse the process because the cause of the disease is perceived as unnatural: someone bewitched the woman while she was sleeping. The magic has blocked menstruation and reversed the normal flow of blood, like "an evil spell." While the normal function of menstrual blood is to descend and leave the body, the spell forces it to go back up into the womb and through the body. It is therefore trapped and causes excess heating throughout and evacuation through the mouth. The mention of vomiting is noteworthy here because, as we will see, a real physiological connection between the uterus and mouth exists. It should be noted that the term  (*ḥbb.t*)[30] refers to the primordial waters—to the Nile—but also to the amniotic liquids in the womb. Thus, in the case discussed, this uterine fluid, essential to the pregnancy process, cannot function properly because of the spell. Therefore, the body evacuates it through another orifice.

Misplaced Uterine Substances

Blood is not the only substance that threatens women's health by being trapped and ascending within the body. Gynecological formulas, especially in the first seventeen cases in the Kahun papyrus, also enumerate a multitude of symptoms, such as pain, cramps, infections, respiratory problems, and harmful secretions, all due to a dysfunctional blocked uterus. These manifestations seem to have the ability to migrate throughout the body. Their nature is difficult to define because they may not have a physical reality; they are the expression of a woman's specific condition, which could almost be compared to the premenstrual syndrome or endometriosis much discussed nowadays.[31] But, for an Egyptian, like bodily fluids or air, these agents were real and they could move freely, transported by the channels throughout the body. The ability of the organic components to travel spontaneously is an important aspect in the understanding of the body in ancient Egypt. Some texts also mention that the uterus itself can move, deviate, or even migrate upward in the body, like the heart.[32]

Here, we will consider only a few cases that are particularly enlightening. First of all, a diffusion of symptoms in the surrounding areas close to the uterus is regularly described. The entire pelvic region can be affected, which includes the bladder and the rectum and anus. Pain may even spread to the buttocks and thighs, as in formula no. 3 (1, 8–12), in which "a woman has pain in her rectum, her pubic region, and both of her inner thighs."[33] In that case, the pathological agent responsible for the disease is called the "*khâau*-substance of the uterus." The  (*ḫ3ʿw*), which originally meant "throw, cast off, eject," is probably an abnormal excretion discharged from the sickly womb.[34] The symptoms are considered as the manifestation of these discharges, which dangerously spreads down into the lower limbs of the body.

Sometimes the echoes of uterine pathologies are physically visible elsewhere on the body, such as the head, where they attack the natural orifices (eyes, ears, mouth, and nose) in their search for a way out. In formula no. 5, the woman is described with "toothache and with pain in her gums and (that) she cannot [open] her mouth. *You should conclude:* it is *tiau*—substance of the uterus. *You should treat this* (. . .)".[35] This expression has been further discussed because the word  *(tj3w)* is precisely determined by the elephant tusk, while the woman suffers pain from her teeth and gums. According to W. Westendorf,[36] the patient suffers from strong cramps of her chewing apparatus, but for Th. Bardinet,[37] it is a typical case of tetanus that infects the mouth. Toothache and swollen gums are also known symptoms of premenstrual syndrome; they are due to hormonal variations. The consequences of painful childbirth, during which the woman clenches her jaws tightly, can also be considered.[38]

The senses (sight, hearing, smell, taste) are often affected by diseases of the uterus. In formula no. 2 (1, 5, 8) from the Kahun papyrus,[39] a woman suffers from uterine pain when she moves and she perceives an odor of burning flesh. The physician says: "it is the *nemsu*-substance of the uterus. *You should treat this* by fumigating her with everything that she smells like a roast." A putrid uterine secretion:  (*nmsw*),[40] determined by a pustule, is responsible for the pain, but has also incurred the release of a bad efflux emanating from the uterus, which the woman can detect through her nose. The smell has migrated from the ailing sexual organs to the patient's face. In Formula no. 8 (1, 25–27), the woman has pains in her neck, in her pubic region, and also in her ears "so much so that she cannot hear a word." In that case, the diagnostic says: "it is the *neryu*-substance. *You should treat this:* the same prescription as for removing the *sehau*-substance."[41] The  (*nryw*)[42] is related to shivering and twitching sensations in the womb and causes pain in the closed pubic area, but also in the neck and ears to the extent that the patient goes deaf. The remedy is the same as for  (*sḥ3w*), which is known from other formulas and can be identified as some kind of mucous membrane mixed with blood.[43] Finally, blindness can also be caused by a woman's failing uterus, as in the formula Kahun no. 16 (1, 51–54): "*Examination* of a woman suffering pain in her limbs and eye sockets [...] *kemetu*-substance. *You should conclude*: it is *kemet*-substance of the uterus. (. . .)."[44] The word *kmt*  can, of course, be linked to the term *km*, "black," because it causes the darkening of vision—attacking the limbs, but also the sockets of the eyes.

In these texts, the cause of the disease is a pathological condition of the uterus. The pain, the symptoms, and the secretions spread throughout the body, sometimes in a relatively limited area, but more often the substances travel upward through the whole body and migrate to the face. They colonize other body orifices such as the mouth, eyes, or ears, and cause pain, disability, and even internal bad smells. The cause is a defective opening of the womb which prevents the uterine substances from evacuating properly. Thus, when an obstruction occurs, fluids accumulate in the womb or nearby places, or they totally reverse their flow (this is known as "fausse-route" in French). [45] This dysfunction leads them to move upward via a system of channels, the locations of which are unknown. According to Egyptian conceptions, the body is crossed by a multitude of these *mtw* ("channels"), which all converge toward the heart in one large main tube. This tube connects the facial orifices at the top with the anus and sexual organs at the bottom.[46] If women's bodies are imagined as a long pipe, pathological agents can travel in the wrong direction within the body (upstream) in order to find a way out.[47]

Fertility tests confirm this theory, as they are based on the concept of good "upstream/downstream circulation" of liquids and air. For example, the physician can introduce an element into the patient's vagina and wait for a digestive reaction, as noted in the Carlsberg IV (1 *x*+4 à *x*+6) papyrus: "*[Another way to know one who] will give birth to one will not [give birth]*: You should place an onion inside her flesh (vagina) until the morning. Then, if you find a smell in her mouth, she will give birth. If not, she will not [give birth and] forever."[48] This procedure ensures that there are no obstructions blocking the upward flow of fluids and air, which are essential for the viability of the fetus. The Egyptian seems to believe that "the reproductive system was also connected to the digestive tract."[49] Moreover, other tests recommend putting mixtures into the vagina and waiting for emesis, which is another indication that the fluid is flowing back up.[50] Mythology often mentions conceptions due to the prior ingestion of a fertilizing element that would then go down to the womb, making the woman or goddess immediately pregnant.[51]

The Link between Womb and Milk

The question of milk must also be considered, as there is an obvious link between the menstrual blood, stored in the uterus during pregnancy, and the milk present in the body before breastfeeding ex-utero. For ancient Egyptians, both the man and the woman bring some elements to the fetus through the joining of their fluids during the sexual act. Indeed, as shown by Serge Sauneron[52] and Jean Yoyotte,[53] the sperm comes from the father's bones and flows to the phallus during intercourse. In the womb, this seed creates new bones for the baby. Milk, on the other hand, comes from the mother's flesh and acts as "a female seed" inside the womb during the child's conception.[54] It will form the new flesh of the fetus. Semen and milk mix in the womb through the action of menstrual blood, which has stopped flowing and stays inside the body to shape and cook the embryo.[55]

The vessels going through the breasts were well known to the ancient Egyptians, which is not surprising since they are particularly superficial in that zone. A passage from a physiology treatise says that "two vessels are for her two breasts."[56] The rest of the passage explains that these ducts can "carry heat to the *pḥwy* (of the woman)"—translated as "anus," but also "vaginal entrance."[57] This suggests a physiological connection between the chest and the lower body. The heat, which enters the breasts, probably reaches the heart before it goes down to the pelvic region.[58] Furthermore, a link seems to exist between the breasts and the reproductive system, as some texts highlight the rising and convergence of blood in the breasts during pregnancy. The veins are visible, dilated, and form a relief on the surface of the breasts. The gradual passage of blood through the woman's body to her breasts is a guarantee of good fetal growth and also of good future milk production, as we can read in the fertility test: "If you find her veins flourishing and perfect, not sunken, the birth will be calm. If you find them sunken and like the color of her body, it is miscarriage."[59] If the presence of channels is no longer visible, the prognosis is negative because it implies that the blood may still be blocked somewhere, possibly in the uterine zone. If this is the case, milk production will not start, and blood clogging may cause spontaneous abortion.

The connection between menstrual blood and milk, uterus and breasts, is obvious in another formula in which the fluid of one cures the fluid of the other: "*The beginning of a remedy for not having the nipples go down*: bathe them in the blood of one whose menstruation has just come (for the first time?). Rub it on her belly and both of her thighs so that the *gsw*-disease[60] does not appear on her."[61] The sentence insists on the fact that the menstrual blood has just begun to flow, so it could be the very first menstruation of a young girl. Therefore, this blood is not dirty or impure; on the contrary, it is a symbol of fertility, a promise of pregnancy and birth. Applied to the areas involved, it will bring new vigor and better circulation to the breast whose nipples have gone down and, subsequently, will solve the patient's lactation problems. According to R.A. Jean and A.M. Loyrette,[62] the nature of menstrual blood and milk would be similar: the blood helps in the creation and development of the fetus in the uterus and then transmutes into milk in order to continue, after the birth, to feed and make the child grow.

On the other hand, untransformed blood could suddenly reach the breasts, rendering them incapable of fulfilling their breastfeeding function. Thus, in the "conjuration of the breast," the physician must directly ask the breast not to produce dangerous secretions: "Do not urinate! Do not produce gnawing substances! Do not produce blood!"[63] The first word, *wšš*, has not been well defined, but it is often used for urine and feces in medical documents.[64] Like blood that can rise in the body when the womb is abnormally closed, urine and excrement can be trapped inside the body when the intestines are blocked. Thus, waste flows back in the wrong (upward) direction, up to the chest.[65] In this passage, substances would ascend to the breasts via the channels and would affect their production of milk.

Therefore, several areas are interconnected in women's bodies. If, as for men, the mouth and the anus are connected by a long digestive duct that runs through the whole body, we need to add a secondary channel for the female network carrying substances between the womb, the breasts, and the facial orifices. This channel is also connected to the digestive pathways and can influence their functioning. A formula from the London papyrus transcribes the speech that Isis made while Horus suffered severe burns: "Water is in my mouth, a Nile flood between my thighs. Herewith I come to extinguish the fire! Flow out, burn! This incantation is to be spoken over [1] the milk of a woman who has given birth to a boy, [2] with resin and [3] cat's hair. [All of this] to be placed on burn."[66] Here, it is clear that there is a triple relationship between the goddess's saliva, the blood/flood that escapes from her thighs, and the milk of the male child's mother in the medication. In that context, these orifices and their fluids are similar in their generative and protective functions. Indeed, the act of spitting is also a well-known powerful act of creation in the ancient Egyptian religion.[67]

Conclusion

In conclusion, as with the Mesopotamian texts studied by Ulrike Steinert, ancient Egyptian documents treated contrasting processes in connection with bodily fluids: an overabundance in case of miscarriage on the one hand, and the abnormal retention of fluids inside on the other. The information gained from the study of gynecological texts provides a better understanding of how the Egyptians viewed the internal physiology of women's bodies. The Egyptians perceived a route between the uterus and the face, through which fluids flowed either up or down. Steinert demonstrated that "the 'natural' route for the motion of substances in the body is 'downstream': food and drink enter the body at the top end and come out at the bottom ends of the channel. In extension, the 'natural' route for the purging of gynecological fluids was perceived in the same way"[68]—blood and secretions need to go down through the womb, but when they cannot, they find an alternate out. Thus, the physiology of women is thought of in a different way from that of men, as their sexual fluids (menstrual blood, milk, female secretions), which are essential for procreation, circulate throughout their bodies. Women's illnesses can then be generated by pathological uterine conditions, which can cause her to suffer throughout her body. In the same way, a woman is very dependent on the functioning of her uterus, which she is unable to control: the uterus can open during pregnancy or, alternatively, can remain closed when the blood needs to be evacuated.

The comparison with Near Eastern medicine does not end there. Texts also use the same hydrographic metaphors to describe the human body, especially that of women.[69] Furthermore, there seems to be a connection between the reproductive system and the digestive system in ancient thought, whereby they are seen as operating in parallel. However, unlike in Mesopotamian medicine, Egyptian doctors also saw a channel between the uterus and the breasts, containing blood and milk. Indeed, milk must also circulate in the body to help embryonic creation, and blood must reach the breasts to encourage lactation. At the end of this study, it becomes clear that there is a real and complex system of representation of the woman's body and its fluids that echoes from one ancient culture to another, and it would be beneficial to pursue such investigations in a multidisciplinary way. This type of study tries to integrate medical analysis and ancient physiological conceptions into the broader field of gender studies. Of course, gender is a cultural issue, but perceptions of the body are also intellectual and social creations, and need to be considered further to understand the status of women in ancient Egypt.

Notes

1 On gender studies in Egyptology, see (non-exhaustive list): Gay Robins, *Women in Ancient Egypt* (Cambridge, MA: Harvard University Press, 1993); Janet H. Johnson, "The Legal Status of Women in Ancient Egypt," in *Mistress of the House, Mistress of Heaven: Women in Ancient Egypt*, ed. A.K. Capel and G.E. Markoe (New York: Hudson Hills Press, 1996), 175–86; Ann Macy Roth, "Gender Roles in Ancient Egypt," in *A Companion to the Ancient Near East*, ed. D.C. Snell (Malden: Blackwell, 2005), 211–18; Carolyn Graves-Brown, ed., *Sex and Gender in Ancient Egypt: "Don Your Wig for a Joyful Hour"* (Swansea: Classical Press of Wales, 2008) ; Carolyn Graves-Brown, *Dancing for Hathor: Women in Ancient Egypt* (London and New York: Continuum, 2010); Suzanne Onstine, "Gender and the Religion of Ancient Egypt," *Religion Compass* 4, no. 2 (2010): 1–11; Terry G. Wilfong, "Gender in Ancient Egypt," in *Egyptian Archaeology*, ed. W. Wendrich (Malden: Wiley-Blackwell, 2010), 164–79; Jean Li, *Women, Gender and Identity in Third Intermediate Period Egypt: The Theban Case Study* (London and New York: Routledge, 2017); Uros Matić and Bo Jensen, eds., *Archaeologies of Gender and Violence* (Oxford and Philadelphia: Oxbow Books, 2017).

2 Robert K. Ritner, "A Uterine Amulet in the Oriental Institute Collection," *JNES* 43, no. 3 (1984): 209–21; Wolfhart Westendorf, "Beitrage aus und zu den medizinischen Texten II: Das Isis-Blut Symbol," *ZÄS* 92 (1966): 128–54; Richard-Alain Jean and Anne-Marie Loyrette, *La*

mère, l'enfant et le lait en Égypte ancienne, Collection KUBABA, Série Antiquité (Paris: Harmattan, 2010).

3 All the documents are published and commented in: Hermann Grapow, ed., *Grundriss der Medizin der Alten Ägypter,* vols. 1–8 (Berlin: Academie, 1957–62); Ange-Pierre Leca, *La médecine égyptienne au temps des Pharaons* (Paris: Éditions Roger Dacosta, 1971); Thierry Bardinet, *Les papyrus médicaux dans l'Égypte pharaonique* (Paris: Fayard, 1995); John F. Nunn, *Ancient Egyptian Medicine* (London: British Museum Press, 1996); Wolfhart Westendorf, *Handbuch der altägyptischen Medizin* (Leiden and Boston: Brill, 1999); Eugene Strouhal, Bretislav Vachala, and Hana Vymazalová, *The Medicine of the Ancient Egyptians,* vol. 1, *Surgery, Gynecology, Obstetrics, and Pediatrics* (Cairo: American University in Cairo Press, 2010).

4 Mark Collier and Stephen Quirke, *The UCL Lahun Papyri: Religious, Literary, Legal, Mathematical and Medical* (Oxford: Archaeopress, 2004).

5 John W.B. Barns, *Five Ramesseum Papyri* (Oxford: Oxford University Press, 1956).

6 First editions: Georg Ebers, *Papyros Ebers, Das Hermetische Buch über die Arzeneimittel der Alten Ägypter in hieratischer Schrift* (Leipzig: Osnabrück, 1875); Walter Wreszinski, *Der Papyrus Ebers, Umschrift, Übersetzung und Kommentar* 1 (Leipzig: J.C. Hinrichs'sche Buchhandlung, 1913); Bendix Ebbell, *The Papyrus Ebers: The Greatest Egyptian Medical Document* (Copenhagen: Levin and Munksgaard, 1937).

7 P.Smith verso 3, 13–17. First edition: James Henry Breasted, *The Edwin Smith Surgical Papyrus* (Chicago: University of Chicago Press, 1930), 487–90, pls. XX–XXA, XXI–XXIA.

8 Christian Leitz, *Magical and Medical Papyri of the New Kingdom,* Hieratic Papyri in the British Museum 7 (London: British Museum Press, 1999).

9 Naoko Yamazaki, *Zaubersprüche für Mutter und Kind: Papyrus Berlin 3027. Schriften zur Ägyptologie,* Achet B2 (Berlin: Achet, 2003).

10 First edition: Erik Iversen, *Papyrus Carlsberg no. VIII: With Some Remarks on the Egyptian Origin of Some Popular Birth Prognoses* (Copenhagen: Munksgaard, 1939).

11 First edition: Walter Wreszinski, *Der grosse medizinische Papyrus des Berliner Museums (Pap. Berl 3038)* (Leipzig: J.C. Hinrichs'sche Buchhandlung, 1909–13).

12 Bardinet, *Papyrus médicaux,* 17.

13 Strouhal, Vachala, and Vymazalová, *The Medicine of the Ancient Egyptians,* 98.

14 For a medical interpretation of these symptoms, see Richard-Alain Jean and Anne-Marie Loyrette, "À propos des textes médicaux des papyrus du Ramesseum nos III et IV. II: la gynécologie (1)," in *Encyclopédie religieuse de l'univers végétal, croyances phytoreligieuses de l'Égypte ancienne,* ed. S. Aufrere (Montpellier: Université Paul Valéry–Montpellier III, 2005), 351–489.

15 The same topics are treated in the Hippocratic Corpus (*Diseases of Women* I and II, *On Sterile Women* and *Nature of Woman*); see Hippocrates, vol. 10, *Generation. Nature of the Child. Diseases 4. Nature of Women and Barrenness,* ed. and trans. Paul Potter, Loeb Classical Library 520 (Cambridge, MA: Harvard University Press, 2012); Hippocrates, vol. 11, *Diseases of Women 1–2,* ed. and trans. Paul Potter, Loeb Classical Library 538 (Cambridge, MA: Harvard University Press, 2018). See also the similarities with Chinese medicine in A.K.C. Leung, ed., *Medicine for Women in Imperial China* (Leiden and Boston: Brill, 2006).

16 Ulrike Steinert, "Fluids, Rivers, and Vessels: Metaphors and Body Concepts in Mesopotamian Gynaecological Texts," *Le Journal des Médecines Cunéiformes* 22 (2013): 1–23.

17 On the *mtw* and the Egyptian physiological conception of the human body, see below, p. 287, and Bardinet, *Papyrus médicaux,* 63ff. Identical conceptions are developed by Steinert in "Fluids, Rivers, and Vessels," 10. For the womb seen as a container, see Cathie Spieser, "Vases et peaux d'animaux à fonction matricielle dans l'Égypte ancienne," *BiOr* 63, no. 3/4 (2006): col. 219–34.

18 Ritner, "A Uterine Amulet in the Oriental Institute Collection," 209–21; Westendorf, "Beitrage aus und zu den medizinischen Texten II," 128–54.

19 Bardinet, *Papyrus médicaux,* 147–53; Clémentine Audouit, *Le sang en Égypte ancienne. Représentations et fonctions* (forthcoming).

20 The italicized text corresponds to the passages written in red on the papyrus.

21 P.London no. 29 (IX,14–X,1); translation based on Leitz, *Magical and Medical Papyri of the New Kingdom*, 69.

22 Leitz, *Magical and Medical Papyri of the New Kingdom*, 67–70.

23 P.Louvre [E. 32847] Rx+22,5–22,7; Thierry Bardinet, *Médecins et magiciens à la cour de Pharaon: Une étude du papyrus médical Louvre E 32847* (Paris: Louvre; Khéops, 2018), 145; Clémentine Audouit, "Bodily Fluids in Ancient Egypt: Vital Waters but Dangerous Flows. Concerning an Ongoing Research Project," in *Flesh and Bones: The Individual and His Body in the Ancient Mediterranean Basin*, ed. A. Mouton (Turnhout: Brepols, 2020). In Mesopotamian texts, some metaphors are very similar, as in this incantation from F. Köcher, *Die babylonisch-assyrische Medizin in Texten und Untersuchungen* (Berlin: De Gruyter, 1963–80), 235: 10–16 "Her blood is a carnelian river"; Steinert, "Fluids, Rivers, and Vessels," 10.

24 P.London no. 25 (IX, 1–3); translation based on Leitz, *Magical and Medical Papyri of the New Kingdom*, 67.

25 See examples in Richard Parkinson, *The Tale of the Eloquent Peasant: A Reader's Commentary*, LingAegSM 10 (Hamburg: Widmaier, 2012), 217.

26 P.Ebers no. 828 (96, 13–14).

27 P.Smith v° 3, 13–3,17.

28 Hippocrates, *Diseases of Women*, II, 1.

29 P.Ebers no. 833 (97, 1–7).

30 *Wb* III, 63.1–5; William A. Ward, *The Fourth Egyptian Homographic Roots B-3, Etymological and Egypto-Semitic Studies, Studia-Pohl: series maior* 6 (Rome: Biblical Institute Press, 1978), 103–105; Audouit, "Body Fluids in Ancient Egypt," 47.

31 Paula K. Braverman, "Premenstrual Syndrome and Premenstrual Dysphoric Disorder," *Journal of Pediatric and Adolescent Gynecology* 20, no. 1 (2007): 3–12.

32 Andrew Bednarski, "Hysteria Revisited: Women's Public Health in Ancient Egypt," in *Current Research in Egyptology 2000*, ed. A. McDonald and C. Riggs (Oxford: Archaeopress, 2000), 11–17; Rachel Rodabaugh Suvorov, "The Kahun Papyrus in Context: The 'Floating Uterus,'" in *Current Research in Egyptology 2004*, ed. R.J. Dann (Oxford: Oxbow, 2006), 138–46. See also the uterus spell in *Papyri Graecae Magicae (PGM)* VII. 260–71: "You (uterus) do not turn into the right part of the ribs, or into the left part of the ribs, and that you do not gnaw into the heart . . . ," in Hans Dieter Betz, ed., *The Greek Magical Papyri in Translation Including the Demotic Spells* (Chicago: University of Chicago Press, 1986), 123–24. The uterus could be compared to the heart, an organ that can also move in the body; see Richard-Alain Jean and Anne-Marie Loyrette, *La mère, l'enfant et le lait en Égypte ancienne*, 34–35.

33 Strouhal, Vachala, and Vymazalová, *The Medicine of the Ancient Egyptians*, 107.

34 Hildegard von Deines and Wolfhart Westendorf, *Grundriss der Medizin der Alten Ägypter* 7, pt. 2 (Berlin: Akademie, 1961), 648; Nunn, *Ancient Egyptian Medicine*, 197.

35 Strouhal, Vachala, and Vymazalová, *The Medicine of the Ancient Egyptians*, 108.

36 Deines and Westendorf, *Grundriss der Medizin der Alten Ägypter* 7, pt. 2, 937–38; Wolfhart Westendorf, *Handbuch der altägyptischen Medizin* 1, 413.

37 Bardinet, *Papyrus médicaux*, 222.

38 P.Kahun no. 33 (3, 25–26): "Preventing toothache of a woman (. . .) on the day she gives birth. [It is] really effective for driving out *tjau*."

39 Strouhal, Vachala, and Vymazalová, *The Medicine of the Ancient Egyptians*, 107.

40 Deines and Westendorf, *Grundriss der Medizin der Alten Ägypter* 7, pt. 1, 462. There could be a connection with the word *mns3/nms3* ("effusion"); see Hermann Kees, "Ein alter Götterhymnus als Begleittext zur Opfertafel," *ZÄS* 57 (1922): 111. There could also be an "enveloping" substance, perhaps a pathological membrane (*nms*, "to wrap" or "to cover"; *Wb* II, 269.5).

41 Strouhal, Vachala, and Vymazalová, *The Medicine of the Ancient Egyptians*, 108.

42 Deines and Westendorf, *Grundriss der Medizin der Alten Ägypter* 7, pt. 1, 467.

43 See P.Kahun [UC32057] no.17 (2,25–30).
44 Strouhal, Vachala, and Vymazalová, *The Medicine of the Ancient Egyptians*, 109.
45 Steinert, "Fluids, Rivers, and Vessels," 10.
46 Bardinet, *Papyrus médicaux*, 63–68.
47 About the link between uterus and facial orifices, see also Paul Frandsen, "The Menstrual 'Taboo' in Ancient Egypt," *JNES* 66 (2007): 84. For a comparison with the Greek world, see Helen King, *Hippocrates' Woman: Reading the Female Body in Ancient Greece* (London and New York: Routledge, 1998), 28, 79.
48 Parallel in P.Kahun no. 28 (3, 17–19).
49 Strouhal, Vachala, and Vymazalová, *The Medicine of the Ancient Egyptians*, 162.
50 For example, P.Berlin no. 194 (verso 1, 5–6) and P.Kahun no. 27 (3, 15–17).
51 Of course, Nut is the best example since she swallows the sun every night to give birth to him again every morning. In "The Tale of the Two Brothers" (18, 4–5), a woman also becomes pregnant after swallowing a splinter of wood; cf. William K. Simpson, *The Literature of Ancient Egypt* (New Haven: Yale University Press, 2003), 89.
52 Serge Sauneron, "Le germe dans les os," *BIFAO* 60 (1960): 19–27.
53 Jean Yoyotte, "Les os et la semence masculine à propos d'une théorie physiologique égyptienne," *BIFAO* 61 (1962): 139–46.
54 Jean and Loyrette, *La mère, l'enfant et le lait en Égypte ancienne*, 99; Cathie Spieser, "De l'embryon humain à l'embryon divin en Égypte ancienne," in *L'embryon humain à travers l'histoire: Images, savoirs et rites. Actes du colloque international de Fribourg 27–29 octobre 2004*, ed. V. Dasen (Gollion: In Folio, 2007), 23–24.
55 Bardinet, *Papyrus médicaux*, 139–53; Clémentine Audouit, *Le sang en Égypte ancienne.*
56 P.Berlin, 163c.
57 Leitz, *Magical and Medical Papyri of the New Kingdom*, 67n151; Jens Bl. Joergensen, "Myths, Menarche and the *Return of the Goddess*," in *Lotus and Laurel: Studies on Egyptian Language and Religion in Honour of Paul John Frandsen*, ed. R. Nyord and K. Ryholt, CNI Publications 39 (Copenhagen: Museum Tusculanum Press, 2015), 139–40.
58 Bardinet, *Papyrus médicaux*, 116.
59 P.Berlin no. 196, 1,9–1,11.
60 *Wb.* V, 203, 7, related to *gsgs* ("overflow" or "submerge"); *Wb.* V, 207, 8–9.
61 P.Ebers no. 808 (95, 1–3).
62 Jean and Loyrette, *La mère, l'enfant et le lait en Égypte ancienne*, 323–35.
63 P.Ebers no. 811 (95, 7–14) = P.Louvre rx+10, 6–11.
64 Deines and Westendorf, *Grundriss der Medizin der Alten Ägypter* 7, pt. 1, 218–22 (*wšš* and *wššt*).
65 See P.Ebers no. 854o in which the body is drowned in excrement. See Steinert, "Fluids, Rivers, and Vessels," 7.
66 P.London no. 35 (r° 10,14–11,2); see Leitz, *Magical and Medical Papyri of the New Kingdom*, 72.
67 Robert K. Ritner, *The Mechanics of Ancient Egyptian Magical Practice*, SAOC 54 (Chicago: Oriental Institute of the University of Chicago, 1993), 75–78.
68 Steinert, "Fluids, Rivers, and Vessels," 14.
69 About this specific topic, see Audouit, "Body Fluids in Ancient Egypt," 39–67.

22

Women's Health Issues as Seen in Theban Tomb 16

Suzanne Onstine, Jesús Herrerín López, Nataša Šarkić, Miguel Sanchez, and Rosa Dinarès Solà

THEBAN TOMB 16,[1] belonging to Panehsy and his wife Tarenu, is a Nineteenth Dynasty tomb located in Dra Abu-l-Naga, the northern part of the cemetery of Theban elites in Luxor. It is a small T-shaped chapel with a long sloping corridor, typical of Ramesside tombs.[2] This corridor was extensively used for secondary burials in the Third Intermediate Period and later, most likely until the Greco-Roman Period. In modern times, the secondary burials were heavily looted so that the jumbled and broken remains are not individually datable, nor are we able to reassemble bodies or burial assemblages. However, the distinctive styles of the burial equipment, also heavily damaged in the looting, are what allow us to make assumptions about the dates of the secondary burial phase of use. It should be noted that the full analysis of human remains from the tomb is not yet complete, so the findings presented here are preliminary, but should provide insight into how women's health issues in ancient Egypt were not so different from our own.[3]

For this paper, I will use the fields of Egyptology, gender studies, and bioarchaeology as reference points to discuss the lives of women and, in particular, their health, with reference to and illustrated by the diagnoses of conditions found in the women of TT 16.[4] This paper contextualizes those medical findings in terms of both how we study women in antiquity and how these women in TT 16 fit into ancient Egyptian society.

Women's health issues are often thought of as largely reproductive-age problems, or the medical conditions surrounding menstruation, pregnancy, and childbirth.[5] While reproductive organs and pregnancy are certainly a visible way in which men and women differ, they are not the only ways. Current approaches to medicine recognize that men's and women's bodies experience disease and aging differently; for example, symptoms of heart attack often present differently in women than men. Similarly, our approach to studying the bodies found in ancient Egyptian contexts should receive this kind of attention, aware of the biological realities associated with the different life stages of being male or female and the different ways any person would have experienced a particular pathology. Sex is only one factor among many that may simultaneously affect how a person experiences health; age, social class, and geographic setting all interact with individuals with respect to health issues. This leads to a very complex set of factors that should be considered with every diagnosis made in the field. Even when those factors cannot be known with certainty, the act of asking questions in this way ensures that human remains are treated with a thoughtfulness that respects their lived experience. It is simply not enough to ask of the material whether they were male or female, and to assign an age range or cause of death.

Discussing women's health means looking beyond reproductive health issues, although these will always be important to include, and in fact TT 16 has some dramatic examples related to this subject. Menopausal women's issues and the other ways that women generally experienced health issues should be investigated and added to the dialogue. Additionally, it should be recognized that differences in pathologies could result from both biological causes and gendered cultural practices. In any given physical anthropology report from an excavation, these kinds of issues might be noted, but the larger generalities rarely make it into Egyptological narratives about the life cycles of women.

With this perspective then, the University of Memphis mission to TT 16 has been collecting data on the human remains present in the tomb. There are a number of research questions that address the idea of women's health as a specific topic within the larger population. The most general area of inquiry is to ascertain the general health conditions of the Theban people in the first millennium BCE: what are the common pathologies we can observe? From this, we can be more specific and look at whether there are differences in pathologies between men and women, and whether those differences are due to biological factors, cultural factors, or a combination of the two. Presented here are a few interesting cases that illustrate some women's health concerns from TT 16.

Reproductive Health

In ancient Egypt, women's cultural identities had a strong base in the biological ability to bear children. The role of mother was not only special to the family unit, but also religiously codified through the role of the mother goddesses and through an emphasis on fertility in religious ideology. There were protective deities specifically for protecting women and babies during this time (for example, Bes and Taweret) because the act of creation is messy, dangerous, and terrifying; childbirth can kill mothers. And while it is a truism to say that mortality rates for women in the childbearing years are much higher than men in the same age group, rarely do we have such obvious examples of this phenomenon as the two cases presented here.[6]

Case #1

The first case consists of a pelvis only. It can be determined that the pelvis belonged to a woman between twenty and twenty-five years of age. There were no signs of further pathologies. However, at the pubic bone junction the two halves of the pelvis are tied together with a linen rope that goes through the membrane that would normally hold the two sides of the pelvis in the correct position in the body. It is clear it was tied from inside the pelvic cavity. This area of the body is not normally interfered with in the mummification process, and in order to achieve this maneuver a larger abdominal incision would have been necessary. So why was this done? The hypothesis we suggest is that after the death of the woman, the embalmers removed a fetus and, in doing so, the ligaments that join the two halves of the pelvis were broken. Although we did not determine a cause of death, the young age of the woman is consistent with maternal mortality rates. Tying the pelvis back together seems to have served to restore symbolic functionality to the woman so that she could be whole in the afterlife. In a previous publication, we have noted several instances, including this one, of emendations to the body in the mummification process that we have called "prostheses for the afterlife."[7] These prostheses consisted of postmortem fixtures that addressed problems in the body and aimed to restore appearance or functionality to a specific part of the body. In this case, the practice helped ensure the woman would be able to act as a mother in the afterlife. Since motherhood was an important aspect of women's identities, this repair might have been deemed an important part of her mummification.

Case #2

The second case is part of a mummified woman consisting of an abdomen, pelvis, and part of the spinal column. The most noteworthy aspect of this woman's body is the preserved genitalia. The clitoris is still intact, and there is no sign of trauma related to female genital mutilation. The vagina also appears to be in a distended state. The diameter of the vaginal opening measures approximately 32 x 43 mm. This wide opening suggests that the woman died during or shortly after a birth event. The vagina would have shrunk back to its normal smaller diameter within approximately twenty-four hours of the birth. Based on the spinal measurements and a lack of arthritis in the spinal column, it is estimated that she was between twenty and twenty-five years old, prime child-bearing years. The pelvic cavity was packed with a sandy concrete-like hard substance. The reason for this packing is unclear and has been found in mummies of both sexes in TT 16. In addition to aesthetic reasons to fill out the abdominal cavity, in this case there may be a reason related to the removal of a child; the packing would have replaced the volume of the child during the mummification process. Although we cannot be certain about the cause of death, if she does represent a childbirth-related death, it is certainly one of the most striking pieces of evidence illustrating the dangers of pregnancy in the ancient world.

Menopausal Women

Queen Tiye's famous wooden head, now in Berlin, is so memorable partly because there are few representations of older women in art. Egyptians rarely portrayed women at different stages of life, preferring to stick close to the ideal of young adulthood, or childbearing years. Many Egyptological studies about women also concentrate on these years and, in particular, the symbolic aspects of fertility and sexual arousal are themes mentioned in nearly every study dealing with women. However, works like Deborah Sweeney's articles[8] on older women and aging at Deir al-Medina help to fill the gap, exploring women's lives beyond those fertile years. TT 16 can also contribute to this body of work on older women. Three metabolic conditions are present that are pathologies associated with post-menopausal women and can help us think about the lived experiences of life beyond pregnancy. These conditions are hyperostosis frontalis interna, parietal thinning, and osteoporosis.

Hyperostosis frontalis interna is a thickening of the frontal bone of the skull, most commonly found in women over sixty-five.[9] In most cases the individual is unaware of the condition as it presents no serious threat to health or activity. Parietal thinning is a progressive disease that affects the density of bone in the parietal bones of the skull.[10] It is most often associated with middle-aged people and encountered more often in women than men. On its own, it is not a serious condition leading to symptoms or problems. Like hyperostosis frontalis interna, it was probably a condition the individual did not know they had, although if the bone became extremely thin, it could be a contributing factor to head injuries.

Osteoporosis is the most common of these three, with several examples present in the TT 16 population. Osteoporosis is the loss of bone density; it increases the likelihood of broken bones and secondary problems associated with broken bones. This pattern correlates well to what we know of modern populations where osteoporosis is most commonly associated with older women. It is also corroborated in at least one ancient population by the study of Zaki, Hussein, and El Banna that confirms a higher rate of osteoporosis in elite women from Giza.[11] Both biological and cultural components of behavior are cited; the predisposition of women to getting the disease and the sedentary lifestyle of elites at Giza could both have been contributing factors to the disease.

These three examples are a good reminder that, although a specific disease may be found in both men and women, the disease may affect men and women in disproportionate ways and may present differently and have different outcomes.

Cultural Practices

Arthritis is an extremely common pathology in TT 16, affecting both men and women, with causes that could be related to age or to behavioral choices. It is well established that lifestyle and work habits can produce specific patterns of arthritis. In TT 16, many individuals showed signs of arthritis consistent with age and with normal activities, such as walking a lot. When specific traumas are seen predominantly in one sex or the other, we can speak of gendered behavioral habits that caused this trauma. One interesting pattern that is emerging in some female remains is arthritis in the neck vertebrae and at the base of the skull. These are consistent with carrying heavy objects on the head, as is known from ancient and modern Egypt. And while men and women can both be seen doing this in ancient depictions, like the offering-bearer processions in tomb scenes where both men and women carry things on their heads,[12] the bones with this problem in TT 16 are largely female.

Conclusions

This brief, nonmedical overview of some of the findings of physical anthropologists is meant to reach a wider, nonanthropological audience in order to increase Egyptological awareness of the value of such studies and how they can fit with established narratives and push those narratives further. The lived experiences of gender happen in the body, so focusing attention on the actual bodies is a natural place to start. By thinking about human remains not just as biologically sexed individuals, but rather as gendered individuals, we can think more critically about what artistic portrayals mean as lived experiences, and we can correlate statistics with common tropes, such as the anxiety associated with childbirth. The real value of interdisciplinarity is the ability to formulate new and more meaningful historical narratives from these observations.

Notes

1 PM I[1], 28–29; KRI III, 396–99; G. Foucart, M. Baud, and E. Droiton, *Le Tombeau de Panehsy*, in *Tombes Thébaines. Nécropole de Dira' Abu'n-Naga*, MIFAO 57.2 (Cairo: IFAO, 1932).

2 Publications related to various aspects of the tomb include: S. Onstine, "University of Memphis Mission to Theban Tomb 16: The Life of Panehsy, Chanter and Priest," *JARCE* 47 (2011): 231–36; S. Onstine, "A Brief Report on the University of Memphis Mission to Theban Tomb 16 in Dra Abu el-Naga," *NSSEA* (summer 2012), 4–5; S. Onstine, "A Preliminary Report on the Clearance of Theban Tomb 16 in Dra Abu el-Naga at Thebes," in *Archaeological Research in the Valley of the Kings and Ancient Thebes*, ed. Pearce Paul Creasman (Tucson: University of Arizona, 2013), 227–40; J. Herrerín, M. Sanchez, S. Onstine, V. Reckard, E. Warkentin, and T. Redman, "Prosthesis for the Afterlife in TT16, Luxor, Egypt," *JARCE* 50 (2014): 127–45.

3 Full publications of the tomb and the human remains are in preparation.

4 Thanks to the great work of my physical anthropology team and coauthors, much of this data was presented at the American University in Cairo in the "Bioarchaeology in Ancient Egypt" conference, January 2019, and has been published as Suzanne Onstine et al., "Women's Health Issues Reflected in Case Studies from Theban Tomb 16," in *The Ancient Egyptians and Their Natural World: Flora, Fauna, and Science*, edited by Salima Ikram, Jessica Kaiser, and Stéphanie Porcier (Leiden: Sidestone Press, 2021), 191–98.

5 Some authors have made attempts at covering a more comprehensive life cycle for women. See, for example, Rosalind M. Janssen and Jac. J. Janssen, *Growing Up and Getting Old in Ancient Egypt* (London: Golden House Publications, 2007); and Jaana Toivari-Viitala, *Women at Deir el-Medina: A Study of the Status and Roles of the Female Inhabitants in the Workmen's Community during the Ramesside Period* (Leiden: NINO, 2001).

6 Onstine et al., "Women's Health Issues."

7 See J. Herrerín et al., "Prosthesis for the Afterlife," for more on this aspect of research in TT 16.

8 See Deborah Sweeney, "Forever Young? The Representation of Older and Ageing Women in Ancient Egyptian Art," *JARCE* 41 (2004): 67–84; Deborah Sweeney, "Women Growing Older in Deir el-Medina," in *Living and Writing in Deir el-Medine: Socio-historical Embodiment of Deir el-Medine Texts*, ed. Andreas Dorn and Tobias Hofmann (Basel: Schwabe, 2006), 135–53.

9 https://radiopaedia.org/articles/hyperostosis-frontalis-interna?lang=us, accessed 1 March 2020.

10 https://radiopaedia.org/articles/bilateral-thinning-of-the-parietal-bones?lang=us, accessed 1 March 2020.

11 Moushira E. Zaki, F.H. Hussein, and R. Abd El-Shafy El Banna, "Osteoporosis among Ancient Egyptians," *International Journal of Osteoarchaeology* 19, no. 1 (2009): 78–89.

12 For male examples, see TT 13 (Shuroy), PM I[1], 25 wall 9 register I, depicting a row of men with boxes balanced on their heads as part of the funerary procession, and a similar one on the relief from TT 319 of Neferu, now in the Metropolitan Museum of Art, accession number 26.3.353p, https://www.metmuseum.org/art/collection/search/552055 (accessed 20 June 2020). For female examples, see female offering bearers such as the relief from TT 312 now in the Metropolitan Museum of Art, accession number 1997.137.6, https://www.metmuseum.org/art/collection/search/550441 (accessed 20 June 2020), and the statuette of a similar figure, Metropolitan Museum of Art, accession number 20.3.7, https://www.metmuseum.org/art/collection/search/544210 (accessed June 20, 2020).

23

Shifting Perceptions of Tattooed Women in Ancient Egypt

Anne Austin

While the earliest evidence for tattooing on a mummy from ancient Egypt was found well over a century ago,[1] it has only been in the past decade that we have seen incredible growth in physical evidence for ancient Egyptian tattooing. This disparity between initial evidence for tattooing in the early twentieth century and more recent evidence allows us to compare how scholars have approached the topic over time. With both changes in evidence and broader changes in social attitudes toward tattooing today, the perceptions of tattoos in ancient Egypt have also shifted. As most evidence for tattooing has been specifically found on women, these shifting perceptions have in particular changed our attitudes around tattooed women in the past.

This essay offers an overview of the previous interpretations of tattooing in ancient Egypt and Nubia. After a brief description of existing evidence in human remains and art,[2] I review the various functions of tattooing discussed in previous literature along with the problems and limitations of the conclusions of these earlier authors. I then review more recent evidence and interpretations to show the status of current research on tattooing and its possible functions in ancient Egypt.

Early Evidence in Human Remains for the Practice of Tattooing in Ancient Egypt and Nubia

The first human remains from Egypt identified with tattoos belonged to a woman named Amunet, who was discovered in 1891 during excavations by Grébaut in the funerary enclosure of Mentuhotep II at Deir al-Bahari.[3] Over

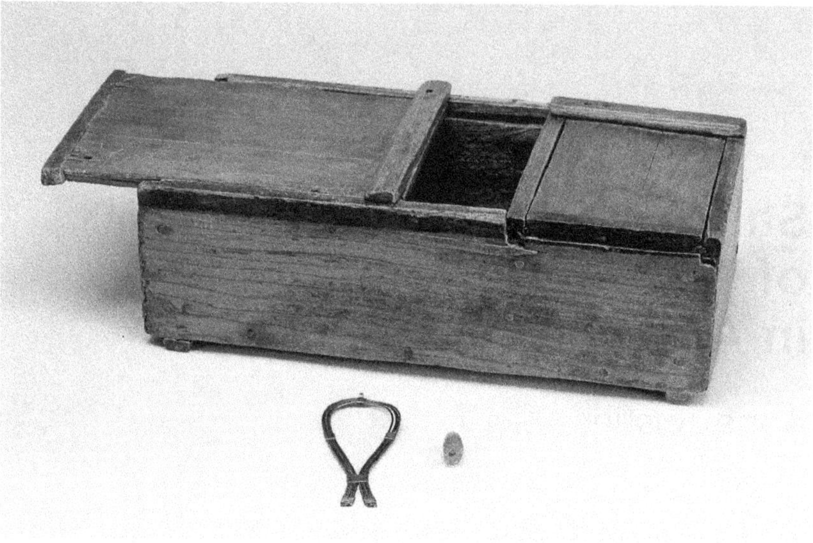

Fig. 23.1. Electrum and silver *sa* amulet (25.3.253), carnelian *seweret* bead (25.3.252), and wooden box (25.3.255a–c) found associated with an unnamed tattooed woman buried in pit 23 of the North Triangular Court of the Temple of Mentuhotep II in Deir al-Bahari. Discovered during the 1922–23 MMA excavations

three decades later, Winlock discovered two tattooed human remains and a figurine with decorations of tattoos from the same region. While early scholars suggested that, given the predominant number of women buried in this area,[4] it was reserved for a royal harem (defined as multiple wives or concubines) of Mentuhotep II,[5] more recent scholarship has suggested that the women were elite members of the royal court, serving as the royal retinue of the queen[6] and/or as royal performers in the cult of Hathor.[7] Roehrig recently revisited earlier publications of these women to collate what is known about their burial contexts.[8] All three were found in Eleventh Dynasty pit tombs in the north triangular court of the Temple of Mentuhotep II at Deir al-Bahari. The two unidentified women were found with valuable grave goods, including a *sa* amulet made of electrum and a carnelian *seweret* bead found in an intricate wooden box (fig. 23.1).

Amunet was found in a decorated coffin bearing the titles "Priestess of Hathor" and "Sole Ornament of the King," or as recently preferred, "Sole Lady-in-Waiting."[9] Soon after these discoveries, Firth identified tattoos on the abdomen of a woman from a Nubian C-group rectangular pit grave in Kubban. Her burial included a "quantity of white shell beads threaded on leather thong,"[10] and he notes that the patterned dots look similar to those found on a previously excavated wooden "doll."[11] In addition to this evidence from human remains, twentieth-century excavations have revealed similar geometric motifs on truncated figurines and paddle dolls from broader Thebes[12] which were interpreted as possible tattoos. Finally, both Vandier d'Abbadie[13] and Bruyère[14] identified possible tattoos of Bes on the thighs of a woman in a *lit clos* fresco from Deir al-Medina. In addition to this example, Keimer identified several other pictorial representations of Bes tattoos on the thighs of women from the New Kingdom.[15]

This evidence, discovered in the twentieth century, suggested that tattooing was either completely a Nubian tradition or derived from Nubia, especially given that several early scholars proposed that the three tattooed women from Deir al-Bahari could have been of Nubian descent.[16] Tattooing also appeared to have been practiced exclusively on women since all of the tattooed mummified bodies and artistic depictions of tattoos were found on women. Artistic depictions of tattoos have been primarily found on nude figures, and while tattoos in the Middle Kingdom were primarily geometric, those found in the New Kingdom emphasized the god Bes and were frequently associated with female musicians. While more recent evidence has broadened our interpretations of tattooing (see below), this initial evidence has had a major influence on the perceptions of ancient Egyptian tattooed women throughout the twentieth century.

Early Perceptions of the Functions of Tattooing in Ancient Egypt

There are several key themes that emerge when reviewing nineteenth- and twentieth-century scholarship on tattooing based on this early evidence. In the earliest writings, tattooed women were seen as dancers, concubines, and sex workers. Their tattoos were interpreted as primarily decorative, functioning to provoke carnal desire from a male gaze. These interpretations suggest that tattoos were perceived as both advertising and manifesting erotic desire. Importantly, these early hypotheses around the functions of tattoos often explicitly divorced sexual desire from fertility, motherhood, and the family.

Early Egyptologists used circumstantial arguments to suggest ancient Egyptian tattooed women were concubines based on the burial context of the three tattooed mummified bodies. They were among a group of women buried in the North Court of Mentuhotep II's burial enclosure, some of whom had the title "wife of the king." Scholars had suggested that these women were a royal harem, and those without royal titles, including the three tattooed mummified bodies, were the king's concubines.[17] The association of dancing girl and concubine with tattooed women was also based on the connections scholars made between tattooed mummified bodies and female figurines, the latter of which were often viewed and described as specifically designed to sexually arouse a male tomb owner either for general pleasure or for his rebirth in the afterlife.[18]

For example, in his publication of the two unnamed, tattooed mummified bodies from Deir al-Bahari, Winlock described them thus: "two nearly complete mummies turned out to be those of dancing girls tattooed exactly like the little faience figure from the living bodies."[19] He assumed they were dancing girls based on his discovery of a tattooed female figurine in the same year found in the tomb of Neferhotep, of which he wrote: "In the passages there was a fragment of a magnificent blue faience hippopotamus rearing up and roaring mightily—quarry for Neferhotep's chase in the Elysian fields—and with it a little faience dancing girl, clad in a cowrie shell girdle and tattooing, to amuse him after the hunt."[20] In both cases, Winlock does not provide additional evidence explaining why these particular women should be dancers, but this association has continued to be made with these particular tattooed women for decades. In subsequent publications about them, these women were similarly labeled as dancing girls, and their tattoos were seen as decorative.[21] While there is additional evidence suggesting tattooing could be linked to dancing (see below), these are not mentioned in discussions of tattooed women. Instead, the focus is on dancing as a means of entertaining, and this is often linked with more explicit references to tattooed women's bodies serving an erotic male gaze.

Vandier d'Abbadie[22] suggested that tattoos of Bes on the thighs of a woman dancing in a *lit clos* fresco at Deir al-Medina may have indicated she was a sex worker. Keimer takes this interpretation with more certainty and offers the strongest and clearest interpretation of tattooed women as functioning for erotic male pleasure, viewing tattooing as a signal of sex work. In discussing the three tattooed mummified bodies, he states:

> pour être attachées à quelque service divin n'en étaient pas moins des péripatéticiennes. Quant aux statuettes montrant l'indication de tatouages, elles représentent sans aucun doute possible,—nous l'avons déjà souligné plus haut (p. 26 et 27)—, des femmes appartenant au même "milieu" que celles dont nous possédons les momies tatouées, parce que les motifs des marques cutanées en question, surtout les points disposés en losanges, sont exactement les mêmes sur les momies et sur les statuettes. J'ajouterai encore que je ne connais aucun exemple, remontant à l'Égypte ancienne, d'une femme de bonne société ornée de tatouages.[23]

Keimer's disdain for tattooed women is palpable. He indicates that even if they were affiliated with priestly titles, they were still sex workers, and uses his own cultural context to argue that tattooed women from the ancient past to the present cannot be a part of "good society." In addition to the above quotes, he mocks Bruyère for attempting to do "l'impossible pour sauver l'honneur" of tattooed "ladies" (note his use of sarcastic quotation marks) by interpreting tattoos as part of the cultic celebration of the family.[24] He suggests that Bruyère's interpretation of tattooing being related to maternity and fertility is erroneous because they can be both mothers and sex workers, possibly even implying that motherhood is a consequence of their occupation, but not the objective of tattooing. Even when he refers to tattoos associated with the goddess Taweret, a goddess known as a protector of childbirth and fertility, he uses it as proof that the figurines with decorations of tattoos represent concubines, sex workers, and/or dancers, even if they were also pregnant or mothers.[25]

By using his views of the morality and social standing of tattooed women in modern Europe as further proof for the status of these women, Keimer demonstrates how early twentieth-century views of tattooing influenced his perceptions of tattooing in the past. Keimer and other early twentieth-century scholarship on tattooing demonstrate an overall bias in the perception of tattooed women and Egyptian mummified bodies that reflects broader views in the United States and Europe during the twentieth century. Tattoos were most publicly affiliated with eroticized circus performances in the 1880s through the 1920s, with socially marginalized groups such as sex workers in the 1920s through the 1950s, and with prisoners and gangs in the 1950s through the 1970s.[26] Academic discourse during these times more broadly reflects these ethnocentric biases and stigmas, labeling tattooing as an indicator of social and psychological disorder. Tattooing was discussed as a sign of social deviancy,[27] and with that, tattooing was seen as a sign of sex work and sexual promiscuity among women.[28] Keimer's, Winlock's, Derry's, and Vandier d'Abbadie's perceptions of Egyptian women's tattooed bodies as not only erotic, but also consumable for the male tomb owner as a figurine or person, align with these broader trends in European and American interpretations of tattoos during this time.

Additionally, the eroticization of ancient Egyptian women may have been partially informed by the broader tendency in Egyptomania to eroticize females mummified during this same period. During the late nineteenth and early twentieth centuries, media representations of mummies "deal not with the vengeful mummies popularized by Hollywood, but with male collectors and Egyptologists who fall in love with revitalized female mummies."[29] Indeed, in his opening discussion of tattooed women from Egypt, Keimer says, "Les lecteurs de ce Mémoire seront probablement surpris d'avoir à étudier les anciens tatouages d'Égypte,—qui présentent essentiellement un intérêt décoratif—sur la peau desséchée de charmantes danseuses et concubines royales du Moyen Empire devenues momies grimaçantes."[30] Keimer repeats the idea that the women were concubines and dancers while also making it clear that the tattoos were intended only for decoration. Keimer is focused on both the idea that these women would have been attractive in the past and his own disgust at their current mummified state. His comments about their transformation from charming dancers to grimacing mummies are mirrored by the next quote he gives by Maspero: "A voir telle momie de Turin ou d'une autre collection européenne, —un paquet d'os desséchés à peine recouverts d'une peau brune, et des traits contractés par l'embaumement en une grimace lamentable ou grotesque, —il faut une certaine force d'imagination pour recomposer la jeune fille élégante et frêle dont le charme subtil enivra les galants de Thèbes durant sa verte nouveauté."[31] Keimer not only promotes the assumption that the tattooed women were dancers and concubines, but, by quoting Maspero, emphasizes that their nude bodies were intended for an erotic male gaze, the function of which has since been lost due to the ravages of time and mummification. He goes on to say that the female figurines "présentant un aspect plus amiable que nos pauvres momies tatouées,"[32] even redirecting their role as manifesting enjoyment for a male gaze to himself. These quotes also reveal how Keimer and others continually describe these women in the past as youthful (for example, referring to them as girls), regardless of their actual estimated age at death.[33]

This tendency to eroticize tattooed mummies and figurines while divorcing them from the related topics of fertility and family has continued in more recent decades. Cherpion agrees with Keimer's assertion that tattoos of the god Bes advertised a woman as being a sex worker, going on to say that "les dames dont la cuisse est tatouée à l'effigie du dieu Bès sont bien des dames aux mœurs dévergondées et libertines."[34] Cherpion's assertions are based on the fact that tattooed women are nude adults and musicians, linking both to eroticism and ultimately advertising themselves as a woman who is "ready to give herself" to her husband, lover, or client.[35]

Additional evidence indicates that later in the twentieth century, scholars clearly continued to believe that the purpose of interred tattooed bodies, whether physical or as figurines, was the sexual pleasure of deceased male tomb owners. In describing tattooed figures, Bianchi states:

> Small in scale, easily fondled, and intentionally rendered physically helpless, such statuettes were interred with the deceased to arouse his primitive

> sexual instincts . . . The priestess Amunet and the figurines in question are all associated with Hathor, the most lascivious of all Egyptian goddesses . . . . Consequently the tattoos of this group of figurines and of the mummy of Amunet have an undeniably carnal overtone.[36]

His comments are echoed by Goelet's interpretation of nude, female bodies: "It is not surprising that the depictions of unclothed females should be overwhelmingly connected with male pleasure, sex, and fertility."[37] Despite having more evidence to contradict these claims—namely, the presence of figurines with decorations of tattoos in a variety of contexts and not exclusively deposited in male tombs—Goelet doubles down on their need to be seen as exclusively erotic, and on the role of tattooing in advertising these women's bodies as lower class:

> Even when they are associated with female burials, these figurines probably do not represent the tomb owners themselves, for the statuettes usually have no feet and often the wigs are not the types worn by noble ladies. Furthermore, a number of both types of figurine seem to be adorned with tattoos, a practice limited to servants and the lower social classes.[38]

In some examples in early scholarship, tattooing moves beyond the focus on identifying women as concubines, sex workers, and dancers for amusement. Most notably, Bernard Bruyère states:

> Il nous semble plutôt qu'elles personnifient toujours la femme, mais avec le but bien précisé de la reproduction et cette précision de fonction a pour expression l'absence de costume et la présence de bijoux et de tatouages parce que la femme qui veut plaire, dans l'Orient ancien (Bible) se dévêt pour danser . . . La toilette particulière des figurines nues, tatouées et parées, n'est d'ailleurs pas exclusivement réservée a la danse, c'est ici, plutôt celle d'amour qui doit assurer la lignée familiale et il est intéressant de constater que le culte de la famille est ainsi élevé dès les origines à la hauteur d'un principe et qu'il se joint au culte funéraire pour constituer le germe de la religion des ancêtres et des dieux.[39]

While Bruyère still emphasizes that tattooing eroticizes a female body, he shifts the function of this to serving the cult of the family. Bruyère thus bridges the artificial divide between eroticism and female fertility. This same idea is reiterated in later scholarship. Robins[40] suggests that the naked imagery of women was intended to symbolize family continuity in domestic contexts and regeneration in mortuary contexts. This shift in perception of tattooed women moves them away from male amusement to a model on functional fertility.

The earliest publication on tattooing in ancient Egypt is quite distinct from the scholarship discussed above. Fouquet[41] proposes that scarification and tattoos on the mummy of Amunet served as a kind of medical treatment for a chronic ailment near the pelvis. He uses his research on recent medical tattoos on Coptic Egyptians as a link between ancient and modern practices. Despite the early date of his work, however, Fouquet is infrequently cited, and his suggestion has had comparatively less influence over later scholarship.

In summary, twentieth-century scholarship on tattooing often focused on the perception that tattoos function to eroticize female bodies and serve to emphasize their sexuality. What shifted was the role eroticism played. Earlier interpretations link it with sex work and male amusement while later interpretations tend to focus on its role in ensuring fertility for the tomb owner and, in some cases, his family. Recent evidence and research have greatly expanded our ideas about tattooing, but discourse focusing exclusively on eroticism is still visible in some of the most recent publications on tattooing. Renaut[42] reviews evidence for tattooing in Nubia and Egypt, suggesting two separate traditions: type A (TA), primarily from Nubia, and type B (TB), primarily from Egypt. In Egypt, he concludes that "the paintings and artifacts depicting pretty tattooed girls might suggest that TB tattooing was fashionable in Egypt only among female musicians, dancers and courtesans" and that all tattooed women "considered tattooing as an appropriate way to enhance their carnal beauty." Renaut's assertions, while engaging more complexly with recent evidence for tattooing (see below), still demonstrate an overall argument that the objective of tattooing was exclusively to decorate women's bodies in order to enhance their sexual desirability.

Problems and Limitations with Perceptions of Tattooed Women

While the presence of tattoos on nude figures and in association with musical performance viably link the latter with eroticism, there are several problems with some of the above arguments around the functions and perceptions of tattooed women: (1) a lack of evidence, or even contradictory evidence, from the small number of examples of tattooed women identified in the twentieth century; (2) selective perception of archaeological and Egyptological data; and (3) ethnocentric approaches to tattooed women.

First, in the quotes above, both Keimer and Goelet exclude women with high social status from having tattoos despite evidence that tattooed women came from a royal burial context containing high-value grave goods and were given honorific titles. Derry's and Keimer's assertions that tattooed women served as sex workers and/or concubines are made with minimal or no corroborating evidence for these roles, often ignoring and erasing additional information. For example, Derry refers to Amunet as a concubine[43] based on her title as "Sole Ornament of the King"[44] while neglecting to mention her other title as priestess of Hathor. More recent reviews of the evidence for women's burials in the North Court of Mentuhotep II indicate that the assumption the women served as concubines is very dubious.[45] The assumption that tattooed women were sex workers is based solely on their association with cultural indications of eroticism (for example, nudity, Bes, and music). More broadly, there is no clear evidence for sex work during pharaonic Egypt.[46] Despite this lack of evidence, articles written in the past ten years still refer to tattooed women as sex workers and courtesans.[47]

This previous scholarship also often conflates tattooing with nudity, implying that only women shown nude were tattooed. For example, Derry suggests that the tattoos give weight to the postulation that the two unnamed tattooed mummified bodies were nude dancers.[48] These previous interpretations of tattoos do not account for the possibility that tattoos could be present on non-nude figures. Tassie points out that it is difficult to know whether there were any class differences in who received tattoos during the New Kingdom since we, by default, are more likely to see tattoos on servants, who were more often portrayed as nude.[49] The reality is even more complex. So far, the only tattooed figures in tomb scenes are dancers or musicians, and none of the nude women interpreted as doing serving work display tattoos.

Moreover, this scholarship often only acknowledges or prioritizes the location of the tattoos when they elicit an erotic reaction. Renaut[50] suggests that the presence of a tattoo on the lower back of the tattooed mummy from Deir al-Medina was sexually charged and therefore lessens the interpretation that her tattoos functioned for cult ritual and performance (see below). This assumes, however, that the two interpretations must be in contradiction to each other rather than the possibility that tattoos could be multifunctional. It is notable that, beyond brief description, he does not discuss the location of the other dozens of tattoos on her body. Keimer carefully photographed and discussed the locations of Amunet's tattoos, including a series of dots just below her navel, yet his discussion of their function focuses entirely on her role as sexually arousing men, intentionally dismissing a meaningful connection between tattoos

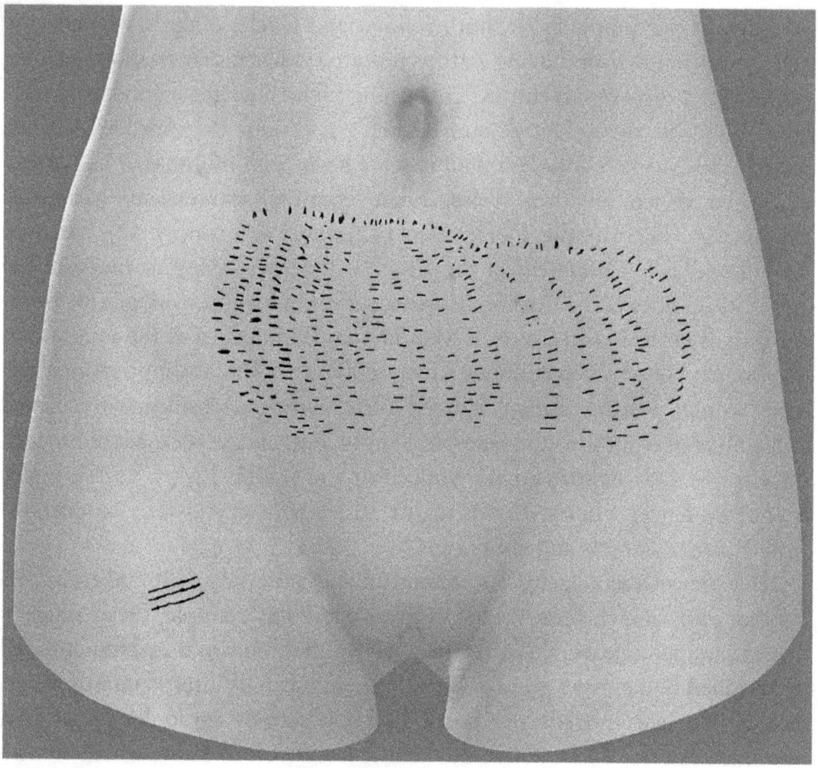

Fig. 23.2. A reconstruction of tattoos found on the abdomen of Amunet based on photographs in Keimer, *Remarques sur le tatouage dans l'Egypte Ancienne*

and her own fertility. Yet given their location and design—which encircle and emphasize her lower abdomen (fig. 23.2)—should we really favor interpreting her tattoos as appealing exclusively to the king's regenerative fertility in death without considering their role in Amunet's own fertility in life?

Second, when reviewing previous literature, many of these scholars often take previous perceptions of tattooed Egyptian women at face value without consideration of previous evidence. After quoting Winlock's interpretation of a figurine with decorations of tattoos as a dancing girl meant to amuse the tomb owner after the hunt, Keimer says that "cette interprétation de la trouvaille donnée par H.E. Winlock me paraît logique,"[51] adding that the same applies for Winlock's assumption that the two unnamed tattooed women from Deir al-Bahari must therefore be dancers. His easy acceptance of Winlock is noticeably in contrast to his reticence to consider Bruyère's interpretation of tattooing as a sign of the cult celebration of family.

Third, previous scholarship that identifies tattoos as exclusively eroticizing often carries ethnocentric attitudes with it about sexual morality that are not adequately supported by archaeological and historical evidence. By describing tattooed Egyptian women as "dames aux mœurs dévergondées et libertines"[52] and "des femmes de moralité douteuse,"[53] Keimer and Cherpion both make it clear that tattooed women were lascivious and immoral. Here, eroticism is linked with depravity, yet again there is no evidence presented that the Egyptians viewed sexuality with the same moral codes as modern Europe.

Finally, broader ethnographic surveys of tattooing practices suggest that across cultures it is extremely rare for tattoos to only function as eroticizing and/or decorative. This was already known in the early twentieth century. The first major ethnographic study on tattooing and its history was completed in 1925 by Hambly, who suggests that, beginning in Egypt, "the art of painting and tattooing became incorporated with a complex of social and religious usages and beliefs of a kind fundamental in human society."[54] More recently, Krutak reviewed gendered tattooing practices among cultures worldwide,[55] and in each example he offers, tattooing on women extended far beyond mere decoration: "The indigenous need to adorn the skin with tattoos was not simply, as many early ethnnographers have put it, 'to make a person more beautiful."[56] For example, while tattoos on the thighs are often seen as being intended for an erotic male gaze in Egyptology, across cultures they have more complex functions. In the Arctic, tattoos along a woman's thigh "ensured that the first thing a newborn infant saw would be something of beauty."[57] We cannot, therefore, assume that even tattoos with the strongest evidence for an erotic function would have functioned exclusively as decoration intended to evoke carnal desire.

Shifting Perceptions of Tattooing in Egypt in the Twentieth and Twenty-first Centuries

Researchers over the past few decades have identified many more examples of tattoos in iconography.[58] These tattoos appear in similar contexts (that is, on female figurines and paddle dolls) and show similar motifs to those identified by earlier researchers, including geometric motifs along the thighs and abdomen. Improved archaeological methods, however, allow recent scholars to more carefully discuss provenience in interpreting the functions of tattoos in iconography. Additionally, there has been a relative surge in published evidence for tattooing in human remains from Egypt and Nubia over the past decade.[59] These new discoveries have included several identifications of tattoos among Nubian C-group and Pan-Grave cemeteries,[60] but additionally included new evidence in Egyptian burials that breaks many of the trends seen previously.

In an investigation of archival photographs of the 1920–21 excavations of the Metropolitan Museum of Art, Morris[61] recently identified a tattoo of paired birds on the upper right arm of a mummy in Asasif. This tattoo is figural, unlike the geometric motifs identified earlier. Friedman additionally found tattoos on predynastic mummified bodies from Gebelein, currently housed in the British Museum, including "Ginger" or Gebelein Man 1 (EA 32751), who has been on public display to millions of visitors over the past century. This discovery marks the first physical evidence for tattooing on a man from an Egyptian cemetery. Finally, our work at Deir al-Medina revealed a heavily tattooed mummy of a woman. She has over thirty tattoos placed along her arms, shoulders, back, and neck, several of which are clearly associated with the cult of Hathor.[62] Not only are her tattoos predominantly figural, but they also are distributed in different regions of the body from those of the Middle Kingdom, with many of her tattoos placed in highly public and visible locations such as her arms, shoulders, and neck. Each of these examples redefines the rules established around tattooing, which had assumed tattoos were geometric motifs visible only on women's nude bodies, to include examples of tattoos that were figural, found on men, and in highly visible areas of the body.

With a shift in new discoveries, so too have scholars shifted their arguments around the nature and function of tattooing in ancient Egypt. During the late twentieth century, feminist critiques began to deconstruct past interpretations that treated women as sexual objects with little or no agency. Simultaneously, tattooing became an increasingly popular phenomenon and scholarship on tattooing began to deconstruct the idea that tattooing is exclusively socially deviant. Burgeoning research on both women in ancient Egypt and tattooing have led to new discoveries that have expanded our data set of tattooed human remains, as discussed above. More recent interpretations, therefore, have shifted away from viewing the tattooed body as exclusively erotic by proposing more diverse functions for tattooing in ancient Egypt.

Tattooing as Indicators of Social Identity

As noted above, much of the previous evidence for tattooing found in Egypt has been associated with Nubian cemeteries and iconography, and many scholars argue that tattooing in Egypt may have originated from Nubian traditions. Renée Friedman has identified both male and female mummified bodies with tattoos in Nubian C-Group and Pan Grave burials in Hierakonpolis.[63] Friedman argues that these tattoos "were culturally specific and understood as indicative of ethnicity,"[64] based not only on their patterning, but on their association with other clear markers of ethnicity, including leather clothing depicted in dance and performance. Tassie suggested that C-group people "developed the practice of tattooing to culturally identify themselves from the Egyptian civilization to the north and the growing Kerma (Kushite) civilization to the south in Upper Nubia."[65] Ashby argues that "tattooing may well have served as a cultural marker for many Nubian tribes, which was incorporated later into the attire of Egyptian Hathoric dancers. Employing the Nubian tradition of tattooing effectively linked Hathoric dancers with the goddess because Hathor was so closely associated with Nubia, as a goddess who originated/sojourned in Nubia and returned to Egypt with a retinue of worshippers from the many tribes of Nubia."[66] Similarly, Renaut suggests that tattooing may have originated from a Nubian tradition through the introduction of Nubian dancers, musicians, and possibly sex workers into Egypt. It then would have disseminated into Egypt as a broader representation of their professional affiliation, connoting both social markers of ethnicity and profession.[67] All four scholars therefore argue that tattooing functioned to indicate ethnic cultural affiliations. Importantly, there remains ambiguity about whether and when tattoos shifted from indicating that someone was of Nubian descent to being a Nubianized motif, potentially worn by women identified as Egyptian, but affiliated with Nubia and related cultic practices, such as Nubian dances for Hathor.

Tattooing as Cult Practice

Through linking multiple lines of evidence found in local tomb scenes, Egyptian mythology, mummified human remains, figurines, and paddle dolls, Morris[68] argues that tattooed women acted as *khener* dancers, who danced not only *for* Hathor but *as* her, by revealing their vulvas to the sun. This act, referencing the *Myth of the Contendings of Horus and Seth*, harnessed the goddess's sexuality to rejuvenate the sun god, raising him up. In performance, Hathoric dancers embodied the goddess in order to rejuvenate the king, linking this mythological precedent with other associations with Hathor and divine rebirth, including her role as king's wife, mistress of the West, and Lady of the Vulva. Morris places tattooing squarely within the cult of Hathor by directly linking tattoos on paddle dolls with tattooed *khener* dancers. This also explains the presence of tattoos among the burials of women in the funerary complex of Nebhepetre Mentuhotep II, who, Morris argues, were his key cultic staff as the *khener* troupe. While Morris does not offer a more specific suggestion for the function of the tattoos, she goes further than previous scholars[69] in associating tattooing specifically with the cult of Hathor. Ashby[70] similarly focuses on the role of dance within the cult of Hathor and the link between tattooing

Fig. 23.3. Tattoo of two Hathoric cows wearing *menat* necklaces found on the lower left arm of the heavily tattooed mummy from Deir al-Medina

and Hathoric dancing. Ashby connects tattooing with the depiction of tattooed dancers performing the *ksks*-dance. This links Hathor with her role as the Distant Goddess who returned to Egypt from Nubia, bringing with her the inundation, celebrated through rituals of dance and drunkenness. In both cases, Morris and Ashby identify how iconographic depictions of tattoos and tattooed human remains are connected to myths and rituals involving Hathor.

Our discovery of a tattooed mummy from Deir al-Medina further suggests that tattooing was linked with cult worship of Hathor.[71] Cédric Gobeil and I have argued that the heavily tattooed mummy from Deir al-Medina was not only a part of local cult worship of Hathor, but may have even embodied the goddess through the public and permanent placement of Hathoric tattoos (for example, Hathoric cows with *menat* necklaces; fig. 23.3).

We have identified shared themes between imagery in the tattoos and local cult practice to Hathor evidenced in temple graffiti and votive offerings. This mirrors other scholarship suggesting that in performance and ritual, women impersonated Hathor.[72] Additionally, her numerous divine eye tattoos may have operated under a logic similar to cultic indwelling,[73] where the cult image channels divine presence directly. The placement of divine eyes on her neck, shoulders, and back meant that no matter from what direction you looked at her, a pair of divine eyes could be looking back at you.

Additionally, the tattoo of a Hathoric handle on her right arm (fig. 23.4) would have linked her movements with ritual movements of the sistrum or mirror, objects affiliated with dances and performances for Hathor. In this case, every movement of her arm also would have moved the tattooed handle.

Friedman and colleagues[74] similarly suggested that the tattoo of a ritual object on the right arm of a predynastic woman from Gebelein may have represented her continuous use of a ritual instrument. Moreover, they suggest that the tattoos on the Gebelein mummified bodies may have "denoted status through magical empowerment or cult knowledge."[75]

Fig. 23.4. Tattoo of a Hathoric handle found on the upper right arm of the heavily tattooed mummy from Deir al-Medina. Note that the handle is upside-down and facing distally (away from the shoulder)

Tattooing as Protective

Tassie associates tattooing with fertility, based on the presence of tattooed figures on toiletry items and the recurring presence of Bes in depictions of tattoos, but he further indicates that these could have served a protective function.

> The placement of the tattoo and Bes' principal function would seem to indicate its primary symbolic role as being that of protection and secondarily of sexuality . . . . Thus, tattooing predominantly of women, and the positioning of some tattoos, such as dot-dash designs, as well as Bes and earlier Taweret figures, on the thighs and/or the abdomen, strongly indicate that the tattooing practice was closely linked to female spheres of life, and indicate their possible protective functions to aid fertility or to protect the wearer from death in childbirth.[76]

Similarly, we have suggested that the tattooed mummy from Deir al-Medina had tattoos that could have had a protective function. Specifically, a *wedjat* eye placed between two seated baboons on her neck (fig. 23.5) may have served as a protection, given the prominent use of the *wedjat* eye as a protective symbol in general, and more specifically as an amuletic protection worn on the neck.[77] The symbolism of the tattoo and its location on the body are key to our interpretations.

Tattooing as Divine Enhancers

The tattooed mummy from Deir al-Medina has one tattooed design that is repeated in three places on her body: the placement of two or three *nefer* signs between a pair of *wedjat* eyes. These are placed on her neck (fig. 23.5) and the tops of both shoulders. This combination of signs is otherwise attested in Deir al-Bahari and used to create the phrase "to do good, to do good,"[78] though more frequently employing the normal eye (ir). Cédric Gobeil and I have suggested that the purposeful and symmetrical placement of this tattoo over the voice box as well as on both shoulders could have acted as divine enhancers, allowing her to "do good" with every movement of her arm or in speech or song: "The placement of the permanent tattoos on her body would have not only linked her with the divine through Hathoric symbolism, but also empowered her to take on important cultic or magical roles. This suggests that the tattoos served a dual purpose: to protect as well as to help in the performance of actions that played a significant role in the life of the communities."[79]

We have hypothesized that the tattooed woman from Deir al-Medina may have thus served as a cult performer of Hathor, a wise woman, and/or a

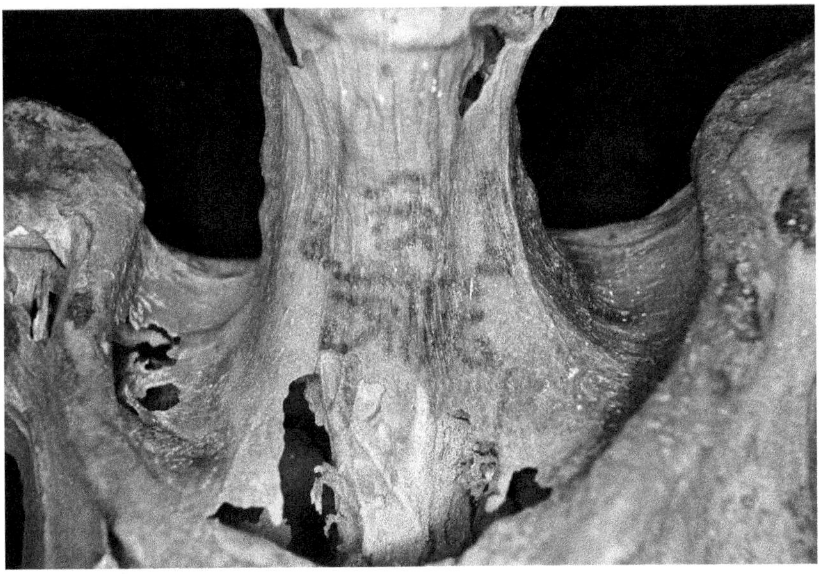

Fig. 23.5. Tattoos found on the neck of the heavily tattooed mummy from Deir al-Medina

magico-medical healer due to the functions of her tattoos as both magico-medical protections and divine enhancers. Not all scholars agree with this interpretation. Renaut believes our hypothesis is "very unconvincing" because these functions do not have any parallel in the ethnography of tattooing.[80] As a brief response, there are a variety of ethnographic parallels that suggest tattoos can and do act as magico-medical protections and divine enhancers, and in turn, that these functions enable their wearers to perform key duties associated with the roles discussed above.

In a variety of cultures, tattoos are a key protection for their wearers, but a more detailed review of these suggests variation in the ways tattoos can protect an individual. In Japan, tattoos placed at the mouth are intended to prevent evil entering the body,[81] functioning in a way similar to known functions of Egyptian amulets and proposed functions of *wedjat* eye tattoos at the neck because they prevent disease-bearing entities from entering the body. Apotropaic tattoos that harness power from the divine are also documented in the Arctic.[82] These tattoos connected a person to the spiritual world and could allow an ancestor to spiritually visit an individual, similar to the concept of indwelling in Egyptology. In both Gran Chaco (a region in South America) and among the Amazigh of North Africa, tattoo pigment is mixed with the tattooist's saliva. When impregnated into the skin during tattooing, these serve to repel malevolent spirits.[83] In Iraq, Muslim women were tattooed during oral readings of the Qur'an to make the tattoos more effective as both protective and prophylactic treatments.[84] This practice is similar to the use of oral recitation during the production of Egyptian amulets in order to make them effective. These examples show us that tattoos can serve as divine protections due to their symbolism, but also because they create a physical connection between the visible and invisible worlds during their creation. The ritual of being tattooed can be as important for magical protection as the resulting tattoo itself. In considering the functionality of tattoos, we should be open to considering how the process of receiving and giving a tattoo could include ritual interactions, sounds, and substances that carry equally important functions to the tattoo itself. While these may be less visible in the archaeological record, they are nonetheless important factors to a holistic study on the possible functions of tattoos in ancient Egypt.

Tattoos are used not only as medicine, but also by medico-magical practitioners for interactions with the divine. Simon Forman, a seventeenth-century medical astrologer, believed his tattoos "would be able to harness the power of his horoscope, and alter the course of his life," and his example is part of a broader practice in early modern Europe of using permanent markings on the body to take on supernatural powers.[85] The Salvatori, an Italian group that claimed descent from St. Paul, used the figure of a serpent inscribed on their skin to have power over animals and give them immunity over venomous serpents and scorpions,[86] the same attributes that we have suggested could explain the abundance of snake tattoos and their relationship to the possible role of a *Kherep-Serqet* (scorpion charmer), one of the magico-medical healers documented at Deir al-Medina. This example illustrates the possibility that in other cultures tattoos can operate under principles similar to homeopathic magic, where like affects like. Moreover, medical practitioners use body marking to perform magico-medical rituals in North America, Australia, and Papua New Guinea as well,[87] with these examples illustrating that tattoos could be used to act as a guardian for medical practitioners and as a means to interact with divine forces.

Conclusions

Earlier scholarship focused on tattoos as having the sole function of eroticizing women's bodies for a male gaze. These assumptions were often based on minimal or even contradictory evidence, and frequently divorced eroticism from fertility, pregnancy, and childbirth. These earlier assumptions also frequently integrated ethnocentric ideas about tattooed women, projecting early twentieth-century stigmas and morality around tattooing into the past. The consequence is research that suggested that tattoos only functioned to advertise and manifest erotic desire for a male gaze, culminating in the assumption that ancient Egyptian tattooed women served as sex workers. Such ideas still exist in more recent literature from the past decade.

Recent scholarship offers more varied approaches to the role of tattoos in ancient Egypt based on critical approaches to both the study of women and tattooing. Recent scholarship also benefits from new discoveries which have expanded the period in which tattoos are attested in ancient Egypt as well as the symbolism associated with tattooing. New interpretations suggest that tattooing can also serve as indicators of ethnic identities, cult worship, magico-medical protections, and even divine enhancers. An important point is that these more recent interpretations do not divorce tattooing from eroticism, but rather embrace eroticism as one facet to the role that tattooing can play. This allows tattooing to be multifunctional, a conclusion that has been more broadly evidenced in cross-cultural studies of tattooing. Finally, as new discoveries have consistently forced us to reevaluate our assumptions, it is likely that we will need to rewrite the rules of tattooing in ancient Egypt in coming years as more figurines, tattooed bodies, and evidence in tomb paintings are revealed. These could expand known functions of tattooing or provide a clearer picture of the primary ways they were seen and used in ancient Egypt.

Notes

1 G. Daressy, "Notes et Remarques, LVI," *RecTrav* 14 (1893): 166–68.

2 This discussion does not include any overviews of textual evidence for tattooing, as previous scholarship has found few or no examples. The verb *mtn* (TLA lemma 77610) is used in Papyrus Bremner Rhind to describe names of Isis and Nepthys being inscribed, but it remains ambiguous whether this refers to tattooing or not. In the same papyrus, *mtn* is used to describe inscribing on a wax figure of Apep, a context which clearly does not use the verb to describe permanently marking skin with pigment. For further discussion, see Robert S. Bianchi, "Tattoo in Ancient Egypt," in *Marks of Civilization: Artistic Transformation of the Human Body*, ed. A. Rubin (Los Angeles: Museum of Cultural History, University of California, 1988), 27, and Louis Keimer, *Remarques sur le tatouage dans l'Egypte Ancienne* (IFAO, 1948), 52–53.

3 Daressy, "Notes et Remarques, LVI," 166–68.

4 It should be noted that earlier scholarship on age and sex estimation in human remains was frequently inaccurate. Unfortunately, we do not have detailed discussions of methods used to determine sex on these individuals, though in this case, photographs and descriptions make it clear that secondary sexual characteristics were often preserved and observable. For a more detailed description of these individuals, see Douglas E. Derry, "Mummification II—Methods Practiced at Different Periods," *ASAE* 41 (1942): 240–65.

5 For example, William Christopher Hayes, *The Scepter of Egypt: A Background for the Study of the Egyptian Antiquities in the Metropolitan Museum of Art*, vol. 1, *From the Earliest Times to the End of the Middle Kingdom* (New York: Metropolitan Museum of Art, 1953), 158.

6 William A. Ward, *Essays on Feminine Titles of the Middle Kingdom and Related Subjects* (Beirut: American University of Beirut, 1986).

7 Ellen Morris, "Paddle Dolls and Performance," *JARCE* 47 (2011): 71–103.

8 Catharine Roehrig, "Two Tattooed Women from Thebes," in *The Art and Culture of Ancient Egypt: Studies in Honor of Dorothea Arnold*, BES 19 (New York: Oxbow/David Brown, 2015), 527–36.

9 "Hofdame," in Rosemarie Drenkhahn, "Bemerkungen zu dem Titel *Ḫkr.t Nswt*," *SAK* 4 (1976): 59–67.

10 Cecil Firth, *The Archaeological Survey of Nubia: Report for 1910–11* (Cairo: National Print Department, 1927), 54.

11 Firth, *The Archaeological Survey of Nubia: Report for 1910–11*, pl. 25.

12 Morris, "Paddle Dolls and Performance," 79–80.

13 Jeanne Vandier d'Abbadie, "Une fresque civile de Deir El-Médineh," *RdE* 3 (1938): 27–35.

14 Bernard Bruyère, *Rapport sur les Fouilles de Deir el-Médineh 1934–1935* 3, FIFAO 16 (Cairo: IFAO, 1939), 60, 132, 274.

15 Keimer, *Remarques sur le tatouage dans l'Egypte Ancienne*, 104–105.

16 For an overview, see Solange Ashby, "Dancing for Hathor: Nubian Women in Egyptian Cultic Life," *Dotawo: A Journal of Nubian Studies* 5 (2018), https://digitalcommons.fairfield.edu/djns/vol5/iss1/2.

17 Ward has more recently demonstrated that it is unlikely these women were all buried together as a royal harem. Ward, *Essays on Feminine Titles*, 102–14.

18 For an overview, see Geraldine Pinch, *Votive Offerings to Hathor* (Oxford: Griffith Institute, 1993), 211–19.

19 Herbert Winlock, "The Museum's Excavations at Thebes," *BMMA* 18, no. 12 (December 1, 1923): 26, https://doi.org/10.2307/3254661.

20 Winlock, "The Museum's Excavations at Thebes" (1923), p. 20. Winlock makes a similar type of argument around paddle dolls: "Most of the Eleventh Dynasty tombs at Thebes contained dolls. Some of them already mentioned in these reports undoubtedly represented dancing girls and were put in the tomb in order that their spirits might while away the time of the Theban grandees in the tedious hours of eternity" (Herbert Winlock, "The Museum's Excavations at Thebes," *BMMA* 27, no. 3 [1932]: 36, https://doi.org/10.2307/3255360).

21 Douglas E. Derry, "Note on Two Mummies of the Eleventh Dynasty from Deir El Bahary" (December 31, 1938), in *Remarques sur le tatouage dans l'Egypte Ancienne*, ed. Louis Keimer (Cairo: IFAO, 1948), 14–15; Hayes, *The Scepter of Egypt* 1, 162, 230; Ward, *Essays on Feminine Titles*, 114; Herbert Winlock, "The Museum's Excavations at Thebes," *BMMA* 21, no. 3 (1 March 1926): 5–32, https://doi.org/10.2307/3254817.

22 Vandier d'Abbadie, "Une fresque civile de Deir El-Médineh."

23 Keimer, *Remarques sur le tatouage dans l'Egypte Ancienne*, 98.

24 Keimer, *Remarques sur le tatouage dans l'Egypte Ancienne*, 98.

25 Keimer, *Remarques sur le tatouage dans l'Egypte Ancienne*, 98.

26 Michael Atkinson, *Tattooed: The Sociogenesis of a Body Art* (Toronto: University of Toronto Press, 2003), 33–42.

27 Norman Goldstein, "V. Psychological Implications of Tattoos," *Journal of Dermatologic Surgery and Oncology* 5, no. 11 (November 1, 1979): 883–88, https://doi.org/10.1111/j.1524-4725.1979.tb00771.x; D.W. McKerracher and R.A. Watson, "Tattoo Marks and Behaviour Disorder," *British Journal of Criminology* 9 (1969): 167–72.

28 Albert Parry, "Tattooing among Prostitutes and Perverts," *Psychoanalytic Quarterly* 3 (1934): 476–82.

29 Nicholas Daly, "That Obscure Object of Desire: Victorian Commodity Culture and Fictions of the Mummy," *NOVEL: A Forum on Fiction* 28, no. 1 (1994): 42, https://doi.org/10.2307/1345912.

30 Keimer, *Remarques sur le tatouage dans l'Egypte Ancienne*, 7.

31 Gaston Maspero, *Causeries d'Egypte* (Paris: Goutte d'or, 1907), 151.

32 Keimer, *Remarques sur le tatouage dans l'Egypte Ancienne*, 7.

33 For example, Derry estimated Amunet to have died in middle age; see Roehrig, "Two Tattooed Women from Thebes." Daniel Fouquet also asserts this in "Le tatouage médical en Égypte dans l'antiquite et à l'époque actuelle," *Archives d'Anthropologie Criminalle*, vol. 13 (Lyon, 1899), 270–79. Neither example provides a description of aging methods. I am unaware of any age estimates for the two unnamed tattooed women.

34 Nadine Cherpion, "La danseuse de Deir El-Médîna et les prétendus 'lits clos' du village," *Association des Archéologues et Historiens d'Art de Louvain. Revue* 4 (2011): 20.

35 Nadine Cherpion, "La danseuse de Deir El-Médîna," 20.

36 Bianchi, "Tattoo in Ancient Egypt," 22–23.

37 Ogden Goelet, "Nudity in Ancient Egypt," *Source: Notes in the History of Art* 12, no. 2 (1993): 25.

38 Goelet, "Nudity in Ancient Egypt," 26.

39 Bruyère, *Rapport sur les Fouilles de Deir el-Médineh 1934–1935* 3:131.

40 Gay Robins, "Dress, Undress, and the Representation of Fertility and Potency in New Kingdom Egyptian Art," in *Sexuality in Ancient Art*, ed. N.B. Kampen (Cambridge: Cambridge University Press, 1996), 30.

41 Fouquet, "Le tatouage médical en égypte dans l'antiquite et à l'époque actuelle."

42 Luc Renaut, "Tattooed Women from Nubia and Egypt: A Reappraisal," in *Flesh and Bones: The Individual and His Body in the Ancient Mediterranean Basin*, ed. Alice Mouton, Semitica et Classica Supplementa (Turnhout: Brepols, 2020), 69–87.

43 Douglas Derry, "Mummification II—Methods Practiced at Different Periods," 249.

44 While during Derry's time this title had been affiliated with the royal harem, more recent scholarship suggests it should instead be translated as "lady in waiting." See Carolyn Graves-Brown, *Dancing for Hathor: Women in Ancient Egypt* (London: Continuum, 2010), 115; Ward, *Essays on Feminine Titles*, 114.

45 Ward, *Essays on Feminine Titles.*

46 Graves-Brown, *Dancing for Hathor*, 80–82. This is not to argue that sex work did not exist, but rather to emphasize that our conclusions about the past must be based on evidence.

47 Cherpion, "La danseuse de Deir El-Médîna"; Renaut, "Tattooed Women from Nubia and Egypt: A Reappraisal."

48 Derry, "Note on Two Mummies of the Eleventh Dynasty from Deir El Bahary."

49 Geoffrey Tassie, "Identifying the Practice of Tattooing in Ancient Egypt and Nubia," *Papers from the Institute of Archaeology* 14 (2003): 85–101, https://doi.org/10.5334/pia.200.

50 Renaut, "Tattooed Women from Nubia and Egypt: A Reappraisal."

51 Keimer, *Remarques sur le tatouage dans l'Egypte Ancienne*, 19.

52 Cherpion, "La danseuse de Deir El-Médîna," 20.

53 Keimer, *Remarques sur le tatouage dans l'Egypte Ancienne*, 98.

54 Wilfrid Dyson Hambly, *The History of Tattooing* (Mineola, NY: Dover Publications, 1925; reprint 2009), 326.

55 Lars Krutak, *The Tattooing Arts of Tribal Women* (London: Bennett and Bloom/Desert Hearts, 2007).

56 Krutak, *The Tattooing Arts of Tribal Women*, 229.

57 Bernadette Driscoll, "The Inuit Parka as an Artistic Tradition," in *The Spirit Sings: Artistic Traditions of Canada's First Peoples*, ed. D.F. Cameron (Toronto: McClelland and Stewart, 1987), 198.

58 Important works on recent discoveries of iconographic evidence of tattooing include Morris, "Paddle Dolls and Performance"; Pinch, *Votive Offerings to Hathor*; Angela M.J. Tooley, "Notes on Type 1 Truncated Figurines: The Ramesseum Ladies," in *Company of Images: Modelling the Imaginary World of Middle Kingdom Egypt (2000–1500 BC)*, ed. G. Miniaci, M. Betrò, and S. Quirke (Leuven: Peeters, 2017), 421–56. For a more comprehensive overview of evidence, see Vittoria Rapisidara, "'Indossare' i tatuaggi: Studio del tatuaggio nell'Antico Egitto sui resti umani, archeologici e iconografici" (MA thesis, Università di Pisa, 2019).

59 For a more detailed discussion, see Aaron Deter-Wolf, "Tattooed Human Mummies, List Version 3.0," March 7, 2019, https://doi.org/10.6084/m9.figshare.5738439.v3; Renée Friedman, "New Tattoos from Ancient Egypt: Defining Marks of Culture," in *Ancient Ink: The Archaeology of Tattooing*, ed. Lars Krutak and Aaron Deter-Wolf (Seattle: University of Washington Press, 2017), 11–36; Renaut, "Tattooed Women from Nubia and Egypt: A Reappraisal."

60 Renée Friedman, "Excavations of the C-Group Cemetery at KH27C," *Sudan & Nubia* 8 (2004): 47–51; Friedman, "New Tattoos from Ancient Egypt: Defining Marks of Culture"; Anna Pieri and Daniel Antoine, "A Tattooed Trio at HK27C," *Nekhen News* 26 (2014): 28–29.

61 Morris, "Paddle Dolls and Performance," 83.

62 Anne Austin and Cédric Gobeil, "Embodying the Divine: A Tattooed Female Mummy from Deir El-Medina," *BIFAO* 116 (2017): 23–46.

63 Friedman, "New Tattoos from Ancient Egypt: Defining Marks of Culture."

64 Friedman, "New Tattoos from Ancient Egypt: Defining Marks of Culture," 33.

65 Tassie, "Identifying the Practice of Tattooing in Ancient Egypt and Nubia," 93.

66 Ashby, "Dancing for Hathor," 74.

67 Luc Renaut, "Marquage corporel et signation religieuse dans l'Antiquité" (PhD diss., École pratique des hautes études, Paris, 2004), 196–97, https://tel.archives-ouvertes.fr/tel-00275245.

68 Morris, "Paddle Dolls and Performance."

69 For example, Pinch, *Votive Offerings to Hathor*, 213.

70 Ashby, "Dancing for Hathor."

71 Austin and Gobeil, "Embodying the Divine."

72 Graves-Brown, *Dancing for Hathor*, 96–97.

73 Jan Assmann, "Semiosis and Interpretation in Ancient Egyptian Ritual," in *Interpretation in Religion (Philosophy and Religion 2)*, ed. Shlomo Biderstein and Ben-Ami Scharfstein (Leiden: Brill, 1992), 87–109; Jan Assmann, "Einwohnung," in *Menschenbilder-Bildermenschen: Kunst und Kultur im Alten Ägypten*, ed. Tobias Hofmann and Alexandra Sturm (Norderstedt: Books on Demand, 2003), 1–14.

74 Renée Friedman et al., "Natural Mummies from Predynastic Egypt Reveal the World's Earliest Figural Tattoos," *Journal of Archaeological Science* 92 (2018): 116–25, https://doi.org/10.1016/j.jas.2018.02.002.

75 Friedman et al., "Natural Mummies from Predynastic Egypt," 121.

76 Tassie, "Identifying the Practice of Tattooing in Ancient Egypt and Nubia," 96.

77 Austin and Gobeil, "Embodying the Divine," 28; for an example of such an amulet at Deir el-Medina, see Jacco Dieleman, "The Materiality of Textual Amulets in Ancient Egypt," in *The Materiality of Magic*, ed. D. Boschung and J.N. Bremmer, Morphomata 20 (Paderborn: Wilhelm Fink, 2015), 23–58.

78 Marek Marciniak, "Quelques remarques sur la formule 'Ir Nfr, Ir Nfr,'" *Études et Travaux* 2 (1968): 26–31.

79 Austin and Gobeil, "Embodying the Divine," 33.

80 Renaut, "Tattooed Women from Nubia and Egypt: A Reappraisal," 79. In part, his argument against our hypothesis is based on his interpretation that we suggest tattoos are required for these professions, though we never make such an argument.

81 Krutak, *The Tattooing Arts of Tribal Women*, 133.

82 Krutak, *The Tattooing Arts of Tribal Women*, 156.

83 Krutak, *The Tattooing Arts of Tribal Women*, 30–31, 214.

84 Krutak, *The Tattooing Arts of Tribal Women*, 39–41.

85 Jennifer Allen Rosecrans, "Wearing the Universe: Symbolic Markings in Early Modern England," in *Written on the Body: The Tattoo in European and American History*, ed. Jane Caplan (Princeton: Princeton University Press, 2000), 46–60.

86 Rosecrans, "Wearing the Universe," 59.

87 Hambly, *The History of Tattooing*, 132–37.

Abbreviations

ÄA	Ägyptische Abhandlungen
ÄAT	Ägypten und Altes Testament
ACE	Australian Centre for Egyptology
ACER	Australian Centre for Egyptology: Reports
ACHET	Achet Schriften zur Ägyptologie
ADAIK	Abhandlungen des Deutschen Archäologischen Instituts Kairo. Ägyptologische Reihe
AfO	Archiv für Orientforschung/Archiv für Orientforschung. Internat. Zeitschrift für die Wissenschaften vom Vorderen Orient
AfP	*Archiv für Papyrusforschung und verwandte Gebiete*
AJA	*American Journal of Archaeology*
AJP	*American Journal of Philology*
Ä&L	Ägypten und Levante
AncSoc	*Ancient Society*
ANSMN	*American Numismatic Society Museum Notes*
AOAT	Alter Orient und Altes Testament
AoF	*Altorientalische Forschungen*
ASAE	*Annales du Service des Antiquités de l'Égypte*
ASE	Archaeological Survey of Egypt
AUC	American University in Cairo
AV	Archäologische Veröffentlichungen
AVDAIK	Archäologische Veröffentlichungen/Deutsches Archäologisches Institut, Kairo
BACE	*Bulletin of the Australian Centre for Egyptology*

BAe	Bibliotheca Aegyptiaca
BAR	British Archaeological Reports
BARIS	British Archaeological Reports. International Series
BASP	*Bulletin of the American Society of Papyrologists*
BdE	Bibliothèque d'Étúde
BEJ	*Birmingham Egyptology Journal*
BES	*Bulletin of the Egyptological Seminar of New York*
BEStud	Brown Egyptological Studies
BIE	*Bulletin de l'Institut d'Égypte*
BIFAO	*Bulletin de l'Institut Français d'Archéologie Orientale*
BiOr	*Bibliotheca Orientalis*
BM	British Museum, London
BMMA	*Bulletin of the Metropolitan Museum of Art*
BMSAES	*British Museum Studies in Ancient Egypt and Sudan*
BOREAS	Boreas. Uppsala Studies in Ancient Mediterranean and Near Eastern Civilizations
BSA	British School of Archaeology in Egypt
BSAK	Studien zur Altägyptischen Kultur, Beihefte
BSEA	British School of Egyptian Archaeology
BSFE	*Bulletin de la Société française d'égyptologie*
CAENL	Contributions to the Archaeology of Egypt, Nubia and the Levant
CahKarn	*Cahiers de Karnak*. Centre franco-égyptien d'étude des temples de Karnak (CFEETK)
CdE	*Chronique d'Égypte*
CFEETK	Centre franco-égyptien d'étude des temples de Karnak (http://www.cfeetk.cnrs.fr)
CG	*Catalogue Générale des Antiquités égyptiennes du musée du Caire*
CHANE	Culture and History of the Ancient Near East
CSEG	Cahiers de la Société d'Égyptologie
CP	*Classical Philology*
CRAIBL	*Comptes rendus des séances de l'Académie des Inscriptions et Belles-Lettres*
CSCT	Columbia Studies in the Classical Tradition
CT	de Buck, Adriaan. *The Egyptian Coffin Texts* 7. *Texts of Spells 787–1185*. OIP 87. Chicago: University of Chicago Press, 1961.
DE	*Discussions in Egyptology*
DÖAW	Denkschriften der Österreichischen Akademie der Wissenschaften Wien

EA	*Egyptian Archaeology, The Bulletin of the Egypt Exploration Society*
EAO	*Égypte—Afrique et Orient*
EEF	Egypt Exploration Fund
EES	Egypt Exploration Society
EGU	Egyptologische Uitgaven
EM	Egyptological Memoirs
EME	Études et Mémoires d'Égyptologie
ERA	Egyptian Research Account
FIFAO	Fouilles de l'Institut français d'archéologie orientale
FuB	Forschungen und Berichte—Staatliche Museen Berlin
GHP	Golden House Publications
GM	*Göttinger Miszellen. Beiträge zur ägyptologischen Diskussion*
GOF IV	Göttinger Orientforschungen (IV. Reihe: Ägypten)
HdO	Handbuch der Orientalistik
IBAES	Internet-Beiträge zur Ägyptologie und Sudanarchäologie
IdS	Jansen-Winkeln, Karl. *Inschriften der Spätzeit.* Teil 3: *Die 25. Dynastie (Nubierzeit).* Wiesbaden: Harrassowitz, 2009.
IFAO	Institut Français d'Archéologie Orientale
IG	*Inscriptionum Graecarum*
JAC	*Jahrbuch für Antike und Christentum*
JAEI	*Journal of Ancient Egyptian Interconnections*
JAOS	*Journal of the American Oriental Society*
JARCE	*Journal of the American Research Center in Egypt*
JBL	*Journal of Biblical Literature*
JEA	*Journal of Egyptian Archaeology*
JEGH	*Journal of Egyptian History*
JES	*Journal of Egyptian Studies*
JESHO	*Journal of the Economic and Social History of the Orient*
JNES	*Journal of Near Eastern Studies*
JSSEA	*Journal of the Society of the Studies of Egyptian Antiquities*
Kêmi	*Kêmi: Revue de philologie et d'archéologie égytiennes et coptes*
KIU	Karnak Identifiant Unique
KRI	Kenneth A. Kitchen, *Ramesside Inscriptions: Historical and Biographical.* 8 vols. Oxford: Blackwell, 1968–99.
KSGH	Königtum, Staat und Gesellschaft früher Hochkulturen
KVAB	Koninklijke Vlaamse Academie van België
LÄ	Wolfang Helck, Eberhard Otto, and Wolfhart Westendorf, eds., *Lexikon der Ägyptologie.* 7 vols. Wiesbaden: Harrassowitz, 1972–92.

LD	Richard Lepsius, *Denkmäler aus Aegypten und Aethiopien.* 12 vols. Berlin: Nicolaische Buchhandlung, 1849–56.
LGG	Christian Leitz, ed., *Lexikon der ägyptischen Götter und Götterbezeichnungen.* 8 vols. OLA 110–116 and 129. Leuven: Peeters, 2002–2003.
LingAeg	*Lingua Aegyptia*
LingAegSM	Lingua Aegyptia, Studia Monographica
LSJ	Henry George Liddell, *A Greek–English Lexicon.* Oxford: Clarendon Press, 1961
MAJA	Münchner Arbeitskreises Junge Aegyptologie
MÄS	Münchner ägyptologische Studien
MDAIK	*Mitteilungen des Deutschen Archäologischen Instituts, Abteilung Kairo*
MFA	Museum of Fine Arts, Boston
MIFAO	Mémoires publiés par les membres de l'Institut français d'archéologie orientale
MittSAG	*Mitteilungen der Sudanarchäologischen Gesellschaft zu Berlin*
MMJ	*Metropolitan Museum Journal*
NINO	Nederlands Instituut voor het Nabije Oosten
NSSEA	*Newsletter of the Society for the Study of Egyptian Antiquities*
OBO	Orbis Biblicus et Orientalis
OGIS	*Orientis Graeci Inscriptiones Selectae*
OIP	Oriental Institute Publications, University of Chicago
OLA	Orientalia Lovaniensia Analecta
OLZ	*Orientalische Literaturzeitung*
ORA	Orientalische Religionen in der Antike
PAM	*Polish Archaeology in the Mediterranean*
PES	*Prague Egyptological Studies*
Philippika	Philippika. Marburger altertumskundliche Abhandlungen
PM I^1	B. Porter and R.L.B. Moss, *Topographical Bibliography of Ancient Egyptian Hieroglyphic Texts, Reliefs, and Paintings.* Vol. I, *The Theban Necropolis.* Part 1, *Private Tombs.* 2nd. ed. Oxford: Clarendon Press, 1960.
PM I^2	B. Porter and R.L.B. Moss, *Topographical Bibliography of Ancient Egyptian Hieroglyphic Texts, Reliefs, and Paintings.* Vol. I, *The Theban Necropolis.* Part 2, *Royal Tombs and Smaller Cemeteries.* Oxford: Clarendon Press, 1964.
PM II^2	B. Porter and R.L.B. Moss, *Topographical Bibliography of Ancient Egyptian Hieroglyphic Texts, Reliefs and Paintings.* Vol.

	II, *Theban Temples*. 2nd ed. Revised and augmented. Oxford: Clarendon, 1972.
PM III[1]	B. Porter and R.L.B. Moss, *Topographical Bibliography of Ancient Egyptian Hieroglyphic Texts, Reliefs and Paintings*. Vol. III, *Memphis*. Part 1: *Abû Rawâsh to Abûsîr*. 2nd ed., revised and augmented by J. Mälek. Oxford: Griffith Institute, 1974.
PM III[2]	B. Porter and R.L.B. Moss, *Topographical Bibliography of Ancient Egyptian Hieroglyphic Texts, Reliefs and Paintings*. Vol. III, *Memphis*. Part 2: *Saqqâra to Dahshûr*. 2nd ed., revised and augmented by J. Málek. Oxford: Griffith Institute, 1979.
PM VII	B. Porter and R.L.B. Moss, *Topographical Bibliography of Ancient Egyptian Hieroglyphic Texts, Reliefs and Paintings*. Vol. VII, *Nubia, the Deserts, and Outside Egypt*. Oxford: Griffith Institute, 1952.
PN	Hermann Ranke, *Die ägyptischen personennamen*. Vol. 1, *Verzeichnis der Namen*. Glückstadt: J.J. Augustin, 1935.
Pyr.	Kurt Sethe, *Die altägyptischen Pyramidentexte nach den Papierabdrücken und Photographien des Berliner Museums* 1.1: *Spruch 1–468 (Pyr. 1–905)*. Hildesheim: Olms, 1987.
RBN	*Revue Belge de Numismatique*
RdE	*Revue d'égyptologie*
RecTrav	*Recueil de travaux relatifs à la philologie et à l'archéologie égyptiennes et assyriennes*
SAA	Studia Antiqua Australiensia
SAK	*Studien zur altägyptischen Kultur*
SAOC	Studies in Ancient Oriental Civilization
SASAE	Supplément aux Annales du Service des Antiquités de l'Égypte
SAT	Studien zum altägyptischen Totenbuch
SBL	Society of Biblical Literature
SIG	*Sylloge Inscriptionum Graecarum*
SRaT	Studien zu den Ritualszenen altägyptischer Tempel
SSR	Studien zur Spätägyptischen Religion
StudEgypt	Studies in Egyptology
TAPA	*Transactions of the American Philological Association*
TLA	Thesaurus Linguae Aegyptiae
UEE	UCLA Encyclopedia of Egyptology. Los Angeles, 2010–. https://escholarship.org/uc/nelc_uee
UÖAI	Untersuchungen der Zweigstelle Kairo des Österreichischen Archäologischen Instituts der Akademie der Wissenschaften

Urk. I	Kurt Sethe, *Urkunden des Alten Reichs* I. Leipzig: J.C. Hinrichs, 1933.
Urk. IV	Kurt Sethe, *Urkunden der 18. Dynastie, IV [1–314], Urkunden des Ägyptischen Altertums IV (1–4 [= Band 1])*. Leipzig, 1905–1906.
USE	Uppsala Studies in Egyptology
WAW	Writings from the Ancient World
Wb.	Adolf Erman and Hermann Grapow, *Wörterbuch der ägyptischen Sprache*. 7 vols. Leipzig and Berlin: Akademie/Hinrichs 1926–63.
WGRWSup	Writings from the Greco-Roman World Supplement
WVDOG	Wissenschaftliche Veröffentlichung der Deutschen Orient-Gesellschaft
ZAR	*Zeitschrift für altorientalische und biblische Rechtsgeschichte/Journal for Ancient Near Eastern and Biblical Law*
ZÄS	*Zeitschrift für ägyptische Sprache und Altertumskunde*
ZPE	*Zeitschrift für Papyrologie und Epigraphik*

Bibliography

Abdallah, Aly O.A. "An Unusual Private Stela of the Twenty-first Dynasty from Coptos." *JEA* 70 (1984): 65–72.

Abd el-Qader, Adel Mahmoud, and Sylvie Donnat. *Catalogue of Funerary Objects from the Tomb of the Servant in the Place of Truth Sennedjem (TT1): Ushabtis, Ushabtis in Coffins, Ushabti Boxes, Canopic Coffins, Canopic Chests, Cosmetic Chests, Furniture, Dummy Vases, Pottery Jars, and Walking Sticks, Mainly from Egyptian Museum in Cairo and Metropolitan Museum of Art of New York.* Cairo: IFAO, 2011.

Adams, Matthew Joel. "The Title *ḫnty-š* in the Old Kingdom." MA thesis, Pennsylvania State University, 2003.

Ager, Sheila L. "The Power of Excess: Royal Incest and the Ptolemaic Dynasty." *Anthropologica* 48, no. 2 (2006): 165–86.

Ahrens, A. "The Egyptian Objects from Tell Hizzin in the Beqa'a Valley (Lebanon): An Archaeological and Historical Reassessment." *Ä&L* 25 (2015): 201–22.

Ahrens, Alexander. "A Stone Vessel of Princess Itakayet of the Twelfth Dynasty from Tomb VII at Tell Misrife/Qatna (Syria)." *Ä&L* 20 (2010): 15–30.

Albert, Florence. "Quelques observations sur les titulatures attestées dans les Livres des Morts." In *Herausgehen am Tage. Gesammelte Schriften zum altägyptischen Totenbuch*, edited by Rita Lucarelli, Marcus Müller-Roth, and Annik Wüthrich, 1–66. SAT 17. Wiesbaden: Harrassowitz, 2012.

Aldred, Cyril. *Akhenaten: King of Egypt.* London: Thames and Hudson, 1996.

———. *Egyptian Art in the Days of the Pharaohs 3100–320 BC.* London: Thames and Hudson, 1980.

Alexander, R.L. "A Great Queen on the Sphinx Piers at Alaca Hüyük." *Anatolian Studies* 39 (1989): 151–58.

Allam, S. "L'apport des documents juridiques de Deir el-Médineh." In *Le droit égyptien ancien: Colloque organisé par l'Institut des Hautes Etudes de Belgique 18 et 19 mars*

1974, edited by A. Theodorides, 139–62. Brussels: Institut des Hautes Etudes de Belgique, 1974.

———. *Beiträge zum Hathorkult (bis zum Ende des Mittleren Reiches).* MÄS 4. Berlin: B. Hessling, 1963.

———. "Egyptian Law Courts in Pharaonic and Hellenistic Times." *JEA* 77 (1991): 109–27.

———. *Hieratische Ostraka und Papyri aus der Ramessidenzeit.* Tübingen: Selbstverlag des Herausgebers, 1973.

———. "A New Look at the Adoption Papyrus (Reconsidered)." *JEA* 76 (1990): 189–91.

———. "Les obligations et la famille dans la société égyptienne ancienne." *Oriens Antiquus* 16 (1977): 89–97.

———. "Papyrus Turin 2021: Another Adoption Extraordinary." In *Individu, société et spiritualité dans l'Égypte pharaonique et copte: mélanges égyptologiques offerts au Professeur Aristide Théodoridès*, edited by C. Cannuyer and J.-M. Kruchten, 23–28. Brussels and Mons: Association Montoise d'Égyptologie, 1993.

———. "Quelques aspects du mariage dans l'Égypte ancienne." *JEA* 67 (1981): 116–35.

———. "Women as Holders of Rights in Ancient Egypt (during the Late Period)." *JESHO* 32 (1990): 1–34.

———. "Women as Owners of Immovables." In *Women's Earliest Records from Ancient Egypt and Western Asia: Proceedings of the Conference on Women in the Ancient Near East, Brown University, November 5–7, 1987*, edited by B.S. Lesko, 123–35. Atlanta: Scholars Press, 1989.

———. "Zur Stellung der Frau in Alten Ägypten in der Zeit des Neuen Reiches." *BiOr* 26 (1969): 155–59.

Allen, J.P. *Middle Egyptian: An Introduction to the Language and Culture of Hieroglyphs.* 3rd ed. Cambridge: Cambridge University Press, 2014.

———. "The Role of Amun." In *Hatshepsut: From Queen to Pharaoh*, edited by C.H. Roehrig, 83–84. New York: Metropolitan Museum Press, 2005.

Alliot, Maurice. *Le culte d'Horus à Edfou au temps des Ptolémées* 1. BdE 20.1. Cairo: IFAO, 1949.

Allon, Niv, and Hana Navratilova. *Ancient Egyptian Scribes: A Cultural Exploration.* London and New York: Bloomsbury, 2017.

Almansa-Villatoro, Victoria. "Renaming the Queens: A New Reading for the Crossed Arrows Sign and a Religious Approach to the Early Dynastic Onomastics." *SAK* 48 (2019): 35–51.

Altenmüller, Hartwig. *Die Wanddarstellungen im Grab des Mehu in Saqqara.* AVDAIK 42. Mainz am Rhein: Philipp von Zabern, 1998.

———. "Zur Bedeutung der Harfnerlieder des Alten Reiches." *SAK* 6 (1978): 1–24.

Altenmüller, H., and A.M. Moussa. "Die Inschrift Amenemhets II. aus dem Ptah-Tempel von Memphis. Ein Vorbericht." *SAK* 18 (1991): 1–48.

Althoff, Eva Barbara. *Kronen und Kopfputz von Königsfrauen im Neuen Reich.* Hildesheimer Ägyptologische Beiträge 49. Hildesheim: Verlag Gebrüder Gerstenberg, 2009.

el-Amir, Mustafa. *A Family Archive from Thebes: Demotic Papyri in the Philadelphia and Cairo Museums from the Ptolemaic Period.* Cairo: Government Printing Offices, 1959.

Ancient Egypt Research Associates. "Khafre's Giza Monuments as a Unit." The Sphinx Project, part. 4. Accessed 23 October 2017. http://www.aeraweb.org/sphinx-project/khafres-monuments/

Andreu, Guillemette. *Les artistes de Pharaon. Deir el-Médineh et la Vallée des Rois, Paris, Musée du Louvre, 15 avril–5 août 2002, Bruxelles, Musées royaux d'art et d'histoire, 11 septembre 2002–12 janvier 2003, Turin, Fondation Bricherasio, 11 février–18 mai 2003.* Paris and Turnhout: Réunion des musées nationaux, 2002.

———. *La statuette d'Ahmès Néfertari.* Paris: Éditions de la Réunion des musées nationaux, 1997.

Andrews, Carol A. *Catalogue of Demotic Papyri in the British Museum.* Vol. 4, *Ptolemaic Legal Texts from the Theban Area.* London: British Museum Press, 1990.

Arafa, E. "The Legitimacy of Shajar al-Durr Reign as Represented in Light of a Rare Dinar." *Egyptian Journal of Archaeological and Restoration Studies* 6, no. 1 (2016): 65–70.

Arnold, Dieter. "The Middle Kingdom and Changing Notions of Kingship." In *Egyptian Treasures from the Egyptian Museum in Cairo,* edited by Francesco Tiradritti, 90–99. Vercelli: White Star Publishers, 1999.

———. *The Pyramid Complex of Senwosret III at Dahshur: Architectural Studies.* Publications of The Metropolitan Museum of Art Egyptian Expedition 26. New York: The Metropolitan Museum of Art, 2002.

———. *Der Pyramidenbezirk des Königs Amenemhet III. in Dahschur.* Vol. 1, *Die Pyramide.* AV 53. Mainz am Rhein: Philipp von Zabern, 1987.

———. *The South Cemeteries of Lisht.* Vol. 3, *The Pyramid Complex of Senwosret I.* Publications of The Metropolitan Museum of Art Egyptian Expedition 25. New York: The Metropolitan Museum of Art, 1992.

Arnold, Dorothea. "Amenemhat I and the Early Twelfth Dynasty at Thebes." *MMJ* 26 (1991): 5–48.

———. "Aspects of the Royal Female Image during the Amarna Period." In *The Royal Women of Amarna: Images of Beauty from Ancient Egypt,* edited by D. Arnold, 85–119. New York: Metropolitan Museum of Art, 1996.

———. "An Egyptian Bestiary." *BMMA* 52 (1995): 1–71.

———. "Plaque with Sphinx." In *Beyond Babylon: Art, Trade, and Diplomacy in the Second Millennium B.C.,* edited by J. Aruz, K. Benzel, and J. Evans, 144–46. New York: The Metropolitan Museum of Art, 2008.

———. "Recumbent Lion." In *Recent Acquisitions. A Selection: 2001–2002, BMMA* 60, no. 2 (Fall 2002): 6.

Aruz, J. "The Art of Exchange." In *Beyond Babylon: Art, Trade, and Diplomacy in the Second Millennium B.C.,* edited by J. Aruz, K. Benzel, and J. Evans, 387–94. New York: The Metropolitan Museum of Art, 2008.

———. "Central Anatolian Ivories." In *Beyond Babylon: Art, Trade, and Diplomacy in the Second Millennium B.C.,* edited by J. Aruz, K. Benzel, and J. Evans, 82–90. New York: The Metropolitan Museum of Art, 2008.

———. "Imagery and Interconnections." *Ä&L* 5 (1995): 33–38.

———. "Ritual and Royal Imagery." In *Beyond Babylon: Art, Trade, and Diplomacy in the Second Millennium* B.C., edited by J. Aruz, K. Benzel, and J. Evans, 136–37. New York: The Metropolitan Museum of Art, 2008.

———. "Seals and the Imagery of Interaction." In *Cultures in Contact: From Mesopotamia to the Mediterranean in the Second Millennium* B.C., edited by J. Aruz, S. Graff, and Y. Rakic, 216–25. New York: The Metropolitan Museum of Art, 2013.

Aruz, J., K. Benzel, and J. Evans, eds. *Beyond Babylon: Art, Trade, and Diplomacy in the Second Millennium* B.C. New York: The Metropolitan Museum of Art, 2008.

Aruz, J., S. Graff, and Y. Rakic, eds. *Cultures in Contact: From Mesopotamia to the Mediterranean in the Second Millennium* B.C. New Haven and New York: The Metropolitan Museum of Art, 2013.

Ashby, Solange. "Dancing for Hathor: Nubian Women in Egyptian Cultic Life." *Dotawo: A Journal of Nubian Studies* 5 (2018): 63–90. https://digitalcommons.fairfield.edu/djns/vol5/iss1/2 17.01.2020.

Assmann, Jan. "Death and Initiation in the Funerary Religion of Ancient Egypt." In *Religion and Philosophy in Ancient Egypt*, edited by W.K. Simpson, 135–59. New Haven: Yale University Press, 1989.

———. "Einwohnung." In *Menschenbilder-Bildermenschen: Kunst und Kultur im Alten Ägypten*, edited by Tobias Hofmann and Alexandra Sturm, 1–14. Norderstedt: Books on Demand, 2003.

———. *Grabung im Asasif 1963–1970*. Vol. 6, *Das Grab der Mutirdis*. AV 13. Mainz am Rhein: Philip von Zabern, 1977.

———. "Semiosis and Interpretation in Ancient Egyptian Ritual." In *Interpretation in Religion (Philosophy and Religion 2)*, edited by Shlomo Biderstein and Ben-Ami Scharfstein, 87–109. Leiden: Brill, 1992.

Aston, David A. *Burial Assemblages of Dynasty 21–25*. DÖAW 56. Vienna: Verlag der Österreichischen Akademie der Wissenschaften, 2009.

———. "TT 320 and the *k3y* of Queen Inhapi: A Reconsideration Based on Ceramic Evidence." *GM* 236 (2013): 7–20.

———. "TT 358, TT 320 and KV 39: Three Early Eighteenth Dynasty Queens' Tombs in the Vicinity of Deir-el-Bahari." *PAM* 24, no. 2 (2015): 15–42.

Atkinson, Michael. *Tattooed: The Sociogenesis of a Body Art*. Toronto: University of Toronto Press, 2003.

Audouit, Clémentine. "Bodily Fluids in Ancient Egypt: Vital Waters but Dangerous Flows. Concerning an Ongoing Research Project." In *Flesh and Bones: The Individual and His Body in the Ancient Mediterranean Basin*, edited by Alice Mouton, 39–67. Turnhout: Brepols, 2020.

———. *Le sang en Égypte ancienne. Représentations et fonctions* (forthcoming).

Austin, Anne, and Cédric Gobeil. "Embodying the Divine: A Tattooed Female Mummy from Deir el-Medina." *BIFAO* 116 (2016): 23–46.

Awadallah, Atef, and Ahmed El-Sawy. "Un sarcophage de Nsi-Ptah dans la tombe de Montouemhat." *BIFAO* 90 (1990): 29–39.

El Awady, Tarek. *Abusir XVI: Sahure—The Pyramid Causeway: History and Decoration Program in the Old Kingdom*. Prague: Charles University, 2009.
Ayad, Mariam. "The Female Scribe Irtieru and Her Tomb (TT 390) in South Asasif." In *The South Asasif Project*, edited by E. Pischikova, 273–83. Cairo: American University in Cairo Press, 2021.
———. "Gender, Ritual, and Manipulation of Power: The God's Wife of Amun (Dynasty 23–26)." In *Prayer and Power: Proceedings of the Conference on the God's Wives of Amun in Egypt during the First Millennium* BC, edited by Meike Becker, Anke Ilona Blöbaum, and Angelika Lohwasser, 89–106. ÄAT 84. Münster: Ugarit-Verlag, 2016.
———. *God's Wife, God's Servant: The God's Wife of Amun (c. 740–525* BC*)*. London and New York: Routledge, 2009.
———. "Some Thoughts on the Disappearance of the Office of the God's Wife of Amun." *JSSEA* 28 (2001): 1–14.
———. "The Transition from Libyan to Nubian Rule: The Role of the God's Wife of Amun." In *The Libyan Period in Egypt: Historical and Chronological Problems of the Third Intermediate Period*, edited by G.P.F. Broekman, R.J. Demarée, and O.E. Kaper, 29–49. Leiden: NINO, 2009.
———. "Women's Self-presentation in Pharaonic Egypt." In *Living Forever: Self-presentation in Ancient Egypt*, edited by Hussein Bassir, 221–46. Cairo: American University in Cairo Press, 2019.
El-Ayedi, Abdel-Rahman. *Index of Egyptian Administrative, Religious and Military Titles of the New Kingdom*. Ismailia: Obelisk Publications, 2006.
Ayrton, Edward R., Charles Trick Currelly, and Arthur Weigall. *Abydos* 3. London: EEF, 1904.
El-Azhari, Taef. "The Ayyubids: Their Two Queens and Their Powerful Castrated Atabegs." In *Queens, Eunuchs and Concubines in Islamic History, 661–1257*. Edinburgh: University Press, 2019.
Azim, M. "La structure des pylones d'Horemheb à Karnak." *CahKarn* 7 (1982): 127–34.
Backe-Dahmen, Annika. "Sandals for the Living, Sandals for the Dead: Roman Children and Their Footwear." In *Shoes, Slippers, and Sandals: Feet and Footwear in Classical Antiquity*, edited by Sadie Pickup and Sally Waite, 263–82. New York: Routledge, 2018.
Baer, Klaus. *Rank and Title in the Old Kingdom: The Structure of the Egyptian Administration in the Fifth and Sixth Dynasties*. Chicago: University of Chicago Press, 1960.
Bagnall, Roger S. "An Owner of Literary Papyri." *CP* (1992): 137–40.
———. *Reading Papyri, Writing Ancient History*. London: Routledge, 1995 and 2019. Both editions cited.
———. "Religious Conversion and Onomastic Change in Early Byzantine Egypt." *BASP* 19, no. 3/4 (1982): 108–109.
Bagnall, Roger S., and Raffaella Cribiore. *Women's Letters from Ancient Egypt, 300* BC–AD *800*. Ann Arbor: University of Michigan Press, 2006.
Bagnall, Roger S., and Bruce W. Frier. *The Demography of Roman Egypt*. Cambridge Studies in Population, Economy, and Society in Past Time 23. Cambridge: Cambridge University Press, 1994.

Baines, John. *Visual and Written Culture in Ancient Egypt*. Oxford: Oxford University Press, 2007.

Baines, John, and C.J. Eyre. "Four Notes on Literacy." *GM* 61 (1983): 65–96.

Bakir, Abd el-Mohsen. *Slavery in Pharaonic Egypt*. SASAE 18. Cairo: IFAO, 1952.

Balme, Jane, and Chilla Bulbeck. "Engendering Origins: Theories of Gender in Sociology and Archaeology." *Australian Archaeology* 67 (2008): 3–12.

Bandy, A.C. *Ioannes Lydus: On Powers or the Magistracies of the Roman State*. Philadelphia: American Philosophical Society, 1983.

Bardinet, Thierry. *Médecins et magiciens à la cour de Pharaon. Une étude du papyrus médical Louvre E 32847*. Paris: Louvre; Khéops, 2018.

———. *Les papyrus médicaux dans l'Égypte pharaonique*. Paris: Fayard, 1995.

Barguet, Paul. *Le temple d'Amon-Re à Karnak: essai d'exégèse*. Cairo: IFAO, 1962.

Barnett, R.D. "The Nimrud Ivories and the Art of the Phoenicians." *Iraq* 2, no. 2 (1935): 179–210.

Barns, John W.B. *Five Ramesseum Papyri*. Oxford: Oxford University Press, 1956.

Barrett-Lennard, R.J.S. *Christian Healing after the New Testament: Some Approaches to Illness in the Second, Third, and Fourth Centuries*. Lanham, MD: University Press of America, 1994.

Bárta, Miroslav. *Journey to the West: The World of the Old Kingdom Tombs in Ancient Egypt*. Prague: Charles University, 2011.

———. "Kings, Viziers, and Courtiers: Executive Power in the Third Millennium B.C." In *Ancient Egyptian Administration*, edited by Juan Carlos Moreno García, 153–76. Leiden: Brill, 2013.

———. "The Title 'Property Custodian of the King' during the Old Kingdom Egypt." *ZÄS* 126 (1999): 79–89.

Bassir, Hussein, "The Self-presentation of Payeftjauemawyneith on Naophorous Statue BM EA 83." In *Decorum and Experience: Essays in Ancient Culture for John Baines*, edited by Elizabeth Frood and Angela McDonald, 6–13. Oxford: Griffith Institute, 2013.

Baud, Michel. *Famille royale et pouvoir sous l'Ancien Empire égyptien*. 2 vols. BdE 126. Cairo: IFAO, 1999.

———. "The Old Kingdom." In *A Companion to Ancient Egypt*, edited by Alan B. Lloyd, 63–80. Chichester and Malden: Wiley-Blackwell, 2010.

Bayer, C. *Die den Herrn Beider Länder mit ihrer Schönheit erfreut. Teje. Eine ikonographische Studie*. Ruhpolding: Verlag Franz Philipp Rutzen, 2014.

Beaucamp, Joëlle. *Le statut de la femme à Byzance, 4e–7e siècle*. Travaux et mémoires du Centre de recherche d'histoire et civilisation de Byzance. Monographies 5–6. Paris: De Boccard, 1990.

Beaux, Nathalie, Nicholas Grimal, and Gael Pollin. *La chapelle d'Hathor: Temple d'Hatchepsout à Deir el-Bahari* 1: *Vestibule et sanctuaires*. MIFAO 129. Cairo: IFAO, 2012.

Beck, Susanne, and Kathrin Gabler. "Die Überlieferung von Text und Befund in Deir el-Medine am Beispiel des Wächters Khawy *Ḫwj* (ii)." In *En détail—Philologie und Archäologie im Diskurs. Festschrift für Hans-Werner Fischer-Elfert*, edited by Marc Brose, Peter Dils, Franziska Naether, Lutz Popko, and Dietrich Raue, 29–78. ZÄS Beihefte 7. Berlin and Boston: De Gruyter, 2019.

Becker, Meike. "Female Influence, aside from That of the God's Wives of Amun, during the Third Intermediate Period." In *Prayer and Power: Proceedings of the Conference on the God's Wives of Amun in Egypt during the First Millenium* BC, edited by M. Becker, A.I. Blöbaum, and A. Lohwasser, 21–46. ÄAT 84. Münster: Ugarit-Verlag, 2016.

Becker, Meike, Anke Ilona Blöbaum, and Angelika Lohwasser, eds. *Inszenierung von Herrschaft und Macht im ägyptischen Tempel. Religion und Politik im Theben des frühen 1. Jahrtausends v. Chr.* ÄAT 95. Münster: Zaphon-Verlag, 2020.

———. *Prayer and Power: Proceedings of the Conference on the God's Wives of Amun in Egypt during the First Millennium* BC. ÄAT 84. Münster: Ugarit-Verlag, 2016.

Beckerath, Jürgen von. "Ein Torso des Mentemḥēt in München." *ZÄS* 87 (1962): 1–8.

Bednarski, Andrew. "Hysteria Revisited: Women's Public Health in Ancient Egypt." In *Current Research in Egyptology 2000*, edited by Angela McDonald and Christina Riggs, 11–17. Oxford: Archaeopress, 2000.

Beinlich, Horst. "Das Totenbuch bei Tutanchamun." *GM* 102 (1988): 7–18.

Benaissa, Amin, and Sofie Remijsen. "A Sound Body and Mind." In *A Companion to Greco-Roman and Late Antique Egypt*, edited by Katelijn Vandorpe, 381–93. Blackwell Companions to the Ancient World. Hoboken, NJ: Wiley Blackwell, 2019.

Ben Shitrit, Lihi. *Righteous Transgressions: Women's Activism on the Israeli and Palestinian Religious Right.* Princeton: Princeton University Press, 2016.

Benzel, Kim, and Diana Craig Patch. "Activating the Divine." In *Jewelry: The Body Transformed*, edited by Melanie Holcomb et al., 79–80, 255. New York: Metropolitan Museum of Art, 2018.

Berman, Laurence M. "Amenemhat I." In *Dictionary of African Biography*, vol. 1, edited by Emmanuel Kwaku Akyeampong and Henry Louis Gates, 203–204. Oxford and New York: Oxford University Press, 2012.

———. "Overview of Amenhotep III and His Reign." In *Amenhotep III: Perspectives on His Reign*, edited by David B. O'Connor and Eric H. Cline, 1–25. Ann Arbor: University of Michigan Press, 1998.

Bernhauer, Edith. *Innovationen in der Privatplastik: Die 18. Dynastie und ihre Entwicklung.* Philippika 27. Wiesbaden: Harrassowitz, 2010.

Betz, Hans Dieter, ed. *The Greek Magical Papyri in Translation Including the Demotic Spells.* Chicago: The University of Chicago Press, 1986.

Bevan, Edwyn. *The House of Ptolemy: A History of Egypt under the Ptolemaic Dynasty.* Chicago: Argonaut, Inc., 1927; reprint 1968.

Bianchi, R.S. "Tattoo in Ancient Egypt." In *Marks of Civilization: Artistic Transformations of the Human Body*, edited by Arnold Rubin, 21–28. Los Angeles: Museum of Cultural History, University of California, 1988.

Bickel, Susanne. "Individuum und Rollen: Frauen in den thebanischen Gräbern des Neuen Reiches." In *Images and Gender: Contributions to the Hermeneutics of Reading Ancient Art*, edited by Silvia Schroer, 83–105. Fribourg: Academic Press; Göttingen: Vandenhoeck and Ruprecht, 2006.

Bielman-Sánchez, Anne. "Régner au féminin. Réflexions sur les reines attalides et séleucides." In *L'Orient méditerranéen de la mort d'Alexandre aux campagnes de Pompé: Cités et royaumes à l'époque hellénistique*, edited by F. Prost, 41–64. Paris: Rennes, 2015.

Bielman-Sánchez, Anne, and Giuseppina Lenzo. "Deux femmes de pouvoir chez les Lagides: Cléopâtre I et Cléopâtre II (IIe siècle av. J.-C.)." In *Femmes influentes dans le monde hellénistique et à Rome: IIIe siècle av. J.-C.–Ier siècle apr. J.-C*, edited by Anne Bielman, Isabelle Cogitore, and Anne Kolb, 157–74. Grenoble: ELLUG, 2016.

———. "Réflexions à propos de la régence féminine hellénistique: l'exemple de Cléopâtre I." *Studi ellenistici* 29 (2015): 145–73.

Bierbrier, Morris L. "Geneaology and Chronology: Theory and Practice." In *Village Voices: Proceedings of the Symposium "Texts from Deir el-Medîna and Their Interpretation," Leiden, 31.05.–01.06.1991*, edited by Robert J. Demarée and Arno Egberts, 1–7. Leiden: CNWS, 1992.

———. "More Light on the Family of Montemhat." In *Orbis Aegyptiorum Speculum: Glimpses of Ancient Egypt. Studies in Honor of H.W. Fairman*, edited by John Ruffle, G.A. Gaballa, and Kenneth A. Kitchen, 116–18. Warminster: Aris and Phillips, 1979.

———. "Terms of Relationship at Deir el-Medina." *JEA* 66 (1980): 100–107.

———. *The Tomb-builders of the Pharaohs*. London: American University in Cairo Press, 1982.

———. "Udjarenes Rediscovered." *JEA* 79 (1993): 274–75.

Billing, Nils. *Nut: The Goddess of Life*. USE 5. Uppsala: Uppsala Universitet, 2002.

Bingen, Jean. *Hellenistic Egypt: Monarchy, Society, Economy, Culture*, edited by Roger S. Bagnall. Edinburgh: Edinburgh University Press, 2007.

Bissing, F.W., Freiherr von. *Der Tote vor dem Opfertisch*. Munich: Verlag der Bayerischen Akademie der Wissenschaften, 1952.

Bleeker, C.J. *Hathor and Thoth: Two Key Figures of the Ancient Egyptian Religion*. Studies in the History of Religions 26. Leiden: Brill, 1973.

Blöbaum, Anke Ilona. "Monthemhet—Priester des Amun und Gouverneur von Theben: Die Selbstpräsentation eines Lokalherrschers im sakralen Raum." In *Inszenierung von Herrschaft und Macht im ägyptischen Tempel. Religion und Politik im Theben des frühen 1. Jahrtausends v. Chr.*, edited by Meike Becker, Anke Ilona Blöbaum, and Angelika Lohwasser. ÄAT 95. Münster: Zaphon-Verlag, 2020.

———. "The Nitocris Adoption Stela: Representation of Royal Dominion and Regional Elite Power." In *Prayer and Power: Proceedings of the Conference about the God's Wives of Amun in Egypt during the First Millennium BC*, edited by Meike Becker, Anke Ilona Blöbaum, and Angelika Lohwasser, 183–204. ÄAT 84. Münster: Ugarit-Verlag, 2016.

Blok, Josine H. "Sexual Asymmetry: A Historiographical Essay." In *Sexual Asymmetry in Ancient Society*, edited by Josine Henriëtte Blok and Peter Mason, 1–58. Amsterdam: Gieben, 1987.

Blumell, Lincoln H. *Lettered Christians: Christians, Letters, and Late Antique Oxyrhynchus*. New Testament Tools, Studies, and Documents 39. Leiden and Boston: Brill, 2012.

Blumell, Lincoln H., and Thomas A. Wayment, eds. *Christian Oxyrhynchus: Texts, Documents, and Sources*. Waco, TX: Baylor University Press, 2015.

Bogoslovskij, Eugenij. *Drevneegipetskie mastera: Po materialam iz Der èl'-Medina: Altägyptische Meister anhand Materialien aus Deir el-Medina*. Translated by Tatjana Waimer and Kathrin Gabler. Moscow: Springer, 1983.

Bolshakov, V. "Princess *ḥm.t-Rʿ(W)*: The First Mention of Osiris?" *CdE* 67 (1992): 203–10.
Bomann, Anne H. *The Private Chapel in Ancient Egypt*. London and New York: Kegan Paul International, 1991.
Bonhême, Marie-Ange. *Pharaon: Les secrets du pouvoir*. Paris: Armand Colin, 1988.
Borchardt, Ludwig. *Denkmäler des alten Reiches (ausser den Statuen) im Museum von Kairo, nr. 1295–1808 [57001–57100]*. CG. Berlin: Reichsdruckerei, 1937; reprint 1964.
———. *Das Grabdenkmal des Königs Ne-User-Re*. Ausgrabungen der Deutschen Orient-Gesellschaft in Abusir 1902–1904. WVDOG 7. Osnabrück: Otto Zeller Verlag, 1984.
———. *Das Grabdenkmal des Königs S'aḥu-Re*. Ausgrabungen der Deutschen Orient-Gesellschaft in Abusir 1902–1908. WVDOG 14. Osnabrück: Otto Zeller Verlag, 1982. First published 1913 by Hinrichs (Leipzig).
Borghouts, Joris F. "Divine Intervention in Ancient Egypt and Its Manifestation (*b3w*)." In *Gleanings from Deir el-Medina*, edited by Robert J. Demarée and Jacobus J. Janssen, 1–70. EGU 1. Leiden: NINO, 1982.
Bosse-Griffiths, Kate. "A Beset-amulet from the Amarna Period." *JEA* 63 (1997): 98–106.
Botti, Giuseppe. *L'Archivio demotico da Deir el-Medineh*. Catalogo del Museo Egizio di Torino. Serie prima. Monumenti e Testi 1. Florence: Le Monnier, 1967.
Bouché-Leclerq, Auguste. *Histoire des Lagides*. Paris: E. Leroux, 1903.
Bouillon, H. "A New Perspective on the So-called 'Hathoric Curls.'" *Ä&L* 24 (2014): 209–26.
Bowman, Alan K., R.A. Coles, N. Gonis, D. Obbink, and P.J. Parsons. *Oxyrhynchus: A City and Its Texts*. Graeco-Roman Memoirs 93. London: EES, 2007.
Bracke, Sara. "Conjugating the Modern/Religious, Conceptualizing Female Religious Agency: Contours of a Post-secular Conjecture." *Theory, Culture & Society* 25, no. 6 (2008): 51–67.
Brand, Peter J., Rosa Erika Feleg, and William J. Murnane. *The Great Hypostyle Hall in the Temple of Amun at Karnak*. Vol. 1, part 2. OIP 106. Chicago: The Oriental Institute of the University of Chicago, 2018.
———. *The Great Hypostyle Hall in the Temple of Amun at Karnak*. Vol. 1, part 3. OIP 142. Chicago: The Oriental Institute of the University of Chicago, 2018.
Braverman, Paula K. "Premenstrual Syndrome and Premenstrual Dysphoric Disorder." *Journal of Pediatric and Adolescent Gynecology* 20, no. 1 (2007): 3–12.
Breasted, James Henry. *The Edwin Smith Surgical Papyrus*. Chicago: University of Chicago Press, 1930.
Bresciani, Edda. *L'Archivio demotico del tempio di Soknopaiu Neso nel Griffith Institute di Oxford*. Testi e Documenti per lo Studio dell'Antichità 49. Milan: Istituto Editoriale Cisalpino, 1975.
Bresciani, Edda, and Antonio Giammarusti. *I Templi di Medinet Madi nel Fayum*. Pisa: Edizioni Plus–Pisa University Press, 2012.
Brosius, Maria. *Women in Ancient Persia, 559–331 BC*. Oxford: Clarendon Press, 1996.
Brunner, Hellmut. *Die Geburt des Gottkönigs: Studien zur Überlieferung eines altägyptischen Mythos*. ÄA 10. Wiesbaden: O. Harrassowitz, 1986.

———. *Die südlichen Räume des Tempels von Luxor*. AV 18. Mainz am Rhein: Philipp von Zabern, 1977.
Brunton, G. *Mostagedda and the Tasian Culture: British Museum Expedition to Middle Egypt, First and Second Years, 1928, 1929*. London: British Museum, 1937.
Bruyère, Bernard. "Journal de fouilles. Deir el Médineh," *Archives de Bernard Bruyère (1879–1971)*. http://www.ifao.egnet.net/bases/archives/bruyere/.
———. *Rapport sur les fouilles de Deir el Médineh (1934–1935). Troisième Partie. Le village, les décharges publiques, la station de repos du col de la Vallée des Rois*. FIFAO 16. Cairo: IFAO, 1939.
———. *La Tombe n° 1 de Sen-nedjem à Deir el Médineh*. MIFAO 88. Cairo: IFAO, 1959.
Bryan, Betsy M. "The Etymology of *ḫnr* 'Group of Musical Performers.'" *BES* 4 (1982): 35–54.
———. "Evidence for Female Literacy from Theban Tombs of the New Kingdom." *BES* 6 (1984): 17–32.
———. "Hatshepsut and Cultic Revelries in the New Kingdom." In *Creativity and Innovation in the Reign of Hatshepsut: Papers from the Theban Workshop 2010, edited by José M. Galán and Betsy Morrell Bryan*, 93–124. Occasional Proceedings of the Theban Workshop. SAOC 69. Chicago: Oriental Institute of the University of Chicago, 2014.
———. "In Women Good and Bad Fortune Are on Earth: Status and Roles of Women in Egyptian Culture." In *Mistress of the House, Mistress of Heaven: Women in Ancient Egypt*, edited by Anne E. Capel and Glenn E. Markoe, 25–46, 189–91. New York: Hudson Hills Press, 1996.
———. "Property and the God's Wives of Amun." In *Women and Property*, edited by D. Lyons and R. Westbrook, 1–15. Cambridge, MA: Harvard University Center for Hellenic Studies, 2005.
———. "The Temple of Mut: New Evidence on Hatshepsut's Building Activity." In *Hatshepsut: From Queen to Pharaoh*, edited by Catherine H. Roehrig, 181–83. New York: Metropolitan Museum Press, 2005.
Buck, Adriaan de. *The Egyptian Coffin Texts*. Vol. 7, *Texts of Spells, 787–1185*. OIP 87. Chicago: University of Chicago Press, 1961.
Budge, Ernest A.W. *The Book of the Dead: Facsimiles of the Papyri of Hunefer, Anhai, Kerâsher and Netchemet with Supplementary Text from the Papyrus of Nu*. London: British Museum, 1899.
Burgos, Franck, and François Larché. *La chapelle Rouge: Le sanctuaire de barque d'Hatshepsout*. Vol. 1, *Facsimilés et photographies des scenes*. Paris: Recherche sur les Civilisations, 2007.
Burstein, Stanley. "Arsinoe II Philadelphos: A Revisionist View." In *Philip II, Alexander the Great, and the Macedonian Heritage*, edited by W. Lindsay Adams and Eugene N. Borza, 197–212. Washington, DC: University Press of America, 1982.
Callender, Vivienne Gae. "A Contribution to the Burial of Women in the Old Kingdom." *Archív Orientální* 70, no. 3 (2002): 301–308.
———. "Female Officials in Ancient Egypt." In *Stereotypes of Women in Power: Historical Perspectives and Revisionist Views*, edited by Barbara Garlick, Suzanne Dixon, and Pauline Allen, 11–35. Westport, CT: Greenwood Press, 1992.

———. *El-Hawawish: Tombs, Sarcophagi, Stelae. Palaeography*. Cairo: IFAO, 2019.
———. *In Hathor's Image* 1: *The Wives and Mothers of Egyptian Kings from Dynasties I–VI*. Prague: Charles University, Faculty of Arts, 2011.
———. "Materials for the Reign of Sebekneferu." In *Proceedings of the Seventh International Congress of Egyptologists, Cambridge, 3–9 September 1995*, edited by C.J. Eyre, 227–36. OLA 82. Leuven: Peeters, 1998.
———. "The Nature of the Egyptian 'Harim': Dynasties 1–20." *BACE* 5 (1994): 7–25.
———. "Non-royal Women in Old Kingdom Egypt." *Archív Orientální* 68, no. 2 (2000): 219–36.
———. "The Wives of the Egyptian Kings: Dynasties I–XVII." PhD diss., Macquarie University, 1992.
Caltabiano, Maria C. "Berenice II: Il Ruolo di una *basilissa* rivelato dalle sue monete." In *La Cirenaica in Età Antica: Atti del Convegno Internazionale di Studi*, edited by Enzo Catani and Silvia M. Marengo, 97–115. Macerata: Università degli studi di Macerata, 1998.
Camino, Luc. *Literary Fragments in the Hieratic Script*. Oxford: Griffith Institute, 1956.
Caminos, Ricardo A. "The Nitocris Adoption Stela." *JEA* 50 (1964): 71–101.
Candelas Fisac, Juan. "Presence of Lithic Industry in the C2 Wadi at West Thebes." In *Proceedings of the Congress "In Thy Arms I Lost Myself": Images, Perceptions and Productions in/of Antiquity, Lisbon 2019*. Cambridge: Cambridge Scholarly Publishers, in press.
Caneva, Stefano G. "Queens and Ruler Cults in Early Hellenism: Festivals, Administration, and Ideology." *Kernos* 25 (2012): 75–101.
Capart, Jean. "Note sur un fragment de bas-relief au British Museum." *BIFAO* 30 (1931): 73–75.
Capel, A.K., and G.E. Markoe, eds. *Mistress of the House, Mistress of Heaven: Women in Ancient Egypt*. New York: Hudson Hills Press, 1996.
Carlotti, Jean-François, and Philippe Martinez. "Nouvelles observations architecturales et épigraphiques sur la grande salle hypostyle du temple d'Amon-Rê à Karnak." *CahKarn* 14 (2013): 231–77.
Carney, Elizabeth D. *Arsinoë of Egypt and Macedon: A Royal Life*. Oxford: Oxford University Press, 2013.
———. "Being Royal and Female in the Early Hellenistic Period." In *Creating a Hellenistic World*, edited by Andrew Erskine and Lloyd Llewellyn-Jones, 195–220. Swansea: The Classical Press of Wales, 2010.
———. "The Initiation of Cult for Royal Macedonian Women." *CP* 95 (2000): 21–43.
———. "The Reappearance of Royal Sibling Marriage in Ptolemaic Egypt." *Parola del Passato* 237 (1987): 420–39.
———. "What's in a Name? The Emergence of a Title for Royal Women in the Hellenistic Period." In *Women's History and Ancient History*, edited by Sarah B. Pomeroy, 154–72. Chapel Hill: University of North Carolina Press. 1991.
Carter, Howard. *The Tomb of Tut.Ankh.Amen* 3. London: Cassell and Co, 1933.
Cenival, Françoise de. "Un acte de renonciation consécutif à un partage de revenus liturgiques memphites (P. Louvre E 3266)." *BIFAO* 71 (1972): 11–65.

———. *Les associations religieuses en Égypte d'dprès les documents demotiques.* BdE 46. Cairo: IFAO, 1972.

———. *Cautionnements démotiques du début de l'époque ptolémaïque (P. Dém. Lille 34 à 96).* Paris: Éditions Klincksieck, 1973.

———. "Deux papyrus inédits de Lille, avec une révision du P.dém.Lille 31." *Enchoria* 7 (1977): 1–49.

Černý, Jaroslav. *A Community of Workmen at Thebes in the Ramesside Period.* 2nd ed. BdE 50. Cairo: IFAO, 2001. (Originally published 1973.)

———. "Consanguineous Marriages in Pharaonic Egypt." *JEA* 40 (1954): 23–29.

———. *Egyptian Stelae in the Bankes Collection.* Oxford: Oxford University Press, 1958.

———. *Graffiti hieroglyphiques et hieratiques de la nécropole thébaine. Nos. 1060 a 1405.* Cairo: IFAO, 1956.

———. *Late Ramesside Letters.* BAe 9. Brussels: Fondation Égyptologique Reine Élisabeth, 1939.

———. "The Will of Naunakhte and the Related Documents." *JEA* 31 (1945): 29–53.

Černý, Jaroslav, and Alan H. Gardiner. *Hieratic Ostraca.* Oxford: University Press, 1957.

Černý, J., and T.E. Peet. "A Marriage Settlement of the Twentieth Dynasty: An Unpublished Document from Turin." *JEA* 13, no. 1/2 (1927): 30–39.

Černý, Jaroslav, and Abdel Aziz Sadek. *Graffiti de la Montaigne Thébaine.* Cairo: Antiquities Department, 1974.

Champollion, Jean-François. *Monuments de l'Égypte et de la Nubie: Notices descriptives conformes aux manuscrits autographes.* Paris: F. Didot Frères, 1834.

Chaniotis, Angelos. "The Divinity of Hellenistic Rulers." In *A Companion to the Hellenistic World,* edited by Andrew Erskine, 431–45. Malden, MA: Blackwell, 2005.

Cherpion, Nadine. "La danseuse de Deir El-Médîna et les prétendus 'lits clos' du village." *Association des Archéologues et Historiens d'Art de Louvain. Revue* 4 (2011): 11–34.

Chevrier, Henri. "Rapport sur les travaux de Karnak 1950–1951." *ASAE* 51 (1951): 549–72.

———. "Rapport sur les travaux de Karnak 1953–1954." *ASAE* 53 (1955): 21–42.

Choat, Malcolm. *Belief and Cult in Fourth-century Papyri.* SAA 1. Sydney: Ancient History Documentary Research Centre, 2006.

Choo, Hae Yeon, and Myra Marx Ferree. "Practicing Intersectionality in Sociological Research: A Critical Analysis of Inclusions, Interactions, and Institutions in the Study of Inequalities." *Sociological Theory* 28, no. 2 (2010): 129–49.

Clarysse, Willy. "Deeds of Last Will: Demotic, Greek, and Latin; Donation of the Woman Eschonsis to Her Son." In *Law and Legal Practice in Egypt from Alexander to the Arab Conquest: A Selection of Papyrological Sources in Translation, with Introductions and Commentary,* edited by James G. Keenan, J.G. Manning, and U. Yiftach-Firanko, 202–205. Cambridge: Cambridge University Press, 2014.

———. "Ptolemaic Wills." In *Legal Documents of the Hellenistic World,* edited by Markham J. Geller and Herwig Maehler, 88–98. London: The Warburg Institute, in cooperation with the Institute of Jewish Studies, University College London, 1995.

———. "Some Greeks in Egypt." In *Life in a Multi-cultural Society: Egypt from Cambyses *to Constantine and Beyond*, edited by Janet H. Johnson, 51–56. SAOC 51. Chicago: Oriental Institute of the University of Chicago, 1992.

Clayman, Dee L. "Berenice and Her Lock." *TAPA* 141, no. 2 (2011): 229–46.

———. *Berenice II and the Golden Age of Ptolemaic Egypt*. Oxford: Oxford University Press, 2014.

Clère, Jaques Jean. *Les Chauves d'Hathor*. OLA 63. Leuven: Peeters, 1995.

Clère, J.J., and J. Vandier. *Textes de la Première Période Intermédiare et de la XIeme dynastie*. BAe 10. Brussels: Fondation Egyptologique Reine Elisabeth, 1948.

Cline, Eric H., and David O'Connor, eds. *Thutmose III: A New Biography*. Ann Arbor: University of Michigan Press, 2006.

Collier, Mark, and Stephen Quirke. *The UCL Lahun Papyri: Religious, Literary, Legal, Mathematical and Medical*. BARIS 1209. Oxford: Archaeopress, 2004.

Collier, Sandra A. "The Crowns of Pharaoh: Their Development and Significance in Ancient Egyptian Kingship." PhD diss., University of California, 1996.

Collin, F. "Les prêtresses indigènes dans l'Égypte hellénistique et romaine: Une question à la croisée des sources grecques et égyptiennes." In *Le rôle et le statut de la femme en Egypte hellénistique, romaine et byzantine: Actes du Colloque International, Bruxelles et Louvain, 27–29 novembre 1997*, edited by Henri Melaerts and Leon Mooren, 41–122. Studia Hellenistica 37. Leuven: Peeters, 2002.

Collombert, Philippe. "Hout-sekhem et le septième nome de Ḥaute-Égypte: La divine Oudjarenes." *RdE* 46 (1995): 55–79.

———. *Le tombeau de Mérérouka: Paléographie*. Cairo: IFAO, 2010.

Connor, Simon, and Luc Delvaux. "Ehnasya (Heracleopolis Magna) et les colosses en quartzite de Sésostris III." *CdE* 92 (2017): 247–65.

Cooney, J.D. *Amarna Reliefs from Hermopolis in American Collections*. Mainz am Rhein: Philipp von Zabern, 1965.

Cooney, K.M. *The Cost of Death: The Social and Economic Value of Ancient Egyptian Funerary Art in the Ramesside Period*. EGU 22. Leiden: NINO, 2007.

———. *When Women Ruled the World*. Washington, DC: National Geographic, 2018.

———. *The Woman Who Would Be King*. New York: Crown, 2014.

Coulon, Laurent. "Padiaménopé et Montouemhat. L'apport d'une statue inedite à l'analyse des relations entre les deux personnages." In *Aere Perennius. Mélanges égyptologiques en l'honneur de Pascal Vernus*, edited by Philippe Collombert, Dominique Lefèvre, Stéphane Polis, and Jean Winand, 91–119. OLA 242. Leuven: Peeters, 2016.

Crenshaw, Kimberlé. "Demarginalizing the Intersection of Race and Sex: A Black Feminist Critique of Antidiscrimination Doctrine, Feminist Theory and Antiracist Politics." In *University of Chicago Legal Forum*, 139–68. Chicago: University of Chicago Law School, 1989.

Cribiore, Rafaella. *Gymnastics of the Mind: Greek Education in Hellenistic and Roman Egypt*. Princeton: Princeton University Press, 2005.

Critchlow, Donald T. *Phyllis Schlafly and Grassroots Conservatism: A Woman's Crusade*. Princeton: Princeton University Press, 2005.

Cwiek, Andrejz. "Relief Decoration in the Royal Funerary Complexes of the Old Kingdom." PhD diss., Warsaw University, 2003.

Daly, Nicholas. "That Obscure Object of Desire: Victorian Commodity Culture and Fictions of the Mummy." *NOVEL: A Forum on Fiction* 28, no. 1 (1994): 42. https://doi.org/10.2307/1345912.

Daressy, Georges. *Cercueils des cachettes royales*. Cairo: IFAO, 1909.

———. "Notes et remarques." *RecTrav* 14 (1893): 20–38.

———. "Notes et remarques, LVI." *RecTrav* 14 (1893): 166–68.

———. "Remarques et notes." *RecTrav* 19 (1897): 13–22.

Darnell, J.C. "Hathor Returns to Medamûd." *SÄK* 22 (1995): 47–94.

Darnell, J.C., D. Darnell, R. Friedman, and S. Hendrickx. *Theban Desert Road Survey in the Egyptian Western Desert*. Vol. 1, *Gebel Tjauti Rock Inscriptions 1–45 and Wadi el-Hôl Rock Inscriptions 1–45*. OIP 119. Chicago: The Oriental Institute of the University of Chicago, 2002.

Darnell, J.C., and C. Manassa. *Tutankhamun's Armies: Battle and Conquest during Ancient Egypt's Late Eighteenth Dynasty*. Hoboken, NJ: John Wiley and Son, 2007.

David, A. *The Legal Register of Ramesside Private Law Instruments*. Wiesbaden: Harrassowitz, 2010.

David, A. Rosalie. *Handbook to Life in Ancient Egypt*. Oxford: Oxford University Press, 2007.

Davies, Benedict G. *Life within the Five Walls: A Handbook to Deir el-Medina*. Wallasey: Abercromby Press, 2018.

———. *Who's Who at Deir el-Medina: A Prosopographic Study of the Royal Workmen's Community*. EGU 13. Leiden: NINO, 1999.

Davies, Norman de Garis. *The Mastaba of Ptahhetep and Akhethetep at Saqqareh*. Vol. 2. ASE Memoir 9. London: Kegan Paul and Co., 1901.

———. *Rock Tombs of Amarna* 2. London: EEF, 1905.

———. *Rock Tombs of Amarna* 6. London: EEF, 1908.

Davies, V. "Hatshepsut's Use of Tuthmosis III in Her Program of Legitimation." *JARCE* 41 (2004): 55–66.

Davis, N. Zemon. "Women's History in Transition: The European Case." *Feminist Studies* 3, no. 3/4 (1976): 83–103.

Davis, Theodore M., ed. *The Tomb of Iouiya and Touiyou. Theodore M. Davis' Excavations: Bibân el Molûk*. London: Constable, 1907.

Dee, Michael, David Wengrow, Andrew Shortland, Alice Stevenson, Fiona Brock, Girdland Linus Flink, and Christopher Bronk Ramsey. "An Absolute Chronology for Early Egypt Using Radiocarbon Dating and Bayesian Statistical Modelling." *Proceedings of the Royal Society A, Mathematical Physical and Engineering Sciences* 469 (2013): 1–10.

Deines, Hildegard von, and Wolfhart Westendorf. *Grundriss der Medizin der Alten Ägypter*. Berlin: Akademie-Verlag, 1957–62.

———. *Grundriss der Medizin der Alten Ägypter*. Vol. 7, no. 1, *Wörterbuch der medizinischen Texte. Erste Hälfte*. Berlin: Akademie-Verlag, 1961.

Delechuk Campello, Rocío. "Tumba de Mentuemhat, ushebtis." In *Novos trabalhos de Egiptologia Ibérica: IV Congresso Ibérico de Egiptologia*, edited by Luís Manuel de Araújo and José das Candeias Sales, 1. Lisbon: Instituto Oriental e Centro de História da Facultade de Letras da Universidade de Lisboa, 2012.

Demarée, Robert, Kathrin Gabler, and Stéphane Polis. "A Family Affair in the Community of Deir el-Medina: Gossip Girls in Two 19th Dynasty Letters." In *Ägyptologische "Binsen"-Weisheiten IV. Hieratisch des Neuen Reiches: Akteure, Formen und Funktionen. Akten der internationalen Tagung in der Akademie der Wissenschaften und der Literatur, Mainz, im Dezember 2019*, edited by Svenja Gülden, Tobias Konrad, and Ursula Verhoeven. Abhandlungen der Geistes- und sozialwissenschaftlichen Klasse. Einzelveröffentlichung. Stuttgart: Steiner, 2022 (forthcoming).

de Meulenaere, Hermann. "Nesptah. Fils et successeur de Montouemhat." *CdE* 83 (2008): 98–108.

———. "Le papyrus de Brooklyn, trente ans après." In *Essays on Ancient Egypt in Honour of Herman Te Velde*, edited by Jan van Dijk, 243–49. EMs 1. Groningen: STYX, 1997.

Depauw, Mark. *A Companion to Demotic Studies*. Papyrologica Bruxellensia 28. Brussels: Fondation Égyptologique Reine Élisabeth, 1997.

Depauw, Mark, and Tom Gheldof. "Trismegistos: An Interdisciplinary Platform for Ancient World Texts and Related Information." In *Theory and Practice of Digital Libraries—TPDL 2013 Selected Workshops*, edited by Łukasz Bolikowski, Vittore Casarosa, Paula Goodale, Nikos Houssos, Paolo Manghi, and Jochen Schirrwagen, 40–52. Communications in Computer and Information Science 416. Cham: Springer, 2014.

Derry, Douglas E. "Mummification II—Methods Practiced at Different Periods." *ASAE* 41 (1942): 240–65.

———. "Note on Two Mummies of the Eleventh Dynasty from Deir El Bahary" (from December 31, 1938)." In *Remarques sur le Tatouage dans l'Egypte Ancienne*, edited by Louis Keimer, 14–15. Cairo: IFAO, 1948.

Desroches-Noblecourt, Christiane. *La femme au temps des pharaons*. Paris: L. Pernoud, 1986.

Dessenne, A. *Le Sphinx, Étude iconographique* 1: *Des origines à la fin du second millénaire*. Bibliothèque des Écoles françaises d'Athènes et de Rome, fasc. 186. Paris: E. de Broccard, 1957.

Deter-Wolf, Aaron. "Tattooed Human Mummies, List Version 3.0." March 7, 2019. https://figshare.com/articles/dataset/Tattooed_Human_Mummies_List_Version_2_0/5738439/6.

Dickey, Eleanor. "Literal and Extended Use of Kinship Terms in Documentary Papyri." *Mnemosyne* 57, no. 2 (2004): 131–76.

Dieleman, Jacco. "The Artemis Liturgical Papyrus." In *Ägyptische Rituale der griechisch-römischen Zeit*, edited by Joachim Friedrich Quack, 171–83. Tübingen: Mohr Siebeck, 2014.

———. "The Materiality of Textual Amulets in Ancient Egypt." In *The Materiality of Magic*, edited by D. Boschung and J.N. Bremmer, 23–58. Morphomata 20. Paderborn: Wilhelm Fink Verlag, 2015.

Dimand, M.S. "A Gift of Syrian Ivories." *BMMA* 31, no. 11 (1936): 221–61.
Di Teodoro, M. *Labour Organisation in Middle Kingdom Egypt.* Middle Kingdom Studies 7. London: Golden House Publications, 2018.
Dodson, Aidan. *Amarna Sunset: Nefertiti, Tutankhamun, Ay, Horemheb, and the Egyptian Counter-Reformation.* Cairo: American University in Cairo Press, 2009.
———. "The Tombs of the Queens of the Middle Kingdom." *ZÄS* 115 (1988): 131.
Dodson, Aidan, and Dyan Hilton. *The Complete Royal Families of Ancient Egypt: A Genealogical Sourcebook of the Pharaohs.* London: Thames and Hudson, 2004.
Dolansky, Fanny. "Playing with Gender: Girls, Dolls, and Adult Ideals in the Roman World." *Classical Antiquity* 31, no. 2 (2012): 256–92.
Donker van Heel, Koenraad. "Abnormal Hieratic and Early Demotic Texts Collected by the Theban Choachytes in the Reign of Amasis: Papyri from the Louvre Eisenlohr Lot." PhD diss., Leiden University, 1995–96.
———. *Mrs. Naunakhte and Family: The Women of Ramesside Deir al-Medina.* Cairo: American University in Cairo Press, 2016.
———. *Mrs. Tsenhor: A Female Entrepreneur in Ancient Egypt.* Cairo: American University in Cairo Press, 2014.
———. "P. Louvre E 7858: Another Abnormal Hieratic Puzzle." In *The Workman's Progress: Studies in the Village of Deir el-Medina and Other Documents from Western Thebes in Honor of Rob Demarée*, edited by B.J.J. Haring, O.E. Kaper, and R. van Walsem, 43–55. Leiden: NINO; Leuven: Peeters, 2014.
Donker van Heel, Koenraad, Ben Haring, Robert Demarée, and Jana Toivari-Viitala, comps. "The Deir el-Medina Database." https://dmd.wepwawet.nl.
Donnat, Sylvie, and Johan Beha. "Du référent au signifié: réflexions autour de deux figurines (*paddle doll* et apode) de l'Institut d'Égyptologie de Strasbourg." In *Figurines féminines nues: Proche-Orient, Egypte, Nubie, Méditerranée orientale, Asie centrale (VIIIe millénaire av. J.-C– IV e siécle av. J.-C.)*, edited by Sylvie Donnat, Régine Hunziker-Rodewald, and Isabell Weygand. Strasbourg: Collection Etudes d'archéologie et d'histoire ancienne, 2020.
Donnat, Sylvie, and Juan Carlos Moreno Garcia. "Intégration du mort dans la vie sociale égyptienne à la fin du troisième millénaire." In *Life, Death and Coming of Age in Antiquity: Individual Rites of Passage in the Ancient Near East and Adjacent Regions*, edited by Alice Mouton and Julie Patrier, 179–87. Leiden: NINO, 2014.
Donnat Beauquier, Sylvie. *Écrire à ses morts. Enquête sur un usage rituel de l'écrit dans l'Égypte pharaonique.* Grenoble: Éditions Jérôme Million, 2014.
Dorman, P.F. "The Career of Senenmut." In *Hatshepsut: From Queen to Pharaoh*, edited by C.H. Roehrig, 107–94. New York: Metropolitan Museum Press, 2005.
Dorn, Andreas. *Arbeiterhütten im Tal der Könige. Ein Beitrag zur altägyptischen Sozialgeschichte aufgrund von neuem Quellenmaterial aus der Mitte der 20. Dynastie (ca. 1150 v. Chr.).* Aegyptiaca Helvetica 23. Basel: Schwabe, 2011.
———. "Ostraka aus der Regierungszeit Sethos' I. aus Deir el-Medineh und dem Tal der Könige. Zur Mannschaft und zur Struktur des Arbeiterdorfes vor dem Bau des Ramesseums." *MDAIK* 67 (2011): 31–52.

Drenkhahn, Rosemarie. "Bemerkungen zu dem Titel *Ḫkr.t Nswt*." *SAK* 4 (1976): 59–67.

Dreyer, Günter. "Funde." In *Umm el-Qaab. Nachuntersuchungen im frühzeitlichen Königsfriedhof: 11./12. Vorbericht*, edited by Günter Dreyer et al. *MDAIK* 56 (2000): 125–28.

Drioton, Étienne. "A. Hermann, *Altägyptische Liebesdichtung* (compte-rendu)." *RdE* 13 (1961): 138–41.

Driscoll, Bernadette. "The Inuit Parka as an Artistic Tradition." In *The Spirit Sings: Artistic Traditions of Canada's First Peoples*, edited by D.F. Cameron, 170–200. Toronto: McClelland and Stewart, 1987.

Dubiel, Ulrike. "'Dude Looks like a Lady . . . .' Der zurechtgemachte Mann." In *Sozialisationen: Individuum—Gruppe—Gesellschaft: Beiträge des ersten Münchner Arbeitskreises Junge Aegyptologie*, edited by Gregor Neunert, Kathrin Gabler, and Alexandra Verbovsek, 61–78. MAJA 1. Wiesbaden: Harrassowitz, 2012.

Duell, P. *The Mastaba of Mereruka* 1–2. Chicago: University of Chicago Press, 1938.

Dulíková, Veronika, Mařík Radek, Miroslav Bárta, and Matej Cibuľa. "Invisible History: Hidden Markov Model of Old Kingdom Administration Development and Its Trends." In *Old Kingdom Art and Archaeology 7: Proceedings of the International Conference Università Degli Studi di Milano 3–7 July 2017*, edited by Patrizia Piacentini and Alessio Delli Castelli, 226–37. Milan: Sala Napoleonica, Palazzo Greppi, 2019.

Du Mesnil du Buisson, R. "L'ancienne Qatna ou les ruines d'el-Meshrifé au N.-E. de Homs (Émèse): Deuxième campagne de fouilles (1927)." *Syria* 9 (1928): 6–24.

Dunham, Dows. *Naga-ed-Dêr Stelae of the First Intermediate Period.* London: Oxford University Press, 1937.

Dunham, D., and W. K. Simpson. *The Mastaba of Queen Mersyankh III (G 7530–7540).* Giza Mastabas 1. Boston: Dept. of Egyptian and Ancient Near Eastern Art, MFA, 1974.

Dziobek, Eberhard. *Die Gräber des Vezirs User-Amun. Theben Nr. 61 und 131.* AV 84. Mainz am Rhein: Philipp von Zabern, 1994.

Eaton-Krauss, Marianne. *Post–Amarna Period Statues of Amun and His Consorts Mut and Amunet.* Harvard Egyptological Studies 9. Leiden and Boston: Brill, 2020.

Ebbell, Bendix. *The Papyrus Ebers: The Greatest Egyptian Medical Document.* Copenhagen: Levin and Munksgaard, 1937.

Ebers, Georg. *Papyros Ebers. Das Hermetische Buch über die Arzeneimittel der Alten Ägypter in hieratischer Schrift.* Osnabrück: Osnabrück Verlag, 1987. First published 1875 by Engelmann (Leipzig).

Edel, E. *Hieroglyphische Inschriften des Alten Reiches.* Opladen: Westdeutscher Verlag, 1981.

Edgar, Campbell Cowan. "Recent Discoveries at Kom el Hisn." In *Le Musée Égyptien: Recueil de monuments et de notices sur les fouilles d'Égypte*, ed. M.G. Maspero, 54–63. Vol. 3. Cairo: IFAO, 1890–1915.

Eigner, Diethelm. *Die monumentalen Grabbauten der Spätzeit in der thebanischen Nekropole.* UÖAI 6. Vienna: Verlag der Österreichischen Akademie der Wissenschaften, 1984.

Emerit, Sibylle. "Music and Musicians." In *UEE*, edited by Elizabeth Frood and Willeke Wendrich (Los Angeles: University of California), https://escholarship.org/uc/item/6x587846.

Emery, Walter B. *Archaic Egypt*. Harmondsworth: Penguin Books, 1961.
———. *Great Tombs of the First Dynasty* 3. London: EES, 1958.
Engel, Eva-Maria. "The Early Dynastic Neith." *SAK* 50 (2021): 69–85.
———. *Private Rollsiegel der Frühzeit und des frühen Alten Reiches. Versuch einer Einordnung*. Menes 8. Wiesbaden: Harrassowitz, 2021.
———. "Review of Geoffrey Thorndike Martin, *Umm el-Qaab VII. Private Stelae of the Early Dynastic Period from the Royal Cemetery at Abydos*. AV 123 (Wiesbaden: Harrassowitz Verlag, 2011)." *BiOr* 70 (2013): 659–63.
———. "Die Rollsiegel und Siegelabrollungen." In *Elephantine* 24. *Funde und Befunde aus der Umgebung des Satettempels*, edited by Peter Kopp, 127–44. AV 104. Wiesbaden: Harrassowitz Verlag, 2018.
———. "Siegelabrollungen." In *Umm el-Qaab. Nachuntersuchungen im frühzeitlichen Königsfriedhof: 16./17./18. Vorbericht*, edited by Günter Dreyer et al. *MDAIK* 62 (2006): 115–22.
———. *Umm el-Qa'ab VI: Das Grab des Qa'a. Architektur und Inventar*. AV 100. Wiesbaden: Harrassowitz, 2017.
———. "Why Can't a Woman Be More Like a Man? Frauen (und Männer) in den Nebenkammern der königlichen Grabanlagen in Umm el-Qa'ab." *ZÄS* 148 (2021): 124–36.
Epigraphic Survey. *Medinet Habu* 5: *The Temple Proper*. Part 1, *The Portico, the Treasury and Chapels Adjoining the First Hypostyle Hall with Material from the Forecourts*. OIP 83. Chicago: University of Chicago, 1957.
———. *Medinet Habu* 6: *The Temple Proper*. Part 2, *The Re Chapel, the Royal Mortuary Complex and Adjacent Rooms with Miscellaneous Material from the Pylons, the Forecourts, and the First Hypostyle Hall*. OIP 84. Chicago: University of Chicago, 1963.
———. *Reliefs and Inscriptions at Karnak: Ramses III's Temple within the Great Inclosure of Amon*, 1. OIP 25. Chicago: University of Chicago, 1936.
———. *Reliefs and Inscriptions at Karnak. Ramses III's Temple Within the Great Inclosure of Amon*, 2; *and Ramses III's Temple in the Precinct of Mut*. OIP 35. Chicago: University of Chicago, 1936.
———. *The Temple of Khonsu* 1: *Plates 1–110. Scenes of King Herihor in the Court. With Translations of Texts*. OIP 100. Chicago: University of Chicago, 1979.
———. *The Temple of Khonsu* 2: *Scenes and Inscriptions in the Court and the First Hypostyle Hall with Translations of Texts and Glossary for Volumes 1 and 2*. OIP 103. Chicago: University of Chicago, 1981.
———. *The Tomb of Kheruef: Theban Tomb 192*. OIP 102. Chicago: Oriental Institute of the University of Chicago, 1980.
Epp, Eldon Jay. "The Jews and the Jewish Community in Oxyrhynchus: Socio-religious Context for the New Testament Papyri." In *New Testament Manuscripts: Their Texts and Their World*, edited by Thomas J. Kraus and Tobias Nicklas, 13–52. Texts and Editions for New Testament Study 2. Leiden and Boston: Brill, 2006.
———. "The Oxyrhynchus New Testament Papyri: 'Not Without Honor Except in Their Hometown'?" *JBL* 123, no. 1 (2004): 5–55.
———. *Perspectives on New Testament Textual Criticism: Collected Essays, 1962–2004*. Leiden and Boston: Brill, 2005.

Erman, Adolf, and Hermann Grapow. *Wörterbuch der ägyptischen Sprache.* Vols. 1–7. Berlin: Akademie-Verlag, 1971. http://aaew.bbaw.de/tla

Ertman, E.L. "Smiting the Enemy in the Reign of Akhenaten: A Family Affair." *KMT: A Modern Journal of Ancient Egypt* 17, no. 4 (2007): 59–65.

Evers, H. G. *Staat aus dem Stein. Denkmäler, Geschichte und Bedeutung der ägyptischen Plastik während des mittleren Reichs.* Munich: F. Bruckmann, 1929.

Exell, Karen. *Soldiers, Sailors and Sandalmakers: A Social Reading of Ramesside Period Votive Stelae.* GHP Egyptology 10. London: Golden House Publications, 2009.

Eyre, Christopher J. "The Adoption Papyrus in Social Context." *JEA* 78 (1992): 207–21.

———. "Egyptian Self-presentation Dynamics and Strategies." In *Living Forever: Self-presentation in Ancient Egypt*, edited by Hussein Bassir, 9–23. Cairo: American University in Cairo Press, 2019.

———. "The Evil Stepmother and the Rights of a Second Wife." *JEA* 93 (2007): 223–43.

———. "Feudal Tenure and Absentee Landlords." In *Grund und Boden (Rechtliche und socio-ökonomische Verhältnisse)*, edited by S. Allam, 107–33. Tübingen: Im Selbstverlag des Herausgebers, 1994.

———. "Funerals, Initiation and Rituals of Life in Pharaonic Egypt." In *Life, Death and Coming of Age in Antiquity: Individual Rites of Passage in the Ancient Near East and Adjacent Regions*, edited by Alice Mouton and Julie Patrier, 287–309. Leiden: NINO, 2014.

———. "Village Economy in Pharaonic Egypt." In *Agriculture in Egypt: From Pharaonic to Modern Times*, edited by Alan K. Bowman and Eugene L. Rogan, 33–60. Oxford: Oxford University Press, 1999.

———. "Women and Prayer in Pharaonic Egypt." In *Decorum and Experience: Essays in Ancient Culture for John Baines*, edited by Elizabeth Frood and Angela McDonald, 109–16. Oxford: Griffith Institute, 2013.

Fakhry, A. "A Note on the Tomb of Kheruef at Thebes." *ASAE* 42 (1943): 449–508.

Falke, Sylvia. *Die Frau im Alten Aegypten.* Didaktische Informationen. Berlin: PZ, 1992.

Fantham, Elaine, Helene Peet Foley, Natalie Boymel Kampen, Sarah B. Pomeroy, and H. Alan Shapiro. *Women in the Classical World: Image and Text.* New York: Oxford University Press. 1994.

Farag, N., and Z. Iskander. *The Discovery of Neferuptah.* Cairo: General Organization for Government Printing Offices, 1971.

Farge, Arlette. *The Allure of the Archives.* New Haven, CT: Yale University Press, 2013.

Faulkner, R.O. *A Concise Dictionary of Middle Egypt.* Oxford: Griffith Institute, 1981.

Fay, Biri. "Another Statue of Montuemhat." *GM* 189 (2002): 23–31.

———. *The Louvre Sphinx and Royal Sculpture from the Reign of Amenemhat II.* Mainz am Rhein: Philipp von Zabern, 1996.

———. "Royal Women as Represented in Sculpture During the Old Kingdom." In *Les critères de datation stylistiques à l'Ancien Empire*, edited by Nicolas Grimal, 159–86. BdE 120. Cairo: IFAO, 1998.

———. "Royal Women as Represented in Sculpture During the Old Kingdom, Part II: Uninscribed Sculptures." In *L'art de l'Ancien Empire égyptien: Actes du colloque organisé au Musée du Louvre par le Service culturel les 3 et 4 avril 1998*, edited by Christiane Ziegler with Nadine Palayret, 99–147. Paris: La Documentation Française, 1999.

Fazzini, Richard A. "Aspects of the Mut Temple's Contra-temple at South Karnak, Part II." In *Offerings to the Discerning Eye: An Egyptological Medley in Honor of Jack A. Josephson*, edited by Sue H. D'Auria, 83–101. CHANE 38. Leiden: Brill, 2010.

———. *Egypt: Dynasty XXII–XXV.* Iconography of Religions 16. Leiden and New York: Brill, 1988.

———. "More Montuemhat at South Karnak." In *The 62nd Annual Meeting of the American Research Center in Egypt—April 1–3, 2011.* Chicago Marriott Downtown Chicago, Illinois (Book of Abstracts). https://www.arce.org/sites/default/files/documents/2011.pdf.

———. "Report on the 1983 Season of Excavation at the Precinct of the Goddess Mut." *ASAE* 70 (1984–85): 287–307.

Fazzini, Richard A., Robert S. Bianchi, and James F. Romano. *Nefrut Net Kemit: Egyptian Art from The Brooklyn Museum.* Brooklyn: Brooklyn Museum, 1983.

Fazzini, Richard A., Robert S. Bianchi, James F. Romano, and Donald B. Spanel. *Ancient Egyptian Art in The Brooklyn Museum.* Brooklyn: Brooklyn Museum, 1989.

Fazzini, Richard A., and Paul O'Rourke. "Aspects of the Mut Temple's Contra-temple at South Karnak, Part I." In *Hommages à Jean-Claude Goyon offerts pour son 70e anniversaire*, edited by Luc Gabolde, 139–50. BdE 143. Cairo: IFAO, 2008.

Fazzini, Richard A., and William H. Peck. "The Precinct of Mut during Dynasty XXV and Early Dynasty XXVI: A Growing Picture." *JSSEA* 11 (1981): 115–26.

Fekri, M.M. "Les Khekerout nesout dans l'Égypte ancienne." PhD diss., Paris–Sorbonne, 1986.

Feldman, M.H. "The Art of Ivory Carving in the Second Millennium B.C." In *Cultures in Contact: From Mesopotamia to the Mediterranean in the Second Millennium B.C.*, edited by J. Aruz, S. Graff, and Y. Rakic, 248–57. New York: The Metropolitan Museum of Art, 2013.

Firth, C. *The Archaeological Survey of Nubia: Report for 1910–11.* Cairo: National Print Department, 1927.

Fischer, Henry George. "Administrative Titles of Women in the Old and Middle Kingdom." In *Egyptian Studies*, vol. 1, *Varia*, 69–79. New York: Metropolitan Museum of Art, 1976.

———. *Dendera in the Third Millennium B.C., down to the Theban Domination of Upper Egypt.* New York: J.J. Augustin, 1968.

———. *Egyptian Studies.* Vol. 1, *Varia.* New York: Metropolitan Museum of Art, 1976.

———. *Egyptian Studies.* Vol. 3, *Varia Nova.* New York: Metropolitan Museum of Art, 1996.

———. *Egyptian Titles of the Middle Kingdom: A Supplement to Wm. Ward's Index.* 2nd rev. ed. New York: Metropolitan Museum of Art, 1997.

———. *Egyptian Women of the Old Kingdom and of the Heracleopolitan Period.* 2nd ed., revised and augmented. New York: Metropolitan Museum of Art, 2000.

———. "A Memphite High Priest and His Sisters." In *Egyptian Studies*, vol. 1, *Varia*, 59–67. New York: Metropolitan Museum of Art, 1976.

———. "Women in the Old Kingdom and the Heracleopolitan Period." In *Women's Earliest Records from Ancient Egypt and Western Asia*, edited by Barbara S. Lesko, 5–24. Atlanta: Scholars' Press, 1989.

Fondazione Museo della Antichità Egizie di Torino. *Museo Egizio*. Turin: Fondazione Museo della Antichità Egizie di Torino, 2015.

Foucart, G., M. Baud, and E. Droiton. *Le Tombeau de Panehsy. Tombes Thébaines. Nécropole de Dira' Abu'n-Naga*. MIFAO 57.2. Cairo: IFAO, 1932.

Fouquet, D. "Le tatouage médical en Égypte dans l'antiquite et à l'époque actuelle." In *Archives d'Anthropologie Criminalle* 13: 270–79. Lyon, 1899. https://criminocorpus.org/bibliotheque/livre/13/.

Fournet, J.-L. "Homère et les papyrus non littéraires: Le Poète dans le contexte de ses lecteurs." In *I papiri omerici: Atti del Convegno Internazionale di Studi, Firenze, 9–10 giugno 2011*, edited by G. Bastianini and A. Casanova, 140–41. Studi et Testi di Papirologia NS 14. Florence: Instituto papirologico G. Vitelli, 2012.

Frandsen, Paul. "The Menstrual 'Taboo' in Ancient Egypt." *JNES* 66, no. 2 (2007): 81-105.

Franke, D. *Altägyptische Verwandtschaftsbezeichnungen im Mittleren Reich*. Hamburg: Verlag Borg, 1983.

Franke, Detlef. "Middle Kingdom Hymns, and Other Sundry Religious Texts—An Inventory." In *Egypt—Temple of the Whole World: Studies in Honor of Jan Assmann*, edited by Sibylle Meyer, 95–135. Leiden: E.J. Brill, 2003.

Fraser, P.M. *Ptolemaic Alexandria*. Oxford: Oxford University Press, 1972.

Freed, Rita. "Art in the Service of Religion and the State." In *Pharaohs of the Sun: Akhenaten, Nefertiti, Tutankhamen*, edited by Rita E. Freed, Sue D'Auria, and Yvonne Markowitz, 110–30. Boston: MFA, 1999.

Freed, Rita E., Sue D'Auria, and Yvonne Markowitz, eds. *Pharaohs of the Sun: Akhenaten, Nefertiti, Tutankhamen*. Boston: MFA, 1999.

Freed, Rita E., and Jack A. Josephson. "A Middle Kingdom Masterwork in Boston: MFA 2002.609." In *Archaism and Innovation: Studies in the Culture of Middle Kingdom Egypt*, edited by David P. Silverman, William Kelly Simpson, and Josef Wegner, 1–15. New Haven: Department of Near Eastern Languages and Civilizations, Yale University; Philadelphia: University of Pennsylvania Museum of Archaeology and Anthropology, 2009.

Friedman, Renée. "Excavations of the C-Group Cemetery at KH27C." *Sudan & Nubia* 8 (2004): 47–51.

———. "New Tattoos from Ancient Egypt: Defining Marks of Culture." In *Ancient Ink: The Archaeology of Tattooing*, edited by Lars Krutak and Aaron Deter-Wolf, 11–36. Seattle: University of Washington Press, 2017.

Friedman, Renée, Daniel Antoine, Sahra Talamo, Paula J. Reimer, John H. Taylor, Barbara Wills, and Marcello A. Mannino. "Natural Mummies from Predynastic Egypt Reveal the World's Earliest Figural Tattoos." *Journal of Archaeological Science* 92 (2018): 116–25. https://doi.org/10.1016/j.jas.2018.02.002.

Gabler, Kathrin. *Homes through Time: The Inhabitants of Deir el-Medina and Their Houses Revisited* (in preparation).

———. "Rezension Davies, Benedict G.: *Life within the Five Walls. A Handbook to Deir el-Medina* (Wallasey: Abercromby Press, 2018 . . .)." *OLZ* 115, no. 3 (2020): 210–14.
———. "Stele Turin CGT 50057 (= cat. 1514) im ikonografischen und prosopografischen Kontext Deir el-Medines. *Nb.t-pr Mw.t(-m-wjꜣ)* (vi) im Spannungsfeld der Mächte der Taweret und des Seth?" *Rivista del Museo Egizio* 1 (2017): 1–39. https://rivista.museoegizio.it/article/stele-turin-cgt-50057-cat-1514-im-ikonografischen-und-prosopografischen-kontext-deir-el-medines-nb-t-pr-mw-t-m-wja-vi-im-spannungsfeld-der-machte-der-taweret-und-des-seth/ [DOI: 10.29353/rime.2017892].
———. *Who's Who around Deir el-Medina. Untersuchungen zur Organisation, Prosopographie und Entwicklung des Versorgungspersonals für die Arbeitersiedlung und das Tal der Könige*. EGU 31. Leiden and Leuven: Peeters, 2018.
Gabler, Kathrin, and Anne-Claire Salmas. "'Make Yourself at Home': Some 'House Biographies' from Deir el-Medina, with a Special Focus on the Domestic (and Funerary) Spaces of Sennedjem's Family." In *Proceedings of the Conference "Deir el-Medina Through the Kaleidoscope,"* edited by Paolo del Vesco, Christian Greco, Federico Poole, and Susanne Töpfer. Turin: Rivista del Museo Egizio, forthcoming.
Gabler, Kathrin, and Daniel Soliman. "P. Turin Provv. 3581: An Eighteenth Dynasty Letter from the Valley of the Queens in Context." *Rivista del Museo Egizio* 2 (2018): 1–26. https://rivista.museoegizio.it/article/p-turin-provv-3581-an-eighteenth-dynasty-letter-from-the-valley-of-the-queens-in-context/. DOI: https://doi.org/10.29353/rime.2018.1671
Gabolde, Luc. *Karnak, Amon-Rê: La genèse d'un temple, la naissance d'un dieu*. BdE 167. Cairo: IFAO, 2018.
Galán, José, Betsy M. Bryan, and Peter F. Dorman, eds. *Creativity and Innovation in the Reign of Hatshepsut*. SAOC 69. Chicago: Oriental Institute, 2014.
Gamer-Wallert, Ingrid. *Die Wandreliefs des zweiten Lichthofs im Grab des Monthemhat (TT 34): Versuch einer zeichnerischen Rekonstruktion*. CAENL 2/DÖAW 75. Vienna: Verlag der Österreichischen Akademie der Wissenschaften, 2013.
Gardiner, Alan H. "Adoption Extraordinary." *JEA* 26 (1941): 23–29.
———. "Davies's Copy of the Great Speos Artemidos Inscription." *JEA* 32 (1946): 43–56.
———. *Egyptian Grammar: Being an Introduction to the Study of Hieroglyphs*. Oxford: Griffith Institute, 1957.
———. *Egypt of the Pharaohs: An Introduction*. Oxford: Clarendon Press, 1961.
———. *The Ramesseum Papyri*. Oxford: Oxford University Press, 1955.
Gardiner, A. H., and Sethe, K. *Egyptian Letters to the Dead, Mainly from the Old and Middle Kingdoms*. London: EES, 1928.
Gavin, M. "The Hereditary Status of the Titles of the Cult of Hathor." *JEA* 70 (1984): 42–49.
Gayet, A. *Musée du Louvre. Stèles de la XIIe Dynastie*. Paris: F. Vieweg, 1886.
———. *Le Temple de Louxor*. Paris: Leroux, 1894.
George, Matthew W.B. "'Going Govern-mental for Administration': An Investigation of the Evolution of the Structure and Function of the Egyptian Administration in the Pre- and Early Dynastic Periods." PhD diss., Macquarie University, 2019.

———. "Those Documents Are Sealed: A Study of the Evolution of the Structure and Function of the Egyptian Administration in the Late Predynastic and Early Dynastic Period, with Special Attention to Seals and Seal Impressions." MA thesis, Macquarie University, 2014.

Germer, Renate, and Claudia Näser. "Sie wurden in alle Winde verstreut. Das Schicksal der Mumien aus dem Grab des Sennedjem." In *Ägyptische Mumien. Unsterblichkeit im Land der Pharaonen*, 94–105. Mainz am Rhein: Philipp von Zabern; Stuttgart: Landesmuseum Württemberg, 2007.

Gestermann, Louise, and Farouk Gomaà. "Remarks on the Decoration and Conception of the Theban Tomb of Montuemhat (TT 34)." In *Thebes in the First Millennium BC: Art and Archaeology of the Kushite Period and Beyond*, edited by Elena Pischikova, Julia Budka, and Kenneth Griffin, 152–61. GHPE 27. London: Golden House Publications, 2018.

———. "The Tomb of Montuemhat (TT 34) in the Theban Necropolis: A New Approach." In *Thebes in the First Millenium BC*, edited by Elena Pischikova, Julia Budka, and Kenneth Griffin, 201–203. Cambridge: Cambridge Scholars Publishing, 2014.

Gestermann, Louise, Carolina Teotino, and Mareike Wagner. *Die Grabanlage des Monthemhet (TT 34) I. Der Weg zur Sargkammer (R 44.1 bis R 53), mit einem Beitrag von Farouk Gomaà† und Zeichnungen von Natalie Schmidt*. SSR 31. Wiesbaden: Harrassowitz, 2020.

Ghalioungui, Paul. "Les plus anciennes femmes-médecins de l'Histoire." *BIFAO* 75 (1975): 159–64.

Ghedini, Giuseppe. *Lettere cristiane dai papiri greci del III e IV secolo*. Supplementi ad "Aegyptus," ser. Divulgazione, sez. greco-romana, no. 3. Milan: Aegyptus, 1923.

Gillam, Robyn A. "Priestesses of Hathor: Their Function, Decline and Disappearance." *JARCE* 32 (1995): 211–37.

Gitton, Michel. *Les divines épouses de la XVIIIème dynastie*. Paris: Belles-Lettres, 1984.

———. *L'épouse du Dieu, Ahmes Néfertary: Documents sur sa vie et son culte posthume*. Paris: Belles-Lettres, 1975.

———. "La résiliation d'une fonction religieuse: Nouvelle interprétation de la stèle de donation d'Ahmès Néfertary." *BIFAO* 76 (1976): 65–89.

Glanzmann, Rahel. "The Shabti of the Lady of the House Iahhetep and the Emergence of Female Shabtis in the New Kingdom." *ZÄS* (forthcoming).

Goedicke, Hans. "Reviewed Work(s): *Untersuchungen zur Ägyptischen Provinzialverwaltung bis zum Ende des Alten Reiches* by Eva Martin-Pardey." *JARCE* 14 (1977): 121–24.

———. *The Speos Artemidos Inscription of Hatshepsut and Related Discussions*. Oakville, CT: HALGO, 2004.

Goelet, Ogden. "Nudity in Ancient Egypt." *Source: Notes in the History of Art* 12, no. 2 (1993): 20–31.

Goldstein, Norman. "V. Psychological Implications of Tattoos." *Journal of Dermatologic Surgery and Oncology* 5, no. 11 (November 1, 1979): 883–88. https://doi.org/10.1111/j.1524-4725.1979.tb00771.x.

Gomaà, Farouk. "Die Darstellungen an der Südwand des Zweiten Hofes." In *Die Grabanlage des Monthemhet (TT 34) I. Der Weg zur Sargkammer (R 44.1 bis R 53), mit einem Beitrag von Farouk Gomaà† und Zeichnungen von Natalie Schmidt*, edited by Louise Gestermann, Carolina Teotino, and Mareide Wagner, 20–22. SSR 31. Wiesbaden: Harrassowitz, 2020.

Gombert-Meurice, Florence, and Frédéric Payraudeau, eds. *Servir les dieux d'Égypte: Divine adoratrice, chanteuses et prêtres d'Amon à Thèbes*. Paris: Musée de Grenoble and Somogy éditions d'art, 2018.

Gorre, Gilles. "*Rḫ-nswt*: titre aulique ou titre sacerdotal 'spécifique'?" *ZÄS* 136 (2009): 8–18.

Gosselin, Luc. *Les divines épouses d'Amon dans l'Egypte de la XIXe à la XXIe dynastie*. EME 6. Paris: Cybèle, 2007.

Goyette, Michael. "Ptolemy II Philadelphus and the Dionysiac Model of Political Authority." *JAEI* 2 (2010): 1–13.

Gozzoli, Roberto. "Self-presentation in the Third Intermediate Period." In *Living Forever: Self-presentation in Ancient Egypt*, edited by Hussein Bassir, 177–90. Cairo: American University in Cairo Press, 2019.

Graefe, Erhart. *Untersuchungen zur Verwaltung und Geschichte der Institution der Gottesgemahlin des Amun vom Beginn des neuen Reiches bis zur Spätzeit*. Wiesbaden: Harrassowitz, 1981.

Graefe, Erhart, and Galina Belova, eds. *The Royal Cache TT 320: A Re-examination*. Cairo: Supreme Council of Antiquities Press, 2010.

Grajetzki, Wolfram. *Ancient Egyptian Queens: A Hieroglyphic Dictionary*. London: Golden House Publications, 2005.

———. "La place des reines et des princesses." In *Sésostris III: Pharaon de légende*, edited by Fleur Morfoisse and Guillemette Andreu-Lanoë, 48–57. Ghent: Éditions Snoek, 2014.

Grallert, Silke. *Bauen—Stiften—Weihen. Ägyptische Bau- und Restaurierungsinschriften von den Anfängen bis zur 30. Dynastie*. ADAIK 18. Berlin: Achet Verlag, 2001.

Grapow, Hermann, ed. *Grundriss der Medizin der Alten Ägypter*. Vols. 1–8. Berlin: Academie, 1957–62.

Grassart-Blésès, Amandine. "Les représentations des déesses dans le programme décoratif de la chapelle rouge d'Hatchepsout à Karnak: Le rôle particulier d'Amonet." *CahKarn* 16 (2017): 253–68.

Graves-Brown, Carolyn. *Dancing for Hathor: Women in Ancient Egypt*. London: Continuum, 2010.

———, ed. *Sex and Gender in Ancient Egypt: "Don Your Wig for a Joyful Hour."* Swansea: Classical Press of Wales, 2008.

Greene, Elizabeth M. "If the Shoe Fits: Style and Status in the Assemblage of Children's Shoes from Vindolanda." In *Life in the Limes: Studies of the People and Objects of the Roman Frontiers*, edited by Rob Collins and Frances McIntosh, 30–31. Oxford: Oxbow Books, 2014.

Grenfell, Bernard P., and Arthur S. Hunt. *The Oxyrhynchus Papyri*. Vol. 6. London: EEF, 1908.

Gribetz, Sarit Kattan. "Women as Readers of the Nag Hammadi Codices." *Journal of Early Christian Studies* 26, no. 3 (2018): 463–94.

Griffith, Francis Ll. *Catalogue of the Demotic Papyri in the Rylands Library Manchester.* Manchester and London: University Press, 1909.
———. "Greek Papyri from Gebelên." In *The Adler Papyri,* edited by Elkan N. Adler, John G. Tait, Fritz M. Heichelheim, and Francis Ll. Griffith, 1–59. London: Humphrey Milford, Oxford University Press, 1939.
Grimal, Nicolas. *A History of Ancient Egypt,* translated by Ian Shaw. Oxford: Blackwell, 1992.
Grimal, Nicholas, and François Larché. "Karnak 1994–1997." *CahKarn*11 (2003): 7–64.
Großmann, Franziska. *Die Rolle der Frau und die Erziehung im Alten Ägypten.* Hamburg: Diplomica Verlag, 2012.
Grunert, Stefan. "Danse macabre. Ein altägyptischer 'Totentanz' aus Saqqara." *SAK* 40 (2011): 113–36.
———. *Thebanische Kaufverträge des 3. und 2. Jahrhunderts v. u. Z.* Demotische Papyri aus den Staatlichen Museen zu Berlin 2. Berlin: Akademie Verlag, 1981.
Gunn, B. "Review of *Egyptian Letters to the Dead, Mainly from the Old and Middle Kingdoms* by Alan H. Gardiner and Kurt Sethe." *JEA* 16, no. 1/2 (1930): 147–55.
Gutgesell, Manfred. *Die Datierung der Ostraka und Papyri aus Deir el-Medineh und ihre ökonomische Interpretation. Teil I. Die 20. Dynastie I.* Hildesheimer ägyptologische Beiträge 19. Hildesheim: Gerstenberg, 1983.
Gutzwiller, Kathryn. "Callimachus' Lock of Berenice: Fantasy, Romance, and Propaganda." *AJP* 133, no. 3 (1992): 359–85.
Habachi, Labib. "Notes on the Altar of Sekhemrĕ'-Sewadjtowĕ Sebkhotpe from Sehēl." *JEA* 37 (1951): 17–19.
———. *The Obelisks of Egypt: Skyscrapers of the Past.* New York: Charles Scribner's Sons, 1977.
———. "La reine Touy, femme de Séthi I, et ses proches parents inconnus." *RdE* 21 (1969): 27–47.
———. *Die unsterblichen Obelisken Ägyptens.* Mainz am Rhein: Philipp von Zabern, 2000.
Hagen, Fredrik. "New Kingdom Sandals: A Philological Perspective." In *Tutankhamun's Footwear: Studies of Ancient Egyptian Footwear,* edited by Andre Veldmeijer, 193–97. Norg: DrukWare; Sidestone Press, 2010.
Hall, E.S. *The Pharaoh Smites His Enemies: A Comparative Study.* Munich: Deutscher Kunstverlag, 1986.
Hambly, Wilfrid Dyson. *The History of Tattooing.* Mineola, NY: Dover Publications, 1925. Reprint 2009.
Haring, Ben J.J. "From Oral Practice to Written Record in Ramesside Deir el-Medina." *JESHO* 46, no. 3 (2003): 249–72.
———. "Workmen's Marks and the Early History of the Theban Royal Necropolis." In *Deir el-Medina Studies: Helsinki June 24–26, 2009 Proceedings,* edited by Jaana Toivari-Viitala, Turo Vartiainen, and Saara Uvanto, 87–100. The Finnish Egyptological Society—Occasional Publications 2. Vantaa: Multiprint, 2014.
Harpur, Yvonne. *Decoration in Egyptian Tombs of the Old Kingdom: Studies in Orientation and Scene Content.* StudEgypt 14. London and New York: Routledge and Keegan Paul, 1987.

Harpur, Yvonne, and Paolo Scremin. *The Chapel of Ptahhotep: Scene Details*. Egypt in Miniature 2. Oxford: Oxford Expedition to Egypt, 2008.
Hartman, Saidiya. "Venus in Two Acts." *Small Axe* 12, no. 2 (2008): 1–14.
Hartwig, Melinda K. *The Tomb Chapel of Menna (TT69): The Art, Culture and Science of Painting in an Egyptian Tomb*. Cairo: American University in Cairo Press, 2013.
Hassan, Selim. *Excavations at Giza* 1: *1929–1930*. Oxford: Oxford University Press, 1932.
———. *Excavations at Gîza* 2: *1930–1931*. Cairo: Faculty of Arts of the Egyptian University; Government Press, Bulâq, 1936.
———. *Excavations at Gîza* 6 (3): *1934–1935. The Mastabas of the Sixth Season and Their Description*. Cairo: Service des Antiquités de l'Égypte, 1950.
———. *The Great Sphinx and Its Secrets: Historical Studies in the Light of Recent Excavations*. Cairo: Government Press, 1953.
———. *The Mastaba of Neb-Kaw-Her: Excavations at Saqqara 1937–1938*. Vol. 1. Cairo: U.S. Government Printing Office, 1975.
Hauben, Hans. "Arsinoé II et la politique extérieure de l'Égypte." In *Egypt and the Hellenistic World: Proceedings of the International Colloquium Leuven, 24–26 May 1982*, edited by E. van't Dack and P. van Dessel, 99–128. Leuven: Peeters, 1983.
———. "Ptolémée III et Bérénice II, divinités cosmiques." In *More than Men, Less than Gods: Studies on Royal Cult and Imperial Worship*, edited by P.P. Iossif, A.S. Chanikowski, and C.C. Lorber, 357–88. Leuven: Peeters, 2011.
Hawass, Zahi A. *Builders of the Pyramids*. Giza: Nahdet Misr, 2008.
———. *Silent Images: Women in Pharaonic Egypt*. Cairo: Ministry of Culture, 1995.
Hayes, William C. *A Papyrus of the Late Middle Kingdom in the Brooklyn Museum*. New York: The Brooklyn Museum, 1955.
———. *The Scepter of Egypt: A Background for the Study of the Egyptian Antiquities in the Metropolitan Museum of Art*. Vol. 1, *From the Earliest Times to the End of the Middle Kingdom*. New York: Metropolitan Museum of Art, 1953.
———. *The Scepter of Egypt: A Background for the Study of the Egyptian Antiquities in the Metropolitan Museum of Art*. Vol. 2, *The Hyksos Period and the New Kingdom (1675–1080 B.C.)*. Cambridge, MA: Metropolitan Museum of Art, 1959.
Hazzard, R.A. *Imagination of a Monarchy: Studies in Ptolemaic Propaganda*. Toronto: University of Toronto Press, 2000.
Heindl, Patrizia. "Monumentale Feindvernichtung: die Felidenfellträgerstatuen des Monthemhat." In *Funktion/en: Materielle Kultur—Sprache—Religion. Beiträge des siebten Berliner Arbeitskreises Junge Aegyptologie (BAJA 7) 2.12.–4.12.2016*, edited by Alexandra Verbovsek, Burkhard Backes, and Jan Aschmoneit, 45–64. GOF IV, vol. 64. Wiesbaden: Harrassowitz, 2018.
Heise, Jens. *Erinnern und Gedenken: Aspekte der biographischen Inschriften der ägyptischen Spätzeit*. OBO 226. Fribourg: Vandenhoeck and Ruprecht, 2007.
Helck, Wolfgang. "Ägyptische Statuen im Ausland, ein chronologisches Problem." *Ugarit Forschungen* 8 (1976): 101–15.
———. *Die datierten und datierbaren Ostraka, Papyri und Graffiti von Deir el-Medineh. Bearbeitet von Adelheid Schlott.* ÄA 63. Wiesbaden: Harrassowitz, 2002.

———. "Qatna." *LÄ* 5 (1984), cols. 46–47.
Hendrickx, Stan, Heiko Reimer, Frank Förster, and John C. Darnell. "Late Predynastic/Early Dynastic Rock Art Scenes of Barbary Sheep Hunting in Egypt's Western Desert: From Capturing Wild Animals to the Women of the 'Acacia House.'" In *Desert Animals in the Eastern Sahara: Status, Economic Significance, and Cultural Reflection in Antiquity. Proceedings of an Interdisciplinary ACACIA Workshop Held at the University of Cologne, December 14–15, 2007*, edited by Heiko Riemer et al. Cologne: Heinrich-Barth-Institut, 2009.
Herrerín, J., M. Sanchez, S. Onstine, V. Reckard, E. Warkentin, and T. Redman. "Prosthesis for the Afterlife in TT16, Luxor, Egypt." *JARCE* 50 (2014): 127–45.
Herrmann, Sabine. "Monthemhat, der Stadtgraf von Theben." *Sokar* 23 (2011): 90–95.
Hickey, T.M. *Wine, Wealth, and the State in Late Antique Egypt: The House of Apion at Oxyrhynchus*. New Texts from Ancient Cultures. Ann Arbor: University of Michigan Press, 2012.
Hickmann, H. "La danse aux miroirs: essai de reconstitution d'une danse pharaonique de l'Ancien empire." *BIE* 37, no. 1 (1955): 151–90.
Hippocrates. Volume 10, *Generation. Nature of the Child. Diseases 4. Nature of Women and Barrenness*, edited and translated by Paul Potter. Loeb Classical Library 520. Cambridge, MA: Harvard University Press, 2012.
Hippocrates. Volume 11, *Diseases of Women 1–2*, edited and translated by Paul Potter. Loeb Classical Library 538. Cambridge, MA: Harvard University Press, 2018.
Hobson, Deborah. "The Role of Women in the Economic Life of Roman Egypt: A Case Study from First Century Tebtunis." *Echos du Monde Classique/Classical Views* 28, no. 3 (1984): 373–90.
———. "Woman as Property Owners in Roman Egypt." *TAPA* 113 (1983): 311–21.
Hofmann, Tobias. *Zur sozialen Bedeutung zweier Begriffe für "Diener": bꜣk und ḥm. Untersucht an Quellen vom Alten Reich bis zur Ramessidenzeit.* Aegyptiaca Helvetica 18. Basel: Schwabe, 2005.
Hölbl, Gunther. *A History of the Ptolemaic Empire*, translated by Tina Saavedra. London: Routledge, 2001.
Hollis, Susan T. *Five Egyptian Goddesses: Their Possible Beginnings, Actions, and Relationships in the Third Millennium* BCE. London: Bloomsbury Academic, 2019.
Hornung, Erik, Rolf Krauss, and David A. Warburton. *Ancient Egyptian Chronology*. HdO 83. Leiden: Brill, 2006.
Horvath, Z. "Hathor and Her Festivals at Lahun." In *The World of Middle Kingdom Egypt (2000–1550* BC*)*, vol. 1, edited by Gianluca Miniaci, 125–44. London: Golden House Publications, 2015.
Hübner, Sabine. *Der Klerus in der Gesellschaft des spätantiken Kleinasiens*. Altertumswissenschaftliches Kolloquium 15. Stuttgart: Franz Steiner, 2005.
Hudáková, Ľubica. *The Representations of Women in the Middle Kingdom Tombs of High Officials: Studies in Iconography*. Harvard Egyptological Studies 6. Leiden and Boston: Brill, 2019.
Hughes, George R., and Richard Jasnow. *Oriental Institute Hawara Papyri: Demotic and*

Greek Texts from an Egyptian Family Archive in the Fayum (Fourth to Third Century B.C.). OIP 113. Chicago: Oriental Institute of the University of Chicago, 1997.

Illin-Tomich, Alexander. "Female Titles Specific to Southern Upper Egypt in the Late Middle Kingdom and the Second Intermediate Period." *BACE* 26 (2016–18): 19–36.

———. "Theban Administration in the Late Middle Kingdom." *ZÄS* 142 (2015): 120–53.

Iversen, Erik. *Papyrus Carlsberg no. VIII, with Some Remarks on the Egyptian Origin of Some Popular Birth Prognoses*. Copenhagen: Ejnar Munksgaard, 1939.

Iwaszczuk, Jadwiga. *Sacred Landscape of Thebes during the Reign of Hatshepsut: Royal Construction Projects*. Vol. 2, *Topographical Bibliography of the West Bank*. Warsaw: Institut des Cultures Méditerranéennes et Orientales de l'Académie Polonaise des Sciences, 2016.

Jacquet, J. "Fouilles de Karnak Nord: neuvième et dixième campagnes (1975–1977)." *BIFAO* 78 (1978): 41–52.

Jacquet-Gordon, Helen. *Graffiti on the Khonsu Temple Roof*. Chicago: OIP, 2003.

———. *Les noms des domaines funéraires sous l'Ancien empire égyptien*. BdE 34. Cairo: IFAO, 1962.

Jamen, France. "La société thébaine sous la XXIe dynastie (1069–945 av. J.-C.)." PhD diss., Université Lumière Lyon, 2012.

James, Peter, and Robert Morkot. "Herihor's Kingship and the High Priest of Amun Piankh." *JEGH* 3, no. 2 (2010): 231–60.

Jánosi, Peter. "Die Pyramidenanlage der 'Anonymen Königin' des Djedkare-Isesi." *MDAIK* 45 (1989): 187–202.

———. *Die Pyramidenanlagen der Königinnen: Untersuchungen zu einem Grabtyp des Alten und Mittleren Reiches*. Österreichische Akademie der Wissenschaften: Denkschriften der Gesamtakademie 13. UÖAI 13. Vienna: Verlag der Österreichischen Akademie der Wissenschaften, 1996.

Jansen-Winkeln, Karl. "Bemerkungen zu den Frauenbiographien der Spätzeit." *AoF* 31, no. 2 (2004): 358–73.

———. "Das Ende des Neuen Reiches." *ZÄS* 119 (1992): 22–37.

———. "Die Entwicklung der genealogischen Informationen nach dem Neuen Reich." In *Genealogie—Realität und Fiktion von Identität*, edited by Martin Fitzenreiter, Steffen Kirchner, and Olaf Kriseleit, 137–46. IBAES 5. London: Golden House Publications, 2005.

———. *Inschriften der Spätzeit*. Teil 1, *Die 21. Dynastie*. Wiesbaden: Harrassowitz, 2007.

———. *Inschriften der Spätzeit*. Teil 3, *Die 25. Dynastie (Nubierzeit)*. Wiesbaden: Harrassowitz, 2009.

Janssen, J.J. "Debt and Credit in the New Kingdom." *JEA* 80 (1994): 129–36.

———. *Donkeys at Deir el-Medîna*. EGU 19. Leiden: NINO, 2005.

———. "Foreword: Earning a Living in a New Kingdom Village." In *Commerce and Economy in Ancient Egypt: Proceedings of the Third International Congress of Young Egyptologists 25–27 September 2009, Budapest*, edited by A. Hudecz and M. Petrik, 1–4. Oxford: Archaeopress, 2010.

———. "Gift-giving in Ancient Egypt as an Economic Feature." *JEA* 68 (1982): 253–58.
Janssen, J.J., and P.W. Pestman. "Burial and Inheritance in the Community of the Necropolis of Workmen at Thebes." *JESHO 11* (1968): 137–70.
Janssen, R.M. "The Old Women of Deir el-Medina." *Buried History* 42 (2006): 3–10.
Janssen, Rosalind M., and Jac. J. Janssen. *Growing Up and Getting Old in Ancient Egypt*. London: Golden House Publications, 2007.
Jaroš-Deckert, B. *Kunsthistorisches Museum Wien, Lieferung 1: Statuen des Mittleren Reichs und der 18. Dynastie*. Corpus Antiquitatum Aegyptiacarum. Museum Wien, Ägyptisch-Orientalische Sammlung. Mainz am Rhein: Philipp von Zabern, 1987.
Jasnow, Richard. "New Kingdom." In *A History of Ancient Near Eastern Law*, edited by R. Westbrook, 289–359. Leiden and Boston: Brill, 2003.
Jasnow, Richard, and Mark Smith. "New Fragments of the Demotic Mut Text in Copenhagen and Florence." In *Joyful in Thebes: Egyptological Studies in Honor of Betsy M. Bryan*, edited by K. Cooney and R. Jasnow, 239–82. Atlanta: Lockwood Press, 2015.
Jay, Jacqueline E. "The *Petition of Petiese* Reconsidered." In *Mélanges offerts à Ola el-Aguizy*, edited by Fayza Haikal, 229–47. BdE 164. Cairo: IFAO, 2015.
Jean, Richard-Alain, and Anne-Marie Loyrette. "À propos des textes médicaux des papyrus du Ramesseum nos III et IV. II: la gynécologie (1)." In *Encyclopédie religieuse de l'univers végétal, croyances phytoreligieuses de l'Égypte ancienne*, ed. S. Aufrere, 351–488. Montpellier: Université Paul Valéry-Montpellier III, 2005. https://independent.academia.edu/RichardAlainJean
———. *La mère, l'enfant et le lait en Égypte ancienne*. Collection KUBABA. Série Antiquité. Paris: Harmattan, 2010.
Joergensen, Jens Bl. "Myths, Menarche and the *Return of the Goddess*." In *Lotus and Laurel: Studies on Egyptian Language and Religion in Honour of Paul John Frandsen*, edited by R. Nyord and K. Ryholt, 133–64. CNI Publications 39. Copenhagen: Museum Tusculanum Press, 2015.
Johnson, Janet H. "The Legal Status of Women in Ancient Egypt." In *Mistress of the House, Mistress of Heaven: Women in Ancient Egypt*, edited by Anne K. Capel and Glenn E. Markoe, 175–86. New York: Hudson Hills Press in association with Cincinnati Art Museum, 1996.
———. "Social, Economic, and Legal Rights of Women in Ancient Egypt." In *The Life of Meresamun: A Temple Singer in Ancient Egypt*, edited by E. Teeter and J.H. Johnson, 82–97. Chicago: The Oriental Institute of the University of Chicago, 2009.
Johnson-DeBaufre, Melanie. "'Gazing upon the Invisible': Archaeology, Historiography, and the Elusive Wo/Men of I Thessalonians." In *From Roman to Early Christian Thessalonike: Studies in Religion and Archaeology*, edited by Laura Nasrallah, Charalambos Bakirtzis, and Steven J. Friesen, 73–108. Cambridge, MA: Harvard University Press, 2010.
Jones, Dilwyn. *An Index of Ancient Egyptian Titles, Epithets and Phrases of the Old Kingdom*. 2 vols. BARIS 866. Oxford: Archaeopress, 2000.
Jones, Jana. "Pre- and Early Dynastic Textiles: Technology, Specialisation and Administration during the Process of State Formation." In *Egypt at Its Origins* 2:

Proceedings of the International Conference "Origin of the State: Predynastic and Early Dynastic Egypt," Toulouse (France), 5th–8th September 2005, edited by B. Midant-Reynes and Y. Tristant, 99–132. OLA 172. Leuven, Paris, and Dudley: Peeters, 2008.

Jørgensen, M. *Catalogue Egypt I (3000– 1550 B.C.).* Copenhagen: Ny Carlsberg Glyptotek, 1996.

Josephson, Jack A. "La période de transition à Thebes 663–648 avant J.-C." *EAO* 28 (2003): 39–46.

———. "Sacred and Profane: The Two Faces of Mentuemhat." In *Egyptian Museum Collections around the World*, edited by Mamdouh Eldamaty and May Trad, 619–27. Cairo: American University in Cairo Press, 2001.

Josephson, J.A., and R.E. Freed. "The Brooklyn Sphinx Head (56.85)." In *Zeichen aus dem Sand: Streiflichter aus Ägyptens Geschichte zu Ehren von Günter Dreyer*, edited by Eva-Maria Engel, Vera Müller, and Ulrich Hartung, 295–306. Menes 5. Wiesbaden: Harrassowitz, 2008.

———. "The Status of the Queen in Dynasty XII." In *Studies in Memory of James F. Romano*, edited by James P. Allen. *BES* 17 (2007): 135–43.

Judge, Edwin A., and Stewart R. Pickering. "Papyrus Documentation of Church and Community in Egypt to the Mid-fourth Century." *JAC* 20 (1977): 47–71.

Junker, Hermann. *Gîza.* 1, *Bericht über die von der Akademie der Wissenschaften in Wien auf gemeinsame Kosten mit Dr. Wilhelm Pelizaeus unternommenen Grabungen auf dem Friedhof des Alten Reiches bei den Pyramiden von Gîza. Die Maṣṭabas der IV. Dynastie auf dem Westfriedhof.* Vienna and Leipzig: Hölder-Pichler-Tempsky, 1929.

———. *Gîza.* 7, *Bericht über die von der Akademie der Wissenschaften in Wien auf gemeinsame Kosten mit Dr. Wilhelm Pelizaeus unternommenen Grabungen auf dem Friedhof des Alten Reiches bei den Pyramiden von Gîza.* Vienna: Hölder-Pichler-Tempsky, 1944.

———. *Gîza.* 11, *Bericht über die von der Akademie der Wissenschaften in Wien auf gemeinsame Kosten mit Dr. Wilhelm Pelizaeus unternommenen Grabungen auf dem Friedhof des Alten Reiches bei den Pyramiden von Gîza. Der Friedhof südlich der Cheopspyramide, Ostteil.* Vienna: Rudolf M. Rohrer, 1953.

Kahl, Jochem. *Das System der ägyptischen Hieroglyphenschrift in der 0.–3. Dynastie.* GOF IV, vol. 29. Wiesbaden: Harrassowitz Verlag, 1994.

Kamal, Ahmed. *Tables d'offrandes. CG nos. 23001–23256.* Cairo: IFAO, 1906.

Kanawati, Naguib. "The Vizier Nebet and the Royal Women of the Sixth Dynasty." In *Thebes and Beyond: Studies in Honor of Kent R. Weeks*, edited by Zahi A. Hawass and Salima Ikram, 115–25. Cairo: Conseil Suprême des Antiquités de l'Égypte, 2010.

Kanawati, Naguib, and Mahmud Abdel Raziq. *Mereruka and His Family.* 2, *The Tomb of Waatetkhethor.* ACER 26. London: Aris and Phillips, 2008.

———. *The Unis Cemetery at Saqqara.* Vol. 2, *The Tombs of Iynefert and Ihy (reused by Idut).* ACER 19. Warminster: Aris and Phillips, 2003.

Kanawati, Naguib, and Anne McFarlane. *Deshasha: The Tombs of Inti, Shedu and Others.* Sydney: ACE, 1993.

Kanawati, Naguib, Alexandra Woods, Sameh Shafik, and Effy Alexakis. *Mereruka and His Family.* Part 3.1, *The Tomb of Mereruka.* ACER 29. Oxford: Aris and Phillips, 2010.

———. *Mereruka and His Family.* Part 3.2, *The Tomb of Mereruka.* ACER 30. Oxford: Aris and Phillips, 2011.

Kantor, H.J. "Syro–Palestinian Ivories." *JNES* 15 (1956): 153–74.

Kapiec, Katarzyna. *The Southern Room of Amun.* Part 1: *History and Epigraphy.* Deir el-Bahari 10. Warsaw: Institute of Mediterranean and Oriental Cultures, Polish Academy of Science; Wiesbaden: Harrassowitz, 2021.

———. "The Southern Room of Amun in the Temple of Hatshepsut at Deir el-Bahari: Epigraphic Work between 2014 and 2015." *PAM* 26, no. 1 (2017): 207–20.

Kaplony, Peter. *Die Inschriften der ägyptischen Frühzeit.* ÄA 8. Wiesbaden: Harrassowitz, 1963.

———. *Die Inschriften der ägyptischen Frühzeit, Suppl.* ÄA 9. Wiesbaden: Harrassowitz, 1964.

———. *Kleine Beiträge zu den Inschriften der ägyptischen Frühzeit.* ÄA 15. Wiesbaden: Harrassowitz, 1966.

———. "Toter am Opfertisch." *LÄ* 6, 711–26.

Kaplony-Heckel, Ursula. "Die demotischen Gebelên-Papyri der Berliner Papyrussammlung." *FuB* 8 (1967): 70–87, pls. 23–30.

———. *Die demotischen Tempeleide.* ÄA 6.1. Wiesbaden: Harrassowitz, 1963.

———. "Die demotischen Tempeleide der Berliner Papyrussammlung." *FuB* 10 (1968): 133–84.

———. "Das Getreide-Darlehn P. Haun. Inv. Demot. 2 in Kopenhagen." In *Acts of the Seventh International Conference of Demotic Studies, Copenhagen, 23–27 August 1999,* edited by Kim Ryholt, 229–48. CNI Publications 27. Copenhagen: Carsten Niebuhr Institute of Near Eastern Studies, University of Copenhagen, Museum of Tusculanum Press, 2002.

Katary, Sally L.D. "The Administration of Institutional Agriculture in the New Kingdom." In *Ancient Egyptian Administration,* edited by Juan Carlos Moreno García, 719–84. Leiden: Brill, 2013.

Kayser, Hans. *Die Mastaba des Uhemka: Ein Grab in der Wüste.* Hannover: Fackelträger, 1964.

Kees, H. "Ein alter Götterhymnus als Begleittext zur Opfertafel." *ZÄS* 57 (1922): 92–120.

———. *Das Re-Heiligtum des Königs Ne-woser-re (Rathures).* Vol. 3, *Die grosse Festdarstellung,* edited by Friedrich Wilhelm von Bissing. Leipzig: J.C. Hinrichs, 1928.

Keimer, Louis. *Remarques sur le tatouage dans l'Egypte Ancienne.* Cairo: IFAO, 1948.

———. "Sur un fragment de statuette en calcaire ayant la forme d'un oiseau (vautour?) à tête de reine." *ASAE* 35 (1935): 182–92.

Kelly, Susan Anne. "Identifying the Women of Early Dynastic Egypt: An Analysis of the Women's Funerary Stelae/Slabs from Abu Rawash, Helwan and Abydos." Master's thesis, Macquarie University, 2016.

———. "Women's Work in the Early Dynastic Period." *PES* 23 (2019): 92–105.

Keydell, R. *Nonni Panopolitani Dionysiaca.* 2 vols. Berlin: Weidmann, 1959.

Khaled, Mohamed Ismail. *Abusir XXVI. The Funerary Domains in the Pyramid Complex of Sahura: An Aspect of the Economy in the Late 3rd Millennium* BCE. Prague: Charles University, Faculty of Arts, 2020.

———. "The Donation of Royal Funerary Domains in the Old Kingdom." In *Rich and Great: Studies in Honour of Anthony J. Spalinger on the Occasion of His 70th Feast of Thoth*, edited by Renata Landgráfová and Jana Mynářová, 169–85. Prague: Charles University, Faculty of Arts, 2016.

el-Khouli, Ali, and Naguib Kanawati. *The Old Kingdom Tombs of El-Hammamiya*. Sydney: ACE, 1990.

———. *Quseir el-Amarna: The Tombs of Pepy-ankh and Khewen-wekh*. Sydney: ACE, 1989.

King, Helen. *Hippocrates' Woman: Reading the Female Body in Ancient Greece*. London and New York: Routledge, 1998.

———. "Women's Health and Recovery in the Hippocratic Corpus." In *Health in Antiquity*, edited by H. King, 150–61. London and New York: Routledge, 2005.

Kinney, Lesley. "Butcher Queens of the Fourth and Fifth Dynasties: Their Association with the Acacia House and the Role of Butchers as Ritual Performers." In *Ancient Memphis: "Enduring Is the Perfection." Proceedings of the International Conference Held at Macquarie University, Sydney on August 14–15, 2008*, edited by Linda Evans, 253–66. Leuven: Peeters, 2012.

———. *Dance, Dancers and the Performance Cohort in the Old Kingdom*. BARIS 1809. Oxford: Archaeopress, 2008.

Kitchen, Kenneth A. KRI III. Oxford: Blackwell: 1980.

———. KRI V. Oxford: B.H. Blackwell, 1983.

———. KRI VI. Oxford: B.H. Blackwell, 1983.

———. *Ramesside Inscriptions, Translated and Annotated: Translations*. Vol. 5, *Setnakht, Ramesses III, and Contemporaries*. Malden, MA and Oxford: Blackwell, 2008.

———. *Ramesside Inscriptions, Translated and Annotated: Translations*. Vol. 6, *Ramesses IV to XI, and Contemporaries*. Malden, MA and Oxford: Wiley-Blackwell, 2012.

———. *The Third Intermediate Period in Egypt (1100–650 BC)*. 3rd ed. Warminster: Aris and Phillips, 1996.

Knapp, A. Bernard. "Boys Will Be Boys: Masculinist Approaches to a Gendered Archaeology." In *Reader in Gender Archaeology*, edited by Kelly Hays-Gilpin and David S. Whitley, 365–73. London and New York: Routledge, 1998.

Koch, Carola. *"Die den Amun mit ihrer Stimme zufriedenstellen." Gottesgemahlinnen und Musikerinnen im thebanischen Amunstaat von der 22. bis zur 26. Dynastie*. SRaT 27. Dettelbach: J.H. Röll Verlag GmbH, 2012.

Köcher, F. *Die babylonisch-assyrische Medizin in Texten und Untersuchungen*. Berlin: De Gruyter, 1963–80.

Koenen, Ludwig. "The Ptolemaic King as a Religious Figure." In *Images and Ideologies: Self-definition in the Hellenistic World*, edited by A. Bulloch, 25–115. Berkeley: University of California Press, 1993.

Köhler, E. Christiana. "Early Dynastic Society in Memphis." In *Streiflichter aus Ägyptens Geschichte zu Ehren von Günter Dreyer*, edited by E.-M. Engel, V. Müller, and U. Hartung, 381–99. Wiesbaden: Harrassowitz, 2008.

———. "Ursprung einer langen Tradition. Grab und Totenkult in der Frühzeit." In *Grab*

und Totenkult im Alten Ägypten, edited by Heike Guksch, Eva Hofmann, and Martin Bommas, 11–26. Menes 5. Munich: C.H. Beck, 2003.
Köhler, E. Christiana, and Jana Jones. *Helwan 2: The Early Dynastic and Old Kingdom Funerary Relief Slabs*. Rahden/Westf: Verlag Marie Leidorf, 2009.
Kóthay, Katalin Anna. "Categorisation, Classification, and Social Reality: Administrative Control and Interaction with the Population." In *Ancient Egyptian Administration*, edited by Juan Carlos Moreno García, 479–520. HdO 104. Leiden: Brill, 2013.
Kramer, B., J.C. Shelton, and G.M. Browne, eds. *Das Archiv des Nepheros und verwandte Texte*. Aegyptiaca Treverensia 4. Mainz am Rhein: Philipp von Zabern, 1987.
Krauss, Rolf. "Der Oberbildhauer Bak und sein Denkstein in Berlin." *Jahrbuch der Berliner Museen* 28 (1986): 5–46.
Krutak, Lars F. *The Tattooing Arts of Tribal Women*. London: Bennett and Bloom/Desert Hearts, 2007.
Krzyszkowska, O., and R. Morkot. "Ivory and Related Materials." In *Ancient Egyptian Materials and Technology*, edited by P.T. Nicholson and I. Shaw, 320–31. Cambridge: Cambridge University Press, 2000.
Kuhlmann, Klaus-Peter, and Wolfgang Schenkel. *Das Grab des Ibi, Obergutsverwalters der Gottesgemahlin des Amun (Thebanisches Grab Nr. 36)*. Vol. 1, *Beschreibung der unterirdischen Kult- und Bestattungsanlage*. AV 15. Mainz am Rhein: Philipp von Zabern, 1983.
Küllmer, Hella. "Marktfrauen, Priesterinnen und Elde des Königs. Untersuchung über die Position von Frauen in der sozialen Hierarchie den Alten Ägypten bis zum Ende der 1. Zweischenzeit." PhD diss., Universität Hamburg, 2007.
Kurz, Marcel. *Graffiti de la Montagne Thébaine*. Cairo: Centre de documentation et d'études sur l'ancienne Egypte, 1973.
Labrousse, Audran. "Huit épouses du roi Pépi I." In *Egyptian Culture and Society: Studies in Honour of Naguib Kanawati* 2, edited by A. Woods, A. McFarlane, and S. Binder, 297–314. SASAE 38. Cairo: Conseil Suprême des Antiquités de l'Égypte, 2010.
———. *Les pyramides des reines: Une nouvelle nécropole à Saqqâra*. Paris: Éditions Hazan, 1999.
———. *Le temple funéraire du roi Pépy Ier: Le temps de la construction*. 2 vols. Cairo: IFAO, 2019.
Labrousse, Audran, and Jean-Philippe Lauer. *Les complexes funéraires d'Ouserkaf et de Néferhétepès*. BdE 130. Cairo: IFAO, 2000.
Lacau, Pierre, and Henri Chevrier. *Une chapelle d'Hatshepsout à Karnak* 1. Cairo: IFAO, 1977.
———. *Une chapelle de Sésostris Ier à Karnak*. Cairo: IFAO, 1956–69.
Larché, François. *L'anastylose des blocs d'Amenhotep Ier à Karnak*. Études d'égyptologie 18. Paris: Soleb, 2019.
Larkin, D.B. "Titles and Epithets of Kheruef." In *The Tomb of Kheruef: Theban Tomb 192*, edited by Ch.F. Nims et al., 78–80. OIP 102. Chicago: Oriental Institute of Chicago Press, 1980.
Larsen, M.T. "The Old Assyrian Merchant Colonies." In *Beyond Babylon: Art, Trade, and Diplomacy in the Second Millennium B.C.*, edited by J. Aruz, K. Benzel, and J. Evans, 70–73. New York: The Metropolitan Museum of Art, 2008.

Leahy, A. "The Adoption of Ankhnesneferibre at Karnak." *JEA* 82 (1996): 145–65.

Leca, Ange-Pierre. *La médecine égyptienne au temps des Pharaons*. Paris: Dacosta, 1971.

Leclant, Jean. *Montouemhat, quatrième prophète d'Amon*. BdE 35. Cairo: IFAO, 1961.

———. "Le rôle du lait et l'allaitement d'après les textes des pyramides." *JNES* 10 (1951): 123–27.

———. "The Suckling of Pharaoh as a Part of the Coronation Rites in Ancient Egypt. Le rôle de l'allaitement dans le cérémonial pharaonique du couronnement." In *Proceedings of the IXth International Congress for the History of Religion*, 135–45. Tokyo: Maruzen, 1960.

Legrain, Georges. "Achats à Louqsor." *ASAE* 4 (1903): 133–35.

———. *Statues et statuettes de rois et de particuliers* 1. Cairo: IFAO, 1906.

———. *Statues et statuettes de rois et de particuliers* 3. Cairo: IFAO, 1914.

———. "Le temple et les chapelles d'Osiris à Karnak I: Le temple d'Osiris, Hiq-Djeto ." *RecTrav* 22 (1900): 125–36, 146–49.

Leitz, Christian. *Magical and Medical Papyri of the New Kingdom*. Hieratic Papyri in the British Museum 7. London: British Museum Press, 1999.

———, ed. *Lexikon der ägyptischen Götter und Götterbezeichnungen*, 110–16, 129. OLA. Leuven: Peeters, 2002–2003.

Lekov, Teodor. "The Shadow of the Dead and Its Representation." *JES* 3 (2010): 43–61.

Lelong, Mélanie. "Néférousobek ou comment concevoir la royauté au féminin." *Égypte, Afrique & Orient* 69 (March–May 2013): 47–54.

Lenzo, Giuseppina. "The Two Funerary Papyri of Queen Nedjmet (P. BM EA 10490 and P. BM EA 10541 + Louvre E. 6258)." *BMSAES* 15 (2010): 63–83.

Lepsius, Karl Richard. *Denkmäler aus Aegypten und Aethiopien: nach den Zeichnungen der von seiner Majestät dem Koenige von Preussen Friedrich Wilhelm IV nach diesen Ländern gesendeten und in den Jahren 1842–1845 ausgeführten wissenschaftlichen Expedition*. Berlin: Nicolaische Buchhandlung, 1849–56.

Lesko, Barbara S. *The Great Goddesses of Egypt*. Norman: University of Oklahoma Press, 1999.

———. "'Listening' to the Egyptian Woman: Letters, Testimonials, and Other Expression of Self." In *Gold of Praise: Studies on Ancient Egypt in Honor of Edward F. Wente*, edited by Emily Teeter and John A. Larson, 247–54. SAOC 58. Chicago: Oriental Institute, 1999.

———. *The Remarkable Women of Ancient Egypt*. Berkeley: B.C. Scribe Publications, 1978.

———. "Women's Monumental Mark on Ancient Egypt." *The Biblical Archaeologist* 54, no. 1 (March 1991): 4–15.

———, ed. *Women's Earliest Records from Ancient Egypt and Western Asia: Proceedings of the Conference on Women in the Ancient Near East, Brown University, November 5–7, 1987*. Atlanta: Scholars' Press, 1989.

Lesko, Leonard H. "Literature, Literacy, and Literati." In *Pharaoh's Workers*, edited by L.H. Lesko, 131–44. Ithaca: Cornell University Press, 1994, 2018.

———. "Some Comments on Ancient Egyptian Literacy and Literati." In *Studies in Egyptology Presented to Miriam Lichtheim* 2, edited by Sarah Israelit-Groll, 656–67. Jerusalem: Magness Press, Hebrew University, 1990.

Letellier, Bernadette, and François Larché. *La cour à portique de Thoutmosis IV*. Études d'égyptologie 12. Paris: Soleb, 2013.

Leung, A.K.C., ed. *Medicine for Women in Imperial China*. Leiden and Boston: Brill, 2006.

Lewis, Naphtali. "The Demise of the Demotic Document: When and Why." *JEA* 79 (1993): 276–81.

Li, Jean. "Elite Theban Women of the Eighth–Sixth Centuries BCE in Egypt: Identity, Status and Mortuary Practice." PhD diss., University of California, Berkeley, 2010.

———. *Women, Gender and Identity in Third Intermediate Period Egypt: The Theban Case Study*. Routledge StudEgypt 4. London and New York: Routledge, 2017.

Lichtheim, Miriam. *Demotic Ostraca from Medinet Habu*. OIP 80. Chicago: University of Chicago Press, 1957.

Liddell, Henry George. *A Greek–English Lexicon*, edited by Robert Scott, Henry Stuart Jones, and Roderick McKenzie. New rev. ed. Oxford: Clarendon Press, 1961.

Lilyquist, Christine. "Egypt and the Near East: Evidence of Contact in the Material Record." In *Hatshepsut: From Queen to Pharaoh*, edited by C.H. Roehrig, 60–67. New York: The Metropolitan Museum of Art, 2005.

———. "Royal Head." In *The Metropolitan Museum of Art Annual Report 1977–1978*. New York: Metropolitan Museum of Art, 1978.

———. "Royal Head, Middle Kingdom." In *The Metropolitan Museum of Art Notable Acquisitions 1975–1979*. New York: Metropolitan Museum of Art, 1979.

Lion, Brigitte. "La notion de genre en assyriologie." In *Problèmes du genre en Grèce ancienne*, edited by Violaine Sebillotte Cuchet and Nathalie Ernoult, 51–64. Paris: Éditions de la Sorbonne, 2007.

Lipkin, Bron, and Gary Dibley. *A Compendium of Egyptian Funerary Cones*. London: Bron Lipkin and Gary Dibley, 2009.

Lippert, Sandra L. "Begegnungen und Kollisionen: Das Recht in Ägypten von der Spätzeit bis in die römische Zeit." *ZAR* 16 (2010): 157–71.

———. *Einführung in die altägyptische Rechtsgeschichte*. 2nd ed. Einführungen und Quellentexte zur Ägyptologie 5. Münster: LIT Verlag, 2012.

———. "Inheritance." In *UEE*, edited by Elizabeth Frood and Willeke Wendrich, 1–20. Los Angeles: University of California, 2013. http://digital2.library.ucla.edu/viewItem.do?ark=21198/zz002hg0w1.

Lippert, Sandra L., Maren Schentuleit, and Karl-Theodor Zauzich. *Dokumente aus Dime*. Vol. 3, *Urkunden. Mit Beiträgen von Fabian Reiter*. Wiesbaden: Harrassowitz Verlag, 2010.

Llewellyn-Jones, Lloyd, and Stephanie Winder. "A Key to Berenike's Lock? The Hathoric Model of Queenship in Early Ptolemaic Egypt." In *Creating a Hellenistic World*, edited by Andrew Erskine and Lloyd Llewellyn-Jones, 247–70. Swansea: Classical Press of Wales, 2010.

Lloyd, Alan B. "The Ptolemaic Period (332–30 BC)." In *The Oxford History of Ancient Egypt*, edited by Ian Shaw, 388–413. 2nd ed. Oxford and New York: Oxford University Press, 2003.

Loeben, Christian E. "Nefertiti's Pillars: A Photo Essay of the Queen's Monument at Karnak." *Amarna Letters* 3 (1994): 41–45.

Logan, Tom. "The *Jmyt-pr* Document: Form, Function, and Significance." *JARCE* 37 (2000): 49–73.

Lohwasser, Angelika. *Die königlichen Frauen im antiken Reich von Kusch. 25. Dynastie bis zur Zeit des Nastasen.* Meroitica 19. Wiesbaden: Harrassowitz, 2001.

———. "'Nubianess' and the God's Wives of the 25th Dynasty: Office Holders, the Institution, Reception and Reaction." In *Prayer and Power: Proceedings of the Conference on the God's Wives of Amun in Egypt during the First Millennium BC*, edited by M. Becker, A.I. Blöbaum, and A. Lohwasser, 121–36. ÄAT 84. Münster: Ugarit-Verlag, 2016.

Loring, Edward. "The Dynasty of Piankh and the Royal Cache." In *The Royal Cache TT 320: A Re-examination*, edited by Erhart Graefe and Galina Belova, 61–76. Cairo: Supreme Council of Antiquities Press, 2010.

Lucarelli, Rita. *The Book of the Dead of Gatseshen: Ancient Egyptian Funerary Religion in the 10th Century BC.* EGU 21. Leiden: NINO, 2006.

———. "L'uso dei papiri funerari presso il clero femminile di Amon a Tebe nella XXI dinastia." In *Sacerdozio e società civile nell'Egitto antico. Atti del terzo Colloquio di Egittologia e di Antichita Copte, Bologna—30/31 maggio 2007*, edited by S. Pernigotti and M. Zecchi, 105–13. Pisa: La Mandragora, 2008.

Lüddeckens, Erich. *Demotische Urkunden aus Hawara: Umschrift, Übersetzung, und Kommentar.* Stuttgart: F. Steiner, 1998.

Luijendijk, AnneMarie. "Books and Private Readers in Early Christian Oxyrhynchus: 'A Spiritual Meadow and a Garden of Delight.'" In *Books and Readers in the Pre-modern World*, edited by Karl Shuve, 101–35. WGRWSup 12. Atlanta: SBL, 2018.

———. "A Gospel Amulet for Joannia (P. Oxy. VIII 1151)." In *Daughters of Hecate: Women and Magic in the Ancient World*, edited by Kimberly B. Stratton and Dayna S. Kalleres, 418–43. Oxford: Oxford University Press, 2014.

———. *Greetings in the Lord: Early Christians and the Oxyrhynchus Papyri.* Harvard Theological Studies 60. Cambridge, MA: Harvard University Press, 2008.

———. "A New Testament Papyrus and Its Documentary Context: An Early Christian Writing Exercise from the Archive of Leonides (P. Oxy. II 209/P10)." *JBL* 129 (2010): 575–96.

———. "On and beyond Duty: Christian Clergy at Oxyrhynchus (c. 250–400)." In *Beyond Priesthood: Religious Entrepreneurs and Innovators in the Roman Empire*, edited by Richard L. Gordon, Georgia Petridou, and Jörg Rüpke, 103–26. Berlin and Boston: De Gruyter, 2017.

———. "'Twenty Thousand Nuns': The Domestic Virgins of Oxyrhynchos." In *Christianity and Monasticism in Middle Egypt: Al-Minya and Asyut*, edited by Gawdat Gabra and Hany Takla, 57–67. Cairo: American University in Cairo Press, 2015.

Luiselli, Maria M. "Early Mut(s): On the Origins of the Theban Goddess Mut and Her Cult." *RdE* 66 (2015): 111–29.

———. *Die Suche nach Gottesnähe: Die altägyptische "persönliche Frömmigkeit" von der Ersten Zwischenzeit bis zum Ende des Neuen Reiches.* Wiesbaden: Harrassowitz Verlag, 2011.

Macadam, M.F. Laming. "A Royal Family of the Thirteenth Dynasty." *JEA* 37 (1951): 20–28.

———. *The Temples of Kawa* 1: *The Inscriptions.* Oxford: Oxford University Press, 1949.

Mack-Canty, Colleen. "Third-wave Feminism and the Need to Reweave the Nature/Culture Duality." *National Women's Studies Association* 16, no. 3 (Autumn 2004): 154–79.

Macramallah, R. *Le Mastaba d'Idout.* Fouilles à Saqqarah. Cairo: IFAO, 1935.

Macurdy, Grace Harriet. *Hellenistic Queens: A Study of Woman-Power in Macedonia, Seleucid Syria, and Ptolemaic Egypt.* Baltimore: The Johns Hopkins Press, 1932.

Mahaffy, J.P. *A History of Egypt under the Ptolemaic Dynasty.* London: Methuen and Co., 1899.

Mahmood, Saba. "Feminist Theory, Embodiment, and the Docile Agent: Some Reflections on the Egyptian Islamic Revival." *Cultural Anthropology* 16, no. 2 (2001): 202–36.

———. *Politics of Piety: The Islamic Revival and the Feminist Subject.* Princeton: Princeton University Press, 2011.

Mahmoud, Adel. "Ii-neferti, a Poor Woman." *MDAIK* 55 (1999): 315–23.

Mann, Michael. *The Sources of Social Power.* Vol. 1, *A History of Power from the Beginning to AD 1760.* Cambridge: Cambridge University Press, 2012.

Manniche, L. *Music and Musicians in Ancient Egypt.* London: British Museum, 1991.

Manning, Joseph G. "Demotic Law." In *A History of Ancient Near Eastern Law,* edited by Raymond Westbrook, 819–62. Handbook of Oriental Studies/Handbuch der Orientalistik, Section 1: The Near and Middle East, 72. 2 vols. Leiden and Boston: Brill, 2003.

———. *The Hauswaldt Papyri: A Third Century B.C. Family Dossier from Edfu.* Demotische Studien 12. Sommerhausen: Gisela Zauzich, 1997.

———. *Land and Power in Ptolemaic Egypt: The Structure of Land Tenure.* Cambridge: Cambridge University Press, 2003.

———. "Ptolemaic Demotic Marriage Contract." In *Law and Legal Practice in Egypt from Alexander to the Arab Conquest: A Selection of Papyrological Sources in Translation with Introductions and Commentary,* edited by James G. Keenan, Joseph G. Manning, and Uri Yiftach-Firanko, 150–51. Cambridge: Cambridge University Press, 2014.

———. "The Ptolemaic Period (332–30 BC)," in *Law and Legal Practice in Egypt from Alexander to the Arab Conquest: A Selection of Papyrological Sources in Translation, with Introductions and Commentary,* edited by James G. Keenan, Joseph G. Manning, and Uri Yiftach-Firanko, 5–6. Cambridge: Cambridge University Press, 2014.

Manuelian, Peter Der. "An Essay in Reconstruction: Two Registers from the Tomb of Mentuemhat at Thebes (no. 34)." *MDAIK* 39 (1984): 131–50.

———. "A Fragment of Relief from the Tomb of Mentuemhat Attributed to the Fifth Dynasty." *JSSEA* 12 (1982): 185–88.

———. "Two Fragments of Relief and a New Model for the Tomb of Mentemhēt." *JEA* 71 (1985): 98–121.

Maragioglio, Vito Giuseppe, and Celeste Ambriogio Rinaldi. *L'architettura delle piramidi menfite* 8. Turin: Artale, 1977.

———. *Notizie sulle piramidi di Zedefra, Zedkara Isesi, Teti.* Turin: T. Artale, 1962.

Marciniak, Marek. "Quelques remarques sur la formule 'Ir Nfr, Ir Nfr.'" *Études et Travaux* 2 (1968): 26–31.

Marcus, E. "Amenemhet II and the Sea: Maritime Aspects of the Mit Rahina (Memphis) Inscription." *Ä&L* 17 (2007): 137–90.

Mariette, Auguste. *Catalogue général des monuments d'Abydos découverts pendant les fouilles de cette ville.* Paris: L'imprimerie nationale, 1880.

———. *Les mastabas de l'ancien empire.* Paris: F. Vieweg, 1885.

———. *Les papyrus égyptiens du Musée de Boulaq.* Vol. 3, *Papyrus Nos 21 & 22.* Paris: F. Vieweg, 1876.

Martin, Geoffrey T. *Egyptian Administrative and Private-name Seals, Principally of the Middle Kingdom and Second Intermediate Period.* Oxford: Griffith Institute, 1971.

———. *The Memphite Tomb of Horemheb, Commander-in-Chief of Tutankhamun.* Vol. 1. London: EES, 1989.

———. *Umm el-Qaab VII: Private Stelae of the Early Dynastic Period from the Royal Cemetery at Abydos.* AV 123. Wiesbaden: Harrassowitz, 2011.

Martin-Pardey, Eva. "Kopf einer Sphinx." In *Nofret—die Schöne II. Die Frau im Alten Ägypten. "Wahrheit" und Wirklichkeit,* edited by Arne Eggebrecht, 46–47. Mainz am Rhein: Philipp von Zabern, 1985.

———. "Neferuptah." In *LÄ* 4, col. 382.

Maspero, Gaston. *Causeries d'Egypte.* Paris: Goutte d'or, 1907.

———. *Les momies royales de Deir el-Bahari.* Cairo, 1889.

Mathieson, Erica A. *Christian Women in the Greek Papyri of Egypt to 400 CE.* SAA 6. Turnhout: Brepols, 2014

Matić, Uroš. "(De)queering Hatshepsut: Binary Bind in Archaeology of Egypt and Kingship beyond the Corporeal." *Journal of Archaeological Method and Theory* 23, no. 3 (September 2016): 810–31.

———. "Her Striking but Cold Beauty: Gender and Violence in Depictions of Queen Nefertiti Smiting the Enemies." In *Archaeologies of Gender and Violence,* edited by Uroš Matić and Bo Jensen, 103–21. Oxford and Philadelphia: Oxbow Books, 2017.

Matić, Uroš, and Bo Jensen, eds. *Archaeologies of Gender and Violence.* Oxford and Philadelphia: Oxbow Books, 2017.

Mattha, Girgis. *Demotic Ostraca.* Cairo: IFAO, 1945.

Mattha, G., and G.R. Hughes. *The Demotic Legal Code of Hermopolis West.* Cairo: IFAO, 1975.

Matthiae, Paolo. "Ebla." In *Beyond Babylon: Art, Trade, and Diplomacy in the Second Millennium B.C.,* edited by J. Aruz, K. Benzel, and J. Evans, 34–41. New York: The Metropolitan Museum of Art, 2008.

McClure, Laura K. *Women in Classical Antiquity: From Birth to Death.* Newark: John Wiley and Sons, 2019.

McDowell, A.G. *Jurisdiction in the Workmen's Community of Deir el-Medîna.* Leiden: NINO, 1990.

McKerracher, D.W., and R.A. Watson. "Tattoo Marks and Behaviour Disorder." *British Journal of Criminology* 9 (1969): 167–72.

Megahed, Mohamed. "Neue Forschungen im Grabbezirk des Djedkare-Isesi." *Sokar* 22 (2011): 25–35.

———. "The Pyramid Complex of Djedkare-Isesi at South Saqqara and Its Decorative Program." PhD diss., Charles University, Prague, 2016.
———. "The Pyramid Complex of 'Djedkare's Queen' in South Saqqara Preliminary Report 2010." In *Abusir and Saqqara in the Year 2010*, edited by Miroslav Bárta, Filip Coppens, and Jaromír Krejčí, 616–34. Prague: Czech Institute of Egyptology, Charles University, Faculty of Arts, 2011.
———. "Die Wiederentdeckung des Pyramidenbezirks des Djedkare-Isesi in Sakkara-Süd." *Sokar* 28 (2014): 6–19.
Megahed, Mohamed, and Peter Jánosi. "The Pyramid Complex of Djedkare at Saqqara South: Recent Results and Future Prospects." In *Abusir and Saqqara in the Year 2015*, edited by Miroslav Bárta, Filip Coppens, and Jaromír Krejčí, 237–56. Prague: Czech Institute of Egyptology, Faculty of Arts, Charles University, 2017.
Megahed, Mohamed, Peter Jánosi, and Hana Vymazalová. "Exploration of the Pyramid Complex of King Djedkare: Season 2018." *PES* 19 (2017): 37–52.
———. "Djedkare's Pyramid Complex: Preliminary Report of the 2017 Season." *PES* 21 (2018): 34–44.
———. "Exploration of the Pyramid Complex of King Djedkare: Season 2018." *PES* 23 (2019): 12–36.
Megahed, Mohamed, and Hana Vymazalová. "Notes on the Newly Discovered Name of Djedkare's Queen." In *Guardian of Ancient Egypt: Studies in Honor of Zahi Hawass*, edited by Janice Kamrin, Miroslav Bárta, Salima Ikram, Mark Lehner, and Mohamed Megahed, 1024–41. Prague: Charles University, Faculty of Arts, 2020.
———. "South-Saqqara Circumcision Scene: A Fragment of an Old Kingdom Birth-legend?" In *Royal versus Divine Authority: Acquisition, Legitimization and Renewal of Power. Prague, June 26–28, 2013. 7. Symposion zur ägyptischen Königsideologie/7th Symposium on Egyptian Royal Ideology*, edited by Filip Coppens, Jiří Janák, and Hana Vymazalová, 275–87. Wiesbaden: Harrassowitz, 2015.
———. "The Tomb of Khuwy at Djedkare's Royal Cemetery at South Saqqara: Preliminary Report on the 2019 Spring Season." *PES* 23 (2019): 37–48.
Megahed, Mohamed, Hana Vymazalová, Vladimír Brůna, and Marek Zdeněk. "Die Pyramide des Djedkare-Isesi in 3-D. Neue Methoden zur Dokumentation der Königlichen Grabkammer." *Sokar* 32, no. 1 (2016): 38–49.
Mélèze-Modrzejewski, Joseph. "Law and Justice in Ptolemaic Egypt." In *Legal Documents of the Hellenistic World*, edited by Markham J. Geller and Herwig Maehler, 1–19. London: The Warburg Institute, in cooperation with the Institute of Jewish Studies, University College London, 1995.
Mellink, M.J. "The Pratt Ivories in the Metropolitan Museum of Art: Kerma-chronology and the Transition from Early Bronze to Middle Bronze." *AJA* 73 (1969): 285–87.
Menu, Bernadette. "Considérations sur le droit pénal au Moyen Empire égyptien dans le p. Brooklyn 35.1446 (texte principal du recto): Responsables et dépendants." *BIFAO* 81 (1981): 57–76.
———. "Women and Business Life in the First Millennium B.C." In *Women's Earliest Records from Ancient Egypt and Western Asia*, edited by B.S. Lesko, 193–205. Atlanta: Scholars' Press, 1989.

Meskell, Lynn. *Archaeologies of Social Life: Age, Sex, Class et cetera in Ancient Egypt.* Social Archaeology. Oxford: Blackwell, 1999.

———. "Deir el Medina in Hyperreality: Seeking the People of Pharaonic Egypt." *Journal of Mediterranean Archaeology* 7, no. 2 (1994): 193–216.

———. "Intimate Archaeologies: The Case of Kha and Merit." *World Archaeology* 29, no. 3 (1998): 363–79.

———. *Object Worlds in Ancient Egypt: Material Biographies Past and Present.* Oxford and New York: Berg, 2004.

Michel, Cécile. "The Kārum Period on the Plateau." In *The Oxford Handbook of Ancient Anatolia,* edited by S.R. Steadman and G. McMahon, 313–36. Oxford: Oxford University Press, 2011.

———. "The Old Assyrian Trade in the Light of Recent Kültepe Archives." *Journal of the Canadian Society for Mesopotamian Studies* (2008): 71–82.

Millet, Nicholas B. "Ancient Cylinder Seals." MA thesis, University of Chicago, 1959.

Minas, Martina. "Macht und Ohnmacht. Die Repräsentation ptolemäischer Königinnen in ägyptischen Tempeln." *AfP* 51 (2005): 127–54.

Moje, Jan. *Untersuchungen zur hieroglyphischen Paläographie und Klassifizierung der Privatstelen der 19. Dynastie.* ÄAT 67. Wiesbaden: Harrassowitz, 2007.

Möller, Georg. *Die beiden Totenpapyrus Rhind des Museums zu Edinburg.* Demotische Studien 6. Leipzig: J.C. Hinrichs, 1913.

Montembault, Véronique, and Christiane Ziegler, eds. *Catalogue des chaussures de l'antiquité égyptienne.* Paris: Réunion des Musées Nationaux, 2000.

Montet, Pierre. *Les constructions et le tombeau de Psousennès à Tanis.* Vol. 2, *La nécropole de Tanis.* Paris: n.p., 1951.

Moreno García, Juan Carlos. "The Territorial Administration of the Kingdom in the 3rd Millennium." In *Ancient Egyptian Administration,* edited by Juan Carlos Moreno García, 85–152. Leiden: Brill, 2013.

Morenz, L. "Fremde als potentielle Feinde. Die prophylaktische Szene der Erschlagung der Fremden in Altägypten." In *Annäherung an des Fremde. XXVI. Deutscher Orientalistentag vom 25 bis 29.9.1995 in Leipzig,* edited by H. Preissler and H. Stein, 93–103. Stuttgart: Franz Steiner Verlag, 1998.

Morenz, Ludwig D., and Robert Kuhn. "Ägypten in der Vor- und Frühzeit. Vorspann oder formative Phase? Ein kurzer Überblick." In *Vorspann oder formative Phase? Ägypten und der Vordere Orient 3500–2700 v. Chr.*, edited by Ludwig D. Morenz and Robert Kuhn, 3–17. Philippika 48. Wiesbaden: Harrassowitz Verlag, 2011.

Moret, A. "L'éducation d'un prince royal égyptien de la IXe dynastie." *CRAIBL* 71, no. 4 (1927): 267–79.

Morfoisse, F., and G. Andreu-Lanoë. *Catalogue de l'exposition Sésostris III, pharaon de légende, Lille/Heule, Palais des beaux-arts de Lille.* Lille: Snoeck Éditions, 2014.

Mori, Anatole. "Personal Favor and Public Influence: Arete, Arsinoë II, and the *Argonautica.*" *Oral Tradition* 16, no. 1 (2001): 85–106.

Morris, Ellen F. "Paddle Dolls and Performance." *JARCE* 47 (2011): 71–103.

———. "Propaganda and Performance at the Dawn of the State." In *Experiencing Power,*

Generating Authority: Cosmos, Politics, and the Ideology of Kingship in Ancient Egypt and Mesopotamia, edited by Jane A. Hill, Phillip Jones, and Antonio J. Morales, 33–64. Philadelphia: University of Pennsylvania, 2013.

———. "Sacred and Obscene Laughter in 'The Contendings of Horus and Seth,' in Egyptian Inversions of Everyday Life, and in the Context of Cultic Competition." In *Egyptian Stories: A British Egyptological Tribute to Alan B. Lloyd on the Occasion of His Retirement*, edited by Thomas Schneider and Kasia Szpakowska, 197–224. AOAT 347. Münster: Ugarit-Verlag, 2007.

Motte, Aurore. "*Reden und Rufe*, a Neglected Genre? Towards a Definition of the Speech Captions in Private Tombs." *BIFAO* 117 (2017): 293–317.

Moursi, Mohamed. "Die Ausgrabungen in der Gegend um die Pyramide des *Ḏd-kꜣ-Rʿ 'Ỉssj'* bei Saqqara." *ASAE* 71 (1987): 185–93.

Muhlestein, Kerry. *Violence in the Service of Order: The Religious Framework for Sanctioned Killing in Ancient Egypt*. BARIS 2299. Oxford: Archaeopress, 2011.

Muhs, Brian P. "A Demotic Donation Contract from Early Ptolemaic Thebes (P. Louvre N. 3263)." In *Millions of Jubilees: Studies in Honor of David P. Silverman*, edited by Zahi A. Hawass and Jennifer Houser, 439–55. Cairo: Supreme Council of Antiquities, 2010.

———. "Gender Relations and Inheritance in Legal Codes and Legal Practice in Ancient Egypt." In *Structures of Power: Law and Gender across the Ancient Near East and Beyond*, edited by I. Peled, 15–25. Chicago: The Oriental Institute of the University of Chicago, 2017.

———. "The Girls Next Door: Marriage Patterns among the Mortuary Priests in Early Ptolemaic Thebes." *Journal of Juristic Papyrology* 35 (2005): 169–94.

———. *Tax Receipts, Taxpayers, and Taxes in Early Ptolemaic Thebes*. OIP 126. Chicago: Oriental Institute of the University of Chicago, 2005.

Müller, Vera. "Do Seal Impressions Prove a Change in the Administration during the Reign of King Den." In *Seals and Sealing Practices in the Near East: Developments in Administration and Magic from Prehistory to the Islamic Period. Proceedings of an International Workshop at the Netherlands–Flemish Institute in Cairo on December 2–3, 2009*, edited by Ilona Regulski, Kim Duistermaat, and Peter Verkinderen, 17–32. Leuven: Peeters, 2012.

Müller, Wolfgang. "Der 'Stadtfürst' von Theben, Monthemhêt." *Münchener Jahrbuch für Bildende Kunst* 26 (1975): 7–12.

Munro, Peter. *Der Unas-Friedhof Nord-West* 1. *Topographisch-historische Einleitung. Das Doppelgrab der Königinnen Nebet und Khenut*. Mainz am Rhein: Philipp von Zabern, 1993.

Münster, Maria. *Untersuchungen zur Göttin Isis vom Alten Reich bis zum Ende des Neuen Reiches*. MÄS 11. Berlin: Verlag Bruno Hessling, 1968.

Murnane, William J. *Texts from the Amarna Period in Egypt*. WAW 5. Atlanta: SBL, 1995.

Musée des beaux-arts, Lille. *Sésostris III, pharaon de légende: Exposition au Palais des beaux-arts de Lille, du 10 octobre 2014 au 26 janvier 2015*. Heule: Éditions Snoeck, 2014.

Myśliwiec, Karol. "Les couronnes à plumes de Thoutmosis III." In *Mélanges Gamal Eddin Mokhtar* 2, edited by Paule Posener-Kriéger. BdE 97, vol. 2. Cairo: IFAO, 1985.

———. *The Eighteenth Dynasty before the Amarna Period*. Iconography of Religions 16. Leiden: E.J. Brill, 1985.

Naguib, Saphinaz-Amal. *Le clergé féminin d'Amon thébain à la 21e dynastie.* OLA 38. Leuven: Peeters, 1990.

Nasr, Mohammed. "The Excavation of the Tomb of Montuemhat at Thebes." *Memnonia* 8 (1997): 211–23.

Nasrallah, Laura Salah. *Archaeology and the Letters of Paul.* Oxford: Oxford University Press, 2018.

Naunton, Christopher H. "Regime Change and the Administration of Thebes during the Twenty-fifth Dynasty." PhD diss., Swansea University, 2011.

———. "Titles of Karakhamun and the Kushite Administration of Thebes." In *Tombs of the South Asasif Necropolis: Thebes, Karakhamun (TT 223), and Karabasken (TT 391) in the Twenty-fifth Dynasty*, edited by Elena Pischikova, 103–107. Cairo: American University in Cairo Press, 2014.

Naville, Edouard. *The Temple of Deir el-Bahari.* Part 2, *The Ebony Shrine and the Middle Platform.* London: EEF, 1896.

———. *The Temple of Deir el-Bahari.* Part 3, *End of the Northern Half and the Southern Half of the Middle Platform.* London: EEF, 1898.

———. *The Temple of Deir el-Bahari.* Part 5, *The Upper Court and Sanctuary.* London: EEF, 1906.

Navrátilová, Hana. "Gender and Historiography (in Deir el-Medina)?" In *Sozialisationen: Individuum—Gruppe—Gesellschaft. Beiträge des ersten Münchner Arbeitskreises Junge Aegyptologie (MAJA 1), 3.–5.12.2010*, edited by Gregor Neunert, Kathrin Gabler, and Alexandra Verbovsek, 149–67. GOF 4, vol. 51. Wiesbaden: Harrassowitz, 2012.

Nelson, Harold H., and William J. Murnane. *The Great Hypostyle Hall at Karnak.* Vol. 1, pt. 1, *The Wall Reliefs.* OIP 106. Chicago: The Oriental Institute of the University of Chicago, 1981.

Nelson-Hurst, Melinda. "Spheres of Economic and Administrative Control in Middle Kingdom Egypt: Textual, Visual and Archaeological Evidence for Female and Male Sealers." In *Structures of Power: Law and Gender Across the Ancient Near East and Beyond*, edited by Ilan Peled, 131–41. Chicago: The Oriental Institute of the University of Chicago, 2017.

Neunert, Gregor. *Mein Grab, mein Esel, mein Platz in der Gesellschaft: Prestige im Alten Ägypten am Beispiel Deir el-Medine.* Manetho 1. Berlin: Manetho, 2010.

Newberry, P.E., and F.Ll. Griffith. *Beni Hasan.* Vols. 1–4. ASE 1–2, 5, 7. London: EEF, 1893–1900.

Nilsson, Maria. "The Crown of Arsinoë II: The Creation and Development of an Imagery of Authority." PhD diss., University of Gothenburg, 2010.

Nims, Ch.F. "*Amarna Reliefs from Hermopolis in American Collections* by John D. Cooney, Review." *JAOS* 88, no. 3 (1968): 544–46.

Niwiński, Andrzej, Mikolaj Budzanowski, Maciej Pawlikowski, and Slawomir Rzepka. "Deir el-Bahari Cliff Mission, 2000." *PAM* 12 (2001): 221–35.

Nongbri, Brent. *God's Library: The Archaeology of the Earliest Christian Manuscripts.* New Haven: Yale University Press, 2018.

Nord, Del. "The Term *ẖnr*: 'Harem' or 'Musical Performers'?" In *Ancient Egypt, the Aegean and the Sudan: Essays in Honor of Dows Dunham on the Occasion of His 90th Birthday,*

June 1, 1980, edited by W.K. Simpson and W.M. Davis, 137–45. Boston: Dept. of Egyptian and Ancient Near Eastern Art, MFA, 1981.

———. "'Xkrt-nsw' = 'King's Concubine'?" *Serapis* 2 (1976): 1–16.

Nourse, Kyra L. "Women and the Early Development of Royal Power in the Hellenistic East." PhD diss., University of Pennsylvania, 2002.

Nunn, John F. *Ancient Egyptian Medicine*. London: British Museum Press, 1996.

Nur El-Din, 'Abd al-Ḥalīm. *The Demotic Ostraca in the National Museum of Antiquities at Leiden*. Collections of the National Museum of Antiquities at Leiden 1. Leiden: Brill, 1974.

O'Brien, Alexandra A. "Private Tradition, Public State: Women in Demotic Business and Administrative Texts from Ptolemaic and Roman Thebes." PhD diss., University of Chicago, 1999.

———. "Women in Ptolemaic and Roman Thebes." In *Acts of the Seventh International Conference of Demotic Studies, Copenhagen, 23–27 August 1999*, edited by Kim Ryholt, 273–81. CNI Publications 27. Copenhagen: Carsten Niebuhr Institute of Near Eastern Studies, University of Copenhagen, Museum of Tusculanum Press, 2002.

Ockinga, Boyo G. *A Concise Grammar of Middle Egyptian: An Outline of Middle Egyptian Grammar by Hellmut Brunner Revised and Expanded*. Mainz am Rhein: Philipp von Zabern, 2005.

Ockinga, Boyo, et al. *The Tomb of Amenemope at Thebes (TT 148)*. Oxford: Aris and Phillips, 2009.

O'Connor, David. "The Eastern High Gate: Sexualized Architecture at Medinet Habu?" In *Structure and Significance: Thought on Ancient Egyptian Architecture*, edited by Peter Jánosi, 439–54. Vienna: Verlag der Österreichischen Akademie der Wissenschaften, 2005.

———. "Egypt's View of 'Others.'" In *Never Had the Like Occurred: Egypt's View of Its Past*, edited by J. Tait, 213–23. London: University College London Press, 2003.

O'Connor, David B., and Eric H. Cline. *Amenhotep III: Perspectives on His Reign*. Ann Arbor: University of Michigan Press, 1998.

Ogden, Daniel. *Polygamy, Prostitutes, and Death: The Hellenistic Dynasties*. London: Duckworth with The Classical Press of Wales, 1999.

Olabarria, L. "Formulating Relations: An Approach to the *smyt*-formula." *ZÄS* 145, no. 1 (2018): 57–70.

———. *Kinship and Family in Ancient Egypt: Archaeology and Anthropology in Dialogue*. Cambridge: Cambridge University Press, 2020.

Olivier, Julien, and Catharine Lorber. "Three Gold Coinages of Third-century Ptolemaic Egypt." *RBN* 159 (2013): 49–150.

Olson, Stacie Lynn. "New Kingdom Funerary Figurines in Context: An Analysis of the Cemeteries of Aniba, Gurob, and Soleb." PhD diss., University of Pennsylvania, 1996. Ann Arbor: UMI, 1997.

Onstine, Suzanne L. "A Brief Report on the University of Memphis Mission to Theban Tomb 16 in Dra Abu-l-Naga." *NSSEA* (summer 2012): 4–5.

———. "Gender and the Religion of Ancient Egypt." *Religion Compass* 4, no. 1 (2010): 1–11.

———. "A Preliminary Report on the Clearance of Theban Tomb 16 in Dra Abu el-Naga at Thebes." In *Archaeological Research in the Valley of the Kings and Ancient Thebes:*

Papers Presented in Honor of Richard H. Wilkinson, edited by Pearce Paul Creasman, 227–40. Tucson: University of Arizona, 2013.

———. *The Role of the Chantress (Smay.t) in Ancient Egypt.* BARIS 140. Oxford: Hadrian Books, 2005.

———. "The Role of the *šmʿyt* Chantress in Ancient Egypt." PhD diss., University of Toronto, 2001.

———. "University of Memphis Mission to Theban Tomb 16: The Life of Panehsy, Chanter and Priest." *JARCE* 47 (2011): 231–36.

———. "Women's Participation in the Religious Hierarchy of Ancient Egypt." In *Women in Antiquity: Real Women Across the Ancient World*, edited by Stephanie Lynn Budin and Jean MacIntoch Turfa, 218–28. London and New York: Routledge, 2016.

Onstine, Suzanne, Jesús Herrerín López, Miguel Sanchez, and Rosa Dinarès Solà. "Women's Health Issues Reflected in Case Studies from Theban Tomb 16." In *The Ancient Egyptians and Their Natural World: Flora, Fauna, and Science*, edited by Salima Ikram, Jessica Kaiser, and Stéphanie Porcier, 191–98. Leiden: Sidestone Press, 2021.

Oppen de Ruiter, Branko F. van. *Berenice II Euergetis: Essays in Early Hellenistic Queenship.* New York: Palgrave Macmillan, 2015.

———. "The Death of Arsinoe II Philadelphus: The Evidence Reconsidered." *ZPE* 174 (2010): 139–50.

Oppenheim, Adela. "The Royal Treasures of the Twelfth Dynasty." In *Egyptian Treasures from the Egyptian Museum in Cairo*, edited by Francesco Tiradritti, 136–41. Vercelli: White Star Publishers, 1999.

Oppenheim, Adela, Dorothea Arnold, Dieter Arnold, and Kei Yamamoto, eds. *Ancient Egypt Transformed: The Middle Kingdom.* New York: The Metropolitan Museum of Art, 2015.

Özgüç, Nimet. *Acemhöyük Kazilari/Excavations at Acemhöyük.* Ankara: Türk Tarih Kurumu Basimevi, 1966.

———. "The Composite Creatures in Anatolian Art during the Period of the Assyrian Trading Colonies." In *Near Eastern Studies: Dedicated to H.I.H. Prince Takahito Mikasa on the Occasion of His Seventy-fifth Birthday*, edited by Masao Mori et al., 293–317. Wiesbaden: Harrassowitz, 1991.

———. "New Light on the Dating of the Levels of the Karum of Kanish and of Acemhöyük near Aksaray." *AJA* 72 (1968): 318–20.

Paget, Rosalind F.E., and Annie A. Pirie. *The Tomb of Ptah-hetep.* ERA 2. London: Bernard Quaritch, 1989.

Palmer, Jennifer. "The High Priests of Amun at the End of the Twentieth Dynasty." *BEJ* 2, no. 1 (2014): 1–22.

Panagiotopoulos, Diamantis. "Foreigners in Egypt in the Time of Hatshepsut and Thutmose III." In *Thutmose III: A New Biography*, edited by Eric H. Cline and David O'Connor, 370–412. Ann Arbor: University of Michigan Press, 2006.

Pany-Kucera, Doris, Michaela Spannagl-Steiner, Stanislaus Argeny, Barbara Maurer-Gesek, Wolfgang J. Weninger, and Katharina Rebay-Salisbury. "Sacral Preauricular Extensions, Notches and Corresponding Iliac Changes: New Terms and the Proposal of a Recording System." *International Journal of Osteoarchaeology* 29 (2019): 1013–21. https://onlinelibrary.wiley.com/doi/full/10.1002/oa.2814.

Papazian, Hratch. "The Central Administration of the Resources in the Old Kingdom: Departments, Treasuries, Granaries and Work Centers." In *Ancient Egyptian Administration*, edited by Juan Carlos Moreno Garciá, 41–84. Leiden: Brill, 2013.

———. "Domain of Pharaoh: The Structure and Components of the Economy of Old Kingdom Egypt." PhD diss., University of Chicago, 2005.

———. "The Temple of Ptah and Economic Contacts between Memphite Cult Centers in the Fifth Dynasty." In *8. Ägyptologische Tempeltagung: Interconnections between Temples*, edited by Monika Dolińska and Horst Beinlich, 137–53. KSGH 3.3. Wiesbaden: Harrassowitz, 2010.

Parker, Richard A. *A Saite Oracle Papyrus from Thebes*. BEStud 4. Providence: Brown University Press, 1962.

Parkinson, Richard. "'Boasting about Hardness': Constructions of Middle Kingdom Masculinity." In *Sex and Gender in Ancient Egypt: "Don Your Wig for a Joyful Hour,"* edited by Carolyn Graves-Brown, 115–42. Swansea: Classical Press of Wales, 2008.

———. *The Tale of the Eloquent Peasant: A Reader's Commentary*. LingAegSM 10. Hamburg: Widmaier, 2012.

Parrot, A. *Musée de Louvre: Le département des Antiquités orientales: Guide sommaire*. Paris: Réunion des Musées nationaux, 1947.

Parry, Albert. "Tattooing among Prostitutes and Perverts." *Psychoanalytic Quarterly* 3 (1934): 476–82.

Parsons, P.J. *City of the Sharp-nosed Fish: Greek Lives in Roman Egypt*. London: Weidenfeld and Nicolson, 2007.

Patch, Diana Craig. "Excursus: Considering Middle Kingdom Pectorals." In *Ancient Egypt Transformed: The Middle Kingdom*, edited by Adela Oppenheim, Dorothea Arnold, Dieter Arnold, and Kei Yamamoto, 112–14. New York: The Metropolitan Museum of Art, 2015.

Pätznick, Jean-Pierre. *Die Siegelabrollungen und Rollsiegel der Stadt Elephantine im 3. Jahrtausend v. Chr. Spurensicherung eines archäologischen Artefaktes*. BARIS 1339. Oxford: Oxbow Books, 2005.

Payraudeau, Frédéric. *Administration, société et pouvoir à Thèbes sous la XXIIe dynastie bubastite*. BdE 160. Cairo: IFAO, 2014.

———. "Nesptah, père de Montouemhat, à Karnak-Nord." In *A True Scribe of Abydos: Essays on First Millennium Egypt in Honour of Anthony Leahy*, edited by Claus Jurman, Bettina Bader, and D. Aston, 319–26. OLA 265. Leuven: Peeters, 2017.

Pearson, Karl. "On the Criterion that a Given System of Deviations from the Probable in the Case of a Correlated System of Variables Is Such That It Can Be Reasonably Supposed to Have Arisen from Random Sampling." In *Breakthroughs in Statistics*. Vol. 2, *Methodology and Distribution*, edited by Samuel Kotz and Norman L. Johnson, 11–28. Springer Series in Statistics. New York: Springer, 1992.

Pécoil, Jean-François. *L'Akh-menou de Thoutmosis III à Karnak: La Heret-ib et les chapelles attenantes. Relevés épigraphiques*. Paris: Éditions Recherche sur les civilisations, 2001.

Peden, Alexander. *The Graffiti of Pharaonic Egypt: Scope and Role of Informal Writings (c. 3100–332 BC)*. Leiden and Boston: Brill, 2001.

Peled, Ilan, ed. *Structures of Power: Law and Gender across the Ancient Near East and Beyond*. Chicago: The Oriental Institute of the University of Chicago, 2017.

Pemler, Doris. "Nubian Women in New Kingdom Tomb and Temple Scenes and the Case of TT 40 (Amenemhet Huy)." *Dotawo: A Journal of Nubian Studies* (2018): 25–46.

Perdu, O. "Khenemet-nefer-hedjet: une princesse et deux reines du Moyen Empire." *RdE* 29 (1977): 68–85.

———. "Statue assise sur un siège de Montouemhat." In *Le crépuscule des Pharaons. Chefs-d'œuvre des dernières dynasties égyptiennes*. Brussels: Fonts Mercator, 2012.

Perrin, B., trans. *Plutarch's Lives*. 11 vols. Loeb Classical Library. Cambridge, MA: Harvard University Press, 1914 (repr. 1967).

Pestman, Pieter W. "Appearance and Reality in Written Contracts: Evidence from Bilingual Family Archives." In *Legal Documents of the Hellenistic World: Papers from a Seminar Arranged by the Institute of Classical Studies, the Institute of Jewish Studies and the Warburg Institute, University of London, February to May 1986*, edited by M.J. Geller and H. Maehler, 79–87. London: Warburg Institute, University of London, 1995.

———. *The Archive of the Theban Choachytes (Second Century B.C.): A Survey of the Demotic and Greek Papyri Contained in the Archive*. Studia Demotica 2. Leuven: Peeters, 1993.

———. *Marriage and Matrimonial Property in Ancient Egypt: A Contribution to Establishing the Legal Position of the Woman*. Papyrologica Lugduno-Batava 9. Leiden: Brill, 1961.

———. *Recueil de textes démotiques et bilingues*. 3 vols. Leiden: E.J. Brill, 1977.

Petrie, W.M. Flinders. *Kahun, Gurob and Hawara*. London: K. Paul, Trench, Trübner, 1890.

———. *Medum*. London: Nutt, 1892.

Petrie, W.M. Flinders, and J H. Walker. *Qurneh*. BSA 16. London: BSA/Bernard Quaritch, 1909.

Petrie, Hilda Flinders, and Margaret A. Murray. *Seven Memphite Tomb Chapels*. BSEA 65. London: B. Quaritch, 1952.

Pfeiffer, S. "The God Serapis, His Cult, and the Beginnings of the Ruler Cult in Ptolemaic Egypt." In *Ptolemy II Philadelphus and His World*, edited by Paul McKechnie and Philippe Guillaume, 387–408. Leiden: Brill, 2008.

Piacentini, Patrizia. *Les scribes dans la société égyptienne de l'Ancien Empire*. Vol. 1, *Les premières dynasties: Les nécropoles memphites*. Paris: Cybele, 2002.

Pieri, Anna, and Daniel Antoine. "A Tattooed Trio at HK27C." *Nekhen News* 26 (2014): 28–29.

Pinch, G. *Votive Offerings to Hathor*. Oxford: Griffith Institute, 1993.

Pischikova, Elena, ed. *Tombs of the South Asasif Necropolis, Thebes: Karakhamun (TT 223) and Karabasken (TT 391) in the Twenty-fifth Dynasty*. Cairo: American University in Cairo Press, 2014.

Pomeroy, Sarah B. *Goddesses, Whores, Wives, and Slaves: Women in Classical Antiquity*. New York: Schocken Books, 1995.

———. *Women in Hellenistic Egypt: From Alexander to Cleopatra.* Detroit: Wayne State University Press, 1990.

Poole, Federico. "Flawed and Fine? The Statue of Hel in the Museo Egizio, Turin (Cat. 7352)." *Rivista del Museo Egizio* 3 (2019): 1–24.

Porter, B., and R.L.B. Moss. *Topographical Bibliography of Ancient Egyptian Hieroglyphic Texts, Reliefs, and Paintings.* Vol. 1, *The Theban Necropolis.* Part 2, *Royal Tombs and Smaller Cemeteries.* Oxford: Claredon Press, 1964.

———. *Topographical Bibliography of Ancient Egyptian Hieroglyphic Texts, Reliefs, and Paintings.* Vol. 2, *Theban Temple.* 2nd rev. and aug. ed. Oxford: Clarendon Press, 1972.

———. *Topographical Bibliography of Ancient Egyptian Hieroglyphic Texts, Reliefs and Paintings.* Vol. 3, *Memphis.* Part 2, *Saqqâra to Dahshûr.* Oxford: Griffith Institute, 1978.

———. *Topographical Bibliography of Ancient Egyptian Hieroglyphic Texts, Reliefs and Paintings.* Vol. 7, *Nubia, the Deserts, and Outside Egypt.* Oxford: Griffith Institute, 1952.

Posener, G. "Maquilleuse en Égyptien." *RdE* 21 (1969): 150–51.

Posener-Kriéger, Paule. *Les archives du temple funéraire de Néferirkarê-Kakaï.* BdE 65. Cairo: IFAO, 1976.

Postel, Lilian. "Un homme de cour de Sésostris Ier: le préposé au diadème royal Emhat (Louvre C 46 et Leyde AP 67)." In *Ex Aegypto Lux et Sapientia: Homenatge al professor Josep Padró Parcerisa*, edited by Núria Castellano, Maite Mascort, Concepció Piedrafita, and Jaume Vivó, 489–99. Barcelona: Universitat de Barcelona, 2015.

———. "Quand réapparaît la forme *ms(w).n*? Réflexions sur la formule de filiation maternelle à la fin du Moyen Empire." In *Verba manent: recueil d'études dédiées à Dimitri Meeks par ses collègues et amis*, edited by Isabelle Régen and Frédéric Servajean, 331–54. Montpellier: Université Paul Valéry, 2009.

Preisigke, Friedrich, and Emil Kiessling, eds. *Wörterbuch der griechischen Papyrusurkunden: mit Einschluss der griechischen Inschriften, Aufschriften, Ostraka, Mumienschilder usw. aus Ägypten.* Berlin: Selbstverlag der Erben, 1925.

Quack, Joachim. *Menschenbilder und Körperkonzepte im Alten Israel, in Ägypten und im Alten Orient.* ORA 9. Tübingen: Mohr Siebeck, 2012.

Quaegebeur, Jan. "Cleopatra VII and the Cults of the Ptolemaic Queens." In *Cleopatra's Egypt: Age of the Ptolemies*, edited by R.S. Bianchi, 41–54. Brooklyn: Brooklyn Museum, 1988.

———. "The Egyptian Clergy and the Cult of the Ptolemaic Dynasty." *AncSoc* 20 (1989): 93–116.

———. "Ptolémée II en adoration devant Arsinoé II divinisée." *BIFAO* 69 (1969): 191–217.

———. "Reines ptolémaïques et traditions égyptiennes." In *Das ptolemäische Agypten*, edited by H. von Maehler and V.M. Stocka, 245–62. Mainz am Rhein: Akten des Internationalen Symposions, 1978.

Quirke, Stephen. *The Administration of Egypt in the Late Middle Kingdom: The Hieratic Documents.* New Malden, Surrey: SIA Publishing, 1990.

———. "State and Labour in the Middle Kingdom: A Reconsideration of the Term *ẖnrt*." *RdE* 39 (1988): 83–106.

———. *Titles and Bureaux of Egypt 1850–1700 BC.* GHP Egyptology. London: Golden House Publications, 2004.

———. "Women in Ancient Egypt: Temple Titles and Funerary Papyri." In *Studies on Ancient Egypt in Honour of H.S. Smith*, edited by Anthony Leahy and John Tait, 227–35. Occasional Publications 13. London: EES, 1999.

Radini, Anita, Monica Tromp, A. Beach, Elizabeth Tong, Camilla Speller, Michael McCormick, John Dudgeon, Matthew J. Collins, Frank Rühli, Roland Kröger, and Christina Warinner. "Medieval Women's Early Involvement in Manuscript Production Suggested by Lapis Lazuli Identification in Dental Calculus." *Science Advances* 5, no. 1 (2019): 1–8. https://advances.sciencemag.org/content/5/1/eaau7126.

Ranke, Hermann. *Die ägyptischen Personennamen.* Vol. 1, *Verzeichnis der Namen.* Glückstadt: J.J. Augustin, 1935.

Rapisidara, Vittoria. "'Indossare' i Tatuaggi: Studio del Tatuaggio nell'Antico Egitto sui resti umani, archeologici e iconografici." MA thesis, Università di Pisa, 2019.

Raven, Maarten J. *The Tomb of Iurudef: A Memphite Official in the Reign of Ramesses II.* EES Excavation Memoir 57. London: EES, 1991.

Ray, J.D. *Demotic Papyri and Ostraca from Qasr Ibrim.* Texts from Excavations 13. London: EES, 2005.

———. "Papyrus Carlsberg 67 B: A Healing Prayer from the Fayûm." *JEA* 61 (1975): 181–88.

Rebillard, Éric. *Christians and Their Many Identities in Late Antiquity, North Africa, 200–450 CE.* Ithaca, NY and London: Cornell University Press, 2012.

———. "Conversion and Burial in the Late Roman Empire." In *Conversion in Late Antiquity and the Early Middle Ages: Seeing and Believing*, edited by Kenneth Mills and Anthony Grafton, 61–83. Studies in Comparative History. Essays from the Shelby Cullom Davis Center for Historical Studies. Rochester, NY: University of Rochester Press, 2003.

———. "Everyday Christianity in Carthage at the Time of Tertullian." *Religion in the Roman Empire* 2 (2016): 91–102.

———. "Expressing Christianness in Carthage in the Second and Third Centuries." *Religion in the Roman Empire* 3, no. 1 (2017): 119–34.

Redford, Donald B. *Egypt, Canaan and Israel in Ancient Times.* Princeton: Princeton University Press, 1992.

———. *From Slave to Pharaoh: The Black Experience of Ancient Egypt.* Baltimore and London: The Johns Hopkins University Press, 2004.

———. *History and Chronology of the Eighteenth Dynasty of Egypt: Seven Studies.* Toronto: University of Toronto Press, 1967.

———. "Textual Sources for the Hyksos Period." In *The Hyksos: New Historical and Archaeological Perspectives*, edited by E. Oren, 1–44. Philadelphia: University Museum, University of Pennsylvania, 1997.

Reeves, Nicholas. "The Royal Family." In *Pharaohs of the Sun: Akhenaton, Nefertiti, Tutankhamun*, edited by Rita E. Freed, Sue H. D'Auria, and Yvonne J. Markowitz, 81–95. Boston: MFA, 1999.

Regulski, Ilona. "Egypt's Early Dynastic Cylinder Seals Reconsidered." *BiOr* 68 (2011): 5–32.
———. *A Palaeographic Study of Early Writing in Egypt*. OLA 195. Leuven: Peeters, 2010.
———. "Seal Impressions from Tell el-Iswid." In *Tell el-Iswid, 2006–2009*, edited by Ahmed Baher and Beatrix Midant-Reynes, 230–42. FIFAO 73. Cairo: IFAO, 2014.
Reinard, Patrick. *Kommunikation und Ökonomie: Untersuchungen zu den privaten Papyrusbriefen aus dem kaiserzeitlichen Ägypten*. Pharos Studien zur griechisch-römischen Antike 32. Rahden: Marie Leidorf, 2016.
Reiser, Elfriede. *Der königliche Harim im alten Ägypten und seine Verwaltung*. Dissertationen der Universität Wien 77. Vienna: Verlag Notring, 1972.
Reisner, George A. *The Early Dynastic Cemeteries of Naga-ed-Dêr* 1. Leipzig: J.C. Hinrichs, 1908.
Relats Montserrat, Félix. "Le signe D19, à la recherche des sens d'un déterminatif (I): La forme d'un signe." *NeHeT* 1 (2014): 129–67.
———. "Le signe D19, à la recherche des sens d'un déterminatif (II): Les usages d'un signe." *NeHeT* 4 (2016): 77–121.
Renaut, Luc. "Marquage corporel et signation religieuse dans l'Antiquité." PhD diss., Ecole pratique des hautes études, Paris, 2004. https://tel.archives-ouvertes.fr/tel-00275245.
———. "Tattooed Women from Nubia and Egypt: A Reappraisal." In *Flesh and Bones: The Individual and His Body in the Ancient Mediterranean Basin*, edited by Alice Mouton, 69–87. Semitica et Classica Supplementa. Turnhout: Brepols, 2020.
Richards, Janet E. *Society and Death in Ancient Egyptian Mortuary Landscapes of the Middle Kingdom*. Cambridge: Cambridge University Press, 2005.
Riggs, Christina. "Body." In *UEE*, edited by Elizabeth Frood and Willeke Wendrich. Los Angeles: University of California, 2010. https://escholarship.org/uc/nelc_uee.
———. *Unwrapping Ancient Egypt*. London: Bloomsbury, 2014.
Ritner, Robert K. "'And Each Staff Transformed into a Snake': The Serpent Wand in Ancient Egypt." In *Through a Glass Darkly: Magic, Dreams and Prophecy in Ancient Egypt*, edited by Kasia Szpakowska, 205–26. Swansea: Classical Press of Wales, 2006.
———. *The Mechanics of Ancient Egyptian Magical Practice*. SAOC 54. Chicago: The Oriental Institute of the University of Chicago Press, 1993.
———. "A Uterine Amulet in the Oriental Institute Collection." *JNES* 43, no. 3 (1984): 209–21.
Roberts, C.H., and E.G. Turner. *Catalogue of the Greek and Latin Papyri in the John Rylands Library, Manchester*. Vol. 4, *Documents of the Ptolemaic, Roman, and Byzantine Periods*. Manchester: Manchester University Press, 1952.
Robins, Gay. "Composition and the Artist's Squared Grid." *JARCE* 28 (1991): 41–54.
———. "Dress, Undress, and the Representation of Fertility and Potency in New Kingdom Egyptian Art." In *Sexuality in Ancient Art*, edited by N.B. Kampen, 27–40. Cambridge: Cambridge University Press, 1996.
———. "Egyptian Queens in the Eighteenth Dynasty up to the Reign of Amenhotep III." PhD diss., Oxford University, 1981.
———. "Ideal Beauty and Divine Attributes." In *Queens of Egypt: From Hetepheres to Cleopatra*, edited by Christiane Ziegler, 118–30. Monaco: Grimaldi Forum 2008.

———. *Proportion and Style in Ancient Egyptian Art*. London: Thames and Hudson, 1994.
———. "The Relationships Specified by Egyptian Kinship Terms of the Middle and New Kingdoms." *CdE* 54, no. 108 (1979): 197–209.
———. "Some Principles of Compositional Dominance and Gender Hierarchy in Egyptian Art." *JARCE* 31 (1994): 33–40.
———. *Women in Ancient Egypt*. London: British Museum Press, 1993a.
———. *Women in Ancient Egypt*. Cambridge, MA: Harvard University Press, 1993b.
Roche, Aurélie. "Des scènes de danse dans l'iconographie prédynastique? Essai d'identification et d'interprétation à la lumière de la documentation pharaonique." *Archéo-Nil* 24 (2014): 161–89.
Roeder, Günther. *Aegyptische Inschriften aus den Königlichen Museen zu Berlin*. Vol. 1, *Inschriften von der Ältesten Zeit bis zum Ende der Hyksoszeit*. Leipzig: J.C. Hinrichs, 1969.
———. *Amarna-Reliefs aus Hermopolis*. Hildesheim: Verlag Gebrüder Gertenberg, 1969.
Roehrig, Catherine H. "The Eighteenth Dynasty Titles Royal Nurse (*mnꜥt nsw*), Royal Tutor (*mnꜥ nswt*), and Foster Brother/Sister of the Lord of the Two Lands (*sn/snt mnꜥ n nb tꜣwy*)." PhD diss., University of Berkeley, 1990.
———, ed. *Hatshepsut: From Queen to Pharaoh*. New York: Metropolitan Museum Press, 2005.
———. "Two Tattooed Women from Thebes." In *The Art and Culture of Ancient Egypt: Studies in Honor of Dorothea Arnold*, 527–36. BES 19. New York: Oxbow, 2015.
———. "Women's Work: Some Occupations of Nonroyal Women as Depicted in Ancient Egyptian Art." In *Mistress of the House, Mistress of Heaven: Women in Ancient Egypt*, edited by Anne K. Capel and Glenn E. Markoe, 13–24. New York: Hudson Hills Press, 1996.
Romano, James. "The Bes-image in Pharaonic Egypt." PhD diss., New York University, 1989. Ann Arbor: UMI, 1989.
Rosecrans, Jennifer Allen. "Wearing the Universe: Symbolic Markings in Early Modern England." In *Written on the Body: The Tattoo in European and American History*, edited by Jane Caplan, 46–60. Princeton: Princeton University Press, 2000.
Roth, Ann Macy. "The Absent Spouse: Patterns and Taboos in Egyptian Tomb Decoration." *JARCE* 36 (1999): 37–53.
———. *A Cemetery of Palace Attendants including G 2084–2099, G 2230+2231, and G 2240*. Giza Mastabas 6. Boston: Department of Ancient Egyptian, Nubian, and Near Eastern Art, MFA, 1995.
———. "Gender Roles in Ancient Egypt." In *A Companion to the Ancient Near East*, edited by Daniel C. Snell, 211–18. Newark and Malden, MA: Blackwell, 2005.
———. "Harem." In *UEE*, edited by Elizabeth Frood and Willeke Wendrich. Los Angeles: University of California, 2010. https://escholarship.org/uc/nelc_uee.
———. "The Meaning of Menial Labor: 'Servant Statues' in Old Kingdom Serdabs." *JARCE* 39 (2002): 103–21.
———. "Models of Authority: Hatshepsut's Predecessor in Power." In *Hatshepsut: From Queen to Pharaoh*, edited by Catharine H. Roehrig, 9–14. New York: The Metropolitan Museum of Art, 2005.

———. "The *psš-kf* and the 'Opening of the Mouth' Ceremony: A Ritual of Birth and Rebirth." *JEA* 78 (1992): 113–47.
———. "The Social Aspects of Death." In *Mummies and Magic: The Funerary Arts of Ancient Egypt*, edited by Sue D'Auria, Peter Lacovara, and Catharine H. Roehrig, 52–59. Boston: MFA, 1988.
———. "The Usurpation of Hem-Re: An Old Kingdom 'Sex-Change Operation.'" In *Egyptian Museum Collections around the World*, edited by Mamdouh Eldamaty and May Trad, 1011–23. Cairo: Supreme Council of Antiquities, 2002.
Roth, Silke. *Gebieterin aller Länder: Die Rolle der königlichen Frauen in der fiktiven und realen Aussenpolitik des ägyptischen Neuen Reiches*. OBO 85. Freiburg, Switzerland: Universitätsverlag, 2002.
———. "Harem." In *UEE*, edited by Elizabeth Frood and Willeke Wendrich. Los Angeles: 2010. https://escholarship.org/uc/item/1k3663r3.
———. *Die Königsmütter des Alten Ägypten von der Frühzeit bis zum Ende der 12. Dynastie*. ÄAT 46. Wiesbaden: Harrassowitz, 2001.
Rowlandson, Jane. *Landowners and Tenants in Roman Egypt: The Social Relations of Agriculture in the Oxyrhynchite Nome*. Oxford Classical Monographs. Oxford: Clarendon Press; New York: Oxford University Press, 1996.
———, ed. *Women and Society in Greek and Roman Egypt: A Sourcebook*. Cambridge and New York: Cambridge University Press, 1998.
Roy, Jim. "The Masculinity of the Hellenistic King." In *When Men Were Men: Masculinity, Power and Identity in Classical Antiquity*, edited by Lin Foxhall and John Salmon, 111–35. London: Routledge, 1998.
Ruffini, Giovanni. "Genealogy and the Gymnasium." *BASP* 43 (2006): 71–99.
———. *Social Networks in Byzantine Egypt*. Cambridge: Cambridge University Press, 2008.
Rupp, L. "Review: Women Worthies and Women's History." *Reviews in American History* 12, no. 3 (1984): 409–13.
Russmann, Edna R. "Art in Transition: The Rise of the Eighteenth Dynasty and the Emergence of the Thutmoside Style in Sculpture and Relief." In *Hatshepsut: From Queen to Pharaoh*, edited by Catharine Roehrig, 23–44. New York: Metropolitan Museum Press, 2005.
———. *Eternal Egypt: Masterworks of Ancient Art from the British Museum*. Berkeley: University of California Press, 2001.
———. "Mentuemhat's Kushite Wife: Further Remarks on the Decoration of the Tomb of Mentuemhat 2." *JARCE* 34 (1997): 21–39.
———. "The Motif of Bound Papyrus Plants and the Decorative Program in Mentuemhat's First Court: Further Remarks on the Decoration of the Tomb of Mentuemhat, 1." *JARCE* 32 (1995): 117–26.
———. "Relief Decoration in the Tomb of Mentuemhat (TT 34)." *JARCE* 31 (1994): 1–19.
Russo, Simona. *Le calzature nei papiri di età greco-romana*. Florence: Istituto papirologico G. Vitelli, 2004.
Rzepka, Slawomir. "Graffiti of Nubkheperre Intef in Deir el Bahari." *MDAIK* 60 (2004): 149–58.

———. *Who, Where and Why: The Rock Graffiti of Members of the Deir el-Medina Community.* Warsaw: University of Warsaw Publications, 2014.
Saad, Zaki Youssef. *Ceiling Stelae in Second Dynasty Tombs: From the Excavations at Helwan*. Cairo: IFAO, 1957.
Sabbahy, Lisa Kuchman. "The Development of the Titulary and Iconography of the Ancient Egyptian Queen from Dynasty One to Early Dynasty Eighteen." PhD diss., University of Toronto, 1982.
———. "The Female Family of Amenemhat II: A Review of the Evidence." In *Hommages à Fayza Haikal*, edited by N. Grimal, 439–44. BdE 138. Cairo: IFAO, 2002.
El-Sabban, Sherif. "Nesptah: The Heir to Power." *DE* 62 (2005): 33–41.
El Saddik, Wafaa. "A Head for Amenemhat III's *Heb-sed* Triad?" In *The Art and Culture of Ancient Egypt: Studies in Honor of Dorothea Arnold*, edited by Adela Oppenheim and Ogden Goelet, 553–56. *BES* 19 (2015).
Said, Edward. *Orientalism*. London: Penguin, 1977.
Sakr, Fakri. "New Foundation Deposits of Kom el-Hisn." *SAK* 33 (2005): 349–55.
Şare-Ağtürk, Tuna. "Headdress Fashions and Their Social Significance in Ancient Western Anatolia: The Seventh through Fourth Centuries BCE." *Anatolia* 40 (2014): 45–85.
Sarris, Peter. *Economy and Society in the Age of Justinian*. Cambridge: Cambridge University Press, 2006.
Sauneron, Serge. "Le germe dans les os." *BIFAO* 60 (1960): 19–27.
Sauneron, Serge, and J. Vérité. "Fouilles dans la zone axiale du IIIe pylon." *Kêmi* 19 (1969): 249–76.
Savalli-Lestrade, Ivana. "La place des reines à la cour et dans le royaume à l'époque hellénistique." In *Les femmes antiques entre sphère privée et sphère publique*, edited by Regula Frei-Stolba, Anne Bielman, and Olivier Bianchi, 59–76. Bern: P. Lang, 2003.
———. "Il ruolo pubblico delle regine ellenistiche." In *Historie: Studie offerti dagli Allievi Giuseppe Nenci in occasione del suo settantesimo compleanno*, edited by Salvatore Allessandri, 415-32. Congedo: Galatina LE, 1994.
Säve-Söderbergh, T. *Four Eighteenth Dynasty Tombs: Private Tombs at Thebes* 1. Oxford: Oxford University Press, 1957.
el-Sayed, Ramadan. *La déesse Neith de Saïs: Importance et rayonnement de son culte*. BdE 86. Cairo: IFAO, 1982.
Scandone Matthiae, Gabriella. "Art et politique: les images de pharaon à l'étranger." *Ä&L* 10 (2000): 187–93.
———. "La dea e il gioiello." *La parola del passato* 40 (1985): 321–37.
———. "Les rapports entre Ebla et l'Egypte à l'Ancien et au Moyen Empire." In *Egyptology at the Dawn of the Twenty-first Century: Proceedings of the Eighth International Congress of Egyptology*, edited by Z. Hawass and L. Pinch-Brock, 487–94. Cairo: AUC Press, 2003.
Schaeffer, C.F.A. "Fouilles de Minet-el-Beida et de Ras-Shamra. Troisiéme campagne (printemps 1931). Rapport sommaire." *Syria* 13 (1932): 1–27.
Schäfer, Heinrich. *Principles of Egyptian Art*, translated by John Baines. Oxford: Griffith Institute, 1986.

Scharff, A. "Ein Rechnungsbuch des königlichen Hofes aus der 13. Dynastie (Papyrus Boulaq Nr. 18)." *ZÄS* 57 (1922): 51–68.
Scheele-Schweitzer, Katrin. *Die Personennamen des Alten Reiches. Altägyptische Onomastik unter lexikographischen und sozio-kulturellen Aspekten*. Philippika 28. Wiesbaden: Harrassowitz, 2014.
Schmitz, Bettina. *Untersuchungen zum Titel S3–NJŚWT "Königssohn."* Bonn: Rudolf Habelt Verlag, 1976.
Schneider, Hans D. *Shabtis: An Introduction to the History of Ancient Egyptian Funerary Statuettes with a Catalogue of the Collection of Shabtis in the National Museum of Antiquities at Leiden, [3 parts]*. Leiden: Rijksmuseum van Oudheden, 1977.
Schoske S. "Das Erschlagen der Feinde. Ikonographie und Stilistik der Feindvernichtung im alten Ägypten." PhD diss., Heidelberg University, 1982.
Schott, Siegfried. "Die Bitte um ein Kind auf einer Grabfigur des frühen Mittleren Reiches." *JEA* 16 (1930): 23.
Schwaller de Lubicz, René A. *The Temples of Karnak*. London: Thames and Hudson, 1999.
Scott, Joan Wallach. "Gender: A Useful Category of Historical Analysis." *American Historical Review* 91, no. 5 (1986): 1053–75.
Sealey, Raphael. *Women and Law in Classical Greece*. Chapel Hill and London: University of North Carolina Press, 1990.
Seipel, Wilfried. "Sphinxkopf einer Königin oder Prinzessin." In *Gott, Mensch, Pharao. Viertausend Jahre Menschenbild in der Skulptur des Alten Ägypten*. Vienna: Kunsthistorisches Museum, 1992.
Sethe, K. *Die altägyptischen Pyramidentexte nach den Papierabdrücken und Photographien des Berliner Museums*. Vol. 1. Leipzig: J.C. Hinrichs, 1908.
———. *Urkunden der 18. Dynastie*. Leipzig: J.C. Hinrichs, 1906.
Sewell-Lasater, Tara. "Becoming Kleopatra: Ptolemaic Royal Marriage, Incest, and the Path to Female Rule." PhD diss., University of Houston, 2020.
Shalomi-Hen, Racheli. "The Two Kites and the Osirian Revolution." In *Edal: Egyptian & Egyptological Documents Archives Libraries*, edited by Patrizia Piacentini, 372–79. Milan: Pontremoli editore, 2009.
Sharpe, Donald. "Your Chi-square Test Is Statistically Significant: Now What?" *Practical Assessment, Research & Evalulation* 20, no. 8 (2015): 2–10.
Siesse, Julien. *La XIIIe dynastie: Histoire de la fin du Moyen Empire égyptien*. Paris: Sorbonne Université Presses, 2019.
Silverman, David P. *The Tomb Chamber of Ḫsw the Elder: The Inscribed Material at Kom El-Hisn*. Vol. 1, *Illustrations*. Winona Lake, IN: Eisenbrauns, 1988.
Simpson, E. "An Early Anatolian Ivory Chair: The Pratt Ivories in the Metropolitan Museum of Art." In *AMILLA: The Quest for Excellence. Studies Presented to Guenter Kopcke in Honor of His 75th Birthday*, edited by Robert B. Koehl, 221–61. Philadelphia: INSTAP Academic Press, 2013.
Simpson, William Kelly. *The Literature of Ancient Egypt*. 3rd ed. New Haven: Yale University Press, 2003.
———. *The Mastabas of Kawab, Khafkhufu I and II: G 7110–20, and 7150 and*

Subsidiary Mastabas of Street G 7100. Boston: Dept. of Egyptian and Ancient Near Eastern Art, MFA, 1978.

———. *The Mastabas of Qar and Idu, G 7101 and 7102.* Giza Mastabas 2. Boston: MFA, 1976.

Skumsnes, R. "Patterns of Change and Disclosures of Difference: Family and Gender in New Kingdom Egypt: Titles of Non-royal Women." PhD diss., University of Oslo, 2018.

Smith, H.S. "Marriage and Family Law." In *Legal Documents of the Hellenistic World*, edited by M.J. Geller and H. Maehler. London: Warburg Institute, University of London, 1995.

Smith, Mark. "Egyptian Elite Self-presentation in the Context of Ptolemaic Rule." In *Ancient Alexandria between Egypt and Greece*, edited by W.V. Harris and Giovanni Ruffini, 33–66. CSCT 26. Boston: Brill, 2004.

———. *The Liturgy of Opening the Mouth for Breathing.* Oxford: Griffith Institute, Ashmolean Museum, 1993.

———. "Papyrus Harkness." *Enchoria* 18 (1991): 95–105.

Smith, Mark, and Richard Jasnow. "'As for Those Who Have Called Me Evil, Mut Will Call Them Evil': Orgiastic Cultic Behavior and Its Critics in Ancient Egypt (PSI Inv. [provv.] D114a + PSI Inv. 3056 verso)." *Enchoria* 32 (2010/2011): 9–53.

Smith, Ray Winfield, and Donald Redford. *The Akhenaten Temple Project* 1. Warminster: Aris and Philips, 1976.

Smith, Stuart Tyson. "Intact Tombs of the 17th and 18th Dynasties from Thebes and the New Kingdom Burial System." *MDAIK* 48 (1992): 193–231.

Smith, W.S. *A History of Egyptian Sculpture and Painting in the Old Kingdom.* London: Oxford University Press, 1946.

———. *Interconnections in the Ancient Near East: A Study of the Relationships Between the Arts of Egypt, the Aegean, and Western Asia.* New Haven: Yale University Press, 1965.

Soliman, Daniel. "Workmen's Marks in Pre-Amarna Tombs at Deir el-Medina." In *Non-textual Marking Systems in Ancient Egypt (and Elsewhere)*, edited by Julia Budka, Frank Kammerzell, and Slawomir Rzepka, 109–32. LingAegSM 16. Berlin: Widmaier, 2015.

Sourouzian, Hourig. "Lion and Sphinx Varia in the Egyptian Museum, Cairo." In *The Art and Culture of Ancient Egypt: Studies in Honor of Dorothea Arnold*, edited by Adela Oppenheim and Ogden Goelet. *BES* 19 (2015): 597–612.

———. "Les sphinx dans les allées processionelles." In *Sphinx: Les gardiens de l'Égypte*, 99–111. Brussels: ING Belgique and Fonds Mercator, 2006.

Spanel, Donald B. "Palaeographic and Epigraphic Distinctions between Texts of the So-called First Intermediate Period and the Early Twelfth Dynasty." In *Studies in Honor of William Kelly Simpson* 2, edited by Peter Der Manuelian, 765–86. Boston: Dept. of Ancient Egyptian, Nubian and Near Eastern Art, MFA, 1996.

Speidel, M. Alexander. *Die Friseure des ägyptischen alten Reiches: eine historisch-prosopographische Untersuchung zu Amt und Titel (jr-šn).* Konstanz: Hartung-Gorre Verlag, 1990.

Spencer, A.J. *Brick Architecture in Ancient Egypt.* Warminster: Aris and Phillips, 1979.

Spencer, Neal. "Sustaining Egyptian Culture? Non-royal Initiatives in Late Period Temple Building." In *Egypt in Transition: Social and Religious Development of Egypt in the First Millennium* BCE, edited by L. Bareš, F. Coppens, and K. Smoláriková, 441–90. Prague: Oxbow Books, 2010.

Spiegelberg, Wilhelm. *Ägyptische und andere Graffiti (Inschriften und Zeichnungen) aus der Thebanischen Nekropolis. Text und Atlas.* Heidelberg: Carl Winter, 1921.

Spieser, Cathie. "De l'embryon humain à l'embryon divin en Égypte ancienne." In *L'embryon humain à travers l'histoire. Images, savoirs et rites. Actes du colloque international de Fribourg 27–29 octobre 2004*, edited by V. Dasen, 23–39. Gollion: In Folio, 2007.

———. "Vases et peaux d'animaux à fonction matricielle dans l'Égypte ancienne." *BiOr* 63, no. 3/4 (2006): col. 219–234.

Springborg, Patricia. *Royal Persons: Patriarchal Monarchy and the Feminine Principle.* London: Unwin Hyman, 1990.

Spruill, Marjorie J. *Divided We Stand: The Battle over Women's Rights and Family Values that Polarized American Politics.* New York: Bloomsbury Publishing, 2017.

Stadelmann, Rainer. *Die ägyptischen Pyramiden. Vom Ziegelbau zum Weltwunder.* Mainz am Rhein: Philipp von Zabern, 1997.

Staring, Nico. "Interpreting Figural Graffiti: Case Studies from a Funerary Context." In *Current Research in Egyptology* 11, edited by Maarten Horn et al., 145–56. Oxford: Oxbow Books, 2010.

Stefanović, Danijela. *The Non-royal Regular Feminine Titles of the Middle Kingdom and Second Intermediate Period: Dossiers.* London: Golden House Publications, 2009.

———. "The *ẖkrt-nswt* on the Monuments of the *3ṯw n tt ḥḳ3*." In *Proceedings of the Tenth International Congress of Egyptologists, University of the Aegean, Rhodes, 22–29 May 2008*, edited by Panagiotis Kousoulis and Nikolaos Lazardis, 861–73. OLA 241. Leuven: Peeters, 2015.

Stefanović, Danijela, and Helmut Satzinger. "I Am a *Nbt-pr*, and I Am Independent." In *The World of Middle Kingdom Egypt (2000–1550* BC*): Contributions on Archaeology, Art, Religion, and Written Sources* 1, edited by Gianluca Miniaci and Wolfram Grajetzki, 333–38. Middle Kingdom Studies 1. London: Golden House Publications, 2015.

Steinert, Ulrike. "Fluids, Rivers, and Vessels: Metaphors and Body Concepts in Mesopotamian Gynaecological Texts." *Le Journal des Médecines Cunéiformes* 22 (2013): 1–23.

Stevens, Marissa. "Family Associations Reflected in the Materiality of the 21st Dynasty Funerary Papyri." In *Invisible Archaeologies: Hidden Aspects of Daily Life in Ancient Egypt and Nubia*, edited by Loretta Kilroe, 26–56. Oxford: Archaeopress, 2019.

———. "Illustrations of Temple Rank on 21st Dynasty Funerary Papyri." In *Current Research in Egyptology 2018*, edited by M.P. Hlouchová, D. Bělohoubková, J. Honzl, and V. Nováková, 162–228. Oxford: Archaeopress, 2019.

Stewart, Harry M. *Egyptian Shabtis.* Shire Egyptology 23. Princes Risborough: Shire Publications, 1995.

Stowers, Stanley K. *Letter Writing in Greco-Roman Antiquity*. Library of Early Christianity 5. Philadelphia: Westminster Press, 1986.

Strouhal, Eugene, Bretislav Vachala, and Hana Vymazalová. *The Medicine of the Ancient Egyptians*. Vol. 1: *Surgery, Gynecology, Obstetrics, and Pediatrics*. Cairo: American University in Cairo Press, 2010.

Strudwick, Nigel. *The Administration of Egypt in the Old Kingdom: The Highest Titles and Their Holders*. London: KPI, 1985.

———. *Texts from the Pyramid Age*. WAW 16. Atlanta: SBL, 2005.

Stünkel, Isabel. *The Decoration of the North Chapel of Khenemetneferhedjet Weret I at Dahshur*. Bonn: Rheinische Friedrich-Wilhelms-Universität, 2018. https://bonndoc.ulb.uni-bonn.de/xmlui/handle/20.500.11811/7451.

———. "Notes on Khenemet-nefer-hedjet Weret II." In *The Art and Culture of Ancient Egypt: Studies in Honor of Dorothea Arnold*, edited by Adela Oppenheim and Ogden Goelet. *BES* 19 (2015): 631–40.

———. "Royal Women: Ladies of the Two Lands." In *Ancient Egypt Transformed: The Middle Kingdom*, edited by Adela Oppenheim, Dorothea Arnold, Dieter Arnold, and Kei Yamamoto, 92–95, 332. New York: The Metropolitan Museum of Art, 2015.

Suvorov, Rachel Rodabaugh. "The Kahun Papyrus in Context: The 'Floating Uterus.'" In *Current Research in Egyptology 2004*, edited by Rachael J. Dann, 138–46. Oxford: Oxbow, 2006.

Sweeney, Deborah. "Forever Young? The Representation of Older and Ageing Women in Ancient Egyptian Art." *JARCE* 41 (2004): 67–84.

———. "Gender and Language in Ramesside Egyptian." *LingAeg* (2006) 14: 433–50.

———. *Gender and Religious Activities at Deir el-Medina*. OBO. Leuven: Peeters, forthcoming.

———. "Walking Alone Forever, Following You: Gender and Mourner's Laments from Ancient Egypt." *NIN: Journal of Gender Studies in Antiquity* 2 (2001): 27–48.

———. "Women and Language in the Ramesside Period or, Why Women Don't Say Please." In *Proceedings of the Seventh International Congress of Egyptologists, Cambridge, 3–9 September 1995*, edited by Christopher J. Eyre, 1109–17. Leuven: Peeters, 1998.

———. "Women at Deir el-Medîna." In *Women in Antiquity: Real Women across the Ancient World*, edited by Stephanie L. Budin and Jean M. Turfa, 243–54. London and New York: Routledge, 2016.

———. "Women at Worship on Deir el-Medina Stelae." In *Deir el-Medina Studies: Helsinki June 24–26, 2009 Proceedings*, edited by Jaana Toivari-Viitala, Turo Vartiainen, and Saara Uvanto, 179–90. The Finnish Egyptological Society—Occasional Publications 2. Vantaa: Multiprint, 2014.

———. "Women Growing Older in Deir el-Medina." In *Living and Writing in Deir el-Medine: Socio-historical Embodiment of Deir el-Medine Texts*, edited by Andreas Dorn and Tobias Hofmann, 135–53. Aegyptiaca Helvetica 19. Basel: Schwabe, 2006.

Szafrański, Zbigniew E. "The Exceptional Creativity of Hatshepsut." In *Creativity and Innovation in the Reign of Hatshepsut*, edited by J. Galán, B.M. Bryan, and P.F. Dorman. SAOC 69. Chicago: Oriental Institute, 2014.

———. "Tombs of the Third Intermediate Period on the Upper Terrace of the Temple of Hatshepsut." *PAM* 24, no. 2 (2015): 183–201.
Szpakowska, K. *Daily Life in Ancient Egypt.* Oxford: Blackwell, 2008.
Tassie, Geoffrey J. "Identifying the Practice of Tattooing in Ancient Egypt and Nubia." *Papers from the Institute of Archaeology* 14 (2003): 85–101. https://doi.org/10.5334/pia.200.
Tawfik, Sayed. "Aton Studies." *MDAIK* 31 (1975): 159–68.
Taylor, John H. *Egyptian Coffins.* Shire Egyptology 11. Princes Risborough: Shire Publications, 1989.
———. "A Note on the Family of Montemhat." *JEA* 73 (1987): 229–30.
Tefnin, Roland. "La date de la statuette de la dame Toui au Louvre." *CdE* 46, no. 91 (1971): 35–49.
Teissier, B. *Egyptian Iconography on Syro-Palestinian Cylinder Seals of the Middle Bronze Age.* Fribourg: University Press, 1996.
Théodoridès, A. "Le testament d'Imenkhâou." *JEA* 54 (1968): 149–54.
Thiers, Christophe. "Civils et militaires dans les temples. Occupation illicite et expulsion." *BIFAO* 105 (2005): 493–516.
Thijs, Ad. "Nodjmet A, Daughter of Amenhotep, Wife of Piankh and Mother of Herihor." *ZÄS* 140 (2013): 54–69.
———. "Two Books for One Lady: The Mother of Herihor Rediscovered." *GM* 163 (1998): 101–10.
Thomas, Siân E. "Ptolemaic Gebelein: An Exploration of Legal, Social and Topographical Themes Based on Unpublished Documents for Money and Cessions in the British Museum. Volume I." PhD diss., University of Cambridge, 2009.
Tibiletti, Giuseppe. *Le lettere private nei papiri greci del III e IV secolo d.C.: Tra paganesimo e cristianesimo.* Scienze Filologiche e Letteratura 15. Milan: Vita e Pensiero, 1979.
Toivari-Viitala, Jaana. "Marriage at Deir el-Medina." In *Proceedings of the Seventh International Congress of Egyptologists*, edited by C J. Eyre, 1157–63. Leuven: Peeters, 1995.
———. "O. DeM 764: A Note Concerning Property Rights." *GM* 195 (2003): 87–96.
———. *Women at Deir el-Medina: A Study of the Status and Roles of the Female Inhabitants in the Workmen's Community during the Ramesside Period.* EGU 15. Leiden: NINO, 2001.
Tooley, Angela M.J. "Notes on Type 1 Truncated Figurines: The Ramesseum Ladies." In *Company of Images: Modelling the Imaginary World of Middle Kingdom Egypt (2000–1500 BC)*, edited by Gianluca Miniaci, Marilina Betrò, and Stephen Quirke, 421–56. Leuven: Peeters, 2017.
Traunecker, Claude. "Un document inédit sur une famille de contemporains de la XXIIe dynastie." *BIFAO* 69 (1971): 219–37.
Traunecker, Claude, and Isabelle Régen. "La tombe d'un intellectuel dans la Thèbes des divines adoratrices." In *Servir les dieux d'Égypte. Divines adoratrices, chanteuses et prêtres d'Amon à Thebes*, edited by Florence Gombert-Meurice and Frédéric Payraudeau, 60–63. Paris: Somogy, 2018.
Trigger, Bruce. "The Rise of Egyptian Civilization." In *Ancient Egypt: A Social History*, edited by B.G. Trigger, B.J. Kemp, D. O'Connor, and A.B. Lloyd, 1–70. Cambridge: Cambridge University Press, 1983.

Trigger, Bruce, G., Barry J. Kemp, David O'Connor, and Alan B. Lloyd. *Ancient Egypt: A Social History*. Cambridge: Cambridge University Press, 1983.

Troxell, H.A. "Arsinoe's Non-era." *ANSMN* 28 (1983): 35–70.

Troy, Lana. *Patterns of Queenship in Ancient Egyptian Myth and History*. Acta Universitatis Upsaliensis. BOREAS 14. Uppsala and Stockholm: Almquist and Wiksell International, 1986.

———. "The Queen as a Female Counterpart of the Pharaoh." In *Queens of Egypt: From Hetepheres to Cleopatra*, edited by Christiane Ziegler, 154–70. Monaco: Grimaldi Forum, 2008.

Turner, Victor. *The Ritual Process: Structure and Anti-structure*. Chicago: Aldine, 1969.

Tyldesley, Joyce A. *Chronicle of the Queens of Egypt: From Early Dynastic Times to the Death of Cleopatra*. London: Thames and Hudson, 2006.

———. *Daughters of Isis: Women of Ancient Egypt*. London and New York: Penguin, 1995.

———. "Foremost of Women: The Female Pharaohs of Ancient Egypt." In *Tausret: Forgotten Queen and Pharaoh of Egypt*, edited by Richard H. Wilkinson, 5–24. Oxford: Oxford University Press, 2012.

———. "The Role of Egypt's Dynastic Queens." In *Women in Antiquity: Real Women across the Ancient World*, edited by S. Budin and J. Turfa, 271–80. London and New York: Routledge, 2016.

Upton, Graham J.G. "Fisher's Exact Test." *Journal of the Royal Statistical Society. Series A (Statistics in Society)* 155, no. 3 (1992): 395–402. https://doi.org/10.2307/2982890.

Valbelle, Dominique. *Ouchebtis de Deir El-Médineh*. Cairo: IFAO, 1972.

———. *Les Ouvriers de la tombe: Deir-el-Médineh à l'époque Ramesside*. BdE 96. Cairo: IFAO, 1985.

Valloggia, Michel. *Abou Rawash* 1: *Le complexe funéraire royal de Rêdjedef*. 2 vols. FIFAO 63. Cairo: IFAO, 2011.

———. "Amenemhat IV et sa corégence avec Amenemhat III." *RdE* 21 (1969): 107–33.

Vandekerckhove, Hans, and Renate Müller-Wollermann. *Die Felsinschriften des Wadi Hilâl*. Vol. 6, *Elkab*. Turnhout: Brepols, 2001.

Vandier, J. *Manuel d'archéologie égyptienne, Tome III. Les Grandes époques: La Statuaire*. Paris: Picard, 1958.

Vandier d'Abbadie, J. "Une fresque civile de Deir El-Médineh." *RdE* 3 (1938): 27–35.

Van Dijk, L. "The Amarna Period and the Later New Kingdom (c. 1352–1069 BC)." In *Oxford History of Ancient Egypt*, edited by I. Shaw, 265–307. Oxford: Oxford University Press, 2000.

Vandorpe, Katelijn. "Apollonia, a Businesswoman in a Multicultural Society (Pathyris, 2nd–1st Centuries B.C.)." In *Le rôle et le statut de la femme en Égypte hellénistique, romaine et byzantine. Actes du colloque international, Bruxelles–Leuven 27–29 November 1997*, edited by Henri Melaerts and Leon Mooren, 325–36. Studia Hellenistica 37. Paris, Leuven, and Sterling, VA: Peeters, 2002.

———. "Archives and Dossiers." In *The Oxford Handbook of Papyrology*, edited by Roger S. Bagnall, 216–54. Oxford and New York: Oxford University Press, 2009.

———. *The Bilingual Family Archive of Dryton, His Wife Apollonia and Their Daughter*

Senmouthis (P. Dryton). Collectanea Hellenistica 4. Brussels: Comite Klassieke Studies, Subcomité Hellenisme, KVAB, 2002.

———. "City of Many a Gate, Harbour for Many a Rebel: Historical and Topographical Outline of Greco-Roman Thebes." In *Hundred-gated Thebes: Acts of a Colloquium on Thebes and the Theban Area in the Graeco-Roman Period*, edited by Sven P. Vleeming, 203–39. P. L. Bat. 27. Leiden, New York, and Cologne: Brill, 1995.

———. "The Ptolemaic Period." In *A Companion to Ancient Egypt*, edited by Alan B. Lloyd, 159–79. Chichester, West Sussex and Malden, MA: Wiley-Blackwell, 2010.

———. "A Successful, but Fragile Biculturalism: The Hellenization Process in the Upper Egyptian Town of Pathyris under Ptolemy VI and VIII." In *Ägypten zwischen innerem Zwist und äußerem Druck. Die Zeit Ptolemaios' VI. bis VIII. Internationales Symposium Heidelberg 16.–19.9.2007*, edited by Andrea Jördens and Joachim F. Quack, 292–308. Wiesbaden: Harrassowitz Verlag, 2011.

Vandorpe, Katelijn, W. Clarysse, and Herbert Verreth. *Graeco-Roman Archives from the Fayum*. Collectanea Hellenistica. KVAB 6. Leuven: Peeters, 2015.

Vandorpe, Katelijn, and Sofie Waebens. "Women and Gender in Roman Egypt: The Impact of Roman Rule." In *Tradition and Transformation: Egypt under Roman Rule*, edited by Katja Lembke, Martina Minas-Nerpel, and Stefan Pfeiffer, 415–35. Leiden: Brill, 2010.

Van Genepp, Arnold. *Les rit es de passage*. Paris: Picard, 1909.

Van Lepp, Jonathan. "The Role of Dance in Funerary Ritual in the Old Kingdom." In *Akten des vierten Internationalen Aegyptologen Kongresses* 3, edited by S. Schoske, 386–94. Hamburg: Helmut Buske, 1989.

van Minnen, Peter. "The Volume of the Oxyrhynchite Textile Trade." *Münstersche Beiträge zur antiken Handelsgeschichte* 5 (1986): 88–95.

VanPool, Todd L., and Robert D. Leonard. *Quantitative Analysis in Archaeology*. Chichester: Wiley-Blackwell, 2011.

Van Walsem, René. *MastaBase: The Leiden Mastaba Project*. Leuven: Peeters, 2008.

Vasiljević, Vera. "Female Owners of Carrying Chairs: *Sitzsänfte* and *Hocksänfte*." *SAK* 41 (2012): 395–406.

———. "Der Grabherr und seine Frau: zur Ikonographie der Status- und Machtverhältnisse in den Privatgräbern des Alten Reiches." *SAK* 36 (2007): 333–45.

———. "Hierarchy of Women within Elite Families: Iconographic Data from the Old Kingdom." In *Art and Society: Ancient and Modern Contexts of Egyptian Art. Proceedings of the International Conference Held at the Museum of Fine Arts, Budapest, 13–15 May 2010*, edited by Katalin A. Kóthay, 139–49. Budapest: Museum of Fine Arts Budapest, 2012.

———. *Untersuchungen zum Gefolge des Grabhernn in den Gräbern des Alten Reiches*. Belgrade: Filozofski Fakultet, 1995.

Veenhof, K. R., and Jesper Eidem. *Mesopotamia: The Old Assyrian Period*. Fribourg: Academic Press; Göttingen: Vandenhoeck and Ruprecht, 2008.

Veldmeijer, André J. *The Ancient Egyptian Footwear Project: Final Archaeological Analysis*. Leiden: Sidestone Press, 2019.

———. *Excavations of Gebel Adda (Lower Nubia): Ancient Nubian Leatherwork*. Vol. 1: *Sandals and Shoes*. Leiden: Sidestone Press, 2016.

———. *Sandals, Shoes and Other Leatherwork from the Coptic Monastery Deir El-Bachit: Analysis and Catalogue*. Leiden: Sidestone Press, 2011.

Veldmeijer, André J., and Salima Ikram. *Catalogue of the Footwear in the Coptic Museum (Cairo)*. Leiden: Sidestone Press, 2014.

Vergnieux, Robert. *Recherches sur les monuments thébains d'Amenhotep IV à l'aide d'outils informatiques: Méthodes et résultats*. CSEG 4. Geneva: Société d'Égyptologie, 1999.

Verner, Miroslav. *Abusir III: The Pyramid Complex of Khentkaus*. Prague: Karolinum, 1995.

———. *Sons of the Sun: Rise and Decline of the Fifth Dynasty*. Prague: Charles University, Faculty of Arts, 2014.

Vernus, Pascal. "Comment l'élite se donne à voir dans le programme décoratif de ses chapelles funéraires. Stratégie d'épure, stratégie d'appogiature et le frémissement du littéraire." In *Élites et pouvoir en Égypte ancienne: Actes du colloque Université Charles-de-Gaulle–Lille 3, 7 et 8 juillet 2006*, edited by Juan Carlos Moreno García, 67–116. Lille: Université Charles-de-Gaulle–Lille III, 2009–10.

———. "Omina calendériques et comptabilité d'offrandes sur une tablette hiératique de la XVIIIe dynastie." *RdE* 33 (1981): 89–124.

Vischak, Deborah. *Community and Identity in Ancient Egypt: The Old Kingdom Cemetery at Qubbet el-Hawa*. New York: Cambridge University Press, 2015.

Vittmann, Günter. *Der demotische Papyrus Rylands 9*. AÄT 38. Wiesbaden: Harrassowitz, 1998.

———. "A Question of Names, Titles, and Iconography: Kushites in Priestly, Administrative and Other Positions from Dynasties 25 to 26." *MittSAG* 18 (2007): 139–61.

———. "Ein thebanischer Verpfrundungsvertrag aus der Zeit Ptolemaios' III, Euergetes, P. Marseille 298 + 299." *Enchoria* 10 (1980): 127–40.

Vymazalová, Hana. "The Administration and Economy of the Pyramid Complexes and Royal Funerary Cults in the Old Kingdom." Habilitation thesis, Charles University, Prague, 2015.

———. "The Administration of the Royal Funerary Complexes." In *Ancient Egyptian Administration*, edited by Juan Carlos Moreno García, 177–98. Leiden: Brill, 2013.

Ward, William A. *Essays on Feminine Titles of the Middle Kingdom and Related Subjects*. Beirut: American University of Beirut, 1986.

———. *The Fourth Egyptian Homographic Roots B-3, Etymological and Egypto-Semitic Studies, Studia-Pohl: series major 6*. Rome: Biblical Institute Press, 1978.

———. *Index of Egyptian Administrative and Religious Titles of the Middle Kingdom*. Beirut: American University of Beirut, 1982.

———. "Non-royal Women and Their Occupations in the Middle Kingdom." In *Women's Earliest Records from Ancient Egypt and Western Asia*, edited by Barbara S. Lesko, 33–43. Atlanta: Scholars Press, 1989.

Watterson, Barbara. *Women in Ancient Egypt*. New York: St. Martin's Press, 1991.

Weiner, A.B. *Inalienable Possesions: The Paradox of Keeping While Giving*. Berkeley, Los Angeles, and Oxford: University of California Press, 1992.

Weiss, Lara. *Religious Practice at Deir el-Medina*. EGU 29. Leiden: NINO, 2015.
Weissner, P. "Alienating the Inalienable: Marriage and Money in a Big Man Society." In *The Scope of Anthropology: Maurice Godelier's Work in Context*, edited by L. Dousset and S. Tcherkézoff, 67–85. New York and Oxford: Berghahn Books, 2012.
Wenig, S. *Die Frau im Alten Ägypten*. Leipzig: Helmut Heyne, 1967.
———. *The Woman in Egyptian Art*. New York: McGraw-Hill, 1969.
Wente, Edward F. "Hathor at the Jubilee." In *Studies in Honor of J.A. Wilson*, edited by E.B. Hauser, 83–91. SAOC 35. Chicago: University of Chicago Press, 1969.
———. *Letters from Ancient Egypt*. Edited by Edmund S. Meltzer. Atlanta: Scholars Press, 1990.
———. "Some Graffiti from the Reign of Hatshepsut." *JNES* 43, no. 1 (1984): 47–54.
Wenzel, G. "Ein Sphinxkopf aus der 12. Dynastie (München ÄS 7110)." In *From Illahun to Djeme: Papers Presented in Honour of Ulrich Luft*, edited by Eszter Bechtold, András Gulyás, and Andrea Hasznos, 343–54. BARIS 2311. Oxford: BAR, 2011.
Westendorf, Wolfhart. "Beitrage aus und zu den medizinischen Texten II. Das Isis-Blut Symbol." *ZÄS* 92 (1966): 128–54.
———. *Handbuch der altägyptischen Medizin*. Leiden and Boston: Brill, 1999.
Whitehorne, John. "The Pagan Cults of Roman Oxyrhynchus." In *Aufstieg und Niedergang der Römischen Welt*, edited by W. Haase and H. Temporini, vol. 18.5, 3050–91. Berlin: Walter de Gruyter, 1995.
Wiener, M. "Contacts: Crete, Egypt, and the Near East circa 2000 B.C." In *Cultures in Contact: From Mesopotamia to the Mediterranean in the Second Millennium B.C.*, edited by J. Aruz, S. Graff, and Y. Rakic, 34–45. New York: The Metropolitan Museum of Art, 2013.
Wikander, Charlotte. "Religion, Political Power and Gender: The Building of Cult-image." In *Religion and Power in the Ancient Greek World: Proceedings of the Uppsala Symposium 1993*, edited by Pontus Hellström and Brita Alroth, 183–88. Uppsala: Uppsala University, 1996.
Wild, H. "A Bas-relief of Sekhemrē'-Sewadjtowē Sebekhotpe from Sehēl." *JEA* 37 (1951): 12–16.
Wildung, Dietrich. *Sesostris und Amenemhet: Aegypten im Mittleren Reich*. Fribourg: Hirmer, 1984.
Wilfong, Terry G. "Gender in Ancient Egypt." In *Egyptian Archaeology*, edited by W. Wendrich, 164–79. Chichester and Malden: Wiley-Blackwell, 2010.
———. "Menstrual Synchrony and the 'Place of Women' in Ancient Egypt (Oriental Institute Museum Hieratic Ostracon 13512)." In *Gold of Praise: Studies on Ancient Egypt in Honor of Edward F. Wente*, edited by Emily Teeter and John A. Larson, 419–34. Chicago: Oriental Institute of the University of Chicago, 1999.
Wilkinson, Richard H., and Kent R. Weeks, eds. *The Oxford Handbook of the Valley of the Kings*. Oxford: Oxford University Press, 2016.
Wilkinson, Toby A.H. *Early Dynastic Egypt*. London: Routledge, 1999.
———. "The Early Dynastic Period." In *A Companion to Ancient Egypt*, edited by Alan B. Lloyd, 48–62. Chichester and Malden: Wiley-Blackwell, 2010.

Willems, Harco. *Historical and Archaeological Aspects of Egyptian Funerary Culture: Religious Ideas and Ritual Practice in Middle Kingdom Elite Cemeteries*. Leiden and Boston: Brill, 2014.

Williamson, Jacquelyn. "Alone Before the God: Gender, Status, and Nefertiti's Image." *JARCE* 51 (2015): 179–92.

———. "Evidence for Innovation and Experimentation on the Akhenaten Colossi." *JNES* 78, no. 1 (2019): 25–36.

———. "Nefertiti: Agency and the Individual." Unpublished paper presented at a conference on "Women in Ancient Egypt: Current Research and Historical Trends," Cairo, October 31, 2019.

———. "The Sunshade of Nefertiti." *EA* 33 (2008): 5–7.

Wilson, J.A. "Akh-en-aton and Nefert-iti." *JNES* 32 (1973): 235–41.

Winand, Jean. "Les décrets oraculaires pris en l'honneur d'Henouttaouy et de Maâtkarê (Xe et VIIe pylônes)." *CahKarn* 11 (2003): 603–710.

Winlock, Herbert E. "Assyria: A New Chapter in the Museum's History of Art." *BMMA* 28, no. 2 (1933): 17–24.

———. "The Egyptian Expedition 1918–1920: Excavations at Thebes 1919–20." *BMMA* 15 (1920): 12–32.

———. *Excavations at Deir el Bahari, 1911–1931*. New York: Metropolitan Museum, 1942.

———. "The Museum's Excavations at Thebes." *BMMA* 18, no. 12 (December 1, 1923): 11–39. https://doi.org/10.2307/3254661.

———. "The Museum's Excavations at Thebes." *BMMA* 21, no. 3 (March 1, 1926): 5–32. https://doi.org/10.2307/3254817.

———. "The Museum's Excavations at Thebes." *BMMA* 27, no. 3 (1932): 4–37. https://doi.org/10.2307/3255360.

Wipszycka, Ewa. "Del buon uso delle lettere private. Commento a *SB* III, 7243 e *P. Oxy.* XIV, 1774." In *"Humana sapit": Études d'antiquité tardive offertes à Lellia Cracco Ruggini*, edited by Jean-Michel Carrié and Rita Lizzi Testa, 469–73. Bibliothèque de l'antiquité tardive 3. Turnhout: Brepols, 2002.

Wreszinski, Walter. *Atlas zur altaegyptischen Kulturgeschichte*. Leipzig: J.C. Hinrichs, 1914.

———. *Atlas zur altaegyptischen Kulturgeschichte*. 2 vols. Geneva and Paris: Slatkine Reprints, 1988.

———. *Der grosse medizinische Papyrus des Berliner Museums*. Leipzig: J.C. Hinrichs, 1909–13.

———. *Der Papyrus Ebers, Umschrift, Übersetzung und Kommentar* 1. Leipzig: J.C. Hinrichs, 1913.

Wüthrich, Annik. "L'expression de la filiation à la XXIème dynastie: Reflet d'une réalité historique ou simple effet de mode? L'exemple du Livre des Morts." *BSFE* 204 (2021): 114–40.

Yamazaki, Naoko. *Zaubersprüche für Mutter und Kind: Papyrus Berlin 3027. Schriften zur Ägyptologie*. ACHET B2. Berlin: Achet Verlag, 2003.

Yoyotte, Jean. "Une monumentale litanie de granit. Les Sekhmet d'Amenophis III et la conjuration permanente de la Déesse dangereuse." *BSFE* 87–88 (1980): 46–75.

———. "Les os et la semence masculine à propos d'une théorie physiologique égyptienne." *BIFAO* 61 (1962): 139–46.
———. *Tanis. L'or des pharaons.* Paris: Association française d'action artistique, 1987.
Yoyotte, Marine. "Le 'harem' dans l'Égypte ancienne." In *Reines d'Égypte: d'Hétephérès à Cléopâtre*, edited by Christiane Ziegler, 76–90. Monaco: Grimaldi Forum; Paris: Somogy éditions d'Art, 2008.
———. "Le 'harem,' les femmes de l'entourage royal et leurs lieux de résidence aux époques tardives: espace social ou espace clos?" *Topoi Orient-Occident* 20, no. 1 (2015): 25–45.
Zaki, Moushira E., F.H. Hussein, and R. Abd El-Shafy El Banna. "Osteoporosis among Ancient Egyptians." *International Journal of Osteoarchaeology* 19, no. 1 (2009): 78–89.
Zauzich, Karl-Theodor. *Die ägyptische Schreibertradition in Aufbau, Sprache und Schrift der demotischen Kaufverträge aus ptolemäischer Zeit.* Vol. 1: *Text.* ÄA 19. Wiesbaden: Harrassowitz, 1968.
———. "Akten II." *LÄ* 1, 126–29. Wiesbaden: Harrassowitz, 1975.
———. "Kaufurkunden, demotische." *LÄ* 3, 370–71. Wiesbaden: Harrassowitz, 1980.
———. *Papyri von der Insel Elephantine.* Berlin: Akademie-Verlag, 1978.
Zenihiro, Kento. *The Complete Funerary Cones.* Toyko: Maruzen, 2009.
Ziegler, Christiane, ed. *Queens of Egypt: From Hetepheres to Cleopatra.* Monaco: Grimaldi Forum, 2008.
Zivie, C.M. "Sphinx." In *LÄ* 5, ed. W. Helck and E. Otto, 1139–47. Wiesbaden: Harrassowitz, 1984.
Zivie-Coche, Christiane. *Sphinx: History of a Monument.* Ithaca and London: Cornell University Press, 2002.

Ancient Sources

Aelian. *Varous History.*
Athenaeus. *Deipnosophistae.*
Catullus. Poem 66.
Diogenes Laërtius. *Lives of Eminent Philosophers.*
Justin. *Epitome of Pompeius Trogus' Philippic Histories.*
Kallimachos, *Coma Berenices.*
Major Rock Edict 13
Pausanias. *Description of Greece.*
Plutarch. *Parallel Lives.*
Polybius. *Histories.*
Posidippos. Epigrams.
Scholia on Theokritos.
Theokritos. *Idylls.*

Online Resources

Bernard Bruyère's Archives, IFAO, Cairo. https://www.ifao.egnet.net/bases/archives/bruyere/.

The Brooklyn Museum. https://www.brooklynmuseum.org/opencollection/objects/4157.

Deir el-Medina Database, Leiden. https://dmd.wepwawet.nl.

Demotic and Abnormal Hieratic Texts. https://www.trismegistos.org/daht/.

The Metropolitan Museum of Art in New York. https://www.metmuseum.org/art/collection/search/549536.

The R Project for Statistical Computing. https://www.r-project.org.

Trismegistos. An interdisciplinary portal of the ancient world. https://www.trismegistos.org/.